Communications in Computer and Information Science   2703

Series Editors

Gang Li ⓘ, *School of Information Technology, Deakin University, Burwood, VIC, Australia*

Joaquim Filipe ⓘ, *Polytechnic Institute of Setúbal, Setúbal, Portugal*

Ashish Ghosh ⓘ, *Indian Statistical Institute, Kolkata, West Bengal, India*

Zhiwei Xu, *Chinese Academy of Sciences, Beijing, China*

Rationale

The CCIS series is devoted to the publication of proceedings of computer science conferences. Its aim is to efficiently disseminate original research results in informatics in printed and electronic form. While the focus is on publication of peer-reviewed full papers presenting mature work, inclusion of reviewed short papers reporting on work in progress is welcome, too. Besides globally relevant meetings with internationally representative program committees guaranteeing a strict peer-reviewing and paper selection process, conferences run by societies or of high regional or national relevance are also considered for publication.

Topics

The topical scope of CCIS spans the entire spectrum of informatics ranging from foundational topics in the theory of computing to information and communications science and technology and a broad variety of interdisciplinary application fields.

Information for Volume Editors and Authors

Publication in CCIS is free of charge. No royalties are paid, however, we offer registered conference participants temporary free access to the online version of the conference proceedings on SpringerLink (http://link.springer.com) by means of an http referrer from the conference website and/or a number of complimentary printed copies, as specified in the official acceptance email of the event.

CCIS proceedings can be published in time for distribution at conferences or as post-proceedings, and delivered in the form of printed books and/or electronically as USBs and/or e-content licenses for accessing proceedings at SpringerLink. Furthermore, CCIS proceedings are included in the CCIS electronic book series hosted in the SpringerLink digital library at http://link.springer.com/bookseries/7899. Conferences publishing in CCIS are allowed to use Online Conference Service (OCS) for managing the whole proceedings lifecycle (from submission and reviewing to preparing for publication) free of charge.

Publication process

The language of publication is exclusively English. Authors publishing in CCIS have to sign the Springer CCIS copyright transfer form, however, they are free to use their material published in CCIS for substantially changed, more elaborate subsequent publications elsewhere. For the preparation of the camera-ready papers/files, authors have to strictly adhere to the Springer CCIS Authors' Instructions and are strongly encouraged to use the CCIS LaTeX style files or templates.

Abstracting/Indexing

CCIS is abstracted/indexed in DBLP, Google Scholar, EI-Compendex, Mathematical Reviews, SCImago, Scopus. CCIS volumes are also submitted for the inclusion in ISI Proceedings.

How to start

To start the evaluation of your proposal for inclusion in the CCIS series, please send an e-mail to ccis@springer.com.

Jorge Bernardino · Ana Fred · Antonella Poggi ·
Le Gruenwald · Frans Coenen · Elio Masciari ·
David Aveiro
Editors

Knowledge Discovery, Knowledge Engineering and Knowledge Management

16th International Joint Conference, IC3K 2024
Porto, Portugal, November 17–19, 2024
Revised Selected Papers

Editors
Jorge Bernardino
Polytechnic University of Coimbra
Coimbra, Portugal

Antonella Poggi
Università di Roma "La Sapienza"
Rome, Italy

Frans Coenen
University of Liverpool
Liverpool, UK

David Aveiro
University of Madeira
Funchal, Portugal

NOVA-LINCS
Funchal, Portugal

ARDITI
Funchal, Portugal

Ana Fred
University of Lisbon
Lisbon, Portugal

Le Gruenwald
University of Oklahoma
Norman, OK, USA

Elio Masciari
University of Naples Federico II
Naples, Italy

ISSN 1865-0929   ISSN 1865-0937 (electronic)
Communications in Computer and Information Science
ISBN 978-3-032-06877-4   ISBN 978-3-032-06878-1 (eBook)
https://doi.org/10.1007/978-3-032-06878-1

© The Editor(s) (if applicable) and The Author(s), under exclusive license
to Springer Nature Switzerland AG 2026

This work is subject to copyright. All rights are solely and exclusively licensed by the Publisher, whether the whole or part of the material is concerned, specifically the rights of translation, reprinting, reuse of illustrations, recitation, broadcasting, reproduction on microfilms or in any other physical way, and transmission or information storage and retrieval, electronic adaptation, computer software, or by similar or dissimilar methodology now known or hereafter developed.
The use of general descriptive names, registered names, trademarks, service marks, etc. in this publication does not imply, even in the absence of a specific statement, that such names are exempt from the relevant protective laws and regulations and therefore free for general use.
The publisher, the authors and the editors are safe to assume that the advice and information in this book are believed to be true and accurate at the date of publication. Neither the publisher nor the authors or the editors give a warranty, expressed or implied, with respect to the material contained herein or for any errors or omissions that may have been made. The publisher remains neutral with regard to jurisdictional claims in published maps and institutional affiliations.

This Springer imprint is published by the registered company Springer Nature Switzerland AG
The registered company address is: Gewerbestrasse 11, 6330 Cham, Switzerland

If disposing of this product, please recycle the paper.

Preface

This book includes revised and extended versions of selected papers from the 16th International Joint Conference on Knowledge Discovery, Knowledge Engineering and Knowledge Management (IC3K 2024), held in Porto, Portugal, from November 17 to 19, 2024.

The purpose of IC3K is to bring together researchers, engineers and practitioners in the areas of Knowledge Discovery, Knowledge Engineering, and Knowledge Management to exchange ideas on research, development, and implementation.

IC3K 2024 received 175 paper submissions from 47 countries, 17 (10%) of which are included in this book.

The papers were selected by the event chairs based on several criteria, including the classifications and comments provided by the program committee members, the assessments of the session chairs, and the program chairs' overall view of all papers in the technical program. The authors of the selected papers were invited to submit revised and extended versions, with at least 30% new material compared to their original conference papers.

The papers selected for inclusion in this book contribute to understanding current research trends in Knowledge Discovery, Knowledge Engineering, and Knowledge Management. Topics include Information Extraction, Tools and Technologies for Knowledge Management, Deep Learning, Knowledge Management Projects, Machine Learning, Large Language Models, Database Integration, Applications of Knowledge Discovery and Information Retrieval, Knowledge Management Strategies and Implementations, Natural Language Processing, Uncertainty Analysis, Data Processing and Exploratory Data Analysis, and Bioinformatics and Pattern Discovery.

We would like to thank all the authors for their contributions. We also would like to thank the reviewers who helped ensure the quality of this publication.

November 2024

Jorge Bernardino
Ana Fred
Antonella Poggi
Le Gruenwald
Frans Coenen
Elio Masciari
David Aveiro

Organization

Conference Chair

IC3K

Jorge Bernardino   Polytechnic University of Coimbra, Portugal

Program Co-chairs

KDIR

Frans Coenen   University of Liverpool, UK
Ana Fred   Instituto de Telecomunicações and Instituto Superior Técnico (University of Lisbon), Portugal

KEOD

David Aveiro   University of Madeira, NOVA-LINCS and ARDITI, Portugal
Antonella Poggi   Università di Roma "La Sapienza", Italy

KMIS

Le Gruenwald   University of Oklahoma, USA
Elio Masciari   University of Napoli Federico II, Italy

Program Committee

KDIR

Amir Ahmad   United Arab Emirates University, UAE
Mayer Aladjem   Ben-Gurion University of the Negev, Israel
Eva Armengol   IIIA CSIC, Spain

Mohamed Ben Aouicha	University of Sfax, Tunisia
Marko Bohanec	Jožef Stefan Institute, Slovenia
Mohamed-Rafik Bouguelia	Halmstad University, Sweden
Alina Campan	Northern Kentucky University, USA
Jesús Carrasco-Ochoa	INAOE, Mexico
Luigi Cerulo	University of Sannio, Italy
Sharma Chakravarthy	University of Texas at Arlington, USA
Chih-Ming Chen	National Chengchi University, Taiwan
Chong Chen	Beijing Normal University, China
Zhiyuan Chen	University of Maryland Baltimore County, USA
Patrick Ciarelli	Universidade Federal do Espírito Santo, Brazil
Justin Dauwels	Nanyang Technological University, Singapore
Tai Dinh	Kyoto College of Graduate Studies for Informatics, Japan
Mihaela Dinsoreanu	Technical University of Cluj-Napoca, Romania
Thanh-Nghi Do	Can Tho University, Vietnam
Bilel Elayeb	Yncréa Ouest, L@bISEN, ISEN de Nantes, France
Iaakov Exman	Holon Institute of Technology, Israel
Dayne Freitag	Artificial Intelligence Center, SRI International, USA
Susan Gauch	University of Arkansas, USA
Josephine Griffith	University of Galway, Ireland
Gerhard Heyer	Leipzig University, Germany
Dorit Hochbaum	University of California-Berkeley, USA
Victoria Hodge	University of York, UK
Beatriz de la Iglesia	University of East Anglia, UK
Arti Jain	Jaypee Institute of Information Technology, India
Yogan Jaya Kumar	Universiti Teknikal Malaysia Melaka, Malaysia
Uzay Kaymak	Eindhoven University of Technology, Netherlands
Ron Kenett	Technion, Israel
Roman Kern	Know-Center GmbH, Austria
Ikuo Keshi	Fukui University of Technology, Japan
Margita Kon-Popovska	Ss Cyril and Methodius University, North Macedonia
Constantine Kotropoulos	Aristotle University of Thessaloniki, Greece
Jean-Charles Lamirel	LORIA, University of Strasbourg, France
Jie Liu	Western Oregon University, USA
Jake Luo	University of Wisconsin-Milwaukee, USA
Xiao Luo	Oklahoma State University, USA
Christos Makris	University of Patras, Greece
Saadia Malik	King Abdulaziz University, Saudi Arabia

J. Martínez-Trinidad	Instituto Nacional de Astrofísica, Óptica y Electrónica, Mexico
Dulani Meedeniya	University of Moratuwa, Sri Lanka
Enza Messina	University of Milano-Bicocca, Italy
Manuel Montes y Gómez	INAOE, Mexico
Agnieszka Mykowiecka	Institute of Computer Science, Polish Academy of Sciences, Poland
Simon O'Keefe	University of York, UK
Elias Oliveira	Universidade Federal do Espírito Santo, Brazil
Farhad Oroumchian	University of Wollongong in Dubai, UAE
Gaurav Pradhan	Mayo Clinic Arizona, USA
Alfredo Pulvirenti	University of Catania, Italy
Marcos Quiles	Federal University of São Paulo, Brazil
Chotirat Ratanamahatana	Chulalongkorn University, Thailand
Georg Rehm	Deutsches Forschungszentrum für Künstliche Intelligenz GmbH, Germany
Leonardo Ribeiro	Federal University of Goiás, Brazil
Marcela Ribeiro	Universidade Federal de São Carlos, Brazil
Farag Saad	FIZ Karlsruhe – Leibniz Institute for Information Infrastructure, Germany
Diana Santos	University of Oslo, Norway
Rui Santos	Polytechnic Institute of Leiria, CEAUL - Center of Statistics and Applications, Portugal
Alessia Sarica	Magna Graecia University of Catanzaro, Italy
Abeed Sarker	Emory University, USA
Claudio Sartori	Università di Bologna, Italy
Milos Savic	University of Novi Sad, Serbia
Filippo Sciarrone	Universitas Mercatorum, Italy
Asadollah Shahbahrami	University of Guilan, Iran
Dana Shapira	Ariel University, Israel
Marek Sikora	Silesian University of Technology, Poland
Wei Song	North China University of Technology, China
Julian Szymanski	Gdańsk University of Technology, Poland
Maguelonne Teisseire	INRAE, France
Marco Temperini	Sapienza University of Rome, Italy
Kar Toh	Yonsei University, South Korea
Suppawong Tuarob	Mahidol University, Thailand
Domenico Ursino	Università Politecnica delle Marche, Italy
Ishan Verma	Tata Consultancy Services, India
Manuel Vilares Ferro	University of Vigo, Spain
Jie Wang	University of Massachusetts Lowell, USA
Xing Wei	Pinterest Inc., USA

Albert Weichselbraun	University of Applied Sciences of the Grisons, Switzerland
Nicola Zeni	University of Trento, Italy
Yan Zhang	California State University, San Bernardino, USA

Additional Reviewers

KDIR

Roberto Asín	Universidad Técnica Federico Santa María, Chile
Abdelhalim Dahou	Independent Researcher, Germany
Zheng Fang	Pinterest, USA
Giacomo Frisoni	Universita di Bologna, Italy
Andrew Mackey	University of Arkansas, USA
Quan Mai	University of Arkansas, USA
Uttamasha Oyshi	University of Arkansas, USA
Juliana Wolf Pereira	UFMS, Brazil

Program Committee

KEOD

Mara Abel	Universidade Federal do Rio Grande do Sul, Brazil
Yuan An	Drexel University, USA
Stephen Balakirsky	Georgia Tech Research Institute, USA
Teresa Basile	Università degli Studi di Bari, Italy
Ralph Bergmann	University of Trier, Germany
Rafael Berlanga	Universitat Jaume I, Spain
Fernando Bobillo	University of Zaragoza, Spain
Rafik Braham	ISITCom, University of Sousse, Tunisia
Arif Canakoglu	Policlinico di Milano, Italy
Dickson Chiu	University of Hong Kong, China
Simona Colucci	Politecnico di Bari, Italy
João Costa	University of Coimbra, Portugal
Massimo De Santo	Unversità degli Studi di Salerno, Italy
Marne De Vries	University of Pretoria, South Africa
Mihaela Dinsoreanu	Technical University of Cluj-Napoca, Romania
Erdogan Dogdu	Angelo State University, USA

John Edwards	Aston University, UK
Faezeh Ensan	Ryerson University, Canada
Francisco García-Sánchez	University of Murcia, Spain
John Gennari	University of Washington, USA
Ronald Giachetti	Naval Postgraduate School, USA
Krzysztof Goczyla	Gdańsk University of Technology, Poland
Jane Greenberg	Drexel University, USA
Tiago Guimarães	University of Minho, Portugal
Anne Håkansson	UiT The Arctic University of Norway, Norway
Xudong He	Florida International University, USA
Stijn Hoppenbrouwers	HAN University of Applied Sciences, Netherlands
Martina Husáková	University of Hradec Králové, Czech Republic
Giovambattista Ianni	University of Calabria, Italy
Junichi Iijima	Tokyo Institute of Technology, Japan
Petar Jovanovic	Polytechnic University of Catalonia, Spain
Dimitris Kiritsis	EPFL, Switzerland
Jakub Klímek	Charles University, Czech Republic
Mitch Kokar	Northeastern University, USA
Tomislava Lauc	University of Zagreb, Croatia
Ulrike Lechner	University of the Bundeswehr Munich, Germany
Paulo Maio	Polytechnic Institute of Porto, Portugal
Jean-Luc Maire	Université Savoie Mont-Blanc, France
Kazuyuki Matsumoto	Tokushima University, Japan
Nives Mikelic Preradovic	University of Zagreb, Croatia
Michele Missikoff	ISTC-CNR, Italy
Owen Molloy	University of Galway, Ireland
Alessandro Mosca	Institute of Cognitive Sciences and Technologies, National Research Council (Italy), Italy
Olga Nevzorova	Kazan Federal University, Russian Federation
Jørgen Nilsson	Technical University of Denmark, Denmark
Alex Norta	Tallinn University of Technology, Estonia
Barbara Oliboni	University of Verona, Italy
Mihaela Oprea	Petroleum-Gas University of Ploieşti, Romania
Carlos Periñán-Pascual	Universitat Politècnica de València, Spain
Yehoshua Perl	New Jersey Institute of Technology, USA
Andreas Prinz	University of Agder, Norway
Thomas Risse	Goethe University Frankfurt, Germany
Colette Rolland	Université Paris 1 Panthéon-Sorbonne, France
Aires Rover	Federal University of Santa Catarina, Brazil
Duncan Ruiz	Pontifical Catholic University of Rio Grande do Sul, Brazil
Kurt Sandkuhl	University of Rostock, Germany

xii   Organization

Stefan Schlobach	VU Amsterdam, Netherlands
Johannes Schönböck	Upper Austrian University of Applied Sciences, Austria
Nuno Silva	Polytechnic Institute of Porto, Portugal
Derek Sleeman	University of Aberdeen, UK
Dagobert Soergel	University at Buffalo, USA
Víctor Sosa-Sosa	Centro de Investigación y de Estudios Avanzados del IPN, Mexico
Daniele Spoladore	National Research Council of Italy, Italy
Francesco Taglino	CNR-IASI, Italy
Giorgio Terracina	University of Calabria, Italy
Nico Van de Weghe	Ghent University, Belgium
Ludger van Elst	German Research Center For Artificial Intelligence (DFKI), Germany
Azeddine Zahi	Sidi Mohamed Ben Abdellah University, Morocco
Fu Zhang	Northeastern University, China
Nianjun Zhou	IBM, USA
Qiang Zhu	University of Michigan, Dearborn, USA

Additional Reviewers

KEOD

Antonio De Nicola	ENEA, Italy
Alexandr Kormiltsyn	Tallinn University of Technology, Estonia
Marco Manna	University of Calabria, Italy

Program Committee

KMIS

Leon Abdillah	Bina Darma University, Indonesia/INTI International University, Malaysia
Nekane Aramburu	University of Deusto, Spain
Michael Arias	Universidad de Costa Rica, Costa Rica
Benjamin Aziz	Buckinghamshire New University, UK
Giuseppe Berio	University of South Brittany, France
Claudio Biancalana	Roma Tre University, Italy
Kelly Braghetto	University of São Paulo, Brazil

Adriana Burlea-Schiopoiu	University of Craiova, Romania
Marcirio Chaves	Pontifical Catholic University of Rio Grande do Sul, Brazil
Eric Cheng	Education University of Hong Kong, China
Vincent Cheutet	Université de Lyon, INSA Lyon, DISP (EA4570), France
Chin Wei Chong	Multimedia University, Malaysia
Ritesh Chugh	Central Queensland University, Australia
Mikael Collan	Lappeenranta University of Technology, Finland
Laurent d'Orazio	University of Rennes, France
James Denford	Royal Military College of Canada, Canada
Mihaela Dinsoreanu	Technical University of Cluj-Napoca, Romania
Michael Dzandu	University of Westminster, UK
Kurt Engemann	Iona College, USA
Rik Eshuis	Eindhoven University of Technology, Netherlands
Benoit Eynard	University of Technology of Compiègne, France
Joan-Francesc Fondevila Gascón	CECABLE (Centre d'Estudis sobre el Cable), UPF, URL, UdG (EU Mediterrani) and UOC, Spain
Matteo Gaeta	University of Salerno, Italy
Francisco García-Sánchez	University of Murcia, Spain
Severin Grabski	Michigan State University, USA
Gabriel Guerrero-Contreras	University of Cádiz, Spain
Keith Harman	Liberty University, USA
Anca Daniela Ionita	University Politehnica of Bucharest, Romania
Dimka Karastoyanova	University of Groningen, Netherlands
Marite Kirikova	Riga Technical University, Latvia
Erhun Kundakcioğlu	Özyeğin University, Turkey
Dominique Laurent	ETIS Laboratory CNRS UMR 8051 - CY Cergy Paris University - ENSEA, France
Fernando Laurindo	University of São Paulo, Brazil
Michael Leyer	University of Rostock, Germany
Kecheng Liu	University of Reading, UK
Carlos Malcher Bastos	Universidade Federal Fluminense, Brazil
Ra'ed Masa'deh	University of Jordan, Jordan
Nada Matta	University of Technology of Troyes, France
Sally McClean	University of Ulster, UK
Brahami Menaouer	National Polytechnic School of Oran (ENPOran), Algeria
Birendra Mishra	Anderson Graduate School of Management, USA
Michele Missikoff	ISTC-CNR, Italy
Owen Molloy	University of Galway, Ireland

Oswaldo Moscoso-Zea   Universidad Tecnológica Equinoccial, Ecuador
Rohana Ngah   Universiti Teknologi MARA, Malaysia
Pham Ngoc   National Economics University, Vietnam
Alex Norta   Tallinn University of Technology, Estonia
Mazni Omar   Universiti Utara Malaysia, Malaysia
Faizuniah Pangil   Universiti Utara Malaysia, Malaysia
Iraklis Paraskakis   South East European Research Centre, Greece
Wilma Penzo   University of Bologna, Italy
Quoc Trung Pham   HCMC University of Technology, Vietnam
Dara Pir   City University of New York, USA
Pedro Luiz Pizzigatti Correa Universidade de São Paulo, Brazil
Nicolas Prat   Essec Business School Paris, France
Arkalgud Ramaprasad   University of Illinois Chicago, USA
Nataša Rupcic   University of Rijeka, Croatia
Higor Santos   Pernambuco University, Brazil
Stanko Škec   University of Zagreb, Croatia
Alessandro Stefanini   University of Pisa, Italy
Costas Vassilakis   University of the Peloponnese, Greece
Anthony Wensley   University of Toronto, Canada
Wei Zhang   University of Massachusetts Boston, USA

Additional Reviewers

KMIS

Sowelu Avanzo   University of Turin, Italy
Aihua Han   University of Reading, UK
Alexandr Kormiltsyn   Tallinn University of Technology, Estonia
Hadi Novandish   Tallinn University, Estonia

Invited Speakers

Carlo Sansone   University of Naples Federico II, Italy
Nirmalie Wiratunga   Robert Gordon University, UK
João Gama   University of Porto, Portugal

Contents

Knowledge Discovery and Information Retrieval

Identification of Sex-Specific Gene Signatures for Atopic Dermatitis
Using Machine Learning Models 3
  Ana Duarte and Orlando Belo

Subset Pretraining for Enhancing Neural Network Training Efficiency 22
  *Bernhard Bermeitinger, Tomas Hrycej, Jan Spörer,
  and Siegfried Handschuh*

Enhancing Text Embeddings for Emotion Detection: A Study
on Dimensionality Reduction and Lexicon Filtering 37
  Hande Aka Uymaz and Senem Kumova Metin

Knowledge Graph Mining-Based Personalized Learning Path
Recommendation for English Learning: Leveraging Adaptive Techniques
for Improved Outcomes 57
  Duong Nguyen and Thu Nguyen

Enhanced Prediction of Post-Myocardial Infarction Complications:
Dual-Modality Analysis with Optimized Flow Cytometry Preprocessing
and Feature Visualization 93
  Nada Al-Dausari, Frans Coenen, Anh Nguyen, and Eduard Shantsila

A Generative Framework for Web Pages Classification Using Multi-modal
Topic Fusion 106
  *Domenico Benfenati, Antonio Maria Rinaldi, Cristiano Russo,
  and Cristian Tommasino*

A Systematic Literature Review on LLM-Based Content Classification 121
  Diogo Cosme, António Galvão, and Fernando Brito e Abreu

Enhanced Document and Database Integration for Advanced
Question-Answering in Enterprise Contract Management with LLMs
and Agents 150
  *Antony Seabra, Claudio Cavalcante, Joao Nepomuceno,
  Nicolaas Ruberg, and Sergio Lifschitz*

Knowledge Engineering and Ontology Development

Enhancing Bilateral International Trade Flow Analysis with Knowledge Graph Embeddings 177
Durgesh Nandini, Simon Blöthner, Mirco Schönfeld, and Mario Larch

Knowledge Management and Information Systems

Semantic Support in Standardized Environments 199
Daniel Spieldenner, André Antakli, Torsten Spieldenner, and Harkiran Sahota

From Lessons Learned to Project Triumph: Unveiling the Enablers and Barriers in Construction 229
Jeffrey Boon Hui Yap

How Does Automation Impact Healthcare Operations? A Model to Describe the Impact of Robotic Process Automation and AI-Enhanced Intelligent Automation in Healthcare 249
Jani Kaitosalmi and Milla Ratia

Uncertainty Analysis in Socio-economic Dynamic Microsimulation Models: A Literature Review 279
Miia Rissanen and Jyrki Savolainen

Utilizing ER Model Extraction for an Industry Data Validation Use Case 301
Philipp Schmurr, Andreas Schmidt, Maiko Friedrich, Karl-Uwe Stucky, Wolfgang Suess, and Veit Hagenmeyer

Design and Validation of a Digital Mindset Model: A Combination of Organizational Culture Theory and Design Science 326
Seyma Kocak and Jan Pawlowski

Artificial Intelligence for Improving Drivers' Emotional Intelligence: An Innovative Approach for Safer Roads 360
Ana Todorova, Irina Kostadinova, and Svetlana Stefanova

Systemic View on Creating Knowledge Maps: Putting the Pieces Together 386
Tatiana Gavrilova, Anna Kuznetsova, and Irina Leshcheva

Author Index 403

Knowledge Discovery and Information Retrieval

Identification of Sex-Specific Gene Signatures for Atopic Dermatitis Using Machine Learning Models

Ana Duarte(✉) and Orlando Belo

Algoritmi R&D Centre/LASI, University of Minho, Campus of Gualtar, 4710-057 Braga, Portugal
`id9618@alunos.uminho.pt, obelo@di.uminho.pt`

Abstract. Atopic dermatitis is a common chronic disease that affects the quality of life of patients and their families and is marked by cyclical periods of flare-ups and remissions. Although there is no cure for the disease, its symptoms can be alleviated with proper management. However, atopic dermatitis is a complex disease that manifests differently in men and women, and the molecular mechanisms behind flare-ups are not yet fully understood. Identifying the genes that characterise lesional and non-lesional skin could improve the current understanding of the key molecular mechanisms and facilitate the development of new targeted therapies. In this paper, we present a machine learning approach aimed at discovering candidate sex-specific biomarkers for the disease. First, we selected the differentially expressed genes and applied feature selection techniques and machine learning methods to reduce the number of features. After a backward feature elimination step, we obtained an 11-gene male signature, a 10-gene female signature and an 8-gene general signature. Based on an independent test and using a soft-voting classifier, we obtained an AUC of 0.839 and accuracy of 0.7222 for the male signature and an AUC of 0.650 and accuracy of 0.6667 for the female signature. For the general signature, the AUC and accuracy values obtained were 0.783 and 0.8, respectively. The results suggest the potential existence of sex-specific biomarkers for atopic dermatitis. Consequently, our proposed gene signatures could serve as a starting point for scientific investigations aimed at understanding how the molecular mechanisms of the disease differ between males and females.

Keywords: Machine learning · Atopic dermatitis · Gene · Sex-specific · Biomarkers · Precision medicine

1 Introduction

Atopic dermatitis (AD), also referred to as atopic eczema, is the most common chronic inflammatory skin disease [1]. The disorder is characterised by alternating periods of flare-ups and remissions, accompanied by symptoms such as redness, inflammation, severe itching, and excessive dryness of the skin [2]. The rashes can occur anywhere, but usually appear in skin fold areas, including the arms and neck [3]. Although nonfatal, AD is a debilitating condition that leaves an indelible mark on quality of life, with significant negative impacts on sleep, work productivity, daily activities and overall well-being [4]. Children are particularly affected by the disease, given that AD onset occurs before the age of 5 in 85% of cases and the symptoms tend to diminish or even disappear with increasing age [5]. Nevertheless, in many cases, they persist into adulthood. In high-income countries, around 20% of children and 10% of adults are affected by AD [6, 7]. The high prevalence in developed countries is possibly related to a higher degree of industrialisation and urbanisation [8–10]. In these countries, however, the prevalence of AD has stabilised, in contrast to low- and middle-income countries, where the number of new cases has increased in recent years [11, 12]. In addition to differences in the level of development between countries, the prevalence and severity of the disease vary widely depending on geographical region and culture, age, sex and ethnic background [8, 11, 13]. Despite significant progress in the management and treatment of AD in recent years, the underlying heterogeneity of the condition remains not fully understood. Both genetic and environmental factors are believed to play a decisive role in its pathogenesis [14]. However, the underlying mechanisms involved in the disease remain elusive, and a deeper understanding of the complex, multidimensional interactions is a major research priority [15].

Complex diseases such as AD are characterised not only by a broad spectrum of clinical manifestations, but also by their unpredictable course and response to treatment. The effective treatment of these diseases currently requires a strategy based on precision medicine. By combining molecular, demographic, environmental, lifestyle and disease symptom information, precision medicine aims to personalise the treatment and prevention of diseases to ensure that the right intervention is provided to the right patient at the right time [16, 17]. Although it is seen as the future of healthcare, the application of precision medicine to AD remains in its infancy and the management of the disease is still predominantly based on a "one-size-fits-all" approach [18, 19]. The development of new therapies tailored to each patient's profile has the potential to revolutionise current medical treatment. However, the prescription of personalised therapies depends on a thorough understanding of the molecular mechanisms involved in the onset and progression of AD [20]. As this is an incurable disease, scientific research should focus on the development of therapies that successfully control the lesions and shorten flare-up periods. In this sense, the identification of biomarkers able to distinguish lesional skin (AD-L) from non-lesional skin (AD-NL) in patients with AD may lead to a better understanding of the critical molecular mechanisms and to the development of new medicines specifically targeting these mechanisms. In particular, biomarkers based on omics, such as genomics, transcriptomics and metabolomics, offer enormous potential for AD research since they provide information at different pathological and molecular levels [21]. Omics data objectively quantify the entire population of any biological system of interest. Transcriptomic data, for example, measure the amount of messenger RNA molecules in a tissue or cell [22, 23]. The exponential advances in omics technologies have led to the increasing availability of omics data in biobanks, such as the UK Biobank [24] and the Estonian Biobank [25], as well as in public databases such as Gene Expression Omnibus (GEO) [26]. These repositories have been used extensively in recent studies and have contributed to groundbreaking advances in biomedical research.

The integration of omics with demographic data such as sex, age or comorbidities can be of great benefit for more accurate biomarker detection. Accurate biomarkers support the creation of complex and complete patient profiles, which are essential for effective disease management and treatment [19].

This paper is an extended version of our previous work [27]. Our goal is to help bridge the existing gap in the literature by advancing precision medicine in the management and treatment of AD. We applied machine learning (ML) algorithms to transcriptomic data with the aim of finding sex-specific biomarkers for AD. Our work was based on the hypothesis that sex plays a key role in the manifestation of the disease and that the development of eczema lesions is triggered by molecular mechanisms that differ between males and females. Based on these assumptions, we found two specific gene signatures, one for males and one for females, which could allow a more individualised analysis of the manifestation of the disease. We used ML techniques as they have proven to be particularly effective for processing high-dimensional data and capturing complex interactions between attributes [28, 29]. In this extended version, we give a more detailed description of our methodology and include the determination of a general gene signature without sex differentiation, which we have analysed and compared with the male and female signatures.

The remaining part of this paper is organised as follows. Section 2 begins with an overview of some ML applications for biomarker discovery in AD based solely on omics information. We then discuss some studies that emphasise the influence of the patients' sex on the disease and conclude with some research that uses ML algorithms to discover sex-specific biomarkers for Alzheimer's disease and tuberculosis. The third section describes in detail the methodology used in our study. First, we give a brief overview of the datasets used and explain how we performed the identification of differentially expressed genes. The next part deals with the data preparation and feature selection processes, as well as our strategy for ML modelling to identify specific and general gene signatures. The results are presented and examined in Sect. 4, including a brief analysis of some of the genes found and their association with AD. The final section summarises our main findings and possible directions for future research.

2 Potential of Sex-Specific Biomarkers in AD

The identification of disease-specific biomarkers represents a major challenge in precision medicine. Despite the enormous potential of gene-based biomarkers to improve disease detection, prognosis and treatment, the literature in this area is still at an early stage. Moreover, most of the work using ML focuses on life-threatening diseases, namely cancer [30–32]. In dermatology, melanoma and other skin cancers have been the main targets of ML applications for biomarker discovery, followed by systematic lupus erythematosus and psoriasis. On the other hand, only a small number of researchers have explored other diseases such as AD. Specifically, Zhong et al. [33] analysed expression profile datasets from the GEO database, including 129 lesion samples and 114 samples from non-lesional tissue. Using LASSO, the authors identified the genes GZMB, CXCL1 and CD274 as potential biomarkers to distinguish lesions from non-lesions. Additionally, the study conducted by Möbus and colleagues [34] enabled the stratification of AD patients into two different endotypes with different clinical characteristics.

The authors used the Boruta algorithm and a random forest model to identify relevant genes and predict the endotype to which the patients belong. Both papers point to potential biomarkers for AD that may have a significant impact on the management of the disease. However, these biomarkers may not be accurate enough as the phenotypic data of the patients such as sex, age or ethnicity were not considered in the studies, although they play an important role in the manifestation of AD.

Statistical studies have shown the influence of demographic data on the development of AD. Several investigations state that sex has an impact on the pathophysiology of the disease. For example, in a Swedish population-based study involving 3055 individuals, Johansson et al. [35] observed that the 12-month prevalence at 24 years was higher in females (20.5%) than in males (14.8%). A similar study in England [36] showed that the incidence of the disease is higher in males among patients under 2 years and patients over 70 years. However, for all other age groups, the authors concluded that the incidence is higher in females. Further investigations in different populations also concluded that the sex of the patients may affect the prevalence of the disease [37–39].

To date, there is no published scientific research on AD that has examined both the sex of the patients and omics data with ML algorithms. However, some studies have already been published in this area for other diseases. Bourquard et al. [40], for example, used nine different ML techniques to identify potential sex-specific biomarkers for Alzheimer's disease. The results suggest that separate analysis by sex leads to more sensitive results compared to combined sex cohorts. In addition, certain biological pathways appear to affect men and women differently. The authors argue that a ML approach to calculating the risk of developing Alzheimer's disease provides better results than using statistical methods. A study conducted by Krishnan and colleagues [41] describes the identification of a male and female gene signatures for tuberculosis in pediatric population from Kenya, South Africa and Malawi. The authors employed Boruta and the Random Forest algorithms for feature selection and ranking, respectively, and discovered four specific genes for males and females. Compared to previously reported gene signatures, the researchers concluded that performance improves following a sex-stratified analysis.

Despite the tremendous potential of sex-specific omics biomarkers, there exists a limited body of literature in this field, especially in the context of dermatological diseases. To fill this gap, this paper aims to propose sex-specific gene signatures for AD that can distinguish between lesions and non-lesions. To the best of our knowledge, this is the first attempt to apply ML algorithms to gene expression data to discover specific AD genes for males and females. These gene-specific signatures could improve the existing understanding of the disease and reveal sex differences in the molecular mechanisms that drive the manifestation of the disease. This understanding could lead to new insights and support the advancement of precision medicine in dermatology.

3 Methods

To achieve the proposed research objectives, we adopted a methodology that is organised into two main stages (Fig. 1). In the first phase, we focused on the identification of differentially expressed genes (DEGs) for males and females separately and for both profiles, using two datasets from the same platform. In the second step, we constructed ML models using the selected DEGs to determine both specific and general signatures.

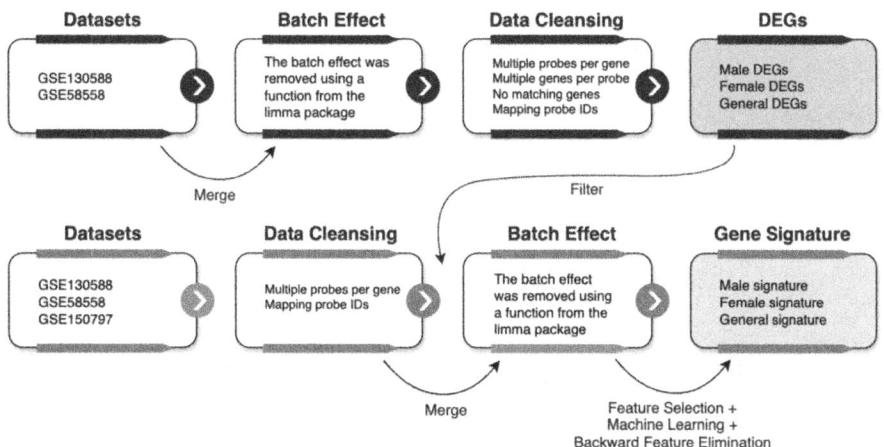

Fig. 1. Methodology of the proposed work (adapted from [27]).

3.1 Datasets Overview and Identification of DEGs

The datasets used in our study were retrieved from the public repository GEO[1]. Since combining datasets from multiple platforms may lead to data distortions [42, 43], we searched for transcriptome datasets from the same manufacturer (Affymetrix) that contained information on patient sex. Datasets GSE130588 and GSE58558 from platform GPL570 and GSE150797 from platform GPL23159 were selected for analysis. All selected datasets contain microarray data of skin biopsies from lesional and non-lesional skin, collected from AD patients before and after specific treatments. Since our aim is to find gene signatures to distinguish non-lesional from lesional skin, we only considered samples from patients before treatment. In total, the three datasets contain 175 samples, of which 100 are AD-L and 75 AD-NL samples. The AD-L samples correspond to 49 female and 51 male samples. The AD-NL samples in turn refer to 39 female and 36 male samples. Table 1 shows the distribution of the datasets.

Each dataset contains a gene expression matrix with more than 25,000 gene probes, i.e. fragments of RNA used to identify specific genes. The rows of each matrix correspond to the samples and the columns to the probes. Since the number of probes far exceeds the number of samples, ML techniques cannot be processed efficiently. Therefore, to reduce the initial feature set, we selected only the DEGs. DEGs correspond to genes that are expressed significantly differently when comparing lesional samples with non-lesional skin. For example, a gene that has a low average count in the AD-L samples and a considerably higher average count in the AD-NL samples is considered a DEG. These differences suggest that the gene may play an important role in the occurrence of

---

[1] [1]https://www.ncbi.nlm.nih.gov/geo/.

Table 1. Properties of the selected datasets.

Dataset	Requirements	Sex	AD-L samples	AD-NL samples
GSE130588	Week 0 LS or NL	Female	22	21
		Male	29	21
		Total	51	42
GSE58558	Day 1	Female	6	7
		Male	12	10
		Total	18	17
GSE150797	Untreated	Female	21	11
		Male	10	5
		Total	31	16

lesions. On the other hand, genes that do not show differential expression between the two conditions can be excluded from the analysis.

The DEG identification process was based only on datasets GSE130588 and GSE58558, which use the same platform. Considering datasets from different platforms increases the risk of introducing bias into the data [44]. In order to find specific DEGs for males and females as well as DEGs for a general signature, we combined the samples from each dataset into three profiles. The female samples from both datasets were grouped into one profile, the male data into a second profile and the entire data into a third profile, as shown in Fig. 2. In total, the first profile contained 28 AD-L and 28 AD-NL samples, the second profile 41 AD-L and 31 AD-NL samples, and the third profile 69 AD-L and 59 AD-NL samples. The datasets were merged into profiles and the DEGs were identified using the R software (version 4.3.1) and the limma package. The "removeBatchEffect" function from the limma package was used to eliminate possible biases resulting from the consideration of different datasets. In microarray experiments, probe sets are used to measure the expression levels of genes. Typically, a probe targets a single gene, but some probes may target multiple genes or no gene at all. Additionally, different probes may target the same gene. Before processing the data, all these situations were considered and corrected. Probes that matched more than one gene [45] and probes that did not match a specific gene were removed [46]. On the other hand, if different probes matched the same gene, we kept the probe with the highest average expression. In case of a tie in average expression values, we selected one probe and discarded the others [47]. Finally, all probes, expressed by their probe IDs, were converted to their corresponding gene symbols and the DEGs were determined. Genes with an absolute $\log_2(\text{fold change}) \geq 1$ and $p_{adj} < 0.05$ were considered as DEGs. The p-values were adjusted using the Benjamini & Hochberg method.

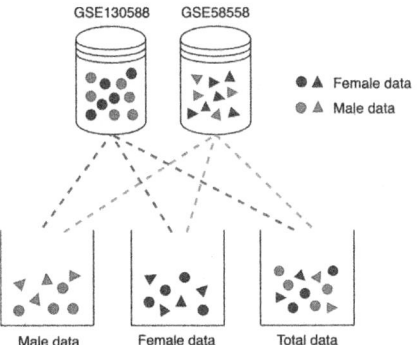

Fig. 2. Creation of male, female and general profiles for the identification of DEGs.

3.2 Data Preparation and Feature Selection

After identifying the DEGs, we proceeded to a second step to find gene signatures. Using the R software and considering all the three datasets, we created three profiles for each dataset – one that contained only male data (profile 1), one that contained only female data (profile 2), and one that contained both male and female data (profile 3), resulting in a total of 9 subsets. In each subset, only the probe with the highest average expression was retained when multiple probes matched the same gene, following the strategy described in Sect. 3.1. Probe IDs were also converted to their gene symbols and the features were filtered to include only the identified DEGs. By combining the subsets corresponding to the same profile into a single dataset, we obtained three datasets – one specifically for males, one specifically for females and one for both sexes. Since each of these datasets contained data from different experiments, we removed the batch effect for each.

Once the initial sets were prepared, each dataset was processed independently using Python 3.6 and the scikit-learn library. The processing included a first step of stratified splitting of the data (80% for training and 20% for testing). The stratified split preserves the original distribution of AD-L and AD-NL classes in the training and test data. To reduce further the gene set and promote a more effective use of the ML techniques, we added a second feature reduction step. Boruta, Support Vector Machine Recursive Feature Elimination (SVM-RFE), and Least Absolute Shrinkage and Selection Operator (LASSO) were the feature selection methods chosen to extract the most important gene sets. To avoid discarding important genes that might not be identified by a given method, our strategy was to identify the most relevant genes in different scenarios (Boruta, SVM-RFE and LASSO).

3.3 Machine Learning Models

The feature selection techniques yielded three different gene sets for each profile. The Random Forest (RF), XGBoost, linear Support Vector Machine (SVM), Logistic Regression (LR) and AdaBoost methods were applied to each of these sets separately and the accuracy and area under the ROC curve (AUC) values were obtained. To evaluate the ML models, we used a shuffled and stratified 5-fold cross-validation (CV) and optimised the hyperparameters of the models with BayesSearchCV (30 iterations). The hyperparameter values to be optimised for each ML technique are listed in Table 2. The ML methods used have the advantage of providing the importance values for each feature. New models were created based on the same techniques, varying the set of features and discarding the least relevant features. The set with fewer features and identical (or higher) predictive power was selected in order to prioritise the most important features. This procedure led to a further reduction in the number of features. The importance values of each feature were extracted and normalised to a value between 0 and 1 to facilitate the comparison of the importance values of the different methods. For each technique, all features that were not considered relevant were assigned importance values of 0 and the features with the highest importance value were assigned a value of 1. By summing the importance values obtained in the five ML techniques, we calculated the score of each gene and extracted only the top genes with the highest scores in each scenario. This process resulted in three distinct sets containing the top genes. By combining these three sets, we obtained our candidate genes for the signatures.

Table 2. Hyperparameter values to be optimised for each ML technique.

ML technique	Parameters
RF	n_estimators: [50, 80, 100, 250, 500] min_samples_split: (4,9) max_depth: (1,9) criterion: ["gini", "entropy"]
XGBoost	max_depth: (3, 10) gamma: (0, 1) subsample: (0.5, 1, 'uniform') n_estimators:(50, 100, 200) reg_alpha: [1e-5, 1e-2, 0.1, 1, 100] reg_lambda: [1e-5, 1e-2, 0.1, 1, 100] colsample_bytree: (0.5, 1, 'uniform') objective: ('binary:logistic','reg:squarederror','binary:logitraw') eta: (0.01, 0.3, 'log-uniform')
SVM	C: [0.1, 1, 100, 1000] gamma: [0.0001, 0.001, 0.01, 1] kernel: 'linear'
LR	penalty: ['l1', 'l2'] C: np.logspace(-4, 4, 20) solver: ['liblinear', 'saga'] max_iter: [100, 250, 1000]
AdaBoost	n_estimators: [1, 2, 3, 4, 5, 6, 7, 8, 9, 10, 11, 12, 20, 30] learning_rate: [(0.97 + x / 100) for x in range (0, 8)] algorithm: ['SAMME', 'SAMME.R']

To determine the gene signatures, we followed a backward feature elimination strategy. First, we constructed new ML models based on the same techniques and ranked the genes according to their importance value. Based on the AUC and accuracy, the feature that was considered least relevant by the set of five techniques was removed and the models were reconstructed. The metrics were recalculated and if their values did not deteriorate, the process was repeated iteratively, removing the gene with the lowest average importance. If the metrics deteriorate, the process ends, and the less important gene is not removed. All remaining genes form the gene signature of the profile under analysis.

The gene signatures were validated against the test data to determine the AUC and accuracy values. A soft-voting classifier that combines the predictions of the models was used for this evaluation. According to some researchers, this classifier leads to better results than using a single predictive ML method [48, 49]. Each of the gene signatures was not only applied to the data of the corresponding profile but also tested with the data of the other two profiles. These tests are important to compare the results and assess whether male and female specific gene signatures provide more accurate results when applied to the corresponding data profile. The answer to this research question is particularly important to understand whether gene signatures for AD should be sex specific.

4 Results

In the DEG identification phase, the combination of the GSE130588 and GSE58558 datasets resulted in a significant difference between the expression values of the samples in each profile. For example, Fig. 3 (left) clearly shows that the samples from the two datasets were divided into two different groups. After removing the batch effect, these differences were no longer visible (Fig. 3, right) and the DEGs were determined. In total, we obtained 188 DEGs for the male profile, 764 DEGs for the female profile and 394 DEGs for the general profile.

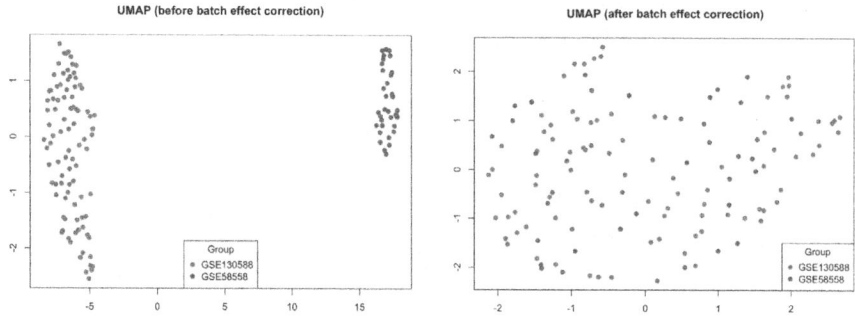

Fig. 3. UMAP for the male samples before (left) and after (right) batch effect correction.

Since the dataset GSE150797 was generated with a different platform, some DEGs did not match the probe IDs. Therefore, when we combined the data from the three datasets and filtered the columns by DEGs, we obtained 172, 700 and 394 DEGs in the male, female and general scenarios, respectively. For each scenario, after splitting the data into training and test sets, we obtained the following distribution:

- Male dataset: 70 samples for training (41 AD-L and 29 AD-NL) and 17 samples for testing (10 AD-L and 7 AD-NL).
- Female dataset: 70 samples for training (39 AD-L and 31 AD-NL) and 18 samples for testing (10 AD-L and 8 AD-NL).
- General dataset: 140 samples for training (80 AD-L and 60 AD-NL) and 35 samples for testing (20 AD-L and 15 AD-NL).

Applying Boruta, SVM-RFE and LASSO to the training data reduced the gene set to 12, 90 and 62 features in the male dataset; 23, 75 and 92 in the female dataset; and 13, 70 and 28 in the general dataset. Since the number of DEGs in the male dataset is relatively small, we included an additional scenario that considers all of these genes without applying any feature selection method. For each scenario, RF, XGBoost, linear SVM, LR and AdaBoost methods were constructed, and the importance values of each feature were obtained, as shown in Fig. 4.

By eliminating the least relevant features, we created new models and selected the optimal feature set for each technique. Table 3 lists the values obtained for AUC and accuracy in the general profile for each technique. An identical strategy was followed for the other two profiles. For example, in this case Boruta reduced the gene set to 13 features. The AUC and accuracy values were 0.8323 and 0.7786, respectively. The optimised feature set consisted of 3 features and the values of the metrics improved slightly (AUC of 0.8385 and accuracy of 0.7857).

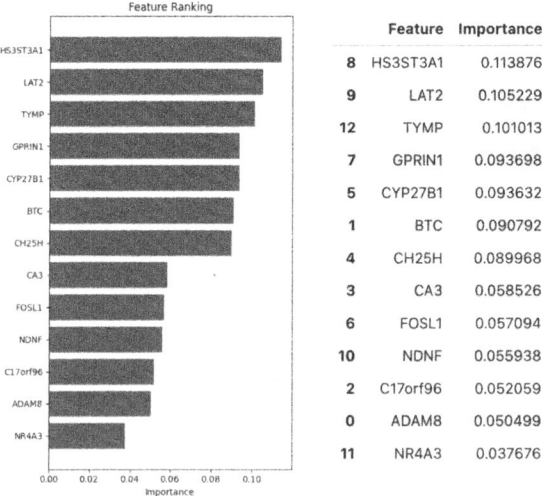

Fig. 4. Importance values obtained by the RF model with all features (13) in the Boruta scenario (general signature).

Table 3. AUC and accuracy values obtained for each ML technique for i) all features of the scenarios and ii) the optimised feature sets.

		RF		XGBoost		SVM		LR		AdaBoost	
		all	optimised	all	optimised	all	optimised	all	optimised	all	optimised
Boruta	Features	13	3	13	12	13	8	13	6	13	2
	AUC	0.8323	0.8385	0.8156	0.8510	0.8188	0.8615	0.8104	0.8479	0.7427	0.8115
	Accuracy	0.7786	0.7857	0.7929	0.8071	0.7786	0.7929	0.7929	0.8214	0.7357	0.7429
SVM-RFE	Features	28	12	28	15	28	12	28	27	28	1
	AUC	0.8385	0.8594	0.8344	0.8323	0.8563	0.8979	0.8854	0.8865	0.7125	0.7901
	Accuracy	0.8000	0.7929	0.7929	0.8000	0.7786	0.8357	0.8214	0.8857	0.7429	0.8000
LASSO	Features	70	9	70	8	70	65	70	61	70	8
	AUC	0.7865	0.8563	0.7865	0.8354	0.9427	0.9458	0.9354	0.9635	0.7255	0.8443
	Accuracy	0.7646	0.8286	0.7500	0.7929	0.8643	0.8714	0.8857	0.8929	0.6857	0.7929

From the models created considering the optimised feature sets, the importance values of each gene were normalised, and a score was calculated. Table 4 shows the final score for each gene in the general profile for the Boruta scenario. The score made it possible to select the most important genes in each scenario. Considering the scores obtained, the following genes were selected for the male profile:

- **Boruta scenario:** KIF2C, AKR1B10, PHYHIP, FOSL1, FPR1, and HS3ST3A1.
- **SVM-RFE scenario:** KIF2C, FOSL1, FPR1, MX1, KANK4, and PPARG.
- **LASSO scenario:** FOSL1, KIF2C, MX1, PHYHIP, HS3ST3A1, KANK4, and BCL2A1.
- **All DEGs scenario:** KIF2C, FOSL1, PHYHIP, AKR1B10, KLHDC7B, FPR1, and HS3ST3A1.

Similarly, the following genes were selected for the female profile:

- **Boruta scenario:** CEP126, FCHSD1, C17orf96, GNA15, IL18RAP, and P2RY10.
- **SVM-RFE scenario:** FCHSD1, C17orf96, IL18RAP, PTAFR, WIF1, STRIP2, PLAG1, MS4A14, and ANKFN1.
- **LASSO scenario:** C17orf96, IL18RAP, MS4A14, STRIP2, TBX18, P2RY2, AEN, GNA15, HSD11B1.

Finally, the following genes were selected for the general profile:

- **Boruta scenario:** HS3ST3A1, CYP27B1, CA3, NDNF, FOSL1, LAT2, TYMP, C17orf96, BTC, and NR4A3.
- **SVM-RFE scenario:** TYMP, LRRC20, SGCG, MSMB, CYP27B1, RGS18, CLC, CDH3, AGR3, CA3, ACOT11, WIF1, KIF2C, CLEC10A, ELOVL3, MYRIP, and ENPP5.
- **LASSO scenario:** HS3ST3A1, SERPINB3, SGCG, BTC, LRRC20, WIF1, FOSL1, PCSK1, and IGFL1.

Table 4. Raw and normalised values for each gene and technique in the general profile for the Boruta scenario, and the scores obtained.

Gene	RF		XGB		LR		SVM		AdaBoost		Score
	Raw	Norm.	Raw	Norm.	Raw	Norm.	Raw	Norm.	Raw	Norm.	
HS3ST3A1	0.340	0.994	0.093	0.801	0.229	0.790	0.388	0.760	0.556	1.000	4.345
CYP27B1	–	0.000	0.076	0.659	0.289	1.000	0.401	0.786	0.444	0.799	3.245
CA3	–	0.000	0.078	0.671	0.250	0.864	0.510	1.000	–	0.000	2.535
NDNF	–	0.000	0.060	0.519	0.286	0.989	0.379	0.743	–	0.000	2.251
FOSL1	–	0.000	0.073	0.629	0.199	0.687	0.317	0.621	–	0.000	1.937
LAT2	0.318	0.930	0.116	1.000	–	0.000	–	0.000	–	0.000	1.930
TYMP	0.342	1.000	0.082	0.709	–	0.000	–	0.000	–	0.000	1.709
C17orf96	–	0.000	0.101	0.868	0.144	0.497	–	0.000	–	0.000	1.366
BTC	–	0.000	---	0.000	0.222	0.766	0.252	0.494	–	0.000	1.261
NR4A3	–	0.000	0.066	0.566	0.184	0.636	–	0.000	–	0.000	1.203
CH25H	–	0.000	0.104	0.901	–	0.000	–	0.000	–	0.000	0.901
ADAM8	–	0.000	0.095	0.824	–	0.000	–	0.000	–	0.000	0.824
GPRIN1	–	0.000	0.056	0.487	–	0.000	–	0.000	–	0.000	0.487

Combining the top genes from the three scenarios for each profile led to the identification of the genes indicated in Fig. 5. C17orf96 and WIF1 were identified in both the female and general profiles, and FOSL1, KIF2C and HS3ST3A1 were found simultaneously in the male and general profiles. Accordingly, we selected an initial set of 11 candidate genes for males, 16 for females and 27 for the general scenario.

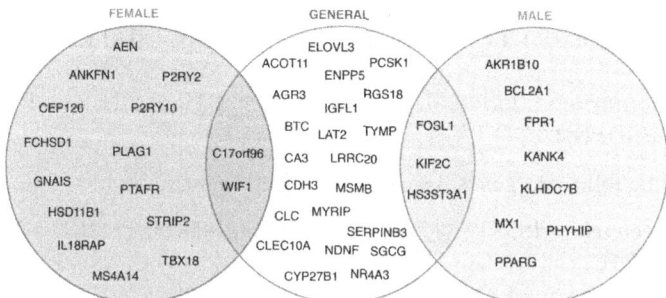

Fig. 5. Identified top genes for each profile.

Table 5. AUC and accuracy values obtained with the backward feature elimination strategy for the general, female and male gene signatures.

		RF		XGB		SVM		LR		ADA	
	Top	AUC	Accuracy	AUC	Accuracy	AUC	Accuracy	AUC	Accuracy	AUC	Accuracy
General	27	0.8385	0.7857	0.8260	0.8143	0.8229	0.7500	0.8646	0.8000	0.7958	0.7286
	26	0.8219	0.7857	0.8458	0.8000	0.8260	0.7714	0.8667	0.8000	0.7990	0.7500
	25	0.8531	0.8000	0.8570	0.8143	0.8292	0.7857	0.8698	0.8071	0.8115	0.7571
	24	0.8406	0.8071	0.8427	0.7929	0.8240	0.7929	0.8698	0.8071	0.8167	0.7500
	23	0.8490	0.8000	0.8490	0.8000	0.8250	0.7929	0.8688	0.8071	0.8115	0.7643
	22	0.8354	0.8000	0.8146	0.7929	0.8344	0.7929	0.8729	0.8071	0.8063	0.7500
	21	0.8458	0.8071	0.8479	0.7929	0.8469	0.8000	0.8719	0.8071	0.7958	0.7357
	20	0.8417	0.8000	0.8333	0.7929	0.8531	0.7857	0.8802	0.8000	0.8036	0.7500
	19	0.8563	0.8214	0.8583	0.8071	0.8490	0.7714	0.8740	0.8000	0.8036	0.7571
	18	0.8677	0.8071	0.8740	0.8000	0.8552	0.8698	0.8146	0.7500	0.8750	0.8214
	17	0.8885	0.8286	0.8552	0.8286	0.8563	0.8143	0.8781	0.7929	0.8052	0.7571
	16	0.8469	0.8143	0.8573	0.8143	0.8573	0.8000	0.8792	0.8143	0.8172	0.7857
	15	0.8458	0.8143	0.8583	0.8143	0.8573	0.8000	0.8750	0.8071	0.8130	0.7643
	14	0.8604	0.8143	0.8594	0.8143	0.8688	0.8071	0.8604	0.8286	0.8031	0.7714
	13	0.8500	0.8143	0.8568	0.8143	0.8740	0.8429	0.8708	0.8357	0.8281	0.7929
	12	0.8542	0.8000	0.8490	0.8214	0.8771	0.8214	0.8708	0.8357	0.8292	0.7786
	11	0.8521	0.8071	0.8552	0.8214	0.8875	0.8143	0.8740	0.8357	0.8260	0.7929
	10	0.8552	0.8143	0.8552	0.8071	0.8917	0.8214	0.8760	0.8286	0.8271	0.7714
	9	0.8583	0.8214	0.8573	0.8143	0.8833	0.8429	0.8771	0.8286	0.8536	0.8071
	8	0.8583	0.8214	0.8486	0.8214	0.8865	0.8357	0.8813	0.8429	0.8464	0.8000
Female	16	0.9208	0.8714	0.8625	0.8857	0.9708	0.9571	0.9542	0.8857	0.9375	0.8714
	15	0.9458	0.8714	0.8917	0.8714	0.9833	0.9143	0.9333	0.8857	0.9375	0.8714
	14	0.9208	0.8714	0.9167	0.8714	0.9792	0.9429	0.9250	0.8714	0.9167	0.8571
	13	0.9417	0.8714	0.8875	0.8714	0.9833	0.9571	0.9250	0.8714	0.9458	0.9000
	12	0.9417	0.8714	0.9167	0.8714	0.9833	0.9143	0.9375	0.9000	0.9418	0.9000
	11	0.9271	0.8714	0.9083	0.8857	0.9958	0.9429	0.9708	0.9143	0.9209	0.8571
	10	0.9500	0.8714	0.9000	0.8857	0.9917	0.9571	0.9667	0.9429	0.9709	0.9143
Male	11	0.8800	0.7956	0.8383	0.7956	0.9067	0.8242	0.9200	0.8242	0.8217	0.7956

With our backward feature elimination strategy, we obtained the AUC and accuracy values shown in Table 5. For the general profile, we obtained an 8-gene signature containing the genes AGR3, BTC, CA3, CDH3, FOSL1, LRRC20, NR4A3, and SGCG. For the male profile, we identified an 11-gene signature containing the genes KIF2C, AKR1B10, PHYHIP, FOSL1, FPR1, HS3ST3A1, MX1, KANK4, PPARG, BCL2A1, and KLHDC7B. For the female profile, a 10-gene signature with the genes CEP126, FCHSD1, C17orf96, IL18RAP, P2RY10, PTAFR, ANKFN1, TBX18, P2RY2, and AEN was found.

The signatures found do not show common genes between male and female profiles, suggesting that different molecular processes are involved in the manifestation of the disease in males and females. In the male profile, the genes KANK4, PHYHIP and PPARG were downregulated in the lesions, while the other genes were upregulated. In the female profile, the expression levels of ANKFN1, CEP126 and TBX18 were reduced in the lesions, while all other genes were overexpressed. In the general profile, the genes AGR3, BTC, CA3 and SGCG were downregulated, while the remaining genes CDH3, FOSL1, LRRC20 and NR4A3 were upregulated.

For some genes in the signatures, there are already some lines of evidence in the literature of a possible association with AD. For the genes in the male signature, for example, some authors argue that PPARG is related to the epidermal barrier function and that the expression of this gene is reduced in inflamed skin lesions. Its downregulation may also be related to keratinisation and sebaceous gland function [50, 51]. The overexpression of AKR1B10 has been noticed in several skin diseases, including AD [52]. Regarding the female signature, P2Y receptors, including the P2RY10 and P2RY2 genes, are believed to participate in skin inflammation [53]. Some authors also suggest that the IL18RAP gene is associated with AD [54, 55]. On the other hand, the BTC gene, which belongs to the general signature, is involved in skin regeneration and repair. Low expression of this gene increases the predisposition to the disease [56]. In a previous work, we conducted a study [57] to identify potential candidate genes for AD using RNA-Seq data instead of microarray data. Interestingly, BTC was also found in this study and proved to be one of the top 2 genes with the strongest predictive power for distinguishing between lesional and non-lesional skin. In turn, the results of a study conducted by Kagaya *et al.* suggest that the severity of AD correlates with higher expression of NR4A3, which is also part of the general signature.

Each gene signature was properly evaluated using the soft-voting classifier applied to the independent test of each profile. The results obtained are shown in Table 6.

Table 6. AUC and accuracy values obtained for each gene signature when testing with male, female and total independent test data.

		male data		female data		total data	
		AUC	accuracy	AUC	accuracy	AUC	accuracy
male signature	train	0.9737	0.8099	0.8543	0.8429	0.8063	0.75
	test	0.839	0.7222	0.575	0.6111	0.792	0.8
female signature	train	0.76	0.6659	0.975	0.9286	0.8219	0.7643
	test	0.552	0.6111	0.65	0.6667	0.775	0.8
general signature	train	0.8642	0.7813	0.8625	0.8286	0.8813	0.8357
	test	0.695	0.7222	0.7	0.7222	0.783	0.8

From Table 6, we can observe that the male signature has high AUC values (0.839) and high accuracy (0.7222) when applied to the male dataset only. When this signature is tested with female data, the metric values deteriorate significantly (AUC = 0.575 and accuracy = 0.6111). When we test with the entire data, the AUC decreases (0.792) and the accuracy improves (0.8). The significant difference between the results when using only male data and only female data suggests that there may be male-specific genes involved in the development of AD. Conversely, the female signature has relatively low predictive power in the independent test (AUC = 0.65 and accuracy = 0.6667) when tested with female data. Nevertheless, when tested against male data, it performs worse (AUC = 0.552 and accuracy = 0.6111). However, when the female signature is tested against the entire data, the results improve (AUC = 0.775 and accuracy = 0.8). This difference could be explained by the fact that the number of independent test samples in the total data (20 AD-L and 15 AD-NL) is significantly greater than the number of test samples in the female data (10 AD-L and 8 AD-NL). The limited number of test samples in the female data could have led to some kind of data bias. In addition, the number of samples used to identify the DEGs in the female profile (28 AD-L and 28 AD-NL) was significantly lower than the number of samples used to identify the male-specific DEGs (41 AD-L and 31 AD-NL) and the DEGs without sex differentiation (69 AD-L and 59 AD-NL). This aspect could lead to a poorer performance of the female signature compared to the other two signatures. Finally, when we test our general signature, we find that the metric values are high (AUC = 0.783 and accuracy = 0.8). However, the fact that the models for the general signature were created and validated with twice as many training and test samples as the male and female signatures may influence the results and not allow a fair comparison. The general signature loses predictive power when applied only to male or female data. Regarding the training data, this signature does not achieve the same high results as sex-specific signatures.

Overall, the results seem to show that there may be sex-specific genes for AD. However, the number of training (70 in both male and female datasets) and test samples (17 in the male profile and 18 in the female profile) is limited. Ideally, this study should be supplemented with more samples to increase the robustness of the conclusions.

5 Conclusions and Future Research

AD is a complex disease that is difficult to treat, and the incidence rates differ between men and women. Understanding the molecular mechanisms involved in the development of lesions could enable a better understanding and clinical management of the disease. Despite the potential of ML techniques and the considerable progress made in the field of omics technologies in recent decades, few researchers have investigated ML applications for AD based on omics data. In particular, we found no scientific studies aimed at using ML algorithms to identify sex-specific biomarkers for the disease. Considering this, this paper presents a ML approach based on transcriptomic data to identify general as well as male- and female-specific biomarkers capable of discriminating between lesional and non-lesional skin in patients with AD.

Our research led to the identification of a gene signature with 8 genes for the general profile, a specific 11-gene male signature and a 10-gene female signature. An analysis focusing on these genes and the mechanisms in which they are involved could lead to new insights allowing a better understanding of the disease and more personalised and effective treatment. For some of the genes in the signatures, there is already evidence in the literature of a possible association with the disease. In a previous work, we applied ML algorithms to RNA-Seq data and highlighted BTC as one of the most important genes for distinguishing between lesional and non-lesional samples. Interestingly, this work also led to the identification of the BTC gene in the general signature.

The results of our study support the idea that sex-specific gene signatures may contribute to improve the clinical management of AD. The signatures found do not share common genes between male and female profiles, suggesting that different pathways may participate in the development of lesions in males and females. Furthermore, the male signature performs considerably better when applied to the male data than when applied to the female data. The same is true for the female signature, which performs better on female data than on male data. The general signature loses predictive power when applied exclusively to male or female data.

Despite the promising results, some potential weaknesses need to be considered and addressed in future research. The most important limitation is due to the small number of samples analysed. Current public biobanks still have a limited number of samples containing both omics and demographic information, such as the sex of the patients. Given the small sample size, the results must be interpreted with caution. Ideally, it would be beneficial to repeat the study with a larger sample size to ensure greater confidence in the results obtained. In future work, it would also be interesting to investigate the influence of additional demographic data beyond patients' sex and to apply the proposed methodology to other diseases. The genes identified in each signature need to be clinically validated. Moreover, these genes should be analysed in scientific studies to understand how the molecular mechanisms involved in AD differ between males and females.

Acknowledgments. This work has been supported by FCT – Fundação para a Ciência e Tecnologia within the R&D Unit Project Scope UID/00319/Centro ALGORITMI (ALGORITMI/UM), and the PhD grant: 2022.12728.BD.

Disclosure of Interests. The authors have no competing interests to declare that are relevant to the content of this article.

References

1. Chu, D.K., Koplin, J.J., Ahmed, T., Islam, N., Chang, C.L., Lowe, A.J.: How to prevent atopic dermatitis (Eczema) in 2024: theory and evidence. J. Allergy Clin. Immunol. In Pract. **12**, 1695–1704 (2024). https://doi.org/10.1016/j.jaip.2024.04.048
2. Chovatiya, R.: Atopic dermatitis (Eczema). JAMA **329**, 268 (2023). https://doi.org/10.1001/jama.2022.21457
3. Siegfried, E.C., et al.: Dupilumab treatment leads to rapid and consistent improvement of atopic dermatitis in all anatomical regions in patients aged 6 months to 5 years. Dermatol. Ther. (Heidelb). **13**, 1987–2000 (2023). https://doi.org/10.1007/s13555-023-00960-w
4. Koszorú, K., Borza, J., Gulácsi, L., Sárdy, M.: Quality of life in patients with atopic dermatitis. Cutis **104**, 174–177 (2019)

5. Pyun, B.Y.: Natural history and risk factors of atopic dermatitis in children. Allergy Asthma Immunol. Res. **7**, 101–105 (2015). https://doi.org/10.4168/aair.2015.7.2.101
6. Bylund, S., Von Kobyletzki, L.B., Svalstedt, M., Svensson, Å.: Prevalence and incidence of atopic dermatitis: a systematic review. Acta Derm. Venereol. **100**, 320–329 (2020). https://doi.org/10.2340/00015555-3510
7. Laughter, M.R., et al.: The global burden of atopic dermatitis: lessons from the global burden of disease study 1990–2017. Br. J. Dermatol. **184**, 304–309 (2021). https://doi.org/10.1111/bjd.19580
8. Schuler, C.F., Billi, A.C., Maverakis, E., Tsoi, L.C., Gudjonsson, J.E.: Novel insights into atopic dermatitis. J. Allergy Clin. Immunol. **151**, 1145–1154 (2023). https://doi.org/10.1016/j.jaci.2022.10.023
9. Skevaki, C., Ngocho, J.S., Amour, C., Schmid-Grendelmeier, P., Mmbaga, B.T., Renz, H.: Epidemiology and management of asthma and atopic dermatitis in Sub-Saharan Africa. J. Allergy Clin. Immunol. **148**, 1378–1386 (2021). https://doi.org/10.1016/j.jaci.2021.10.019
10. Tsai, T.-F., et al.: Burden of atopic dermatitis in Asia. J. Dermatol. **46**, 825–834 (2019). https://doi.org/10.1111/1346-8138.15048
11. Nutten, S.: Atopic dermatitis: global epidemiology and risk factors. Ann. Nutr. Metab. **66**, 8–16 (2015). https://doi.org/10.1159/000370220
12. Faye, O., et al.: Atopic dermatitis: a global health perspective. J. Eur. Acad. Dermatol. Venereol. **38**, 801–811 (2024). https://doi.org/10.1111/jdv.19723
13. Mesjasz, A., Kołkowski, K., Wollenberg, A., Trzeciak, M.: How to understand personalized medicine in atopic dermatitis nowadays? Int. J. Mol. Sci. **24**, (2023). https://doi.org/10.3390/ijms24087557
14. Chovatiya, R., Silverberg, J.I.: The heterogeneity of atopic dermatitis. J. Drugs Dermatol. **21**, 172–176 (2022). https://doi.org/10.36849/JDD.6408
15. Nakamura, T., Haider, S., Custovic, A.: Understanding the heterogeneity of atopic dermatitis in childhood. Curr. Allergy Clin. Immunol. **31**, 124–130 (2018)
16. Wang, R.C., Wang, Z.: Precision medicine: disease subtyping and tailored treatment. Cancers (Basel). **15**, (2023). https://doi.org/10.3390/cancers15153837
17. Steele, R., Paardekooper, C., Steenhuis, S., Boonen, L.: Talking value: a taxonomy on value-based healthcare (2022)
18. Mastraftsi, S., et al.: Atopic dermatitis: striving for reliable biomarkers. J Clin. Med. **11**, (2022). https://doi.org/10.3390/jcm11164639
19. Muraro, A., et al.: Precision medicine in patients with allergic diseases: airway diseases and atopic dermatitis - PRACTALL document of the European academy of allergy and clinical immunology and the American academy of Allergy, asthma & immunology. J. Allergy Clin. Immunol. **137**, 1347–1358 (2016). https://doi.org/10.1016/j.jaci.2016.03.010
20. Arkwright, P.D., Koplin, J.J.: Challenging best practice of atopic dermatitis. J. Allergy Clin. Immunol. Pract. **11**, 1391–1393 (2023). https://doi.org/10.1016/j.jaip.2023.03.023
21. He, X., Liu, X., Zuo, F., Shi, H., Jing, J.: Artificial intelligence-based multi-omics analysis fuels cancer precision medicine. Semin. Cancer Biol. **88**, 187–200 (2023). https://doi.org/10.1016/j.semcancer.2022.12.009
22. Poinsignon, T., Poulain, P., Gallopin, M., Lelandais, G.: Working with omics data: an interdisciplinary challenge at the crossroads of biology and computer science. In: NeuroMethods, pp. 313–330. Humana Press Inc. (2023). https://doi.org/10.1007/978-1-0716-3195-9_10
23. Vailati-Riboni, M., Palombo, V., Loor, J.J.: What are omics sciences? In: Periparturient Diseases of Dairy Cows: A Systems Biology Approach, pp. 1–7. Springer (2017). https://doi.org/10.1007/978-3-319-43033-1_1
24. UK Biobank, https://www.ukbiobank.ac.uk/, Accessed 03 May 2022
25. Estonian Biobank, https://genomics.ut.ee/en/content/estonian-biobank, Accessed 27 Dec 2024

26. Edgar, R., Domrachev, M., Lash, A.E.: Gene expression Omnibus: NCBI gene expression and hybridization array data repository. Nucleic Acids Res. **30**, 207–210 (2002)
27. Duarte, A., Belo, O.: Machine learning unravels sex-specific biomarkers for atopic dermatitis. In: Proceedings of the 16th International Joint Conference on Knowledge Discovery, Knowledge Engineering and Knowledge Management, pp. 27–35. SCITEPRESS - Science and Technology Publications (2024). https://doi.org/10.5220/0012890700003838
28. Karthik, S., Sudha, M.: A survey on machine learning approaches in gene expression classification in modelling computational diagnostic system for complex diseases. Int. J. Eng. Adv. Technol. (IJEAT). **8**, 182–191 (2018)
29. Liu, J., Liu, L., Antwi, P.A., Luo, Y., Liang, F.: Identification and validation of the diagnostic characteristic genes of ovarian cancer by bioinformatics and machine learning. Front Genet. **13**, (2022). https://doi.org/10.3389/fgene.2022.858466
30. Koppad, S., Basava, A., Nash, K., Gkoutos, G. V., Acharjee, A.: Machine learning-based identification of colon cancer candidate diagnostics genes. Biology (Basel). **11**, (2022). https://doi.org/10.3390/biology11030365
31. Mirza, Z., et al.: Identification of novel diagnostic and prognostic gene signature biomarkers for breast cancer using artificial intelligence and machine learning assisted transcriptomics analysis. Cancers (Basel). **15**, (2023). https://doi.org/10.3390/cancers15123237
32. Tian, L., et al.: A cancer associated fibroblasts-related six-gene panel for anti-PD-1 therapy in melanoma driven by weighted correlation network analysis and supervised machine learning. Front Med (Lausanne). **9**, (2022). https://doi.org/10.3389/fmed.2022.880326
33. Zhong, Y., Qin, K., Li, L., Liu, H., Xie, Z., Zeng, K.: Identification of immunological biomarkers of atopic dermatitis by integrated analysis to determine molecular targets for diagnosis and therapy. Int J Gen Med. **14**, 8193–8209 (2021). https://doi.org/10.2147/IJGM.S331119
34. Möbus, L., et al.: Blood transcriptome profiling identifies 2 candidate endotypes of atopic dermatitis. J. Allergy Clin. Immunol. **150**, 385–395 (2022). https://doi.org/10.1016/j.jaci.2022.02.001
35. Johansson, E.K., et al.: Prevalence and characteristics of atopic dermatitis among young adult females and males - report from the Swedish population-based study BAMSE. J. Eur. Acad. Dermatol. Venereol. **36**, 698–704 (2022). https://doi.org/10.1111/JDV.17929
36. de Lusignan, S., et al.: The epidemiology of eczema in children and adults in England: a population-based study using primary care data. Clin Exp Allergy **51**, 471–482 (2021). https://doi.org/10.1111/cea.13784
37. Kiiski, V., Salava, A., Susitaival, P., Barnhill, S., Remitz, A., Heliovaara, M.: Atopic dermatitis in adults: a population-based study in Finland. Int. J. Dermatol. **61**, 324–330 (2022). https://doi.org/10.1111/ijd.15912
38. Pesce, G., et al.: Adult eczema in Italy: prevalence and associations with environmental factors. J. Eur. Acad. Dermatol. Venereol. **29**, 1180–1187 (2015). https://doi.org/10.1111/jdv.12784
39. Silverberg, J.I., Hanifin, J.M.: Adult eczema prevalence and associations with asthma and other health and demographic factors: a US population-based study. J. Allergy Clin. Immunol. **132**, 1132–1138 (2013). https://doi.org/10.1016/j.jaci.2013.08.031
40. Bourquard, T., et al.: Functional variants identify sex-specific genes and pathways in Alzheimer's Disease. Nat Commun. **14**, (2023). https://doi.org/10.1038/s41467-023-38374-z
41. Krishnan, P., Bobak, C.A., Hill, J.E.: Sex-specific blood-derived RNA biomarkers for childhood tuberculosis. Sci. Rep. **14**, (2024). https://doi.org/10.1038/s41598-024-66946-6
42. Liu, L., Wang, T., Huang, D., Song, D.: Comprehensive analysis of differentially expressed genes in clinically diagnosed irreversible pulpitis by multiplatform data integration using a robust rank aggregation approach. J. Endod. **47**, 1365–1375 (2021). https://doi.org/10.1016/j.joen.2021.07.007

43. Serio, P.: Gene expression microarray merging, https://rpubs.com/Karksus/1013177, Accessed 12 Feb 2024
44. Campain, A., Yang, Y.H.: Comparison study of microarray meta-analysis methods. BMC Bioinf. **11**, (2010). https://doi.org/10.1186/1471-2105-11-408
45. Hu, Y., et al.: Identification of diagnostic immune-related gene biomarkers for predicting heart failure after acute myocardial infarction. Open Med. **18**, (2023). https://doi.org/10.1515/med-2023-0878
46. Ji, W., An, K., Wang, C., Wang, S.: Bioinformatics analysis of diagnostic biomarkers for Alzheimer's disease in peripheral blood based on sex differences and support vector machine algorithm. Hereditas. **159**, (2022). https://doi.org/10.1186/s41065-022-00252-x
47. Miller, J.A., et al.: Strategies for aggregating gene expression data: the collapseRows R function. BMC Bioinf. **12**, (2011). https://doi.org/10.1186/1471-2105-12-322
48. Kumari, S., Kumar, D., Mittal, M.: An ensemble approach for classification and prediction of diabetes mellitus using soft voting classifier. Int. J. Cogn. Comput. Eng. **2**, 40–46 (2021). https://doi.org/10.1016/j.ijcce.2021.01.001
49. Srinivas, A., Mosiganti, J.P.: A brain stroke detection model using soft voting based ensemble machine learning classifier. Measure. Sens. **29**, (2023). https://doi.org/10.1016/j.measen.2023.100871
50. Konger, R.L., et al.: Epidermal pparγ is a key homeostatic regulator of cutaneous inflammation and barrier function in mouse skin. Int. J. Mol. Sci. **22**, (2021). https://doi.org/10.3390/ijms22168634
51. Blunder, S., Krimbacher, T., Moosbrugger-Martinz, V., Gruber, R., Schmuth, M., Dubrac, S.: Keratinocyte-derived IL-1β induces PPARG downregulation and PPARD upregulation in human reconstructed epidermis following barrier impairment. Exp. Dermatol. **30**, 1298–1308 (2021). https://doi.org/10.1111/exd.14323
52. Endo, S., Matsunaga, T., Nishinaka, T.: The role of AKR1B10 in physiology and pathophysiology. Metabolites. **11**, (2021). https://doi.org/10.3390/metabo11060332
53. Pastore, S., et al.: Stimulation of purinergic receptors modulates chemokine expression in human keratinocytes. J. Investig. Dermatol. **127**, 660–667 (2007). https://doi.org/10.1038/sj.jid.5700591
54. Vaher, H., et al.: Skin Colonization with S. aureus can lead to increased NLRP1 inflammasome activation in patients with atopic dermatitis. J. Invest. Dermatol. **143**, 1268–1278.e8 (2023). https://doi.org/10.1016/j.jid.2023.01.013
55. Hirota, T., et al.: Genome-wide association study identifies eight new susceptibility loci for atopic dermatitis in the Japanese population. Nat. Genet. **44**, 1222–1226 (2012). https://doi.org/10.1038/ng.2438
56. Zhu, J., Wang, Z., Chen, F.: Association of key genes and pathways with atopic dermatitis by bioinformatics analysis. Med. Sci. Monit. **25**, 4353–4361 (2019). https://doi.org/10.12659/MSM.916525
57. Duarte, A., Belo, O.: A novel signature for distinguishing non-lesional from lesional skin of atopic dermatitis based on a machine learning approach. In: Maglogiannis, I., Iliadis, L., Macintyre, J., Avlonitis, M., Papaleonidas, A. (eds.) IFIP Advances in Information and Communication Technology, pp. 3–16. Springer, Cham (2024). https://doi.org/10.1007/978-3-031-63211-2_1

Subset Pretraining for Enhancing Neural Network Training Efficiency

Bernhard Bermeitinger[1(✉)], Tomas Hrycej[2], Jan Spörer[2], and Siegfried Handschuh[2]

[1] Institute of Computer Science in Vorarlberg, University of St. Gallen (HSG), Dornbirn, Austria
`{bernhard.bermeitinger}@unisg.ch`
[2] Institute of Computer Science, University of St. Gallen (HSG), St. Gallen, Switzerland
`{tomas.hrycej,jan.spoerer,siegfried.handschuh}@unisg.ch`

Abstract. We propose a novel alternative to traditional randomly sampled mini-batches for gradient computation: using a fixed subset for complete pretraining of a neural network model. This approach enables deterministic convergence instead of a merely probabilistic one, as proven by the stochastic approximation theory, whose prerequisites are frequently violated by popular optimization algorithms. The approach is justified by the hypothesis that the loss minimum of the training set can be expected to be well-approximated by the minima of its subsets. Such subset minima can be computed in a fraction of the time necessary for optimizing with the whole training set. They are also compatible with efficient second-order optimization methods, such as the conjugate gradient optimizer. These methods are particularly efficient in the convex environment of the loss minimum. The image classification datasets MNIST, CIFAR-10, and CIFAR-100, (optionally extended by augmentation of training data) test this hypothesis. The experiments confirm that the models achieve performance equivalent to that when trained with the conventional training scheme. In conclusion, if the overdetermination ratio for the given model and dataset sufficiently exceed unity, even small subsets are representative. This results in a possible reduction of the computing expense to a tenth or less.

This paper is an extended version of Spörer et al. [13].

Keywords: Deep neural network · Convolutional network · Computer vision · Efficient training · Resource optimization · Training strategies · Overdetermination ratio · Stochastic approximation theory

1 Introduction

The rapidly growing size of deep neural networks (such as those used for image or language processing) motivates striving for a maximum computing economy. The computations consist of minimizing a loss function expressing the discrepancy between the reference data and the model's prediction. By far, most minimization algorithms use the gradient of the loss function. Gradient computation is a critical operation that is responsible for most of the computing expenses. This is why efforts to enhance the computing economy focus on efficient gradient computation.

One widespread approach is determining the loss function gradient from subsets of the training data, called batches (or mini-batches). Different batches are used alternately to cover all training data during training.

Some arguments support this approach. Goodfellow et al. [3] refer to the statistical fact that the random standard deviation decreases with the square root of the number of samples (assuming a random distribution of gradient components). Consequently, the gradients computed from $1/k$ training samples ($k \in \mathbb{N}, k > 1$) have a standard deviation equal to the factor $\sqrt{k}$ of those gradients that would have been computed over the full training data. This is a valid idea.

Another popular justification arises from the stochastic approximation theory. Its principle applies when drawing training samples from a stationary population generated by a fixed but unknown model. Robbins and Monro [10] discovered this principle in the context of finding the *root* of a function $g(x)$, which cannot be directly observed. Instead, randomly fluctuating values $h(x)$ can be observed where the mean value equals the value of the unobservable function:

$$E\left[h(x)\right] = g(x) \tag{1}$$

The task is to find parameters of the underlying model that maps input features (here: image pixels) to output values (here: class probability distribution) by gradient descent. For the parameter vector ω of this mapping, it is expected that the mean of the gradient $h(\omega)$ with respect to the loss function computed for a single training sample will be equal to the gradient $g(\omega)$ across the whole data population. The local minimum of the loss function is where the gradient $g(\omega) = 0$, i.e. the mean value of $h(\omega)$. Under certain conditions, the root is found with probability one, however, with a concrete time upper bound, as proven by Robbins and Monro [10].

However, there are some shortcomings of this approach. One flaw is that the gradients of different batches could point in different directions. This can lead to an optimization direction that is a descent for one batch while being an ascent for another. Robbins and Monro [10] formulated the convergence conditions to cope with this. They require that for the update rule of the parameter vector ω in typical gradient descent with a learning rate α_t:

$$\omega_{t+1} = \omega_t - \alpha_t h(\omega_t) \tag{2}$$

the learning rate sequence α_t has to satisfy the two conditions:

$$\sum_{t=1}^{\infty} \alpha_t = \infty \tag{3}$$

and

$$\sum_{t=1}^{\infty} \alpha_t^2 < \infty \tag{4}$$

The first condition in (3) is necessary for the learning rate not to vanish prematurely before reaching the optimum with sufficient precision. The second condition from (4) provides a decreasing learning rate. With a constant learning rate, the solution would fluctuate infinitely around the optimum. This is because, in the context of error minimization, its random instance $h(\omega)$ will not diminish for individual samples. However, the gradient $g(\omega) = E[h(x)]$ will gradually vanish as it approaches the minimum. In other words, the gradients of individual samples will not vanish even if their mean over the training data is zero. At the minimum, $g(\omega) = 0$ will result from a balance between individual nonzero vectors $h(\omega)$ pointing in various directions.

Other shortcomings of this approach are addressed in Sect. 2. An alternative approach consisting of a complete pre-training of the model with the help of a fixed subset is proposed in Sect. 3. Computing experiments confirming the efficiency of the proposed approach are described in Sects. 4 and 5.

This paper is an extended version of the initial publication by Spörer et al. [13].

2 Shortcomings of the Batch-Oriented Approach

Utilizing a small portion of the training data to calculate gradients is generally acceptable. However, several deficiencies from theoretical viewpoints suggest potential improvements.

2.1 Violating the Conditions of Stochastic Approximation

The two conditions (3) and (4) for convergence of the stochastic approximation procedure to a global (or at least local) minimum stem from the stochastic approximation theory. Unfortunately, they are almost always neglected in the current practice of training neural networks. This may lead to bad convergence or even divergence. The common *Stochastic Gradient Descent* (SGD) with a fixed learning step size violates the stochastic approximation principles. However, even popular sophisticated algorithms do not satisfy the conditions. The widespread and successfully applied *Adam* optimizer [6] uses a weight consisting of the quotient of the exponential moving average derivative and the exponential moving average of the square of the derivative

$$\omega_{t+1,i} = \omega_{t,i} - \frac{\alpha m_{t,i}}{\sqrt{d_{t,i}}} \frac{\partial E(\omega_{t,i})}{\partial \omega_{t,i}}$$

$$m_{t,i} = \beta_1 d_{t-1,i} + (1 - \beta_1) \frac{\partial E(\omega_{t-1,i})}{\partial \omega_{t-1,i}} \quad (5)$$

$$d_{t,i} = \beta_2 d_{t-1,i} + (1 - \beta_2) \left(\frac{\partial E(\omega_{t-1,i})}{\partial w_{t-1,i}}\right)^2$$

with hyperparameters α, β_1, and β_2, network weights $\omega_{t,i}$, and the loss function E. β_1 is the decay factor of the exponential mean of the error derivative, β_2 is the decay factor of the square of the error derivative, and α is the scaling parameter of the learning rate. Their values have been set to the sensible defaults of the implementation framework $\alpha = 0.001$, $\beta_1 = 0.9$, and $\beta_2 = 0.999$ in the following computing experiments.

Normalizing the gradient components by the moving average of their square via $\sqrt{d_{t,i}}$ is the opposite of the decreasing learning rate required in stochastic approximation theory. If the gradients become small (as expected at the proximity of the minimum), the normalization increases them. This may or may not be traded off by the average gradient $m_{t,i}$.

2.2 A Good Approximation of the Gradient is Not Enough

The argument quoted in Goodfellow et al. [3, Section 8.1.3] that the standard deviations of the gradient components decrease with the square root $\sqrt{k}$ of the number of samples used while the computing expense increases with k is, of course, accurate for independent samples drawn from a population.

However, this relationship is only valid if the whole statistical population (a generally unavailable superset of the training data) is considered. This does not account for the nature of numerical optimization algorithms. The more sophisticated among them follow the descent direction. The gradient's statistical deviation is relatively small in respect to the statistical population, but this does not guarantee that a so-determined estimated descent direction is not, in fact, an ascent direction. The difference between descent and ascent may easily be within the gradient estimation error—the batch-based gradient is always a sample estimate, with a standard deviation depending on the unknown variance of the individual derivatives within the training data. In contrast, when the entire training data is used for optimization, the training data gradient is computed deterministically with zero deviation. This can be referred to as an *epoch-wise* gradient descent. Then, the descent direction is guaranteed to lead to a lower loss in the next epoch.

The sole objective of the optimization algorithm is to minimize the loss for the training data. If the goal of optimizing for the entire (explicitly unknown) population is adopted, the appropriate means would be biased estimates that can have lower errors on the population, such as ridge regression for linear problems [14]. The biased estimate theory provides substantial results concerning this goal, but also shows that it is difficult to reach. The superiority to the unbiased estimate is given only for a narrow range of regularization parameters. This range can only be determined empirically with the help of computationally expensive experiments using at least one validation dataset. The result may be substantially worse than the unbiased solution without careful determination of the appropriate regularization parameters.

Even if the loss is extended with regularization terms to allow the model to generalize to the whole population (represented by validation data), the optimized regularized fit is reached at the minimum of the extended loss function once again for the *given training data*. Thus, as mentioned above, it is incorrect from the optimization algorithm's viewpoint to compare the precision of the gradient of the full training data with that of the mini-batches, which are subsamples drawn from the training dataset. The former is precise, while the latter are approximations.

A related and frequently cited argument is that what is genuinely sought is the minimum for the population and not for the training dataset. However, this argument is somewhat misleading. There is no method for finding the exact minimum for this population, only based on a subsample such as the training data—the training data is the best and only information available. In addition, the loss function values used in the algorithm to decide whether to accept or reject a solution are explicit values for the given training data. The examples in [5] show that no law guarantees computing time savings by incremental learning for the same performance.

2.3 Convexity Around the Minimum is Not Exploited

Another flaw of batch-wise gradient descent is that in a specific environment of the local minimum, every smooth function is convex—this directly results from the definition of a minimum. Then, the location of the minimum is not determined solely by the gradient; the Hessian matrix also captures the second derivatives. Although using an explicit estimate of the Hessian is infeasible for large problems with millions to billions of parameters, there are second-order algorithms that exploit the curvature information implicitly. One of them is the *Conjugate Gradient* algorithm [1,4], thoroughly described in [9]. It requires only the storage of an additional vector with a dimension equal to the length of the plain gradient. However, batch sampling substantially distorts second-order information more than the gradient [3]. This leads to a considerable loss of efficiency and convergence guarantee of second-order algorithms, which is why they are scarcely used in the neural network community, possibly sacrificing the benefits of their computing efficiency.

Second-order algorithms cannot be used with the mini-batch paradigm for another reason: they are usually designed for a continuous descent of loss values. Reaching a specific loss value with one batch cannot guarantee that this value will not become worse with another batch. This violates assumptions for which second-order algorithms have been developed. Mediocre computing results with these algorithms in the batch-wise scheme confirm this hypothesis.

3 Substituting the Training Data with a Subset

In summary, training with batch-wise gradient descent suffers from three shortcomings:

1. It is not fully consistent with the requirements of the stochastic approximation theory and thus cannot claim convergence guarantees.
2. It does not guarantee the strict loss function descent in every iteration.
3. Its stochastic character prevents a meaningful use of the second-order algorithms, which are superior in convex regions of the loss function domain. Such convex regions are encountered with certainty in an environment around the minimum.

We propose a different approach, not suffering from the latter two shortcomings. It is also not stochastic, making the loan from stochastic approximation theory (the first of the shortcomings from Sect. 2.1) obsolete.

3.1 Hypothesis About the Loss for a Subset of the Training Data

In contrast to the gradient computation on random batches, the hypothesis followed here is related but essentially different. It adopts a fixed subset of the training data. It is assumed that *the optimum of the loss for the selected subset is close to the optimum of the full training data.*

Adopting this assumption provides important benefits for optimization. An outstanding property of the procedure using a fixed subset of the training data instead of varying batches is that both the gradient and the intermediary loss relate to each other for a fixed subset. This allows fast second-order optimization methods, such as the conjugate gradient (CG) method [9]. These methods exhibit superlinear convergence for convex functions, unlike simple first-order methods whose convergence may take an exponentially growing time with the number of optimized parameters. An important component of CG is the line search in the direction of the conjugate gradient. Line search is crucial for two reasons:

1. It ensures strict minimization in the descent direction.
2. The reliability of finding the line minimum is a prerequisite for the search directions to be conjugate. If the directions are conjugate, the progress made in the past directions is guaranteed to be unspoiled by the current update.

Line search requires deterministic loss values to embrace the minimum unambiguously. Such deterministic loss values are provided in the training with a fixed subset.

3.2 Properties of Subset Training

The loss computed over the subset is only an approximation of that over the full training data. Consequently, its minimum of the former is only an approximation of the latter. However, even if the minimum approximation is imperfect, it can be expected to be a very good initial point for fine-tuning over the full training data so that a few iterations may suffice to reach the true minimum. This principle is illustrated in Fig. 1. The subset loss function (dotted line) is not identical to the training data loss function (solid line). Reaching the minimum of the subset loss function (diamond) delivers an initial point for fine-tuning on the training data (circle). This initial point is close to the training data loss minimum (cross) and is very probably within a convex region around the minimum.

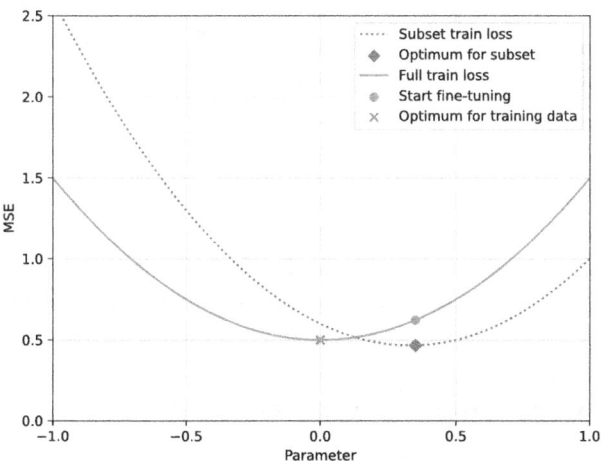

Fig. 1. Optima for a subset and the full training data.

Whether this expectation is justified depends on two factors:

1. the steepness of the side walls of the "bowl" formed by the convex loss function; and
2. the estimation error of the true loss minimum for both the subset and the full training data.

If the loss function is broad, that is, has a moderate slope, even imprecise minimum estimates will remain close to the minimum of the loss function. For narrow loss functions with steep slopes, the accuracy of minimum estimates is more critical.

We consider the mean squared error (MSE) as a loss measure for simplicity. The steepness of the loss function directly results from the Jacobian matrix of the model parameters

$$J = \frac{\partial y}{\partial \omega} \tag{6}$$

computed at the local minimum. Models strongly sensitive to the parameters will deliver steep and narrow loss functions, while resilient ones will deliver a broad loss function.

In linear regression models, the estimation error of the true parameters p depends on the training data via the formula for covariance of regression coefficients:

$$C_p = s^2 (X'X)^{-1} \tag{7}$$

with s^2 as the estimate of random residual error and X as the input data matrix.

The covariance matrix of output estimation errors is

$$C_y = s^2 X'(X'X)^{-1} X \tag{8}$$

The numbers on the diagonal of C_y correspond to the variances of the output estimates. With a larger variance, the loss minimum found in a subset may be more distant from the true minimum. The term $(X'X)^{-1}$ shrinks with the growing size of the training dataset X. So, for larger subsets, the estimate of the loss function is close to the true one, while the bias grows for smaller subsets.

Of course, the question is how large the subset has to be for the approximation to be sufficiently good. As noted, a smooth function is always locally convex around a minimum. If the approximate minimum over the training subset is in this environment, the conditions for efficient minimization for the second-order algorithms are satisfied. Then, a fast convergence to the minimum can be expected throughout the full training data.

Consequently, it would be desirable for the minimum of the subset loss to be within the convex region of the training data loss. According to the criteria mentioned above, this is the case for sufficiently large subsets and not excessively steep gradients.

4 Setup of Computing Experiments

The following computing experiments investigate the support of these hypotheses. The experimental method substitutes the training data with representative subsamples of various sizes. Subsequently, a short fine-tuning on the full training data is performed to finalize the optimum solution. The model is trained in the subsamples for exactly 1,000 epochs, whereas the fine-tuning on the full training data fixed to 100 epochs.

4.1 Dataset Selection

The benchmarks for the evaluation are chosen from the domain of computer vision. They are medium-sized problems that can be run for a sufficient number of experiments. This would not be feasible for large models and very large datasets, such as those used in language modeling.

Three image classification datasets are chosen: MNIST [8], CIFAR-10 [7], and CIFAR-100 [7]. MNIST contains grayscale images of handwritten digits (0–9) while CIFAR-10 contains color images of exclusively ten different mundane objects like "horse", "ship", or "dog". CIFAR-100 contains the same images as CIFAR-10; however, they are classified into 100 fine-grained classes. They contain 60,000 (MNIST) and 50,000 (CIFAR-10 and CIFAR-100) training examples. Their respective preconfigured test splits of each 10,000 examples are used as validation data. Although both CIFAR-10 and CIFAR-100 are evenly distributed among the classes, MNIST can be considered roughly evenly distributed. No further action is taken to handle this slight class imbalance.

4.2 The Model Architecture

The model is a convolutional network inspired by the *VGG* architecture [12]. It uses three consecutive convolutional layers with the same kernel size of 3×3, 32/64/64 filters, and the ReLU activation function. Each convolutional layer is followed by a maximum pooling layer of size 2×2. The last feature map is flattened and after a classification block with a 64-unit dense layer and the ReLU activation function, a linear dense layer classifies it into a softmax vector. The trainable parameters of all layers are randomly initialized from a uniform Glorot [2] distribution with a random but fixed seed per layer such that all trained models throughout the experiments have a guaranteed identical starting point. The biases of each trainable layer are initialized to zero. The number of parameters for the models only differs because MNIST has one input channel, while CIFAR-10 and CIFAR-100 have three, and CIFAR-100 has 100 class output units instead of 10.

4.3 Preventing Underdetermination of Model Parameters

An important criterion is that the size of the training data is sufficient for this procedure. The size of the training subsets (as related to the number of model parameters) must be large enough for the model not to be underdetermined. The underdetermination or overdetermination of the model results from the relationship between the number of constraints imposed by the task and the number of free model parameters. A classification task with N training examples and M classes imposes NM constraints (i.e., equalities that would be satisfied if all data were perfectly fitted). The model parameters in neural network structures with hidden layers are not necessarily completely independent as some redundancies (e.g., by permutation of hidden layer units or scaling of inputs and outputs of a layer) may and will appear. However, the number of model parameters P is at least the upper bound of the number of free parameters.

With $NM > P$, there are more constraints than parameters, so the former can be satisfied only approximately. For example, this is a typical case in linear regression and can be called the *overdetermined case*.

In contrast, the constraints can be satisfied with $NM < P$, and the number of equivalent parameter solutions is infinite. This is the *underdetermined case*. In this case, the parameters with perfect fit to the data are redundant; some attain arbitrary values. This leads to poor generalization, as these values are fitted to the training data but lead to arbitrary outputs for the validation data. This is the main reason for *overfitting*.

The *overdetermination ratio* Q [5] is a meaningful characteristic for this:

$$Q = \frac{NM}{P} \qquad (9)$$

For linear models, it can be shown that the fitting to additive noise depends on Q. It was shown in [5, Chapter 4] that fitting to the additive noise and thus the influence of the noise from the training data on the prediction of the model is reduced to the fraction $1/Q$. In other words, keeping the overdetermination ratio Q significantly greater than 1 is sensible.

This is the reason why the overdetermination ratio of each benchmark candidate are evaluated. The evaluated datasets must have the potential for training on a relatively small subset of the training data. However, subsequent fine-tuning on the full training data can "repair" a moderate underdetermination.

The two datasets MNIST and CIFAR-10 each have ten classes. This makes the number of constraints NM in (9) too small for subsets with $b > 4$. This is why the training datasets for these two are optionally enriched tenfold by random image augmentation. This procedure implies slight random rotations, translations, and contrast variations. The randomness is fixed for the experiments, resulting in equally augmented subsets throughout all training runs.

This problem does not occur on CIFAR-100 and its 100 classes, so these images were not augmented.

4.4 Processing Steps

The processing steps for each given benchmark task and an algorithm tested have been the following:

- The number of subsets b such that a subset is the fraction $1/b$ of the training data has been defined. These numbers have been: $b \in B$ with $B = \{2, 4, 8, 16, 32, 64, 128\}$. With a training data size N, a subset contains N/b samples. For example, a value of $b = 2$ results in two subset with each half of the samples from the original training data.
- All b subsets of size N/b are built to support the results statistically. Each subset N_{bi}, $i \in \{1, \ldots, b\}$ consists of training samples with index i selected so that the subsets partition the entire training data. For larger values of b, the number of experiments is excessive, so only three random subsets are selected. All randomness is seeded so that each experiment receives the same subset.

- For every $b \in B$ and every $i \in \{1, \ldots, b\}$, the subset loss E_{bi} is minimized using the selected training algorithm. The number of epochs is set to 1,000. Furthermore, losses are calculated for the complete training data E_{BTbi} and the validation data E_{BVbi}. Subsequently, fine-tuning is performed on the full training data for 100 epochs, and the metrics for the training data E_{Tbi} and the validation data E_{Vbi} are evaluated. In summary, the set of loss characteristics E_{bi}, E_{BTbi}, E_{BVbi}, E_{Tbi}, and E_{Vbi} represents the final results.
- For comparison, conventional training on the original training data is given by choosing $b = 1$.

The conjugate gradient algorithm would be the favorite for optimizing the subset (because of its relatively small size) and fine-tuning (because of its expected convexity in the region containing the initial point delivered by the subset training). Unfortunately, this algorithm is unavailable in popular deep learning frameworks such as *Keras* or *PyTorch*. This is why the above-mentioned Adam optimizer has been used. For reproducibility and removal of additional hyperparameters, a fixed learning rate of 0.001 was used for all training steps.

5 Empirical Results on Various Datasets

5.1 Dataset MNIST

The results for the non-augmented dataset MNIST are shown in Figs. 2a and 2b. The training has two phases:

1. In the *subset training* phase, only a fraction of the training data is used.
2. In the *fine-tuning* phase, the optimized parameters of the subset training phase are fine-tuned by a (relatively short) training over the full training data.

On the x-axis, the fractions of the complete training data are shown as used for the subset training. The subset variants are $1/2$, $1/4$, $1/8$, $1/16$, $1/32$, $1/64$, and $1/128$, as well as the baseline (fraction equal to unity). This baseline corresponds to the conventional training procedure over the full training data. The y-axis shows the evaluated metrics: the loss (categorical cross-entropy) and the accuracy, respectively.

The plotted magnitudes in Figs. 2a and 2b refer to

- *Subset (pretraining)*: Loss and accuracy reached for the given subset regarding the respective subset fraction $1/b$
- *Full data (pre-training)*: Loss and accuracy over the full training data at the subset training optimum after 1000 epochs
- *Validation data (pre-training)*: Loss and accuracy over the validation data at the subset training optimum after 1000 epochs
- *Full data (fine-tuning)*: Loss and accuracy over the full training data attained through fine-tuning after fine-tuning on the full training data for 100 epochs
- *Validation data (fine-tuning)*: Loss and accuracy over the validation data at the fine-tuning optimum after fine-tuning on the full training data for 100 epochs

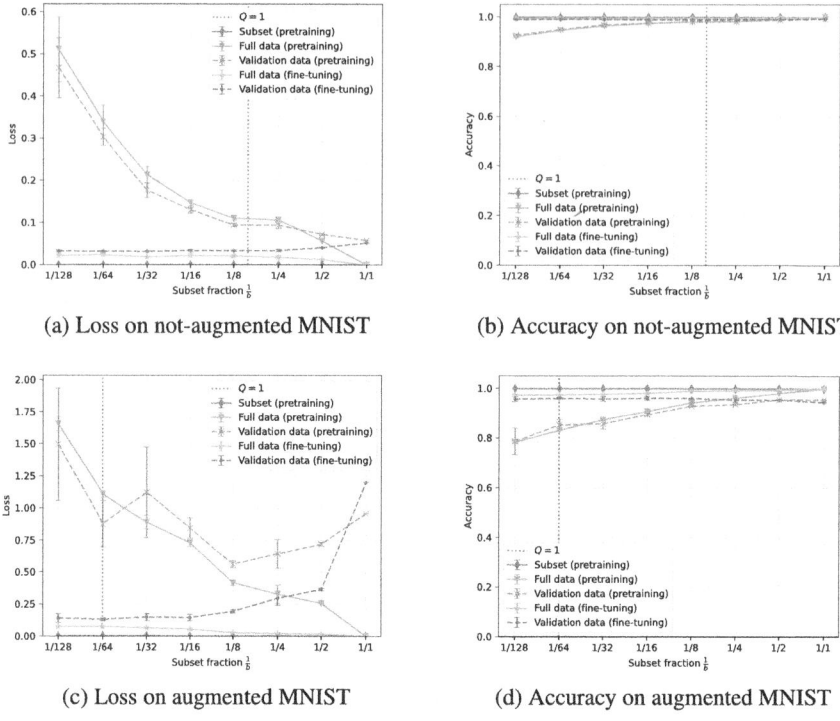

Fig. 2. Dataset MNIST: loss and accuracy for pre-training on the subset and the full training data in dependence on the subset size as a fraction of the training data.

All of them are average values over the individual runs with disjoint subsets, as can be observed by the error bars.

The vertical dotted line marks the subset fraction with an overdetermination ratio (9) equal to unity. To the left of this line, the subsets are underdetermined; to the right, they are overdetermined.

Both loss (Fig. 2a) and accuracy (Fig. 2b) suggest similar conjectures:

- Training with small subsets leads to poor losses for both the full training data and the validation data. This gap decreases with increasing subset size.
- Fine-tuning essentially closes the performance gap between the training and validation data. The optimum value for the training data tends to be lower for large fractions—since they have an "advance" from the subset training—but this does not lead to a better validation data performance. The baseline loss (the rightmost point) exhibits the highest validation data loss.

The overdetermination ratio, as shown by the dotted vertical lines in Figs. 2a and b, gives an additional finding: the gap between the performance on the subset and on the full training data after the subset pre-training is very large for $Q < 1$ (the left side of the plot) and shrinks for $Q > 1$ (the right side).

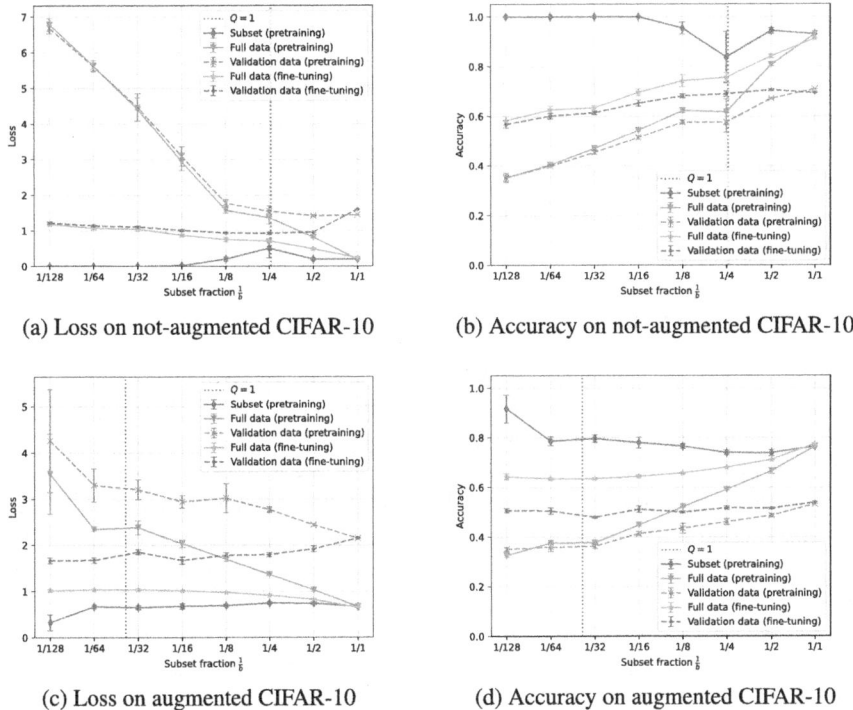

Fig. 3. Dataset CIFAR-10: loss and accuracy for pre-training on the subset and the full training data in dependence on the subset size as a fraction of the training data.

The results for the augmented data on MNIST are shown in Figs. 2c and d. As the augmented data are more challenging to fit, their performance characteristics are generally worse than those of the non-augmented dataset. However, an important point can be observed: the performance after the pre-training (particularly for the validation data) does not differ to the same extent as it did with non-augmented data. As with the non-augmented dataset, the baseline loss (the rightmost point) exhibits the highest validation data loss. There, the difference between the lowest and the highest subset losses has been tenfold, while it is roughly the same for all subset fractions with the augmented data.

The tenfold larger size of the augmented dataset leads to overdetermination ratios Q mainly (except for the fraction $1/128$) over unity. Then, even the small-fraction subsets lead to acceptable generalization performance (which is the goal of sufficient overdetermination).

5.2 Dataset CIFAR-10

The results for the non-augmented CIFAR-10 dataset are shown in Figs. 3a and 3b, those for the augmented data in Figs. 3c and 3d. Due to the size of CIFAR-10 being close to MNIST, the overdetermination ratios are also very similar. Since CIFAR-10 is substantially more challenging to classify, the losses are higher and the accuracies are lower, respectively.

However, the conclusions are similar to those of MNIST. The gap between the performances on the subset and the entire training data diminishes as the subset grows. This gap is large with non-augmented data in Fig. 3a because of low to overdetermination ratios Q but substantially smaller for augmented data in Fig. 3c where overdetermination ratios are sufficient. The validation data performance after both training phases is generally better with subsets of most sizes than with the full training data.

5.3 Dataset CIFAR-100

The results of the not-augmented CIFAR-100 dataset are shown in Figs. 4a and 4b. This classification task differentiates 100 classes so that there are only 500 examples per class. Optimum losses for this benchmark are higher than for the previous ones.

For small subset sizes, the representation of classes is probably insufficient. This may explain the large gap between subset loss and training data loss after subset training with small subset fractions. These may contain, on average, even as few examples per class as four. Nevertheless, the loss for the validation data with various subset sizes is close to the baseline loss for the conventional full-size training.

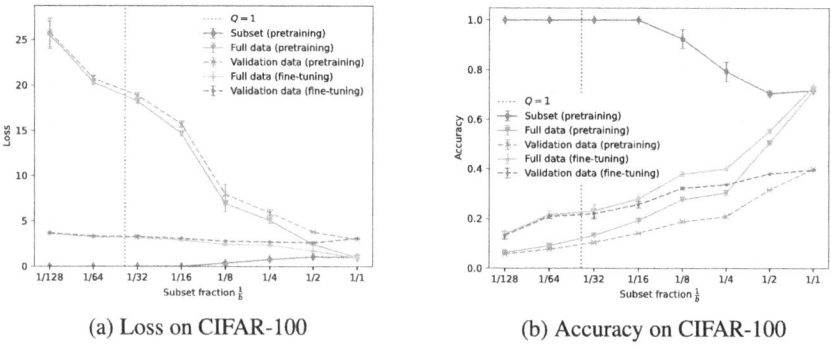

Fig. 4. Dataset CIFAR-100: loss and accuracy optima for pre-training on the subset and the full training data in dependence from the subset size as a fraction of the training data.

6 Conclusion

In contrast to batch-oriented processing with alternating, randomly drawn batches, the subset pre-training performs a complete optimization with a single, fixed subset of the training set.

We conclude that pre-training on a subset rather than the full training data will achieve comparable results with substantially reduced runtime.

The size of the subset is the main driving factor and has to be deliberately selected. For a larger subset, the efficiency gain decreases, while for a smaller subset, the model's number of trainable parameters might be excessive, resulting in overfitting. Preferably, the overdetermination ratio Q should be greater than 1, giving a good indication for the size of the subset. The corresponding definition is given in (9). However, even models with an underdetermined subset could lead to acceptable results, with the caveat that the fine-tuning phase may then require more computing resources.

Reducing the required computing resources is the main achievement. The numbers of optimization steps of the pre-training phase on one hand and the fine-tuning phase on the other are different: the pre-training phase takes a substantially higher number of forward and backward passes. This is intentional and justified by the fact that the subset is only a fraction of the full training data with a lower computing time per epoch. We invested ten times more epochs in training on the subset than fine-tuning on the full training data. The relative speed-up against the baseline is shown in Fig. 5. The cost of training is reduced to 10% of the baseline cost.

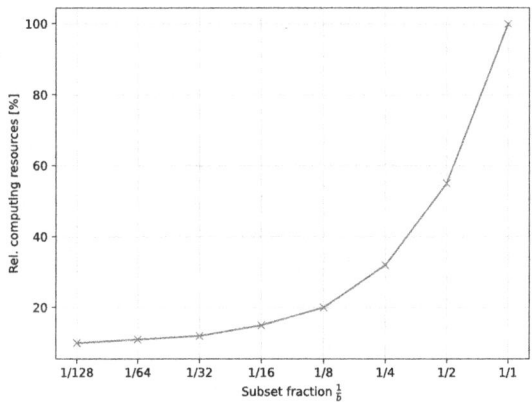

Fig. 5. Training time on a subset, relative to conventional training on the full training data in percent, quantifying the computational savings achieved by pre-training on the subset as a function of the chosen subset size.

This empirical assessment with five benchmarks for image classification is not enough to draw broad conclusions and generalize to any data and model setup. Future evaluations should include larger datasets like *ImageNet* [11], which have been excluded due to the high number of experiments required to generate adequate statistics. Moreover, these experiments have the potential to be expanded to cover a variety of different model architectures and domains, especially language models.

Another important feature could be examining the performance of second-order optimization algorithms, such as the conjugate gradient [1,4]. Their effectiveness becomes evident with a large enough number of training data iterations (epochs), which poses a challenge when training with large datasets. Carefully selected subset sizes could contain the increasing training time while achieving comparable (or even better) performance.

References

1. Fletcher, R., Reeves, C.M.: Function minimization by conjugate gradients. Comput. J. **7**(2), 149–154 (1964). https://doi.org/10.1093/comjnl/7.2.149
2. Glorot, X., Bengio, Y.: Understanding the difficulty of training deep feedforward neural networks. In: Proceedings of the 13th International Conference on Artificial Intelligence and Statistics, vol. 9, pp. 249–256. PMLR, Sardinia, Italy (2010-05-13/2010-05-15)
3. Goodfellow, I., Bengio, Y., Courville, A.: Deep Learning. Adaptive Computation and Machine Learning, The MIT Press, Cambridge, Massachusetts (2016)
4. Hestenes, M.R., Stiefel, E.: Methods of Conjugate Gradients for Solving Linear Systems, vol. 49. NBS Washington, DC (1952)
5. Hrycej, T., Bermeitinger, B., Cetto, M., Handschuh, S.: Mathematical Foundations of Data Science. Texts in Computer Science, Springer, Cham, March 2023. https://doi.org/10.1007/978-3-031-19074-2
6. Kingma, D.P., Ba, J.: Adam: a method for stochastic optimization. In: 3rd International Conference on Learning Representations (2015)
7. Krizhevsky, A.: Learning Multiple Layers of Features from Tiny Images. University of Toronto, Dataset (2009)
8. LeCun, Y., Bottou, L., Bengio, Y., Haffner, P.: Gradient-based learning applied to document recognition. Proc. IEEE **86**(11), 2278–2324 (1998). https://doi.org/10.1109/5.726791
9. Press, W.H., Teukolsky, S.A., Vetterling, W.T., Flannery, B.P.: Numerical Recipes in C (2nd ed.): The Art of Scientific Computing. Cambridge University Press, USA (1992)
10. Robbins, H., Monro, S.: A stochastic approximation method. Ann. Math. Stat. **22**(3), 400–407 (1951). https://doi.org/10.1214/aoms/1177729586
11. Russakovsky, O., et al.: ImageNet large scale visual recognition challenge. Int. J. Comput. Vision **115**(3), 211–252 (2015). https://doi.org/10.1007/s11263-015-0816-y
12. Simonyan, K., Zisserman, A.: Very deep convolutional networks for large-scale image recognition. In: ICLR (2015)
13. Spörer, J., Bermeitinger, B., Hrycej, T., Limacher, N., Handschuh, S.: Efficient neural network training via subset pretraining. In: Proceedings of the 16th International Joint Conference on Knowledge Discovery, Knowledge Engineering and Knowledge Management, pp. 242–249. SCITEPRESS, Porto, Portugal, November 2024. https://doi.org/10.5220/0012893600003838
14. van Wieringen, W.N.: Lecture notes on ridge regression, May 2021

Enhancing Text Embeddings for Emotion Detection: A Study on Dimensionality Reduction and Lexicon Filtering

Hande Aka Uymaz[✉] and Senem Kumova Metin

Department of Software Engineering, İzmir University of Economics, İzmir, Turkey
{hande.aka,senem.kumova}@ieu.edu.tr

Abstract. Emotion detection in textual data is a crucial task in Natural language processing (NLP), yet standard word embeddings often fail to capture emotional nuances. This study explores an emotion-enrichment approach that refines text representations by integrating emotional information into word embeddings. In the study, two key challenges are primarily addressed: limitations of emotion lexicons, which may include ambiguous or misclassified words, and high-dimensional vector representations, which may increase computational complexity. To improve lexicon quality, which is an important data source in emotion enrichment studies, a filtering mechanism is introduced aiming to remove the words with inconsistent emotional associations, enhancing lexicon precision. Additionally, a sliding window-based dimensionality reduction method is applied to BERT embeddings to identify emotion-rich vector segments, reducing computational cost while preserving emotional information. Experiments are conducted in both English and Turkish to evaluate the impact of lexicon filtering and dimensionality reduction on emotion detection. Results show that filtering improves the accuracy of emotion-enriched representations, while sub-vector selection gives the possibility of finding more representative parts about emotional content. By focusing on emotion-relevant vector dimensions, the proposed method achieves superior performance compared to full-dimensional embeddings. This research contributes to multilingual emotion representation by refining lexicon-based enrichment strategies and optimizing embedding spaces for emotion detection. The findings highlight the importance of structured lexicon filtering and targeted dimensionality reduction in improving sentiment and emotion analysis models.

Keywords: Natural language processing · NLP · Emotion detection · Emotion enrichment · Dimensionality reduction · Emotion Lexicon · BERT

1 Introduction

Natural Language Processing (NLP) is an interdisciplinary domain bridging computer science, artificial intelligence, and linguistics, focused on equipping machines to comprehend and produce human language. In text-based NLP, the foundational step involves transforming textual data into numerical forms computable by machines.

These numerical representations must encapsulate linguistic intricacies such as syntax, lexicon, and semantic structures. This transformation, known as vectorization, produces a vector space model [12]—a mathematical framework based on linear algebra that supports operations like vector arithmetic and similarity measures, including cosine similarity and Euclidean distance, which help quantify relationships between text representations.

Vectorization techniques are broadly categorized into three groups: traditional (e.g., TF-IDF, bag-of-words (BoW)), semantic (e.g., Word2Vec [14], GloVe [21]), and context-aware methods (e.g., BERT [5], DistilBERT [26], GPT [19]). Traditional approaches generate sparse vectors that lack semantic depth. These methods rely on word frequency and statistical weighting to represent text without considering word meaning or contextual nuances. Semantic embeddings produce static and dense vectors that capture meaning but overlook polysemy (multiple meanings of words). In contrast, context-aware models can assign different vectors to the same word depending on its usage in a sentence, allowing them to capture meaning more accurately. Due to the computational inefficiency of conventional methods (e.g., scalability issues with vocabulary size) and semantic embeddings' inability to handle context-dependent word senses, context-aware techniques have become dominant in modern NLP, achieving superior performance in several tasks.

Unlike static embeddings, models like ELMo [22], BERT [5], and DistilBERT [26] generate context-sensitive representations that resolve polysemy by analyzing word usage within specific sentences. For example, ELMo employs bidirectional long short-term memory to create context-dependent vectors, enhancing tasks like sentiment analysis and named entity recognition by capturing word meaning based on the surrounding context. BERT, built on transformers and masked language modeling, captures deeper semantic relationships, leading to more refined variants like RoBERTa [11] and ALBERT [10], which optimize efficiency and accuracy. Additionally, models like ULMFit, XLNet, and GPT excels in complex applications such as emotion detection, conversational AI, and text generation.

Although vector representations effectively capture syntactic and semantic aspects of language, they frequently fail to account for the emotional or affective dimensions that are naturally present in human communication. Recognizing the emotional nuances in textual data is essential for enhancing model performance, especially in applications like emotion detection. Nevertheless, most traditional and even context-sensitive embeddings are primarily designed for broad language comprehension tasks rather than focusing on the explicit modeling of emotions. To bridge this limitation, emotion enrichment techniques improve text representations by integrating emotional attributes into these vectors (e.g. [2,9,27]). This approach involves enhancing embeddings with emotion-specific data obtained from external sources, such as emotion lexicons or sentiment analysis scores. By incorporating emotion-focused vectors into embeddings, models become better equipped to identify subtle emotional signals in text, leading to more accurate emotion classification.

In the emotion enrichment studies from the literature and in our studies, it is realized that some limitations may affect the results of emotion/sentiment-based classification or similarity tasks. These limitations can be explained as follows:

- **Limitations of emotion lexicons:** The quality of the emotion lexicon plays a critical role in the success of emotion enrichment studies. This is because, in most studies, an emotion lexicon is used to measure the similarity between a text unit and words belonging to different emotion categories. Emotion lexicons can be constructed in various ways, such as through manual human annotation, translation from lexicons in other languages, or automatic methods like clustering. However, each of these methods can introduce issues related to the quality of the words assigned to emotion categories. Common problems include incorrect categorization of words, the presence of ambiguous words, the assignment of the same word to multiple emotion categories, and low relevance of words to a specific category.
- **Limitations of high dimensional vector representations:** The vectors generated to represent text units are typically high-dimensional. For instance, vectors produced by BERT-base and BERT-large models have dimensions of 768 and 1024, respectively. While these high-dimensional vectors are useful for tasks like classification, similarity measurement, and other operations, they can also result in substantial memory usage and computational expenses, particularly when dealing with large datasets. High-dimensional vectors contain rich and detailed information, but not all dimensions may be relevant or necessary for solving a specific problem.

Considering these limitations, we proposed *lexicon filtering* and *dimensionality reduction* approaches. And we based our experimental study on the following three research questions (RQ):

RQ1. Can dimensionality reduction of embeddings reveal underlying emotional patterns and improve efficiency in emotion-enriched representations?

In order to improve efficiency and address the computational challenges of working with high-dimensional vectors, especially in large-scale datasets, we systematically analyzed recurring patterns within these vectors using a sliding-window technique.

RQ2. How can emotion lexicons be refined by filtering, and how does this refinement impact the precision of emotion-enriched vectors?

To enhance quality, we applied a filtering process to emotion lexicons by evaluating the contextual relevance of words within emotion-rich datasets. This refinement aimed to remove ambiguous, irrelevant, or misclassified words, improving the accuracy of emotion enrichment studies.

RQ3. What are the differences or similarities between the application of a lexicon filtering and optimization approach on vectors in the English and Turkish languages?

By applying the same lexicon filtering and vector optimization methods to both Turkish and English datasets, we compared the effectiveness of these methods across languages and aimed to understand their impact on emotion enrichment quality in those languages.

In our approach to lexicon filtering, our objective is to refine emotion lexicons by examining how words are used in emotion-rich texts compared to general contexts. If a word's meaning in emotional sentences significantly diverged from its general usage, we considered there may be a potential inconsistency (the word may not be used correctly in emotional sentences) and filtered it out to enhance lexicon accuracy. For dimensionality reduction, we employed a sliding window technique to segment BERT vectors, allowing us to detect consistent patterns in vector representation that may include more emotive knowledge. This method aims to provide deeper insights into how emotions are embedded in language and offering a novel perspective on emotion modeling. The contributions of the study can be listed as follows:

1. To address possible shortcomings in emotion lexicons, a new approach is introduced to develop a more precise and well-structured lexicon. By considering contextual variations, words within the lexicon are filtered to enhance overall accuracy.
2. A sliding window-based dimensionality reduction technique is presented, which segments high-dimensional text vector representations into smaller sub-vectors. This approach enhances computational efficiency while preserving or even improving representational effectiveness.
3. Certain sub-vectors within BERT embeddings have been found to encode emotional information, indicating that emotional cues are concentrated in specific vector dimensions.
4. Experiments on enriching sentence vectors were conducted using all possible input combinations, including different vector types (full vectors and sub-vectors) and lexicon variations (filtered and non-filtered emotion lexicons) in both English and Turkish. The results demonstrated significant performance improvements, highlighting the effectiveness of the proposed method across languages with distinct grammatical structures.

In the following sections, we comprehensively discuss the research background, methodology, and findings. Section 2 presents a literature review, summarizing previous work. Section 3 details our proposed method, including lexicon filtering and dimensionality reduction techniques. Section 4 describes the experimental setup and evaluates the results obtained from various configurations. Finally, we conclude with a discussion of key insights and future research directions.

2 Literature Review

Natural Language Processing (NLP) has experienced significant advancements over the past decades, largely driven by the development of text representation techniques. Vector space models describe the process of representing textual elements, such as words or phrases, as numerical vectors within a multidimensional space. As illustrated in Fig. 1, these models can be categorized into two distinct types: those that operate independently of context and those that incorporate contextual information.

Traditional context-free models, such as one-hot encoding, tf-idf, and co-occurrence matrix representations, lack the ability to capture semantic meaning. For example, while the co-occurrence matrix captures word co-occurrence patterns by positioning words based on their statistical relationships in a vector space, it fails to encode deeper semantic connections or contextual meanings. As a result, these approaches face challenges in tasks demanding profound linguistic understanding, such as document summarization, question answering, and emotion analysis. To address this limitation, semantic embedding techniques like Word2Vec and GloVe represent words with similar meanings as closely positioned vectors in a shared space. These models improve performance in

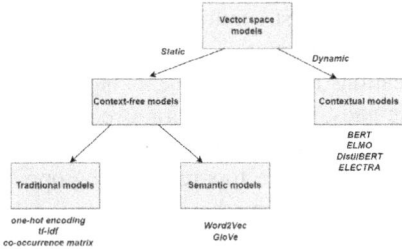

Fig. 1. Vector space models [30].

tasks like word analogy and semantic similarity detection by encoding semantic relationships. Despite being a major advancement in NLP, they generate only a fixed and static vector for each word. In other words, since these models create static word representations, they fail to account for polysemy or contextual variations.

Contextual models, such as BERT [5], RoBERTa [11], and ELMO [22], generate word embeddings that vary depending on their surrounding context, allowing them to differentiate between words with multiple meanings. For example, the same word can have different vectors according to the sentence in which it is used. These models are designed to capture intricate linguistic patterns and represent complex word relationships across different contexts. However, their embeddings exist in high-dimensional spaces, generally ranging from 512 to 1024 dimensions. For example, BERT is available in two versions: BERT-base with 768 dimensions and BERT-large with 1024 dimensions. Likewise, ELMO embeddings have a dimensionality of 1024. Similarly, GPT-based embedding models, such as *text-embedding-3-small* and *text-embedding-3-large*, produce vectors with lengths of 1536 and 3072, respectively. Although these high-dimensional embeddings encode rich linguistic features, they also introduce challenges, including increased computational cost and memory consumption. To mitigate these issues while maintaining model performance, researchers frequently apply dimensionality reduction techniques like PCA (Principal Component Analysis) and t-SNE (t-Stochastic Neighbor Embedding) [3,6,8,25,32].

Zhang et al. explore the impact of dimensionality reduction on high-dimensional sentence embeddings while evaluating multiple unsupervised techniques, including Principal Component Analysis (PCA), truncated Singular Value Decomposition (SVD), Kernel PCA (KPCA), Gaussian Random Projections (GRP), and autoencoders, to compress these embeddings [32]. The primary objective is to lower storage and computational demands while maintaining effectiveness across various NLP tasks. The results highlight PCA as the most effective approach, achieving a 50% reduction in dimensionality with only a minor 1% decline in performance.

A study by Su et al. introduces a strategy known as "whitening" rooted in PCA, to refine BERT-generated sentence embeddings [28]. Compressing the embeddings to dimensions of 256 and 384, this approach targets the challenges of anisotropy and high dimensionality. Evaluations across seven standard datasets reveal that their technique significantly boosts efficiency, decreases vector dimensions, and improves both storage utilization and retrieval performance.

In the literature, one of the most common applications of vectorization methods is text-based emotion/sentiment detection. To better represent the emotional information of texts, various modifications and improvements have been proposed for these vectors. In many of these methods, the proximity of a vector to words containing a certain emotion has been measured; vectors representing similar emotions are placed closer together in the vector space, while vectors representing opposite emotions are pushed further apart. However, some problems have been observed in the lexicons containing words related to these emotion categories. These challenges cover various aspects, such as ensuring precise classification of words into emotion categories, addressing words with ambiguous or overlapping emotional connotations, and terms that may be irrelevant or lack meaningful emotional significance. For example, in the frequently utilized NRC emotion lexicon [18], the term "grim" (tr. "acımasız") is simultaneously linked to the emotion categories *anger, sadness, disgust, fear* and *anticipation*. Effectively handling emotion lexicons requires taking both real-world context and human perception into account. Subjective interpretations, cultural backgrounds, and ethnic variations deeply influence emotional expressions. Given this complexity, it is crucial to recognize the impact of human subjectivity and cultural diversity on the annotation and understanding of emotion lexicons. Furthermore, English, as a language, has an abundance of resources in NLP studies, whereas resources for other languages are more limited. Thus, methods successful in solving NLP problems based on one language may not yield the same results across all languages. When addressing problems in other languages, new data sources must be constructed, or, in some cases, manually or automatically translated sources are utilized. These translations also introduce challenges to the quality of data sources due to the same issues. The problems with these data sources have been discussed in several studies in the literature (e.g., [2,4,16,24]).

3 Proposed Method

In order to overcome the limitations on emotion lexicons and high-dimensional vector representations, two approaches, lexicon filtering and dimensionality reduction, are presented in this work, which are detailed in the following subsections.

3.1 Lexicon Filtering

The process of emotion/sentence enrichment is generally performed using words from an emotion lexicon in the literature. However, certain limitations regarding the quality of such lexicons may affect the precision of emotion recognition and classification in textual content. These issues stem from factors such as the assignment of words to specific emotional categories, potential misclassification of terms, and the inclusion of irrelevant or ambiguous words.

This study introduces a novel approach to refining emotion lexicons by applying a filtering mechanism to words assigned to emotion categories. The methodology is outlined as follows: We constructed two BERT-based vector representations for words appearing in the NRC lexicon [18] and its Turkish translated version, TT-NRC [2]. Since BERT generates contextual embeddings, the meaning of words within their respective contexts plays a crucial role in embedding generation. To obtain vector representations *(VE)* for words within the lexicon, we sampled sentences containing these words from the collection of multiple datasets, all of which were pre-labeled with corresponding emotion categories. The datasets utilized in this process include TEI [17], TEC [15], and TREMO [29]. Next, we computed vectors *(VN)* for each emotion word from unlabeled datasets. For English, we extracted sentences from the OpenWebTextCorpus dataset [7], which comprises randomly shuffled Reddit posts where these words are commonly used in diverse contexts. For Turkish, we relied on the Turkish news dataset [20], which consists of articles from Turkish news sources. We derived *(VN)* BERT embeddings from the OpenWebTextCorpus and the Turkish news dataset to represent the general meaning and contextual usage of words. Consequently, each word in the emotion lexicon was assigned two separate vector representations based on distinct datasets. The process of generating vectors for *(VE)* and *(VN)* followed the same methodology, differing only in the datasets used. The details of how a word's BERT vector is extracted from a specific context (sentence) were determined by following the procedures outlined in our previous study [2]. Subsequently, we evaluated the similarity between word representations from *(VE)* and *(VN)* by computing cosine similarity *(CS)* for each term. An overview of this procedure and further steps are illustrated in Fig. 2.

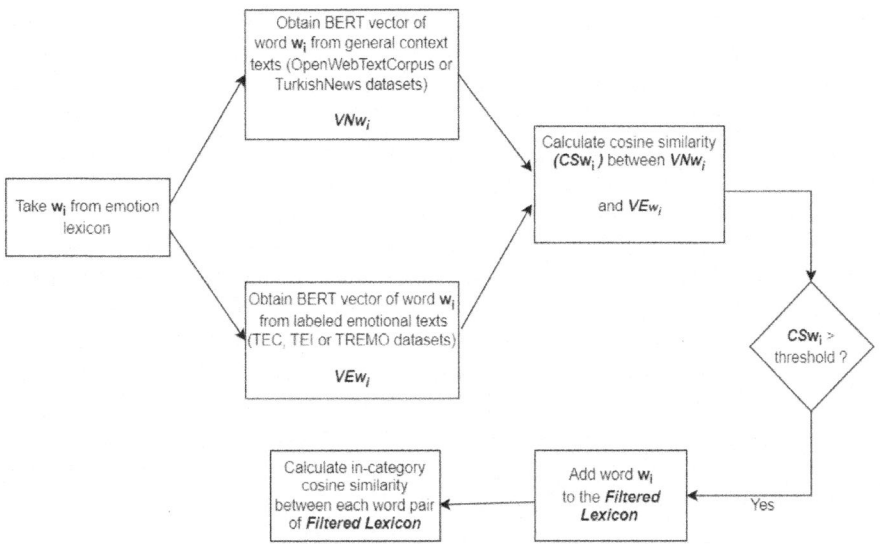

Fig. 2. The overview of the lexicon filtering procedure.

Consider an emotion lexicon represented as $W = \{w_1, w_2, w_3, ..., w_n\}$ where n denotes the total number of words in the lexicon. The process entails generating BERT vector embeddings for each word (w), producing vector pairs for comparison. Specifically, cosine similarity is computed between corresponding vectors, such as VE_{w_1} and VN_{w_1}, VE_{w_2} and VN_{w_2}, VE_{w_3} and VN_{w_3} continuing this pattern for all n words.

Through this systematic evaluation, we gain insights into how word representations are influenced by labeled sentence dataset contexts versus the broader, general context datasets. Once the cosine similarity values were computed for each word using the two datasets, words with similarity scores below a predefined threshold were considered for exclusion from further analysis. A low cosine similarity value indicates that the word may have been used with different meanings in emotion-labeled sentences and might not actually represent the intended emotion. To determine an optimal threshold, we performed several iterations of the experiment, refining the selection process accordingly.

Tables 1 and 2 display the averages in the cosine similarity category before and after the filtering process for English and Turkish, respectively. Initially, the "unfiltered" category reports the average cosine similarity scores for word pairs within each emotion category, along with the total number of words in each category before any filtering is applied. Next, we implemented a filtering mechanism based on various threshold values, removing a word w_i if the cosine similarity between VE_{w_i} and VN_{w_i} is less than a predefined limit. Following this removal process, in-category cosine similarity averages are recalculated using the vector space VE and the revised results are presented. This procedure was repeated across multiple threshold values to determine the most effective filtering criterion. The observed improvements in cosine similarity scores and the corresponding decrease in lexicon size are detailed in Tables 1 and 2.

As can be seen in Tables 1 and 2, while it was feasible to repeat the threshold experiments for English, the same approach could not be applied to Turkish. Even at a minimal threshold of 0.1, the total number of words across the four emotion categories dropped by 30%. Due to this significant reduction, we decided to utilize the 0.1 threshold without performing additional experiments.

Table 3 displays the results of applying different cosine similarity thresholds during the filtering process of the English lexicon. In the table, the first column indicates the cosine similarity thresholds tested, while the second and the third columns show the number of words retained after filtering and the corresponding percentage reduction from the original lexicon size of 2442 words. The fourth column presents the weighted average cosine similarity values across all emotion categories after the filtering process, and the last column shows the percentage increase in cosine similarity compared to the unfiltered dataset. According to the results, it can be seen that as the threshold increases, the number of words in the dataset consistently decreases, and the weighted average cosine similarity steadily rises. Based on the balance between the increase in cosine similarity and the reduction in lexicon size, 0.5 is selected as the threshold for filtering in our further experiments.

3.2 Dimensionality Reduction

While contextual embeddings excel at capturing semantic and contextual information, their high-dimensional nature can lead to substantial storage requirements and computational overhead, particularly when dealing with large datasets. Moreover, certain dimensions or portions of these vectors may encode specific linguistic features or textual properties. In our research, we introduce an alternative method that focuses on detecting patterns within text unit vectors, thereby simplifying the analytical process [30]. This technique is versatile and can be applied to any vectorization model.

Table 1. Variations in word counts across four emotion categories and the corresponding increases in average cosine similarity (CS) values for English lexicon words under different threshold settings.

		Anger	Fear	Sadness	Joy
Unfiltered	CS	0.448	0.447	0.451	0.512
	% Increase in CS	–	–	–	–
	# of words	526	650	526	740
	% Decrease in # of words	–	–	–	–
0.2	CS	0.466	0.469	0.469	0.527
	% Increase in CS	3.936%	4.971%	4.138%	2.880%
	# of words	462	570	464	650
	% Decrease in # of words	−12.167%	−12.308%	−11.787%	−12.162%
0.3	CS	0.484	0.485	0.485	0.537
	% Increase in CS	7.842%	8.391%	7.629%	4.748%
	# of words	376	493	395	576
	% Decrease in # of words	−28.517%	−24.154%	−24.905%	−22.162%
0.4	CS	0.500	0.500	0.499	0.560
	% Increase in CS	11.620%	11.951%	10.964%	9.490%
	# of words	290	402	333	481
	% Decrease in # of words	−44.867%	−38.154%	−36.692%	−35.000%
0.5	**CS**	0.530	0.539	0.5390	0.587
	% Increase in CS	18.313%	20.514%	19.636%	14.671%
	# of words	197	283	240	376
	% Decrease in # of words	−62.548%	−56.462%	−54.373%	−49.189%
0.6	CS	0.573	0.580	0.559	0.607
	% Increase in CS	27.886%	29.783%	24.002%	18.648%
	# of words	120	172	145	253
	% Decrease in # of words	−77.186%	−73.538%	−72.433%	−65.811%
0.7	CS	0.618	0.623	0.597	0.620
	% Increase in CS	37.895%	39.347%	32.598%	21.072%
	# of words	41	57	48	78
	% Decrease in # of words	−92.205%	−91.231%	−90.875%	−89.459%

In this study, experiments were carried out to identify sub-vectors within BERT representations of words and sentences that contain emotional information. Using data labeled with four distinct emotion categories, which are anger, fear, sadness, and joy, the effectiveness of sentence and word embeddings by considering only these extracted sub-vectors are evaluated. To assess the robustness of our approach across languages, we conducted experiments in both English and Turkish.

Table 2. Variations in word counts across four emotion categories and the corresponding increases in average cosine similarity (CS) values for Turkish lexicon words under different threshold settings.

		Anger	Fear	Sadness	Joy
Unfiltered	CS	0.589	0.578	0.577	0.619
	% Increase in CS	–	–	–	–
	# of words	450	536	475	321
	% Decrease in # of words	–	–	–	–
0.1	CS	0.618	0.618	0.604	0.628
	% Increase in CS	5.029%	6.816%	4.763%	1.562%
	# of words	297	376	328	256
	% Decrease in # of words	–34%	–29.851%	–30.947%	–20.249%

Table 3. Variation in English dataset size and average cosine similarity scores within each emotion category.

Threshold	Data set size	% Decrease in data set size	Weighted Average CS	% increase in CS
0.00	2442	–	0.47	–
0.20	2146	12.12%	0.49	3.89%
0.30	1840	24.65%	0.50	7.02%
0.40	1506	38.33%	0.52	11.07%
0.50	1096	55.12%	0.55	18.42%
0.60	690	71.74%	0.58	24.95%
0.70	224	90.83%	0.62	31.59%

Our proposed methodology about dimensionality reduction consists of the following steps:

1. A sliding window approach is utilized to analyze and extract informative patterns from BERT embeddings. This technique segments the vectors into smaller, fixed-length sections (windows) that allow the capture of local contextual details.
2. Cosine similarity is computed for words (in both English and Turkish) within the same emotion category, relying only on specific windows of the BERT vectors for word representations. If certain sub-vectors encode emotion-specific information, an increase in cosine similarity values is expected.
3. The findings and insights obtained from word-level experiments were applied to sentence-level representations.

The appropriate window size for the sliding window method is determined by referencing the study of Su et al., which proposed a dimensionality reduction technique that reduces BERT vectors to sizes of 256 and 384 [28]. Based on this, we set the window size to 256 in our study. Initially, BERT word vectors, each consisting of 768 dimensions and labeled with one of the four emotion categories, were divided into smaller sub-vectors of size 256. To ensure full coverage of all dimensions, a slide size of 64 was selected. For instance, the first sub-vector spans dimensions 1 to 256, while the next covers dimensions 65 to 321, as illustrated in Fig. 3. In summary, we partitioned the 768-dimensional BERT word vectors into nine sub-vectors by applying the sliding window technique.

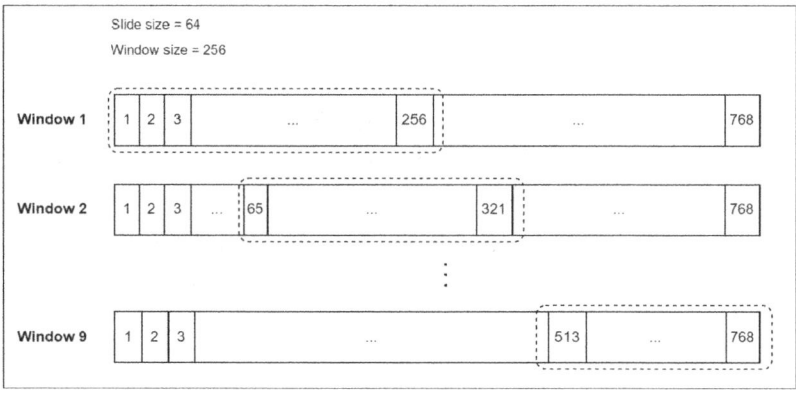

Fig. 3. Proposed sliding window-based method for vector segmentation [30].

4 Experiments

In this research, we employed the NRC English emotion lexicon [18] alongside its Turkish-translated counterpart, the TT-NRC lexicon [2]. Both resources are categorized according to Plutchik's emotion framework [23]. Our experiments focused on lexicon terms that correspond to four specific emotional states in both languages. The process began with extracting BERT embeddings for each lexicon term. Since BERT generates word representations based on contextual information, both individual words and their corresponding sentences were input into BERT for vector computation. To obtain these embeddings, we adopted the same methodology as [2], leveraging three emotion-labeled sentence datasets—TEI [17], TEC [15], and TREMO [29] which classify text into the four selected emotions (anger, fear, sadness, and joy).

Following the application of our proposed sliding window strategy, each BERT based word vector was segmented into nine smaller sub-vectors. These sub-vectors were then individually utilized to represent each word, and we calculated pairwise cosine similarity scores within the same emotion category which is called as in-category cosine similarity. Cosine similarity values range between 0 and 1, where 0 signifies complete dissimilarity between vectors, and 1 denotes high similarity between representations. A high similarity score in this context suggests that certain sub-vectors are more effective in capturing the nuances of a given emotion. As an example, when computing the cosine similarity for two words classified under the anger emotion category, first, we specifically used sub-vectors covering dimensions 1 to 256. This process was systematically repeated across all nine sub-vectors, yielding nine separate cosine similarity analyses for each word representation. Tables 4 and 5 present the results for English and Turkish lexicon words, respectively, in the form of heatmaps

Table 4. Pairwise cosine similarity(CS) results for *English* words within the same category using a single window [30].

		Windows								
		1	2	3	4	5	6	7	8	9
In-category CS	Anger-Anger	0.249	0.597	0.628	0.633	0.630	0.361	0.256	0.244	0.233
	Fear-Fear	0.220	0.607	0.634	0.640	0.637	0.340	0.236	0.226	0.215
	Sadness-Sadness	0.236	0.598	0.629	0.636	0.633	0.357	0.254	0.250	0.242
	Joy-Joy	0.285	0.665	0.687	0.692	0.690	0.403	0.311	0.305	0.283

Table 5. Pairwise cosine similarity (CS) results for *Turkish* words within the same category using a single window [30].

		Windows								
		1	2	3	4	5	6	7	8	9
In-category CS	Anger-Anger	0.288	0.330	0.300	0.324	0.312	0.767	0.766	0.768	0.775
	Fear-Fear	0.276	0.318	0.292	0.321	0.306	0.760	0.760	0.761	0.768
	Sadness-Sadness	0.275	0.317	0.295	0.321	0.302	0.760	0.760	0.762	0.770
	Joy-Joy	0.276	0.318	0.316	0.342	0.341	0.797	0.796	0.798	0.805

The heat maps indicate that specific dimensions within BERT embeddings encode emotional information. As a result, calculating cosine similarity using selected sub-vectors leads to higher similarity scores than using the full vector. This suggests that analyzing certain portions of the vectors can be just as effective as working with the entire 768-dimensional representation. In particular, our analysis of English word embeddings revealed that emotional content is concentrated in windows 2, 3, 4, and 5, whereas for Turkish words, emotional intensity can also be detected in windows 6, 7, 8, and 9.

Subsequently, we introduced filters with thresholds of 0.5 for English and 0.1 for Turkish into our lexicon word experiments and then repeated the previous analysis. Following the filtering process for both English and Turkish lexicon words (as detailed in 3.1), we once again divided the BERT word vectors into 256-dimensional sub-vectors. We then carried out the same experiment by computing cosine similarity between these sub-vectors on filtered lexicon words. The results for English and Turkish are presented in Tables 6 and 7.

Table 6. Pairwise cosine similarity (CS) results for *Filtered English* words within the same category using a single window.

		Windows								
		1	2	3	4	5	6	7	8	9
In-category CS	Anger-Anger	0.301	0.687	0.714	0.717	0.713	0.427	0.308	0.292	0.281
	Fear-Fear	0.279	0.700	0.723	0.728	0.725	0.417	0.301	0.289	0.274
	Sadness-Sadness	0.289	0.697	0.723	0.727	0.723	0.420	0.305	0.304	0.297
	Joy-Joy	0.342	0.739	0.757	0.760	0.757	0.465	0.366	0.362	0.338

Table 7. Pairwise cosine similarity (CS) results for Filtered Turkish words within the same category using a single window.

		Windows								
		1	2	3	4	5	6	7	8	9
In-category CS	Anger-Anger	0.303	0.344	0.316	0.346	0.333	0.792	0.791	0.792	0.799
	Fear-Fear	0.299	0.343	0.318	0.352	0.337	0.794	0.794	0.795	0.801
	Sadness-Sadness	0.284	0.324	0.306	0.334	0.315	0.783	0.783	0.785	0.793
	Joy-Joy	0.279	0.321	0.321	0.346	0.344	0.805	0.805	0.806	0.814

Table 8. Percentage rise in cosine similarity (CS) per window following the filtering of *English* lexicon words.

		Windows								
		1	2	3	4	5	6	7	8	9
In-category CS	Anger-Anger	20.884%	15.075%	13.694%	13.270%	13.175%	18.283%	20.313%	19.672%	20.601%
	Fear-Fear	26.818%	15.321%	14.038%	13.750%	13.815%	22.647%	27.542%	27.876%	27.442%
	Sadness-Sadness	22.458%	16.555%	14.944%	14.308%	14.218%	17.647%	20.079%	21.600%	22.727%
	Joy-Joy	20.000%	11.128%	10.189%	9.827%	9.710%	15.385%	17.685%	18.689%	19.435%
	Average % increase in in-category CS	**22.540%**	**14.520%**	**13.216%**	**12.789%**	**12.729%**	**18.490%**	**21.405%**	**21.959%**	**22.551%**

Table 9. Percentage rise in cosine similarity (CS) per window following the filtering of *Turkish* lexicon words.

		Windows								
		1	2	3	4	5	6	7	8	9
In-category CS	Anger-Anger	5.208%	4.242%	5.333%	6.790%	6.731%	3.259%	3.264%	3.125%	3.097%
	Fear-Fear	8.333%	7.862%	8.904%	9.657%	10.131%	4.474%	4.474%	4.468%	4.297%
	Sadness-Sadness	3.273%	2.208%	3.729%	4.050%	4.305%	3.026%	3.026%	3.018%	2.987%
	Joy-Joy	1.087%	0.943%	1.582%	1.170%	0.880%	1.004%	1.131%	1.003%	1.118%
	Average % increase in in-category CS	**4.475%**	**3.814%**	**4.887%**	**5.417%**	**5.511**	**2.941**	**2.974%**	**2.903%**	**2.875%**

Tables 8 and 9 present the percentage increase in *CS* when each sub-vector is used after filtering the English and Turkish lexicon words, respectively. Analyzing these tables reveals the following observations:

1. When a word is represented solely by a BERT sub-vector corresponding to a single window in both languages, and cosine similarity is calculated among filtered lexicon words within the same emotion category (in-category CS), the similarity scores show an increase compared to those obtained from unfiltered lexicon words.
2. This increase is observed across all emotion categories; however, the emotion *joy* exhibits the smallest rise in both languages.
3. A cross-linguistic comparison indicates that the rise in cosine similarity after filtering is lower in Turkish than in English.

Throughout our experiments thus far, we have explored the effectiveness of lexicon filtering and sub-vector selection techniques on Turkish and English lexicon words. By performing in-category cosine similarity calculations, we examined the impact of utilizing specific vector segments rather than the entire vector. Our findings indicated that this effect became even more pronounced after applying lexicon filtering. Building on these insights, we extended our approach to address the problem of emotion enrichment in sentence representations. The experimental study on emotion enrichment is structured into two main phases:

1. Constructing sentence sub-vectors
2. Enriching sentence vectors with emotional information.

In this stage of the study, we employed the TEI [17], TEC [15], and TREMO [29] sentence datasets. While TEI and TEC contain English sentences, TREMO is a Turkish dataset. To facilitate bilingual experiments, we translated the English datasets into Turkish and the Turkish dataset into English. Next, we randomly selected 500 sentences from each emotion category (anger, fear, sadness, joy) to form the Emotion Sentence Dataset (ESD), which was used in sentence representation based evaluations. For sentence sub-vector construction, instead of utilizing full 768-dimensional BERT vectors for sentence representations, we focused on the sub-vectors previously identified as emotion-rich in our word-based experiments for both languages, as depicted in Fig. 4. We then combined the most informative sub-parts for each language. For example, in English, emotional content was predominantly concentrated in sub-vectors 2, 3, 4, and 5. These segments were merged to form a vector spanning from the beginning of the second window to the end of the fifth window. The method used to assemble these sub-vectors is visualized in Fig. 5.

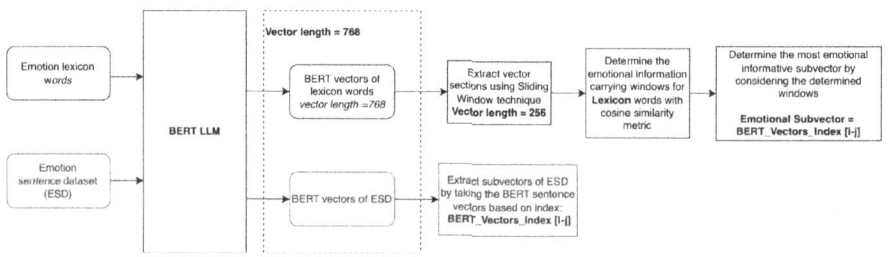

Fig. 4. Diagram illustrating the dimensionality reduction process for *word* and *sentence* vectors [30].

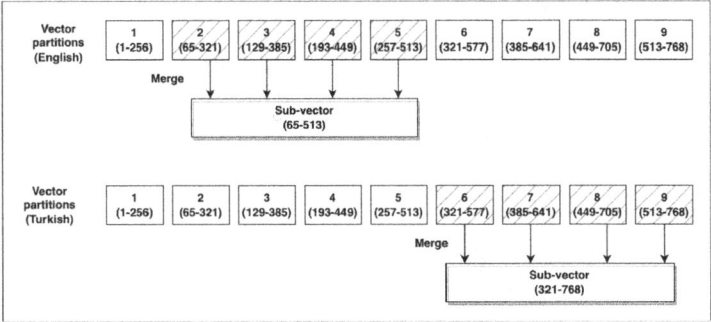

Fig. 5. The process of extracting sub-vectors [30].

Subsequently, we examined the effectiveness of BERT sentence vectors and their sub-vectors in both languages in emotion enrichment process (EEP). Emotion or sentiment enrichment is a widely explored topic in studies focusing on emotion classification and detection (e.g. [1,31] and [13]). According to the literature, while semantic and contextual embeddings are highly effective in capturing textual meaning, they often fall short in conveying emotional nuances. To address this limitation, enhancing these embeddings with emotional information is proposed. Various strategies have been introduced in the literature to implement this enhancement. In this study, we applied the emotion enrichment technique described by [2] to our datasets in English and Turkish. Essentially, this approach involves enriching a given vector by comparing it against the vectors of words from an emotion lexicon. The process computes the cosine similarity between each word and the lexicon's emotional terms. The most similar emotional words are then identified, and their vectors are leveraged to refine the original word's vector through a weighted averaging mechanism based on their emotional association. Ultimately, this results in a hybrid representation that seamlessly integrates semantic/contextual embeddings with emotional features.

In our experiments on the emotion enrichment process, we utilized sentences in both Turkish and English as the textual units to be enhanced with emotional information. Next, we computed the pairwise cosine similarity scores within each emotion category, both before and after the enrichment. For sentence representation, we employed 768-dimensional BERT vectors along with the sub-vectors derived in the preceding phase. The emotion enrichment process was carried out using the NRC [18] and TT-NRC [2] lexicons. We used both the complete set and the filtered versions of the lexicon words in the experiments. To represent the lexicon words as vectors, we adopted the same approach as we did for sentences. Specifically, we first encoded the lexicon words using BERT, then applied the enrichment method described in [2], and finally extracted their sub-vectors. In summary, in our experiments on the emotion enrichment process, we used different configurations for the inputs: (1) for sentence representation, we employed either BERT vectors or BERT sub-vectors, and (2) for the lexicon, we utilized either the complete set of lexicon words or the filtered lexicon words and/or BERT word vectors or BERT word sub-vectors.

Table 10. Enhancement of *English* sentence embeddings using various combinations. (The top-performing results are highlighted in bold).

Sentence embedding	Enrichment method	Enrichment by	In-category similarity (% improvement)				
			Anger	Fear	Joy	Sadness	Average
BERT	–	–	0.610 –	0.593 –	0.623 –	0.597 –	0.606 –
BERT	EEP	Emotion Lexicon Words (BERT + EEP)	0.844 38.36%	0.838 41.32%	0.879 41.09%	0.845 41.54%	0.852 40.57%
BERT	EEP	Filtered Emotion Lexicon Words (BERT)	0.697 14.25%	0.669 12.79%	0.628 0.74%	0.634 6.18%	0.657 8.43%
BERT	EEP	Filtered Emotion Lexicon Words (BERT + EEP)	0.863 41.50%	0.862 45.34%	0.899 44.24%	0.866 45.06%	0.872 44.02%
BERT Subvector	EEP	Emotion Lexicon Words Subvector (BERT + EEP)	0.885 45.09%	0.880 48.44%	0.905 45.28%	0.883 47.88%	0.888 46.65%
BERT Subvector	EEP	Filtered Emotion Lexicon Words Subvector (BERT + EEP)	**0.900 47.55%**	**0.899 51.68%**	**0.922 47.99%**	**0.900 50.83%**	**0.905 49.48%**

Table 11. Enhancement of *Turkish* sentence embeddings using various combinations. (The top-performing results are highlighted in bold).

Sentence embedding	Enrichment method	Enrichment by	In-category similarity (% improvement)				
			Anger	Fear	Joy	Sadness	Average
BERT	–	–	0.752 –	0.747 –	0.758 –	0.747 –	0.751 –
BERT	EEP	Emotion Lexicon Words (BERT + EEP)	0.922 22.61%	0.931 24.63%	0.943 24.41%	0.927 24.10%	0.931 23.93%
BERT	EEP	Filtered Emotion Lexicon Words (BERT)	0.916 21.76%	0.926 23.99%	0.939 23.93%	0.922 23.39%	0.926 23.27%
BERT	EEP	Filtered Emotion Lexicon Words (BERT + EEP)	0.927 23.31%	0.937 25.37%	0.948 25.01%	0.932 24.83%	0.936 24.63%
BERT Subvector	EEP	Emotion Lexicon Words Subvector (BERT + EEP)	0.953 26.67%	0.959 28.45%	0.966 27.45%	0.956 28.03%	0.959 27.65%
BERT Subvector	EEP	Filtered Emotion Lexicon Words Subvector (BERT + EEP)	**0.957 27.24%**	**0.962 28.84%**	**0.968 27.68%**	**0.960 28.50%**	**0.962 28.06%**

The different combinations explored, along with the in-category cosine similarity results for sentences from four distinct emotion categories, are presented in Tables 10 and 11. The first row in both tables shows the baseline results, where sentence embeddings are represented using 768-dimensional BERT vectors without any enrichment. These baseline values were then used as a reference to compare the outcomes of various enrichment techniques, with the percentage improvements provided in the respective tables.

The second lines of the tables present enriching sentence embeddings with lexicon word representations obtained through BERT lexicon word vectors enriched using the EEP method.

Next, as indicated in the third and fourth rows of Tables 10 and 11, sentence vectors were further enhanced using filtered lexicon words, represented by both standard BERT vectors and emotionally enriched BERT vectors (BERT + EEP).

Finally, instead of using full 768-dimensional BERT vectors, we incorporated sub-vectors identified as optimal in our previous experiments for both Turkish and English. These sub-vectors were constructed by concatenating the most informative sub-parts across both languages. For instance, in English, sub-vectors 2, 3, 4, and 5 carried the most emotion-relevant information. These segments were combined into a single vector, spanning from the start of the second window to the final dimension of the fifth window. The extraction process for these sub-vectors is illustrated in Fig. 5. As a final step, we enriched the sentence sub-vectors first using the sub-vectors of enriched emotion lexicon words (BERT+EEP) and then with the sub-vectors derived from filtered lexicon words (BERT+EEP). Here, either for the whole lexicon and the filtered lexicon word representations, enriched representations are utilized.

Analyzing the findings presented in Tables 10 and 11, all configurations exhibit an improvement across all emotion categories when compared to the baseline BERT vectors. The most effective sentence representation enrichment was achieved under the following conditions:

1. Utilizing sub-vectors to represent sentences,
2. Enhancing sentence vectors with filtered lexicon words,
3. Representing lexicon word vectors using emotionally enriched sub-vectors.

5 Conclusion

In this study, we explored the effectiveness of emotion-enriched vector representations by addressing two key challenges: refining emotion lexicons and optimizing high-dimensional embeddings. Our lexicon filtering approach aims to filter ambiguous or misclassified words, leading to more precise emotion categories and improved representation quality. Additionally, by applying a sliding window-based dimensionality reduction technique, we identified specific sub-vectors within BERT embeddings that encode emotional information, enhancing computational efficiency while preserving representational effectiveness.

Our experimental results demonstrate that filtering lexicon words and using emotion-enriched sub-vectors significantly improve the accuracy of sentiment-related tasks in both English and Turkish. Notably, the improvements observed in Turkish highlight the effectiveness of our methods across languages with distinct grammatical structures and resource availability. These findings emphasize the importance of refining both lexicon quality and embedding structures in sentiment analysis and emotion detection applications. To guide our research, we formulated the following research questions:

RQ1. Can dimensionality reduction of embeddings reveal underlying emotional patterns and improve efficiency in emotion-enriched representations?

To address this question, we applied a sliding window-based approach to segment BERT embeddings into smaller sub-vectors. By analyzing cosine similarity within emotion categories, we identified sub-vectors that encode emotional information. Our results demonstrated that using only these emotion-rich sub-vectors maintained, and in some cases improved, classification accuracy. The findings suggest that specific dimensions within high-dimensional embeddings contribute more significantly to emotion representation, allowing for more efficient sentiment analysis models.

RQ2. How can emotion lexicons be refined by filtering, and how does this refinement impact the precision of emotion-enriched vectors?

We developed a lexicon filtering method that evaluates the contextual relevance of words within emotion-labeled datasets. By comparing word representations in emotion-rich contexts to their general usage, we filtered out terms that displayed inconsistencies. Our experiments showed that this process led to a more precise and semantically meaningful lexicon, improving the quality of emotion-enriched embeddings.

RQ3. What are the differences or similarities between the application of a lexicon filtering and optimization approach on vectors in the English and Turkish languages?

By applying our lexicon filtering and sub-vector optimization techniques to both English and Turkish datasets, we examined their effectiveness across languages with distinct linguistic structures.

Subsequent investigations could expand these studies to include other advanced language models, such as GPT variants [19], RoBERTa [11], and ELMO [22], all of which have shown notable effectiveness in prior research. Such an expansion would facilitate a deeper examination of how emotional information is encoded in sub-vectors within these frameworks, potentially yielding novel perspectives. In the current research, we performed comparative evaluations on English, a language with abundant resources, and Turkish, an agglutinative language with fewer NLP resources and a unique grammatical framework. Future studies could widen the focus by integrating languages from various linguistic families that exhibit differing structural traits. Additionally, the proposed methodology could be revisited and tested on different tasks, such as alternative information retrieval challenges, to assess its versatility and efficacy across a range of practical applications.

Disclosure of Interests. The authors have no competing interests to declare that are relevant to the content of this article.

References

1. Agrawal, A., An, A., Papagelis, M.: Learning emotion-enriched word representations. In: Proceedings of the 27th International Conference on Computational Linguistics, pp. 950–961. Association for Computational Linguistics, Santa Fe (2018). https://www.aclweb.org/anthology/C18-1081
2. Aka Uymaz, H., Kumova Metin, S.: Emotion-enriched word embeddings for Turkish. Expert Syst. Appl. **225**, 120011 (2023). https://doi.org/10.1016/j.eswa.2023.120011. https://www.sciencedirect.com/science/article/pii/S0957417423005134
3. Ayesha, S., Hanif, M.K., Talib, R.: Overview and comparative study of dimensionality reduction techniques for high dimensional data. Inf. Fusion **59**, 44–58 (2020). https://doi.org/10.1016/j.inffus.2020.01.005. https://www.sciencedirect.com/science/article/pii/S156625351930377X
4. Bjornsdottir, R.T., Tskhay, K.O., Ishii, K., Rule, N.O.: Cultural differences in perceiving and processing emotions: a holistic approach to person perception. Cult. Brain **5**(2), 105–124 (2017). https://doi.org/10.1007/s40167-017-0053-z

5. Devlin, J., Chang, M.W., Lee, K., Toutanova, K.: Bert: pre-training of deep bidirectional transformers for language understanding (2018)
6. George, L., Sumathy, P.: An integrated clustering and bert framework for improved topic modeling (2022). https://doi.org/10.21203/rs.3.rs-1986180/v1
7. Gokaslan, A., Cohen, V.: Openwebtext corpus (2019). http://Skylion007.github.io/OpenWebTextCorpus
8. Álvaro Huertas-García, Martín, A., Huertas-Tato, J., Camacho, D.: Exploring dimensionality reduction techniques in multilingual transformers (2022)
9. Kasri, M., Birjali, M., Nabil, M., Beni-Hssane, A., El-Ansari, A., El Fissaoui, M.: Refining word embeddings with sentiment information for sentiment analysis. J. ICT Standard. 353–382 (2022)
10. Lan, Z., Chen, M., Goodman, S., Gimpel, K., Sharma, P., Soricut, R.: Albert: a lite bert for self-supervised learning of language representations (2019)
11. Liu, Y., et al.: Roberta: a robustly optimized bert pretraining approach (2019)
12. Manning, C.D., Raghavan, P., Schütze, H.: Introduction to Information Retrieval. Cambridge University Press, Cambridge (2008). http://nlp.stanford.edu/IR-book/information-retrieval-book.html
13. Matsumoto, K., Matsunaga, T., Yoshida, M., Kita, K.: Emotional similarity word embedding model for sentiment analysis. Computación y Sistemas 26(2) (2022)
14. Mikolov, T., Chen, K., Corrado, G., Dean, J.: Efficient estimation of word representations in vector space. In: Proceedings of Workshop at ICLR (2013)
15. Mohammad, S.: #emotional tweets. In: Proceedings of the First Joint Conference on Lexical and Computational Semantics (*SEM) (2012)
16. Mohammad, S.: Challenges in Sentiment Analysis, pp. 61–83 (2017). https://doi.org/10.1007/978-3-319-55394-8_4
17. Mohammad, S., Bravo-Marquez, F.: Emotion intensities in tweets. In: Proceedings of the 6th Joint Conference on Lexical and Computational Semantics (*SEM 2017), pp. 65–77. Association for Computational Linguistics, Vancouver (2017). https://doi.org/10.18653/v1/S17-1007. https://www.aclweb.org/anthology/S17-1007
18. Mohammad, S.M., Turney, P.D.: Crowdsourcing a word-emotion association lexicon. Comput. Intell. 29(3), 436–465 (2013)
19. OpenAI: Gpt-large language model (2023)
20. Özbay, F.: Turkish News Dataset (2019). https://www.kaggle.com/datasets/furkanozbay/turkish-news-dataset/
21. Pennington, J., Socher, R., Manning, C.D.: Glove: global vectors for word representation. In: In EMNLP (2014)
22. Peters, M., et al.: Deep contextualized word representations. In: Proceedings of the 2018 Conference of the North American Chapter of the Association for Computational Linguistics: Human Language Technologies, vol. 1. Association for Computational Linguistics, New Orleans (2018)
23. Plutchik, R.: A general psychoevolutionary theory of emotion. In: Plutchik, R., Kellerman, H. (eds.) Theories of Emotion, pp. 3–33. Academic Press (1980)
24. Poria, S., Gelbukh, A., Cambria, E., Hussain, A., Huang, G.B.: Emosenticspace: a novel framework for affective common-sense reasoning. Knowl.-Based Syst. 69, 108–123 (2014). https://doi.org/10.1016/j.knosys.2014.06.011. https://www.sciencedirect.com/science/article/pii/S0950705114002329 https://www.sciencedirect.com/science/article/pii/S0950705114002329 https://www.sciencedirect.com/science/article/pii/S0950705114002329
25. Raunak, V., Gupta, V., Metze, F.: Effective dimensionality reduction for word embeddings. In: Augenstein, I., et al. (eds.) Proceedings of the 4th Workshop on Representation Learning

for NLP (RepL4NLP-2019), pp. 235–243. Association for Computational Linguistics, Florence (2019). https://doi.org/10.18653/v1/W19-4328. https://aclanthology.org/W19-4328
26. Sanh, V., Debut, L., Chaumond, J., Wolf, T.: Distilbert, a distilled version of bert: smaller, faster, cheaper and lighter. ArXiv arxiv:1910.01108 (2019)
27. Sharma, D.A.: Context-aware Sentiment Analysis on Refined Word Embeddings Word2Vec Model. TechRxiv (2022)
28. Su, J., Cao, J., Liu, W., Ou, Y.: Whitening sentence representations for better semantics and faster retrieval (2021)
29. Tocoglu, M., Alpkocak, A.: Tremo: a dataset for emotion analysis in Turkish. J. Inf. Sci. **44**, 016555151876101 (2018). https://doi.org/10.1177/0165551518761014
30. Uymaz, H.A., Metin, S.K.: Optimizing high-dimensional text embeddings in emotion identification: a sliding window approach. In: Proceedings of the 16th International Joint Conference on Knowledge Discovery, Knowledge Engineering and Knowledge Management, vol. 1: KDIR, pp. 258–266. INSTICC, SciTePress (2024). https://doi.org/10.5220/0012899300003838
31. Wongpatikaseree, K., Kaewpitakkun, Y., Yuenyong, S., Matsuo, S., Yomaboot, P.: Emocnn: encoding emotional expression from text to word vector and classifying emotions–a case study in Thai social network conversation. Eng. J. **25**(7), 73–82 (2021)
32. Zhang, G., Zhou, Y., Bollegala, D.: Evaluating unsupervised dimensionality reduction methods for pretrained sentence embeddings (2024)

Knowledge Graph Mining-Based Personalized Learning Path Recommendation for English Learning: Leveraging Adaptive Techniques for Improved Outcomes

Duong Nguyen[1] and Thu Nguyen[2,3](✉)

[1] Division of Information Technology, Campus in Ho Chi Minh City, University of Transport and Communications, Ho Chi Minh City, Vietnam
duongnt_ph@utc.edu.vn
[2] Faculty of Information Technology, University of Science, Ho Chi Minh City, Vietnam
ntmthu@fit.hcmus.edu.vn
[3] Viet Nam National University, Ho Chi Minh City, Vietnam

Abstract. Everyone may now learn more conveniently by using e-learning platforms to study online. For these systems to offer an initial personalized learning path (PLP), a component must function as a content recommendation system (RS). This component must also be able to continuously modify the path to accommodate the learner's learning characteristics and the available learning materials in real time. The provision of highly tailored suggestions is still beset by problems like cold start concerns and data sparsity. Recently, there has been a lot of interest in RS development based on knowledge graphs (KG). KGs can leverage the properties of users and items within a unified graph structure, utilizing semantic relationships among entities to address these challenges and offer more relevant recommendations than traditional methods. In this paper, we provide a KG-based learning path recommendation system to aid in English language acquisition by producing a series of lessons intended to successfully lead learners from their present proficiency level to their desired level. We created a domain KG architecture that includes important idea classes and their connections, especially for preparing English certification examinations. Next, to develop an initial PLP recommendation (PLPR) model, we investigated and used graph data mining algorithms (GAs). Lastly, we devised a method to modify the original PLP's lesson sequence to accommodate the learners' learning characteristics following each real-time interval. With the help of our gathered dataset, consistent experimental conditions, and a chosen set of weights, we assessed our solution using standards like accuracy, efficiency, stability, and execution time.

Keywords: Knowledge graph · Personalized learning path · Recommendation · English learning · Graph database · Adaptive learning paths

1 Introduction

Users now have to pick between a vast array of goods, services, and content due to the proliferation of information and the variety of online services, which makes it challenging to locate content that meets their interests and needs. To better assist users in locating goods or services that they would find interesting, RSs have been created and incorporated into digital platforms. RS's primary purpose is to offer precise and tailored suggestions, which saves consumers time and enhances their experience. Machine learning, deep learning, and data mining techniques are currently enabling recommender systems to produce increasingly accurate and relevant recommendations, leading to significant advancements in their performance [1]. The core operation of an RS is to analyze user data, including behavioral data like past selections, use frequency, time spent on each product or service, online interactions, and user feedback (likes, shares, and reviews). Furthermore, other data is also used to personalize recommendations, including demographic data (age, gender, region) and social characteristics (friendships, comparable user groups). The recommender system creates models in this way to forecast future user preferences or needs. In a variety of domains, such as e-commerce (e.g., product recommendations), online video streaming services (e.g., Netflix, YouTube), music (e.g., Spotify, Apple Music), and numerous social media platforms, recommender systems have been extensively implemented to enhance user experience and boost business efficiency [52].

The recommendation algorithm or model, which is the most crucial part of an RS, comes in three primary varieties: collaborative filtering, content-based filtering, and hybrid filtering. While content filtering depends on the features of a product or service to provide appropriate recommendations, collaborative filtering uses similar user behavior or preferences. Both techniques are combined in hybrid filtering to improve accuracy. Nevertheless, RSs continue to encounter certain significant issues, such as data sparsity, where user data is too sparse to create a useful model, or cold-start, where the system is unable to provide appropriate recommendations when there is little new user or item data. Scalability is another issue that might make standard algorithms less successful when the system must manage massive volumes of data from millions of users and items. As a result, RS researchers and developers are searching for novel ways to address these issues while managing the possible semantic relationships between users and items and securely storing their characteristics. Recent years have seen the emergence of a new research trend in this area: the use of KGs as side information [17].

A KG is a type of heterogeneous graph in which entities are represented by nodes and relationships between them are represented by edges. In general, KG is represented by triple G as presented in Eq. 1, where h refers to the head entities, r the relations, and t the tail entities [25]. To comprehend the relationships between things, items, and their properties, they may be mapped into KG. Additionally, KG may incorporate users and user-side data, improving the accuracy of capturing user preferences and user-item relationships [17–25].

$$G = \{(h, r, t)\} \tag{1}$$

Figure 1 illustrates KG-based recommendation, in which user u1 is recommended the collection of movies $M = \{v_4, v_5, v_6, v_7, v_8, v_9, v_{10}, v_{11}\}$. Users, films, stars, directors, and genres are all entities in this KG, whereas the interactions between entities are *film. Genre, film. Star, film. Director, and star. Star*. The recommendation accuracy is increased by using the KG, which links users and movies with various latent relations. Explainability of the recommendation outcomes is another advantage of the KG-based recommender system. Following the relation sequences in the user-item graph in the same example will reveal the rationale behind the movie recommendations made to user *u1*. For example, one of the reasons that *v8* is recommended is that it features the same star as *v1*, which *u1* has already seen [17].

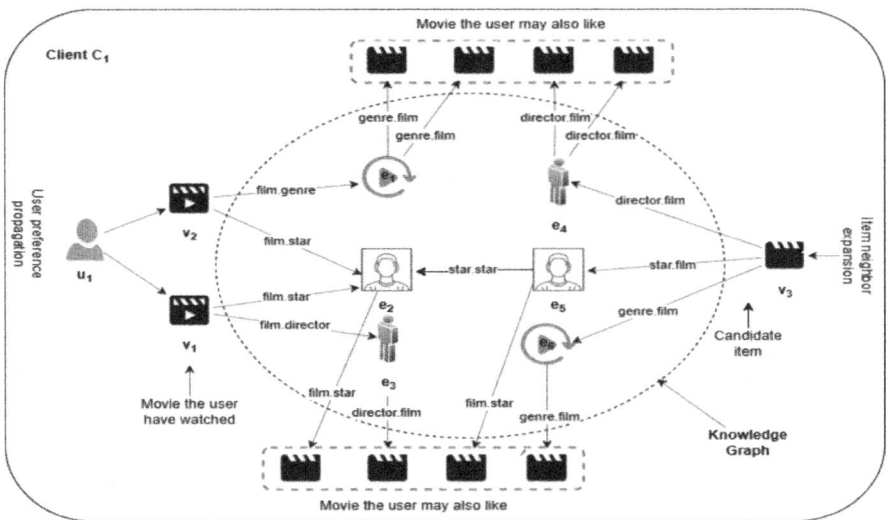

Fig. 1. An illustration of KG-based recommendation.

Significant advancements in education and learning have also been made possible by RS, which has made it easier to create intelligent learning systems that are customized to each learner's needs. By using recommendation approaches, these systems provide PLPs that dynamically adjust to each learner's particular objectives, interests, and skills. By examining learner-specific data, these systems prioritize personalization in contrast to conventional "one-size-fits-all" methods that give all students standardized learning materials and sequences. Such systems continuously evaluate criteria including learning progress, preferred material, and areas for development through data-driven monitoring. The systems can adjust the content and order of learning materials based on these findings, guaranteeing that students are given the most useful and pertinent resources at the appropriate moment. Such advances represent a transformative change in education, paving the way for more comprehensive, effective, and learner-centered approaches that better accommodate diverse learning styles and needs [26–29].

We place a high value on foreign language acquisition since it plays a critical role in job applications, study and research, travel, and involvement in global exchange, among other things. According to a 2023 Statista report [11], English is currently the most widely spoken language in the world, with nearly 1.5 billion speakers, and certification of competency in English with four primary skills—listening, speaking, reading, and writing—is frequently required in job applications and university output standards. As a result, to verify their fluency in English, many people must study and prepare for examinations such as TOEIC, IELTS, TOEFL, and others. The availability of intelligent English learning applications and platforms like Duolingo, Elsa, and others has made it easier for learners to obtain these credentials while also enabling them to study more effectively and save time and money. The results of our survey indicate that these applications typically direct learners to follow a predetermined learning path (LP) based on their goals and current level. However, research is also being done to apply the PLPR models to advise learners on a suitable LP and fulfill the aforementioned goals. This will help learners follow a suitable LP that meets their other personalized requirements, such as time, cost, progress, and learning outcomes [29].

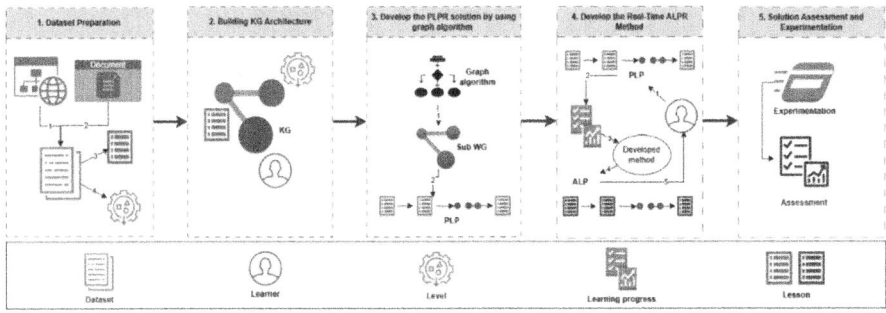

Fig. 2. An overview flowchart illustrating the execution process for the proposed solution [29].

Based on the problem that has been stated, the goal of this study is to propose a solution that can initially recommend PLP for English language learners. To do this, we will use GAs processing on KG architecture and other related approaches. In real time, this PLP may then adjust itself to the learner's learning preferences and the available learning materials. As per the process illustrated in Fig. 2 [29], the proposed solution will proceed through five primary phases of development. Using a variety of websites, papers, and official publications, a dataset pertaining to the format, content, and assessment methods of international English certifications in pertinent exams will first be assembled. Following refinement, this dataset will contain information about entities, their relations, and the attributes that go along with them. Based on the created dataset and the learning needs of the learners, a KG architecture will be developed in the second stage to store and display key concepts of English levels, required knowledge and skills, as well as lessons correlated to those levels. To reduce the execution time, we will next utilize GAs from Neo4j's GDS library in the third phase to generate a weighted subgraph (WG) based on the learner's required learning characteristics data that is kept in the KG. Only the learner's target level-related entities and weighted relational edges, together with the lessons or competencies that correspond to the current level that the learner already possesses, will be included in this produced WG. Next, using GAs to process on the WG created for each individual learner, we suggest a first PLP that consists of a series of lessons that are most appropriate for the learner and must be learned. In step 4, we will create a method for the model to carry out the Adaptive LP Recommendation (ALPR) function, automatically modifying the lessons in the initial PLP to best suit the learners after equal real-time intervals, based on the learning progress data for the initial PLP (including results and learning time for each lesson), as well as the new requirements of the learners. Ultimately, we carefully experimented with various weight sets to find the best set of weights for the proposed solution when implementing the original PLPR so that it meets all evaluation requirements for an LP. Then, using a set of weights that were established in conjunction with the experimental dataset that was generated and consistent testing settings, we assessed our solution according to execution time, accuracy, efficiency, and stability [29].

This paper is organized as follows: Our work and its contributions are described in Sect. 1. An assessment of the state of the art in the subject of research is given in Sect. 2. Section 3 provides a detailed description of the KG architectural development method. The procedures for developing a PLPR solution for students are outlined in Sect. 4. Details regarding the method's development process for the ALPR function for learners in real time will be provided in Sect. 5. The tests, assessments, and data-gathering techniques are detailed in Sect. 6. Lastly, recommendations for future study areas are included in the conclusion of Sect. 7.

2 Related Works

The relevant literature on recommender systems in general and KG-based recommender systems in particular is examined in this section.

2.1 Recommender Systems

In recent years, RS has drawn a lot of interest because of its capacity to improve user experience and tailor information for users. These systems reduce information overload by recommending pertinent goods, services, or resources based on an analysis of user profiles and interests. From a commercial standpoint, RS are essential for drawing in and keeping clients, which eventually increases revenue and content engagement. Applications across a wide range of fields, including social networking [48], e-learning [14–27], entertainment [18–23], and tourism [6], show their adaptability and increasing influence in the digital era [36].

RS has undergone three major phases of development. Using statistical and machine learning models, the first phase was based on three main approaches: content-based filtering (CBF), collaborative filtering (CF), and hybrid approach. To improve suggestions, the second phase added context-aware techniques that considered variables including time, location, and user group ratings. The third, which emphasizes semantic representation and makes use of several knowledge components to improve recommendation quality, has evolved while research on this generation is still ongoing [8].

- CF is widely used to generate recommendations based on users' shared preferences and historical interactions [8]. It can be categorized into memory-based [55] and model-based methods [38–43]. However, CF suffers from challenges like data sparsity, where limited interactions reduce recommendation accuracy, and the cold-start

problem, where new users and items lack sufficient historical data. Additionally, CF does not inherently utilize semantic relationships between items, limiting its effectiveness in some scenarios [8].
- Content-based filtering (CBF), on the other hand, recommends items that share similar features with those previously liked by a user. This approach builds a user profile based on item attributes [4–10]. While effective, CBF faces several issues, including overspecialization (suggesting too similar items), limited content analysis (not capturing deep relationships), and difficulty handling serendipitous recommendations. Like CF, it also struggles with the cold-start problem when new users lack interaction history [8].
- Demographic filtering is another approach that generates recommendations by grouping users based on shared personal attributes such as age, gender, or location. This method is particularly useful when item-related data is limited and does not require explicit user ratings. However, it has notable drawbacks: collecting complete user demographic information raises privacy concerns, and recommendations may become overly generalized, failing to capture individual preferences effectively [8].
- Context-aware recommended systems (CARS) enhance recommendations by incorporating contextual factors like time, location, and social context (e.g., whether the user is alone or with friends). These systems assume that context consists of predefined attributes that remain relatively stable over time [15]. By integrating contextual information, CARS provides more relevant recommendations, especially in dynamic environments where user preferences shift based on situational factors [8].
- Knowledge-based recommender systems utilize domain knowledge to match users with items based on their preferences and needs. These systems rely on three types of knowledge: user preferences, item characteristics, and the relationship between the two. By explicitly modeling this knowledge, they can generate accurate recommendations even when historical user interactions are sparse [8, 34].
- Finally, hybrid recommender systems aim to combine multiple approaches—such as collaborative filtering with content-based filtering or knowledge-based techniques—to leverage the strengths of each method and mitigate their individual limitations [5, 24]. These hybrid approaches improve recommendation accuracy, reduce the cold-start problem, and enhance overall system performance.

In general, RS has generally developed with a variety of models, each with unique benefits and difficulties. Although they improve the user experience by offering tailored suggestions, they frequently have drawbacks such as data sparsity, the cold-start issue, overspecialization, and the incapacity to completely capture intricate user-item relationships. Furthermore, some methods struggle with flexibility and scalability, while others call for either organized data or in-depth topic expertise. In order to overcome these obstacles, new research has been conducted to alleviate these constraints; one notable recent development is the use of KG.

2.2 Methods for Recommender System with Knowledge Graph

As previously noted, KG is simply a structured network of knowledge representations that can hold knowledge entities and relations between entities, with each node representing an entity and each edge representing a set of connections. A relation of r from entity h to entity t is represented by each edge $< h, r, t >$, where h, r, and t stand for the head entity, relation, and tail entity, respectively [53]. Additionally, as noted in [8], KG recommendation takes use of the relationships between entities that represent the users, the suggested products, and their interactions. The system uses links, whether explicit or implicit, to find information that the target user could find interesting or helpful. Accordingly, relationships give the KG-based recommender more useful information that it may use to apply inference between nodes and find new connections. Conversely, traditional feature vector-based recommendation techniques typically ignore these relationships, which can lead to less-than-ideal performance, particularly in cases of sparse data. Researchers have been inspired to study KG-based RSs by the availability of KG in different domains. KG-based recommender systems are classified according to how they use the KG data, as follows: *embedding-based methods, path-based methods, and hybrid methods* [25]. We conducted thorough evaluations of current research in this field and created a succinct synopsis.

Embedding-Based Methods

The embedding approach uses Knowledge Graph Embedding (KGE) to learn the representation of each item and connection by embedding a KG, $G = (V, E)$, into a low-dimensional space. This technique focuses on turning the KG's entities and relationships into high-density spatial vectors, which facilitates the system's processing and reveals previously unnoticed patterns in the data. Item knowledge graphs (IKG) and user-item knowledge graphs (UIKG) that incorporate other variables like user behavior are examples of frequently used KGs. TransE, DistMult, node2vec, Metapath2Vec, ComplEx, and other well-known embedding techniques are used in this method to improve the quality of tailored recommendations by transforming user-item connections into similar vectors [25]. However, current interpretations often do not include the impact of semantic links and the effective use of network information. For instance, Hui et al. [3] proposed ReBKC, a user-tailored RS that integrates KG Embedding (KGE) and user behavior, as a solution to the issue of enhancing the performance of customized RS, particularly with sparse data and cold initiation. Interestingly, it boosts KGE use for in-depth investigation and uses self-attention to identify user preferences. Similarly, Zhang et al. [13] tackled the issue of enhancing RS performance, particularly the sparsity issue in user-item data that frequently arises in collaborative filtering. The suggested technique, known as Collaborative Knowledge Base Embedding (CKE), enhances the quality of recommendations by integrating data from the knowledge base. Three parts make up this approach, which learns hidden representations from collaborative filtering and the knowledge base and extracts semantic representations of things from structural, textual, and visual material. However, the model needs too much additional information outside, which is a difficult condition for most fields. A technique called RippleNet was introduced by Zhao et al. [19]. It predicts the likelihood that a user will click on a potential item by activating "ripples" from the items the user has clicked and propagating user preferences across entities in the knowledge graph. Also, a Deep Knowledge-Aware Network (DKN) model was presented by Wang et al. [39] to enhance click-through rate prediction in news recommendation systems by integrating KGs. Convolutional neural networks (CNNs) with three input channels—entity embedding from news headlines, content embedding, and vocabulary embedding—are used by DKN to integrate knowledge and semantic representations. Wu et al. [44] tackled the session-based recommendation problem, which seeks to forecast user behavior using anonymized sessions. Session-based Recommendation with Graph Neural Networks (SR-GNN), the study's proposed approach, models sessions as graph data, enabling graph neural networks (GNNs) to capture intricate item transitions that conventional linear approaches are unable to. However, SR-GNN regards each user as an anonymous user without taking the interaction among users into account.

Path-Based Methods

Patth-based methods are strategies that concentrate on mining KG pathways to find the relationships between recommendation objectives and users. By evaluating paths according to weight, length, or semantics, the system is better able to comprehend the relationship between things. This approach often creates a UIKG. Specifically, this graph aids in combining relational and semantic data to produce precise recommendations [25]. For instance, Cui et al. [50] proposed a method called RSL-GRU to solve the explanatory recommendation problem in the setting of sequential user activity. To enhance path reasoning, it integrates Gated Recurrent Units (GRUs) and Reinforced Path Reasoning Networks (RPRNs). Using KGs and sequential behavior, the approach makes informative product recommendations. Similarly, Geng et al.'s [31] proposed approach, known as Path Language Modeling Recommendation (PLM-Rec), learns a language model based on the KG's routes, which comprise entities and connections. By decoding the path sequence, PLM-Rec not only makes recommendations but also produces explanations simultaneously, solving the drawbacks of earlier techniques by making elements that are inaccessible through the graph's current connections more accessible. However, the inability to incorporate timestamps into the UIKG restricts the capacity to describe changing user preferences. To maximize the recommendation outcomes, fusion strategies that include both semantic representation and network information in KGs have been developed [25]. In Zhao et al.'s work [46], a technique known as Time-aware Path Reasoning for Recommendation (TPRec) was proposed. TPRec employs temporal information to build a temporally interactive collaborative KG (TCKG), which subsequently generates recommendations with plausible explanations by reasoning on temporal trajectories. There is a spectrum of emotions among entities in KG-based recommendation algorithms. By recognizing these emotional ties, relationships may become richer and more sentiment-aware, improving the interpretability of recommendations [25]. In another study, S.J. Park et al.'s [32] study focused on incorporating sentiment analysis into KGs. Sentiment-Aware Policy Learning (SAPL), the suggested approach, performs route inference and product recommendation by first building a Sentiment-Aware Knowledge Graph (SAKG) using user review and rating analysis and then using reinforcement learning.

The Hybrid Methods

As previously stated, embedding-based approaches extract the implicit information from the item/user KG, whereas path-based methods exploit the semantic link information. The hybrid approaches combine the two aforementioned techniques to obtain more insightful suggestions by utilizing the data in the KG. In particular, this method enriches the vector representations by aggregating multi-hop nearby entity information and propagating entity information on KG using iterative principles [17–25]. He et al.'s work [20] suggested a technique dubbed ERSIF-KR that improves user similarity while lowering exposure bias by using indirect input from things that haven't had direct interaction with the user. Furthermore, by including multi-step neighbor object representations into the target model, this technique enhances the capacity to learn item representations. Also, Wang et al.'s [40] suggested approach, known as the Knowledge Graph-based Intent Network (KGIN), uses KGs to uncover the intentions underlying user-product interactions. It does this by modeling each intention as a weighted combination of relations in the KG, which helps to differentiate between various intentions and enhances modeling power and explainability. Experiments on three benchmark datasets demonstrate that KGIN performs better than current techniques like KGAT, KGNN-LS [41], and CKAN [42] and offers a comprehensible explanation of predictions by identifying relational routes and influencing intents.

Summary of Recommendation Methods Based on KG
Overall, these methods allow for low-dimensional mapping of entity relationships by generalizing the topology of the KG network. The multi-hop transmission of user preferences also allows them to efficiently mine high-order semantic links between things. KG's flexibility has increased, and feature engineering is made simpler with embedding-based methods, which provide an effective way to move vectors from high- to low-dimensional domains. Computational and data storage expenses are decreased by this method. These approaches, however, frequently fall short in mining higher-order information and typically ignore the interactions and linkages between items inside the knowledge network. Path-based approaches, on the other hand, enable the interpretation and tailoring of recommendations by taking message connection into account. The fundamental drawback of the original meta-path is that its practical application range is limited due to the significant domain expertise required for its creation. The drawbacks of the approaches are addressed by hybrid recommendation systems [25].

Furthermore, it is evident from the KG architecture constructed in part three, the insights, and the process of implementing the proposed solution presented in part I (Fig. 2) that the embedding-based approach will not be appropriate. Because when the values of the characteristics between entities and relationships in KG do not clearly indicate continuity or discreteness, it will be hard to put them into feature vectors. This makes it impossible to calculate similarity based on feature vectors to generate recommendations. When using graph traversal algorithms on KG, the Path-based approach will work better in our proposed solution since it can make use of semantic relationships along the path between entities to provide appropriate recommendations.

2.3 KG – Based Personalized Learning Path Recommendations

KGs are widely used in the educational domain for the purpose of planning and recommending LPs because of the particular features of the education sector. By conceptualizing entities like courses and knowledge points and examining the connections between them, knowledge graphs make it easier to derive efficient learning pathways [21].

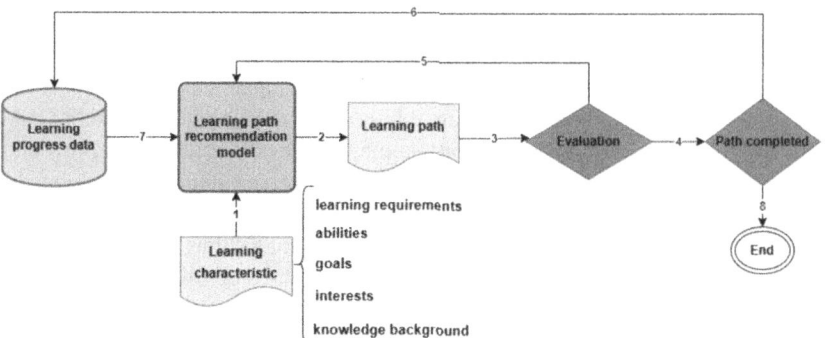

Fig. 3. Workflow of a learning path recommendation system.

And as previously said, PLPR systems, which concentrate on creating LPs that are specific to each learner's requirements, abilities, interests, knowledge background, and goals, are a useful substitute for the "one-size-fits-all" paradigm (Fig. 3). The method not only improves learners' motivation and interest but also helps them absorb information and meet learning objectives more rapidly by monitoring learning progress and modifying the content and arrangement of materials. This is a crucial component of cutting-edge educational programs, which lessen information overload and facilitate learners' more efficient goal-achieving [54].

As a result, numerous studies have been conducted to create RSs for PLPR that use semantic dependency links between learning objects (LOs) and learning materials that are simultaneously stored on a variety of data types to recommend LPs to learners, then utilize data mining models to arrange learning materials into learner-recommended LPs. And it was demonstrated by the study by D. Shi et al. [33] KG has lately been used for PLPR as a significant research domain because it may remove ambiguities in learner learning characteristic descriptions and learning material. Inspired by this characteristic, some researchers tried to create learning systems for KG-based LP recommendations and were able to address the problems that were brought up. For instance, Zhang et al. [54] developed a multidimensional course KG and used graph convolutional networks (GCN) to accurately reflect learner preferences in order to create a PLPR system for e-learning that employs a KG structure. The algorithm reduces the need for human planning and raises learner satisfaction by recommending the best courses based on learners' preferences and the importance of learning resources. H. Yin et al. [49] created a structural KG program for open-source projects using static code analysis. Their deep learning architecture, which combines depth-first and Dijkstra search algorithms with multi-source data and an LP recommendation engine, enables developers to swiftly pick up crucial skills. Y. Sun et al. [35] in the realm of English education provided personalized KG for students using GCN on junior high school English exercises, and they created PLP with the help of Prim and Kruskal algorithms. Chen et al. [7] automated the development of Massive Open Online Courses on KG using pre-knowledge annotation and course similarity calculation. They create a network that combines knowledge and course nodes, enhance TF-IDF calculation, and categorize courses using rule-based and machine learning approaches. Z. Yan et al. [47] proposed a method that suggests personalized activities by utilizing a course knowledge network. The process comprises creating individual knowledge structure diagrams, constructing the graph using deep knowledge tracing, and generating a Q-matrix from the replies of the learners. In line with constructivist learning theory, the model selects customized tasks according to variables including complexity, individuality, and variance. Boya et al. [51] proposed a KG-based LP planning technique for MOOC platforms in order to increase the effectiveness of online learning. To arrange different LPs across courses, this approach combines the Ripplenet algorithm with a KG model. The system gives feedback and modifies the path based on the learner's progress, using Neo4j to store KG data and Echarts for display. G. Xiao's [45] research proposed PLP for university students learning French. These LPs represent the relationships between French knowledge points and are generated using segmentation and correlation techniques, as well as algorithms designed for processing knowledge maps based on big data.

The aforementioned studies all aim to investigate LP recommendation models for each learner using KG by integrating ideas like learning resources, LOs, learners' behaviors, goals, and so on, along with their interrelationships, into the KG architecture. This approach has been shown to produce better PLPR results than traditional ones. However, putting a PLPR system into place can be a difficult and complicated procedure. A thorough grasp of education, assessment, and learning theories is also necessary. Also, according to M. Abed et al.'s research [26], we believe that in order to recommend a more suitable PLP for every learner, other elements of the learner's learning characteristics—such as the learner's current level of knowledge, abilities, desired learning duration, weaknesses and cost, etc.—must be taken into account, as well as the recommended PLP can accommodate the learners' learning characteristics following each real-time interval. Indeed, after examining the research landscape, we have come to the conclusion that current methods for planning and recommending learning paths in online learning scenarios are inadequate for creating paths that correspond with knowledge acquisition sequences based on accurately identifying learners' weak knowledge points. This identifies a critical gap in approaches that might optimize the learning sequence, improving learning effectiveness and the learning experience as a whole. Furthermore, the findings of our study indicate that little research has been done on learning languages other than English. Our research aims at creating a PLPR system for English language learners using KG-based data modeling and processing. By taking into consideration the learners' target level, desired learning time, and current level of knowledge and abilities, this solution will enable them to accomplish their objectives efficiently in the least amount of time while still adhering to an appropriate LP. Finally, based on the learning progress data for the initial PLP (including learning time and results for each lesson) and the new requirements of the learners, we will develop a method for the model to perform the ALPR, automatically adapting the lessons in the initial PLP to best suit the learners after equal real-time intervals.

Section 3 will provide a detailed presentation of the steps involved in developing the KG architecture as well as the proposed solution for this research.

3 KG-Based English Learning Construction

To create a KG architecture for presenting the concept and learning material along with their relationship in preparation for the English certification examinations, we looked at the vocabulary topics, grammar themes, scoring scale, format, assessed skill, and evaluation criteria of the TOEIC, IELTS, and TOEFL test components. This is depicted in Fig. 2 for the second phase. Additionally, in compliance with European standards, we examined the Common European Framework of Reference (CEFR) [30] to evaluate the relationship between English proficiency and certificate scores.

As far as we know, to obtain an international standard English certificate, candidates must first pass a competency test. Upon passing, they will receive the certificate and a score attesting to their proficiency. Although the score on these certificates shows the person's level of English proficiency, it does not indicate whether they passed or failed. To standardize English proficiency levels throughout European and other regional countries, the results can be converted to the level according to CEFR. As a result, the KG architecture will incorporate a *Level class* that is dedicated to storing score information from the learner's current English certificate and the target score of the certificate that the learner hopes to attain in the future to manage learners' test information for international English certificates. Information about each certificate's score and qualification based on the relevant CEFR will be stored as a reference to investigate how English proficiency relates to scores across different certificate kinds.

Additionally, mastery of vocabulary and grammar knowledge, as well as proficiency in speaking, listening, reading, and writing, is necessary for success on international English certificate tests. As a result, the *Competency class* that appeared in KG architecture will cover the required knowledge and abilities. However, since we are aware that this knowledge is only examined in specific sections of the exam, we will build specific vocabulary and pronunciation skills in a different *Lesson class*. Important skills are covered in each section of the test thanks to this individualized approach. Moreover, learners need to completely understand the types of questions, topics, and contexts that will be covered in each section of the test. Create the perfect test-taking strategy by combining your understanding of grammar, vocabulary, pronunciation, and English proficiency. In other words, for every level of English proficiency a learner aspires to, they must be equipped with knowledge from relevant grammar and vocabulary lessons as well as specific lessons on how to comprehend the test's structure, question type, topic context, strategies, and test-taking experience. Consequently, an additional Lesson class will be developed in the KG design to handle data regarding lesson entities that need to be learned to pass the tests. Our proposed comprehensive KG architecture, which is represented in Fig. 4 [29], consists of three fundamental concept classes: *Level, Competency, and Lesson*. Table 1 will provide the list of entities in KG architecture as well as the relations between them, which means the following:

1. "HAS_CURRENT_SCORE": displays the user's current English language certificate score.
2. "WANT_TARGET_SCORE": shows the target score the user hopes to obtain on the target English language certificate.

Table 1. An explanation of the details of the entities in the KG architecture.

Node	Remarks
Learner	The "Learner" entity indicates the basic information of the learner for whom the PLP is to be recommended
	Attribute value: "Learner_id", "Name", "Email"
Current_score	The entity "Current_score", indicates the score on the current English language certificate that the learner has.
	Attribute value: "Cur_Id", "Current_Score", "Certificate"
Target_score	The entity "Target_score", indicates the score on the target English certificate type that the learner wants to achieve
	Attribute value: "Tar_Id", "Target_Score", "Certificate"
CEFR_Level	The "CEFR Level" entity, provides information about the English proficiency level according to the CEFR
	Attribute value: "Level_ID", "Level", "From_score"," To_score"," Certificate"
Skill	The "Skill" entity, which provides information about the skills corresponding to each CEFR English proficiency level
	Attribute value: "Skill_ID", "Name"
Lesson (Grammar, Vocabulary, Listening, Reading, Speaking, Writing, Pronunciation)	The *Lesson class* entity group provides information about the lessons to be learned to achieve the skills corresponding to each CEFR English proficiency level.
	Attribute value: "Lesson_ID", "Lesson", "Theory"," Exercise"," Time_learning", "Category"

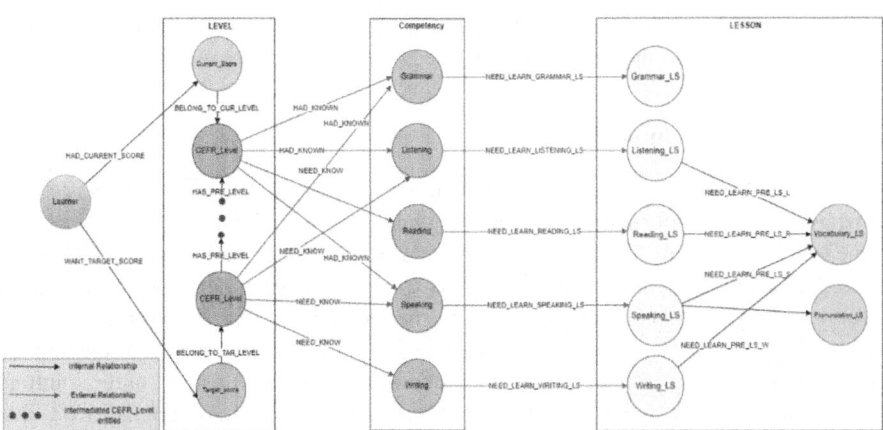

Fig. 4. Complete KG architecture utilized in the proposed solution [29].

3. "BELONG_TO_CUR_LEVEL"/"BELONG_TO_TAR_LEVEL": Indicate which CEFR framework the English proficiency certificate's current or target score falls within.
4. "HAS_PRE_LEVEL": Demonstrates the hierarchy of the English competence levels in the CEFR. Level "A2" would, for instance, come right before level "B1".
5. "NEED_LEARN_PRE_LESSON_L, NEED_LEARN_PRE_LESSON_S, ettc.": Declare that before moving on to the major lectures, a few prerequisite lessons including assigned vocabulary or pronunciation must be finished.
6. "HAD_KNOWN": identify the learner's acquired skills or abilities (lessons) that correspond to their current level as defined by the CEFR.
7. "NEED_KNOW": Determine the skills or knowledge (lessons) that learners must acquire to reach the CEFR target level.
8. "NEED_LEARN_GRAMMAR_LS, NEED_LEARN_LISTENING_LS, etc.": Each skill and knowledge denotes the associated lessons required.

4 A Solution for PLPR

4.1 Description of PLPR Problem

The primary objective of our proposed solution is to provide a suitable PLP for every learner as they work toward getting ready for international English certification exams like the TOEFL, IELTS, and TOEIC (which incorporate the speaking-writing and listening-reading combinations). The first inputs of the solution are the scores that match the learners' current certificates, information about their English proficiency or lessons that match their current level (which will be raised for the learner to choose based on our developed dataset), the desired study time, and the score that matches the desired certificate. As seen in step 2 of Fig. 2, KG architecture will store these inputs. As shown in phase 3 of Fig. 2, our model will next generate an initial PLP for every learner, which will comprise a list of lessons to be learned and advance the learners from their present English proficiency to their target level while considering their preferred schedule.

4.2 End-to-End Solution Processing

As mentioned in Part 3, KG would contain all information on learners' learning characteristics as well as information for obtaining and assessing English certificates. At the same time, we wish to offer answers through a fresh strategy that is easy to use while upholding science and natural reasoning. As a result, we have looked at and evaluated GAs based on a number of criteria, such as the KG architecture, the problem that has to be solved, the desired results at every step of the solution's implementation, and the principles underlying each algorithm's operation. In particular, for step 1 of the solution, we specifically use the graph traversal algorithm BFS so that we may generate a WG that contains only entities that are connected to the learner's target-level entity. The PageRank algorithm is then combined with the LPA_NI algorithm in stage 2 of the solution with the aim of determining the importance of each lesson entity on WG and clustering these entities into clusters corresponding to the list of lessons to be learned from the current level to the target level, then merging into the original LP. Finally, we employed the Min Weighted Sum (MWS) technique to evaluate and choose the best LP as the PLP to recommend to learners to fulfill the optimization objectives in stage 3. Figure 5 [29] will provide details of the processing flow for each stage, precisely as follows:

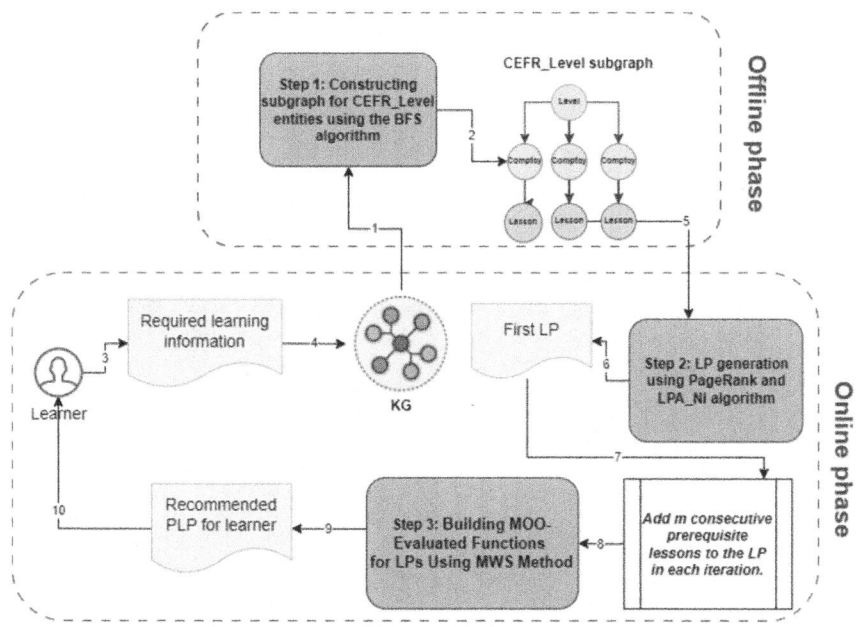

Fig. 5. The execution flows with applied algorithms [29].

Step 1: *Constructing a subgraph for CEFR_Level entities using the BFS algorithm:* This initial step requires offline processing to traverse the KG using the BFS algorithm [22]. Creating subgraphs for every CEFR_Level object is the aim. In doing so, we generate an exhaustive list of all entity categories that are associated with each CEFR_Level entity, either directly or indirectly. This method optimizes the execution time for the following stages by reducing the number of entity interactions.

Step 2: *LP generation using PageRank and LPA_NI algorithms*: This step takes place when processing is done online. Based on data provided by the learner, it first converts the *CEFR_Level* entity subgraph into a WG customized to the learner's target level. The importance of each node within the WG is then assessed using the PageRank algorithm [37]. The LPA_NI algorithm [53] then clusters important nodes according to the lessons and competencies needed for each CEFR_Level entity in WG. These clusters are combined, and the initial LP containing the major lessons is generated by ranking them in ascending order based on the CEFR_Level entity values inside each cluster.

Step 3: *Building Multi-Objective Optimization (MOO)-Evaluated Functions for LPs Using the MWS Method*: This step will also be completed online. The LP made in step 2 is to keep adding m significant nodes in the WG as prerequisite lessons as nodes in the Vocabulary or Pronunciation entity category and then utilize the developed evaluation function to gauge the LP's satisfaction at each kth iteration by using the MWS method.

Then, as the PLP to counsel the learner, select the LP that produces the most optimal outcome while meeting all stated optimization objectives. In the following sections, we will present the details of these main processing steps.

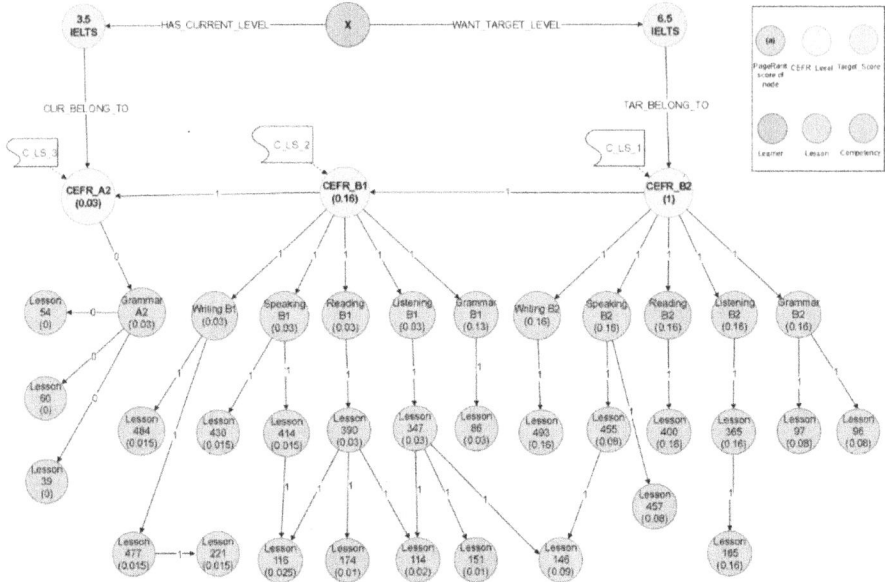

Fig. 6. Full weighted subgraph for the learner's target level after executing step 1 and 2 [29].

Constructing Subgraph for CEFR_Level Entities

The implementation procedure for step 1 is detailed in Algorithm 1. As seen in Fig. 6 [29], for instance, this approach yields a subgraph of the *CEFR_Level* node with the value "CEFR_B2," which denotes learner X's target level. There are nodes in this subgraph that correspond to the learner's present proficiency, current competencies, skills they need to learn, and potential lessons.

Algorithm 1. Constructing subgraph for each CEFR Level entities in KG.

Input:
- G (V, E): The KG includes V vertices and E relationship edges.
- LVL = {LVL_i | i = $\overline{1,n}$}: set of the ith CEFR_Level entity denoted as LVL_i contained in G (V, E).
- n: number of elements in the LVL set.

Output: LV_EN_i (set of entities related to each ith CEFR_Level entity).
1: $LV\_EN_i \leftarrow \emptyset$, i ← 1
2: **while** i ≤ n:
3:   Apply the BFS with each LVL_i as the source vertex → Obtain a set containing k nodes {$v_1, v_2, ..., v_k$}
4:   $LV\_EN_i \leftarrow \{v_1, v_2, ..., v_k\}$
5:   i ← i + 1
6: End while

LP Generation Using PageRank and LPA_NI Algorithms

We present the notations listed in Table 2 and highlight the two main tasks in order to provide a clear explanation of the implementation procedure in step 2. Algorithm 2 describes the PageRank algorithm, which is used in the first job. Furthermore, we computed the PageRank score (PR_score) for every node in the WG using Eq. 2 [37], which is obtained from the subgraph specified in step 1.

$$PR(i) = (1-d) + d \sum_{j \to i} \frac{W_{ji} PR(j)}{\sum_k W_{kj}} + PR'(i) \qquad (2)$$

Note that in Eq. 2, *PR(i)* denotes the PR_score calculated for each node *i* in the *LV_EN* set during the current iteration, while *PR'(i)* represents the existing PR_score of node *i* from the previous iteration, indicating the spread of points among related nodes *PR(j)* refers to the current PR_score of nodes *j* in the *LV_EN* set linked to node *i*. The weight of the edge from node *j* to node *i* is denoted as W_{ji}. Similarly, W_{kj} represents the weight of nodes *k* in the *LV_EN* set, pointing away from node *j*. The damping factor *d*, set as *1*, reflects the probability of the learner accessing node *i* from node *j*, ensuring learning from node *j* to node *i* for pairs with $W_{ji} = 1$. For instance, in Fig. 6, based on the learner's input data, each edge pointing to a node in the subgraph is given a weight value of either 0 or 1. The subgraph will be transformed into WG following this weight assignment procedure. Once Algorithm 2 has run on this WG and assigned a PR_score to each node, we will add these nodes to the *LN_EN_IPT* set in decreasing order of their PR_scores. Figure 7 [29] presents the *LN_EN_IPT* set as an example.

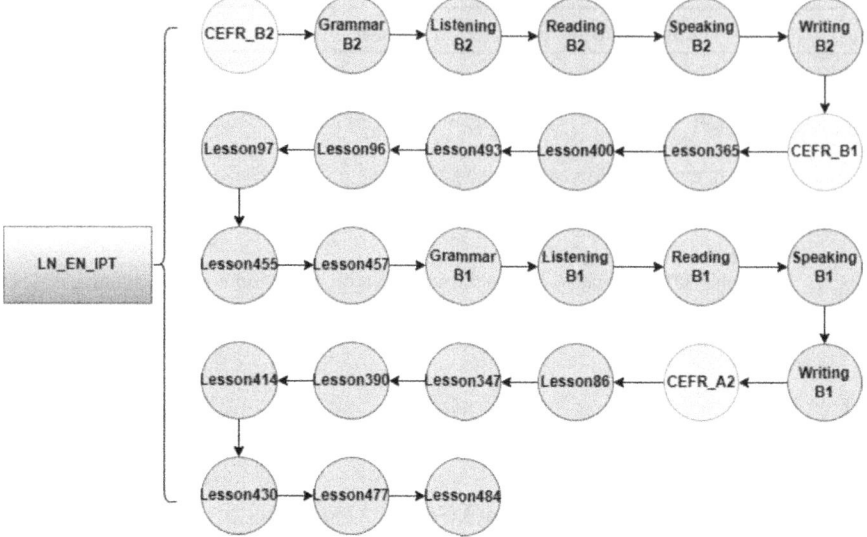

Fig. 7. Entity nodes included in the LN_EN_IPT set [5].

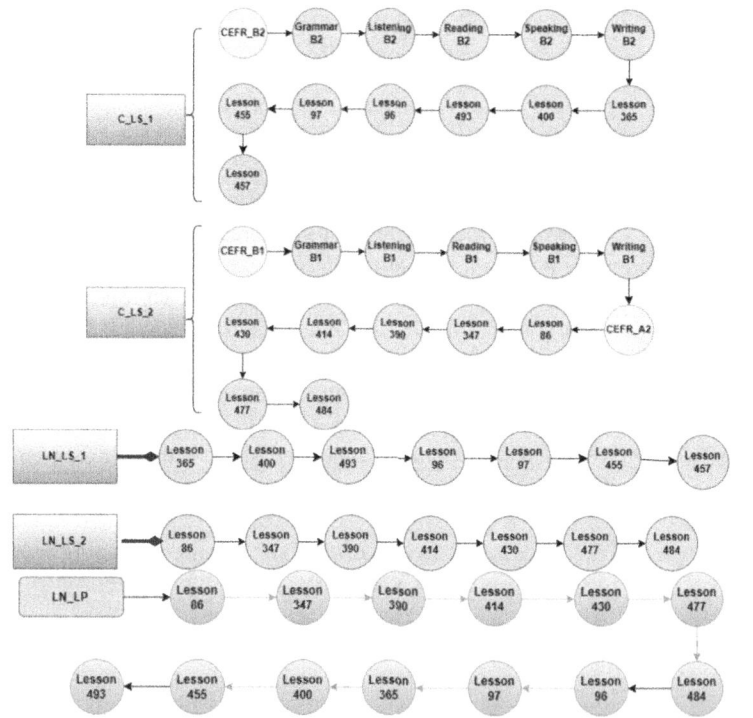

Fig. 8. The LN_LP set construction procedure in step 2 [29].

Algorithm 2. Determine nodes' significance in the WG.

Input: TAR, CUR, subgraph of TAR as G' (v, e), CPT_HAD, LS_KNOWN.
Output: IPT set.
1: $WG \leftarrow G'$
2: **For** each edge e point to node u in WG:
3:    **If** (u ∈ CPT_HAD)||(u ∈ LS_KNOWN)
4:       e. weight ← 0
5:    **Else** e. weight ← 1
6: **For** each node u in WG:
7:    **If** (u == CEFR_Level entity)
8:       PR_score(u) ← 1
9:    **Else** PR_score(u) ← 0
10: **While** not converged:
11:    **For** each node u in WG:
12:       PR_old ← PR_score(u)
13:       Using Eq.1 to calculate PR_score(u)
14:       **If** |PR_score(u) - PR_old| < threshold:
15:          break loop
16: IPT = {u | PR_score(u) > 0 and sort by PR_score(u) decreasing}

Table 2. The meaning of the signs used in Step 2.

Signs	Meaning
LV_EN	Set of entities (competence, previous CEFR level, lesson) related to the learner's target CEFR level
TAR	English proficiency according to the CEFR framework on the target certificate that the learner wants to achieve
CUR	English level on the current certificate according to the CEFR framework that the learner currently has
CPT_HAD	Set of competencies that the learner already has. Equivalent to a competency number belonging to CUR
LS_KNOWN	Set of lessons that the learner has learned before (lessons that the learner can optionally learn) belongs to the competencies of CUR
LN_EN_IPT	Set of CEFR_Level, Competency, and Lesson entities has decreasing importance to learners according to their PR score, which is greater than 0
INTM_LV	The set contains intermediate CEFR_Level nodes between TAR and CUR
CL_EN_u	The uth cluster contains nodes with the same label after each label propagation step
LN_LS_u	The set contains only lesson entities filtered from the corresponding CL_EN_u clusters

Algorithm 3. Building the first LP.

Input: WG of TAR, CUR, EN_IPT, MaxIter (Maximum number of execution loops)
Output: LN_LP.
  1: Initialize seedLabel for CEFR_Level nodes in WG.
  2: t ← 1
  3: **For** each node x ∈ EN_IPT:
  4:      Assign label of most represented connected node.
  5: **If** connected nodes' labels to x are all different:
  6:      Calculate viral influence using Eq. 2.
  7: Choose label satisfying Eq. 3 to update node x.
  8: **If** t = MaxIter or labels of node x match majority connected nodes' labels:
  9:      Assign nodes x to CL_EN_1, CL_EN_2, ..., CL_EN_k with specified labels.
10:      End.
11: **Else**
12:      t ← t + 1;
13:      Repeat steps 3 – 10.
14: **For** each CL_EN_1, CL_EN_2, ..., CL_EN_k:
15:      Initialize LN_LS_u (u = $\overline{1,k}$) containing Lesson entities for each cluster.
16: Create set *LN_LP* = *LN_LS_1* ∪... ∪ *LN_LS_u* containing required lessons.

According to the WG architecture shown in Fig. 6, learners must additionally attain the competencies of the intermediate levels (*INTM_LV*) (for instance, "B1") in order for learner X to go from a *CUR* (for example, level "A2") to a *TAR* (for example, level "B2"). The second job in this stage will cluster the most important lessons to learn (based on the PR_score of each node in the WG) into each cluster at each level of proficiency to ensure that learner X learns enough lessons for the required competencies from *CUR* to *TAR*. A popular clustering algorithm called LPA [9] builds a label propagation mechanism for random nodes using graph structure. However, to increase second job efficiency, we will employ Zhang et al.'s technique [53], known as LPA_NI. On the basis of node significance and label impact, it has been shown that LPA_NI produces better clustering results than standard LPA when propagated. The LPA_NI employs Eqs. 3 and 4 [53] for this job, where *LI(i, lb)* denotes the label's influence *(lb)* on node *i*, *d(j)* denotes the outdegree of node *j*, $N^l(i)$ denotes the set of labels *lb* surrounding node *i*, c_i denotes the most influential label that will be assigned to node *i*, and *l_max* denotes the sets of the maximum number of labels.

$$LI(i, lb) = \sum_{j \in N^l i} \frac{PR(j)}{d(j)} \qquad (3)$$

$$c_i = \underbrace{argmax LI(i, lb)}_{lb \in l\_max} \qquad (4)$$

This job's idea is explained in full in Algorithm 3. The nodes on the WG will also be divided into two clusters, *C_LS_1* and *C_LS_2*, when algorithm 3 is finished, in line with the example in Fig. 8 [29]. To generate the required *LN_LS_1* and *LN_LS_2* additional clusters, entities of the type of Lesson will then be selected from each cluster. The main lessons to be learned from the current level to the target level will be included in the first

LP, known as the *LN_LP* set, which will be created by combining the entities in the two clusters stated above and rearranging them in ascending PR_score values.

Building a MOO Function Using the MWS Method

The PLP not only arranges lessons in a sequence that meets the required competencies but also includes prerequisite lessons—essential lessons that must be learned before engaging in the main lessons. Specifically, in addition to lessons on grammar and the four skills (listening, speaking, reading, and writing), learners need to master a minimum set of vocabulary groups relevant to each skill in the exam. For instance, in the IELTS Listening section, topics such as Transportation and Rooms in a Building frequently appear, so learners should familiarize themselves with these vocabulary groups in advance. Similarly, for the speaking section, learners should first focus on proper pronunciation. Since there is no specific statistical report on the exact vocabulary required for English proficiency exams, the proposed solution optimizes the LP to ensure that learners do not need to study an excessive amount of vocabulary but still cover essential lessons. This approach helps save learning time and prevents overload.

Given these comments, our approach will create an evaluation function in this phase that is based on the MWS technique [16] to evaluate the optimization goals of each *LN_LP* in every iteration. We define the parameter m as a fixed number of consecutive prerequisite lessons selected from the *PRE_LS* set and incorporated into the existing *LN_LP* during each iteration. The assigned weights for optimizing each objective in the evaluation functions are detailed in Table 3 [29]. Using the MWS formula, which integrates information from the weight set and value function for each objective, let x denote the current LN_LP in the kth iteration. As expressed in Eq. 5, the LP with the lowest overall optimization score across all objectives is considered the most optimal.

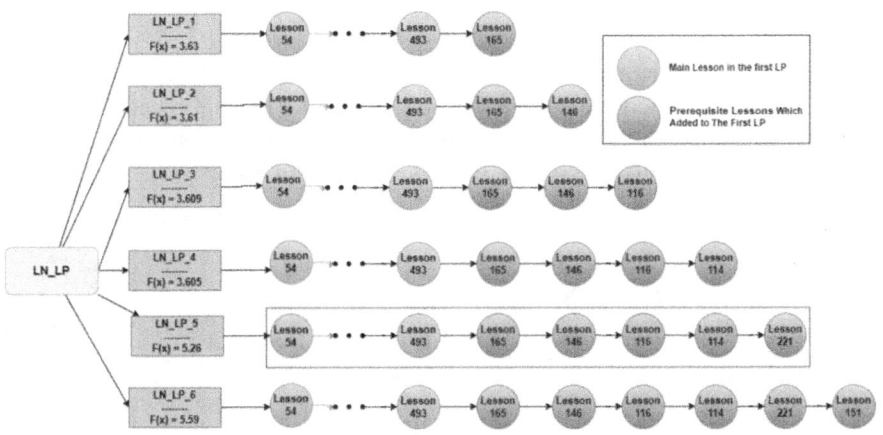

Fig. 9. Illustration of the complete LN_LP construction process in step 3 [29].

Algorithm 4. Building the completed LP as PLP.

Input: WG, LN_LP, EN_IPT, m
Output: LN_LP.
1: Initialize PRE_LS = ∅.
2: **For** each node u in WG:
3: **If** ((u == Vocabulary entity || u == Pronunciation entity) && u ∈ EN_IPT:
4:    PRE_LS ← PRE_LS ∪ {u}.
5: Initialize LN_LP_L = {LN_LP}.
6: **While (PRE_LS ≠ ∅)**
7:    Last_LN_LP = GetLastElement (LN_LP_L).
8:    Add m Lessons entities category from LN_PRE_LS to Last_LN_LP.
9:    Calculate Evaluation Score for Last_LN_LP using MWS with Eq.4.
10:   Add Last_LN_LP to LN_LP_L.
11:   |PRE_LS| = |PRE_LS| - m.
12: Select the best LN_LP from LN_LP_L based on optimal evaluation score.

Table 3. The weights and value functions of objectives [29].

Weight	Function	Meaning
w1	$f_1(x)$	Maximize the number of competency entity types present in the LN_LP set
w2	$f_2(x)$	Minimize the number of prerequisite lesson entities (which are vocabulary or pronunciation lessons) learned enough for the required lessons in LN_LP
w3	$f_3(x)$	Minimize the inverse sum of the PageRank (PR) scores of lessons in LN_LP
w4	$f_4(x)$	Minimize the number of lessons left over in LN_LP after being evaluated

Each LP in every iteration is evaluated based on four optimization goals, with each goal assigned a specific weight representing its priority. The implementation process for step 3 is outlined in Algorithm 4, while Fig. 9 [29] visually presents the phases of execution. Specifically, in each kth iteration, one additional lesson is progressively integrated.

$$minF(x) = \sum_{i=1}^{4} f_i(x).w_i \mid \begin{cases} \sum_{i=1}^{4} w_i = 1 \\ w_3 > 0 \\ 0 \leq w_i \leq 1 where i = \overline{1,4} \end{cases} \quad (5)$$

5 ALPR Solution to Dynamic Initial PLP Adjustment

The learner will begin studying in accordance with the plan after being given a PLP that fits their current level, goals, and desired study time to prepare for the English certificate exam. However, objectives, learning preferences, or learning capacities could alter as a result of the learning process. The learner may become bored or encounter delays in their learning if the previous course is continued. Consequently, the LP must be dynamically modified in real time. Designing a solution to create an ALPR from the initial PLP is the main goal of this section. In order to modify the LP appropriately, a learning trend analysis algorithm is used on the learning progress data (time, number of test attempts, and learning outcomes).

5.1 Execution Sequence of the ALPR Solution

The proposed solution will follow the adaptive learning system development approach known as Micro-Adaptive Learning and follows the principle of algorithm-based sequential systems [12]. The following is the description of the execution sequence of ALPR that will be used in the proposed solution (Fig. 10).

- Steps 1–3: The system will create a learner profile that contains personal information, current level, target level, and learning style - preferences - requirements. The system will recommend an initial PLP as LN_LP for the learner based on this profile. Section 4 provided the specifics of how these actions were implemented.
- Step 4–6: The learner begins studying some lessons in LN_LP. The system will save the lesson data (Learning Progress Log, or LPL for short) in GraphDB each time the student completes a lesson. The Learner entity type and the Lesson entity type have a relation called *HAS_LEARN_LESSON_LOG*, which displays the specifics of the data in LPL.
- Step 7–10: The system's adaptive module will use the algorithm designed to interpret the aforementioned data to recommend an ALP for learners each week based on the LPL data in GraphDB of each lesson learned.
- Until the learner has finished all of the lessons that need to be learnt in LN_LP, the system will keep repeating steps 4 through 10.

5.2 Algorithm Development for ALPR Solution

The following concepts and notations are used to explicitly define the algorithm used in the proposed ALPR solution:

- $A_w = \{[LS_i, I(LS_i)] \mid where\ i = \overline{1, l}\}$: The set containing l lessons learned by the learner in wth week
- $I(LS_i)$: score measuring the importance of ith lesson compared to the remaining lessons in the set A_w corresponding to the learner's results and study time for this lesson
- $S(LS_i)$: the time the learner spends studying for i^{th} lesson in the set A_w ($i \geq 1$)
- $T(LS_i)$: the number of times the learner took the test for i^{th} lesson in the set A_w
- $E(LS_i)$: Time required to complete learning a lesson
- $R(LSi) = \{0\ (Pass),\ 1\ (Fail)\}$: the result the learner achieves after completing i^{th} lesson in the set A_w ($i \geq 1$)
- D_W: The set containing the lessons in the adaptive LP recommended for the learner to study in W^{th} week where $W = w + 1$
- K_w: the number of Lessons to be added to the set D_W is based on the important score of each lesson in the set A_w and satisfies the set of conditions in Eq. 7

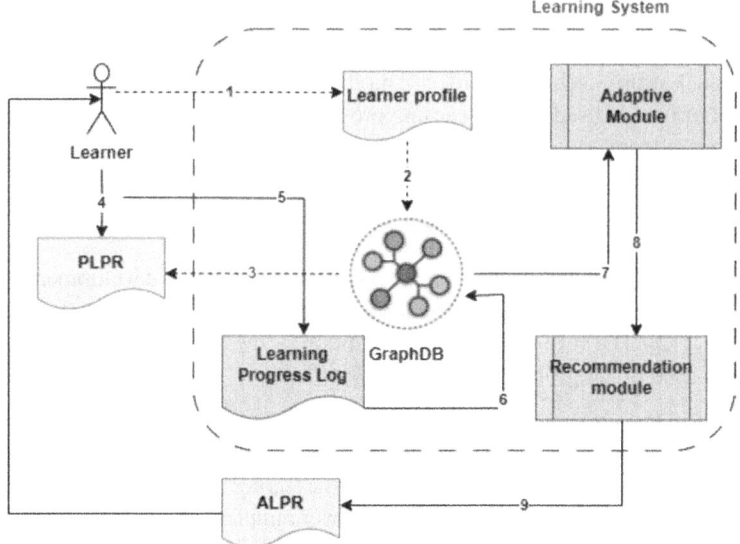

Fig. 10. ALPR operational schematic for the proposed solution.

- L_w: number of lessons with an important score greater than 1 in the set A_w.
- $C_W = \{[LS_i, I(LS_i)] | i = \overline{1, (L_w - K_w)}\}$: The set contains lessons with an important score greater than 1 but are not selected to be included in the D_W set in W^{th} week
- $R_W = (R_w - A_w) \cup D_W \cup C_W = \{[LS_i, I(LS_i)] \mid where\ i = \overline{1, n(LN\_LP)}\}$|: the set containing the remaining lessons that the learner needs to learn in W^{th} week and has fewer Lessons than the initial LN_LP

As shown in Fig. 11, the algorithm that offers learners an adative LP to follow will consist of 12 primary steps and have the following input data (Input) and output outcomes (Output). For the Input:

- Learner identification information
- Learner's LN_LP information
- Number of lessons (l) in the set A_w in the first week ($w = 1$).
- $S(LS_i)$: the time (in days) that the learner has studied for each ith lesson $\left(i = \overline{1, l}\right)$ in the set A_w in the first week
- $R(LS_i)$: the result obtained after completing the tests of each ith lesson $\left(i = \overline{1, l}\right)$ in the set A_w in the first week
- $T(LS_i)$: the number of times the learner has taken the test for i^{th} lesson ($i \geq 1$) in the set A_w

And for the output:

- The lessons in the D_W set
- The lessons in the R_W set.

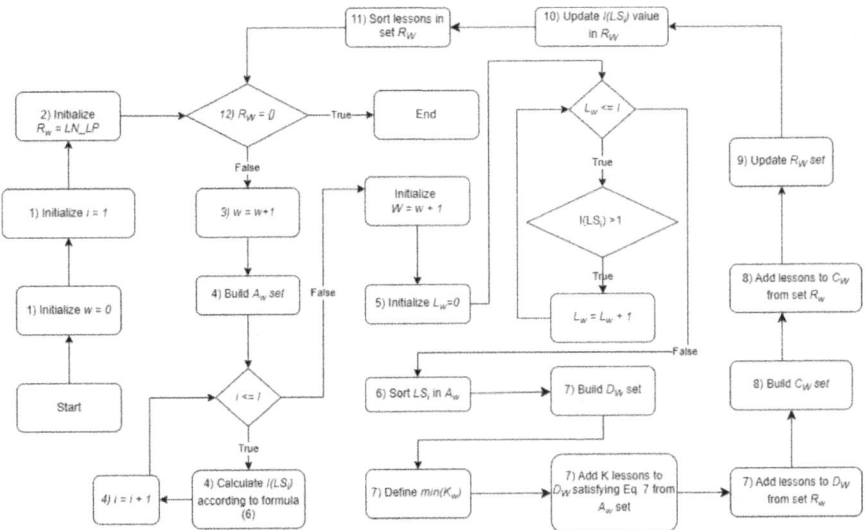

Fig. 11. An illustration of the algorithm used in the suggested ALPR solution.

- Based on the learner's progress and performance each week, this ALP will continually adapt to make sure the most pertinent lessons in the LP are presented.

The following is a description of the specific content of the twelve steps in the proposed algorithm:

- Step 1: Initialize $w = 0$ and $i = 1$
- Step 2: Based on the learner's LN_LP set information, initialize the $R_W = LN\_LP$. Currently, we have $W = w + 1 = 1$, so the $R_1 = LN\_LP$, which means that in the first week when the learner starts learning the first lesson in LN_LP, the information and number of remaining lessons to learn in the R_1 and LN_LP set are the same
- Step 3: Update $w = w + 1$. The algorithm will start processing based on the LPL of the lessons the learner learned in the first week (A_1)
- Step 4: Suppose in A_w set, the learner has learned l lessons consisting of LS_i. Starting with $i = 1$, calculate the $I(LS_1)$ accroding to Eq. 6, continue to increase the value of $i = i + 1$ to calculate the $I(LS_2)$, $I(LS_3)$ … and repeat the operation like that until the value $i > l$.

$$I(LS_i) = \begin{cases} 1 + \frac{E(LS_i)}{S(LS_i)} \times \frac{1}{l}, R(LS_i) = 1 \\ \frac{T(LS_i)}{S(LS_i)} \times \frac{1}{l}, R(LS_i) = 0 \end{cases} \quad (6)$$

- Step 5: Define L_w as the number of lessons with an important score greater than 1 in the set A_w
- Step 6: Rearrange the lessons in the A_w set in order of important score from highest to lowest
- Step 7: Initialize the D_W set to contain the lessons in the ALP that the learner needs to learn in Wth week. The D_W set will contain the top K lessons with the highest

important score selected from the A_w set and the new lessons to be learned will be taken from the R_W set. The criteria for selecting lessons into the D_W set are specified in Eq. 7 as follows:

$$D_W = \{LS_i\} | \begin{cases} I(LS_i) \geq 1 \\ \frac{l_W}{2} \leq \min(K_W) < 6; K_W \in N^* \\ 1 < i \leq 6 \end{cases} \quad (7)$$

- Step 8: Initialize the C_W set. Lessons that are not selected to be added to the D_W set in step 7 will be added to the C_W set. The number of lessons in the C_W set is $(L_W - K_W)$
- Step 9: Update the value for the R_W
- Step 10: Update the important score value for each lesson in the R_W as follows:
  - $I(LS \in R_W) + = I(LS \in A_w)$ (For selected lessons from the A_w set)
  - $I(LS \in R_W) = 0$ (For selected lessons from the R_w set)

- Step 11: Arrange the lessons in the R_W set in descending order of important score
- Step 12: Verify that there are more than zero items in the set R_W. If so, the loop will repeat steps 2 through 10, indicating that the learner still needs to acquire some lessons to finish the LP outlined in the initial LN_LP. If not, the algorithm will end, and the learner's ALP will be generated after it has been determined that the learner has completed all of the lessons outlined in the original LN_LP.

6 Experimentation and Evaluation

Our experiment was conducted on the presumption that the learner's goal is to move up from the lowest current level to the highest target level, which is "TOEIC (L-R)-C1," "TOEIC (S-W)-C1," "IELTS-C2," and "TOEFL-C2," as defined by the CEFR. We start by comparing the results of the suggestions provided on the subgraphs of each instance of a CEFR_Level entity with the whole original KG design, using the procedure outlined in step 1 of the solution building process. Then, utilizing the produced dataset, we focus on step 3 of the solution-building process to determine the optimal weight set for this phase. In the evaluation of the proposed solution, we compare the PageRank algorithm combined with the traditional LPA algorithm (PR_LPA) and the method used in the solution development, applying the PageRank algorithm combined with the LPA_NI method (PR + LPA_NI), to evaluate the performance, stability, accuracy, and efficiency of our proposed solution [12, 26]. The experimental dataset and similarity weights used in the experiment will serve as the basis for this comparison.

6.1 Dataset Building

As per our study done on many websites, official reference papers, and the organizations that administer these examinations, there is presently no standardized dataset that declares the learning content and abilities necessary for these English certifications according to each level. To create a data set suitable for the experimental and evaluation phase, we thus adhered to the process shown in Fig. 12 [29].

Steps 1 and 2 - Data Collection and Processing: We obtain information on the forms, subject matter, and evaluation criteria of English certification examinations from the British Council, the official ETS website, and a few standard documents pertaining to these tests. Create English lesson units using this data, including certification levels, necessary skills, and targeted instruction in grammar, vocabulary, pronunciation, speaking, listening, reading, and writing. Convert the gathered data into properties, relationships, and entities that fit the KG architecture.

Steps 3 and 4 - Saving reprocessed data as a CSV file and importing it into Neo4j: Generate CSV files that include the entity and relationship data from step 2. Use Neo4j's import function to load these files and construct a complete graph database schema based on KG architecture. The number of entities and relationships within the KG architecture is detailed in Table 4 [29], while a sample of the dataset can be seen in Fig. 13 [29]. The full experimental dataset is now accessible on Kaggle.

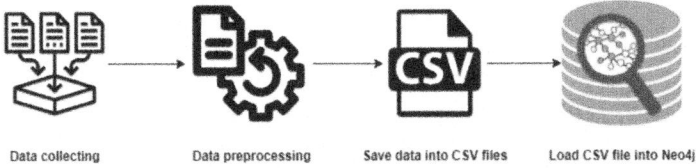

Fig. 12. The process of building an experimental dataset [29].

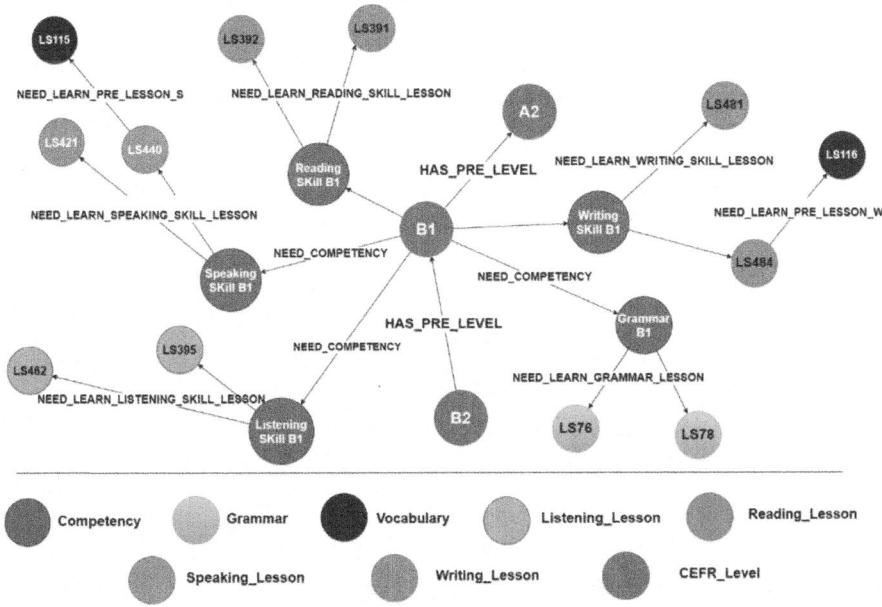

Fig. 13. A part of the nodes and their relations in KG [29].

Table 4. Statistics on the number of entities and relationships in the KG [29].

Entities	Amount	Relations	Amount
		NEED_KNOWN / HAD_KNOW	63
CEFR_Level	22	NEED_LEARN_GRAMMAR	98
Competency	49	NEED_LEARN_LISTEN_SKILL	102
		NEED_LEAN_READING_SKIL	68
Grammar_LS	98	NEED_LEAN_SPEAKING_SKL	115
Listening_LS	79	NEED_LEARN_WRITING_SKIL	54
Pronunciation_LS	7	NEED_LEAN_PRE_LESSON_L	103
Reading_LS	54	NEED_LEARN_PRE_LESSON	59
Speaking_LS	91	NEED_LEAN_PRE_LESSON_S	66
Vocabulary_LS	124	NEED_LEAN_PRE_LESSON_W	12
Writing_LS	39	NEED_LEN_PRONUNCIATION	7

6.2 Post-Experiment Results

For Step 1 of the Solution Building Process

As per the information provided in Sect. 4.2, we will construct a subgraph for every CEFR_Level entity in step 1 to compare the recommendation outcomes of running on the subgraph of each CEFR_Level entity and the full original KG architecture. The LP evaluation function (step 3 of Sect. 4.2) uses a sample weight set of (0.25; 0.25; 0.25; 0.25) to guarantee the stability of the results between executions. The initial default is that the user does not have any competencies or lessons corresponding to the current level to run the test. As demonstrated by the test results in Table 5, the following steps of the solution-building process can be applied to the subgraph of each CEFR_Level entity to produce more optimal execution time results while still producing LP evaluation results that are nearly identical to those on the original graph.

Table 5. Solution Results on Original Graph vs. CEFR-Level entities Subgraphs.

Certificate/Level	Type of graph	No. of vertices	No. of edges	Evaluation score	Time execution (s)
TOEIC L -R (A1-C1)	Sub-graph	215	481	6.55	18.78
	Original graph	570	770	6.55	21.53
TOEIC S –W (A1 – C1)	Sub-graph	178	384	3.89	21.46
	Original graph	570	770	3.90	26.35
IELTS (A1 – C2)	Sub-graph	335	716	10.22	20.35
	Original graph	570	770	10.23	22.04

(*continued*)

Table 5. (*continued*)

Certificate/Level	Type of graph	No. of vertices	No. of edges	Evaluation score	Time execution (s)
TOEFL (A1 – C2)	Sub-graph	170	360	4.0	25.13
	Original graph	570	770	4.03	29.12

Optimal Weight Selection

As stated in Sect. 4.2, an evaluation function for the LP optimization objectives is constructed using the MWS approach in the proposed solution. To assess the impact of the weight sets on the LP recommendation results, we continue testing the proposed algorithm in this section using various weight sets and a fixed number of prerequisite lessons added to the LP under consideration at each kth iteration $(m = 5)$. This method requires weight sets as a priority level of the evaluation criteria. Based on the developed data set, the best set of weights is then chosen for the recommendation procedure.

Using the experimentation method described earlier, we found that all tested weight sets confirmed the sufficiency of lessons in covering the required knowledge, skills, and competencies. Furthermore, the number of prerequisite lessons deemed redundant in the recommended PLP remained consistent across all four types of English certification exams. At the same time, the evaluation function score of the LP tended to decrease as the objective weights showed significant variations. This suggests that when the objective weights are nearly balanced, the optimal LP is achieved by considering all objectives as nearly equally important. Ultimately, we determined that the weight set $\{w1 = 0.28, w2 = 0.27, w3 = 0.25, w4 = 0.2\}$ is the most suitable for this solution, as it best satisfies the evaluation function criteria outlined in Eq. 5.

6.3 Evaluation Findings

To evaluate our solution, we compare the solutions PR + LPA_NI and PR + LPA in terms of accuracy, efficiency, stability, and performance. To show efficiency, a PLP with scores from the evaluation function with the lowest score that meets the requirements in Eq. 5 is utilized. The number of lessons in the learnt PLP is adequate for the number of necessary Competency types, and the two values of these numbers must be fewer than or equal to the number of entities in the Lesson and Competency classes in the original KG design. This is how accuracy is conveyed. The consistency of the output PLP across several runs with the same input data is known as stability, and the time it takes for the learner to be recommended the PLP is a measure of performance. Regarding efficiency, Fig. 14 [29] shows that the PLP evaluation score recommended by the proposed solution for implementation in the PR + LPA_NI or PR + LPA approach consistently satisfies Eq. 5. However, the PR + LPA_NI approach tends to produce an evaluation score closer to the optimal PLP compared to PR + LPA. Additionally, we analyze an example using input data for the "IELTS-C2" certificate to generate a PLP recommendation for learners, as shown in Fig. 15 [29]. The PR + LPA_NI approach maintains a nearly consistent PLP evaluation function score across multiple executions with the same input data, like the PR

+ LPA approach, and this trend is also observed for other certificate types. Furthermore, Fig. 16 [29] highlights that the PLP recommended by the PR + LPA_NI technique has a slightly faster execution time than PR + LPA.

Table 6. The percentage of Lesson entities that meet the Competency entities needed to learn in the recommended PLP [29].

Type of Recommendation (1)	Number of Competency entities required (2)	Number of Lesson entities to learn (3)	Number of Lesson entities in PLP (4)	Number of Competency entities learned in PLP (5)	Compete-ny entity rate is met (6) = (5)/(2)	Lesson entity rate is met (7) = (4)/(3)
TOEIC L-R (A1-C1)	12	198	161	11	91,67%	81,31%
TOEIC S-W (A1-C1)	12	161	124	11	91,67%	77,02%
IELTS (A1-C2)	20	309	272	19	95%	88,03%
TOEFL (A1 – C2)	16	148	111	15	93,76%	75%

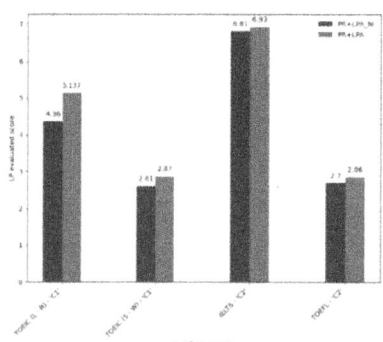

Fig. 14. Evaluation scores of the recommended PLP on two algorithms [29].

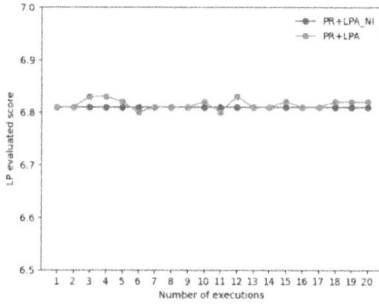

Fig. 15. Execution time when executing on two algorithms for making PLP in "IELTS - C2" [29].

Finally, in terms of accuracy, Fig. 17 [29] and Table 6 [29] demonstrate that both the PR + LPA_NI and PR + LPA approaches recommend a PLP where the proportion of Lesson entities almost fully covers the required Competency entities, while the total number of entities remains smaller than in the original KG. Overall, compared to the PR + LPA technique, the solution created using the PR + LPA_NI approach substantially better satisfied the assessment standards.

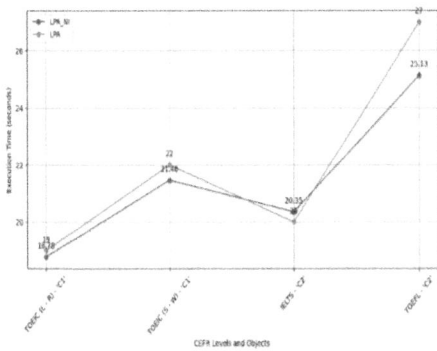

Fig. 16. Results when executed on two algorithms in multiple executions [29].

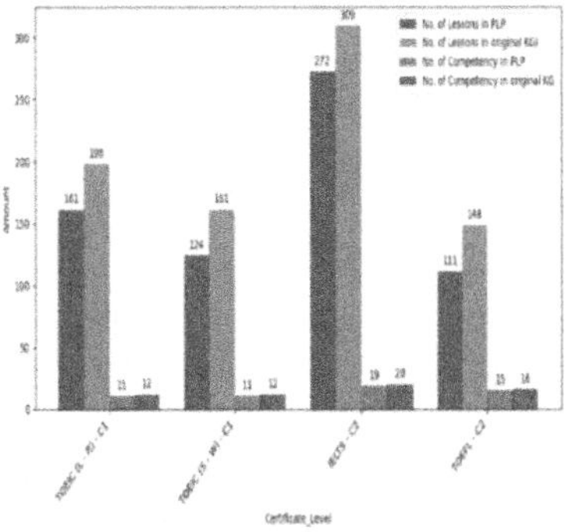

Fig. 17. Number of lessons and competencies of PR + LPA_NI solution [29].

6.4 Illustrative Web Application for the Solution

We have implemented the developed solution, which includes the following primary functional flows, in the first PLP consultation for learners on the online platform. Assume that learner "X" needs to be guided on an LP based on the following information:

- Certificate: IELTS (4 skills).
- Current score: 3.5 (CEFR framework equivalent to level "A2").
- Target score: 7.5 (CEFR framework equivalent to level "C1").
- Desired study time for the recommended LP: 2 years.

The learner must complete the following steps:

- First, the certificate-level information registration screen (Fig. 18) requires the user to enter the necessary data.
- The learner's lessons and competencies at the current level will then be listed (Fig. 19). Each line that corresponds to the competency and associated lessons that the learner wants to retake can be chosen by the learner.
- When the learner hits the "Show your Learning Path" button, the system will create the initial PLP as seen in Fig. 19 using the data the learner has input.

Following the aforementioned procedures, the learner will be presented with a PLP that, as illustrated in Fig. 20, consists of a series of lessons to be learned that most closely correspond to the material supplied. The aforementioned ALPR solution can then be used to modify this PLP in real time.

YOUR IELTS CERTIFICATE INFORMATION

IELTS score belongs to skill *	Learning Start Date *
IELTS (4 skills)	07/03/2024
Your Current TOEIC Score *	Learning End Date *
3.5	07/03/2028
Your Target TOEIC Score *	Your time desired to get the target score
7.5	48

Save And Show Your Current Level Information

Fig. 18. Information registration screen for the learner's level based on their certificate.

Save And Show Your Current Level Information

Select	Competency or Lesson	Name	ID of node
☑	Competency	Grammar for level A2	1147
☐	Grammar	Usage of By and until ,By the time ...	1262
☑	Grammar	Usage of For, during and while	1261
☑	Grammar	Structure of Like/as if /as though	1260
☐	Grammar	Structure of "AS" sentences	1259
☐	Grammar	Structure of Unless , As Long as , Provided/ providing	1258
☑	Grammar	Phrases showing concessions ; Although/though/even though/in spite of/despite	1257
☐	Grammar	Phrases showing reasons: Because of, Due to and Owing to	1256
☑	Grammar	Structure of Superlatives	1255
☐	Grammar	Structure of Comparison	1254
☐	Grammar	Structure of Quite, pretty, rather and fairly	1253
☑	Grammar	Structure of Enough and too	1252
☐	Grammar	Structure of So and such	1251

Fig. 19. The learner's lessons and potential competencies at their current level.

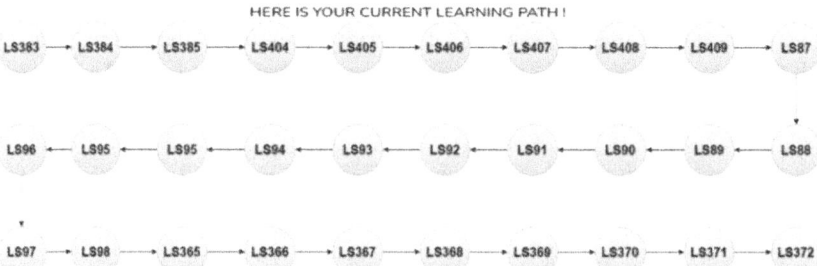

Fig. 20. An initial PLP is recommended to the learner.

7 Conclusion

In this study, we examined how RS are developed and highlighted how KG might enhance RS's accuracy and efficiency in accordance with the most recent state-of-the-art methodology. RSs may better grasp the links between entities, make use of deeper semantic information, and provide suggestions with higher quality by utilizing KG and related approaches. With a case study on English LP recommendation, we specifically looked at the use of RS in the context of personalized learning. To help English language learners, we have developed a tailored LP recommendation system in this study that specifically targets international certification tests like the TOEFL, IELTS, and TOEIC. Numerous noteworthy findings, both theoretical and experimental, have been obtained from the research. To maximize the LP recommendation process, we have examined graph processing algorithms like BFS, PageRank, Label propagation, and the Weighted sum approach. We have also looked at the features of KG and chosen Neo4j as the implementation platform. The approach is based on a KG that shows how each learner's level, abilities, knowledge, and learning needs relate to one another. We finished the English experimental data set, tried the solution with a variety of weight sets, and ultimately chose the best weight set for the experiment. The outcomes demonstrate that the system can provide LP recommendations in an efficient, accurate, stable, and high-performing manner. Additionally, the method has been effectively implemented in a web context, establishing a foundation for future study. Nevertheless, there are still certain obstacles to be addressed, such as the experimental dataset's correctness since it was not thoroughly evaluated, there was no comparison with related research, and learner feedback was not incorporated to enhance the recommendation model. Furthermore, the existing LP's approach of evaluating the lessons' significance is still fixed and not really tailored to each individual student. Hence, real-time dataset updates, system deployment in an actual setting to gather user feedback, and the integration of AI and machine learning models to maximize the adaptive LP for every individual will be the main areas of future development.

References

1. Al-Ghuribi, S.M., Noah, S.A.M.: A comprehensive overview of recommender system and sentiment analysis. arXiv preprint arXiv:2109.08794 (2021)
2. Amara, S., Subramanian, R.R.: Collaborating personalized recommender system and content-based recommender system using TextCorpus. In: 2020 6th International Conference on Advanced Computing and Communication Systems (ICACCS), pp. 105–109. IEEE (2020
3. Hui, B., Zhang, L., Zhou, X., Wen, X., Nian, Y.: Personalized recommendation system based on knowledge embedding and historical behavior. Appl. Intell. **52**, 1–13 (2022)
4. Bahramian, Z., Ali Abbaspour, R., Claramunt, C.: A cold start context-aware recommender system for tour planning using artificial neural network and case based reasoning. Mob. Inf. Syst. **2017**(1), 9364903 (2017)
5. Bhaskaran, S., Marappan, R., Santhi, B.: Design and analysis of a cluster-based intelligent hybrid recommendation system for e-learning applications. Mathematics **9**(2), 197 (2021)
6. Chen, C., Wu, X., Chen, J., Pardalos, P.M., Ding, S.: Dynamic grouping of heterogeneous agents for exploration and strike missions. Front. Inf. Technol. Electron. Eng. **23**(1), 86–100 (2022)

7. Chen, H., Yin, C., Fan, X., Qiao, L., Rong, W., Zhang, X.: Learning path recommendation for MOOC platforms based on a knowledge graph. In: Qiu, H., Zhang, C., Fei, Z., Qiu, M., Kung, S.-Y. (eds.) KSEM 2021. LNCS (LNAI), vol. 12816, pp. 600–611. Springer, Cham (2021). https://doi.org/10.1007/978-3-030-82147-0_49
8. Chicaiza, J., Valdiviezo-Diaz, P.: A comprehensive survey of knowledge graph-based recommender systems: technologies, development, and contributions. Information 12(6), 232 (2021)
9. Čížková, K.: Comparing two main community detection algorithms and their applications on human brains (2022)
10. Drachsler, H., Hummel, H., Koper, R.: Recommendations for learners are different: applying memory-based recommender system techniques to lifelong learning (2007)
11. Dyvik, E.: The most spoken languages worldwide 2023. Statista (2023)
12. Ennouamani, S., Mahani, Z.: An overview of adaptive e-learning systems. In: 2017 Eighth International Conference on Intelligent Computing and Information Systems (ICICIS), pp. 342–347. IEEE (2017)
13. Zhang, F., Yuan, N.J., Lian, D., Xie, X., Ma, W.-Y.: Collaborative knowledge base embedding for recommender systems. In: Proceedings of the 22Nd ACM SIGKDD International Conference on Knowledge Discovery and Data Mining, ser. KDD '16, pp. 353–362. ACM, New York (2016)
14. Fernández-García, A.J., Rodríguez-Echeverría, R., Preciado, J.C., Manzano, J.M.C., Sánchez-Figueroa, F.: Creating a recommender system to support higher education students in the subject enrollment decision. IEEE Access 8, 189069–189088 (2020)
15. Gasmi, I., Anguel, F., Seridi-Bouchelaghem, H., Azizi, N.: Context-aware based evolutionary collaborative filtering algorithm. Lect. Notes Netw. Syst. 156, 217–232 (2021)
16. Gunantara, N.: A review of multi-objective optimization: methods and its applications. Cogent Eng. 5(1), 1502242 (2018)
17. Guo, Q., et al.: A survey on knowledge graph-based recommender systems. IEEE Trans. Knowl. Data Eng. 34(8), 3549–3568 (2020)
18. Gupta, M., Thakkar, A., Gupta, V., Rathore, D.P.S.: Movie recommender system using collaborative filtering. In: 2020 International Conference on Electronics and Sustainable Communication Systems (ICESC), pp. 415–420. IEEE (2020)
19. Wang, H., et al.: Ripplenet: propagating user preferences on the knowledge graph for recommender systems. In: Proceedings of the 27th ACM International Conference on Information and Knowledge Management, pp. 417–426. ACM (2018)
20. He, Z., Hui, B., Zhang, S., Xiao, C., Zhong, T., Zhou, F.: Exploring indirect entity relations for knowledge graph enhanced recommender system. Expert Syst. Appl. 213, 118984 (2023)
21. Hou, B., Lin, Y., Li, Y., Fang, C., Li, C., Wang, X.: KG-PLPPM: a knowledge graph-based personal learning path planning method used in online learning. Electronics 14(2), 255 (2025)
22. Huang, S., Cheng, J., Wu, H.: Temporal graph traversals: definitions, algorithms, and applications. arXiv preprint arXiv:1401.1919 (2014)
23. Kannikaklang, N., Wongthanavasu, S., Thamviset, W.: A hybrid recommender system for improving rating prediction of movie recommendation. In: 2022 19th International Joint Conference on Computer Science and Software Engineering (JCSSE), pp. 1–6. IEEE (2022)
24. Khan, Z. Y., Niu, Z., Nyamawe, A. S., & ul Haq, I. (2021). A deep hybrid model for recommendation by jointly leveraging ratings, reviews and metadata information. Engineering Applications of Artificial Intelligence, 97, 104066
25. Li, D., Qu, H., Wang, J.: A survey on knowledge graph-based recommender systems. In: 2023 China Automation Congress (CAC), pp. 2925–2930. IEEE (2023)
26. Mansouri, N., Soui, M., Abed, M.: Full personalized learning path recommendation: a literature review. In: International Conference on Advanced Intelligent Systems and Informatics, pp. 185–195. Springer, Cham (2023)

27. Marques, G.A., Rigo, S.J., Alves, I.M.D.R.: Graduation mentoring recommender-hybrid recommendation system for customizing the undergraduate student's formative path. In: 2021 XVI Latin American Conference on Learning Technologies (LACLO), pp. 342–349. IEEE (2021)
28. Nabizadeh, A.H., Leal, J.P., Rafsanjani, H.N., Shah, R.R.: Learning path personalization and recommendation methods: a survey of the state-of-theart. Expert Syst. Appl. **159**, 113596 (2020)
29. Nguyen, D.T., Nguyen, T.M.T.: A knowledge map mining-based personalized learning path recommendation solution for english learning (2024)
30. North, B., Piccardo, E.: Developing new CEFR descriptor scales and expanding the existing ones. Zeitschrift Fremdsprachenforschung **30**(2), 142–160 (2019)
31. Geng, S., Fu, Z., Tan, J., Ge, Y., De Melo, G., Zhang, Y.: Path language modeling over knowledge graphsfor explainable recommendation. In: Proceedings of the ACM Web Conference 2022, pp. 946–955 (2022)
32. Park, S.-J., Chae, D.-K., Bae, H.-K., Park, S., Kim, S.-W.: Reinforcement learning over sentiment-augmented knowledge graphs towards accurate and explainable recommendation. In: Proceedings of the Fifteenth ACM International Conference on Web Search and Data Mining, pp. 784–793 (2022)
33. Shi, D., Wang, T., Xing, H., Xu, H.: A learning path recommendation model based on a multidimensional knowledge graph framework for e-learning. Knowl.-Based Syst. **195**, 105618 (2020)
34. Singh, M., Rishi, O.: Event driven recommendation system for E-commerce using knowledge based collaborative filtering technique. Scalable Comput. **21**, 369–378 (2020)
35. Sun, Y., Liang, J., Niu, P.: Personalized recommendation of english learning based on knowledge graph and graph convolutional network. In: International Conference on Artificial Intelligence and Security, pp. 157–166. Springer, Cham (2021)
36. Troussas, C., Krouska, A.: Path-based recommender system for learning activities using knowledge graphs. Information **14**(1), 9 (2022)
37. Turan, E., Arslan, E., Tülü, Ç., Orhan, U.: A comparison of graph centrality algorithms for semantic distance. Lapseki Meslek Yüksekokulu Uygulamalı Araştırmalar Dergisi **1**(2), 61–70 (2020)
38. Valdiviezo-Diaz, P., Ortega, F., Cobos, E., Lara-Cabrera, R.: A collaborative filtering approach based on naïve bayes classifier. IEEE Access **7**, 108581–108592 (2019)
39. Wang, H., Zhang, F., Xie, X., et al.: DKN: deep knowledge-aware network for news recommendation (2018)
40. Wang, X., He, X., Cao, Y., et al.: KGAT: knowledge graph attention network for recommendation (2019)
41. Wang, H., et al.: Knowledge-aware graph neural networks with label smoothness regularization for recommender systems. In: Proceedings of the 25th ACM SIGKDD International Conference on Knowledge Discovery & Data Mining, pp. 968–977 (2019)
42. Wang, Z., Lin, G., Tan, H., Chen, Q., Liu, X.: CKAN: Collaborative knowledge-aware attentive network for recommender systems. In: Proceedings of the 43rd International ACM SIGIR Conference on Research and Development in Information Retrieval, pp. 219–228 (2020)
43. Wen, S., Wang, C., Li, H., Wen, S.: Naïve Bayes regression model and its application in collaborative filtering recommendation algorithm. Int. J. Internet Manuf. **5**, 85–99 (2018)
44. Wu, S., Tang, Y., Zhu, Y., et al.: Session-based Recommendation with Graph Neural Networks (2018)
45. Xiao, G.: A personalized learning path for French study in colleges based on a big data knowledge map. Sci. Program. **2023**(1), 4359133 (2023)
46. Zhao, Y., et al.: Time-aware path reasoning on knowledge graph for recommendation. ACM Trans. Inf. Syst. **41**(2), 1–26 (2022)

47. Yan, Z., Du, H., Lin, Z., Jianhua, Z.: Personalization exercise recommendation framework based on Knowledge Concept Graph. Comput. Sci. Inf. Syst. **20**(2), 857–878 (2023)
48. Yang, X., Dong, M., Chen, X., Ota, K.: Recommender system-based diffusion inferring for open social networks. IEEE Trans. Comput. Social Syst. **7**(1), 24–34 (2019)
49. Yin, H., Sun, Z., Sun, Y., Huang, G.: Automatic learning path recommendation for open source projects using deep learning on knowledge graphs. In: 2021 IEEE 45th Annual Computers, Software, and Applications Conf. (COMPSAC), pp. 824–833. IEEE (2021
50. Cui, Z., et al.: Reinforced KGs reasoning for explainable sequential recommendation. In: World Wide Web, vol. 25, no. 2, pp. 631–654 (2022)
51. Zhang, B., Si, H.: Learning path planning based on knowledge graph on MOOC platform. Open J. Soc. Sci. **11**(3), 457–465 (2023)
52. Zhang, J.C., Zain, A.M., Zhou, K.Q., Chen, X., Zhang, R.M.: A review of recommender systems based on knowledge graph embedding. Expert Syst. Appl. 123876 (2024)
53. Zhang, X.K., Ren, J., Song, C., Jia, J., Zhang, Q.: Label propagation algorithm for community detection based on node importance and label influence. Phys. Lett. A **381**(33), 2691–2698 (2017)
54. Zhang, X., Liu, S., Wang, H.: Personalized learning path recommendation for e-learning based on knowledge graph and graph convolutional network. Int. J. Software Eng. Knowl. Eng. **33**(01), 109–131 (2023)
55. Zhu, B., Hurtado, R., Bobadilla, J., Ortega, F.: An efficient recommender system method based on the numerical relevances and the non-numerical structures of the ratings. IEEE Access **6**, 49935–49954 (2018)

Enhanced Prediction of Post-Myocardial Infarction Complications: Dual-Modality Analysis with Optimized Flow Cytometry Preprocessing and Feature Visualization

Nada Al-Dausari[1(✉)], Frans Coenen[1], Anh Nguyen[1], and Eduard Shantsila[2]

[1] Department of Computer Science, The University of Liverpool, Liverpool, UK
{N.Al-Dausari,coenen,Anh.Nguyen}@liverpool.ac.uk
[2] Institute of Population Health, The University of Liverpool, Liverpool, UK
Eduard.Shantsila@liverpool.ac.uk

Abstract. Cardiovascular disease remains a major global health challenge, and Myocardial Infarction (MI) is among its most critical manifestations. Post-MI complications significantly increase patient morbidity and mortality, underscoring the clinical importance of identifying individuals at high risk. This paper repats on work directed at analysing duel-modality flow cytometry data, specifically, tabular summaries and image-based plots of key markers, to enhance complication prediction. The proposed framework, *FlowCytFuse*, applies data preprocessing techniques optimized for flow cytometry, including the removal of count beads to reduce noise, normalization of fluorescence intensities, and visualization of crucial features as two-dimensional plots. This is combined with a dual neural network architecture: the first network handles tabular data, while the second processes image-based representations (scatter and density plots). A voting mechanism then fuses both outputs to produce a final prediction. In testing on a real-world dataset of 246 patients, the method demonstrates marked improvements in F1 scores for minority-class (complication) cases compared to earlier approaches. These findings highlight the potential of blending numerical and visual representations of flow cytometry data to deliver more accurate and clinically meaningful post-MI risk stratification.

Keywords: Myocardial infarction · Flow cytometry · Dual-Modality · Imbalanced data · Deep learning

1 Introduction

Cardiovascular disease (CVD) remains one of the world's leading health concerns, significantly contributing to global mortality and healthcare burdens [3,6]. Between 2019 and 2021, it was the primary cause of death in the United States [22], while in the United Kingdom, its prevalence surpasses that of cancer [3]. A major manifestation of CVD is myocardial infarction (MI), when obstructed blood flow causes damage to cardiac muscle tissue [32]. Post-MI complications, collectively referred to as Major

Adverse Cardiac Events (MACE), contribute to an approximate 20% mortality rate in the first year, with a considerable fraction of these fatalities occurring within the first 30 days [7,26]. These outcomes underscore the importance of timely detection and refined prognostic methods to reduce long-term morbidity and mortality [12].

Recent research has highlighted the prognostic role of specific white blood cell populations, particularly the $CD14^+$ and $CD16^+$ subsets, in identifying individuals at elevated risk of post-MI complications [5,27,28]. While elevated levels of these markers correlate with a higher incidence of MACE, challenges such as complex flow cytometry calibration, limited sample sizes, and the potential underutilisation of additional clinical variables can undermine the broader applicability of these findings [29]. As a result, an effective framework demands more comprehensive data integration and sophisticated analytic techniques to guide clinically meaningful risk assessment.

Deep learning approaches have increasingly been deployed in the cardiovascular domain, focusing on clinical, demographic, and select biomarker data [11,20,23,24]. While previous studies have explored a wide array of features, their focus has largely been on general clinical and demographic variables, often overlooking the rich, detailed information provided by white blood cell populations. However, a gap remains in effectively exploiting flow cytometry data through multiple representations, specifically, a combination of tabular features and image-based projections of these same features, within a unified deep learning framework.

In this extended study, we address this gap by expanding upon our previous dual-modality approach using flow cytometry data [1]. All features are derived from the same flow cytometry measurements: all are maintained in a tabular format, while some are converted into two-dimensional plots (e.g., scatter or density maps), each of which encodes two specific features. These image-based representations serve to highlight visually discriminative patterns that may be less obvious in a purely numerical format. Our primary goal is to integrate both representations, tabular and image-based, into a single predictive model for post-MI complications.

Our main contributions are:

1. **Enhanced Data Preprocessing and Visualization:** We propose an improved strategy for flow cytometry data handling, including the removal of non-informative features (i.e., count beads) and the use of visualization techniques (e.g., density and scatter plots) to represent pairs of tabular features in image form.
2. **Dual Neural Network Architecture with Voting Mechanism:** We have developed a custom deep learning framework that separately processes tabular and image data streams, both derived from the same flow cytometry dataset. The outputs from these streams are then fused using a voting mechanism to make the final classification. This ensemble approach ensures that both tabular and image-based insights contribute to the decision-making process, improving predictive performance in post-MI complication assessment.

2 Related Works

Previous research has extensively leveraged machine and deep learning methodologies to predict mortality rates and hospital readmissions following MI, often drawing on diverse data sources such as: clinical, demographic, and biological information to improve predictive power [11,20,23,24].

Data Sources, Formats, and Volumes. Prior studies typically employ either tabular or image-based data (or both) to predict CVD complications. Tabular data may include demographic and clinical variables such as age, gender, smoking status, and laboratory biomarkers (e.g., cardiac enzyme levels, renal function tests, liver function tests), all organized into structured tables with numerous features [11,20,23,24]. In contrast, image data often comprises electrocardiograms (ECGs) [2,13], which capture the heart's electrical activity, and echocardiographic (ECHO) images, which assess left ventricular remodelling, a crucial predictor of post-MI outcomes [19,30].

Dataset sizes vary widely across these studies, from hundreds to hundreds of thousands of patient records. Smaller datasets, often including a few hundred to a few thousand patients, provide valuable insights into post-MI complications [2,19,23,24]. In contrast, larger-scale studies with hundreds of thousands of samples facilitate comprehensive model training and greater generalization across diverse patient populations [11,13,30]. Commonly integrated features include patient demographics, clinical markers (e.g., troponin levels), and diagnostic test data (e.g., ECG waveforms). The fusion of these diverse data formats and volumes has significantly enhanced the predictive capabilities of machine learning models for assessing post-MI patient conditions.

Machine Learning Algorithms. A variety of machine learning algorithms have been employed to predict post-MI complications, utilizing both tabular and image-based modalities. For structured tabular data, models such as Random Forest (RF), Support Vector Machines (SVM), and Logistic Regression (LR) are commonly applied, effectively analysing clinical and laboratory variables to forecast patient outcomes [11,23,24]. In the realm of medical imaging, including ECGs and ECHO scans, advanced architectures such as Convolutional Neural Networks (CNNs) and Artificial Neural Networks (ANNs) are frequently leveraged. These models excel at identifying intricate patterns within imagery, thereby enhancing the prediction of adverse events following acute MI [2,13,19,30].

Although prior research has predominantly focused on broad patient data and imaging modalities (e.g., ECG, ECHO), this study takes a different approach by concentrating specifically on white blood cell data collected via flow cytometry. White blood cells play a pivotal role in both cardiovascular damage and repair, making them key indicators of cardiovascular health. To analyse and interpret these data, we employ advanced visualization and neural network techniques. This methodology bridges the gap between machine learning and medical insights by offering a unique perspective on post-MI complication prediction.

3 Flow Cytometry Application Domain

Flow cytometry is a powerful technique that provides high-dimensional immune profiles by measuring the optical and fluorescence properties of cells. In this study, we focus on flow cytometry-derived white blood cell data for predicting MI complications. The method employs lasers to illuminate a fluid stream containing white blood cells,

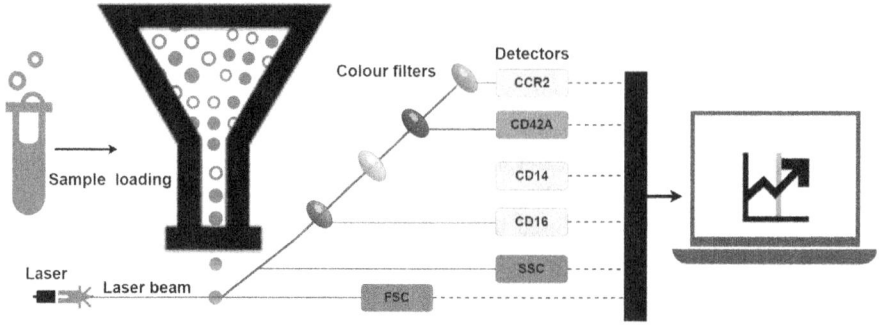

Fig. 1. Data Collection via Flow Cytometry [1].

generating emissions at various wavelengths. Color filters selectively transmit specific wavelengths (e.g., green light) while blocking others, and detectors measure the intensity of both forward scatter (FSC) and side scatter (SSC). FSC correlates with cell size, whereas SSC reflects cell granularity. Fluorescence emissions highlight particular surface molecules labeled according to the Cluster of Differentiation (CD) protocol, including CD14 and CD16, which are linked to immune subsets implicated in post-MI complications [1,8].

To process these measurements, specialized software, such as FlowJo [8], is used to generates detailed immune profiles that elucidate inflammatory responses in post-MI patients. Given the inherently high dimensionality of flow cytometry data, advanced analytic methods and deep neural network models are necessary to integrate these insights with clinical information, there by enhancing the predictive accuracy of patient outcomes. Figure 1 depicts the overall flow cytometry workflow used in this study.

For the study presented here, between November 2009 and November 2012, flow cytometry data was collected from 246 patients across multiple hospitals in Birmingham, UK, including City Hospital, Sandwell General Hospital, Heartlands Hospital, and Queen Elizabeth Hospital. For each patient, the data were provided in two complementary formats: (i) a tabular file in which each row represented a single cell and its associated features (e.g., FSC, SSC, and CD markers), which is the same *FlowCyto-MI* dataset we used in our previous work [1], and (ii) four two-dimensional plots, such as scatter plots and density plots, emphasizing key features.

Scatter plots (dot plots) are commonly used to display individual cell events based on two parameters, such as FSC versus SSC, offering insights into cell size and granularity. Density plots, in contrast, illustrate the concentration of cells in specific regions, allowing researchers to detect populations that differ in marker expression levels. These visualizations provide crucial context for understanding the distribution and behaviour of various immune cell subsets, setting the stage for more advanced, data-driven analyses in post-MI risk prediction.

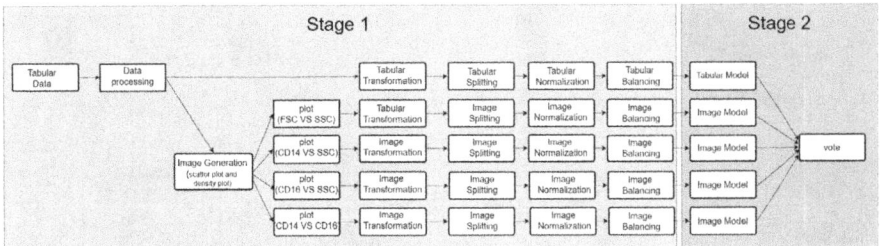

Fig. 2. A schematic depicting FlowCytFuse: a two-stage framework for handling and analyzing flow cytometry data.

4 Method: FlowCytFuse

We propose a two-stage framework, **FlowCytFuse**, designed to improve predictive performance for post-Myocardial Infarction (post-MI) complications. This framework comprises: *(i)* a specialized data handling pipeline for efficient flow cytometry data processing and visualization, and *(ii)* a dual neural network architecture that seamlessly combines tabular and image-based insights. Figure 2 provides an overview of the entire process, illustrating how raw flow cytometry data is processed into actionable inputs for deep learning models. From the Fig. 2 it can be seen that the prposed framwork comprises in two stage process. Each stage is discossed in further details in the following two subsections.

4.1 Data Handling and Visualization (Stage 1)

Data Processing. Our study utilizes the *FlowCyto-MI* dataset, derived from flow cytometry measurements aimed at predicting complications after MI. Building on prior work [1], the dataset was cleansed by removing non-patient-specific elements, such as count beads added during sample processing [5,27], which do not enhance predictive accuracy. After applying necessary filtering, the resulting subset of 246 patients meets the requirements in Eq. 1:

$$FSC < 200 \text{ and } SSC > 300 \text{ and } CD14 > 2000 \text{ and } CD16 > 800 \quad (1)$$

This condition filters out count beads, artificial particles used for flow cytometry calibration that may appear in patient samples due to sample preparation protocols. These beads exhibit distinct optical properties, including low FSC, high SSC, and extreme fluorescence levels (CD14/CD16), which differentiate them from real cells. The thresholds were selected based on experimental validation and previous literature [5,27] to ensure their accurate removal without affecting patient data. By eliminating these artifacts, we enhance the integrity of the dataset and improve the accuracy of downstream predictive models.

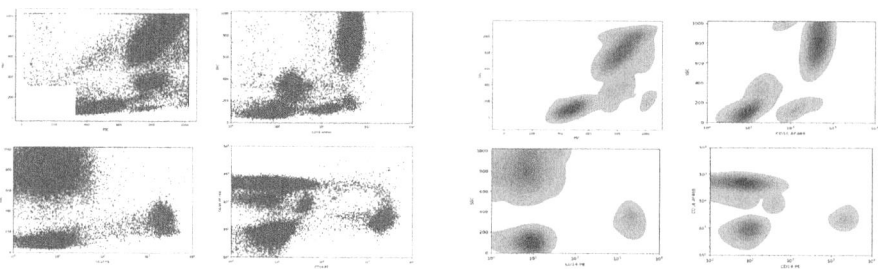

Fig. 3. Examples of scatter plot (left) and density plot (right) for key flow cytometry features.

Image Generation. we generate two-dimensional scatter and density plots for the most pertinent flow cytometry markers: FSC & SSC, CD14 & SSC, CD16 & SSC, and CD14 & CD16. For each patient, four scatter and four density plots were created, as illustrated in Fig. 3. This approach visually underscores critical data patterns relevant to post-MI risk assessment. Parallel to these plots, a tabular summary of all patient-specific features was maintained for comprehensive reference.

Data Transformation. Since each patient's tabular file may contain a varying number of rows (cells), we first identify the maximum row length across the dataset (396,952) in this case. Tabular entries for shorter records was zero-padded to match this dimension, facilitating uniform input shapes for PyTorch-based training. The data was then transformed from `pandas` DataFrames into tensors, forming one master tensor that documents patient counts, row totals, and column dimensions. Notably, the removal of count beads significantly shrinks the original dataset size [1]. For image data, we employ augmentation techniques (e.g., random rotations up to 20 °C, flips with probabilities of 0.4 vertically and 0.5 horizontally) to enhance training data diversity [33]. All images were converted to tensors and standardized to 256×256 pixels.

Data Splitting. Following established protocols [21], we partitioned the dataset into 60% for training, 20% for validation, and 20% for testing. Five-fold cross-validation using Python's `StratifiedKFold` enforces consistent class representation in every split [1]. Crucially, patient-level stratification ensures that all data (both tabular rows and corresponding plots) from the same patient reside either entirely in training or entirely in testing, thus avoiding data leakage. The final distribution is summarized in Table 1.

Data Normalization. Feature scaling is crucial for many classification tasks in medical contexts [9, 15, 31]. For tabular data, we apply `RobustScaler` [14], which transforms each feature X as indicated in Eq. 2:

$$X' = \frac{X - X_{\text{med}}}{IQR} \quad (2)$$

where X_{med} is the median and IQR is the Interquartile Range. For image data, PyTorch's `transforms.ToTensor()` normalizes pixel values from [0,255] to [0,1].

Table 1. Data distribution across training, validation, and testing sets [1].

Fold	Training		Validation		Test		Total
	0	1	0	1	0	1	
1	156	40	39	10	39	11	246
2,3,4,5	156	41	39	11	39	10	246

Data Balancing. The dataset exhibits a 4:1 ratio (195 samples: no complications; 51 samples: complications). To mitigate this imbalance, we combined random oversampling, random under-sampling, and SMOTE [16,34] for tabular data. For images, geometric transformations and random under-sampling are employed. Moreover, we incorporate focal loss [18] with parameters $\alpha = 2$ and $\gamma = 0.80$ to further emphasize minority-class instances. This multi-pronged balancing approach preserves clinically relevant information in both the tabular and image domains.

4.2 Dual Neural Network Architecture (Stage 2)

Tabular Model. We employed a specialized feed-forward neural network, depicted in Fig. 4, for the tabular flow cytometry data. After flattening the zero-padded input into a 2,381,712-dimensional vector, the model passes data through multiple linear layers with batch normalization, ReLU activation, and dropout, culminating in a classifier layer.

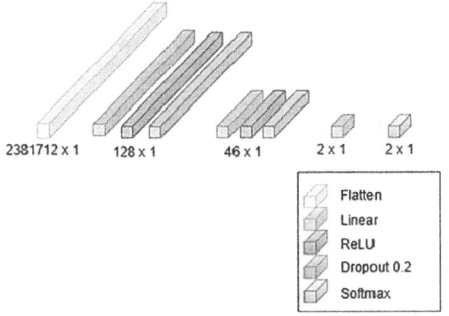

Fig. 4. Architecture of the Tabular Data Feed-Forward Neural Network [1].

For training PyTorch, cross-entropy loss [25] and the Adam optimizer with a learning rate of 1×10^{-3} and a batch size of 8 were used. This approach effectively manages the high dimensionality of tabular data while reducing the risk of overfitting.

Image Model. The image-based component utilized a Convolutional Neural Network (CNN), as shown in Fig. 5. Two convolutional blocks perform feature extraction and downsampling, followed by a fully connected layer for final classification. Input images are consistently resized to 256×256 pixels. Binary cross-entropy loss, combined with the Adam optimizer using a learning rate of 1×10^{-3}, is used to optimize classification accuracy.

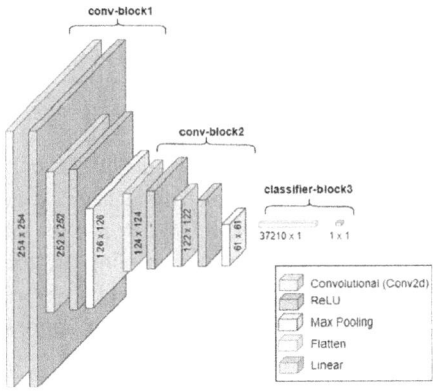

Fig. 5. Architecture of the Image Data CNN [1].

Evaluation Metrics. Following [17], we evaluate both networks using Precision, Recall, and F1 Score:

$$\text{Precision} = \frac{\text{True Positives}}{\text{True Positives} + \text{False Positives}}, \quad (3)$$

$$\text{Recall} = \frac{\text{True Positives}}{\text{True Positives} + \text{False Negatives}}, \quad (4)$$

$$F1 = 2 \times \frac{\text{Precision} \cdot \text{Recall}}{\text{Precision} + \text{Recall}}. \quad (5)$$

These metrics capture the models' abilities to identify post-MI complications accurately and to minimize misclassifications.

Voted Mechanism. To consolidate the tabular and image predictions, we employ a voting mechanis [4,10]. A straightforward method to enhance classifier performance is combining the predictions from multiple classifiers and selecting the class with the highest number of votes. For each patient, the tabular model contributes one vote, while the image model contributes four votes—one for each of the four plots representing two features each resulting in a total of five votes per patient. There is no tie-breaking situation because the total number of votes is odd (five). The final label is assigned to the class with the majority of votes, thereby avoiding ties and enhancing overall classification performance.

5 Results

In both the tabular and image-based models, the same data partitions were used for training, validation, and testing, as summarized in Table 1. Within each fold, only the test set was utilized for evaluation, ensuring no data leakage from the training and validation sets. Various epoch settings were explored: 10 and 15 epochs with different data balancing techniques (random undersampling, random oversampling, and SMOTE) for the tabular model; and 100 and 200 epochs for the image-based model, using techniques such as augmentation, random undersampling, and focal loss. The best results for each data type are detailed in Tables 2, 3, and 4. Specifically, Table 2 presents results for the tabular model, while Table 3 and Table 4 highlight the outcomes for the image-based model using scatter and density plots, respectively.

Tabular Model Results. After removing the count bead feature from the tabular dataset, performance generally improved compared to the prior approach reported in [1]. In earlier study [1], random oversampling with 15 epochs achieved F1 scores of 85 for Class 0 (patients without MI complications) and 15 for Class 1 (patients with MI complications). In contrast, our new experiments demonstrated that random undersampling with 15 epochs yielded the best performance, as shown in Table 2. This configuration achieved F1 scores of 73 for class 0 and 36 for class 1. Although the performance for class 0 was reduced, this approach substantially improved the results for the minority class (class 1), addressing the imbalanced nature of the dataset.

Table 2. Tabular Data Feed Forward Neural Network Results.

Data	Method	Epochs	Class	Prec.	Recall	F1
Tabular	Random under-sampling	15	0	84	68	73
			1	33	51	36

Abbreviations: Prec.= Precision, and Rec.= Recall

Image Model Results. The image-based model consistently outperformed the tabular model in most scenarios, with each plot generally delivering better results than the tabular data with the exception of the CD16 & SSC plot, which performed similarly.

Scatter Plots: The best performance was achieved with the CD16 & SSC scatter plot using 200 epochs. The F1 score for Class 0 was 85, while for Class 1, it was 35. These results demonstrate the strength of this specific feature combination for predicting post-MI complications Table 3.

Density Plots: Similar to the scatter plots, the CD16 & SSC density plot delivered the best performance. However, the performance of the other plots in this category was also comparable to or better than the tabular data results.

Table 3. Scatter Plot Data Convolutional Neural Network Results.

Data	Method	Epochs	Class	Prec.	Recall	F1
CD14 & SSC	Focal loss	200	0	80	83	81
			1	32	21	23
CD16 & SSC	Baseline	200	0	**83**	**88**	**85**
			1	**40**	**31**	**35**
CD14 & CD16	Baseline	200	0	82	87	84
			1	35	27	29
FSC & SSC	Focal loss	200	0	82	80	81
			1	28	33	30

Table 4. Density Plot Data Convolutional Neural Network Results.

Data	Method	Epochs	Class	Prec.	Recall	F1
CD14 & SSC	Focal loss	200	0	82	69	75
			1	27	44	34
CD16 & SSC	Augmentation	100	0	**81**	**89**	**85**
			1	**33**	**21**	**25**
CD14 & CD16	Random undersampling	200	0	85	52	65
			1	26	64	36
FSC & SSC	Focal loss	100	0	80	65	72
			1	23	39	29

Handling Data Imbalance. Across most scenarios, focal loss emerged as the most effective technique for addressing data imbalance in the image-based models. Its ability to emphasize hard-to-classify examples significantly enhanced the performance of the minority class (class 1), providing more balanced predictions compared to other techniques.

Voting. Table 5 presents the voting results between the tabular model, using the best results from tabular data as shown in Table 2, and the image model utilizing the four images with the best results for scatter and density plots, as shown in Tables 3, and 4. The results indicate that the density plot outperforms the scatter plot overall. For the density plot, the F1 score for Class 0 is 83, and for Class 1 is 37. In contrast, for the scatter plot, the F1 score for Class 0 is higher at 88, but significantly lower for Class 1 at 31. While the scatter plot has a higher F1 score for Class 0, the density plot achieves a better average F1 score overall. More importantly, for Class 1, which is particularly critical in medical applications, the density plot demonstrates superior performance, emphasizing its greater significance in this context.

Evaluation of All Models. The results from the experiments for both the density and scatter plots show significant improvement compared to the findings from the previous

Table 5. Comparison of Methods by vote.

Method	Class	Prec.	Recall	F1
Tabular and scatter	0	82	95	88
	1	70	23	31
Tabular and density	0	**84**	**83**	**83**
	1	**36**	**41**	**37**

work [1] as indicated in Table 6. The best result from the previous study produced an F1 score of 75 for Class 0, and 27 for Class 1. In contrast, the current study achieved a best performance using a combination of tabular data and density plots, with a F1 scores of 83 for Class 0, and 37 for Class 1. This reflects an absolute improvement of 8 points for Class 0 and 10 points for Class 1. These results demonstrate a substantial enhancement in performance, particularly for Class 1, which has historically been more challenging to Classify accurately. The observed improvements highlight the effectiveness of integrating both tabular data and density plots within the proposed framework.

Table 6. Comparison of All Works.

Method	Class	Prec.	Recall	F1
Tabular and density	0	**84**	**83**	**83**
	1	**36**	**41**	**37**
Previous study [1]	0	80	71	75
	1	22	34	27

6 Conclusion

In this extended study, we strengthened our dual-modality method for post-MI complication prediction by focusing on flow cytometry data handling and expanding image-based representations. Specifically, we refined our preprocessing pipeline, removing extraneous elements such as count beads, balancing class distributions, and normalizing features, to produce higher-quality data. Alongside these tabular refinements, we introduced additional two-dimensional plots (e.g., scatter, density) to visually highlight key markers. By merging these enriched tabular and image-based data streams within a dual neural network architecture and combining outputs via a voting mechanism, we achieved improved F1 scores, particularly in detecting patients at risk of complications. These results underscore the complementary strengths of numerical and visual marker representations in flow cytometry, as well as their clinical potential. Future directions include incorporating more visualized images or integrating additional clinical data, ultimately aiming to develop more robust, data-driven solutions that enable earlier interventions and improve post-MI patient outcomes.

References

1. ALdausari, N., Coenen, F., Nguyen, A., Shantsila, E.: Predicting post myocardial infarction complication: a study using dual-modality and imbalanced flow cytometry data (2024)
2. Beetz, M., et al.: Post-infarction risk prediction with mesh classification networks. In: International Workshop on Statistical Atlases and Computational Models of the Heart, pp. 291–301. Springer, Heidelberg (2022). https://doi.org/10.1007/978-3-031-23443-9_27
3. Bhatnagar, P., Wickramasinghe, K., Williams, J., Rayner, M., Townsend, N.: The epidemiology of cardiovascular disease in the UK 2014. Heart **101**(15), 1182–1189 (2015). https://doi.org/10.1136/heartjnl-2015-307516
4. Bin Habib, A.Z.S., Tasnim, T.: An ensemble hard voting model for cardiovascular disease prediction. In: 2020 2nd International Conference on Sustainable Technologies for Industry 4.0 (STI), pp. 1–6 (2020). https://doi.org/10.1109/STI50764.2020.9350514
5. Boidin, M., Lip, G.Y., Shantsila, A., Thijssen, D., Shantsila, E.: Dynamic changes of monocytes subsets predict major adverse cardiovascular events and left ventricular function after stemi. Sci. Rep. **13**(1), 48 (2023)
6. Centers for Disease Control and Prevention: Products - data briefs - number 456 - September 2022. National Center for Health Statistics (2022). https://www.cdc.gov/nchs/products/databriefs/db456.htm. Accessed 30 Mar 2024
7. Clinic, C.: Congestive heart failure (2022). https://my.clevelandclinic.org/health/diseases/17069-heart-failure-understanding-heart-failure
8. FlowJo: Flowjo data analysis software (2024). https://www.flowjo.com/solutions/flowjo. Accessed 21 Feb 2024
9. García, S., Luengo, J., Herrera, F.: Data Preprocessing in Data Mining, vol. 72. Springer, Heidelberg (2015)
10. Géron, A.: Hands-On Machine Learning with Scikit-Learn and TensorFlow: Concepts, Tools, and Techniques to Build Intelligent Systems. O'Reilly Media, Sebastopol (2017)
11. Ghafari, R., et al.: Prediction of the fatal acute complications of myocardial infarction via machine learning algorithms. J. Tehran Univ. Heart Center **18**(4), 278–287 (2023)
12. Hall, M., et al.: Health outcomes after myocardial infarction: a population study of 56 million people in England. PLoS Med. **21**(2), e1004343 (2024)
13. Ibrahim, L., Mesinovic, M., Yang, K.W., Eid, M.A.: Explainable prediction of acute myocardial infarction using machine learning and shapley values. IEEE Access **8**, 210410–210417 (2020). https://doi.org/10.1109/ACCESS.2020.3040166
14. Izonin, I., Ilchyshyn, B., Tkachenko, R., Greguš, M., Shakhovska, N., Strauss, C.: Towards data normalization task for the efficient mining of medical data. In: 2022 12th International Conference on Advanced Computer Information Technologies (ACIT), pp. 480–484 (2022). https://doi.org/10.1109/ACIT54803.2022.9913112
15. Jayalakshmi, T., Santhakumaran, A.: Statistical normalization and back propagation for classification. Int. J. Comput. Theory Eng. **3**(1), 1793–8201 (2011)
16. Khushi, M., et al.: A comparative performance analysis of data resampling methods on imbalance medical data. IEEE Access **9**, 109960–109975 (2021). https://doi.org/10.1109/ACCESS.2021.3102399
17. Korkmaz, S.: Deep learning-based imbalanced data classification for drug discovery. J. Chem. Inf. Model. **60**(9), 4180–4190 (2020)
18. Lin, T.Y., Goyal, P., Girshick, R., He, K., Dollár, P.: Focal loss for dense object detection. In: Proceedings of the IEEE International Conference on Computer Vision, pp. 2980–2988 (2017)
19. Logeart, D., et al.: Patterns of left ventricular remodeling post-myocardial infarction, determinants, and outcome. Clin. Res. Cardiol. 1–12 (2024)

20. Mohammad, M.A., et al.: Development and validation of an artificial neural network algorithm to predict mortality and admission to hospital for heart failure after myocardial infarction: a nationwide population-based study. Lancet. Digital health **4**(1), e37–e45 (2022). https://doi.org/10.1016/S2589-7500(21)00228-4
21. Mpanya, D., Celik, T., Klug, E., Ntsinjana, H.: Predicting mortality and hospitalization in heart failure using machine learning: a systematic literature review. IJC Heart Vasculat. **34**, 100773 (2021)
22. Murphy, S.L., Kochanek, K.D., Xu, J., Arias, E.: Mortality in the united states, 2020. National Center for Health Statistics (NCHS), Data Brief Num. **427** (2021)
23. Newaz, A., Mohosheu, M.S., Al Noman, M.A.: Predicting complications of myocardial infarction within several hours of hospitalization using data mining techniques. Inf. Med. Unlocked **42**, 101361 (2023)
24. Oliveira, M., Seringa, J., Pinto, F.J., Henriques, R., Magalhães, T.: Machine learning prediction of mortality in acute myocardial infarction. BMC Med. Inform. Decis. Mak. **23**(1), 1–16 (2023)
25. PyTorch: torch.nn.CrossEntropyLoss (2024). https://pytorch.org/docs/stable/generated/torch.nn.CrossEntropyLoss.html. Accessed 20 Feb 2024
26. Qing Ye, Jie Zhang, L.M.: Predictors of all-cause 1-year mortality in myocardial infarction patients. Medicine **99**(23) (2020)
27. Shantsila, E., Ghattas, A., Griffiths, H., Lip, G.: Mon2 predicts poor outcome in st-elevation myocardial infarction. J. Int. Med. **285**(3), 301–316 (2019)
28. Shantsila, E., Tapp, L.D., Wrigley, B.J., Montoro-Garcia, S., Lip, G.Y.: Cxcr4 positive and angiogenic monocytes in myocardial infarction. Thromb. Haemost. **109**(02), 255–262 (2013)
29. Shantsila, E., et al.: Immunophenotypic characterization of human monocyte subsets: possible implications for cardiovascular disease pathophysiology. J. Thromb. Haemost. **9**(5), 1056–1066 (2011)
30. Shmueli, H., et al.: Echocardiographic predictors of improvement of left ventricular ejection fraction below 35% in patients with st-segment elevation myocardial infarction. J. Clin. Med. **13**(14) (2024)
31. Singh, D., Singh, B.: Investigating the impact of data normalization on classification performance. Appl. Soft Comput. **97**, 105524 (2020)
32. Thygesen, K., Alpert, J.S., Jaffe, A.S., Simoons, M.L., Chaitman, B.R., White, H.D.: Third universal definition of myocardial infarction. Circulation **126**(16), 2020–2035 (2012)
33. Yang, S., Xiao, W., Zhang, M., Guo, S., Zhao, J., Shen, F.: Image data augmentation for deep learning: a survey. arXiv preprint arXiv:2204.08610 (2022)
34. Zhang, Y., Kang, B., Hooi, B., Yan, S., Feng, J.: Deep long-tailed learning: a survey. IEEE Trans. Pattern Anal. Mach. Intell. **45**(9), 10795–10816 (2023). https://doi.org/10.1109/TPAMI.2023.3268118

A Generative Framework for Web Pages Classification Using Multi-modal Topic Fusion

Domenico Benfenati, Antonio Maria Rinaldi(✉), Cristiano Russo, and Cristian Tommasino

Department of Electrical Engineering and Information Technology (DIETI),
University of Naples Federico II, Naples, Italy
{domenico.benfenati,antoniomaria.rinaldi,cristiano.russo,
cristian.tommasino}@unina.it

Abstract. The continuous expansion of web content requires robust methods for systematically categorizing and retrieving web-based multimedia information. While traditional classifiers predominantly focus on textual features, they often overlook the intricate relationships between text and visual content, leading to suboptimal classification performance. In this study, we introduce a multi-modal topic fusion framework to improve semantic consistency between textual and visual data representations. Additionally, we incorporate adaptive relevance weighting mechanisms, allowing for more precise web document classification in different multimedia environments. Our experimental results, conducted on an expanded dataset with complex real-world web content, show a further increase in classification robustness, particularly in dynamic and heterogeneous domains. By refining generative techniques for web crawling and information retrieval, our work contributes a substantial leap forward in multimedia classification efficiency.

Keywords: Web crawler · Web pages classification · Generative AI · Web analysis

1 Introduction

The rapid growth of the web has led to an overwhelming amount of information, with over 5 billion web pages available online [1,2]. Effective web page classification is a crucial task for various applications, including information retrieval, content recommendation, and search engine optimization. However, the diverse and dynamic nature of web content, which includes both textual and multimedia elements, presents significant challenges for traditional classification methods [3]. Previous approaches to web page classification have primarily focused on analyzing textual content, often neglecting the valuable information embedded in visual elements [4,5]. While some methods have attempted to incorporate multimedia data, they typically treat textual and visual content separately, failing to leverage the synergistic potential of combining these modalities [6]. Furthermore, the complexity and resource-intensive nature of processing large volumes of multimedia content necessitate the development of more efficient and scalable solutions [7].

To address these limitations, we introduce a framework for web page classification that integrates textual and visual content analysis to enhance classification accuracy. Our framework leverages a generative, multimedia-focused approach that uses a crawler to collect and process web content efficiently [8]. Building upon our previous work, this study incorporates a multi-modal topic fusion framework, improving the interplay between textual and visual topic representations. Additionally, we introduce adaptive relevance weighting mechanisms, allowing for dynamic adjustments to the importance of text and image data based on content context.

Our primary contributions in this work include:

1. refining the classification framework by introducing a multi-modal topic fusion approach that enhances performance across diverse content types;
2. extending our evaluation to a broader and more complex dataset, demonstrating improved robustness in real-world classification tasks;
3. incorporating adaptive relevance weighting, enabling a more context-aware classification process.

Our advancements significantly improve classification accuracy and ensure a more scalable and efficient processing pipeline. Traditional web classification approaches often rely on static analysis techniques that do not effectively capture the evolving nature of web content [9]. Furthermore, link-based navigation strategies, commonly used in crawlers, may not systematically acquire and process heterogeneous content, limiting their ability to extract meaningful insights and adapt to multimedia-rich web pages [10]. By incorporating a more adaptive and AI-driven framework, leveraging deep learning techniques for context-aware multimedia classification, our approach enhances the effectiveness of web page classification. Our work not only advances classification methodologies but also contributes to more efficient information retrieval and knowledge representation [11].

The paper is organized as follows: in Sect. 2, a literature review is presented and discussed, highlighting the novelties of our approach; the system architecture and the proposed methodology for the web page classification framework and its data acquisition strategy are discussed in Sect. 3; experimental results are presented in Sect. 4; finally, conclusions and future work are outlined in Sect. 5.

2 Related Work

Multimodal fusion techniques have gained significant attention for their ability to integrate multiple sources of information, such as text, images, and structured data, to enhance classification and retrieval tasks [12]. Traditional approaches often rely on single-modality analysis, which can lead to information loss and reduced robustness [13]. Recent studies have demonstrated the effectiveness of Convolutional Neural Networks (CNNs) as general-purpose feature extractors for retrieving multimedia content, highlighting the potential of deep learning for multimodal applications [14].

One key challenge in multimodal fusion is the alignment of heterogeneous data sources. Early research proposed ontology-based methods to structure and integrate different data types, improving retrieval efficiency in various domains [15–17]. These techniques utilize domain-specific knowledge representations to refine selection criteria, ensuring that relevant information is effectively combined and interpreted. Similarly, ontology-based approaches have been explored for document summarization and visualization, increasing the interpretability of multimodal content [18].

Machine learning-based fusion strategies often leverage deep learning models such as LSTMs and CNNs to process and combine textual and visual features [19]. Some studies have proposed Attention-Enhanced Siamese LSTM Networks for relevance prediction in specific fields, such as biomedical information retrieval, demonstrating the potential of attention mechanisms in multimodal analysis [20,21]. Additionally, evolutionary algorithms have been integrated into feature selection and classification processes, optimizing multimodal fusion for more efficient information retrieval [22,23].

Our study introduces a multimodal topic fusion approach that extends the methodology outlined in [24]. Unlike existing models that analyze text and images separately, our framework dynamically adjusts the influence of textual and visual content based on contextual factors, enhancing classification accuracy. Furthermore, we incorporate generative techniques to synthesize visual representations, improving topic extraction and retrieval performance. Comparative evaluations reveal that our model achieves higher recall and better resilience against noisy or irrelevant content, demonstrating its potential for large-scale multimodal classification.

3 Proposed Framework

In this section, we present our multi-modal framework for web page classification. Our approach integrates textual, visual, and topic features to generate a unified representation of web pages.

Our framework operates by systematically analyzing web pages through a multi-modal approach. For each web page, textual content is first extracted and transformed into an embedding representation. Simultaneously, the most relevant image is identified and processed using a convolutional neural network (CNN) to generate a visual embedding. If no suitable image is found, an AI generative model synthesizes an image, which is then embedded using the same CNN. Additionally, topic descriptions from the web page are extracted and encoded into a topic embedding. These three embeddings—textual, visual, and topical—are then fused to create a unified representation. Finally, this integrated representation is used for classification, enabling accurate and context-aware categorization of web content.

Our proposed framework is shown in Fig. 1.

Algorithm 1 shows the proposed framework workflow of web pages classification, using the multi-modal fusion strategy.

3.1 Textual Topic Detection

Our approach utilizes a structured pipeline to extract representative topics from the text by leveraging Sentence-BERT (SBERT) [25] embeddings alongside WordNet synsets [26]. The preprocessing stage ensures consistency by applying lowercasing, sentence

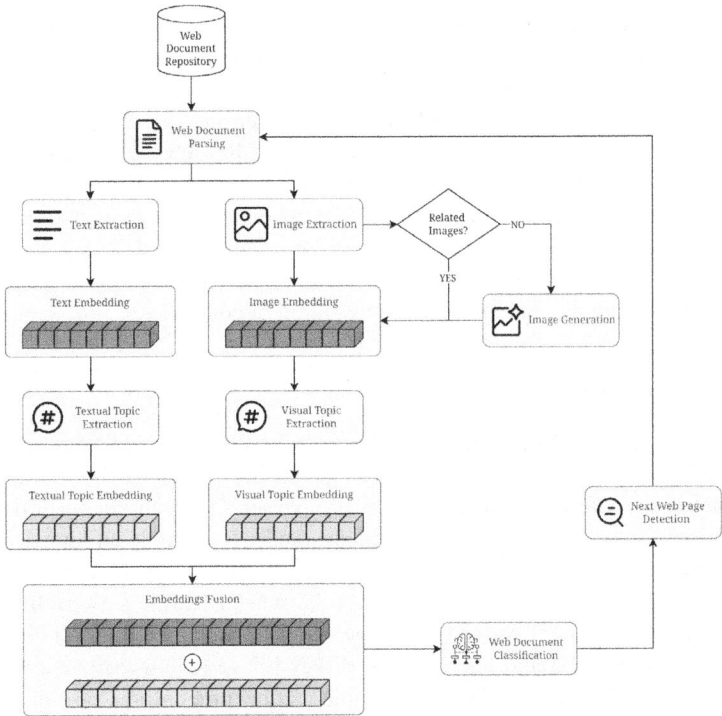

Fig. 1. Schema of the proposed web pages classification framework.

Algorithm 1: General Workflow of Proposed Framework.

Require: Set of web pages P
Ensure: Classification labels for each web page
1: **for** each web page $p \in P$ **do**
2:     Extract textual content T_p from p
3:     Compute text embedding E_T from T_p
4:     Identify most relevant image I_p from p
5:     **if** I_p exists **then**
6:         Compute visual embedding E_I using CNN
7:     **else**
8:         Generate image I'_p using AI generative model
9:         Compute visual embedding E_I from I'_p using CNN
10:     **end if**
11:     Extract topic descriptions D_p from p
12:     Compute topic embedding E_D from D_p
13:     Fuse embeddings: $E_F = f(E_T, E_I, E_D)$
14:     Perform classification using E_F
15: **end for**

tokenization, and the removal of common linguistic artifacts such as stopwords and special characters. SBERT embeddings transform each sentence into a high-dimensional vector space, effectively capturing contextual nuances, and its performances results better that other features extraction methods for topic detection, as we have outlined in Sect. 3. By applying SBERT to the cleaned text, we ensure that the generated vectors remain unaffected by noisy information present in lengthy web pages within the dataset. To identify distinct topics, we employ K-means clustering with a fixed value of k, which is experimentally detected, while WordNet synsets enhance the semantic depth of the extracted topics.

The success of this method depends on the richness and diversity of the input text, enabling a more granular and insightful exploration of content.

3.2 Visual Topic Extraction

Our approach to visual topic detection leverages multimedia elements, particularly images, to identify a document's primary subject, thus enhancing the overall classification framework. Our research emphasizes the extraction of multimedia descriptors to assess the similarity between document images and our multimedia knowledge base. Various descriptor types—local, global, and deep features—are analyzed to optimize performance (see Sect. 3). To facilitate effective transfer learning, we utilize the pre-trained VGG19 model [27], trained on ImageNet [28], and apply it to full images. This enables the identification and visualization of key image regions associated with specific predictions. The model's relatively simple architecture ensures ease of interpretation and seamless implementation.

When multiple images are retrieved from a web page, a selection mechanism is applied to retain only those images most relevant to the extracted textual topic, ensuring a coherent and meaningful representation [29].

3.3 Image Generation

To overcome the limitation of web pages that lack relevant multimedia content, we integrated a Latent Diffusion Model (LDM) into the classification process. This model generates high-quality images that align with the textual description of a web page, ensuring the presence of relevant visual content even when none is initially available. We employ Stable Diffusion as the latent model for converting text into images, leveraging its diffusion-based architecture specifically designed for text-guided image synthesis [30].

Our implementation follows a latent diffusion approach optimized for generating and refining images from textual prompts. The model relies on the pre-trained CLIP ViT-L/14 text encoder, adopting a methodology similar to Imagen's structured diffusion framework [31]. The decision to use Stable Diffusion over alternative generative models is supported by its superior performance in producing high-fidelity and semantically accurate images, as demonstrated in Sect. 3 [32,33].

3.4 Multi-modal Fusion Strategy

Our approach integrates a multi-modal embedding fusion strategy to enhance the representation of web page content by combining textual and visual features. First, we extract high-dimensional embeddings separately from textual content using SBERT and from images using the VGG19 model. To align these modalities, we employ projection techniques that map both embeddings into a common latent space, ensuring that semantic similarities between text and image features are preserved. To further enrich the representation, we integrate WordNet-based topic embeddings. Specifically, we retrieve WordNet synsets corresponding to both the detected textual and visual topics, generating additional topic descriptors. These embeddings are then integrated with the previously fused text-image representation, creating a unified multi-modal vector that encapsulates the semantic relationships between textual descriptions, images, and structured lexical knowledge. This comprehensive fusion strategy enhances classification accuracy by reinforcing topic coherence and improving retrieval efficiency in web classification. Algorithm 2 show the pseudocode for the fusion strategy adopted in detail.

Algorithm 2: Multi-modal Embedding Fusion Strategy.

Require: Web page W with textual content T and images I
Ensure: Unified multi-modal embedding E_{final}
1: **Step 1: Extract Textual Embeddings**
2: Preprocess T (lowercasing, stopword removal, tokenization)
3: Compute SBERT embeddings: $E_T = \text{SBERT}(T)$
4: **Step 2: Extract Visual Embeddings**
5: **for** each image $i \in I$ **do**
6:     Compute deep feature embeddings: $E_I^i = \text{VGG19}(i)$
7: **end for**
8: Compute aggregated visual embedding: $E_I = \text{Aggregate}(E_I^1, \ldots, E_I^n)$
9: **Step 3: Extract WordNet-based Topic Embeddings**
10: Identify textual topic T_{topic} from E_T
11: Identify visual topic I_{topic} from E_I
12: Retrieve WordNet embeddings: $E_W^T = \text{WordNet}(T_{topic})$, $E_W^I = \text{WordNet}(I_{topic})$
13: **Step 4: Fusion of Embeddings**
14: Project E_T and E_I into a common latent space
15: Fuse textual and visual embeddings: $E_{TI} = \text{Fusion}(E_T, E_I)$
16: Fuse with WordNet embeddings: $E_{final} = \text{Fusion}(E_{TI}, E_W^T, E_W^I)$
17: **Return** E_{final} as the unified multi-modal representation

---

4 Experimental Results

4.1 Dataset Description

We used the Curlie[1] repository. Curlie is the largest human-curated directory on the Web, serving as the successor of DMOZ, and is freely available online. Curlie contains

---
[1] https://curlie.org/en.

2,966,795 URLs, divided into 1,031,203 categories and subcategories, organized into a hierarchical taxonomy with a high level of granularity. We use the Curlie repository in English, processing the data using Python to retain unique URLs and homepages. We have heuristically recognized the URLs with an empty path, obtaining 2.28M usable URLs. In Table 1 we have reported the mapping between the categories in Curlie and the related synset in WordNet, and also the percentage of pages included in the Curlie categories.

Table 1. Curlie categories with WordNet Synset and Definition mapping.

Category Name	Web Pages [%]	Synset	Definition	Offset
Arts	9.3	art.n.01	The products of human creativity; works of art collectively	2,743,547
Business	27.6	commercial_enterprise.n.02	The activity of providing goods and services involving financial and commercial and industrial aspects	1,094,725
Computers	6.2	computer.n.01	A machine for performing calculations automatically	3,082,979
Games	1.7	game.n.01	A contest with rules to determine a winner	455,599
Health	5.9	health.n.01	A healthy state of well-being free from disease	14,447,908
Home	1.5	home.n.01	Where you live at a particular time	8,559,508
Kids & Teens	1.1	child.n.01	A young person of either sex	9,917,593
News	1.1	news.n.01	Information about recent and important events	6,642,138
Recreation	8.4	refreshment.n.02	Activity that refreshes and recreates; activity that renews your health and spirits by enjoyment and relaxation	401,783
Reference	4.3	education.n.01	The activities of educating or instructing; activities that impart knowledge or skill	883,297
Science	4.8	science.n.01	A particular branch of scientific knowledge	5,999,797
Shopping	7.4	shopping.n.01	Searching for or buying goods or services	81,836
Society	13.9	society.n.01	An extended social group having a distinctive cultural and economic organization	7,966,140
Sports	6.8	sport.n.01	An active diversion requiring physical exertion and competition	523,513

4.2 Textual Topic Detection

Our framework enhances web page classification by integrating textual, visual, and topical content analysis. To evaluate its effectiveness, we use the Curlie dataset, a comprehensive and structured web directory, as a benchmark for topic detection. We compare our system's performance against established topic modeling algorithms, specifically Latent Semantic Analysis (LSA) and Latent Dirichlet Allocation (LDA). LSA employs a vector-based approach to capture semantic relationships [34], while LDA applies a probabilistic generative model to uncover latent topics in text corpora [35]. Unlike these traditional methods, our system employs a multi-modal topic fusion strategy, leveraging embeddings from text, images, and extracted topic descriptions to improve classification accuracy. Additionally, it incorporates adaptive relevance weighting, dynamically adjusting the importance of different modalities based on content characteristics. The comparison results, presented in Fig. 2, demonstrate the effectiveness of our approach using SBERT compared to the other algorithms.

4.3 Visual Topic Detection

The visual topic detection process leverages multimedia components, particularly images, to identify a document's primary subject, significantly enhancing the effectiveness of our framework. Our extended approach introduces an in-depth evaluation of multiple feature extraction techniques, assessing their contributions to topic detection accuracy. By exploring various configurations, we gain deeper insights into the advantages and limitations of each method, ensuring a more robust and adaptable classification system.

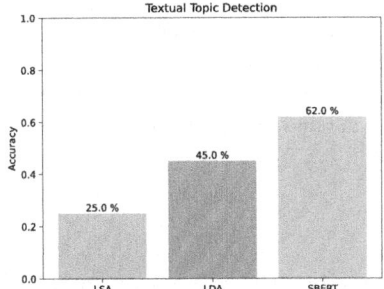

Algorithm	Accuracy	Num. Correct
LSA	0.25	293
LDA	0.45	527
SBERT	**0.62**	**725**

Fig. 2. Accuracy comparison detail about the textual topic detection task.

To achieve this, we experiment with three distinct feature extraction strategies. PHOG [36] provides a global representation of an image, capturing gradient orientation histograms at multiple pyramid levels. This hierarchical structure enhances feature extraction by preserving spatial relationships, making it well-suited for structured visual analysis. SIFT [37], a widely used local descriptor, detects key points across different scales and orientations, offering resilience to transformations and occlusions, which is beneficial for handling diverse web images. VGG19 [27], a deep convolutional neural network, extracts hierarchical feature representations from intermediate layers, particularly leveraging the last max pooling layer to obtain deep embeddings that capture high-level semantic information.

The comparative analysis of these three methods (illustrated in Fig. 3) highlights that the deep features extracted from VGG19 achieve the highest classification accuracy, followed by PHOG and SIFT. This result aligns with expectations, as deep learning-based representations tend to encode richer semantic information compared to hand-crafted features. However, this accuracy comes at the cost of increased computational complexity due to the high dimensionality of deep embeddings. PHOG, while offering a more structured approach to feature extraction, maintains competitive performance, outperforming SIFT due to its ability to integrate both local and global information. Ultimately, the choice of feature extraction method depends on balancing accuracy, computational efficiency, and application-specific constraints, particularly when integrating visual and textual topics in a unified classification pipeline.

4.4 Image Generation

In our proposed strategy, an additional step involves generating multimedia data, prompting us to identify the most suitable models for this task. To this end, we evaluate six generative models: StackGAN [38], AttnGAN [39], Stable Diffusion [30], Big-Gan [40], VQ-VAE-2 [41], and FLUX [42]. StackGAN employs a hierarchical generative adversarial network for multi-stage image synthesis, progressively generating high-resolution images, while AttnGAN incorporates attention mechanisms to refine image generation by focusing on salient regions. Stable Diffusion utilizes diffusion processes to control the gradual evolution of images, achieving high-quality synthesis. BigGan, a class-conditional GAN, is recognized for producing diverse, high-fidelity images through large-scale training, whereas VQ-VAE-2 leverages a hierarchical vector quantized variational autoencoder framework to capture intricate image details. FLUX, a transformer-based model, fuses latent representations with attention mechanisms to synthesize images that are both contextually relevant and visually realistic.

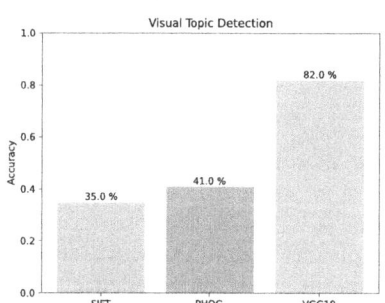

Algorithm	Accuracy	Num. Correct
SIFT	0.35	568
PHOG	0.41	665
VGG19	**0.82**	**1331**

Fig. 3. Accuracy comparison detail about the visual topic detection task.

To assess the fidelity of images generated from textual descriptions, we employ several metrics that address different aspects of image quality. The Fréchet Inception Distance (FID) [43] quantifies the dissimilarity between the distributions of real and generated images, while metrics such as R-precision [39], Semantic Object Accuracy (SOA) [44], and CLIP score [45] evaluate image-text matching. R-precision measures visual-semantic similarity by ranking retrieval results based on image and text features, and SOA assesses object detection performance by providing class (SOA-C) and image (SOA-I) averages. As highlighted in [44], metrics like FID, SOA, and CLIP score align more closely with human visual assessment compared to others such as Inception Score

[46] and R-precision. Consequently, we focus on these three metrics as critical indicators of generative performance. In Table 2, we report a comparison of all the metrics obtained during our evaluation process, with results that indicate that stable diffusion best generates visually accurate images that faithfully represent the textual prompts.

Table 2. Metrics value comparison between different generative models, including GAN-based models, VQ-VAE-2, FLUX, and Stable Diffusion.

Model	FID ↓	CLIP ↑	SOA-C ↑	SOA-I ↑	R-precision ↑
StackGAN [38]	35.40	21.78	19.63	31.21	58.14
AttnGAN [39]	28.93	25.61	24.15	37.98	70.42
BigGAN [40]	26.72	27.89	26.41	40.32	74.11
VQ-VAE-2 [41]	18.35	29.72	28.51	44.89	79.63
FLUX [42]	7.85	31.91	32.74	50.97	91.08
Stable Diffusion [30]	**7.02**	**32.27**	**33.54**	**52.14**	**92.81**

We have reported some examples of generated images based on the textual prompt of WordNet definition in Fig. 4, in order to compare the generative subjective performances.

Fig. 4. Generated images using three WordNet synset as example, with the generative models considered.

4.5 Fusion Strategies

In our study, we explore four distinct combination strategies based on the fusion of different embeddings for classification. Strategy *A* prioritizes the text embedding, ensuring that the semantic content extracted from the web page plays the central role in classification. Strategy *B* shifts the focus to the visual embedding, emphasizing the rich imagery and visual features present on the page. Strategy C combines the text and visual embeddings equally, intentionally excluding the topic embedding to assess the classification performance when relying solely on these two modalities. Finally, Strategy D integrates all available embeddings—textual, visual, and topical—to fully leverage the comprehensive information present in the web pages, aiming for a more robust and context-aware classification.

To achieve effective fusion, we employ a weighted embedding aggregation approach [47]. For Strategy A and B, a dominant weight is assigned respectively to the text or visual embedding, while the remaining embedding is either significantly downweighted or ignored. In Strategy C, text and visual embeddings are concatenated with equal importance, ensuring a balanced contribution from both modalities. Strategy D extends this approach by incorporating the topic embedding alongside text and visual representations. The final fused representation is computed as:

$$E_F = \alpha \cdot E_T + \beta \cdot E_I + \gamma \cdot E_D \qquad (1)$$

where E_T, E_I and E_D represent the textual, visual, and topic embeddings, respectively. The weights α, β and γ are dynamically adjusted based on the chosen strategy, ensuring that each modality contributes optimally to the final classification task. This structured fusion mechanism allows us to systematically analyze the impact of each modality on web page classification performance. In Table 3 we have reported the parameters of the configurations we have made.

Table 3. Strategies combinations parameters and description.

Strategy	α	β	γ	Information
A	1.0	0.2	0.0	Text-Prioritized
B	0.2	1.0	0.0	Visual-Prioritized
C	0.5	0.5	0.0	Text and Visual Equally, No Topics
D	0.4	0.4	0.2	Full Multi-Modal Fusion

Our results demonstrate that Strategy D, which combines all embeddings, yields the best performance, reinforcing the importance of integrating textual, visual, and structured knowledge for robust web page classification. This comprehensive fusion strategy enhances classification accuracy, improves topic coherence, and ensures better retrieval efficiency in web classification. In Fig. 5 the performances obtained using the combinations strategies described are reported.

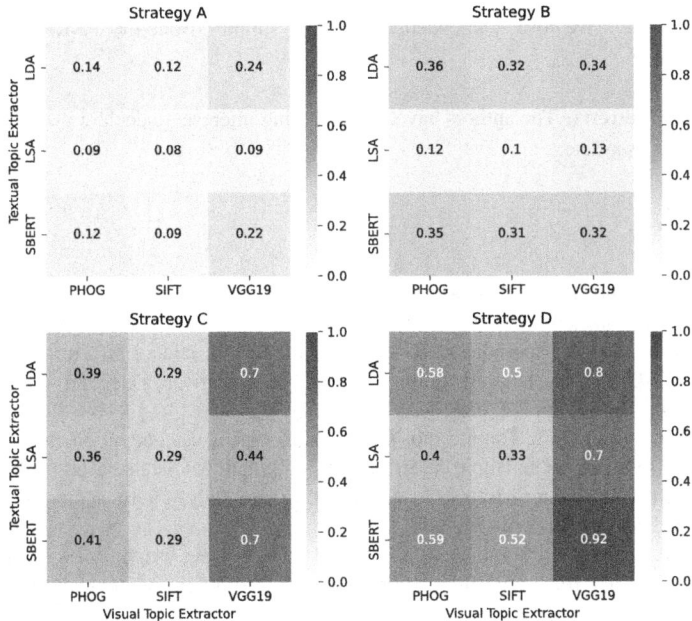

Fig. 5. Accuracy performances comparison using the strategy A, B, C and D.

5 Conclusion

Our experimental results demonstrate that multi-modal fusion significantly enhances web page classification accuracy, with Strategy *D* (full integration of text, visual, and topic embeddings) achieving the best performance. The inclusion of WordNet-based topic embeddings proved beneficial in reinforcing topic coherence, while generative models like Stable Diffusion, BigGAN, VQ-VAE-2, and FLUX effectively supplemented missing visual content, ensuring a more robust representation. The performance improvements highlight the importance of combining structured lexical knowledge with deep learning-based embeddings for more accurate classification. However, challenges remain in optimizing computational efficiency, particularly in handling large-scale web datasets and dynamically adapting weights for embedding fusion. Future work will explore more adaptive fusion mechanisms, such as attention-based weighting for embeddings, and investigate the integration of transformer-based vision models further to improve semantic alignment between textual and visual content, and also explore the usage of Large and Visual Language Models and retrieval techniques to improve classification and topic extraction [48]. Additionally, expanding the dataset to include more diverse and domain-specific web pages will help validate the generalizability of our approach in real-world applications.

Acknowledgments. This research has been partially supported by the Spoke 9 - Digital Society & Smart Cities - Centro Nazionale di Ricerca in High-Performance-Computing, Big Data and Quantum Computing, funded by European Union - NextGenerationEU - CUP:

E63C22000980007. We also acknowledge financial support from the PNRR MUR project PE0000013-FAIR.

Disclosure of Interests. The authors have no competing interests to declare that are relevant to the content of this article.

References

1. Kunder, M.: The size of the world wide web (the internet). Pobrano Z (2018). http://www.worldwidewebsize.com/
2. Bergman, M.: White paper: the deep web: surfacing hidden value. J. Electron. Publ. **7** (2001)
3. Hashemi, M.: Web page classification: a survey of perspectives, gaps, and future directions. Multimedia Tools Appl. **79**, 11921–11945 (2020)
4. Rinaldi, A., Russo, C., Tommasino, C.: Web document categorization using knowledge graph and semantic textual topic detection. In: Computational Science And Its Applications–ICCSA 2021: 21st International Conference, Cagliari, Italy, 13–16 September 2021, Proceedings, Part III 21, pp. 40–51 (2021)
5. Rinaldi, A., Russo, C., Tommasino, C.: Visual query posing in multimedia web document retrieval. In: 2021 IEEE 15th International Conference on Semantic Computing (ICSC), pp. 415–420 (2021)
6. Ahmed, Z., Singh, H.: Text extraction and clustering for multimedia: a review on techniques and challenges. In: 2019 International Conference On Digitization (ICD), pp. 38–43 (2019)
7. Butkiewicz, M., Madhyastha, H., Sekar, V.: Understanding website complexity: measurements, metrics, and implications. In: Proceedings of the 2011 ACM SIGCOMM Conference on Internet Measurement Conference, pp. 313–328 (2011)
8. Benfenati, D., Rinaldi, A.M., Russo, C., Tommasino, C.: GenCrawl: a generative multimedia focused crawler for web pages classification. In: Proceedings of the 16th International Joint Conference on Knowledge Discovery, Knowledge Engineering and Knowledge Management - KDIR, pp. 91–101 (2024)
9. Qi, X., Davison, B.: Web page classification: features and algorithms. ACM Comput. Surv. (CSUR) **41**, 1–31 (2009)
10. Kumar, N., Aggarwal, D.: LEARNING-based focused WEB crawler. IETE J. Res. **69**, 2037–2045 (2023)
11. Martin, P.: Knowledge representation, sharing, and retrieval on the web. Web Intell. 243–276 (2003)
12. Gallo, I., Calefati, A., Nawaz, S.: Multimodal classification fusion in real-world scenarios. In: 2017 14th IAPR International Conference on Document Analysis and Recognition (ICDAR), vol. 5, pp. 36–41 (2017)
13. Lin, R., Hu, H.: Missmodal: increasing robustness to missing modality in multimodal sentiment analysis. Trans. Assoc. Comput. Linguist. **11**, 1686–1702 (2023)
14. Rinaldi, A., Russo, C., Tommasino, C.: A knowledge-driven multimedia retrieval system based on semantics and deep features. Future Internet **12**, 183 (2020)
15. Benfenati, D., Montanaro, M., Rinaldi, A., Russo, C., Tommasino, C.: Using focused crawlers with obfuscation techniques in the audio retrieval domain. In: International Conference on Management of Digital, pp. 3–17 (2023)
16. Liu, J., Li, X., Zhang, Q., Zhong, G.: A novel focused crawler combining web space evolution and domain ontology. Knowl.-Based Syst. **243**, 108495 (2022)
17. Russo, C., Madani, K., Rinaldi, A.: An unsupervised approach for knowledge construction applied to personal robots. IEEE Trans. Cogn. Dev. Syst. **13**, 6–15 (2020)

18. Rinaldi, A., Russo, C.: Using a multimedia semantic graph for web document visualization and summarization. Multimedia Tools Appl. **80**, 3885–3925 (2021)
19. Al-Tameemi, I., Feizi-Derakhshi, M., Pashazadeh, S., Asadpour, M.: Multi-model fusion framework using deep learning for visual-textual sentiment classification. Comput. Mater. Continua **76**, 2145–2177 (2023)
20. Menad, S., Abdeddaim, S., Soualmia, L.: Flexible classification, question-answering and retrieval with siamese neural networks for biomedical texts. In: International Conference on Flexible Query Answering Systems, pp. 27–38 (2023)
21. Mary, J., Balasubramanian, S., Raj, R.: An enhanced focused web crawler for biomedical topics using attention enhanced siamese long short term memory networks. Braz. Arch. Biol. Technol. **64**, e21210163 (2022)
22. Nemati, Z., Mohammadi, A., Bayat, A., Mirzaei, A.: Metaheuristic and data mining algorithms-based feature selection approach for anomaly detection. IETE J. Res. **70**, 6040–6054 (2024)
23. Ali, M., Abdullah, A., Zaki, A., Rizk, F., Eid, M., El-Kenway, E.: Advances and challenges in feature selection methods: a comprehensive review. J. Artif. Intell. Metaheuristics. **1**, 67–77 (2024)
24. Rinaldi, A., Russo, C., Tommasino, C.: A semantic approach for document classification using deep neural networks and multimedia knowledge graph. Expert Syst. Appl. **169**, 114320 (2021)
25. Reimers, N., Gurevych, I.: Sentence-BERT: sentence embeddings using siamese BERT-networks. In: Proceedings of the 2019 Conference on Empirical Methods in Natural Language Processing and the 9th International Joint Conference on Natural Language Processing (EMNLP-IJCNLP), pp. 3982–3992 (2019)
26. Miller, G.: WordNet: a lexical database for English. Commun. ACM **38**, 39–41 (1995)
27. Simonyan, K., Zisserman, A.: Very deep convolutional networks for large-scale image recognition. arXiv Preprint arXiv:1409.1556 (2014)
28. Russakovsky, O., et al.: Imagenet large scale visual recognition challenge. Int. J. Comput. Vis. **115**, 211–252 (2015)
29. Joshi, P., Liu, S.: Web document text and images extraction using DOM analysis and natural language processing. In: Proceedings of the 9th ACM Symposium on Document Engineering, pp. 218–221 (2009)
30. Rombach, R., Blattmann, A., Lorenz, D., Esser, P., Ommer, B.: High-resolution image synthesis with latent diffusion models. In: Proceedings of the IEEE/CVF Conference on Computer Vision and Pattern Recognition, pp. 10684–10695 (2022)
31. Saharia, C., et al.: Photorealistic text-to-image diffusion models with deep language understanding. In: Advances in Neural Information Processing Systems, vol. 35, pp. 36479–36494 (2022)
32. Radford, A., et al.: Learning transferable visual models from natural language supervision. In: International Conference on Machine Learning, pp. 8748–8763 (2021)
33. Architectures, A., et al.: Advancements and challenges in generative AI: architectures, applications, and ethical implications. In: CEUR Workshop Proceedings, vol. 3762, pp. 29–34 (2024)
34. Landauer, T., Foltz, P., Laham, D.: An introduction to latent semantic analysis. Discourse Process. **25**, 259–284 (1998)
35. Blei, D., Ng, A., Jordan, M.: Latent dirichlet allocation. J. Mach. Learn. Res. **3**, 993–1022 (2003)
36. Bosch, A., Zisserman, A., Munoz, X.: Representing shape with a spatial pyramid kernel. In: Proceedings of the 6th ACM International Conference on Image and Video Retrieval, pp. 401–408 (2007)

37. Lowe, G.: Sift-the scale invariant feature transform. Int. J. **2**, 2 (2004)
38. Zhang, H., Xu, T., Li, H., Zhang, S., Wang, X., Huang, X., Metaxas, D.: Stackgan: text to photo-realistic image synthesis with stacked generative adversarial networks. In: Proceedings of the IEEE International Conference on Computer Vision, pp. 5907–5915 (2017)
39. Xu, T., et al.: Attngan: fine-grained text to image generation with attentional generative adversarial networks. In: Proceedings of the IEEE Conference on Computer Vision and Pattern Recognition, pp. 1316–1324 (2018)
40. Brock, A., Donahue, J., Simonyan, K.: Large scale GAN training for high fidelity natural image synthesis. In: International Conference on Learning Representations (2019). https://openreview.net/forum?id=B1xsqj09Fm
41. Razavi, A., Oord, A., Vinyals, O.: Generating diverse high-fidelity images with VQ-VAE-2. In: Advances in Neural Information Processing Systems, vol. 32 (2019)
42. BlackForest. Black forest labs; frontier AI lab (2024). https://blackforestlabs.ai/
43. Heusel, M., Ramsauer, H., Unterthiner, T., Nessler, B., Hochreiter, S.: GANs trained by a two time-scale update rule converge to a local nash equilibrium. In: Advances In Neural Information Processing Systems, vol. 30 (2017)
44. Hinz, T., Heinrich, S., Wermter, S.: Semantic object accuracy for generative text-to-image synthesis. IEEE Trans. Pattern Anal. Mach. Intell. **44**, 1552–1565 (2020)
45. Hessel, J., Holtzman, A., Forbes, M., Bras, R., Choi, Y.: Clipscore: a reference-free evaluation metric for image captioning. arXiv Preprint arXiv:2104.08718 (2021)
46. Szegedy, C., Vanhoucke, V., Ioffe, S., Shlens, J., Wojna, Z.: Rethinking the inception architecture for computer vision. In: Proceedings of the IEEE Conference on Computer Vision and Pattern Recognition, pp. 2818–2826 (2016)
47. Yager, R., Kacprzyk, J.: The ordered weighted averaging operators: theory and applications. Springer (2012)
48. Benfenati, D., De Filippis, G., Rinaldi, A., Russo, C., Tommasino, C.: A retrieval-augmented generation application for question-answering in nutrigenetics domain. Procedia Comput. Sci. **246**, 586–595 (2024). 28th International Conference on Knowledge Based and Intelligent information and Engineering Systems (KES 2024)

A Systematic Literature Review on LLM-Based Content Classification

Diogo Cosme[1(✉)], António Galvão[2], and Fernando Brito e Abreu[1]

[1] ISTAR-IUL, Instituto Universitário de Lisboa (Iscte-IUL),
Av. das Forças Armadas, 40, 1649-026 Lisboa, Portugal
{dfmce,fba}@iscte-iul.pt
[2] CENSE, School of Science and Technology, NOVA University Lisbon,
2829-516 Caparica, Portugal
amg13172@campus.fct.unl.pt

Abstract. This review examines how LLMs, particularly those using transformer architectures, have addressed persistent challenges in text classification through their advanced context understanding and generative capabilities. Despite significant progress, the review highlights gaps in current research, such as the need for greater transparency, reduced computational cost, and better management of model hallucinations. The paper concludes with recommendations for future research to improve the use of LLMs in content classification and ensure their effective use in various domains.

Keywords: Systematic literature review · Large language model · Contents classification

1 Introduction

Due to the immense potential and inherent complexities of LLMs, it is essential to evaluate or conduct literature reviews to support the field of LLM-based content classification, especially for textual content. By understanding the current landscape and methodologies, researchers can realize LLMs' full potential and ensure their applications are innovative and effective in various fields. To check if the characterization of that landscape (aka state of the art) was already performed, we searched for literature reviews on this topic in the SCOPUS database using this search string:

> *"literature review" AND ("information retrieval" OR "contents classification" OR "topics classification") AND (LLM OR "large language model" OR "foundational model" OR GPT)*

We obtained ten hits, but only two corresponded to literature reviews [24,45]. However, none of these were about LLM-based content classification. On [45], a literature review addressed the critical need for guidelines for incorporating LLMs and GenAI into healthcare and medical practice. In contrast, a systematic literature review on [24] identified potential research directions for information extraction from unstructured documents.

In summary, the importance of LLM-based content classification and the lack of previous literature reviews on this topic motivated us to write this paper.

This paper expands upon the literature review on LLM-based content classification presented in a previous conference paper of ours [8]. It includes new studies discovered after the initial submission and a more detailed explanation of the quality assessment performed. It is organized as follows: Sect. 2 describes the methodology used for searching and screening the primary studies; Sect. 3 analyzes the final set of selected studies; and Sect. 4 provides a summary of the existing research and identifies the threats to the validity of this literature review.

2 Methodology

To conduct a rigorous systematic literature review (SLR) on LLM-based content classification, we followed a structured approach to ensure comprehensive coverage of relevant studies. This methodology allowed us to identify key contributions, assess existing research gaps, and evaluate the feasibility of using LLMs to enhance systematic review processes.

2.1 Planning the Review

Research Questions. The research questions (RQs) were designed to capture the breadth and depth of LLM applications in content classification, their contributions to the field, and their potential for evaluating research quality.

RQ1: What empirical studies have been conducted in LLM-based content classification?
RQ2: What were the relevant contributions of the existing studies?
RQ3: Can LLMs be used to assess the structural quality of studies?

Review Protocol. According to [36], Scopus provides a broader subject coverage than Web of Science and Dimensions, including most articles available in these two databases. Therefore, we decided to rely solely on the Scopus database for primary studies in our literature search.

Search String. The search string included the most important terms related to the research questions, as follows:

("Large Language Model" OR "Foundational Model") AND ("Contents Classification" OR "Topic Classification")

Inclusion Criteria. A careful review of the abstracts and overall structure of the primary studies allowed us to determine their relevance to our research. The decision to include a study in our selection was based on the fulfillment of the following inclusion criteria:

- be written in English
- be a primary study
- matches at least one of the literature review questions
- be the most up-to-date and comprehensive version of the document
- be available for download through the Portuguese b-on scheme[1]

Data Extraction. The *Elicit* AI Research Assistant was used to extract details from papers into an organized table. According to its website, it has been used by more than 2 million researchers. Besides, it is claimed that *Elicit* uses various strategies to reduce the rate of hallucinations such as *"process supervision, prompt engineering, ensembling multiple models, double-checking our results with custom models and internal evaluations, and more to reduce the rate of hallucinations"*. In other words, its authors claim that it is a robust and trustworthy AI solution for summarizing, finding, and extracting details from scientific articles.

A dataset containing the following fields, extracted with *Elicit*, is available in [7] as supplementary data: research questions; summary of introduction; dataset; limitations; research gaps; software used; algorithms; methodology; main findings; objectives; study design; intervention effects; hypotheses tested; experimental techniques.

Quality Assessment. The selected studies from the previous phase were evaluated and analyzed to assess their quality using seven questions (see boxes 1 and 2), each rated on an ordinal scale: 0 (strongly disagree), 1 (disagree), 2 (neither agree nor disagree), 3 (agree), and 4 (strongly agree). Since the main objective of our research is about using LLMs for classification, we decided to evaluate how an LLM classifies the quality of articles, taking manual (human) classification as the ground truth.

The information extracted with *Elicit* was then used as the basis for manual and LLM-based quality assessment. For the LLM-based evaluation, we used prompting combined with the ICL zero-shot technique, as this is the fastest and most cost-effective approach compared to fine-tuning and few-shot ICL techniques. Microsoft Copilot was chosen as the foundational model for PDF document analysis due to its prominence at the time of writing.

We then used **Prompt 1** (see Box 1), which is organized as follows: it begins with an introduction to the task, followed by the expected output that the LLM should produce: a JSON object where each key represents a question indicator, and the values are the assigned scores. Finally, for each article, the term *"ARTICLE"* is replaced with the corresponding JSON object, where each key represents a *Elicit* field, and the values are the associated information.

---

[1] This is an initiative that provides access to a wide range of academic journals and publications for researchers and students in Portugal.

Box 1. Prompt 1 of the quality assessment

Prompt 1

Your task is to assess the quality of a study article based on the information provided. You will be given two JSON objects:
1 - One with question indicators as keys and the corresponding questions as values.
2 - Another contains information about the article, where the keys represent specific parameters.
Your goal is to assign each question a score from 0 to 4 (0 - strongly disagree, 1 - disagree, 2 - neither agree nor disagree, 3 - agree, 4 - strongly agree).
Please provide your evaluation in the following JSON format: {"Q1": <score>, "Q2": <score>, ...}.
Questions: {
"Q1": "Were the study's goals and research questions clearly defined?"
"Q3": "Was the research design clearly outlined?"
"Q4": "Were the study limitations evaluated and identified?"
"Q5": "Was the data used for validation described in sufficient detail and made available?"
"Q6": "Were answers to the research questions provided?"
"Q7": "Were negative or unexpected findings reported about the study?"
}
Article:
"""ARTICLE"""
Please provide the requested JSON.

An important note is that none of the available *Elicit* fields refer to related work, so it is impossible to answer Q2 the same way as the other questions. For the latter, the procedure was as follows: via the Copilot sidebar section in the Microsoft Edge browser, we can restrict the relevant information sources to the open page only, which in this case is a PDF opened in Microsoft Edge. We then provided **Prompt 2** as illustrated in Box 2.

Box 2. Prompt 2 of the quality assessment

Prompt 2

Your task is to assign a score from 0 to 4 (0 - strongly disagree, 1 - disagree, 2 - neither agree nor disagree, 3 - agree, 4 - strongly agree) to a question from a study quality assessment about this article. In addition to the score, you must provide a detailed rationale and identify the sections or pages (both, if possible) that contribute to your answer.
The question is: "Was previously published related work exposed and compared with the research results claimed in the study?"

2.2 Conducting the Review

Execute Search. Applying the specified search string and inclusion and exclusion criteria resulted in six new studies not present in the first version of this literature review [8], resulting in nineteen studies. Figure 1 shows the number of studies after each literature review stage.

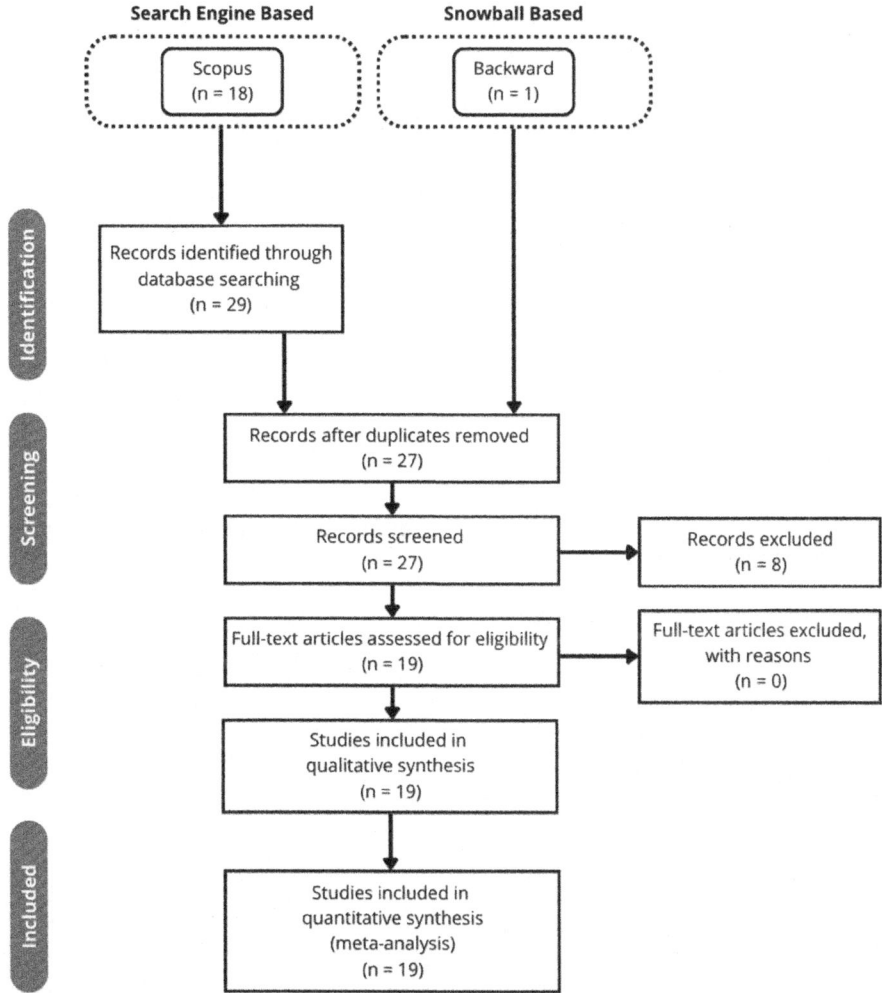

Fig. 1. Stages of the literature review.

Apply Quality Assessment. The performance of each assessment was analyzed based on the mean absolute score difference between the LLM's scores and the manual scores and based on the average scores given to each question by each method (i.e., LLM and manual). Figures 2 and 3 displays the results of the quality assessment performed and presented in the first version of this review, which we named as 1st Search, and Figs. 4 and 5 displays the results for the new six studies, which we named as 2nd Search.

As the graphs of the first and second searches show, the performance was similar except for Q4 and especially Q7. The difference in Q4 could be due to the outlier identified in the first search, which negatively impacted the results. In contrast, Q7 now shows a significant positive performance difference. The mean absolute score difference between the LLM and manual assignments decreased from 1.69 to 0.33. This may indicate an improvement in the model's reasoning capabilities over the three months between the searches (June 2024 and September 2024).

Given the significant improvement in Q7, we evaluated the studies from the first search to determine if the performance improvement extended to all studies.

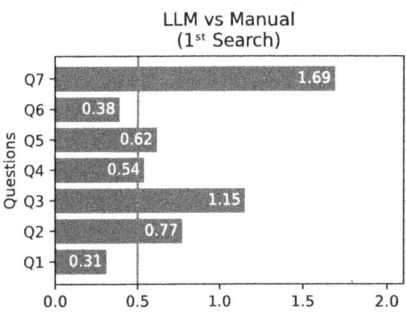

Fig. 2. Mean absolute score difference between methods per question (1st Search), from [8].

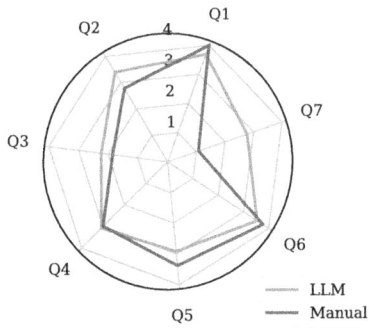

Fig. 3. Average scores given to the studies (1st Search), from [8].

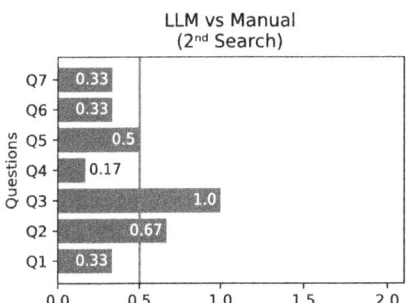

Fig. 4. Mean absolute score difference between methods per question (2nd Search).

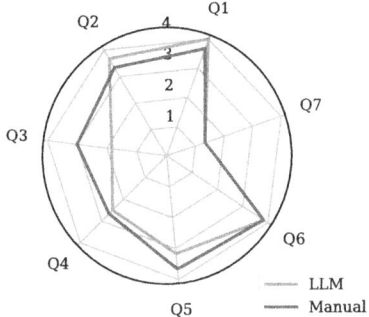

Fig. 5. Average scores given to the studies (2nd Search).

Figure 6 illustrates the mean absolute score difference between the first LLM test and the manual test, and between the second LLM test and the manual test for the 1st Search. From that, it is possible to conclude that:

1. Although not significant, a general improvement is observable.
2. Unexpectedly, the performance in Q7 differed from that observed in the six studies from the second search. One possible explanation is that we used an online model whose performance can be affected by the number of concurrent users. When many users are accessing the model at the same time, the model's reasoning ability may be reduced compared to times of lower usage. This is a limitation because Copilot does not provide information on the capacity of the model at the time of use, making it difficult to identify the reasons for the difference in this question.
3. In the second LLM test, the Q1 scores are exactly the same as the manual test scores.

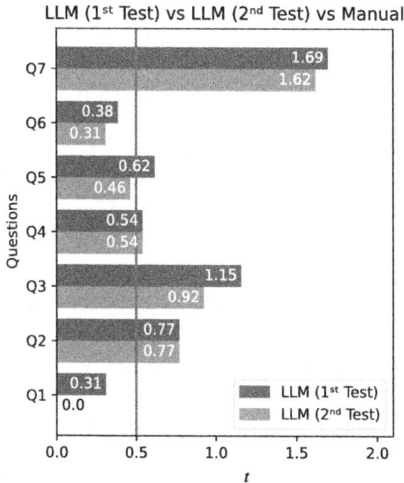

Fig. 6. Mean absolute score difference between the 1st LLM test and the manual test and between the 2nd LLM test and the manual test for the *1st Search*.

A detailed comparison of the scores given to each study from the first search by each LLM test is displayed in Fig. 7. The *n* value next to each question label indicates the number of times the scores were different for the same study.

We decided to draw conclusions using the results from the second LLM test for the first thirteen studies. Figure 8 shows the mean absolute score difference between the LLM assignments (the second LLM test for the *1st Search* and the only LLM test for the *2nd Search*) and the manual assignments. Figures 9 and 10 detail the scores assigned to each question for all nineteen studies. Both graphs show that using Copilot to answer Q1, Q4, Q5, and Q6 is reliable, as the results show. Q2 could also be included, despite the 12 cases where the scores did not match, considering Copilot's slight tendency to be optimistic when answering this question. In 10 out of 12 cases, Copilot scored one unit higher than the manual test.

Despite some improvement in the results compared to the first version of this literature review, we maintain our conclusion: ICL zero-shot is not yet reliable for assessing the full study quality. However, even in a volatile environment and without providing examples to the LLM, we obtained a satisfactory performance for some questions. Thus, we may achieve reasonable performance with a fine-tuned model or by using ICL few-shot examples.

Apart from the limitations of Copilot, there are also restrictions when using information extracted by the *Elicit* AI Research Assistant. As it is an AI system, there is a possibility that the extracted information could be inaccurate or, if presented without full context, could be misinterpreted. An example of this problem is the information extracted from [27] and labeled as *Limitations* by *Elicit*. In fact, the information in this field is about the authors' future work, not about limitations. This incorrect extraction may explain why Copilot gave the question about identifying and evaluating limitations (Q4) a score of 4, while the manual classification gave it a score of 0.

Given the limited number of studies, this task did not exclude any studies and was only helpful in assessing their overall quality.

Overview of Quality Assessment. Figure 11 shows the total score of each study from the manual assignment, along with the corresponding cluster determined by the K-means algorithm. The color of each bar indicates a different cluster. To improve the readability of the graph, a dashed line is drawn at the total score of 19.6, which is 70% of the maximum score, calculated as $(4 \times 7) \times 0.70 = 19.6$. Studies with a score above this threshold are considered good quality. The two clusters containing studies with higher total scores are all above this threshold. Therefore, we categorize the clusters (from top to bottom) as follows: high quality, good quality, high moderate quality, and low moderate quality. The last cluster is still considered moderate, as the scores are around 50% of the maximum score. Some studies are highlighted in red to distinguish those in the 2nd *Search* (red) from those in the 1st *Search* (black).

3 Document the Review

3.1 Demographics

Figure 12 shows that all studies are collaborative efforts with multiple authors, with the majority having two authors. Notably, there are two exceptional cases with many (16). Regarding the authors' affiliations (Fig. 13), the predominant scenario includes one or two institutions. The relatively low number of institutions compared to the number of authors indicates a lack of inter-institutional collaboration, which could improve research outcomes. This is further highlighted by the lack of international partnerships, with only two articles showing collaboration between teams from Indonesia and Turkey [26] and the Faroe Islands and Iceland [9].

Regarding authors' countries of origin, while no single country dominates, Europe stands out as the most active continent (Fig. 14). All demographic data presented so far includes information from both the first and second searches. The most significant differences between these searches pertain to the countries of author affiliations and

A Systematic Literature Review on LLM-Based Content Classification 129

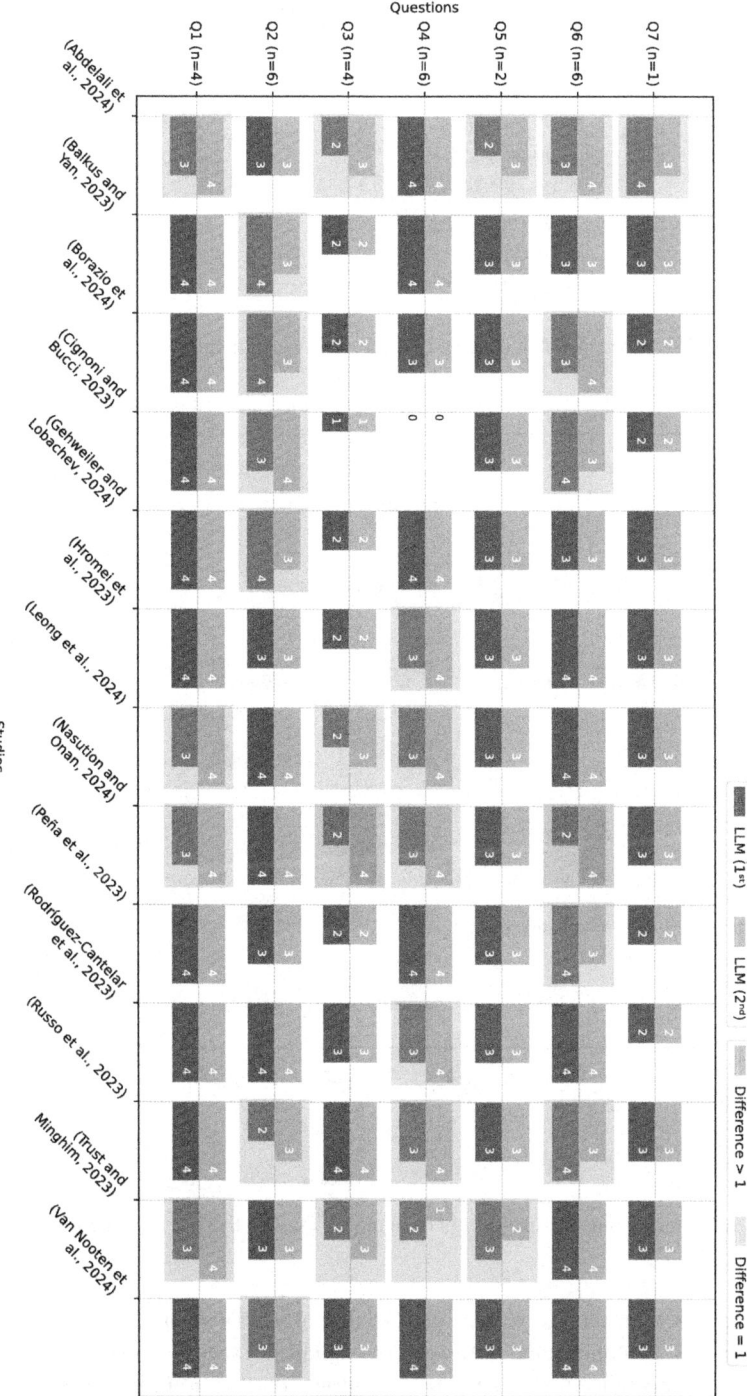

Fig. 7. Scores assigned to each study from the 1st *Search* by each LLM test.

130 D. Cosme et al.

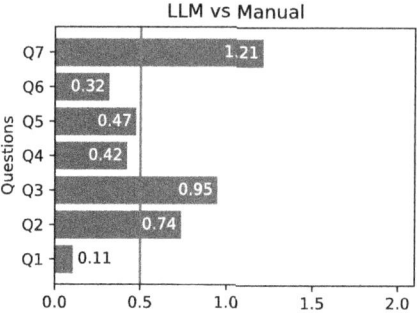

Fig. 8. Mean absolute score difference between methods per question.

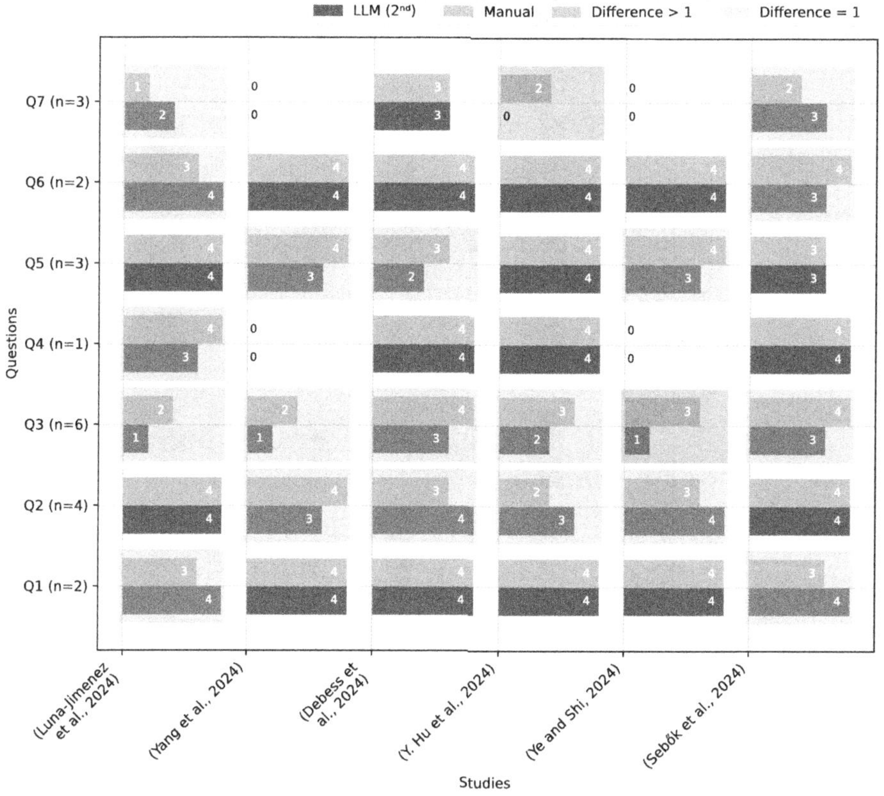

Fig. 9. Scores assigned to each study from the 2nd Search by the LLM and manual tests.

the venue types. In the second search, Chinese affiliations appeared with three studies, while Europe contributed with four new studies. Except for one case (Spain), all these European studies came from new countries. Furthermore, in the second search, the published studies were either related to conferences or journals.

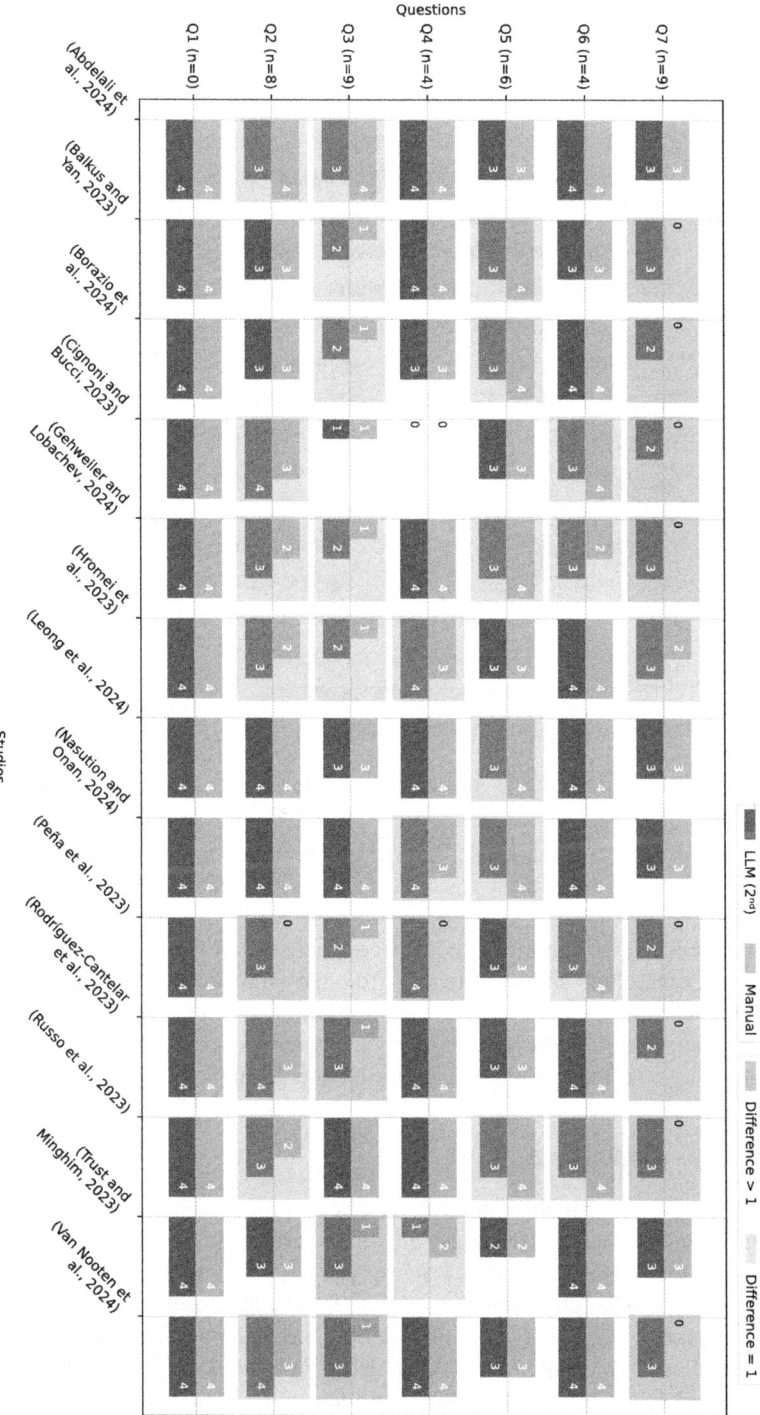

Fig. 10. Scores assigned to each study from the 1st *Search* by the 2nd LLM test and the manual test.

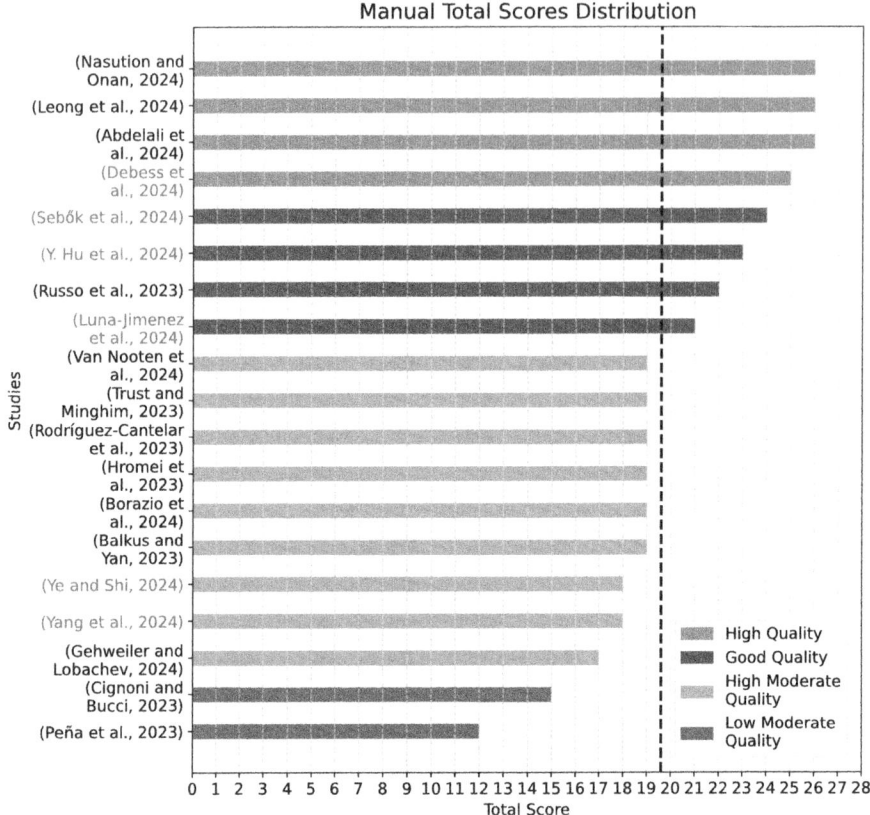

Fig. 11. Study quality clustering of the manual assignment.

Figure 15 indicates that most studies were published in workshops and journals. It is noteworthy that three articles originate from the same workshop (EVALITA 2023). This high concentration may suggest the topic remains niche, with limited venues for broader dissemination. However, it can also be interpreted as an indication of an emerging community with the potential for increased interest in the future.

3.2 Analysis and Findings

A methodology, as described in [30], has been proposed to address the problem of inconsistent responses in chatbots. This methodology involves hierarchical topic/subtopic detection using zero-shot learning (via GPT-4) and identification of inconsistent responses using clustering techniques. The datasets used in the study were the DailyDialog corpus [21] and data collected by the authors' Thaurus bot during the Alexa Prize Socialbot Challenge (SGC5). Using the *DailyDialog* dataset, the authors achieved a weighted F1 score of 0.34 for topic detection and 0.78 for subtopic detection. For the SGC5 dataset, the accuracy was 81% for topic detection and 6% for subtopic

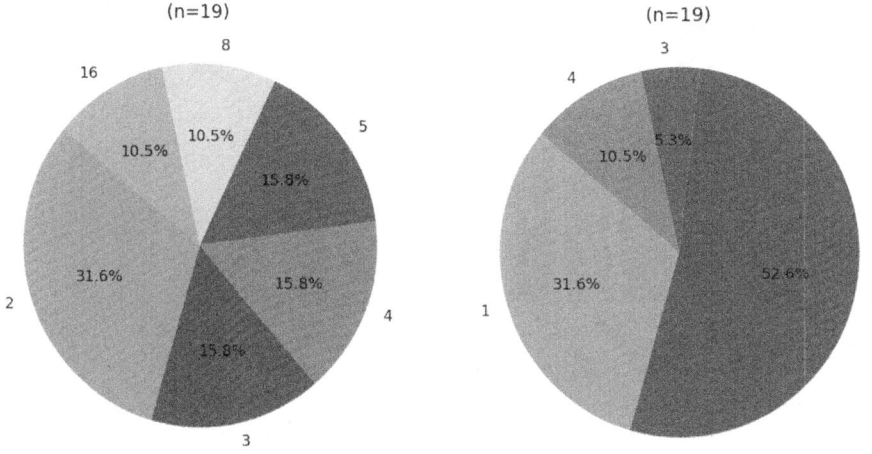

Fig. 12. Frequency by number of authors.   **Fig. 13.** Frequency by affiliation.

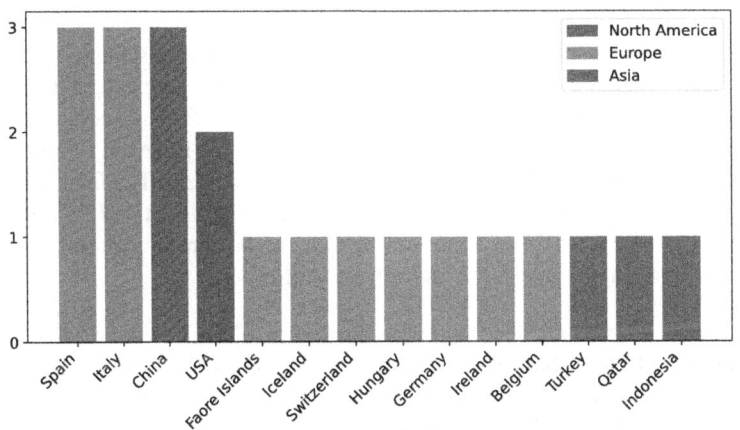

Fig. 14. Frequency by author affiliations' country.

detection. It is noteworthy that there is room for improvement in the *DailyDialog* topic detection, as the lower weighted F1 score suggests a significant number of false positives or false negatives.

An overview of the EVALITA 2023 challenge "Automatic Conspiracy Theory Identification (ACTI)" is detailed in [31]. This challenge aims to identify whether an Italian message contains conspiratorial content (Subtask A) and, if so, classify it into one of four specific conspiracy topics: "*Covid*", "*Qanon*", "*Flat Earth*", or "*Pro-Russia*" (Subtask B). Eight teams participated in Subtask A, while seven teams took part in Subtask B. The dataset provided to each team was identical, consisting of Italian comments scraped from five Telegram channels known for hosting conspiratorial content, collected between January 1, 2020, and June 30, 2020. These comments were manually annotated by two human annotators to identify conspiratorial content (categorized as "*Not Relevant*", "*Non-Conspiratorial*" or "*Conspiratorial*") and to classify

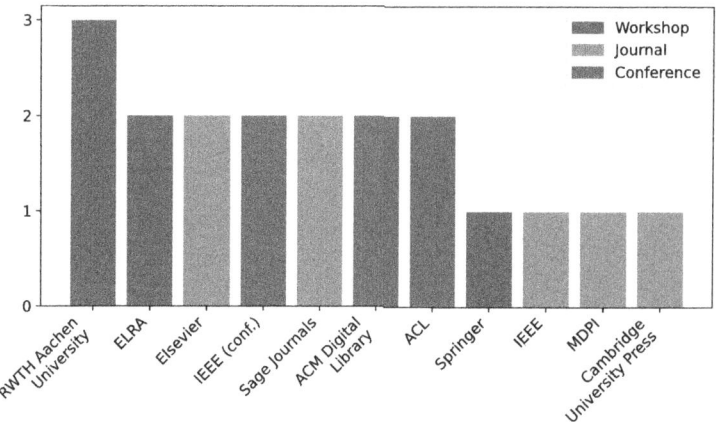

Fig. 15. Frequency by publisher (ACL - Association for Computational Linguistics, ELRA - European Language Resources Association).

them into specific conspiracy theories. The authors used Cohen's Kappa coefficient to measure inter-annotator agreement, achieving high consistency: a Cohen's Kappa of 0.93 for Subtask A and 0.86 for Subtask B. To ensure data integrity, comments that did not receive the same classification were excluded, and "Not Relevant" comments were also discarded to focus solely on relevant conspiratorial content. The final datasets consist of 2,301 comments labeled with a binary label for Subtask A and 1,110 comments labeled with a value from 0 to 3, representing the specific conspiracy topic. The articles in this challenge that are relevant to the subject of this paper are:

- The authors of [5] evaluated the performance of two fine-tuned encoder-only transformer models (bert-base-italian-xxl-cased and XLM-RoBERTa, [6]) against an unfine-tuned decoder-only transformer model (LLaMA 7B, [37]). The BERT models outperformed the LLaMA model in both subtasks. For Subtask A, the scores were 0.83, 0.82, and 0.80, respectively. For Subtask B, the scores were 0.83, 0.85, and 0.74, respectively. The article does not address the limitations of the study or the specific use of LLaMA.
- The authors of [15] employed a distinctive strategy. They initially introduced a model designed to tackle all tasks in the EVALITA 2023 challenge, extending beyond just the ACTI task. As a result, their dataset was considerably larger than the one provided for the ACTI task, encompassing 134,018 examples from various tasks. For each task, the authors evaluated the performance of two models. The first model, *extremIT5*, is an encoder-decoder model based on IT5, with approximately 110 million parameters. This model was fine-tuned by concatenating task names and input texts to generate text that solves the target tasks. The second model, *extremITLLaMA*, is a decoder-only model based on LLaMa 7B. It was initially trained on Italian translations of Alpaca instruction data using LoRA (Low-Rank Adaptation)[2]

---

[2] LoRA fine-tuning significantly reduces the computational and storage costs of training large language models by only adjusting a subset of low-rank parameters.

[16], to enable the model to understand instructions in Italian. Subsequently, it was further fine-tuned using LoRA on instructions specific to the EVALITA tasks. In their final results, the authors achieved an F1 score of 0.82 for Subtask A using *extremIT5* and 0.86 with *extremITLLaMA*. For Subtask B, the F1 scores were 0.81 and 0.86, respectively. Key limitations of this study include the computational cost and inference speed of the larger *extremITLLaMA* model, as well as limited exploration of architectures and hyperparameters due to time constraints. The authors conclude by suggesting that exploring zero-shot or few-shot learning could improve sustainability by reducing the need for large amounts of annotated data.

The methodology outlined in [5] ranked sixth in Subtask A, while the approach presented in [15] ranked second. In Subtask B, their rankings were fourth and fifth, respectively. The team that won both subtasks used a strategy that included data augmentation using large language models (LLMs).

As suggested in [39], query-focused submodular mutual information functions can be utilized to select diverse and representative demonstration examples for in-context learning (ICL) in prompting. Additionally, an interactive tool is introduced to examine the impact of hyperparameters on model performance in ICL. For evaluation, the authors applied their method to the following tasks: two sentiment classification tasks using the Stanford Sentiment Treebank datasets (SST-2 and SST-5) [35], and a topic classification task using the AG News Classification Dataset [48]. Their methodology involves the following two steps:

i. **Retrieval:** The goal is to select representative and diverse in-context demonstration examples from the training data based on the input test. To achieve this, both the input test and the training dataset are embedded using the sentence transformer [29]. Submodular Mutual Information (SMI) functions are then used to select examples from the training data. These selected examples are then incorporated into a prompt template, either with an optional task directive or as independent demonstrations.

ii. **Inference:** The prompt template and input test are fed into a pre-trained language model to infer the corresponding label. They used three open-source pre-trained models: GPT-2 [28], OPT [47], and BLOOM [18].

The authors claim that their approach can lead to performance improvements of up to 20% compared to random selection or traditional prompting methods. Additionally, they note that the size and type of the language model do not necessarily ensure better performance.

A transit-topic-aware language model to classify open-ended text feedback into relevant transit-specific topics based on traditional transit Customer Relationship Management (CRM) feedback is proposed in [19]. The primary dataset consists of approximately 180,000 manually labeled anonymous customer feedback comments from the Washington Metropolitan Area Transit Authority (WMATA) CRM database from January 2017 to December 2022. With 61 different labels, the authors used Latent Dirichlet Allocation (LDA) to group customer feedback into broader themes. Due to the limitation of LDA in detecting significantly less represented topics, these topics were excluded from the CRM dataset prior to applying LDA and grouped according to their original topic (forming two niche groups). LDA failed to identify a primary topic for approximately 62,000 complaints. As a result, the final dataset contained approximately 120,000 complaints grouped into 11 topics (9 LDA-detected topics and two niche topics). The authors evaluated the performance of five machine learning models (Random Forest, Linear SGD, SVM, Naive Bayes, and Logistic Regression) against the proposed language model MetRoBERTA. MetRoBERTA is a fine-tuned version of the RoBERTa language model open-sourced by Meta Research [22] using the CRM dataset. MetRoBERTA outperformed the traditional ML models, achieving a macro average F1 score of 0.80 and a weighted average F1 score of 0.90, compared to the best machine learning model, which scored 0.76 and 0.88, respectively. A significant limitation of this study is the exclusion of approximately 60,000 initial complaints, representing more than one-third of the entire dataset.

A novel framework that leverages LLMs to identify and categorize emergent sociopolitical phenomena during health crises, with a focus on the COVID-19 pandemic, is introduced in [4]. This framework also assists the analyst by generating actionable statements for each identified topic. The dataset used comprises 2,254 news articles, manually categorized by experts from the Istituto Superiore di Sanità (ISS) into five topics: *"Covid Variants," "Nursing Homes Outbreaks," "Hospital Outbreaks," "School Outbreaks,"* and *"Family/Friend Outbreaks,"* collected from February 2020 to September 2022. The system generates linguistic triples to capture detailed concepts, which analysts can refine to correlate themes. For the next step, a model based on BART [20] and previously trained on the Multi-Genre Natural Language Inference corpus [41] is employed. This model uses zero-shot classification to associate news articles with the identified topics without requiring fine-tuning. Preliminary results show accurate mapping of news articles to specific, detailed topics, achieving an accuracy of 67% when proposing a single class, which increases to 88% when considering the top two system suggestions. However, the authors note potential limitations, including hallucinations due to the integration of a decoder LLM (GPT-4) for prompt generation.

The LaraBench benchmarking study [1] addresses the gap in comparing large language models (LLMs) with state-of-the-art models (SOTA) used for Arabic natural language processing and speech processing tasks. The study used 61 publicly available datasets to support nine task groups: Word Segmentation, Syntax and Information Extraction, Machine Translation, Sentiment, Style and Emotion Analysis, News Categorization, Demographic Attributes, Factuality, Disinformation and Harmful Content Detection, Semantics, Question Answering, and Speech Processing. The models used for NLP tasks were GPT-3.5-Turbo, GPT-4, BLOOMZ, and Jais-13b-chat with zero and few-shot learning. Following the recommended format from Azure OpenAI Studio Chat Playground and PromptSource [2], different prompts were tested and the most effective one was selected. The study found that in certain multi-label tasks, such as propaganda detection, the LLMs occasionally produced output that did not match the predefined labels. In addition, the authors found that seamless use of LLMs requires significant effort in creating precise prompts or post-processing to match outputs to reference labels. While GPT-4 has made significant progress in closing the gap with SOTA models, even outperforming them in high-level abstract tasks such as news categorization, achieving consistent SOTA performance in sequence tagging remains a challenge.

In addition, the authors observed an average macro F1 improvement from 0.656 to 0.721 when using few-shot (10-shot) learning instead of zero-shot learning.

The study, described in [27], explored the potential of large language models (LLMs) to improve the classification of public affairs documents. The researchers collected raw data from the Spanish Parliament, covering the period from November 2019 to October 2022. They obtained about 450,000 records, of which about 92,500 were labeled. To address significant class imbalances, they focused on the 30 most frequent topics out of 385 labels. The models used were four transformer models pre-trained from scratch in Spanish by the Barcelona Supercomputing Center as part of the MarIA project [14]: RoBERTa-base, RoBERTa-large, RoBERTalex, and GPT2-base. Their approach involved using transformer models in combination with classifiers. They conducted experiments with four models paired with three classifiers (Neural Networks, Random Forests, and SVMs). The results showed that using an LLM backbone with SVM classifiers is an effective strategy for multi-label topic classification in public affairs, achieving accuracy rates above 85%.

In [3], the authors investigate enhancing the performance of GPT-3 on a short text classification task through data augmentation. The study aims to classify whether a question pertains to data science by comparing two methods: augmenting the GPT-3 Classification Endpoint by expanding the training set and optimizing the GPT-3 Completion Endpoint using a genetic algorithm. Both methods are accessible via the GPT-3 API, each with its own benefits and limitations. The Completion Endpoint relies on a text prompt followed by ICL, either zero-shot or few-shot, but its performance is significantly affected by the specific examples included. Conversely, the Classification Endpoint uses text embeddings and provides more consistent performance, although it requires a large number of examples (hundreds or thousands) to achieve optimal results. The dataset used in the study comprises 72 short text questions collected from the University of Massachusetts Dartmouth Big Data Club's Discord server. For Classification Endpoint Augmentation, GPT-3 was used to generate new questions. Among the methods, the embedding-based GPT-3 Classification Endpoint achieved the highest accuracy, approximately 76%, although this is lower than the estimated human accuracy of 85%. On the other hand, the GPT-3 Completion Endpoint, optimized with a genetic algorithm for in-context examples, showed strong validation accuracy but lower test accuracy, indicating potential overfitting.

The study presented in [26] compares the quality of annotations generated by humans and large language models (LLMs) for NLP tasks in Turkish, Indonesian, and Minangkabau (Topic Classification, Tweet Sentiment Analysis, and Emotion Classification). The authors used three Turkish datasets, each tailored for one of the NLP tasks. In addition, they used two Indonesian datasets: one for Tweet Sentiment Analysis and another for Emotion Classification. They also included two Minangkabau datasets, which were translations of the Indonesian datasets. The LLMs used in the study were ChatGPT-4, BERT [11], BERTurk (a fine-tuned Turkish version of BERT), RoBERTa [22] (fine-tuned to specific datasets), and T5 [25]. Human annotations consistently outperformed LLMs on several evaluation metrics, serving as a benchmark for annotation quality. Although ChatGPT-4 and BERTurk showed competitive performance, they still lagged behind human annotations in certain areas. The study also observed a trade-off between precision and recall among the LLMs, highlighting the need for a better balance between these two metrics.

The use of LLMs for moderating online discussions is investigated in [13], focusing on identifying user intent in various types of content and examining content classification methods. The authors used several datasets, including the One Million Posts Corpus dataset from the Austrian Research Institute for Artificial Intelligence (OFAI), which contains German comments from an Austrian newspaper website [33]. Another dataset used was the New York Times Comments collection, which contains over two million comments on more than 9,000 articles. The LLMs used in their research were obtained from the Detoxify Python library. Their findings highlight the effectiveness of LLM approaches in detecting author intent in online discussions, and suggest that fine-tuned AI models trained on extensive data hold promise for automating this detection.

The authors of [40] report their results on the classification of Corporate Social Responsibility (CSR) themes and topics in a shared task involving cross-lingual multi-class and monolingual multi-label classification. The shared task included two subtasks: cross-lingual multi-class classification to identify CSR topics (using one dataset) and monolingual multi-label text classification of CSR topics related to environment (ENV) and labor and human rights (LAB) topics (using two datasets). For text classification, the authors used LLMs such as GPT-3.5 and GPT-4 (both in zero-shot mode and without fine-tuning), along with fine-tuned versions of DistilBERT [32], BERT [11], RoBERTa, and RoBERTa-large [22]. For the topics dataset, they used fine-tuned versions of Multi-Lingual DistilBERT, XLM-RoBERTa, and XLM-RoBERTa-large [6]. Their zero-shot experiments with GPT models showed that these models still lag behind the fine-tuned models in multi-label classification.

Embeddings in the mental health domain are investigated in [23]. Various feature selection techniques were applied to the embeddings derived from the Llama-2 [38] and MentaLlama [42] models to achieve detailed classification of mental health topics by removing redundant features. The authors used two datasets of requests or responses and the corresponding questions.

- *Counsel-Chat*: Sourced from the HuggingFace library, it contains 3,451 samples across 28 unbalanced topics. The distribution of samples per class is as follows: minimum = 148, maximum = 589, mean (μ) = 123.25, and standard deviation (σ) = 143.71.
- *7Cups*: It contains 142,230 samples across 39 unbalanced topics, with a minimum of 14 and a maximum of 24,891 samples per topic. The μ is 3,646.92 and the σ is 6,091.36. This dataset contains topics similar to those in Counsel-Chat, with some variations in names and additional topics.

Topics with less than three questions and duplicate samples were removed. Finally, the datasets were divided into training, validation, and test sets with proportions of 80%, 10%, and 10%, respectively. To provide more detail about the models, two versions of Llama-2 with 7 billion parameters were used: the original developed by Meta, and a variant trained on ten mental health datasets covering eight mental health tasks (MentaLlama). Using double NF4 quantization (loaded in 4 bits) and 16-bit floating-point format for parameter computation, the authors managed to fit each model on less than 4 GB of GPU. To extract the 4,096 dimensional embeddings from the LLMs, the text of each sample was fed into the Llama-2 model without any modifications. An average over the temporal dimension was then computed to create a compact representation for the feature selection stage. During this stage, ANOVA F-values were used to rank the best feature sets. Two additional stages were then performed:

1. By selecting the optimal combination of hyperparameters and various classifiers (such as SVM, logistic regression, k-NN, etc.) that performed best on each dataset with the full set of 4,096 dimensional features, the authors determined the weighted F1 score, which serves as a benchmark for the next phase.
2. In this phase, the authors selected the classifier that previously achieved the highest weighted F1 score and retrained it using subsets of reduced dimensions based on the ranking from the feature selection strategy. The number of dimensions was incrementally increased until the weighted F1 score reached or approached the reference value.

Their results show that it is possible to reduce the dimensions of the input embeddings by up to 75% (from 4,096 dimensions to about 1,000), thereby reducing the complexity of the models without significantly affecting their performance. Additionally, they discovered other interesting facts. By comparing the selected embeddings from Llama-2 and MentalLlama, they found that the percentage of repetitiveness in the optimal feature set is 81.80% for Counsel-Chat with 1,000 features and 77.60% for 7Cups. This raises the question of whether it is more effective to extract embeddings from a fine-tuned model tailored to a specific task, or to use an open-domain version. When comparing embeddings across different datasets, the overlap percentage for 1,000 features is 46.20% for Llama-2 and 46.40% for MentalLlama. These results indicate that the selected embeddings can vary across different datasets, even when the data and tasks appear similar.

An advanced methodology for classifying financial news topics is proposed in [43]. The dataset used consists of 21,107 financial tweets annotated with twenty different labels. The data is divided into 80% for training and 20% for testing and comes from a Kaggle competition. For LLM, the Chatglm3-6b model [12,46] was used and fine-tuned using LoRA integrated with Noise Enhanced Fine-Tuning (NEFTune). This method aims to mitigate overfitting and improve model performance at no additional computational cost by incorporating uniform noise into the input embeddings. Their experimental settings were as follows: a learning rate of 5e-5, a batch size of 8, gradient accumulation set to 2, and a LoRA rank of 9. The results show that the Chatglm3-6b model outperforms other models, such as Bert-Base, Bert-Large, and Deberta variants, in accurately understanding and classifying financial news content.

Another study in the same research area as [43] that also uses the Chatglm3-6b LLM is [44]. While both studies use the same model, they also appear to use the same dataset. Although [44] states that the data is from the Twitter Financial News dataset, which is available in Kaggle, [43] only mentions that it is from Kaggle. However, the number of samples and features are identical, leading us to believe that they are the same dataset. Despite the similarities in LLM and dataset, the fine-tuning techniques differ. In this study, the authors employed the QLora technique [10]. Their configuration included a batch size of 4, a learning rate of 5e-5, the Adam optimizer, a quantization level of 4, a LoRA rank of 8, and gradient accumulation of 4. They benchmarked their model against others such as *Roberta-Base*, *Roberta-Large*, *Deberta-V2-base*, and *Deberta-V2-large*. The proposed fine-tuned model slightly outperformed the competitors, achieving an accuracy of 0.8815 compared to the lowest accuracy of 0.8615.

The effectiveness of GPT-4 for sentiment analysis and topic classification in low-resource languages, specifically Faroese news texts, is investigated in [9]. The study used the Basic Language Resource Kit 1.0 for Faroese, an open source text corpus. This corpus contains short news articles from the Faroese online news sites Portalurin and Dimmalætting, comprising 44,042 words in 170 articles. For the dataset, one to three complete sentences were randomly selected from these articles for annotation and analysis, resulting in a total of 225 sentences. In the sentiment analysis, each article was scored at both the sentence level (using the randomly selected sentences) and at the full article level. Each sentence and article was classified into one of three classes: positive (1), neutral (0), or negative (-1). In the topic analysis, GPT was instructed to assign one or more topics from a predefined list to each article. Two linguists, native speakers of Faroese, served as human annotators and verified GPT's responses for both tasks. In order to reproduce the annotation results as accurately as possible, the annotators developed a set of guidelines for annotating news items. GPT-4 was prompted with a temperature of 0 using its function API to extract structured information from news articles according to a specified JSON schema. The schema required GPT-4 to split the text into sentences, translate to English each sentence, assign a sentiment, assign one or more topics to the article, and determine an overall sentiment for the article. One variation of the study eliminated the translation requirement. It was found that GPT-4 occasionally failed to split sentences correctly (such errors were omitted), and sometimes suggested topics that were not in the predefined list, which were corrected by the annotators. Moreover, the authors also studied the use of few-shot instructions for sentiment analysis, describing what the task consists of and providing an example for each possible class. Their results showed a moderate inter-annotator agreement between human annotators and GPT-4, suggesting that GPT-4 can reliably classify sentiment in Faroese news texts. Regarding the different approaches used, they did not observe any improvement by translating the news into English. However, they did observe an increase in agreement when using the few-shot sentiment instruction.

The development of a threat intelligence knowledge graph that leverages LLMs to classify topics in collected reports, extract entities and relationships, and identify TTPs (The Tactics, Techniques, and Procedures) from attack descriptions is presented in [17]. The authors gathered the necessary data from various open source threat intelligence platforms, including security company content platforms, security news, and influential personal security blogs. These online resources provide detailed information about malware, vulnerabilities, threat actors, and attack activity, making them valuable sources of threat intelligence. To create a dataset for the tasks *Topic Classification* and *Entity and Relationship Extraction*, GPT-3.5-Turbo with few-shot learning was used to generate data for fine-tuning the Llama2-7B model. Different prompts and few-shot examples were used for each task. Due to the specialized knowledge required for network security and TTP, GPT could not be used for this purpose. Instead, two sources of manually labeled data, MITRE and CTID, were used for fine-tuning. The training dataset follows the format 'instruction+input+output'. The instruction provides a natural language description of the task, the input is the specific segment to be processed, and the output is the expected response. For the *Entity and Relationship Extraction* task, the instruction includes several output examples to ensure higher quality responses. A report only proceeds to the *Entity and Relationship Extraction* task if it successfully passes the *Topic Classification* task. This ensures that only relevant reports that pertain to malware, security vulnerabilities, or attack activities are analyzed further. For cost-effectiveness, the Llama2-7B model was fine-tuned using the LoRA technique on Python 3.9, utilizing 2 × 3090 GPUs. The maximum learning rate was set to 1×10^{-4}, with a maximum of 10 epochs. The maximum sequence length was configured to 1,024 tokens for the entity task and 512 tokens for the other tasks. In addition to the Llama2 model, non-fine-tuned GPT-3.5 and GPT-4 models were also used for comparison, in the *Entity Recognition* task. The Llama2-7B fine-tuned with 1,600 samples achieved the highest precision, GPT-3.5 had the best recall, and GPT-4 obtained the best F1 score. In *TTP Classification*, the Llama model achieved accuracy, precision, recall, and F1 scores above 96% for broad categories. For more specific categories, it achieved an F1 score of 87.50%.

The authors of [34] present *The Babel Machine*, a system for automatically classifying input files based on the 21 major policy topics outlined in the codebook of the Comparative Agendas Project (CAP). The data used for this system come from publicly available datasets on the CAP website and data provided from the international CAP community. According to the authors, the datasets were labeled by human coders and met the quality standards of the CAP project. The training data includes 22 categories (21 major CAP policy topics and one "no policy content" category), spans nine languages, and covers ten domains (e.g., media, legislative, executive speech), totaling 2.66 million records. The data was split into training (80%) and test (20%) sets. The XLM-RoBERTa model [6], which supports 100 languages and has 270 million parameters, was used as the LLM. The model, which accepts up to 512 tokens as input, was accessed via the HuggingFace repository and tuned using the Transformers library. Fine-tuning parameters included a batch size of 8, a learning rate of 5e-6, and a dropout rate of 0.1 in the final classification layer to prevent overfitting. The hardware used was a single NVIDIA A100 GPU with 80 GB of RAM. In total, 61 XLM-RoBERTa models were tuned: 1 pooled model (all data), 10 domain models (one for each domain), 9 language models (one for each language), and 41 language-domain models (one for each language-domain pair). For the language-domain models, 24 achieved a weighted macro F1 score above 0.75, with 6 exceeding 0.90. In general, the language-specific models did not provide any improvement over the pooled model, which had already reached gold standard quality, with the exception of some languages, such as Hungarian. While the domain-specific models also showed improved performance, with the legislative domain achieving the highest average scores. Based on these results, the authors recommend using LLMs as a primary option, while using human coding for validation or active learning processes in more challenging domains or languages.

Table 1 is an extended version of the table presented in [8], that shows the training methods used, the evaluation metrics, and the main results of each study.

Table 1. Articles summary information (extended version of [8])

Article	Method	Evaluation Metrics	Description
[30]	ICL	Weighted F1	Topic: 0.34; Subtopic: 0.78 (DailyDialog)
		Accuracy	Topic: 81%; Subtopic: 62% (SGC5)
[5]	Fine-tuning	Macro-avg F1	Subtask A: 0.83, 0.82 and 0.80, respectively.
			Subtask B: 0.83, 0.85 and 0.74, respectively.
[15]	Fine-tuning	F1	Subtask A: 0.82 (extremIT5) and 0.86 (extrem-ITLLaMA).
			Subtask B: 0.81 (extremIT5) and 0.86 (extrem-ITLLaMA)
[39]	ICL	F1	Sentiment Classification: 88.35%.
			Topic Classification: 90.56%.
[19]	Fine-tuning	Macro-avg F1	0.80 compared to the best ML model with 0.76
		Weighted avg F1	0.90 compared to the best ML model with 0.88
[4]	ICL	Accuracy	Single Class: 67%; Top two system suggestions: 90.56%.
[1]	ICL	Macro-avg F1	Few-shot (10-shot): 0.721; Zero-shot: 0.656.
[27]	Fine-tuning	Accuracy	Accuracies higher than 85%.
[3]	ICL	Accuracy	LLM: 76%; Estimated Human: 85%.
[26]	Fine-tuning; ICL	Avg F1	Human: 0.883; GPT-4: 0.865.
[13]	Fine-tuning	F1	Identifying user intent: 0.755.
[40]	Fine-tuning; ICL	F1	Zero-shot experiments lag behind fine-tuned models.
[23]	Fine-tuning	Weighted F1	In this case, the LLM was not used as a classifier, but rather to extract its embeddings.
[43]	Fine-tuning	Accuracy	88.56%
		Rouge metrics	Rouge-1 = 0.8979, Rouge-2 = 0.5975, Rouge-L = 0.8960
[44]	Fine-tuning	Accuracy	88.15%
[9]	ICL	Accuracy	91.2% in the Topic Annotation
		Cohen's Kappa	Between Humman Annotators and GPT-4: 0.70 at sentence-level; 0.57 at document-level
[17]	Fine-tuning; ICL	Accuracy	97.47% - TPP broad categories; 83.60% - TPP specific categories
		F1	98.21% - TPP broad categories; 87.50% - TPP specific categories; 86.33% - Named Entity Recognition
[34]	Fine-tuning	Weighted macro F1	Various tests performed

4 Conclusions

RQ1: What Empirical Studies Have Been Conducted in LLM-Based Content Classification? Although the current number of approaches to topic/content classification using LLMs is limited, the field is rapidly evolving and is expected to expand and improve significantly, as evidenced by the increase in new studies in 2024 compared to 2023 (Fig. 16).

Despite the limited number of studies, their analysis reveals a wide variety of methodologies, including different approaches (e.g., in-context learning vs. fine-tuning, prompting strategies) and model architectures (encoder-only, encoder-decoder, decoder-only), as well as diverse research areas being explored (Table 2).

Table 2. Research areas explored (extended version of [8]).

Research Area	Articles
Hierarchical topic/subtopic detection in inconsistent chatbot responses	[30]
Socio-political phenomena during health crises	[4]
Public affairs documents	[27]
Customer feedback	[19]
Corporate Social Responsibility themes and topics	[40]
Conspiracy Content	[5, 15]
Sentiment Analysis	[9, 26, 39]
Emotion	[26]
Benchmarking of NLP and speech processing tasks (Arabic)	[1]
Short questions	[3]
User intent in online discussions	[13]
Comparison of annotations generated by Humman and LLM	[9, 26]
Mental-Health	[26]
News	[9, 39, 43, 44]
Threat Intelligence	[17]
Public Policy Analysis	[34]

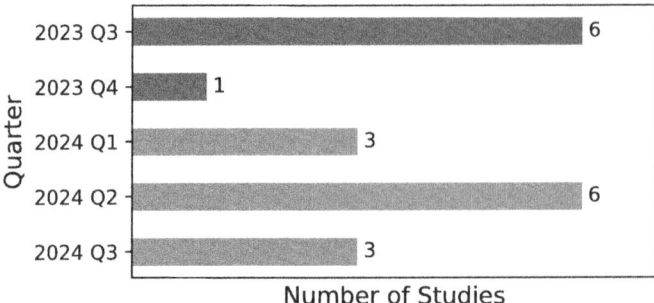

Fig. 16. Number of studies in LLM-based content classification.

RQ2: What Were the Relevant Contributions of the Existing Studies? The significant contributions of the studies are largely consistent with those highlighted in the initial version of this literature review.

Based on the available studies, fine-tuned LLMs generally outperform those trained with ICL techniques [3,40]. When fine-tuning models, it is critical to carefully choose between an encoder-only model, a decoder-only model, or an encoder-decoder model, as each architecture has unique characteristics and implications for model behavior and performance. In addition, analyses by [44] and [43] show that different tuning strategies can yield similar results. Both authors used the same LLM for the same problem but applied different tuning techniques. However, achieving optimal performance requires significant computational resources and a dataset with hundreds or thousands of examples.

LLMs can also be run using zero-shot or few-shot techniques as a less expensive alternative. A comparison of these two methods for a specific case was performed in [1,9] and showed that few-shot learning outperformed zero-shot learning. Importantly, the selection of a few examples is critical [39], and there are inherent limitations in the reasoning abilities of LLMs. Researchers [1,4,9,17] have highlighted issues related to model hallucinations. For example, [9] found that GPT-4, when applied to a classification task, suggested topics that were not in the predefined list.

An important observation highlighted in the new studies identified in this extended version was made by [23]. The authors found significant redundancy in the embeddings derived from Llama models. In addition, they observed that in some cases, extracting embeddings from a fine-tuned version may not be beneficial due to the overlap between the embeddings of the fine-tuned and non-fine-tuned versions. This insight can help reduce computational complexity by using only a small subset of the embeddings or by eliminating the need to fine-tune a model.

RQ3: Can LLMs Be Used to Assess the Structural Quality of Studies? We observed a slight improvement when applying the same framework to newly identified studies, but not enough to be considered reliable. Nevertheless, we maintain the conclusion that evaluating the quality of scientific articles with LLMs could be feasible. This could be accomplished through more extensive research with a fine-tuned model or by employing in-context learning (ICL) with few-shot examples.

4.1 Summary

In summary, this is an emerging field, as indicated by the number of studies and their publication dates. Therefore, further research is necessary to enhance performance, efficiency, transparency, and reasoning while minimizing model hallucination. Potential areas for exploration include examining the impact of architecture, the number of layers and parameters, and the quality of the training dataset used.

4.2 Threats to Validity

The following types of validity issues were considered when interpreting the results from this review.

Construct Validity. A literature database of relevant books, conferences, and journals served as the source for the research found in the systematic review. Therefore, bias in selecting publications is a potential drawback of this strategy, especially considering that three of the thirteen articles were submitted to the same workshop. To address this, we used a research protocol that included the study objectives, research questions, search approach, and search terms. Inclusion and exclusion criteria for data extraction were established to reduce this bias further.

Our dataset only includes studies published in the last two years (2023 and 2024), making it challenging to identify trends due to the recent and limited sample size. Moreover, the studies on LLM-based content classification only used well-established taxonomies, such as news categorization and fake news topics. None of the studies used a taxonomy the model had not encountered during its training process.

Internal Validity. No studies were excluded during the quality assessment due to the low number of documents retrieved in the search, so there is no potential threat to internal validity. In other words, we did not exclude studies that could contribute significantly despite their lower quality.

External Validity. There may be other valid studies in digital libraries that we did not search. However, we attempted to mitigate this limitation using the most relevant literature repository. Additionally, studies not written in English were excluded, which may have omitted important papers that would otherwise have been included.

Conclusion Validity. There may be some bias during the data extraction phase. However, we have addressed this by defining a data extraction form to ensure consistent and accurate data collection to answer the research questions. While there is always a small chance of inaccuracies in the numbers, we mitigate this by publishing our final dataset, allowing for replication and further validation.

References

1. Abdelali, A., et al.: LAraBench: benchmarking Arabic AI with large language models. In: Proceedings of the 18th Conference of the European Chapter of the Association for Computational Linguistics (EACL 2024), vol. 1, pp. 487–520. ACL (2024). https://doi.org/10.48550/arXiv.2305.14982
2. Bach, S., et al.: PromptSource: an integrated development environment and repository for natural language prompts. In: Basile, V., Kozareva, Z., Stajner, S. (eds.) Proceedings of the 60th Annual Meeting of the Assoc. for Computational Linguistics: System Demonstrations, pp. 93–104. ACL (2022). https://doi.org/10.18653/v1/2022.acl-demo.9
3. Balkus, S.V., Yan, D.: Improving short text classification with augmented data using GPT-3. Nat. Lang. Eng. (2023). https://doi.org/10.1017/S1351324923000438
4. Borazio, F., et al.: Semi-automatic topic discovery and classification for epidemic intelligence via large language models. In: Proceedings of the 2nd Workshop on Natural Language Processing for Political Sciences (PoliticalNLP@LREC-COLING), pp. 68–84 (2024). https://www.scopus.com/inward/record.uri?eid=2-s2.0-85195143331&partnerID=40&md5=fdbd936465c630ce6e4818b32757a00f
5. Cignoni, G., Bucci, A.: Cicognini at ACTI: analysis of techniques for conspiracies individuation in Italian. In: CEUR Workshop Proceedings, vol. 3473 (2023). https://www.scopus.com/inward/record.uri?eid=2-s2.0-85173564577&partnerID=40&md5=9284c028d4c4500a7d60667484346379
6. Conneau, A., et al.: Unsupervised cross-lingual representation learning at scale. In: Proceedings of the Annual Meeting of the Association for Computational Linguistics, pp. 8440–8451. ACL (2020). https://doi.org/10.48550/arXiv.1911.02116
7. Cosme, D., Galvão, A., Brito e Abreu, F.: Supplementary Data for 'A Systematic Literature Review on LLM-Based Information Retrieval: The Issue of Contents Classification' (2024). https://doi.org/10.5281/zenodo.13354076
8. Cosme, D., Galvão, A., Brito e Abreu, F.: A systematic literature review on LLM-based information retrieval: the issue of contents classification. In: Proceedings of the 16th International Joint Conference on Knowledge Discovery, Knowledge Engineering and Knowledge Management (KDIR 2024), pp. 135–146. INSTICC, SciTePress (2024). https://doi.org/10.5220/0013062300003838
9. Debess, I.N., Simonsen, A., Einarsson, H.: Good or bad news? Exploring GPT-4 for sentiment analysis for faroese on a public news corpora. In: 2024 Joint International Conference on Computational Linguistics, Language Resources and Evaluation, LREC-COLING 2024 - Main Conference Proceedings, pp. 7814–7824 (2024). https://www.scopus.com/inward/record.uri?eid=2-s2.0-85195997116&partnerID=40&md5=17e8c604738f2655cb7494ee26843ae9
10. Dettmers, T., Pagnoni, A., Holtzman, A., Zettlemoyer, L.: QLoRA: Efficient Finetuning of quantized LLMs. In: Advances in Neural Information Processing Systems, vol. 36 (2023). https://doi.org/10.48550/arXiv.2305.14314
11. Devlin, J., Chang, M.W., Lee, K., Toutanova, K.: BERT: pre-training of deep bidirectional transformers for language understanding. In: Proceedings of the North American Chapter of the Association for Computational Linguistics: Human Language Technologies conference (NAACL HLT), vol. 1, pp. 4171–4186. ACL (2019). https://doi.org/10.48550/arXiv.1810.04805
12. Du, Z., et al.: GLM: general language model pretraining with autoregressive blank infilling. arXiv preprints (2021). https://doi.org/10.48550/arXiv.2103.10360
13. Gehweiler, C., Lobachev, O.: Classification of intent in moderating online discussions: an empirical evaluation. Decis. Anal. J. **10** (2024). https://doi.org/10.1016/j.dajour.2024.100418

14. Gutiérrez-Fandiño, A., et al.: MarIA: Spanish Language Models. Procesamiento del Lenguaje Natural, pp. 39–60 (2022). https://doi.org/10.26342/2022-68-3
15. Hromei, C.D., Croce, D., Basile, V., Basili, R.: ExtremITA at EVALITA 2023: multi-task sustainable scaling to large language models at its extreme. In: CEUR Workshop Proceedings, vol. 3473 (2023). https://www.scopus.com/inward/record.uri?eid=2-s2.0-85173568550&partnerID=40&md5=0d3882fff863f524a297de457d6abb20
16. Hu, E., et al.: LoRA: low-rank adaptation of large language models. In: ICLR 2022 - 10th International Conference on Learning Representations (2022). https://doi.org/10.48550/arXiv.2106.09685
17. Hu, Y., Zou, F., Han, J., Sun, X., Wang, Y.: LLM-TIKG: threat intelligence knowledge graph construction utilizing large language model. Comput. Secur. **145** (2024). https://doi.org/10.1016/j.cose.2024.103999
18. Le Scao, T., et al.: BLOOM: A 176B-Parameter Open-Access Multilingual Language Model. arXiv preprints arXiv:2211.05100 (2022). https://doi.org/10.48550/arXiv.2211.05100
19. Leong, M., et al.: MetRoBERTa: leveraging traditional customer relationship management data to develop a transit-topic-aware language model. Transp. Res. Rec. (2024). https://doi.org/10.1177/03611981231225655
20. Lewis, M., et al.: BART: denoising sequence-to-sequence pre-training for natural language generation, translation, and comprehension. In: Proceedings of the Annual Meeting of the Association for Computational Linguistics, pp. 7871–7880. ACL (2020). https://www.scopus.com/inward/record.uri?eid=2-s2.0-85115443344&partnerID=40&md5=68efdf1732c50aade60d049337fb10e1
21. Li, Y., Su, H., Shen, X., Li, W., Cao, Z., Niu, S.: DailyDialog: a manually labelled multi-turn dialogue dataset. In: Proceedings of the Eighth International Joint Conference on Natural Language Processing (Volume 1: Long Papers) (2017). https://doi.org/10.48550/arXiv.1710.03957
22. Liu, Y., et al.: RoBERTa: A Robustly Optimized BERT Pretraining Approach. arXiv abs/1907.11692 (2019). https://doi.org/10.48550/arXiv.1907.11692
23. Luna-Jimenez, C., Callejas, Z., Griol, D.: Mental-health topic classification employing D-vectors of large language models. In: Proceedings - IEEE Symposium on Computer-Based Medical Systems, pp. 199–204. Institute of Electrical and Electronics Engineers Inc. (2024). https://doi.org/10.1109/CBMS61543.2024.00041
24. Mahadevkar, S.V., Patil, S., Kotecha, K., Soong, L.W., Choudhury, T.: Exploring AI-driven approaches for unstructured document analysis and future horizons. J. Big Data **11**(1) (2024). https://doi.org/10.1186/s40537-024-00948-z
25. Mastropaolo, A., et al.: Studying the usage of text-to-text transfer transformer to support code-related tasks. In: Proceedings of the International Conference on Software Engineering (ICSE), pp. 336–347 (2021). https://doi.org/10.1109/ICSE43902.2021.00041
26. Nasution, A.H., Onan, A.: ChatGPT label: comparing the quality of human-generated and LLM-generated annotations in low-resource language NLP tasks. IEEE Access **12**, 71876–71900 (2024). https://doi.org/10.1109/ACCESS.2024.3402809
27. Peña, A., et al.: Leveraging large language models for topic classification in the domain of public affairs. Lecture Notes in Computer Science (including subseries Lecture Notes in Artificial Intelligence and Lecture Notes in Bioinformatics). LNCS, vol. 14193, pp. 20–33 (2023). https://doi.org/10.1007/978-3-031-41498-5_2
28. Radford, A., Wu, J., Child, R., Luan, D., Amodei, D., Sutskever, I., et al.: Language models are unsupervised multitask learners. OpenAI Blog **1**(8), 9 (2019). https://d4mucfpksywv.cloudfront.net/better-language-models/language-models.pdf
29. Reimers, N., Gurevych, I.: Sentence-BERT: sentence embeddings using siamese BERT-networks. In: Proceedings of the Empirical Methods in Natural Language Processing and

9th International Joint Conference on Natural Language Processing Conference (EMNLP-IJCNLP), pp. 3982–3992 (2019). https://doi.org/10.48550/arXiv.1908.10084
30. Rodríguez-Cantelar, M., Estecha-Garitagoitia, M., D'Haro, L.F., Matía, F., Córdoba, R.: Automatic detection of inconsistencies and hierarchical topic classification for open-domain chatbots. Appl. Sci. **13**(16) (2023). https://doi.org/10.3390/app13169055
31. Russo, G., Stoehr, N., Ribeiro, M.H.: ACTI at EVALITA 2023: automatic conspiracy theory identification task overview. In: CEUR Workshop Proceedings, vol. 3473. CEUR-WS (2023). https://doi.org/10.48550/arXiv.2307.06954
32. Sanh, V., Debut, L., Chaumond, J., Wolf, T.: DistilBERT, a distilled version of BERT: smaller, faster, cheaper and lighter. arXiv preprints (2019). https://doi.org/10.48550/arXiv.1910.01108
33. Schabus, D., Skowron, M., Trapp, M.: One million posts: a data set of German online discussions. In: Proceedings of the 40th International ACM Conference on Research and Development in Information Retrieval (SIGIR), pp. 1241–1244. ACM (2017). https://doi.org/10.1145/3077136.3080711
34. Sebők, M., Máté, A., Ring, O., Kovács, V., Lehoczki, R.: Leveraging open large language models for multilingual policy topic classification: the babel machine approach. Soc. Sci. Comput. Rev. (2024). https://doi.org/10.1177/08944393241259434
35. Socher, R., et al.: Recursive deep models for semantic compositionality over a sentiment treebank. In: Proceedings of the Empirical Methods in Natural Language Processing conference (EMNLP), pp. 1631–1642 (2013). https://www.scopus.com/inward/record.uri?eid=2-s2.0-84926358845&partnerID=40&md5=aee25e7557c51d87ca49204c286b2813
36. Stahlschmidt, S., Stephen, D.: Comparison of Web of Science, Scopus and Dimensions databases. Technical report, KB forschungspoolprojekt, DZHW Hannover, Germany (2020)
37. Touvron, H., et al.: LLaMA: Open and Efficient Foundation Language Models (2023). https://doi.org/10.48550/arXiv.2302.13971
38. Touvron, H., et al.: Llama 2: open foundation and fine-tuned chat models. arXiv preprints (2023). https://doi.org/10.48550/arXiv.2307.09288
39. Trust, P., Minghim, R.: Query-focused submodular demonstration selection for in-context learning in large language models. In: Proceedings of the 31st Irish Conference on Artificial Intelligence and Cognitive Science (AICS) (2023). https://doi.org/10.1109/AICS60730.2023.10470628
40. Van Nooten, J., Kosar, A., De Pauw, G., Daelemans, W.: Advancing CSR theme and topic classification: LLMs and training enhancement insights. In: Proceedings of the Joint Workshop of the 7th Financial Technology and Natural Language Processing, the 5th Knowledge Discovery from Unstructured Data in Financial Services and the 4th Economics and Natural Language Processing (FinNLP-KDF-ECONLP@LREC-COLING), pp. 292–305 (2024). https://www.scopus.com/inward/record.uri?eid=2-s2.0-85195191165&partnerID=40&md5=994484ba62f44f8f5c0352f56a983dbb
41. Williams, A., Nangia, N., Bowman, S.: A broad-coverage challenge corpus for sentence understanding through inference. In: Walker, M., Ji, H., Stent, A. (eds.) Proceedings of the 2018 Conference of the North American Chapter of the Association for Computational Linguistics: Human Language Technologies, Volume 1 (Long Papers), pp. 1112–1122. ACL (2018). https://doi.org/10.18653/v1/N18-1101
42. Yang, K., Zhang, T., Kuang, Z., Xie, Q., Huang, J., Ananiadou, S.: MentaLLaMA: interpretable mental health analysis on social media with large language models. In: Proceedings of the ACM Web Conference 2024, pp. 4489–4500. Association for Computing Machinery (2024). https://doi.org/10.1145/3589334.3648137
43. Yang, L., Huang, Y., Tan, C., Wang, S.: News topic classification base on fine-tuning of ChatGLM3-6B using NEFTune and LORA. In: ACM International Conference Proceeding

Series, pp. 521–525. Association for Computing Machinery (2024). https://doi.org/10.1145/3675249.3675339
44. Ye, C., Shi, X.: Optimizing news topic classification with instructional fine-tuning of Chatglm3. In: ACM International Conference Proceeding Series, pp. 573–577 (2024). https://doi.org/10.1145/3672758.3672851
45. Yu, P., Xu, H., Hu, X., Deng, C.: Leveraging generative AI and large language models: a comprehensive roadmap for healthcare integration. Healthcare **11**(20) (2023). https://doi.org/10.3390/healthcare11202776
46. Zeng, A., et al.: GLM-130b: an open bilingual pre-trained model. arXiv preprints (2022). https://doi.org/10.48550/arXiv.2210.02414
47. Zhang, S., et al.: OPT: Open Pre-trained Transformer Language Models. arXiv preprints, pp. 1–19 (2022). https://doi.org/10.48550/arXiv.2205.01068
48. Zhang, X., Zhao, J., Lecun, Y.: Character-level convolutional networks for text classification. In: Advances in Neural Information Processing Systems, vol. 2015-January, pp. 649–657 (2015). https://doi.org/10.48550/arXiv.1509.01626

Enhanced Document and Database Integration for Advanced Question-Answering in Enterprise Contract Management with LLMs and Agents

Antony Seabra[1,2](✉), Claudio Cavalcante[1,2], Joao Nepomuceno[1], Nicolaas Ruberg[1], and Sergio Lifschitz[2]

[1] BNDES - Área de Tecnologia da Informação, Rio de Janeiro, Brazil
{amede,cfrag,jonep,nic}@bndes.gov.br
[2] Departamento de Informática, PUC-Rio, Rio de Janeiro, Brazil
sergio@inf.puc-rio.br

Abstract. This paper presents an advanced question-answering (QA) system designed to support enterprise contract management by seamlessly integrating document and database information. Leveraging large language models (LLMs) and agent orchestration, our system delivers precise, context-aware responses to complex contract-related queries. We enhance retrieval accuracy through a pipeline incorporating Retrieval-Augmented Generation (RAG) and Text-to-SQL techniques, eliminating the need for LLM retraining. Through targeted Prompt Engineering, we refined the system's ability to extract and synthesize key contractual information, significantly improving response relevance and accuracy. Our evaluation demonstrates the system's potential to significantly reduce time-consuming tasks in contract workflows and provide actionable insights, marking a significant advancement in enterprise contract management systems.

Keywords: Contract management · Information retrieval · Question answer · Large language models · Documents · Databases · Prompt engineering · Retrieval augmented generation · Text-to-SQL

1 Introduction

Contract management in large corporations involves overseeing legally binding agreements from their initiation through to execution and finalization. This process encompasses ensuring that services or products are delivered in accordance with contractual terms, monitoring their execution, and continuously evaluating both operational and financial performance throughout the service or product lifecycle. In the case of public sector companies, this process becomes even more complex due to stringent regulatory frameworks. In Brazil, for instance, Law No. 14,133/2021 mandates that contract management includes a wide range of activities, such as technical and administrative oversight, adherence to contract duration, re-evaluation of economic and financial terms, modifications to service scope, and the enforcement of penalties and fines when necessary. These regulations impose an additional layer of complexity on the contract management process, demanding a robust and systematic approach to ensure compliance and efficiency.

In enterprise contract management, professionals such as contract managers, auditors, lawyers, and administrative staff are central to ensuring efficient contract execution. Their daily tasks involve navigating complex contract documents, including numerous annexes, and retrieving critical information from contract management systems (CMS) stored in databases. These professionals rely on their expertise to interpret contractual language, assess risks, and ensure compliance. For example, contract managers utilize these resources to track obligations and monitor performance, while auditors verify adherence to contractual terms and financial regulations. Lawyers leverage contract data to analyze legal implications and draft amendments, and administrative personnel manage document workflows and update database records. In such a complex service domain, professionals require specialized knowledge to effectively manage the intricate details of contract execution. To streamline these operations, organizations often implement CMS, either developed in-house or sourced from market leaders like SAP Contract Lifecycle Management (CLM) and IBM Emptoris Contract Management.

Although CMS effectively manages core contract metadata, such as contract obligations, expiration dates, payment terms, and contract agents, they often fail to provide access to the granular details essential for proactive contract management. Professionals often find that crucial information remains buried in the original contract documents, including lengthy annexes and technical specifications. For example, traditional CMS struggle to answer nuanced queries regarding specific contractual stipulations, such as the precise conditions triggering penalties, the calculation of discounts based on performance metrics, or the application of fines related to service level agreement breaches. Moreover, these systems lack the analytical capabilities to conduct comparative analyses across contracts, hindering the identification of trends or inconsistencies, such as variations in penalty clauses across database support agreements. This deficiency forces professionals to manually sift through numerous documents, a process that is not only time-consuming but also prone to human error. The need for a system that can bridge the gap between structured database information and unstructured document content is therefore paramount for improving efficiency and accuracy in enterprise contract management.

The primary objective of this study is to develop a Question-Answering (QA) system that significantly reduces the time required for contract management professionals to access and analyze information from both contract documents and traditional Contract Management Systems, thereby streamlining their workflows and enhancing overall efficiency. As previously emphasized, the manual search and retrieval of relevant information from lengthy, complex contract documents and their numerous annexes represent a profoundly time-consuming and labor-intensive process. To directly combat this inefficiency, we leverage state-of-the-art Large Language Models to automate the analysis and extraction of pertinent details from contract documents. This automation not only drastically reduces the time required to locate specific information but also minimizes the risk of human error inherent in manual review. By enabling rapid access to critical data, our solution significantly enhances the productivity of enterprise professionals, freeing them from the tedious and prolonged task of document sifting. Furthermore, our approach seamlessly integrates data from traditional Contract Management Systems, enabling sophisticated operations such as combining information from diverse sources, crossing information between documents and databases to reveal hidden relationships, summarizing extensive contractual clauses into concise overviews, and comparing information among contracts to identify variances in terms and conditions. This unified approach streamlines contract management activities by providing a single, efficient platform for accessing, analyzing, and synthesizing all contract-related information, thereby maximizing time savings and improving overall operational efficiency.

In this work, we evaluated and integrated several Natural Language Processing (NLP) techniques to develop a Question-Answering system specifically designed for contract management, utilizing contract PDF files and data from Contract Management Systems as primary data sources. To enhance the relevance of user queries, we employed Retrieval-Augmented Generation (RAG) techniques and a static approach to text-to-SQL for extracting relevant metadata from contract systems. Building upon this, our approach utilizes agents to dynamically improve the accuracy and contextual relevance of responses, with a particular focus on a context-aware Text-to-SQL agent that interprets user queries more effectively. Furthermore, we applied Prompt Engineering techniques to standardize responses and ensure greater precision in the answers provided. This integration of RAG, Text-to-SQL and agent orchestration allows for a more robust and adaptable system.

The paper is organized as follows: Sect. 2 provides a technical background on LLM and retrieval and orchestration techniques used in our study. Section 3 discusses the methodology of the use of the presented techniques, while Sect. 4 details the architecture of our solution. Section 5 describes how we evaluated the proposed solution and the experimentation of the Q&A application. Finally, Sect. 6 concludes our study and proposes directions for future research in this field.

2 Background

The dissemination of several applications in the area of Natural Language Processing (NLP) was made possible by Large Scale Language Models, including question and answer systems. Recently, the use of agents has been introduced as a key component in LLM-based systems to orchestrate and manage task execution dynamically. Agents, such as router agents, SQL agents, and RAG agents, enable the efficient allocation of tasks by directing queries to the most suitable processing modules, enhancing system adaptability and performance. This approach allows LLMs to better handle complex queries, making responses more accurate and contextually relevant by integrating external data sources and specialized processing routines [1].

2.1 Large Language Models

Large-scale Language Models (LLMs) have revolutionized the field of natural language processing with their ability to understand and generate human-like text. In their architecture, they utilize a specific neural network structure, Transformers, which allows the model to weight the influence of different parts of the input texts at different times [2].

Conversational applications, a specific use case for LLMs, specialize in generating text that is coherent and contextualized. This is achieved through training, in which the models are fed vast amounts of conversational data, allowing them to learn the nuances of dialogue [3]. In this way, LLMs have established a new paradigm for NLP. Moreover, by expanding the search space with external data or specializing through fine-tuning, LLMs become platforms for building specialized applications. In this work, all language models utilized were based on OpenAI's GPT series. Specifically, we employed the *text-davinci-002* model for generating embeddings and the *gpt-4-turbo* model for generating answers to user queries.

2.2 Retrieval-Augmented Generation (RAG)

According to [4], LLMs face significant challenges such as factual hallucination, outdated knowledge, and lack of domain-specific expertise. In response to these challenges, RAG represents a paradigm shift in the way LLMs process and generate text. The principle behind RAG involves using vector storage to retrieve text fragments similar to the input query [5]. This technique converts both the query text and the information database into high-dimensional vectors, allowing one to retrieve similar information, which is then fed to an LLM.

[5] and [6] describe frameworks that exploit the advantages of this technique by providing additional data to the LLM without re-training the model. By dividing the available text into manageable chunks and embedding these chunks in high-dimensional vector spaces, it is possible to quickly retrieve contextually relevant information in response to a query, which informs the next processing steps [7]. As shown in Fig. 1, the first step (1) involves reading the textual content of the PDF documents into manageable chunks, which are then transformed into (2) into high-dimensional vectors (embedding). The text in vector format captures the semantic properties of the text, a format that can have 1536 dimensions and more.

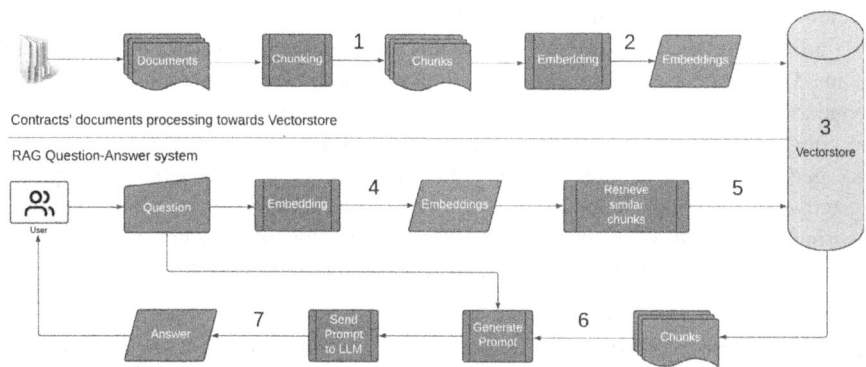

Fig. 1. Retrieval-Augmented Generation. Source: [21].

These vectors are stored in a vectorstore (3), a database specialized in high-dimensional vectors. The vector store allows efficient querying of vectors through their similarities, using the distance for comparison (whether Manhatan, Euclidean or cosine).

Once the similarity metric is established, the query is embedded in the same vector space (4); this allows a direct comparison between the vectorized query and the vectors of the stored chunks, retrieving the most similar chunks (5), which are then transparently integrated into the LLM context to generate a prompt (6). The prompt is then composed of the question, the texts retrieved from the vectorstore, the specific instructions and, optionally, the chat history, all sent to the LLM which generates the final response (7).

Chunking. In Retrieval-Augmented Generation (RAG), the chunking strategy plays a pivotal role, directly impacting the quality and relevance of retrieved information. Chunking refers to the process of dividing large documents into smaller, manageable segments, or "chunks", to be indexed and retrieved. A well-designed chunk generation strategy ensures that these chunks are cohesive and semantically complete, capturing the essence of the information they contain. This is crucial because the retrieval algorithm operates on these chunks, and if a chunk lacks context or is fragmented, the retrieved information may be incomplete or misleading, hindering the LLM's ability to generate accurate responses.

Several factors influence the effectiveness of chunking. One key consideration is the size of the chunks. Smaller chunks may capture fine-grained details but risk losing broader context, while larger chunks may provide more context but increase the likelihood of including irrelevant information. The optimal chunk size often depends on the nature of the documents and the types of queries expected. Another key aspect is the method used for chunking. Simple methods, such as fixed-size chunking or splitting by paragraphs, may not always produce semantically coherent chunks. More advanced techniques, such as semantic chunking or recursive chunking, aim to identify natural boundaries within the text, such as sentences, paragraphs, or sections, to create chunks that are more meaningful and contextually relevant.

Furthermore, the overlap between chunks can significantly impact retrieval performance. Overlapping chunks ensure that important information spanning across chunk boundaries is not lost. However, excessive overlap can lead to redundancy and increase the computational cost of retrieval. Effective chunking strategies must strike a balance between capturing contextual information, minimizing redundancy, and optimizing retrieval efficiency. Ultimately, a well-designed chunking strategy is essential for ensuring that the RAG system retrieves relevant and coherent information, enabling the LLM to generate accurate and contextually appropriate responses.

Vector Similarity and Semantic Relevance. A fundamental challenge in RAG lies in the distinction between similarity and relevance. While vector similarity, often measured by cosine similarity or other distance metrics, excels at identifying passages that are lexically or structurally alike, it doesn't guarantee that these passages contain the information necessary to answer a specific query. This is a very relevant point, as similarity is primarily based on surface-level features, like word overlap or structural patterns, which may not align with the underlying semantic meaning. For instance, two contract clauses might share a high degree of textual similarity due to using similar legal phrasing, but only one might contain the specific information required to address a user's question about liability.

This discrepancy becomes particularly problematic when dealing with large corpora of documents that share structural or lexical similarities, such as a collection of standardized contracts or legal documents. In such cases, retrieval algorithms relying solely on similarity metrics may retrieve numerous passages that are structurally or lexically similar to the query, but lack the semantic relevance needed for accurate answer generation. This can lead to a phenomenon known as "noisy retrieval", where the retrieved context contains irrelevant or misleading information, hindering the LLM's ability to produce accurate and contextually appropriate responses. The challenge is to move beyond mere similarity and develop retrieval mechanisms that can discern the true semantic relevance of passages to a given query.

To address this, advanced RAG systems often incorporate techniques that go beyond simple vector similarity. This includes the use of cross-encoders, which can assess the semantic relevance of a passage to a query by considering the entire context of both. Techniques like query reformulation, where the initial query is expanded or refined based on contextual understanding, can also improve relevance. Furthermore, incorporating knowledge graphs or ontologies can provide a richer semantic understanding of the data, allowing the retrieval algorithm to identify relevant information based on conceptual relationships rather than just surface-level similarity. By integrating such advanced techniques, RAG systems can more effectively bridge the gap between similarity and relevance, leading to more accurate and reliable question-answering.

2.3 Text-to-SQL

Text-to-SQL is a technology that enables the conversion of natural language queries into SQL commands based solely on the database schema, eliminating the need for knowledge of the underlying data [8]. This approach leverages the capabilities of LLMs to understand and interpret human language, allowing users to retrieve data from databases through plain text input without requiring specialized knowledge of SQL syntax [9].

By translating natural language into SQL queries, Text-to-SQL brings complex database structures and end users closer together, making access more intuitive and efficient. This technique is particularly useful because it allows non-expert users to access databases by asking natural language queries. It improves data accessibility, reduces the learning curve associated with database querying, and speeds up data analysis processes, enabling more users to make data-driven decisions.

The main distinction between RAG and Text-to-SQL techniques lies in how information is retrieved. RAG relies on retrieving text segments from a vector store that are similar to the user's question, and using these segments to generate a coherent and contextually relevant answer. This method is effective for questions where the answer can be synthesized from existing text. However, it is not always possible to identify the information expected as the answer. In another aspect, Text-to-SQL translates natural language queries into SQL commands, as demonstrated in [10], which are then executed against a structured database to retrieve exact data matches. This ensures that if the text-to-SQL translation is accurate, the user will receive a highly specific answer directly from the database fields.

Therefore, while RAG operates on the principle of textual similarity and generative capabilities, Text-to-SQL offers a more intrusive mechanism for data retrieval by executing queries that directly match the user's intent, making it particularly effective for data investigations.

2.4 Prompt Engineering

Prompt engineering is the art of designing and optimizing prompts to guide LLMs in generating desired outputs. The goal of prompt engineering is to maximize the potential of LLMs by providing them with instructions and context [11].

In the context of prompt engineering, prompts are a fundamental part of the process. Through prompts, engineers can outline the script for a response, specifying the desired style and format for the LLM response [12,13]. For example, to define the style of a conversation, a prompt could be formulated as "Use professional language and treat the customer with respect" or "Use informal language and emojis to convey a friendly tone." To specify the format of dates in responses, a prompt instruction could be "Use the American format, MM/DD/YYYY, for all dates."

On the other hand, context refers to the information provided to LLMs along with the main prompts. The most important aspect of context is that it can provide additional information to support the response given by the LLM, which is very useful when implementing Q&A systems. This supplemental context can include relevant background details, specific examples, and even previous dialogue exchanges, which collectively help the model generate more accurate, detailed, and contextually appropriate responses. According to [14], prompts provide guidance to ensure that the model generates responses that are aligned with the user's intent. As a result, well-crafted prompts significantly improve the effectiveness and appropriateness of responses.

Recent studies have begun to explore the synergistic integration of these techniques with LLMs to create more sophisticated Q&A systems. For example, [15] reinforces the importance of using Prompt Engineering with RAG to improve the retrieval of relevant documents, which are then used to generate both contextually relevant and information-rich answers. Similarly, [9] explores the integration of Text-to-SQL with Prompt Engineering to enhance the model's ability to interact directly with relational databases, thereby expanding the scope of queries that can be answered accurately.

2.5 Agents

The use of agents in applications built around LLMs is relatively recent but has already became common. Agents act as intelligent intermediaries that route, process, and present information in ways tailored to the context of the query. These agents leverage recent advancements in AI, such as Retrieval-Augmented Generation (RAG) and tool utilization, to perform more complex and contextually aware tasks. They play a pivotal role in orchestrating complex tasks, integrating various data sources, and ensuring that the system responds accurately and efficiently to user queries.

In a complex LLM-based system, different tasks often require specialized handling. Agents enable task orchestration by directing queries to the most appropriate component, whether it's for retrieving data, performing calculations, or generating visualizations. For example, an application may have a Text-to-SQL agent to perform queries over a relational database and a Graph agent to visualize graphs after an answer, if appropriate. According to [16], applying LLMs to text-to-database management and query optimization is also a novel research direction in natural language to code generation task. By converting natural language queries into SQL statements, LLMs help developers quickly generate efficient database query code. In the realm of integrating heterogeneous data sources, Q&A applications often need to access data from documents, databases, APIs, and other repositories. Agents facilitate the seamless integration of these heterogeneous data sources, allowing the system to extract relevant information dynamically.

There are several agent types. As outlined in [17], agent workflows allow LLMs to operate more dynamically by incorporating specialized agents that manage task routing, execution, and optimization. These agents serve as intelligent intermediaries, directing specific tasks—such as data retrieval, reasoning, or response generation—to the most suitable components within the system. One of the most important ones in place are the Router Agents, as they are the decision-makers of the system. When a user poses a query, the router agent analyzes the input and decides the best path forward. For instance, if a query is identified as needing factual data, the router agent might direct it to a RAG agent. If the question involves specific data retrieval from a database, it will engage an SQL agent instead.

As mentioned before, RAG and SQL Agents are very relevant too. According to [18], SQL agents can effectively manage data retrieval tasks by leveraging LLMs. The SQL queries are transformed into prompts for LLMs, allowing the system to interact with unstructured data stored in the model, mimicking traditional database operations. [19] provides a comprehensive overview of the integration of RAG techniques in LLMs but moreover, [20] introduces a novel approach that combines RAG techniques with a drafting-verification process to improve the reasoning capabilities of LLMs when handling retrieved documents. The RAG agent, termed the "drafter", generates multiple answer drafts based on retrieved results, while a larger generalist LLM, the "verifier", assesses these drafts and selects the most accurate one. This approach effectively integrates retrieval and generation, enhancing the overall performance of LLMs in knowledge-intensive tasks such as question answering and information retrieval systems.

3 Methodology

To address the challenges faced by contract managers in terms of complex information retrieval, we propose a QA system supported by an LLM and orchestrated by agents, building upon the foundational work first proposed by [21]. The system employs a range of techniques designed to enhance the relevance of responses while mitigating the risks associated with the standardized textual structures of contracts.

To achieve the goal of increasing the relevance and accuracy of responses, we implemented a comprehensive methodology integrating four key techniques. Firstly,

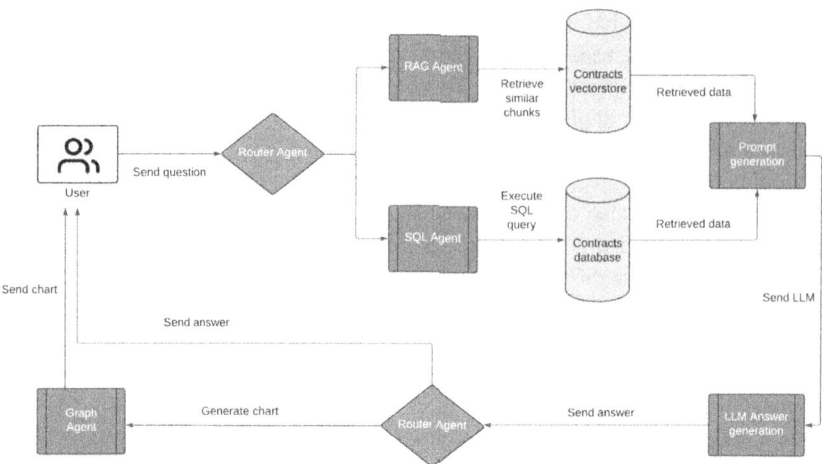

Fig. 2. Methodology Workflow Combining Different Techniques. Source: [21].

we employed RAG to enhance the retrieval of contextually relevant information from contract documents in PDF format. RAG functions by retrieving pertinent text chunks based on the user's query and then feeding these chunks as context to the LLM, enabling it to generate more accurate and contextually grounded responses. This is particularly relevant for navigating the complex and nuanced language often found in legal contracts. Secondly, we utilized intelligent agents to orchestrate and dynamically route the execution flow, allowing for adaptive decision-making based on the query context. These agents act as intelligent intermediaries, selecting the most appropriate processing path and tool for each query, ensuring that the system responds effectively to diverse user needs.

Moreover, we developed a specialized Text-to-SQL agent to retrieve structured data from contract management systems. This agent translates natural language queries into SQL queries, enabling seamless access to database information and integrating it with the document-based context. This integration is essential for providing a holistic view of contract information, combining both textual and structured data. Finally, we applied meticulous Prompt Engineering techniques to standardize and refine the responses generated by the LLM. This involved crafting precise prompts that guide the LLM to produce consistent and accurate outputs, ensuring that the system delivers reliable and trustworthy answers. By combining these four techniques, we created a robust and adaptable Question-Answering system capable of handling the complexities of enterprise contract management.

3.1 Applying RAG

A key initial decision in implementing RAG is, as mentioned before, selecting an effective chunking strategy for segmenting contract documents. Chunking involves dividing PDF files into manageable segments, or "chunks", to be processed by the retrieval system. A common approach employs fixed-size chunks based on a specific number of tokens with a defined overlap. This strategy is particularly useful for sequential texts where maintaining contextual continuity across chunks is paramount. However, while token-based chunking is versatile, it may not always align with the inherent structure of contract documents.

Contract documents typically exhibit a standardized textual structure, organized into distinct contractual sections. This structure implies that sections with similar numbering or proximity often address related contractual aspects, sharing similar semantic content. For instance, the initial section of most contracts consistently outlines the contract's object or purpose. Recognizing this structural consistency, we hypothesized that segmenting chunks by contractual sections would yield a more semantically coherent representation of the document's content. In this scenario, the overlap between chunks naturally occurs at the section level, as queries are likely to be answered by information within the section itself or in adjacent sections. For example, considering the contract page depicted in Fig. 3, we would generate a separate chunk for the contract's object section, another for the term section, and so forth, effectively creating a chunk for each clause and its surrounding context. This section-based chunking strategy ensures that each snippet represents a cohesive semantic unit, enhancing retrieval accuracy and aligning retrieved information with the user's query intent. By aligning chunk boundaries with the inherent structural divisions of the contracts, we ensure that the LLM is provided with contextual information that is most likely to be relevant to the user's query.

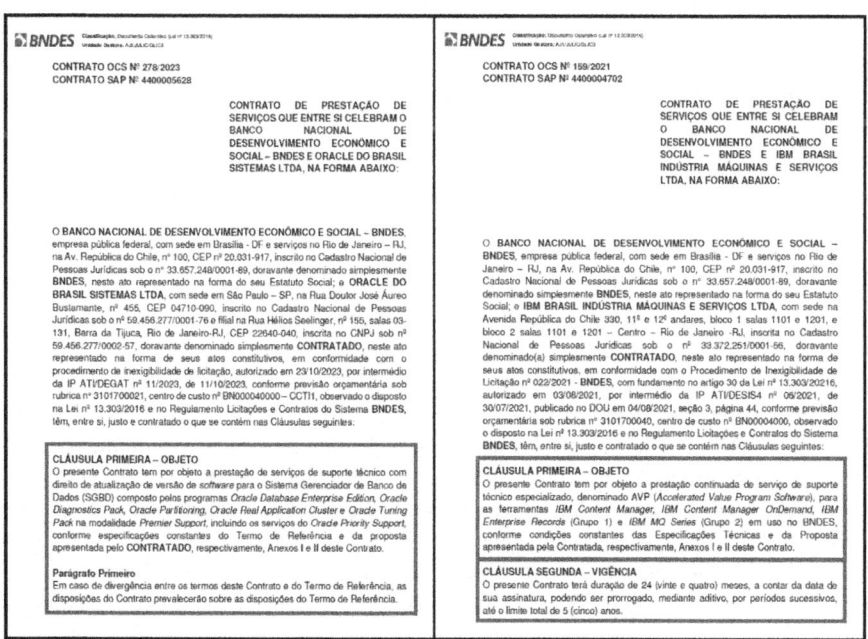

Fig. 3. Chunking applied to Contracts. Source: [21].

While utilizing contract sections as chunk boundaries enhances response relevance within a single contract, a significant challenge arises when scaling the system to handle numerous contracts. Accurately determining the specific contract relevant to a user's query becomes crucial, especially when multiple contracts share similar structures and content. This issue is particularly pronounced in enterprise environments where numerous contracts, often with standardized formats, coexist.

Consider, for example, the service contracts between BNDES (Banco Nacional de Desenvolvimento Econômico e Social) and technology providers, Oracle do Brasil Sistemas Ltda. and IBM Brasil Indústria Máquinas e Serviços Ltda., as illustrated in Fig. 3. These contracts, written in Portuguese, outline technical support and software update provisions. Both contracts feature an object clause detailing the contract's purpose. A common query might be "What is the object of contract OCS 278/2023?". In this scenario, a standard RAG system would likely store vectors representing the object clauses of both contracts, as they share similar structure and content. However, the content within these chunks, as shown in Fig. 3, typically lacks explicit contract identifiers like the contract number. Consequently, a query targeting a specific contract, such as OCS 278/2023, might inadvertently retrieve the object clause from OCS 159/2021 instead. This misidentification occurs because the RAG system, relying solely on semantic similarity of the clause content, fails to differentiate between contracts based on unique identifiers. The system would then return the wrong contract, as the correct response should come from the chunk related to contract OCS 278/2023. This issue highlights the necessity for a retrieval mechanism that goes beyond simple semantic similarity and incorporates contract-specific metadata for accurate identification.

To effectively address the challenge of accurately identifying and retrieving information from specific contracts within a large corpus, it is essential to enrich the chunks with semantic metadata. This involves augmenting each chunk with relevant document attributes, enabling the system to understand the context and origin of the information. When querying the vectorstore, this metadata is then leveraged to filter the retrieved information, ensuring that only chunks matching the desired criteria are considered. This targeted retrieval significantly enhances the relevance and precision of the texts returned. Figure 4 illustrates the most pertinent metadata for our contract documents: "source" (the contract PDF file name), "contract" (the OCS number), and "clause" (the section title). By associating each chunk with this structured metadata, we create a more informative and searchable representation of the contract content.

For instance, when a user poses the query, "What is the object of contract OCS 278/2023?", the system first filters the vectorstore using the metadata "contract: OCS 278/2023". This pre-filtering step ensures that only chunks associated with the specified contract are considered for further processing. Subsequently, a similarity calculation is performed on these filtered chunks, identifying the text segments that are most semantically relevant to the query. Finally, these retrieved text segments, now accurately linked to the correct contract, are passed to the LLM for answer generation. This metadata-driven approach not only prevents the retrieval of irrelevant chunks from other contracts but also significantly improves the system's ability to provide accurate and contextually appropriate responses, particularly in environments with numerous contracts sharing similar content structures.

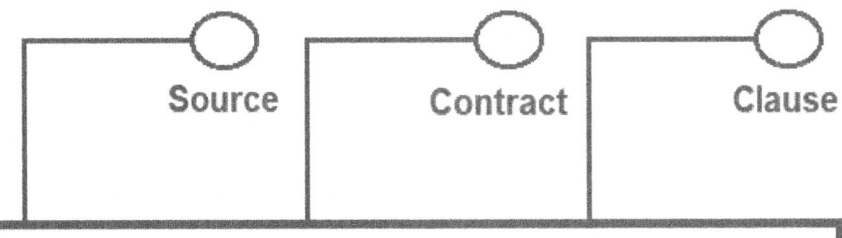

CLÁUSULA PRIMEIRA – OBJETO
O presente Contrato tem por objeto a prestação de serviços de suporte técnico com direito de atualização de versão de *software* para o Sistema Gerenciador de Banco de Dados (SGBD) composto pelos programas *Oracle Database Enterprise Edition, Oracle Diagnostics Pack, Oracle Partitioning, Oracle Real Application Cluster* e *Oracle Tuning Pack* na modalidade *Premier Support*, incluindo os serviços do *Oracle Priority Support*, conforme especificações constantes do Termo de Referência e da proposta apresentada pelo **CONTRATADO**, respectivamente, Anexos I e II deste Contrato.

Parágrafo Primeiro
Em caso de divergência entre os termos deste Contrato e do Termo de Referência, as disposições do Contrato prevalecerão sobre as disposições do Termo de Referência.

Fig. 4. Contracts metadata. Source: [21].

3.2 Applying Text-to-SQL

Contracts, by their very nature, are dynamic entities, subject to a myriad of events throughout their lifecycle, including operational adjustments, management changes, and amendments. To effectively manage this complexity, organizations rely on sophisticated CMS, as outlined before. These systems serve as central repositories for critical contract data, tracking aspects like the assigned technical personnel, changes in contractor representatives, service delivery milestones, and contract expiration dates. These events, occurring throughout the contract term, can profoundly impact contract management and require timely and accurate information retrieval.

To enable the LLM to provide comprehensive and contextually relevant responses, it is essential to integrate data from these CMS. Therefore, a Text-to-SQL technique was implemented, allowing the system to translate natural language queries into structured SQL queries, enabling seamless access to the CMS database. This approach facilitates the retrieval of dynamic contract information, ensuring that the LLM's responses reflect the most up-to-date status of the contract.

Our implementation leverages the capabilities of the LangChain SQL Agent, a versatile tool designed for interacting with relational databases. Upon system initialization, the SQL agent establishes an authenticated connection to the CMS database and retrieves the database schema. This schema information is the basis for accurately mapping natural language entities to database tables and columns. When a user poses a question, the agent initiates a series of processing steps. First, it performs Entity Recognition, identifying key entities within the query. Subsequently, it maps these entities to the corresponding database tables and columns, constructing a structured representation of the query's intent. Finally, it generates the appropriate SQL statement, tailored to retrieve the requested information.

To illustrate the functionality of our Text-to-SQL agent, let's consider a practical scenario. A contract manager queries the system, asking, "What is the expiration date of contract OCS 278/2023?". Upon receiving this query, the agent initiates several processing steps. First, it performs Entity Recognition to identify the key entities: "expiration date" and "contract OCS 278/2023".

Next, the agent maps these entities to the corresponding database schema. Assuming the CMS database contains a table named "Contracts" with columns such as "ContractNumber", "ExpirationDate", and "OtherDetails", the agent recognizes that "OCS 278/2023" refers to the "ContractNumber" column, and "expiration date" refers to the "ExpirationDate" column. Based on this mapping, the agent generates the following SQL query:

```
SELECT ExpirationDate
FROM Contracts
WHERE ContractNumber = 'OCS 278/2023';
```

This query instructs the database to retrieve the "ExpirationDate" from the "Contracts" table where the "ContractNumber" matches "OCS 278/2023".

Before executing the query, the agent performs a security check to ensure it does not contain any harmful commands. In this case, the query is a simple SELECT statement, which is considered safe. The database then executes the query and returns the result, which might be a date value, such as "2025-12-31". This result is then passed to the prompt generation stage, where it is formatted for the LLM. The LLM can then generate a natural language response, such as "The expiration date of contract OCS 278/2023 is December 31, 2025".

Security is a key concern in any system that interacts with databases. To mitigate the risk of unintended or malicious database modifications, our SQL agent incorporates rigorous query validation. Each generated SQL query undergoes a thorough inspection to ensure it does not contain harmful commands. Specifically, the system blocks any query containing "UPDATE", "DROP TABLE", "INSERT", or any other command that could potentially alter the database structure or data integrity. This robust security measure provides assurance about the system's safety and reliability.

Following the execution of the validated SQL query, the resulting output is passed to a prompt generation stage. Here, retrieved data are formatted and incorporated into a prompt that is then fed to the LLM. This allows the LLM to analyze the structured data alongside the unstructured document content, providing a holistic and integrated response to the user's query. This integration ensures that the LLM's responses are not only based on the contract documents but also reflect the dynamic state of the contract as recorded in the CMS database, providing a more comprehensive and accurate understanding of the contract's current status.

3.3 Applying Prompt Engineering

Prompt engineering plays a crucial role in shaping the style, accuracy, and consistency of responses generated by the LLM. By crafting precise instructions and providing relevant context, we can guide the LLM to produce outputs that align with specific requirements and user expectations. In our system, we implemented a series of prompt engineering techniques to enhance the quality of responses related to contract management.

Firstly, we established fundamental guidelines to ensure that the LLM relies solely on the provided contract data, rather than external knowledge. For instance, the instruction "Do not use prior knowledge" explicitly directs the LLM to base its responses exclusively on the information retrieved from the vectorstore contracts or the database. Additionally, we incorporated specific instructions to enhance the clarity and context of responses. For example, "Whenever you answer a question about a contract, provide the OCS number" ensures that contract identifiers are consistently included, facilitating easy reference and verification. Thus, a query like "Do we have an Oracle Support contract?" would elicit a response such as "Yes, we have an Oracle Database Support contract. The OCS number is 278/2023".

Secondly, we focused on maintaining consistency and coherence across conversations by implementing guidelines for chat context management. This included defining the desired tone and style of responses, such as "You should use a formal and objective tone", ensuring that the LLM's outputs align with professional standards. Furthermore, we addressed the issue of context dependency by instructing the LLM to "Given the chat history and the question asked, construct the response completely, without the user needing to review the history". This ensures that the LLM generates self-contained responses that are comprehensible without requiring users to navigate through previous interactions.

Thirdly, we leveraged the context provided to the LLM to tailor responses to the specific roles of users within the contract management workflow. In our system, we defined three distinct roles: contract manager, contract management support, and manager of the contract management support unit. Each role was associated with a unique context prompt, enabling the LLM to adapt its responses to the user's responsibilities and information needs. For example, for the manager of the contract management support unit, we provided the context: "You are an assistant specialized in answering questions about administrative contracts, who provides management and summarized information about the contracts". This contextualization ensures that the LLM delivers responses that are relevant and actionable for each user role.

By implementing these prompt engineering techniques, we significantly improved the relevance, accuracy, and consistency of the LLM's responses. These techniques enabled us to create a more user-friendly and effective Question-Answering system for enterprise contract management, enhancing the productivity and efficiency of contract management professionals.

3.4 Applying Agents

Agents play a key role in our system, orchestrating the execution flow and enhancing the efficiency and precision of the question-answering process. Recognizing the complexity of understanding user queries and generating appropriate responses, we adopted an agent-based approach to manage the various specialized tasks involved. We designed a system incorporating three primary agents: the Router Agent, the RAG Agent, and the SQL Agent.

The Router Agent serves as the central decision-making component, managing the overall workflow and directing tasks based on the nature of the user's question. As depicted in Fig. 2, the Router Agent first determines whether the query falls within the contract management domain. Questions outside this domain, such as general inquiries or unrelated topics, are redirected to the Large Language Model (LLM) with a context prompt that limits its scope to contract-related information. This ensures that the system maintains focus and avoids generating irrelevant responses. For queries within the contract management domain, the Router Agent initiates a more specialized workflow.

Subsequently, the Router Agent can dispatch the user's question to two specialized agents: the RAG Agent and the SQL Agent. The RAG Agent is responsible for retrieving relevant information from the vectorstore, which contains pre-processed chunks of contract documents. Upon receiving a query, the RAG Agent searches for chunks that are semantically similar to the user's question, providing contextual information for the LLM. In parallel, the SQL Agent handles queries that require structured data from the CMS database. This agent translates natural language queries into SQL queries, retrieving specific data points relevant to the user's request. This simultaneous retrieval of structured and textual data enriches the information provided to the LLM, allowing for more comprehensive and accurate responses, as illustrated in Fig. 1.

Following the retrieval of textual and structured data, another instance of the Router Agent initiates the process of crafting a final answer. If the Router Agent determines that a visual representation would enhance the user's understanding, it invokes the Graph Agent. The Graph Agent is responsible for generating visualizations, such as charts and graphs, to present complex data in a clear and accessible format. Simultaneously, the LLM Answer Generation Agent works in conjunction with the prompt generation module to produce coherent and contextually relevant textual responses. This agent leverages the retrieved data and the user's query to generate a natural language answer that addresses the user's needs. By combining data retrieval, visualization, and language generation, our agent-based system provides a multi-faceted approach to question-answering, ensuring that users receive comprehensive and informative responses.

4 Architecture

The architecture of our contract management question-answering system is designed to seamlessly integrate document processing, database interaction, and natural language processing to provide accurate and contextually relevant responses. As illustrated in Fig. 5, the system comprises several key components that work in concert to achieve this goal.

To illustrate the system's functionality within this architecture, let's revisit the example given earlier in the Methodology section: "What is the expiration date of contract OCS 278/2023?". When a user submits this query through the Streamlit interface, the Router Agent recognizes it as a request for structured data and directs it to the SQL Agent. The SQL Agent then interacts with the contracts database, translating the natural language question into an SQL query. The database executes the query and returns

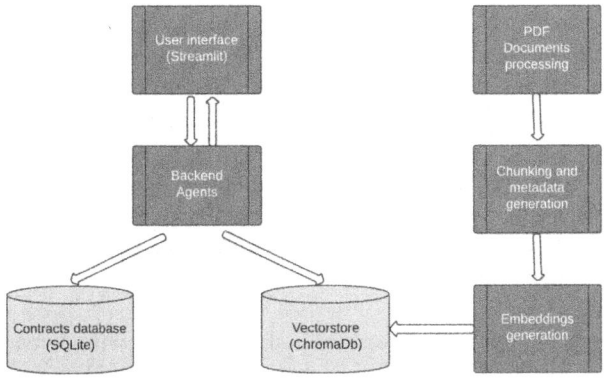

Fig. 5. Application architecture. Source: [21].

the expiration date of the specified contract. This information is then passed to the LLM, which generates a natural language response, such as "The expiration date of contract OCS 278/2023 is December 31, 2025." This response is then displayed to the user through the Streamlit interface, completing the question-answering process. The responsibilities of each component are outlined below.

User Interface (Streamlit): The system features a user-friendly interface built with Streamlit, a Python library for creating web applications. This interface serves as the primary point of interaction for users, allowing them to input natural language queries related to contract management. Streamlit's intuitive design ensures that users can easily interact with the system without requiring technical expertise.

Backend Agents: At the heart of the system lies the backend, which is powered by a network of agents. These agents are responsible for orchestrating the flow of information and processing user queries. As discussed in the methodology section, the agents include a Router Agent, a RAG Agent, and a SQL Agent. The Router Agent directs the query to the appropriate agent(s) based on the query's nature. The RAG Agent retrieves relevant information from the vectorstore, while the SQL Agent fetches data from the contracts database.

PDF Documents Processing: The system begins with the processing of PDF contract documents. This involves extracting text from the PDFs and preparing it for further analysis. This step is crucial for transforming unstructured document content into a format that can be processed by the system.

Chunking and Metadata Generation: Following document processing, the system performs chunking, which involves dividing the contract text into smaller, manageable segments or "chunks". This process is essential for efficient information retrieval. Along with chunking, the system generates metadata for each chunk, including information such as contract number, clause titles, and source document. This metadata is crucial for filtering and retrieving relevant information from the vectorstore.

Embeddings Generation: Once the chunks and metadata are generated, the system creates vector embeddings for each chunk. Embeddings are numerical representations of the text, capturing the semantic meaning of the content. These embeddings are stored in the vectorstore and used for similarity searches during the retrieval process.

Vectorstore (ChromaDB): The vectorstore, implemented using ChromaDB, stores the vector embeddings and metadata of the contract chunks. When a user submits a query, the system uses the vectorstore to retrieve the most semantically similar chunks, providing relevant context for the LLM.

Contracts Database (SQLite): The system also integrates with a contracts database, implemented here using SQLite. This database stores structured information related to contracts, such as expiration dates, responsible parties, and other key details. The SQL Agent interacts with this database to retrieve specific data points in response to user queries.

The integration of these components enables a seamless workflow for processing user queries. When a user enters a question through the Streamlit interface, the Router Agent analyzes the query and determines the appropriate processing path. If the query requires information from the contract documents, the RAG Agent retrieves relevant chunks from the vectorstore. If the query requires structured data from the database, the SQL Agent retrieves the necessary information. The retrieved data is then passed to the LLM, which generates a natural language response. The response is then displayed to the user through the Streamlit interface.

This architecture ensures that the system can handle a wide range of contract-related queries, combining information from both unstructured documents and structured databases. By leveraging intelligent agents and state-of-the-art natural language processing techniques, the system provides accurate, contextually relevant, and comprehensive responses to contract management professionals.

5 Evaluation

To validate the effectiveness of our contract management question-answering system, we conducted an evaluation with two IT contract specialists from BNDES, a major development bank. The system was populated with 75 contracts, encompassing both PDF documents and corresponding data from the contract management system. To assess the system's performance, we prepared a set of benchmark questions categorized into "direct" and "indirect" queries. "Direct" questions were designed to test the system's ability to retrieve information directly from PDF documents and their metadata, while "indirect" questions evaluated its capability to integrate and analyze data from the contract management system (Fig. 6).

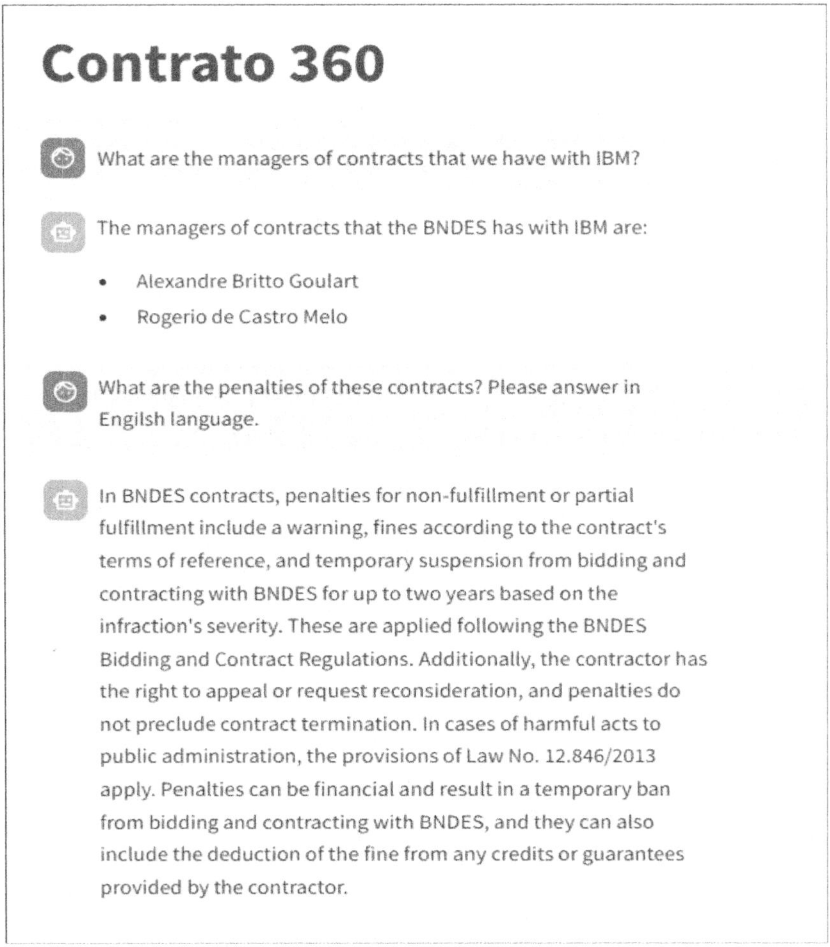

> **Contrato 360**
>
> 👁 What are the managers of contracts that we have with IBM?
>
> 📄 The managers of contracts that the BNDES has with IBM are:
> - Alexandre Britto Goulart
> - Rogerio de Castro Melo
>
> 👁 What are the penalties of these contracts? Please answer in Engilsh language.
>
> 📄 In BNDES contracts, penalties for non-fulfillment or partial fulfillment include a warning, fines according to the contract's terms of reference, and temporary suspension from bidding and contracting with BNDES for up to two years based on the infraction's severity. These are applied following the BNDES Bidding and Contract Regulations. Additionally, the contractor has the right to appeal or request reconsideration, and penalties do not preclude contract termination. In cases of harmful acts to public administration, the provisions of Law No. 12.846/2013 apply. Penalties can be financial and result in a temporary ban from bidding and contracting with BNDES, and they can also include the deduction of the fine from any credits or guarantees provided by the contractor.

Fig. 6. Contracts Q&A Streamlit application. Source: [21].

The users evaluated the relevance of the system's responses, categorizing them as "Correct" or "Incomplete." Notably, no responses were categorized as "Incorrect", indicating a high level of accuracy. The results of the evaluation are presented in Tables 1 and 2.

Table 1 presents the results for "direct" questions. As observed, the system provided "Correct" answers for all questions, except one, demonstrating its proficiency in retrieving information directly from contract documents. This high level of accuracy underscores the effectiveness of our chunking and retrieval strategies in handling document-based queries.

Table 2 displays the results for "indirect" questions, which required the system to integrate data from the contract management system. While the majority of questions were answered "Correct", some questions received "Incomplete" ratings. Specifically,

Table 1. Direct Questions. Source: [21].

Question	Correct	Incomplete
What is the subject of the OCS nnn/yy contract?	10	-
Do we have any contract whose subject is xxxx?	9	1
Do we have any contract with the supplier xxx?	10	-
Who is the manager of the OCS nnn/yy contract?	10	-
Who is the supplier of the nnn/yy contract?	10	-
What is the term of the OCS nnn/yy contract?	10	-

the questions "How many contracts have we signed due to ineligibility?" and "How many DLs (Exemptions from Tenders) were contracted in yy?" received "Incomplete" ratings for one and two responses, respectively. This indicates that these types of questions, which involve more complex semantic understanding and data aggregation, presented a greater challenge. Upon further analysis, we identified that the system struggled to accurately capture the concept of "Waiver of Bidding" (DLs) in these instances. This suggests that further refinements in query processing and prompt engineering are necessary to enhance the system's ability to handle such nuanced queries.

Table 2. Indirect Questions. Source: [21].

Question	Correct	Incomplete
How many active IT contracts do we currently have?	10	-
List the contracts that will end in the year yy?	10	-
How many contracts do we have with supplier xxxx?	10	-
How many contracts have we signed due to inexigibility?	9	1
How many DLs (Exemptions from Tenders) were contracted in yy?	8	2
Who are the managers of the contracts we have with company xxxx?	10	-
How many contracts does employee xxxx have under his/her management?	10	-
Show a summary of contract nnn/yy.	10	-

A key observation from the users was the system's ability to seamlessly combine information from both the structured database and the contract documents. This capability was highly valued, as it significantly reduced the time and effort required to manually search for information across multiple sources. For example, the system could simultaneously identify contract managers and outline penalties associated with non-compliance, providing a comprehensive response without requiring users to sift through lengthy documents. As illustrated in Fig. 8, the system's user interface presents these integrated responses in a clear and concise manner, further enhancing the user experience (Fig. 7).

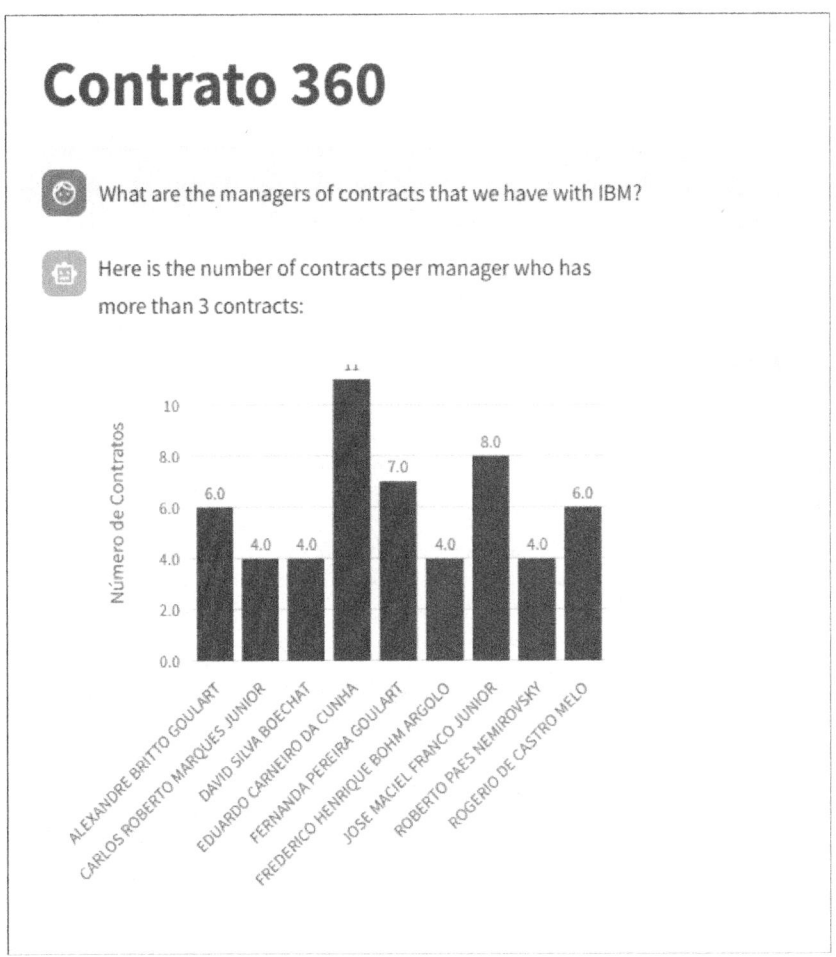

Fig. 7. Plotly Agent. Source: [21].

The users also highlighted the time-saving benefits of the system's ability to directly answer questions with specific details. By providing quick access to critical information, the system eliminates the need for manual document review, improving overall efficiency. Additionally, the system's automatic graph generation feature, powered by the Plotly agent, was positively received. When the system's response includes a table of values, it automatically generates a visual representation, providing immediate insights and supporting the creation of professional presentations. This feature significantly enhances the user's ability to analyze and communicate contract-related information.

The evaluation demonstrated the effectiveness of our contract management question-answering system in providing accurate and relevant responses to both direct and indirect queries. The system's ability to integrate information from diverse sources, automate data retrieval, and generate visual representations significantly enhances the

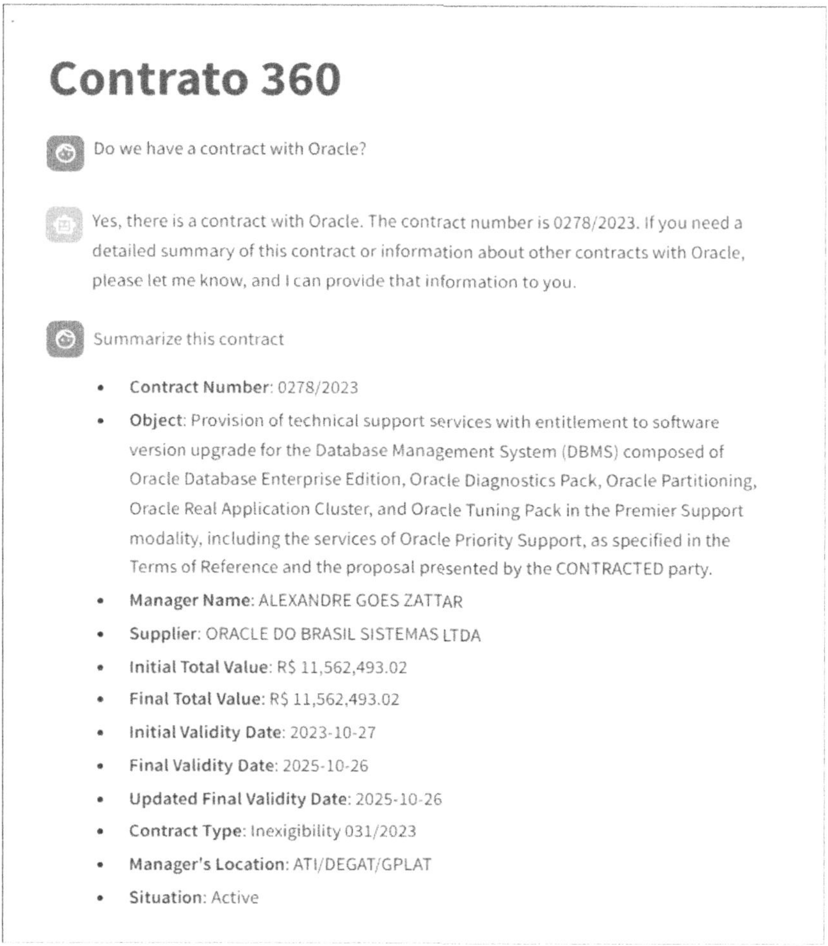

> **Contrato 360**
>
> 👁 Do we have a contract with Oracle?
>
> 📄 Yes, there is a contract with Oracle. The contract number is 0278/2023. If you need a detailed summary of this contract or information about other contracts with Oracle, please let me know, and I can provide that information to you.
>
> 👁 Summarize this contract
>
> - **Contract Number:** 0278/2023
> - **Object:** Provision of technical support services with entitlement to software version upgrade for the Database Management System (DBMS) composed of Oracle Database Enterprise Edition, Oracle Diagnostics Pack, Oracle Partitioning, Oracle Real Application Cluster, and Oracle Tuning Pack in the Premier Support modality, including the services of Oracle Priority Support, as specified in the Terms of Reference and the proposal presented by the CONTRACTED party.
> - **Manager Name:** ALEXANDRE GOES ZATTAR
> - **Supplier:** ORACLE DO BRASIL SISTEMAS LTDA
> - **Initial Total Value:** R$ 11,562,493.02
> - **Final Total Value:** R$ 11,562,493.02
> - **Initial Validity Date:** 2023-10-27
> - **Final Validity Date:** 2025-10-26
> - **Updated Final Validity Date:** 2025-10-26
> - **Contract Type:** Inexigibility 031/2023
> - **Manager's Location:** ATI/DEGAT/GPLAT
> - **Situation:** Active

Fig. 8. Contract Summarization. Source: [21].

user experience and improves the efficiency of contract management tasks. While some areas, such as the handling of complex semantic queries, require further refinement, the overall results indicate that the system is a valuable tool for contract management professionals.

In fact, by directly addressing questions with specific details, the system saves time and improves the user experience, as users can quickly access critical information without sifting through lengthy documents. Finally, the system's ability to automatically generate graphs using its Plotly agent, when a table of values is included in the response, has been positively received by users. This feature not only provides immediate visual insights, enhancing the understanding of the data, but also supports users in creating professional presentations. The integration of dynamic graph generation into the query response process significantly enriches the user experience, allowing for a more comprehensive analysis and efficient communication of contract-related information.

6 Conclusions

This research presented an advanced question-answering system designed to enhance the efficiency and accuracy of contract management by integrating document and database information. By leveraging Large Language Models (LLMs), intelligent agents, and techniques such as Retrieval-Augmented Generation (RAG) and Text-to-SQL, our system provides comprehensive and contextually relevant responses to complex contract-related queries.

The evaluation conducted with contract management professionals demonstrated the system's effectiveness in handling both direct and indirect questions, highlighting its ability to retrieve information from diverse sources and automate time-consuming tasks. The system's ability to combine answers from both structured data and contract texts was particularly valued, as it significantly reduced manual search efforts and provided a holistic view of contract information. Furthermore, the automatic graph generation feature enhanced user understanding and supported efficient communication of data.

While the system demonstrated promising results, there are several avenues for future research and development. Firstly, further investigation is needed to address the challenges encountered with complex semantic queries, particularly those involving nuanced concepts or data aggregation. This could involve refining the query processing and prompt engineering techniques to enhance the system's ability to interpret and respond to such queries accurately.

Secondly, exploring the integration of additional data sources, such as legal databases or industry-specific knowledge bases, could further enrich the system's knowledge and improve its ability to provide comprehensive answers. This expansion could also involve incorporating external APIs to access real-time information, such as market data or regulatory updates, enabling the system to provide more dynamic and context-aware responses.

Moreover, expanding the system's capabilities to support more interactive and conversational interactions could enhance user engagement and facilitate more complex information exploration. This could involve implementing dialogue management techniques and incorporating user feedback mechanisms to personalize the question-answering experience.

Finally, conducting further user studies with a larger and more diverse group of participants could provide valuable insights into the system's usability and identify areas for improvement. This could involve evaluating the system's performance across different contract types, industries, and user roles to ensure its broad applicability and effectiveness.

By pursuing these future research directions, we aim to further enhance the capabilities of our contract management question-answering system and contribute to the development of more intelligent and efficient tools for contract management professionals.

References

1. Mialon, G., et al.: Augmented language models: a survey, arXiv preprint arXiv:2302.07842 (2023)
2. Vaswani, A., et al.: Attention is all you need. In: Advances in Neural Information Processing Systems, vol. 30 (2017)
3. OpenAI, ChatGPT Fine-tune Description. https://help.openai.com/en/articles/6783457-what-is-chatgpt. Accessed 01 Mar 2024
4. Chen, J., Lin, H., Han, X., Sun, L.: Benchmarking large language models in retrieval-augmented generation. In: Proceedings of the AAAI Conference on Artificial Intelligence, vol. 38, pp. 17754–17762 (2024)
5. Gao, Y., et al.: Retrieval-augmented generation for large language models: a survey, arXiv preprint arXiv:2312.10997 (2023)
6. Feng, Z., Feng, X., Zhao, D., Yang, M., Qin, B.: Retrieval-generation synergy augmented large language models. In: ICASSP 2024-2024 IEEE International Conference on Acoustics, Speech and Signal Processing (ICASSP), pp. 11661–11665 (2024)
7. Li, H., Su, Y., Cai, D., Wang, Y., Liu, L.: A survey on retrieval-augmented text generation, arXiv preprint arXiv:2202.01110 (2022)
8. Liu, A., Hu, X., Wen, L., Yu, P.S.: A comprehensive evaluation of ChatGPT's zero-shot Text-to-SQL capability, arXiv preprint arXiv:2303.13547 (2023)
9. Gao, D., et al.: Text-to-SQL empowered by large language models: a benchmark evaluation, arXiv preprint arXiv:2308.15363 (2023)
10. Pinheiro, J., et al.: On the construction of database interfaces based on large language models. In: Proceedings of the 19th International Conference on Web Information Systems and Technologies - Volume 1: WEBIST, pp. 373–380 (2023)
11. OpenAI, ChatGPT Prompt Engineering. https://platform.openai.com/docs/guides/prompt-engineering. Accessed 01 Apr 2024
12. White, J., et al.: A prompt pattern catalog to enhance prompt engineering with chatgpt, arXiv preprint arXiv:2302.11382 (2023)
13. Giray, L.: Prompt engineering with ChatGPT: a guide for academic writers. Ann. Biomed. Eng. **51**(12), 2629–2633 (2023)
14. Wang, M., Wang, M., Xu, X., Yang, L., Cai, D., Yin, M.: Unleashing ChatGPT's power: a case study on optimizing information retrieval in flipped classrooms via prompt engineering. IEEE Trans. Learn. Technol. (2023)
15. Jeong, C.: A Study on the Implementation of Generative AI Services Using an Enterprise Data-Based LLM Application Architecture, arXiv preprint arXiv:2309.01105 (2023)
16. Jin, H., Huang, L., Cai, H., Yan, J., Li, B., Chen, H.: From LLMs to LLM-based Agents for Software Engineering: A Survey of Current, Challenges and Future, arXiv preprint arXiv:2408.02479 (2024)
17. Singh, A., Ehtesham, A., Kumar, S., Khoei, T.T.: Enhancing AI systems with agentic workflows patterns in large language model. In: 2024 IEEE World AI IoT Congress (AIIoT), pp. 527–532 (2024)
18. Saeed, M., De Cao, N., Papotti, P.: Querying large language models with SQL, arXiv preprint arXiv:2304.00472 (2023)
19. Fan, W., et al.: A survey on RAG meeting LLMs: towards retrieval-augmented large language models. In: Proceedings of the 30th ACM SIGKDD Conference on Knowledge Discovery and Data Mining, pp. 6491–6501 (2024)

20. Wang, Z., et al.: Speculative RAG: Enhancing Retrieval Augmented Generation through Drafting, arXiv preprint arXiv:2407.08223 (2024)
21. Seabra, A., Cavalcante, C., Nepomuceno, J., Lago, L., Ruberg, N., Lifschitz, S.: Contrato360 2.0: a document and database-driven question-answer system using large language models and agents. In: Proceedings of the 16th International Joint Conference on Knowledge Discovery, Knowledge Engineering and Knowledge Management, IC3K, Volume 1: KDIR, Porto, Portugal, 17–19 November 2024 (2024)

Knowledge Engineering and Ontology Development

Enhancing Bilateral International Trade Flow Analysis with Knowledge Graph Embeddings

Durgesh Nandini[✉], Simon Blöthner, Mirco Schönfeld, and Mario Larch

University of Bayreuth, Bayreuth, Germany
durgesh.nandini@uni-bayreuth.de

Abstract. Reliably extracting valuable information from economic data is notoriously difficult. They are the result of highly subjective actions driven by contingency and strong non-linearity, driven by high-dimensional influences. These characteristics have long posed a challenge for conventional econometric, regression-based models. To tackle this challenge, we propose using knowledge graph embeddings to analyze economic trade data, with a focus on predicting international trade relationships. We introduce KonecoKG, a knowledge graph representation of economic trade data with multidimensional relationships, built using SDM-RDFizer. We then transform these relationships into knowledge graph embeddings using AmpliGraph. Our results show that the method performs much more accurately when compared to baseline regression models.

Keywords: Knowledge Graph Embedding · Translational embedding · Ontology design · Multidimensional data · International bilateral trade flow data

1 Introduction

Knowledge graphs (KGs) store factual information in the form of triples and have become increasingly common across various fields. The use of knowledge graph embedding models has gained attention as a way to effectively utilize these graphs. These models represent nodes—and sometimes edges—as continuous vectors, offering advantages over traditional graph structures [9,25,50]. As a result, knowledge graphs have supported a wide range of applications, enabling various downstream tasks [1,30]. Additionally, graph-based methods provide a valuable approach for capturing and analyzing relationships between concepts or events, particularly through knowledge graphs that map complex interactions [12,50]. Several studies have demonstrated the effectiveness of these methods in modeling and analyzing economic relationships, highlighting their potential in quantitative economic research [11,52].

This study applies knowledge graph (KG) translational embedding techniques [8] to address fundamental challenges in empirical economic research. Traditionally, economic research represents networks of economic interactions in formats suitable for inferential statistics, often linear, or theoretical algebraic reasoning. However, this transformation can lead to significant information loss and complexity compression, limiting the representativeness of the data by overlooking both interactions and the underlying network structure [51]. Furthermore, economic data is often characterized by high dimensionality, contingency, and strong non-linearity, which stem from multiplicative dynamics [6,17,38]. We explore these challenges and their determinants in greater detail in Sect. 2.1.

To address these problems, we propose that every economic interaction can be represented as a network structure within which we establish the concept of an economic trade network as a system of interconnecting countries based on their trade relations. Our primary aim is to explore the predictive capabilities that such network offer, specifically focusing on forecasting flows between country pairs. To achieve this, we introduce KonecoKG, a downstream knowledge graph (KG) embedding model that incorporates multidimensional translational relationships for international bilateral economic data. In the context of KGs, a multidimensional relationship represents interactions between entities that encompass multiple attributes simultaneously. This approach offers significant advantages, as it captures the combined effect of multiple attributes rather than relying on a single entity-attribute relation. This is especially important for economic data given its high degree of contingency. For instance, a simple binary relationship might only indicate a direct link, such as *"country A trades with country B"*. In contrast, a multidimensional relationship provides a richer representation by integrating additional contextual factors, such as uniquely identifying features of countries, referred to fixed effects in econometric literature, and key economic indicators. These include trade volumes, geographical proximity, gross domestic product (GDP), and population size. By incorporating these diverse dimensions, the KG can offer a more comprehensive and structured representation of economic interactions, ultimately improving the accuracy and representativeness of analysis through the embedding model. By leveraging a trade network dataset, we anticipate future trade opportunities by integrating historical trade patterns with insights into the trading behaviors of neighboring countries within the network. Addressing such multilateral contexts would be of great value to economic analysis that are limited looking at single entities. Additionally, multi-attributes such as trade agreements, geographic proximity and economic similarities act as network features to refine the accuracy of our predictions. The main contributions of this work are as follows:

- Establish network of international trade flows as a graph representation of countries with relationships indicating trade flows, eliminating the problems of non-linearity and non-hierarchical representations in international economic bilateral trade data.
- Introduce the KonecoTradeFlow ontology, which represents the concepts of the international economic bilateral trade data.
- Introduce KonecoKG, a downstream graph embedding model that applies translational techniques to forecast trade flows.

To the best of our knowledge, our study is one of the few pioneering efforts in utilizing a large-scale economic trade network to predict trade flows between countries. The implications of accurately forecasting trade dynamics are significant, offering valuable insights for policymakers, businesses and investors to optimize international trade strategies. The current study is an extended version of conference paper [35], which uses the knowledge graph embedding for prediction of trade volume.

The rest of the paper is organised as follows: First, Sect. 2 gives an overview of the literature on conventional econometric approaches and graph-based methods and underlines the key challenges in economic research, establishing the significance of the current study's contribution. Having outlined the challenges, Sect. 3 focuses on the approach we are using and describes our process to construct the TradeFlow ontology, the embedding methods used, and the learning strategy. Section 4 focuses on the experimental setup and the evaluation metrics used. Section 5 provides insights into the results obtained and discusses their implications. Lastly, we highlight the findings of the research and conclude in Sect. 6, whereby we also layout ideas for future research in this field.

2 State of the Art

In this section, we discuss the challenges associated with the economic data comprising the foundation of this research. Additionally, this section reviews current methods used to address these challenges and identifies gaps in these methods, including those involving KGs, to underscore the necessity of the proposed approach.

2.1 Challenges of Economic Data

Many formal, data-driven efforts do not adequately address the unique characteristics of economic data [43]. Economic exchanges are inherently shaped by subjectivity [33], creating context dependence and contingency, sometimes called localized or contingent knowledge [27]. Combined, these features prevent inquiry into these questions from producing reliable insights from economic data, that offer a high degree of robustness in various settings. Multi- or high-dimensionality requires incorporating many variables into models, which must be capable of untangling all the non-linear interactions between these variables. Beyond this, many economic variables of interest exhibit strong power law behavior, also called heavy- or fat-tailed behavior [3,16,23,29]. This characteristic leads to a slow convergence speed, meaning that the number of observations required to reliably estimate the parameters in question can be extremely high. As a consequence, we are often left in a world of pre-asymptotics in which estimates which have not yet reached stable, reliable values that can be used for business and policy decisions. Even if such a value is reached, it is often unrepresentative of individual observations because of the large difference in magnitude of the effect [47]. Due to the strong degree of contingency, average effects of parameters often mask the variation of the effects that certain changes might have on individual dynamics.

Figure 1 exemplifies this characteristic. Looking at all the bilateral trade flows grouped by year shows that the data has much heavier tails than a Gaussian distribution, also called the normal distribution, under which we would have a much easier time identifying the effects of interests. This can be seen by the mass of probability in the tails, as opposed to that in the body of the distribution. Notably, the distributions in Fig. 1 are on a logarithmic scale, making the problem exponentially more pronounced. The distribution has a tail index $\alpha \approx 1$, leading to slow convergence and imprecise estimates. This observation is in line with current strands of empirical research [41]. The implication for conventional empirical methods is that methods relying on the existence or tangible ability to estimate statistical moments are at the peril of producing unreliable forecasts [34].

The intricacies of human economic action are most challenging when dealing with international trade flows. They are the result of billions of individual choices, that are influenced by each other, thus leading to data of the highest degree of complexity [5].

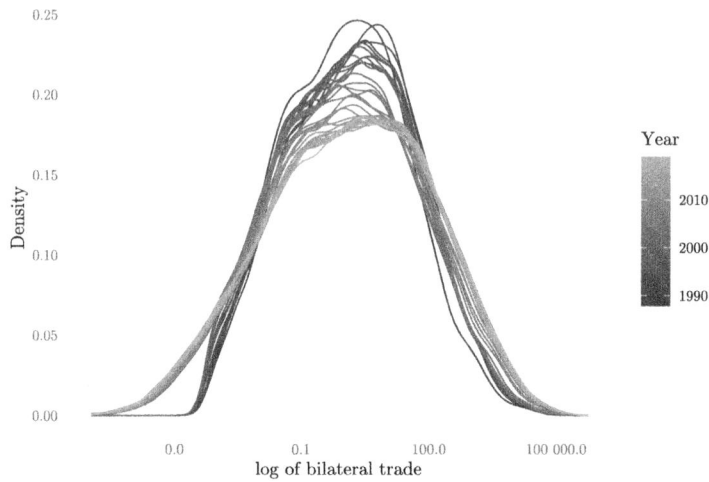

Fig. 1. Log density of bilateral trade flows across time [35].

2.2 Methods for Economic Data Analysis

The standard empirical approach in economic data analysis, a field referred to as econometrics, is a regression model. To explain variations in bilateral international trade flows, the most prevalent way is to estimate the theory-founded gravity equation using the Poisson pseudo-maximum likelihood (PPML) estimator [28,42,53]. This allows for the disentanglement of all the effects that the inputs have on the variable under consideration. Generally, these approaches rely on a large set of fixed effects to control for unobservable effects in various dimensions. This process includes dummy variables for every country, and sometimes for every country pair, as well as exporter-year and importer-year observations [20,21]. We will also rely on this specification when comparing it to our KG model in Sect. 5. Another approach is the descriptive analysis of networks such as in [4,14]. However, such work does not allow for inference or the understanding of factors that drive certain characteristics within the network, nor for the prediction of effects of changes to the data. Recent advances in informatics, especially the combination of machine learning models with graph structures, can provide new insights for the field of economics. However, unlike conventional methods with their focus on causal explanation that have an inbuilt mechanism for interpretation, these emerging approaches have not yet had the same impact as they had in other fields.

2.3 Knowledge Graph for Economic Trade Flow Data

We are building on top of recent advances in the fields of neural networks and KG networks. [44] used a Graph Convolution Network for predicting the trade relation between countries. Elsewhere, [39] used a synthetic triple-generation algorithm for enhancing downstream tasks in KG embeddings based on the graph complement. [40] leveraged KG embeddings for modelling international trade, focusing on link prediction using embeddings, and explored the integration of traditional machine learning methods with KG embeddings. [32] used an enterprise KG to predict China's Free Trade Zone. [24] used a KG to explain trade patterns among various countries. Other approaches to this process have been in the economic trade flow data analysis including economic planning [46], and industrial economic status [37].

3 Methodology

This section explains the creation of KonecoKG, applying embedding techniques, and predicting trade values. KonecoKG takes triples in the form of Subject (s), Predicate (p) and Object (o) as inputs for multiple relationships, and then forms embedding vectors for each relation. The embedding vectors are then combined as an average embedding vector to predict trade flows between countries as the final output. Figure 2 [35] shows a diagrammatic representation of the methodology. The subsections here provide an extensive overview of the methodology followed.

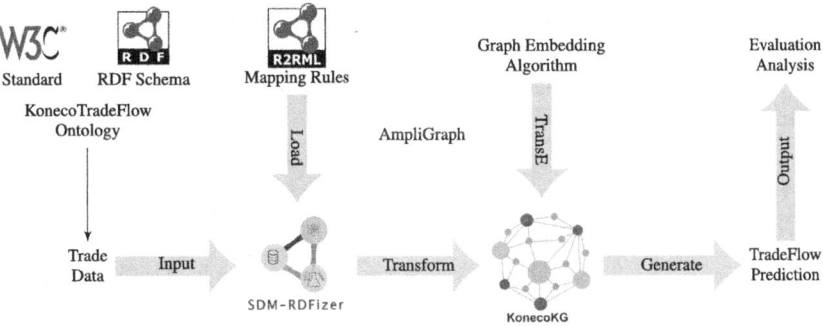

Fig. 2. Trade flow prediction and analysis pipeline [35].

3.1 International Economic Trade Flow Data

The initial step entails identifying relevant aspects of the dataset. Using trade data from [7], spanning 1986 to 2016, and encompassing 170 countries, we tackle the questions of economic drivers of trade flows. To determine this, we added explanatory data from [26] for GDP and population data, and [31] for information on geographic distances between countries. Lastly, we employed data about trade agreements from [19], a strong determinant of international trade flows. We aggregated this data into a tabular format, leaving us with over 2.5 million observations over the whole time frame.

3.2 Data Processing and Feature Selection

A detailed explanation of selected features is given in Table 1, comprising the key determinants of international trade. Economic theory predicts that larger countries, measured using population or economic size (GDP), are more able than smaller countries to trade with each other. Specifically, country size affects a country's division of labor and thus the 'roundaboutness' of production or how many intermediary capital goods for production are employed. This allows a country to specialize in the production of certain goods that are of value to others, leading to mutual gains from trade. As this degree of specialization grows, countries develop greater incentive to trade. In contrast, countries facing high trade costs trade less. These costs can be either direct because they are far apart (distance, geographic position) or indirect due to other trade barriers which increase the transaction cost (triangulation, trust, transfer). One can think of these as factors that increase the cost and hence decrease the gains from trade, like regulatory or political uncertainty, cultural differences, or uncertainty about consumer preferences in far away markets.

3.3 Data Modelling as KonecoTradeFlow Ontology

The next step in building the model was to create a formal semantic representation of the dataset, providing a structured framework for organizing and categorizing concepts, entities, and relationships. The advantage to this approach is that it captures the hierarchical structure and dependencies among these elements, enabling a deeper understanding of how they interact to shape trade dynamics [10,22,49]. Figure 3 [35] represents the hierarchical structure of our data as a class diagram. From the figure, we identify *'trade relation'* as our main class. A complete list of data properties [10,49] and object properties [10,49] is provided in Table 1.

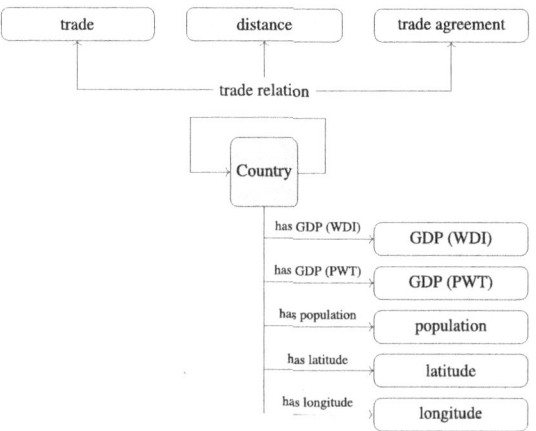

Fig. 3. KonecoKG data model diagram [35].

Table 1. Data & object properties and their description [35].

Data Property	Description
trade	volume of bilateral trade
distance	geodesic distance between exporter and importer
trade agreement	whether a trade agreement exists between two countries
GDP (WDI)	country's GDP measured by the World Development Indicators
GDP (PWT)	country's GDP measured by the Penn World Tables
population	population of a country
latitude	geographical latitude of a country
longitude	geographical longitude of a country
Object Property	Description
tradesWith	indicates whether a trade relation exists between two countries

3.4 Knowledge Graph Construction

In the next step, we use the KonecoTradeFlow ontology formulated in the above step to a structured representation in a KG, producing a set of triples.

To this end, we converted our dataset into KonecoKG using SDM-RDFizer, an open-source tool and interpreter of the W3C Recommendations Standard R2RML[1] and its RDF Mapping Language (RML)[2] extension used for the semantification process and used in KG creation in prior research [45]. The RDF is a standardised data model used to describe resources on the web using subject-predicate-object statements, known as triples. Each triple comprises three components: subject, predicate, and object. The following are the detailed steps used to convert data into KonecoKG:

– **Entity Identification:** We identified the key entities and resources to represent in RDF. For our use case, these entities included countries, specifically exporters and importers, along with their associated data properties and the relationships between them.
– **Ontology:** In the next step, we used the KonecoTradeFlow ontology as a vocabulary to model trade data. For instance, the data property *trade* represents trade (in millions of US$s).
– **Mapping Rule:** Following the steps of SDM-RDFizer, we used R2ML to define mapping rules. We set the base URL as www.koneco.de and used these mapping rules to assign data values to the corresponding subjects, predicates, and objects in RDF triples. Each entity and property was given a unique Uniform Resource Identifier (URI) to establish structured relationships. For example, the trade column in the dataset was mapped as *tradeValue*. A snapshot of the data properties from the KonecoTradeFlow ontology is given below [35].

---
[1] https://www.w3.org/TR/r2rml/.
[2] https://rml.io/specs/rml/.

```
rr:predicateObjectMap [
    rr:predicate kg:tradeValue;
    rr:objectMap [
        rml:reference "trade"
    ]
]
```

- **Serialising as RDF:** We have then serialized the RDF triples into a specific RDF format. For this, we have used a Turtle format to store and exchange RDF data while maintaining the structure and semantics of the triples.

We have represented *Facts* in a KG as relationships between entities—for instance, <ARB_NZL hasTradeValuen>, means Aruba exports, goods and services of value n to New Zealand. We build a series of such statements derived from the raw data collection to represent them as a graph.

3.5 Knowledge Graph Embeddings

After creating KonecoKG, we applied knowledge graph (KG) embeddings to generate embedding scores for each triple, transforming entities and relationships into numerical vectors. This allows the model to process complex patterns and semantic information within a continuous vector space, improving the effectiveness of analysis and inference. We then trained the triples derived from the KG using three embedding models: TransE [8], ComplEx [48], and DistMult [15].

The *TransE* is a deterministic approach that treats the relation as a translation operation from the head entity to the tail entity, using a distance-based scoring function to assess the plausibility of triples. On the other hand, ComplEx extends TransE by using complex-valued embeddings, allowing the model to handle asymmetric relationships more effectively. By leveraging tensor factorization, ComplEx captures richer semantics and interactions between entities, making it well-suited for real-world data with asymmetric and non-reflexive relations. Similarly, DistMult also uses tensor factorization but operates with real-valued vectors. It models relationships through a bilinear scoring function, making it particularly effective for symmetric relationships. Each of these models offers distinct advantages, providing different perspectives on capturing the semantics of the underlying data. In contrast to TransE, ComplEx and DistMult employ tensor factorization, modeling the interaction between entities and relations through vector-matrix products to harness the expressive power of the data. Each of the latter offers unique advantages and facilitates different perspectives on capturing the semantics of the underlying data. On the other hand, the *ComplEx* and *DistMult* utilise tensor factorisation and model the interaction of entities and relations by vector-matrix product to obtain the expressive power of the data.

3.6 Prediction Model

This section explains this study's approach to finding trade relations using link prediction in KonecoKG. Link prediction is the process of exploiting the existing facts in a KG to infer missing ones. For triples <s,p,o> in KonecoKG, where <s> refers to a country pair, <p> represents countries' trade relation, and <o> represents the monetary value of the trade occurring between two countries. Then we used tail prediction to predict the values of o.

Subsequently, we adopted a corruption-based learning strategy [8] to make predictions. This strategy involved deliberately introducing corruptions or perturbations to the input data during the training process to improve the model's ability to generalize and make accurate predictions. The idea behind this approach is that it encourages the model to learn robust representations of the data that are resilient to noise and variations. By exposing the model to a diverse range of corrupted inputs, it becomes better at identifying meaningful patterns and relationships, which ultimately enhances its predictive performance on unseen or noisy data.

Practically, the corruption strategy can be implemented by augmenting the training dataset with artificially corrupted samples or by introducing random perturbations to the input data during each training iteration. The level and type of corruption introduced can be adjusted according to the specific characteristics of the dataset and the desired robustness of the model. Further details on the implementation of the corruption model are provided in Sect. 4.

3.7 Evaluation

We evaluated the quality of the embedding model by measuring how well the model could complete facts. The prediction model predicted the tail of all the possible facts of KonecoKG.

We evaluated the embedding model using the Mean Reciprocal Rank (MRR) and Hits@N. Once the best embedding model was determined, we applied the Mean Squared Error (MSE) metric to calculate the error in the predicted values.

- **MRR** measures how well the model ranks the correct entity or relation among the candidates in the predicted list by measuring the average of the reciprocal ranks of the correct tail entities across all test triples. If the correct tail entity is ranked first, the reciprocal rank is 1; if it is ranked second, the reciprocal rank is 1/2, and so on. MRR is defined as:

$$\text{MRR} = \frac{1}{|\text{Test Triples}|} \sum_{i=1}^{|\text{Test Triples}|} \frac{1}{\text{Rank}_i}$$

- **Hits@N** measures the proportion of test triples where the correct answer appears within the top N predictions. Similar to MRR, we have a set of test triples and a ranked list of candidate tail entities for each test triple. This metric calculates the percentage of test triples for which the correct tail entity appears within the top N ranks in the predicted list. Hits@N is defined as follows:

$$\text{HITS@N} = \frac{\text{Number of Hits at Rank} \leq N}{|\text{Test Triples}|}$$

- **MSE** is used to measure the error in the prediction model by computing the average squared difference between estimated trade values ($\hat{y}_i$) and actual trade values (y_i). MSE is defined as follows:

$$\text{MSE} = \frac{1}{n} \sum_{i=1}^{n} (y_i - \hat{y}_i)^2$$

4 Experimental Setup

To begin with, we employed the Protégé[3] ontology editor, and adopted an ontology design methodology [18] to develop and visualize the KonecoTradeFlow ontology. This foundational step was critical before proceeding with the experimental setup, as it helped in formalizing the concept for mapping trade flow data to the KonecoKG. It played a key role in providing a visual framework of the relationships among entities, offering clarity on how different types are interconnected and ensuring a consistent data structure. Moreover, it facilitated the definition of formal relationships between concepts and established a shared understanding of the domain, enabling effective reasoning over the data.

In the second step, to streamline the experimental process, we began by filtering the data for each year from the entire dataset, as the data contains trade information spanning multiple years. We then created a separate knowledge graph (KG) for each individual year.

TThe third step involved converting the trade flow data into a format suitable for KG embedding. To achieve this, we used the SDM-RDFizer. We began by defining the necessary R2RML mapping rules in Turtle[4]. These rules specified the classes, properties, and relationships that we intended to include in the graph. Using the mapping rules, we generated <s, p, o> triples, also in Turtle format. The final result of all these triples, including subdivisions of classes and relationships, is the KonecoKG, which is also represented in Turtle format.

In the fourth step, we used the generated Turtle output to parse the graph with the RDFLib[5] graph package in our model. Figure 4 [35] provides a simplified view of the trade network. In this figure, the nodes represent the countries, while the edges signify the bilateral trade relationships between them. The labels on the edges indicate the value of the monetary trade exchange in millions of US dollars, with a value of 0.0 denoting no trade relation. The origin of each edge represents the export country, and the direction of the edge points to the import country.

In the fifth step, we used the AmpliGraph [13] Python library[6] to process the graph and transform it into a vectorized multidimensional representation of the statements it contained. The AmpliGraph package provided several potential embedding model

---

[3] https://protege.stanford.edu/.
[4] https://www.w3.org/TR/turtle/.
[5] https://rdflib.readthedocs.io/en/stable/apidocs/rdflib.html.
[6] https://github.com/Accenture/AmpliGraph.

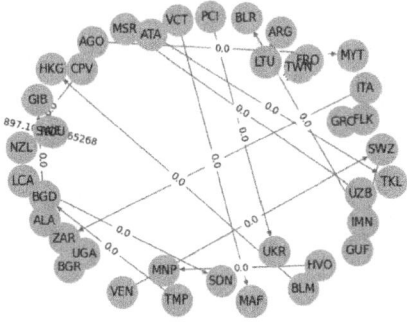

Fig. 4. Sample trade network in KonecoKG [35].

architectures with various parameters. As mentioned in Sect. 3, to evaluate the performance of the KG embedding models, we tested three algorithms: TransE, ComplEx, and DistMult. To optimize the model parameters, we applied a grid search methodology, systematically exploring different combinations to find the most effective settings. The metric performance scores of the models, rounded to the third decimal place, are presented in Table 3.

Notably, our experiments showed that the TransE model consistently outperformed the other models by 10% for our data. While ComplEx performed better than the other models for Hits@1 and Hits@10, further experiments revealed that as the value of N in Hits@N increased, the model's performance steadily declined. In contrast, as N increased, the Hits@N score for TransE consistently improved. Based on these results, we decided to proceed with the TransE model for further experimentation. We then used TransE to predict the trade values and evaluate the performance metrics.

In general, the model trains by comparing statements (s,p,o) known to be true against statements likely to be false based on local closed-world assumptions. This strategy measured the distances between different statements and aimed to minimise the said distance. An essential component of this experimental strategy is the corruption algorithm. The corruption algorithm creates negative triples by corrupting a true triple either by replacing the head or the tail entity with a random incorrect entity. This forces the model to distinguish between true and false facts, thereby enhancing model robustness.

Initially, we used the default corruption method provided by TransE. However, recognizing the potential benefits of incorporating controlled noise into the training process, we modified this strategy by corrupting the trade values by a relative value of 20% of their true values. Through experimentation with different corruption levels (20%, 50%, 70%, 100%, 120%), we found that a 20% corruption level optimally improved the results. This adjustment seemed to simulate real-world variations and uncertainties in trade dynamics, thereby enhancing the model's ability to generalize to unseen data.

Subsequently, we trained our model for 1000 epochs with an embedding size of 150 dimensions. These settings were selected based on preliminary experiments and empirical observations to achieve a balance between model performance and computational efficiency, ensuring both timely convergence and effective learning. A complete overview of the parameter values can be found in Table 2.

However, in our analysis, we noticed that we had to change the hyperparameters for a comparable prediction for the in-sample and out-of-sample methods, most notably in the epoch and batch size. The in-sample method required fewer epochs and lower negative sampling for predicting trade flows.

The trained model works by generalising relationships not yet seen by the neural network to predict the likelihood of a relationship being true with a given confidence.

Table 2. Embedding Parameters [35].

Parameter	Out-of-sample	In-sample
Epochs	1500	1000
Embedding size	150	150
Corruptions	30	10
Batch size	30	50
Loss function	Pairwise	Pairwise
Initialiser	Xavier	Xavier
Regulariser	LP, λ: 0.01, p: 2	LP, λ: 0.01, p: 2
Optimiser	Adam	Adam
Learning rate	0.001	0.001

Table 3. Results of trade flow prediction [35].

(a) ComplEx

Metric	Score
MRR	0.483
Hits@1	**0.428**
Hits@10	**0.513**
Hits@100	0.512
Hits@1000	0.592

(b) TransE.

Metric	Score
MRR	**0.587**
Hits@1	0.298
Hits@10	0.459
Hits@100	**0.576**
Hits@1000	**0.719**

(c) DistMult.

Metric	Score
MRR	0.376
Hits@1	0.311
Hits@10	0.404
Hits@100	0.491
Hits@1000	0.504

5 Results and Discussion

To evaluate the effectiveness of our model on unseen data, we employed leave-one-out cross-validation. In this approach, we iterated over each country relation as the test set, using the remaining data as the training set. The average scores from these runs, each consisting of 1000 epochs, are reported in Table 3. We used the performance metrics MRR [13] and Hits@N [13] to assess the predictions generated by the model. As outlined in Sect. 3, we experimented with the hyperparameters of three KG embedding models: ComplEx, TransE, and DistMult.

Table 4. Mean Squared Error by model [35].

Model	Mean Squared Error (in million)
PPML	2256.65
ComplEx	256.65
DistMult	196.26
TransE	**14.493564**

To place our model within the context of existing trade literature, we fitted a standard PPML model to the same dataset, incorporating country-fixed effects and focusing on the year 2015. We compared the models using the Mean Squared Error (MSE), as shown in Table 4. Our graph-based approaches consistently outperformed the PPML model, regardless of the specific model specification. Among the graph-based models, TransE provided the best fit, being more than 150 times more accurate in its predictions than the conventional PPML model. To visually demonstrate this comparison at the observation level, we plotted the actual trade flow observations against the predictions from both models, as shown in Fig. 5. The black 45° line represents a perfect fit. From this, we observe that PPML performs better for larger trade values, which is a common result. Additionally, Fig. 5a highlights that our model is particularly effective at predicting 0 trade flows, a task that is not possible for PPML, showcasing a key qualitative advantage of our approach over conventional methods. Moreover, KonecoKG delivers consistent predictive performance across the entire range of observations in the out-of-sample case, while outperforming PPML by a factor of 50 in the in-sample case, as measured by MSE.

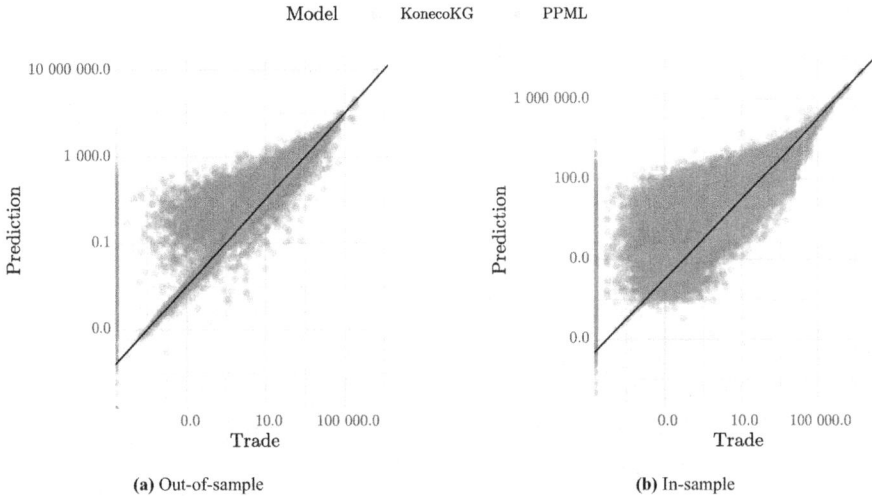

Fig. 5. Comparison of predictions (on log-log scale) [35].

In general, conventional regression-based approaches aim to gauge the average response of a variable of interest to a change, usually in policy. In our case, this process could be represented by the signing a trade agreement between one or multiple countries. As motivated in Sect. 2.1 and reinforced by our results, the influence of certain factors is mediated by a wide variety of contingent factors. Even if such an average response could be estimated, the complex interplay of dependencies would make the individual experience of an economic agent, such as a country, differ wildly from the estimated average. This phenomenon has recently been addressed in economics [36]. For this reason, we see great potential for graph-based learning algorithms to untangle the complexities at the heart of economic processes and to deepen our understanding of economic relationships.

To better grasp the fit of our model and to evaluate the economic factors which are most important to it, we analyze its residuals, defined by $\hat{y}_i - y_i$, where y_i is the true bilateral trade flow value, $\hat{y}_i$ is the prediction and i is the observation. We are then able to disentangle the models performance on the ground of economic arguments. We applied a K-means clustering algorithm to the residuals to render the heterogeneity more clearly. In Fig. 6a we plot each importer-exporter pair and highlight the observations using the clustering and discover that KonecoKG performs well across most of the possible GDP combinations. Only once we look at country pairs where both trading partners are rather large, do we see errors start to gain relevance. Many deviations as indicated by clusters 2 and 6, both positive and negative, occur when the USA (the country with the largest GPD in our 2015 sample) takes the role of an exporter, for which we tend to over-predict. This result is not surprising and commonly observed in the trade literature [2]. Given its size theory and data driven models would predict a much larger openness to trade. However, due to its large domestic market and geopolitical reasons, it is comparatively less open to trade. This, however, is just one piece of the story, as we can see once we also look at the role that the distance between trading partners plays. When looking at Fig. 6b, we see that our model tends to struggle more for pairs that tend to be closer to each other.

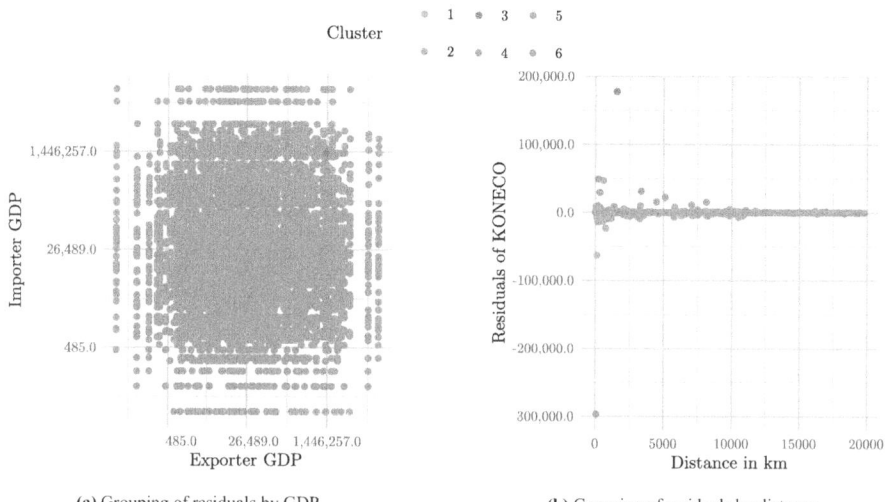

(a) Grouping of residuals by GDP.   (b) Grouping of residuals by distance.

Fig. 6. Exploration of KonecoKG residuals by predictor.

To investigate this further, we aggregate the residuals on a country level, meaning that we collect all residuals associated with a country, either as an exporter or an importer, and extract the maximum as well as the average level. Figure 7 shows the logarithm of the average of each of these residuals per country, while Fig. 8 shows the logarithm of the maximum. In comparing these two results, we again see that the largest deviations tend to occur in countries that are large like China and the USA. Nonetheless, we also notice positive deviations for Russia, northern and southern Africa, western Europe and the Middle East. Interestingly, we can see further clusters emerging that mirror geographical, and hence trade cost features, represented in our data. Among these, are clusters of under prediction for most of South and Middle America, central Africa, north eastern Europe, as well as South East Asia, including Oceania. These tend to be highly connected regions with a high degree of trade openness, which our model fails to capture in its entirety. Switzerland is a noticeable outlier that despite its special status among its neighboring countries is comparatively open to trade, which our model does not take into consideration. Yet, the overall picture offers a vast improvement over existing models and their results.

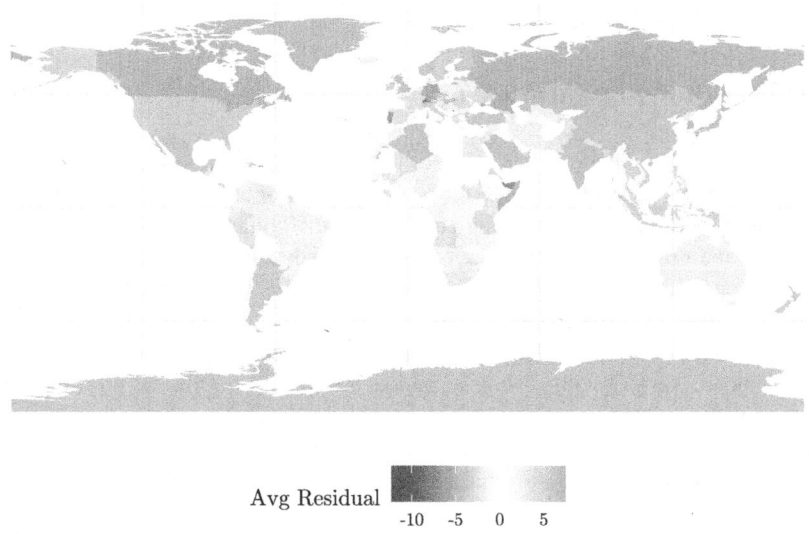

Fig. 7. Logarithm of the average residual of KonecoKG by country.

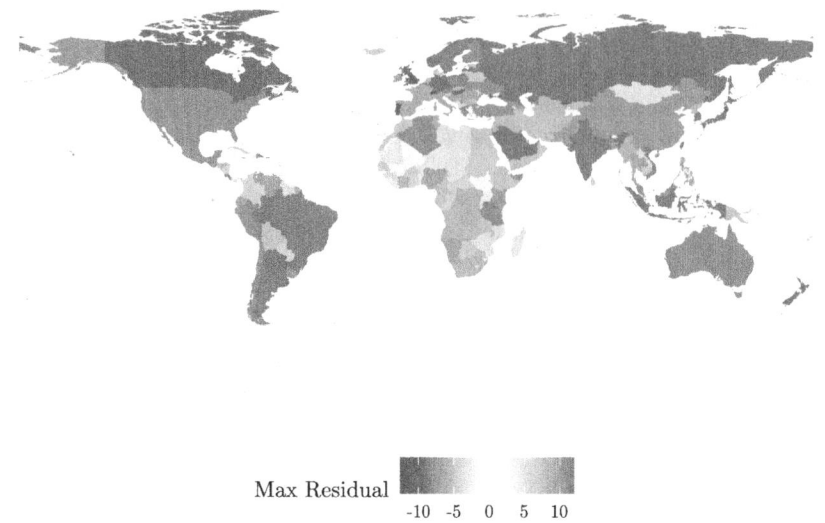

Fig. 8. Logarithm of the maximum residual of KonecoKG by country.

6 Conclusion and Future Work

In this study we have demonstrated the ability of graph-based models to vastly outperform conventional regression-based models used in econometric analysis of bilateral trade flows. Out model produced predictions that are 50 times as accurate for in-sample prediction, and up to 155 times for out-of-sample tasks. We attribute this result to the ability of our model to capture the non-linearity and hierarchical high-dimensionality of processes that shape all economic data.

We posit several promising developments of our current approach. Even though we have enhanced our KG with several attributes and pieces of context information, we believe that this can be intensified to much greater degree. Adding other sources of unstructured data, which conventional methods are incapable of handling, without loss-prone transformation, allows for analysis on even less aggregated levels of economic interactions, such as industry, or even sectoral inquiries.

Additionally, in order to make the insights gained from KG models more actionable for policy decisions, an alternate and subsequent extension of the work would be explaining the embedding and the prediction model to identify the key determinants of the model beyond the mere observational considerations of the previous section.

To leverage the true power of graph-based models, we see great benefit over conventional models in their ability to models not just bilateral, but also multilateral effects. This would extend the ability to extend analysis of economic interactions beyond the strong set of assumptions required today and open a plethora of new insights for other fields in social sciences.

Lastly, we see the need to enhance these models by allowing them to capture the temporal dimension of human action and hence economic data. Time is the medium through which any economic process is realized, requiring most of current empirical research to attribute greatest importance the understanding of its influence. As nonlinearity is most strongly expressed in change, we think that our approach could prove valuable to the current literature.

Supplemental Material

The raw data can be viewed and downloaded from *Mario Larch's* Regional Trade Agreements Database[7], Dynamic Gravity Dataset[8], International Trade and Production Database for Estimation (ITPD-E)[9]. In particular, we will release the ontology model, mapping rules for creating the KonecoTradeFlow ontology, code to tune hyperparameters for the ComplEx, TransE, and DistMult, code to train, and predict model using TransE. The project, data, and the Python Code can also be found on GitHub[10].

Acknowledgments. The work has been done as the part of KONECO project, and it has received funding from the Bundesministerium für Bildung und Forschung (BMBF) under grant No 16DKWN095.

We also thank Rebekka Koch, our student assistant, for her valuable efforts in collecting related literature, and for efforts during various crucial parts of the paper development.

Disclosure of Interests. The authors have no competing interests to declare that are relevant to the content of this article.

References

1. Abu-Salih, B.: Domain-specific knowledge graphs: a survey. J. Netw. Comput. Appl. **185**, 103076 (2021)
2. Aslam, A., Boz, E., Cerutti, E., Poplawski-Ribeiro, M., Topalova, P.: The slowdown in global trade: a symptom of a weak recovery? IMF Econ. Rev. **66**, 440–479 (2018)
3. Axtell, R.L.: Zipf distribution of US firm sizes. Science **293**(5536), 1818–1820 (2001)
4. Basile, R., Commendatore, P., Benedictis, L., Kubin, I.: The impact of trade costs on the European regional trade network: an empirical and theoretical analysis. Rev. Int. Econ. **26**(3), 578–609 (2018)
5. Blöthner, S., Larch, M.: Economic determinants of regional trade agreements revisited using machine learning. Empir. Econ. **63**(4), 1771–1807 (2022)
6. Bolón-Canedo, V., Sánchez-Maroño, N., Alonso-Betanzos, A.: Feature selection for high-dimensional data. Progr. Artif. Intell. **5**(2), 65–75 (2016)
7. Borchert, I., Larch, M., Shikher, S., Yotov, Y.V.: The international trade and production database for estimation (ITPD-E). Int. Econ. **166**, 140–166 (2021)

---

[7] https://www.ewf.uni-bayreuth.de/en/research/RTA-data/index.html.
[8] https://www.usitc.gov/data/gravity/dgd.htm.
[9] https://www.usitc.gov/data/gravity/itpde.htm.
[10] https://github.com/durgeshnandini/Multidimensional-Knowledge-Graph-Embeddings-for-International-Trade-Flow-Analysis.

8. Bordes, A., Usunier, N., Garcia-Duran, A., Weston, J., Yakhnenko, O.: Translating embeddings for modeling multi-relational data. In: Advances in Neural Information Processing Systems, vol. 26 (2013)
9. Cai, H., Zheng, V.W., Chang, K.C.C.: A comprehensive survey of graph embedding: problems, techniques, and applications. IEEE Trans. Knowl. Data Eng. **30**(9), 1616–1637 (2018)
10. Chandrasekaran, B., Josephson, J.R., Benjamins, V.R.: What are ontologies, and why do we need them? IEEE Intell. Syst. Their Appl. **14**(1), 20–26 (1999)
11. Chen, X., Jia, S., Xiang, Y.: A review: knowledge reasoning over knowledge graph. Expert Syst. Appl. **141**, 112948 (2020)
12. Chen, Z., Wang, Y., Zhao, B., Cheng, J., Zhao, X., Duan, Z.: Knowledge graph completion: a review. IEEE Access **8**, 192435–192456 (2020)
13. Costabello, L., Pai, S., Le Van, C., McGrath, R., McCarthy, N., Tabacof, P.: AmpliGraph: a library for representation learning on knowledge graphs. Retrieved Oct **10**, 2019 (2019)
14. Benedictis, L., Tajoli, L.: The world trade network. World Econ. **34**(8), 1417–1454 (2011)
15. Dettmers, T., Minervini, P., Stenetorp, P., Riedel, S.: Convolutional 2D knowledge graph embeddings. In: Proceedings of the AAAI Conference on Artificial Intelligence, vol. 32 (2018)
16. Giovanni, J., Levchenko, A.A., Ranciere, R.: Power laws in firm size and openness to trade: measurement and implications. J. Int. Econ. **85**(1), 42–52 (2011)
17. Donoho, D.L., et al.: High-dimensional data analysis: the curses and blessings of dimensionality. AMS Math Challenges Lect. **1**(2000), 32 (2000)
18. Dutta, B., Nandini, D., Shahi, G.K.: MOD: metadata for ontology description and publication. In: Proceedings of the International Conference on Dublin Core and Metadata Applications. Dublin Core Metadata Initiative (2015)
19. Egger, P.H., Larch, M.: Interdependent preferential trade agreement memberships: an empirical analysis. J. Int. Econ. **76**(2), 384–399 (2008)
20. Egger, P.H., Staub, K.E.: GLM estimation of trade gravity models with fixed effects. Empir. Econ. **50**, 137–175 (2016)
21. Fally, T.: Structural gravity and fixed effects. J. Int. Econ. **97**(1), 76–85 (2015)
22. Fensel, D., Fensel, D.: Ontologies. Springer, Heidelberg (2001)
23. Gabaix, X.: Power laws in economics and finance. Annu. Rev. Econ. **1**(1), 255–294 (2009)
24. Gastinger, J., Steinert, N., Gründer-Fahrer, S., Martin, M.: Dynamic representations of global crises: creation and analysis of a temporal knowledge graph for conflicts, trade and value networks. In: D2R2 (2023)
25. Goyal, P., Ferrara, E.: Graph embedding techniques, applications, and performance: a survey. Knowl.-Based Syst. **151**, 78–94 (2018)
26. Gurevich, T., Herman, P.: The dynamic gravity dataset: 1948-2016. US International Trade Commission, Office of Economics Working Paper (2018)
27. Hayek, F.A.: The use of knowledge in society. Am. Econ. Rev. **35**(4), 519–530 (1945)
28. Head, K., Mayer, T.: Gravity equations: workhorse, toolkit, and cookbook. In: Handbook of International Economics, vol. 4, pp. 131–195. Elsevier (2014)
29. Hinloopen, J., van Marrewijk, C.: Comparative advantage, the rank-size rule, and Zipf's law (2006)
30. Kun, K.W., et al.: WeExt: a framework of extending deterministic knowledge graph embedding models for embedding weighted knowledge graphs. IEEE Access (2023)
31. Mayer, T., Zignago, S.: Notes on CEPII's distances measures: The geodist database (2011)
32. Meng, L.: [retracted] information extraction and knowledge graph construction for enterprises in china's free trade zone. Secur. Commun. Netw. **2022**(1), 2962545 (2022)
33. Menger, C.: Grundsätze der Volkswirtschaftslehre. Braumüller (1871)
34. Nair, J., Wierman, A., Zwart, B.: The Fundamentals of Heavy Tails: Properties, Emergence, and Estimation. Cambridge University Press (2022)

35. Nandini, D., Blöthner, S., Schoenfeld, M., Larch, M.: Multidimensional knowledge graph embeddings for international trade flow analysis. In: Proceedings of the 16th International Joint Conference on Knowledge Discovery, Knowledge Engineering and Knowledge Management - KEOD, pp. 63–73. INSTICC, SciTePress (2024). https://doi.org/10.5220/0013028500003838
36. Peters, O.: The ergodicity problem in economics. Nat. Phys. **15**(12), 1216–1221 (2019)
37. Quan, J.: Visualization and analysis model of industrial economy status and development based on knowledge graph and deep neural network. Comput. Intell. Neurosci. **2022**(1), 7008093 (2022)
38. Raudenbush, S.W., Bryk, A.S.: Hierarchical Linear Models: Applications and Data Analysis Methods, vol. 1. Sage (2002)
39. Rincon-Yanez, D., Mouakher, A., Senatore, S.: Enhancing downstream tasks in knowledge graphs embeddings: a complement graph-based approach applied to bilateral trade. Procedia Comput. Sci. **225**, 3692–3700 (2023)
40. Rincon-Yanez, D., et al.: Accurate prediction of international trade flows: leveraging knowledge graphs and their embeddings. J. King Saud Univ.-Comput. Inf. Sci. **35**(10), 101789 (2023)
41. Rosal, I.: Power laws in EU country exports. Empirica **45**, 311–337 (2018)
42. Santos Silva, J., Tenreyro, S.: The log of gravity. Rev. Econ. Stat. **88**(4), 641–658 (2006)
43. Schumpeter, J.: The common sense of econometrics. Econometrica 5–12 (1933)
44. Sellami, B., Ounoughi, C., Kalvet, T., Tiits, M., Rincon-Yanez, D.: Harnessing graph neural networks to predict international trade flows. Big Data Cogn. Comput. **8**(6), 65 (2024)
45. Shahi, G.K.: Fakekg: a knowledge graph of fake claims for improving automated fact-checking (student abstract). In: Proceedings of the AAAI Conference on Artificial Intelligence, vol. 37, pp. 16320–16321 (2023)
46. Shao, L., Duan, Y., Sun, X., Zou, Q., Jing, R., Lin, J.: Bidirectional value driven design between economical planning and technical implementation based on data graph, information graph and knowledge graph. In: 2017 IEEE 15th International Conference on Software Engineering Research, Management and Applications (SERA), pp. 339–344. IEEE (2017)
47. Taleb, N.N.: Statistical consequences of fat tails: real world preasymptotics, epistemology, and applications. arXiv preprint arXiv:2001.10488 (2020)
48. Trouillon, T., Welbl, J., Riedel, S., Gaussier, É., Bouchard, G.: Complex embeddings for simple link prediction. In: International Conference on Machine Learning, pp. 2071–2080. PMLR (2016)
49. Uschold, M., Gruninger, M.: Ontologies: principles, methods and applications. Knowl. Eng. Rev. **11**(2), 93–136 (1996)
50. Wang, Q., Mao, Z., Wang, B., Guo, L.: Knowledge graph embedding: a survey of approaches and applications. IEEE Trans. Knowl. Data Eng. **29**(12), 2724–2743 (2017)
51. Wolfram, S.: A New Kind of Science, vol. 5. Wolfram Media Champaign, IL (2002)
52. Xia, F., et al.: Graph learning: a survey. IEEE Trans. Artif. Intell. **2**(2), 109–127 (2021)
53. Yotov, Y.V., Piermartini, R., Monteiro, J., Larch, M.: An advanced guide to trade policy analysis: the structural gravity model (2016). https://unctad.org/publication/advanced-guide-trade-policy-analysis-structural-gravity-model-volume-2

Knowledge Management
and Information Systems

Semantic Support in Standardized Environments

Daniel Spieldenner[1](✉)[iD], André Antakli[1][iD], Torsten Spieldenner[2][iD], and Harkiran Sahota[3][iD]

[1] Deutsches Forschungszentrum für Künstliche Intelligenz (DFKI), Campus D3 2, 66123 Saarbrücken, Saarland, Germany
{daniel.spieldenner,andre.antakli}@dfki.de
[2] socialPALS GmbH, Hauptstraße 18a/b, 83607 Holzkirchen, Bavaria, Germany
[3] Lappeenranta-Lahti University of Technology LUT, Yliopistonkatu 34, 53850 Lappeenranta, Finland

Abstract. Integrating data sources and connecting participants in heterogeneous environments is a challenging task that requires extensive expert knowledge about the nature of the systems involved. Even when this knowledge is given in the form of manuals or code documentation, or can be derived by a human expert by interpreting the source code, putting this knowledge to use to actually integrate data sources is mostly entirely left to the human and not exploitable by the system itself. Established standards, such as data spaces or the Asset Administration Shell, aim to provide support with connecting participants in heterogeneous environments, but often fall short when it comes to intuitive interoperability. With this work, we propose an approach to augment existing systems with machine usable expert knowledge via so-called semantic support points: a concept for minimal implementations, adding the power of Semantic Web technologies like semantic queries, as well as the possibility to model expert knowledge in ontologies, to existing systems. One core goal of ours is leaving existing standards untouched, like secure communication between data space participants or industry environments described by Asset Administration Shells, and adding semantic information as an optional, volatile layer on top, generated by externally managed expert knowledge in the form of semantic transformation rules.

Keywords: Intelligent systems · Semantic web · Interoperability · Multi agent systems · Dataspace · Industry 4.0

1 Introduction

With rapidly increasing progress in digitization and digitalization [13,46] and the impact of AI on every aspect of our modern lives, from smart home setups equipped with smart devices ready for the internet of things [31,36,44], smart factories where the assembly processes of autonomous machines need to be efficiently aligned with human workers [28,33,58], to smart cities [29,30,69]. The vision of dataspaces [17,22,24,57,71] promises to provide a secure, controllable and legally binding data exchange, still maintaining these systems and enabling interoperable data exchange has become one of today's core challenges.

This is especially true for complex intelligent systems, which consist of a range of actors working together autonomously. For instance, in a smart home, sensors and control units collaborate to maintain the resident's preferred room temperature and lighting. Similarly, an entire shop floor with machines forming an intricate production line operating in a coordinated manner (Fig. 1).

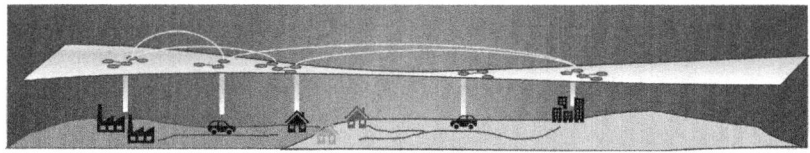

Fig. 1. Our vision of semantic support points, spanning a layer of semantics abstracting from the world below, as introduced in [60].

Such systems often consist of very heterogenous devices, services and data sources, some of them decades old from times long before standardized exchange formats or concepts like interoperability or the *Semantic Web* [34] were are thing. However, these data sources often can't be easily exchanged. Machines in a factory usually run for decades and are expensive to exchange, citizen data in cities with millions of inhabitants stored in distributed, unaligned spread sheets, data bases or text documents, can't just be replaced easily with a more modern representation, let alone change the processes of the responsible offices, and energy suppliers have their established data models and business process optimized for their grid setups rather than being optimized for efficient data exchange.

But no matter how complex a system is, each of its component was designed by an expert with an intention how and what for the component is used, which conditions need to be fulfilled, which restrictions exist, which capabilities a component provides and what the intended outcome of the actions performed by it is. Usually this knowledge is "encoded" in manuals, software documentation, code comments or what we would consider "common knowledge", for example the fact that a thermometer is supposed to measure temperature.

Our goal is to bring this knowledge, which usually is considered to be expert knowledge, held and communicated by humans, to the environment itself, allowing the participants to emanate this "knowledge" when and where needed. Where needed, by minimal additions to the existing systems, a volatile, connected fabric of semantics above the actual system layer, as suggested by [62], is spanned, expressing and encoding expert knowledge concerning the available systems, the intended interpretation of data values, capabilities of actors and the possible connection between participants. The data contained in this volatile fabric is generated and processed with the help of ontologies [12] and principles of the *Semantic Web* [34].

With such a representation at hand, we would allow any system to benefit from concepts like semantic communication [32,48], semantic interoperability [25] as well as reasoning and semantic queries.

In this paper we build upon our approach for *Semantic Support Points* suggested in [60], presenting a method to add a light weight, volatile layer of semantic information to a world consisting of legacy data sources, devices and services, providing human modeled expert knowledge about meaning and intention of available participants and data. This expert knowledge is given in the form of data transform definition files, provided to minimal service implementations that create semantic representations of raw data values on demand, or select data from a knowledge graph and transform it back to non-semantic data representations like JSON.

These *Semantic support points* are realized in the form of distributed, light weight, runtime configurable and non-intrusive micro services, used to read and enrich data generated by the attached systems on the fly and providing knowledge graphs with embedded data values to actors consuming this data. This approach enables concepts like semantic interoperability, semantic queries and reasoning on knowledge graphs in any environment, even if it was initially designed without any attempt to provide semantic capabilities. Pairs of support points allow for bidirectional communication between what we consider the *system layer*, i.e. the collection of participants without any semantic information attached, and arbitrary actors on the *semantic layer*, interacting directly and only with knowledge graphs provided by the semantic support points.

In [60], we already provided a detailed proof of concept by applying the concept of semantic support points to a real life example of an automotive production line. Data from a variety of heterogenous data sources is transformed to a semantic representation and provided to a multi agent system, using the semantic nature of the mapped data values for deriving optimized production plans by using a reasoning engine. In order to further demonstrate the versatility and reusability of the approach, along with the non-intrusive nature, only adding functionality to a system without disrupting working standards, we extend the aforementioned use case to a system that is making heavy use of the standardized *Asset Administraion Shell* [7], and finally we propose a method to seamlessly integrate support points into an existing dataspace according to the EDC^1 specification.

The paper is structured as follows:

An overview over the relevant background and related approaches aiming to realize a concept of a semantic data integration is given in Sect. 2, starting with a brief recap of semantic web concepts like RDF and OWL ontologies. Following that, we introduce the concepts we aim to extend and enrich with our approach, first industry 4.0 environments already making use of the *Asset Administration*

---

[1] https://eclipse-edc.github.io/.

Shell to achieve interoperability, followed by a quick introduction to dataspaces realized by using *Eclipse Dataspace Components (EDC)*.

Having defined our challenges, we introduce our concept of *semantic support points*, minimal service implementations allowing to access transform rules based on semantic concepts about systems and data sources to generate knowledge graphs including knowledge about the system interfaces themselves as well as the data exchanged.

Starting with Sect. 4 we demonstrate how we put the concept into practical use, starting with a recap of how we used semantic support points in an automotive factory environment, as already presented in [60]. This approach is extended to an environment making use of the *Asset Administration Shell*, demonstrating how semantic support points can facilitate communication and data availability as well as discovery and accessibility of information in an already to some extend interoperable environment without much changes to an already running system.

Finally we propose an approach to use semantic support points in an EDC based dataspace environment, adding increased semantic interoperability and providing additional information in the form of optional semantic assets, without violating the security, privacy and data governance requirements or the already existing communication channels within the dataspace.

The results of the exemplary realizations and their relevance as proof of concept are summarized in 7 before we discuss open questions and provide an outlook of possible future work in 7.1.

2 Related Work

The idea of creating a semantic abstraction layer on top of an existing architecture involves a wide range of research domains and technologies. We will make use of semantic web concepts to describe data values and system interfaces, take some inspiration from ambient intelligent systems and employ multi agent systems to interact autonomously with the environment.

In the following, we provide background information to these topics and conclude with a brief overview over existing semantic layer approaches.

2.1 RDF, OWL and the Semantic Web

In order to include expert knowledge directly into our semantic layer, we will make use of *semantic web* [34] technologies, namely *RDF graphs* [38] as data format, making use of *OWL ontologies* [12,39] to define the concepts and relations relevant in a given environment, both well established W3C standards.

RDF allows us to make statements about things in the world in terms of triples, consisting of a subject, predicate and object. The place of the subject position in such a triple is taken by a *resource* with a *unique resource identifier* (URI). This resource does not only represent an entity in the abstract, digital world, but can directly relate to a physical thing in the real world, providing an address where to access information about this entity via the URI.

In order to give actual meaning to a RDF resource, knowledge about the concepts the RDF graph is supposed to described can be modeled in ontologies [66]. By adding the respective namespaces of the ontology we want to use to the identifiers of RDF resources, we tie this resource to the classes and relationships defined in the ontology. This, in our case, gives us the possibility to provide expert knowledge about interfaces and data values of participants in our system by classifying them according to a class in a domain relevant ontology. In order to define these ontologies, we make use of the *Web Ontology Language* (OWL)[2], allowing us to define concepts like sub class relationships, class unions, exclusions, properties and so on.

2.2 The Asset Administration Shell

Within the Industry 4.0 community, the *Asset Administration Shell (AAS)* [7] has emerged as a standard for structured descriptions of *digital twins* [19,56] for data exchange and interoperability. AAS describe *assets*, interactable entities in the real world, referenced by globally unique identifiers, such as URIs. Properties and characteristics of an asset are given in the form of key-value pairs, organized in a hierarchical fashion. Both static properties for pure information storage as well as dynamic ones updated during runtime, e.g. by sensor readings, are supported. With the use of *submodels*, the functionality can be extended, providing concepts standardized by the IDTA[3] to model digital twins according to the user's needs. Extensive research has been done to bring complex features to an AAS powered industrial environment, such as automatic action planning based on PDDL as action language [10].

While the standard format for asset shell or submodel descriptions is the proprietary, binary aasx format, it is also possible to use JSON, XML or RDF representations. While assets, submodels and properties are already providing the option to include a *semantic identifier*, full semantic functionality like reasoning or semantic queries is not yet supported. However, the design of the AAS is based on and AAS structures can be described by using the *Reference Architecture Model Industrie 4.0 (RAMI 4.0)* [55] ontology[4].

2.3 Dataspaces and Dataspace Connectors

Dataspaces [11,18,22,65] have entered the stage in the past years, attempting to define not only a concise but also safe environment to deal with data that shares a similar domain or use case. Adapting recent advances in the field of the *semantic web* [9,27] and *linked data*, the idea of providing such an expressive and flexible way to describe and store data also has become a topic of interest in the dataspace world. [17,40]. However, a dataspace can only be as useful as the data provided, and as dataspaces themselves are not expected to the solve

---

[2] https://www.w3.org/OWL/.
[3] https://industrialdigitaltwin.org/.
[4] https://github.com/i40-Tools/RAMIOntology.

the problem of actually integrating data, additional effort is necessary to unite existing, most likely very heterogenous, data sources under the umbrella of one dataspace.

2.4 Applications of Semantic Web Technologies

Encoding actual expert knowledge within the ambient intelligent environment, making use of semantic web principles in order to increase interoperability or expressiveness of data, is a widely investigated approach [43,45,49,54].

While the semantic, ontology side of view is examined in detail, providing rather a theoretical concept of knowledge encoding, the practical application of these concepts to existing systems is often lacking.

Concepts like the *Semantic Web of Things* [51] aim to bridge the gap between semantically annotated data on the one hand and a real system world on the other hand by introducing the idea of including knowledge about every participant via per device knowledge base generation, united in what Rute et al. refer to as *"ubiquitous knowledge base"*. The most practical approach we are aware of to actually putting the idea of the semantic web of things into action was proposed by Antoniazzi et al. [6]

Building on the W3C vision[5] of the Web of Things [70], Charpenay investigated methods to semantically describe web things [14] and actual semantic data integration. [15]. Semantic data integration is realized by an automatic transform step to JSON-LD, based on the keys of the original JSON object and the ontology to be used for annotation.

While this again shows the interest in and the need for semantic annotation not only on a device interface meta data level, but actual semantic data integration, for our vision this approach is still too limited in two regards: first, the focus on W3C WoT poses a restriction when it comes to system representation as the assumption that participants can be expressed in terms of sensors, actions and so on does not necessarily hold in every case. Furthermore, the key based JSON to JSON-LD approach does not provide the level of freedom we would like to realize when it comes to including actual human expert knowledge into the semantic representation generated.

Further work on introducing some form of *semantic layers* was done, among others, by Vdovjak et al. [67] or Lu and Ashgar [37], showing interest in and the importance of considering the semantics of data and actors in a system to improve usability and interoperability, the solutions suggested are often centered around one specific closed architecture.

Spieldenner introduces the idea of a semantic *medium* in [62], a virtual, semantic reflection of a collection of systems, enhancing the options of multi agent systems to act within the system by exploiting the semantic information available, and making actual changes in the "real world" by directly linking outcomes in the semantic world to actual actions in the real world. [62].

---

[5] https://www.w3.org/WoT/.

Also with regard to the Asset Administration Shell, noticable effort is done to include benefits of the semantic web technologies. Bader et al. motivate the usage of RML, along with a suitable ontology, to create RDF representations of AAS models [8]. Using RML to generate RDF representations of data in an AAS was investigated by Moreno et al. [42], and Rimaz et al. [50] who build on this concept to introduce a method to transform RDF data back to a given JSON representation in order to allow for integration into existing, running AAS, which is not possible with RDF data. Due to shortcomings of RML and design choices, the possibility of editing and maintaining expert knowledge about data and interactions independently of the system is limited.

To summarize, while there is a strong interest in and need for solutions to transform data to and from a semantic representation, to the best of our knowledge, until today there still is a lack of solutions that can be employed with reasonable effort, especially as additions to already existing system environments. Allowing developers to provide an easily accessible and maintainable description of their understanding of data and communication in any system and using this to facilitate data transform and exchange still is an mostly open question.

3   The Semantic Support Point Concept

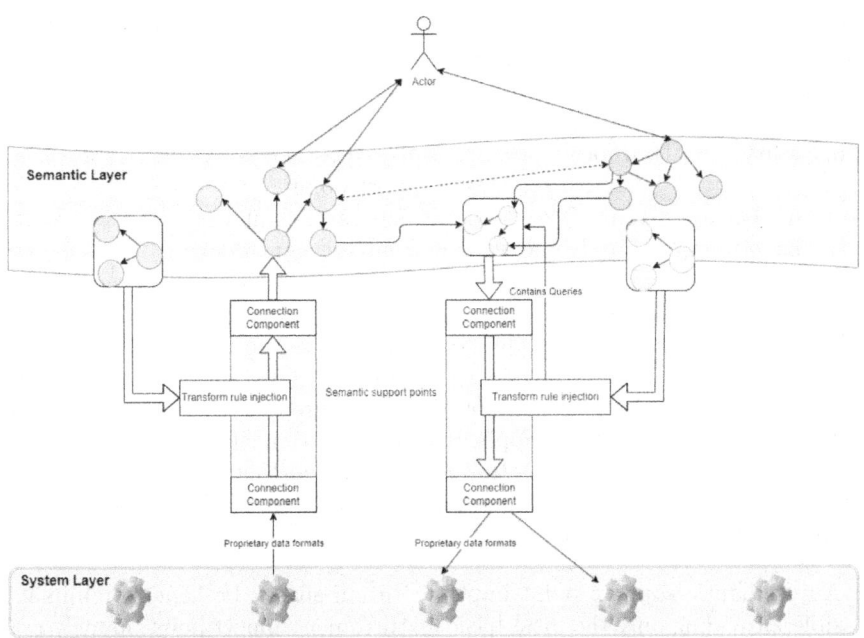

Fig. 2. High level overview of the semantic support point concept as introduced in [60].

As explained in [60], we suggest a concept of *Semantic Support Points* as a possible solution to this problem, minimal implementations that can be easily used as a bridge between an existing system based on data without an explicit semantic representation available, and a semantic abstraction of the underlying data, aggregating information from the non-semantic system layer and providing a volatile semantic fabric that can be queried as needed. Semantic Support Points should follow the following principles:

Distributed. Semantic Support Points should consist of minimal implementations, employed where needed to generate semantic data from one or more aggregated non-semantic data sources on the system layer, rather than one monolithic middleware handling all data transform and transmission on one platform.

Decoupled. Every semantic support should have access to its own required input data, such as transformation rules, and provide interfaces for data in- and output for its specific data source on the system layer. No support point should depend on the existence or availability of other support points to provide its functionality.

Non-invasive. Adding semantic information to an existing system via an abstraction layer should be seen as an optional data offer for actors aiming for exploiting available semantic information, e.g. for reasoning to generate new knowledge, achieving interoperability by working on semantic interface abstractions or to have access of semantic data querying capabilities. To this end, semantic access points should be integrated into existing systems according to the requirements and existing interfaces in these systems.

Non-Persisting. No state and no data should be stored in a specific support point. All data transformation and access should happen on demand, while necessary data transform rules are provided as necessary via *transform rule injection routes* into each semantic support point.

Domain Independent. The semantic support point implementation itself should be minimal and independent from the data domain. All (semantic) information needed to describe the abstracted interface or data point should be provided via external sources. Rules for data transformation should only be provided within the injected transform rules, not hard coded within a specific support point. Domain independence along with the non-invasive, non-persisting and non-invasive properties ensure that the concept of semantic support points can be applied to any environment, in any domain, to an arbitrary extent, without the necessity of hosting or configuring a pre-implemented middleware beyond providing appropriate semantic transform rules to the semantic support points.

Any semantic support point implementation should be kept as minimal as possible, providing only the most basic features per support point, namely reading data from a data source, receiving external transform rules, applying the transform rules to the data and providing the transformed results at its interfaces.

Receiving transform rules from outside sources ensures distributed and non-persisting properties of the support point, as no data relevant for the intended data transform is stored within any support point at any time and can be routed as needed. Transform rules can, and should, be provided per support point, tailored to the underlying data source, thus the distributed property. Further, it ensures the domain independence, as the domain solely depends on the transformation route, not on the support point implementation.

The connection point can implement any communication protocol necessary to connect the systems on the system layer it provides semantic support for as needed, be it HTTP, event driven systems, message buses or whatever else might exist out there.

This is true for both transformation directions. In case of a support point generating RDF from non-RDF sources, the outgoing connection component must provide interfaces for any actors that want to interact with it on a semantic manner. The semantic layer as such is non-persisting and provides data only as needed.

See Fig. 2 for a schematic overview of the semantic support point concept. On the semantic layer side, data is provided on request of an actor by the support points in semantic format. The knowledge graphs generated this way can be processed like any semantic resource, for example by querying the graph for specific information (blue graph), linking data by using transformation results from other support points and connecting them via properties (connection between blue and yellow graph), by deriving additional knowledge via reasoning within an underlying ontology, or include them into reasoning steps, or performing tasks like graph completion or graph embedding into a larger graph or ontology (including the red graph, which is not the result of a support point transformation).

In order to propagate results of computations on the semantic level back to the system layer, again a transform rule is used that may contain additional information on how to query the dataset provided as result of the actor's processes. The sub knowledge graph resulting from this querying step is then routed back through a support point and transformed to a data object according to the transformation rules provided via the injection route.

Notice that transformation rules, as they are written in RDF, can be understood as part of the virtual semantic layer and as such can provide additional information for actors acting on the semantic level, e.g. for service discovery and composition by exploiting information about the handling of certain data values contained in the transform file knowledge graph.

This concept of semantic support points fulfills the intended properties listed above: it is *distributed* in the sense that the minimal support point implementations can be hosted independent from each other where needed and where possible, *decoupled* in the sense that one support point crashing does not affect the runtime of any other support point, or any available transformation rules, *non-invasive* in the sense that existing interfaces do not need to be changed but can connect to support points to send and receive data as-is, *non-persisting* as no knowledge graphs that are results of semantic transformation are stored, and as actors that interact with the semantic layer don't work on a persisted knowledge graph directly, but via the connection components of semantic support points and *domain independent* in the sense that domain is defined by the separately provided transformation rules, not by the support point implementations themselves.

4 Using Semantic Support Points in an Automotive Industry 4.0 Environment

In [60] we have presented a practical use case of using semantic support points in a heterogenous environment in the industry 4.0 domain. On demand transformation of data to and from RDF from a variety of data sources is used to provide a semantic multi agent based operation reasoner with information to generate work plans for human workers in the factory.

Each agent maintains an individual view onto the world in its own knowledge base. This has multiple benefits compared to trying to render the knowledge of the entire world continuously and storing it in one central spot.

First of all it ensures encapsulation between multiple agents acting potentially simultaneously.

Second the we do not need to store a large amount of data representing the entire world at once, eliminating the need of a large, persisting data storage while also reducing the computation times of the queries executed. Instead, each agent can decide when and which data it needs. Imagine it as asking someone who has knowledge you need to explain it to you, or as only looking at the pages of a documentation that cover the points of interest for you.

4.1 Mapping Between Structured Data an RDF

As the multi agent system works on RDF data, exploiting semantic relations between data values, we need to transform data from a variety of data source to an appropriate RDF format, making use of specific ontologies modeling the expert knowledge concerning the manufactoring process and the factory and its machines itself.

For mapping non-semantic data into a RDF knowledge graph, we entirely rely on freely available 3rd party libraries, while for the mapping back from a semantic representation to a explicitly specified interface, we propose our own solution.

From Non-semantic Data Formats RDF. In order to generate RDF graphs from different data formats, several approaches exist [26,41,53], however due to its wide acceptance and the benefit of being able to manage mapping files in a non-central, flexible distributed way, we aim for using *RML* [21].

Mapping files written in RDF allow, in our opinion, the best trade off between complexity and the flexibility for system maintainers or service developers to freely express their intentions and their interpretation of the role of their system in terms of the generated RDF graph. Moreover, the possibility to store mapping files in a separate repository, independent from the running system, allows for easy editing and extending of existing knowledge. This can even happen without stopping a running system. Updating existing mappings to reflect changes in the environment and remove knowledge that is not longer needed at runtime support the idea of a seamless integration of new concepts, fulfilling our properties of support points being distributed, decoupled and non-invasive. We are basically weaving our linked data fabric quilt patch by patch without having to interfere with the underlying physical world.

In order to provide RML mapping functionality to our system, we wrap $CARML^6$ into a micro service offering either an HTTP endpoint for direct calls or capabilities to connect to an event stream. The necessary mapping files are not stored in the service itself, but provided via a separate endpoint we call the *mapping file injection route*. Results are either provided as the response of a HTTP request or can be forwarded to a message bus.

From RDF to Explicitly Specified Non-semantic Data Formats. In order to access the semantic abstraction layer and propagating knowledge from there back to specific systems, we need to be able to generate explicitly specified JSON objects from RDF data.

As the operation of mapping data with RML is not reversible [2], we need a separate solution to generate JSON objects from RDF input. While JSON-LD [64] as standardized serialization format seems like an obvious choice at first glance, it is lacking in means of giving a binding definition of the resulting object structure and key names, a necessary requirement to make an existing API accepting and reading a JSON object properly. Morevover we are not interested in serializing an entire RDF graph but only information that is interesting for us, requiring filtering methods or SPARQL queries as a preprocessing step.

JSON schema [47] on the other hand would allow us to give a better definition of the expected JSON object itself, but tends to be cumbersome to describe larger objects and lacks proper integration of semantic data.

Other approaches to derive non-semantic data objects from RDF knowledge graphs investigated [2,23] did not provide the necessary means for our intentions to enforce restrictions on the structure of the generated JSON or the exact definition of key names to use.

For this reason, we propose our own solution $POSER^7$ [59] to provide data mapping from RDF graphs into a JSON object, following the structure given by transformation rules formulated in terms of a minimal JSON ontology. Both the structure as well as the information we are interested in from a given knowledge graph are described in RDF. For the structure of the JSON object itself we use a slim ontology describing both the hiearchy of the the JSON object as well as the connection to the actual data in terms of OWL classes and properties. A *datatype header* allows for specifying the filters or queries used to extract relevant information from RDF input.

---

[6] https://github.com/carml/carml.
[7] https://github.com/spidan/poser.

These transformation rules can be injected into a semantic support point, analogously to how we provide RML mapping files for mapping non-RDF sources to RDF.

Via connection components in the support points, implementing standard communication methods like HTTP or listening to event streams, RDF data is read from the semantic level only when explicitly asked for by an actor, relevant information is extracted, transformed to JSON according to the transformation rules, and again provided to systems on the system layer via a connection component.

4.2 Integration of a Semantic MAS

As the actor making use of the existence of the semantic fabric, woven by our support points, we integrate a semantic multi agent system into an automotive production system, aggregating data from heterogeneous data sources, exploiting the semantic representation by performing reasoning operations and deriving optimized production plans that are again provided to different elements on the system level.

Examples for agent systems capable of working on semantic data are the semantic web-based MAS platform SEAGENT [20] introduced in 2005, the system of Sabbatini et al. [52], in which OWL and RDF knowledge graphs are used to train machine learning systems to realize learning agents in the Semantic Web or [16] in which a web-based MAS for manufacturing is introduced, interacting with Linked-Data and Web-of-Things environments to develop new behaviors from the semantic environment. However, for our purposes these systems are often too strictly tailored to specific applications and require adaptation to exploit the benefits of working on semantic data sources to an extent that we need. For this reason we decided to use our own semantic Multi Agent System *AJAN* [3].

For additional information on AJAN and its capabilities, we'd like to refer you to previous works where it has been used in various Semantic Web and non-Semantic Web based environments. For example, in an smart living environment in which agents use the W3C Web of Things (WoT) architecture (see [1]), to optimize the production of a virtual factory floor using an AJAN-based MAS (see [63]), to coordinate language courses (see [3]), or to control simulated human-robot collaboration scenarios (see [4]).

4.3 Application Scenario

The EU-funded AIToC[8] project developed an assistance system (see Fig. 3) for on-site workers and production planners in the automotive sector. A key component is the Operation Reasoner (see Fig. 4), an agent-based planner using

---

[8] EU-Project AIToC: aitoc.eu/.

the MAS-framework AJAN[9,10] to generate assembly plans for visualization and verification.

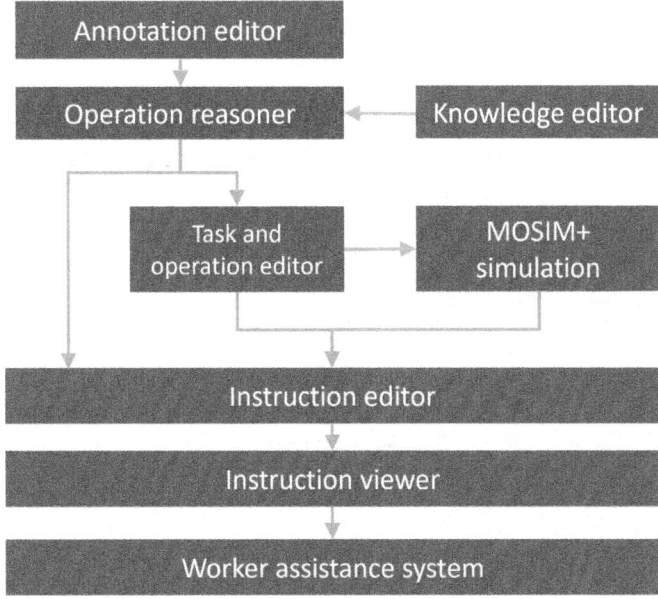

Fig. 3. Assistance Pipelinem as introduced in [60].

The Operation Reasoner is a Web Service combining general process rules and specific product annotations to derive required assembly plans using the Answer Set Programming (ASP) [68] solver clingo[11] Based on previously defined product descriptions as an input for clingo, the Operation Reasoner derives possible assembly plans from resulting stable models. Product descriptions, including annotated 3D models of assembly parts, process definitions and constraints, are given in either JSON, AutomationML[12] (XML), RDF or ASP format. Every input needs to be transformed to RDF in order to be processable by AJAN.

The fact that the required aggregated and homogenized planning problem is contained in the agent's knowledge enables the AJAN-based ASP-reasoning [5] of instructions in the next step. The generated assembly plans are made available to other components and services within the project architecture by translating back into JSON, using the *POSER* approach introduced in 4.1. This

---

[9] AJAN on GitHub: github.com/aantakli/AJAN-service.
[10] Operation Reasoner AJAN-model (ZIP-File) including RML and POSER mapping descriptions: github.com/aantakli/AJAN-packages/blob/main/packages/Operation_Reasoner.ajan.
[11] ASP Solver clingo: https://potassco.org/clingo/.
[12] https://www.automationml.org/.

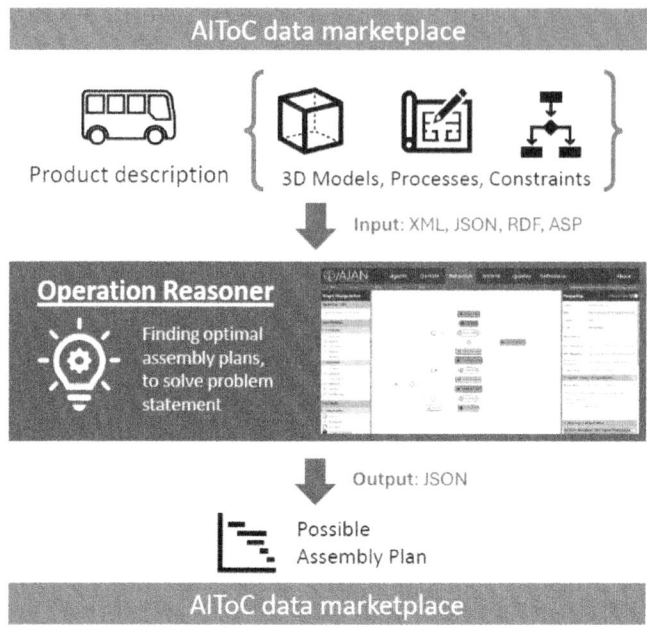

Fig. 4. Operation Reasoner [60].

step is necessary for the generated plans to be usable by other services in our application (see Fig. 3).

The first step of the Operation Reasoner, reading of heterogeneous product descriptions, is a good example to demonstrate the employed data processing steps.

Using a special behavior tree (BT), an operation reasoner agent collects data from the system layer. The agent receives an instruction to generate optimal assembly plans and is refered to the data sources relevant for the reasoning and planning task. Information is then extracted by semantic queries also providing the *transform rule injection routes*, as defined in Sect. 4.1, in BT node property fields: *Data Mapping*, *Endpoint Mapping* and *Response Mapping*. This is done in form of endpoints to read the respective mapping data from. Via a *SPARQL Construct query*, the information relevant for an API call on system level, is collected from the agent's knowledge base, transformed to a proper JSON object matching the recipients API.

An excerpt of the POSER mapping used to extract the correct data from the semantic layer is shown in Fig. 5, an example of the JSON object to be generated is given in Fig. 6. For the sake of brevity, we did not include the full API transform definition. Now we have all necessary information in the correct format to request further context information from a separate data storage, the response of which is again received by the agent and mapped back to RDF via RML, needed for the semantic assembly planning task that follows.

```
: InputDataType_Content {
    json : EntryPoint a ar : Message ;
       ar : action   ar : Action ;
       ar : project  ar : Project ;
       ar : file     ar : File ;
       ar : email    ar : EMail ;
       ar : password ar : Password .

     ar : Action   ar : value   iots : Number .
     ar : Project  ar : value   iots : Number .
     ar : File     ar : value   iots : Number .
     ar : EMail    ar : value   iots : Number .
     ar : Password ar : value   iots : Number .
}
```

Fig. 5. Data types to be used to determine the specific values in a generated JSON object [60].

```
{
        "action": "getFileAsJSON",
        "project": 17,
        "file": "context_information.lp",
        "email": "X.X@example.com",
        "password": "asfkalnknakfsnfjb55"
}
```

Fig. 6. Example of JSON object to be generated [60].

5   Extending the Industry 4.0 Use Case to an AAS Driven Environment

In order to provide the description of and the data provided by an asset in an *Industry 4.0* [33] environment, the Asset Administration shell has emerged as a standardized framework, predominantly for representing tools and machines.

As our goal is to provide proper planning results for work plans intended for human workers, these human workers with their individual skills and limitations should be taken into consideration while planning as well. Describing a human worker is a significantly more complex problem than describing a machine, as no two human beings are exactly the same, and as the skills a human worker has, including their expert knowledge, is much more diverse than the limited skill set of a standardized machine.

While the AAS provides a standardized approach of representing actors in a heterogeneous environment and in theory provides the means to also describe a human worker, setting up an such a complex AAS based environment can be cumbersome. In order to properly following the AAS paradigm, every actor, every data source needs to be described by an AAS, requiring properly served AAS models even for things that are not an asset in the actual sense, like pure data containers. AAS are already designed with exploiting semantics in mind, providing *semantic identifiers* for shells and submodels, and following a general structure that is also reflected in the RAMI ontology[13]. However, accessing and using this semantic information is a difficult task. One major drawback we see in using a collection of separate Asset Administration Shells is the lack of a proper query language and the lack of proper data aggregation.

In our case, human workers, available work places on the shop floor, tools to be used by the workers and the description of the skills and capabilities of a specific worker are, by design, described in separate AAS, each referencing each other. In order for the operation reasoner to do its job, it would be necessary to every time collect data from each separate AAS from the AAS server, traverse the distinct AAS to find the necessary information, potentially find links to other AAS there, aggregate the data, search for relevant information in this aggregated data and then provide it to the operation reasoner in a proper format.

With the use of semantic support points, we can already specify what information we are interested in the corresponding mappings and use the benefits of linked data and semantic queries on the resulting knowledge graphs instead. The data extracted in that way can then easily be provided to the operation reasoner.

5.1 Ontological Representation of AAS

As already briefly introduced in Sect. 2, combining the Asset Administration Shell with semantic information is a widely used concept, starting with the AAS model itself being based on the Reference Architecture Model for Industry 4.0 (RAMI) [55]. The corresponding ontology allows for describing the structure of an AAS in a semantic manner, along with references to other semantic entities. Moreover, the intention of thinking about semantic meaning of AAS models reflects in the existence of a semantic identifier for administration shells, submodels and properties. However, a semantic connection beyond the taxonomy given by the AAS structure is not really made within a plain AAS. Especially information beyond the asset described itself along with its interaction offers and relevant data values, in our case information about the nature of how to perform a certain task including its pre and post conditions, feels counterintuitive to be modeled in an AAS and cumbersome to replicate in every AAS that needs this information. In order to reduce the effort of requesting data concerning concepts shared by multiple AAS, and giving us the option to model knowledge at a central point in our environment in a more natural manner, we replicated the information contained in and needed for worker tasks in form of a separate use case ontology[14] that can easily be connected to relevant RAMI concepts using the corresponding properties.

5.2 Application of the Semantic Support Points Concept

An officially approved and implemented standard of an AAS environment in which various AAS files can be managed, made available in different formats and

---
[13] https://github.com/i40-Tools/RAMIOntology.
[14] https://github.com/spidan/WorkerAASOntology.

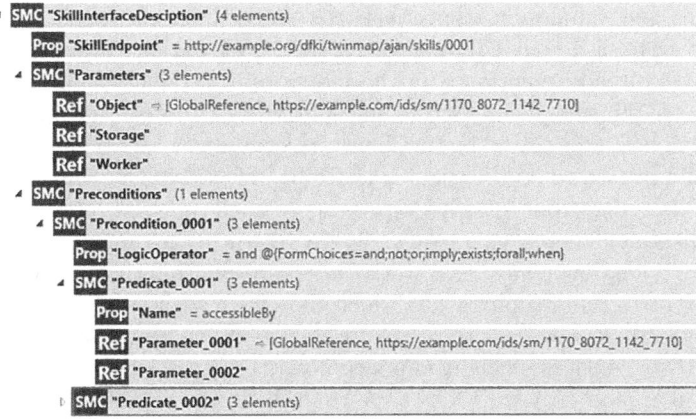

Fig. 7. Asset Administration Shell modeling worker skills and capabilities.

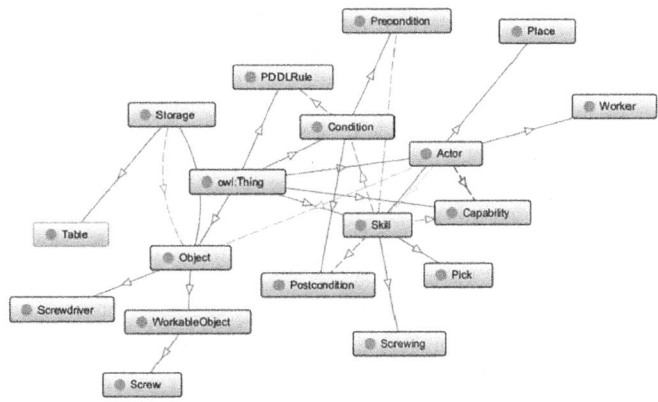

Fig. 8. Ontological representation of the worker AAS.

manipulated is not yet published. As described in the previous chapter, there are official AAS/JSON, AAS/XML, AASX and AAS/RDF ontologies, vocabularies and file formats available to define a AAS, but their respective translations are not yet fully available from official sources. However, there are works or projects that try to fill these gaps and also expand the AAS language space or make proposals for these that are still in the standardization process. The Eclipse BaSyx[15] platform, which has been under development for years to implement an environment for the creation of Industry 4.0 applications, for example, has begun to expand its platform with the advent of the AAS. It offers repositories to store

---

[15] https://github.com/eclipse-basyx.

AAS shells and submodels respectively, to query them via REST or to change states, as well as a web UI to directly view information of the hosted AAS. However, as already mentioned in the motivation, no query language for AAS is offered on the server side, which means that the problem of finding wanted information has to be solved by the client. Accordingly, all AAS information must be read and processed on the client side. To be able to read a complete shell with its submodels, e.g. from a BaSyx repository, a shell must be retrieved and then its linked submodels must be read individually via REST for data aggregation. Here, BaSyx supports only AAS/JSON as the response format. However, if you want to apply a more sophisticated query language such as SPARQL to a AAS repository or link a AAS with other ontologies, it makes sense to describe the AAS in RDF, which is officially supported via the AAS/RDF OWL ontology[16]. Since the mapping of AAS/JSON to AAS/RDF is not yet offered by the official side, third-party solutions must be used. On the one hand, a direct mapping from AAS/JSON to AAS/RDF can be implemented with RML if the mapping files are made available to an agent. In this case, however, the mapping can also be done programmatically, for example, by using the `py-aas-rdf`[17] Python library, which is an open source project to implement this mapping in both directions (Fig. 7).

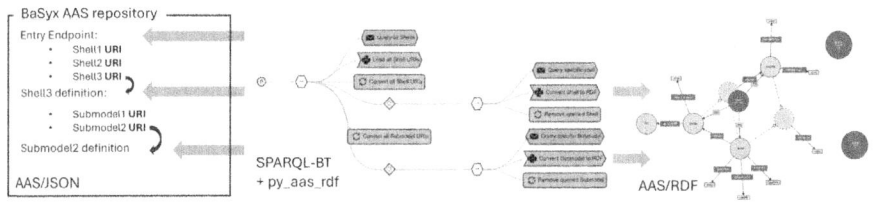

Fig. 9. Translating AAS/JSON to AAS/RDF.

In order to prepare the MAS framework *AJAN* for use with AAS, its existing Python interface was extended with the above-mentioned py-aas-rdf library in order to be able to translate single shells as well as submodels with their properties, etc. from AAS/JSON to AAS/RDF. The logic or SPARQL-BT that in turn queries the AAS repository endpoints successively, for example to read in all AAS files with their linked submodels and then store them in an RDF triplestore, is shown in Fig. 9. As can be seen in the middle section of the figure, the SPARQL-BT first queries all shell endpoints and then translates and saves all

---

[16] https://github.com/admin-shell-io/aas-specs/blob/master/schemas/rdf/rdf-ontology.ttl.
[17] https://github.com/mhrimaz/py-aas-rdf.

shells and submodels to RDF in two loops. To do so, the SPARQL-BT traverses through a respective mapped shell definition and, as soon as a new endpoint, whether to a shell or submodel, is discovered, it is queried, translated and saved into the agents knowledge. As a result, the AJAN agent has access to all queried AAS information via SPARQL. This means that it is no longer necessary to search through all AAS files one after the other for specific values; instead, the aggregated AAS's can be queried and filtered according to specific parameters of interest using a SPARQL query, as shown in Fig. 10. In this example, all workers AAS are read out according to their registered absences. And further narrowed down with a SPARQL FILTER according to absences before the month of May. This simple example is intended to illustrate the more intuitive handling of AAS through SPARQL when they are available in RDF.

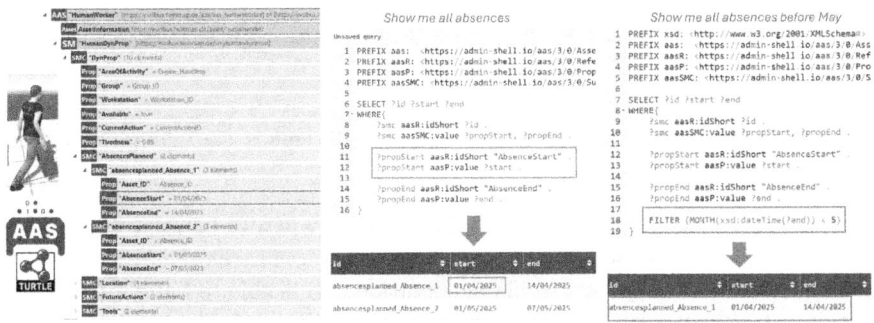

Fig. 10. Query worker AAS/RDF using SPARQL.

For the AJAN agent, it also means that it can now access a new standard, which continues to establish itself in industry, that enables it to interact directly with machines or physical assets as well as logical assets, by, for example interpreting their Assets Interface Description[18] to establish a native communication between the agent and the asset. By following the semantic support point concepts introduced in Sect. 3 we managed to add a semantic layer where needed to a fully standardized environment, without the need to change or extend the system on a level that would interfere with the standard.

---

[18] https://industrialdigitaltwin.org/wp-content/uploads/2024/01/IDTA-02017-1-0_Submodel_Asset-Interfaces-Description.pdf.

5.3 Integrating the Operation Reasoner Into the AAS Environment

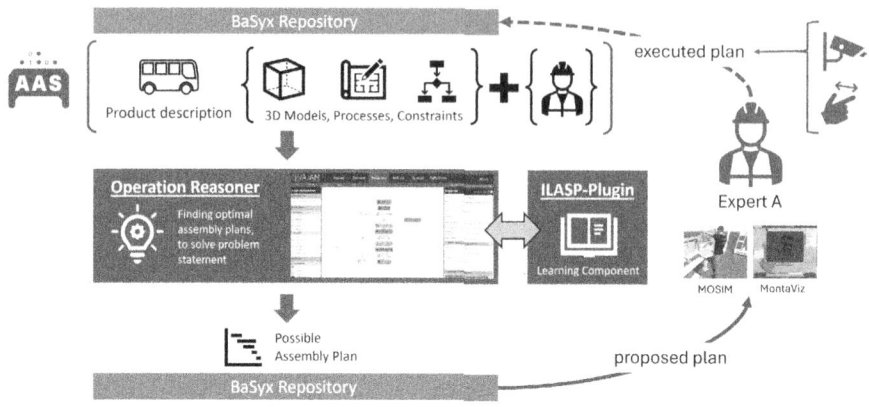

Fig. 11. Extension of the operation reasoner to handle AAS information.

As in the AIToC project, the Operation Reasoner will also be used in the TwinMaP[19,20] project. In TwinMap, as illustrated in Fig. 11, the operation reasoner is extended to include adaptive plan generation and is able to handle AAS information. The adaptation is achieved by learning logical described observations of executed assembly plans:

In the first aspect, the integrated logical machine learning approach ILASP [35] is learning hypotheses or generating ASP rules to realize the dynamic adaptation of assembly plan generation by incorporating expert knowledge from workers into the operation reasoner.

But the latter aspect in particular is of great importance, as AAS is being strongly promoted by the german government and is increasingly being used in productive industries such as automotive, or at least preparations and tests are being carried out for this purpose. In the TwinMaP project in particular, AAS is to be used to describe the manual assembly environment and its processes. The AAS is not only used to describe tools, product parts or the environment, but also the worker who has to carry out the activities. In AIToC the operation reasoner primarily generates work plans by considering only information on the product to be produced and the associated actions, e.g. positioning or screwing, to be carried out. In contrast to AIToC, the information required for planning is to be standardized and made available via the AAS within TwinMaP. This enables the operation reasoner to work on a homogenized data infrastructure and to integrate more relevant data from existing data records into the planning without having to

---

[19] Funded by the German Federal Ministry for Economic Affairs and Climate Action (BMWK).
[20] https://twinmap.de/.

describe them manually in ASP. To access the semantic information of physical as well as logical assets of the manual assembly environment, the operation reasoner uses the SPARQL-BT introduced in the previous subsection. This information is then translated into ASP rules in the same way as the mapping procedure implemented in the AIToC project. In addition, if the required information can only be retrieved directly via the respective asset, the operation reasoner has a description of how it can communicate directly with the asset and request the said information via the Asset Interface Description described in the respective asset AAS. As already mentioned in Sect. 5.1, further semantic information can be linked to an AAS via the semantic identifier, for example. This is advantageous if, for example, a standardized submodel does not contain all the information required for a task. We also use this option in the operation reasoner, for example to provide additional planning information required for the operation reasoner. Thus, we are incorporating the worker AAS ontology (see Fig. 8) into planning to have a deeper knowledge of what a worker is capable of and which input is needed in order to execute a capability. For example, TwinMap does not yet have an AAS for tables, which in turn are a subclass of a storage. However, such class information is relevant for planning if it is planned that an object, for example a screwdriver, must be put down in an intermediate step, for which it requires a storage location.

6 Using the Support Point Concept for Data Alignment in Standardized Dataspaces

Setting up a data space following *Eclipse Dataspace Component (EDC)*[21] specifications already provides a lot of the features we are looking for when it comes to interoperable data exchange: data is easily discoverable via extensive meta data catalogues, communication between participants can securely be negotiated and connections between participants are dynamically established. However, we see a lack in interoperability when it comes to the data exchange itself. While some expert knowledge about the data a certain asset is providing is given via the asset definitions, none of this knowledge is actually used to facilitate data exchange in the sense that data discovered and requested is easily processable on the client's side. Every participant needs to make sure to provide a proper data consumer for every data object they receive.

By applying the semantic support point concept, we go one step further and use the already given meta data information of the assets and embed selected data values into a knowledge graph using that meta data. With that, the meta data describing an asset is not only a means to find the data, but already provides a clear specification of the data format itself.

---

[21] https://eclipse-edc.github.io/.

6.1 EDC Assets

```
{
  "@context": {
    "edc": "https://w3id.org/edc/v0.0.1/ns/"
  },
  "@id": "79d9c360-476b-47e8-8925-0ffbeba5aec2",
  "properties": {
    "somePublicProp": "a very interesting value"
  },
  "privateProperties": {
    "secretKey": "this is secret information, never tell it to
        the dataspace!"
  },
  "dataAddress": {
    "type": "HttpData",
    "baseUrl": "http://localhost:8080/test"
  }
}
```

Fig. 12. Example of simple EDC asset, taken from (https://eclipse-edc.github.io/documentation/for-contributors/control-plane/entities/#1-assets).

In a dataspace environment according to EDC specifications, the access to data is managed via defining *assets*, describing the access point to the data in terms of an endpoint.

This endpoint can be, for example, a simple REST endpoint, a possibility to subscribe to an event stream or execute a call to a more complex service implementation providing the results of sophisticated computations. A catalogue manages the available assets in so called *datasets*, describing their functionality and the data they provide in terms of meta data, giving a user the possibility to search the catalogue for the data they need and, via the asset description received, negotiate the terms and permissions to receive the data.

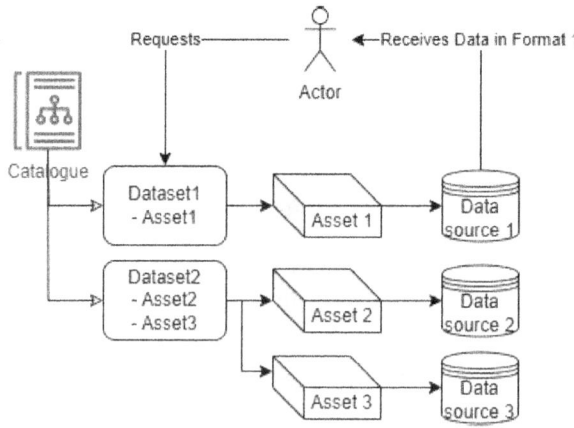

Fig. 13. Simplified communication process with EDC assets.

If a suitable asset is found, however, the communication between the communicating parties is no longer managed by the dataspace environment, nor does it in any way relate to the meta data used in the catalogue to describe the asset, but is happening directly between the parties itself. Any data filtering, alignment and matching needs to be done on client side. Moreover, if a dataset consists of multiple assets, the actor would just receive the separate endpoints of all assets, leaving them with the need to acquire, aggregate and process the data on their own.

See Fig. 12 for a simplified schematic depiction of this process. In this example, the actor requests the catalogue for assets providing the data they need, based on meta data given. Receiving `Dataset 1` as suitable match, the actor is provided with access to `Asset 1`, after making sure to have the necessary permissions, as described by the dataspace data governance and privacy concepts of an EDC environment. After the connection is established, the communication happens between the actor and `Datasource 1` directly. If the actor would have requested data according to the data provided by dataset 2, they would have been provided connections to both `Datasource 2` and `Datasource 3`, referenced by `Asset 2` and `Asset 3` respectively.

6.2 Semantic EDC Assets

In order to facilitate data exchange and processing for an actor using data sources within the data space, we want to provide an actual meaningful view onto the data with the option of on the fly transform to a data format the client can understand. To this end, we introduce semantic support points on top of the raw data sources, registered in the dataspace as a *semantic asset*. These semantic assets follow exactly the same rules and restrictions for assets as given in the EDC specification, especially concerning data access, security and governance, but instead of just receiving data endpoints of relevant data sources, the client is provided with customized data tailored to its needs via semantic transformations. In order to turn an EDC asset into a semantic asset, acting as a semantic support point, the following fields need to be present in the asset description:

Input Transformation. An endpoint that can be used to load an appropriate definition of how to generate the RDF data from the input data, e.g. a RML mapping file

Input Sources. The sources from which to collect the input data

Mapping Endpoint. Instead of using a physical actual data endpoint, we point to the implementation providing mapping functionality

Output Transformation. If needed, a transform rule to generate non-RDF data from the RDF graph generated by the input transformation can be provided.

Instead of pointing to raw data sources as shown in Fig. 13 and the asset definition in listing 12, the `baseUrl` of the `dataAddress` property of the asset refers to the endpoint of the transform service. The transform service then connects to the data sources specified in the asset properties, using the transform rules referenced there, fetches the data and performs the specified transforms. The user then receives the result of this transform to RDF, or, if an output transformation is specified, the result of the corresponding back transform to a non-RDF format.

For the user, the transform service is just an asset like any other asset, providing the data they are looking for and that is discoverable via the catalogue. Non-semantic assets are still available and, from a client perspective, indistinguishable from semantic assets, leaving the original dataspace and its functionality fully intact (Fig. 14).

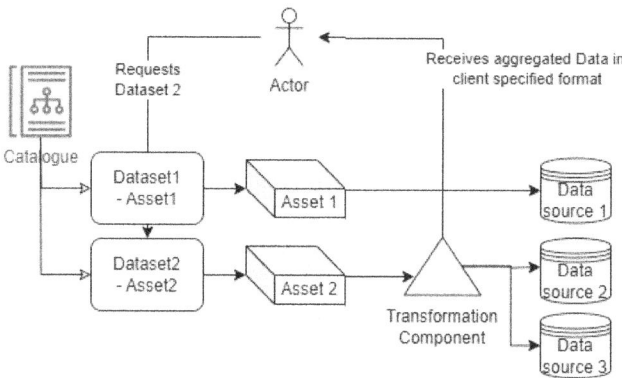

Fig. 14. Using semantic support points as assets to abstract from the underlying data sources.

6.3 Transformation Components

For transforming data from XML, CSV or JSON based formats we use a RML^{22} based Spring service, forwarding requests from the client to a legacy endpoint while reading the mapping file from the *Input Transformation* property of the EDC asset, as suggested in [61]. This results in an RDF graph as the data output of any underlying data source on the system layer, generated on the fly on demand based on a separately managable knowledge representation of the client's data interpretation and intended use, thus complying to non-invasive, non-persisting and domain independent properties introduced in Sect. 3. If an output transformation is needed, we follow the *POSER* [59] approach, again managing transformation files in a separate repository and referencing them via the *output transformation* property of the asset. It's easy to see that semantic assets are decoupled, as each asset only refers to data sources on the system layer and does not depend on the availability of any other EDC assets, and distributed, as an asset only acts as an access point to a data space, leaving

---

[22] http://www.rml.io.

the actual communication between the participants to the respective clients and service, as by design of dataspace connectors and assets according to the EDC specification.

Note that we also used a similar implementation for data mappings in the early use case demonstrated in Sect. 4. This is a nice demonstration of the power of this approach: the actual mapping service implementations are minimal and reusable, and almost domain and architecture independent. Adaption to new environments happens on knowledge modelling level, writing the transformation files, not on implementation level to get data exchange itself running.

7 Conclusion and Discussion

In [60], we introduced the concept of distributed semantic support points, minimal service implementations as optional data offer on top of existing environments to abstract from interfaces and data models of heterogenous systems. Data transform rules used by the transform services are modeled in a semantic fashion, allowing for the use of actual expert knowledge when it comes to the description of data and interfaces. Transform rules and the resulting knowledge graphs are designed in such a way that the line between data and meta data is blurred and explicit, specific data values are immediately embedded into its own meta data and extended knowledge about that data. This semantic data format opens the doors to provide full semantic reasoning and query power on orginially non-semantic data, without changing any existing interface or enforcing a communication or middleware framework. A first proof of concept was given in [60] and summarized in this paper.

On top of that, in order to demonstrate the versatility of the approach and also put emphasis on the claim of being non-invasive and communication paradigm agnostic, we extended the use case of using support points in a purely heterogeneous environment to an environment relying on an established standard, the Asset Administration Shell. Using Semantic Support Points allowed us to fill the gaps we faced in a pure as-is AAS environment by extending the plain AAS world with semantic query- and data aggregation capabilities, resulting in an reduction of complexity and effort when it comes to data discovery and aggregation, and adding powerful semantic query capabilities to our data the AAS does not provide out of the box.

In addition we suggested a concept for semantic dataspace asset, based on the EDC dataspace specification. Without violating dataspace specific architecture, security or data governance principles, we managed to add a semantic interoperability layer on top of the data sources present in a given dataspace, practically invisible to the user and indistinguishable from regular assets within the dataspace.

In all cases, the actual implementation effort to create the transformation service was minimal and existing service implementations could be reused and deployed as is. As intended by our approach of Semantic Support Points, the actual work was mostly shifted to the task of pure knowledge modeling in the shape of semantic transform files.

7.1 Discussion and Future Work

The semantic assets presented in Sect. 6 are still lacking extensive testing concerning the real world applicability, especially concerning security aspects for data sources possibly distributed over several dataspaces. In that case, further methods to ensure access to the underlying data sources only by authorized clients must be investigated and employed.

Writing the transform rules has proven to be a tedious and complicated task. For transforming non-RDF to RDF data, with our current implementations RML mapping files need to be written which turned out to be counterintuitive to understand, even for people with basic RDF experience, and tend to get very large in terms of lines of code, as every relation in the desired RDF graph needs to be explicitly modeled. Furthermore, complex relationships between classes in the desired knowledge graph, or complex hierarchies or collections on source data side, pose a problem due to limitations in RML itself, mostly when it comes to n:m relationships, due to the backwards compatibility to R2RML, and thus restrictions of relational databases. For future work we would like to keep the necessary manually modeled mappings as minimal as possible and investigate possibilities to gather information from the underlying ontologies by methods of graph completion or graph embeddings.

On the side of extracting data from the semantic layer and transforming it back to non-RDF formats, more work needs to be done as *POSER* does not yet support concepts like ordered lists or proper collections. In order to allow for more complex JSON objects to be generated, using query languages like *GraphQL*[23] along with a simple service extracting the data from the semantic layer via SPARQL queries seems like a promising approach and is subject to future work.

As mentioned in our original paper [60], we are eager to bridge the gap between data and its semantics even further by tying meta data catalogues for service discovery and mapping instructions closer together. The concept of dataspaces with an established, standardized service description and discovery functionality seems like a very promising step into this direction and will be investigated further.

Further work is still necessary in terms of runtime behavior and resources needed for time or resource critical applications. While, to our anecdotal findings, mapping instructions provided do have an impact on resources needed, and the mapping procedures themselves as queries to extract interesting data are more time intensive than plain in memory computations, compared to systems based on the AAS we very likely can expect an improvement in terms of computation times. Further work will be done to properly analyse and compare these findings.

Acknowledgments. This work has been supported by the German Federal Ministry for Economic Affairs and Climate Action (BMWK) in the projects *ForeSightNEXT* (01MK23001G) and *TwinMap* (13IK028J).

---

[23] https://graphql.org/.

Disclosure of Interests. The authors have no competing interests to declare that are relevant to the content of this article.

References

1. Alberternst, S., et al.: From things into clouds–and back. In: 2021 IEEE/ACM 21st International Symposium on Cluster, Cloud and Internet Computing (CCGrid), pp. 668–675. IEEE (2021)
2. Allocca, C., Gougousis, A.: A preliminary investigation of reversing RML: from an RDF dataset to its column-based data source. Biodivers. Data J. (3), e5464 (2015)
3. Antakli, A., Kazimov, A., Spieldenner, D., Rojas, G.E.J., Zinnikus, I., Klusch, M.: AJAN: an engineering framework for semantic web-enabled agents and multi-agent systems. In: Mathieu, P., Dignum, F., Novais, P., De la Prieta, F. (eds.) PAAMS 2023. LNCS, vol. 13955, pp. 15–27. Springer, Cham (2023). https://doi.org/10.1007/978-3-031-37616-0_2
4. Antakli, A., et al.: Agent-based web supported simulation of human-robot collaboration. In: Proceedings of the 15th International Conference on Web Information Systems and Technologies (WEBIST), pp. 88–99 (2019)
5. Antakli, A., Vozniak, I., Lipp, N., Klusch, M., Müller, C.: HAIL: modular agent-based pedestrian imitation learning. In: Dignum, F., Corchado, J.M., De La Prieta, F. (eds.) PAAMS 2021. LNCS (LNAI), vol. 12946, pp. 27–39. Springer, Cham (2021). https://doi.org/10.1007/978-3-030-85739-4_3
6. Antoniazzi, F., Viola, F.: Building the semantic web of things through a dynamic ontology. IEEE Internet Things J. **6**(6), 10560–10579 (2019)
7. Bader, S., Barnstedt, E., Bedenbender, H., Berres, B., Billmann, M., Ristin, M.: Details of the asset administration shell-part 1: the exchange of information between partners in the value chain of industrie 4.0 (version 3.0 RC02) (2022)
8. Bader, S.R., Maleshkova, M.: The semantic asset administration shell. In: Acosta, M., Cudré-Mauroux, P., Maleshkova, M., Pellegrini, T., Sack, H., Sure-Vetter, Y. (eds.) SEMANTiCS 2019. LNCS, vol. 11702, pp. 159–174. Springer, Cham (2019). https://doi.org/10.1007/978-3-030-33220-4_12
9. Berners-Lee, T., Hendler, J., Lassila, O.: The semantic web. Sci. Am. **284**(5), 34–43 (2001)
10. Bernhard, A.T., Blumhofer, B., Ruskowski, M., Wagner, A., Luxenburger, A., Porta, D.: Leverage asset administration shells to support artificial intelligence planning. In: 2024 IEEE 29th International Conference on Emerging Technologies and Factory Automation (ETFA). IEEE (2024)
11. Braud, A., Fromentoux, G., Radier, B., Grand, O.: The road to European digital sovereignty with Gaia-X and IDSA. IEEE Netw. **35**(2), 4–5 (2021)
12. Breitman, K.K., Casanova, M.A., Truszkowski, W.: Ontology in computer science. In: Semantic Web: Concepts, Technologies and Applications, pp. 17–34 (2007)
13. Brodny, J., Tutak, M.: Digitalization of small and medium-sized enterprises and economic growth: evidence for the EU-27 countries. J. Open Innov.: Technol. Mark. Complexity **8**(2), 67 (2022)
14. Charpenay, V., Käbisch, S., Kosch, H.: Introducing thing descriptions and interactions: an ontology for the web of things. In: SR+ SWIT@ ISWC, pp. 55–66 (2016)
15. Charpenay, V., Käbisch, S., Kosch, H.: Semantic data integration on the web of things. In: Proceedings of the 8th International Conference on the Internet of Things, pp. 1–8 (2018)

16. Ciortea, A., Mayer, S., Michahelles, F.: Repurposing manufacturing lines on the fly with multi-agent systems for the web of things. In: AAMAS, pp. 813–822 (2018)
17. Curry, E.: Real-Time Linked Dataspaces: Enabling Data Ecosystems for Intelligent Systems. Springer, Cham (2020)
18. Curry, E.: Dataspaces: fundamentals, principles, and techniques. In: Curry, E. (ed.) Real-time Linked Dataspaces, pp. 45–62. Springer, Cham (2020). https://doi.org/10.1007/978-3-030-29665-0_3
19. Deuter, A., Pethig, F.: The digital twin theory. Industrie 4.0 Management. **35**(1), 27–30 (2019)
20. Dikenelli, O., Erdur, R.C., Gumus, O.: Seagent: a platform for developing semantic web based multi agent systems. In: Proceedings of the Fourth International Joint Conference on Autonomous Agents and Multiagent Systems, pp. 1271–1272 (2005)
21. Dimou, A., et al.: Mapping hierarchical sources into RDF using the RML mapping language. In: 2014 IEEE International Conference on Semantic Computing, pp. 151–158. IEEE (2014)
22. Franklin, M., Halevy, A., Maier, D.: From databases to dataspaces: a new abstraction for information management. ACM SIGMOD Rec. **34**(4), 27–33 (2005)
23. Grassi, M., Scrocca, M., Carenini, A., Comerio, M., Celino, I.: Composable semantic data transformation pipelines with chimera (2023)
24. Halevy, A., Franklin, M., Maier, D.: Principles of dataspace systems. In: Proceedings of the Twenty-Fifth ACM SIGMOD-SIGACT-SIGART Symposium on Principles of Database Systems, pp. 1–9 (2006)
25. Heiler, S.: Semantic interoperability. ACM Comput. Surv. (CSUR) **27**(2), 271–273 (1995)
26. Hildebrand, M., Tourkogiorgis, I., Psarommatis, F., Arena, D., Kiritsis, D.: A method for converting current data to RDF in the era of industry 4.0. In: Ameri, F., Stecke, K.E., von Cieminski, G., Kiritsis, D. (eds.) APMS 2019, Part I. IAICT, vol. 566, pp. 307–314. Springer, Cham (2019). https://doi.org/10.1007/978-3-030-30000-5_39
27. Hitzler, P.: A review of the semantic web field. Commun. ACM **64**(2), 76–83 (2021)
28. Hozdić, E.: Smart factory for industry 4.0: a review. Int. J. Mod. Manuf. Technol. **7**(1), 28–35 (2015)
29. Jafari, M., Kavousi-Fard, A., Chen, T., Karimi, M.: A review on digital twin technology in smart grid, transportation system and smart city: challenges and future. IEEE Access **11**, 17471–17484 (2023)
30. Khan, H.H., et al.: Challenges for sustainable smart city development: a conceptual framework. Sustain. Dev. **28**(5), 1507–1518 (2020)
31. Khanna, A., Kaur, S.: Internet of things (IoT), applications and challenges: a comprehensive review. Wireless Pers. Commun. **114**, 1687–1762 (2020)
32. Lan, Q., et al.: What is semantic communication? A view on conveying meaning in the era of machine intelligence. J. Commun. Inf. Netw. **6**(4), 336–371 (2021)
33. Lasi, H., Fettke, P., Kemper, H.-G., Feld, T., Hoffmann, M.: Industrie 4.0. Wirtschaftsinformatik **56**(4), 261–264 (2014). https://doi.org/10.1007/s11576-014-0424-4
34. Lassila, O., Hendler, J., Berners-Lee, T.: The semantic web. Sci. Am. **284**(5), 34–43 (2001)
35. Law, M., Russo, A., Broda, K.: The ILASP system for inductive learning of answer set programs. CoRR abs/2005.00904 (2020). https://arxiv.org/abs/2005.00904
36. Lee, I., Lee, K.: The internet of things (IoT): applications, investments, and challenges for enterprises. Bus. Horiz. **58**(4), 431–440 (2015)

37. Lu, Y., Asghar, M.R.: Semantic communications between distributed cyber-physical systems towards collaborative automation for smart manufacturing. J. Manuf. Syst. **55**, 348–359 (2020)
38. Manola, F., Miller, E., McBride, B., et al.: RDF primer. W3C Recommendation **10**(1-107), 6 (2004)
39. McGuinness, D.L., Van Harmelen, F., et al.: OWL web ontology language overview. W3C Recommendation **10**(10), 2004 (2004)
40. Meckler, S., Dorsch, R., Henselmann, D., Harth, A.: The web and linked data as a solid foundation for dataspaces. In: Companion Proceedings of the ACM Web Conference 2023, pp. 1440–1446 (2023)
41. Méndez, S.J.R., Haller, A., Omran, P.G., Wright, J., Taylor, K.: J2RM: an ontology-based JSON-to-RDF mapping tool. In: ISWC (Demos/Industry), pp. 368–373 (2020)
42. Moreno, T., Sobral, T., Almeida, A., Soares, A.L., Azevedo, A.: Semantic asset administration shell towards a cognitive digital twin. In: Silva, F.J.G., Ferreira, L.P., Sá, J.C., Pereira, M.T., Pinto, C.M.A. (eds) FAIM 2023. LNME, pp. 679–686. Springer, Cham (2023). https://doi.org/10.1007/978-3-031-38165-2_79
43. Ngankam, H.K., Pigot, H., Giroux, S.: OntoDomus: a semantic model for ambient assisted living system based on smart homes. Electronics **11**(7), 1143 (2022)
44. Nižetić, S., Šolić, P., Gonzalez-De, D.L.D.I., Patrono, L., et al.: Internet of things (IoT): opportunities, issues and challenges towards a smart and sustainable future. J. Clean. Prod. **274**, 122877 (2020)
45. Padilla-Cuevas, J., Reyes-Ortiz, J.A., Bravo, M.: Ontology-based context event representation, reasoning, and enhancing in academic environments. Future Internet **13**(6), 151 (2021)
46. Pérez-Martínez, J., Hernandez-Gil, F., San Miguel, G., Ruiz, D., Arredondo, M.T.: Analysing associations between digitalization and the accomplishment of the sustainable development goals. Sci. Total Environ. **857**, 159700 (2023)
47. Pezoa, F., Reutter, J.L., Suarez, F., Ugarte, M., Vrgoč, D.: Foundations of JSON schema. In: Proceedings of the 25th International Conference on World Wide Web, pp. 263–273 (2016)
48. Qin, Z., Tao, X., Lu, J., Tong, W., Li, G.Y.: Semantic communications: principles and challenges. arXiv preprint arXiv:2201.01389 (2021)
49. Razzak, F., et al.: The role of semantic web technologies in smart environments. Ph.D. thesis, Politecnico di Torino (2013)
50. Rimaz, M.H., Plociennik, C., Ruskowski, M.: Semantic asset administration shell for circular economy. In: KG4S@ ESWC (2024)
51. Ruta, M., Scioscia, F., Di Sciascio, E.: Enabling the semantic web of things: framework and architecture. In: 2012 IEEE Sixth International Conference on Semantic Computing, pp. 345–347. IEEE (2012)
52. Sabbatini, F., Ciatto, G., Omicini, A.: Semantic web-based interoperability for intelligent agents with psyke. In: Calvaresi, D., Najjar, A., Winikoff, M., Främling, K. (eds) EXTRAAMAS 2022. LNCS, vol. 13283, pp. 124–142. Springer, Cham (2022). https://doi.org/10.1007/978-3-031-15565-9_8
53. Sahoo, S.S., et al.: A survey of current approaches for mapping of relational databases to RDF. W3C RDB2RDF Incubator Group Report **1**, 113–130 (2009)
54. Santofimia, M.J., Fahlman, S.E., Del Toro, X., Moya, F., Lopez, J.C.: A semantic model for actions and events in ambient intelligence. Eng. Appl. Artif. Intell. **24**(8), 1432–1445 (2011)
55. Schweichhart, K.: Reference architectural model industrie 4.0 (rami 4.0). An Introduction **40** (2016)

56. Singh, M., Fuenmayor, E., Hinchy, E.P., Qiao, Y., Murray, N., Devine, D.: Digital twin: origin to future. Appl. Syst. Innov. **4**(2), 36 (2021)
57. Solmaz, G., et al.: Enabling data spaces: Existing developments and challenges. In: Proceedings of the 1st International Workshop on Data Economy, pp. 42–48 (2022)
58. Soori, M., Arezoo, B., Dastres, R.: Internet of things for smart factories in industry 4.0, a review. Internet Things Cyber-Phys. Syst. **3**, 192–204 (2023)
59. Spieldenner, D.: Poser: A semantic payload lowering service. In: WEBIST, pp. 249–256 (2022)
60. Spieldenner, D., Antakli, A., Spieldenner, T., Sahota, H.: Semantic support points for on the fly knowledge encoding in heterogenous systems. In: Proceedings of the 16th International Joint Conference on Knowledge Discovery, Knowledge Engineering and Knowledge Management - Volume 3: KMIS, pp. 26–37. INSTICC, SciTePress (2024). https://doi.org/10.5220/0012919000003838
61. Spieldenner, D., Spieldenner, T.: A smart integration layer for smart city business applications. In: 2020 4th International Conference on Smart Grid and Smart Cities (ICSGSC), pp. 129–135. IEEE (2020)
62. Spieldenner, T.: Linked data as medium for distributed multi-agent systems. Ph.D. thesis, Universität des Saarlandes (2023)
63. Spieldenner, T., Antakli, A.: Behavior trees as executable representation of milner calculus notations. In: 2022 IEEE/WIC/ACM International Joint Conference on Web Intelligence and Intelligent Agent Technology (WI-IAT). IEEE (2022)
64. Sporny, M., Longley, D., Kellogg, G., Lanthaler, M., Lindström, N.: JSON-LD 1.1. W3C Recommendation (2020)
65. Steinbuss, S., Ottradovetz, K., Langkau, J., Punter, M., et al.: IDSA rule book. Technical report, International Data Spaces Association (2021). https://doi.org/10.5281/zenodo.5658294
66. Taye, M.M.: Understanding semantic web and ontologies: theory and applications. arXiv preprint arXiv:1006.4567 (2010)
67. Vdovjak, R., Houben, G.-J.: Providing the semantic layer for WIS design. In: Pidduck, A.B., Ozsu, M.T., Mylopoulos, J., Woo, C.C. (eds.) CAiSE 2002. LNCS, vol. 2348, pp. 584–599. Springer, Heidelberg (2002). https://doi.org/10.1007/3-540-47961-9_40
68. Vladimir, L.: What is answer set programming. In: AAAI, vol. 8 (2008)
69. Wang, J., Yang, Y., Wang, T., Sherratt, R.S., Zhang, J.: Big data service architecture: a survey. J. Internet Technol. **21**(2), 393–405 (2020)
70. Zeng, D., Guo, S., Cheng, Z.: The web of things: a survey. J. Commun. **6**(6), 424–438 (2011)
71. Zillner, S., et al.: Data economy 2.0: from big data value to AI value and a European data space. In: Curry, E., Metzger, A., Zillner, S., Pazzaglia, J.-C., García Robles, A. (eds.) The Elements of Big Data Value, pp. 379–399. Springer, Cham (2021). https://doi.org/10.1007/978-3-030-68176-0_16

From Lessons Learned to Project Triumph: Unveiling the Enablers and Barriers in Construction

Jeffrey Boon Hui Yap(✉)

Universiti Tunku Abdul Rahman, 43000 Kajang, Selangor, Malaysia
bhyap@utar.edu.my

Abstract. In construction project management, the significance of "lessons learned" (LL) is crucial for effective project management and continuous improvement. This study identifies nine values, seven enablers, and eight barriers to LL practices in the construction industry, based on insights from construction professionals in Malaysia. The aim is to highlight the importance of LL practices in improving project success and fostering a culture of ongoing enhancement. Key LL values include avoiding repeated mistakes, improving performance through past lessons, and promoting collaboration within project teams. By prioritising LL practices, organisations can optimise project outcomes, minimise rework and delays, and enhance future project planning and estimation. The study demonstrates that LL practices help prevent the recurrence of past mistakes and improve project performance. Enablers such as peer recognition, a sharing culture, and honouring commitments are vital for creating knowledge-sharing environments that support communication, collaboration, and trust. However, barriers such as interpersonal skill deficits, resource limitations, and varying levels of education and experience hinder LL implementation. Overcoming these barriers requires targeted interventions, including training and resource allocation. This study offers valuable theoretical and practical insights, providing strategies to enhance knowledge management systems, optimise project outcomes, and achieve sustained success in the competitive construction industry.

Keywords: Lessons learned · Knowledge management · Project management · Construction industry · Enablers · Barriers

1 Introduction

The construction industry is a key driver of socioeconomic growth, particularly in developing countries like Malaysia. It contributes significantly to GDP, generates employment, and supports infrastructure development, ultimately raising living standards and fostering urbanisation [1]. The sector also facilitates urbanisation, industrialisation, and improved connectivity, ultimately raising living standards and stimulating related industries. However, the industry faces increasing pressures to deliver projects on time, within budget, and with high quality, while addressing challenges such as inefficiency, resource scarcity, and sustainability [2, 3].

Despite its importance, construction projects often encounter issues such as delays, cost overruns, safety concerns, and poor-quality outcomes. These challenges highlight the need for better project management practices, particularly in the area of Knowledge Management (KM). KM, which involves the creation, sharing, and application of knowledge, is essential to improving project planning and execution [4]. Recognising the value of KM is crucial for overcoming these industry challenges and gaining a competitive edge [3, 5].

In particular, lessons learned (LL) from past projects offer a valuable opportunity to drive continuous improvement. KM helps organisations systematically capture and apply these lessons to refine processes, manage risks, and enhance collaboration. Evidence from both the Malaysian and Portuguese construction industries demonstrate KM's potential in improving project outcomes and fostering innovation [6, 7]. As Disterer [8] aptly observes, "success of projects depends heavily on the right combination of knowledge and experience". In a similar vein, Meredith et al. [9] emphasise the importance of embedding past knowledge into estimates of future project performance.

Since construction companies are knowledge-intensive, generating valuable insights from completed projects, systematically capturing and applying LL offers a key mechanism to address recurring issues and drive continuous improvement. KM enables organisations to refine planning processes, improve cost estimation, manage risks proactively, and enhance collaboration with stakeholders. Evidence from the Malaysian construction industry highlights KM's value in improving quality, enhancing decision-making, and preventing the recurrence of past mistakes [3]. Similarly, Portuguese practitioners recognise KM as a vital asset that anticipates problems, boosts competitiveness, and fosters innovation, with LL from projects and work meetings being the most effective means of knowledge sharing (KS) [5].

By integrating KM into project workflows, the construction industry can unlock significant opportunities for continuous learning and improvement. Effective LL management enhances competencies, supports better decision-making, improves supply chain integration, and increases client satisfaction. This approach is key to transforming construction practices, ensuring safety, and delivering infrastructure that meets stakeholder expectations. As the industry evolves, leveraging KM is no longer optional but a strategic necessity for sustainable growth and long-term value creation [10–12].

This study explores the role of lessons learned in enhancing construction project delivery, identifying critical enablers and barriers to effective KM practices in the industry. The research questions addressed in this study are:

1. Why is it important to capture LL in construction projects?
2. What are the critical enablers of effective LL practices?
3. What barriers hinder the capturing and implementation of LL?

2 Knowledge Management and Lessons Learned in Construction

The construction industry is inherently project-based and requires extensive collaboration among a variety of stakeholders, including architects, engineers, and contractors. Effective communication and collaboration are essential for successful project outcomes. KM facilitates this by ensuring that valuable knowledge is shared, applied, and used to improve both current and future projects [12]. KM's role in the construction sector is vital, especially considering the industry's highly competitive and fragmented nature, where project teams are often temporary and resources limited [11].

The practice of LL is a cornerstone of KM in construction. LL involves capturing insights from past projects - whether successes or failures - and applying them to future projects. This can include insights into "know-what" (what to do), "know-how" (how to do it), and "know-why" (why it works), thereby improving decision-making, fostering innovation, and enhancing operational efficiency [13, 14]. LL practices contribute directly to improved resource allocation, better risk management, and enhanced project planning [14, 15]. They are essential for preventing mistakes from being repeated and fostering a culture of continuous improvement [16, 17].

KM's integration into construction project workflows is crucial for improving collaboration, decision-making, and overall project outcomes. The systematic application of lessons learned not only strengthens internal processes but also leads to better client satisfaction and increased competitiveness in the market.

The construction industry is more fragmented than many other sectors due to its project-based nature and temporary, project-specific teams. Knowledge, whether tacit or explicit, only adds value when actively used. The effective application of knowledge can spur innovation, enhance business performance, and improve client satisfaction. Failing to capture and reuse LL from previous projects increases the likelihood of redundancy, resource waste, and lost profits. As such, KM is essential for operational efficiency and maintaining a competitive edge in the construction industry [18].

Knowledge management (KM) enables organisations to effectively manage and leverage knowledge resources, optimising learning and enhancing project outcomes. Two critical components of KM are knowledge sharing (KS) and lessons learned (LL), which are intrinsically linked. LL practices involve systematically capturing and disseminating insights from past and ongoing projects to inform future decision-making [13]. By integrating the "know-what," "know-how," and "know-why," decision-making is strengthened, allowing construction organisations to proactively anticipate challenges, refine strategies, and drive innovation [14, 15]. This approach empowers stakeholders to "look back to predict the future," aligning expertise for long-term success [7, 19]. The PMBOK Guide also underscores the importance of effective project knowledge management in fostering continuous learning and maximising the value derived from LL [17].

The inherent complexity of construction projects often results in unforeseen challenges. Leveraging knowledge and experience from past projects helps stakeholders address current issues effectively. Yap & Shavarebi [7] highlight that KM through KS can minimise errors and inefficiencies by sharing critical insights across teams, ensuring that valuable lessons are retained and applied [11, 20].

2.1 Enablers of Lessons Learned Practices in the Construction Context

Table 1 outlines the key enablers of LL practices identified in previous research, specifically relevant to the construction industry. These enablers are categorised into those related to individuals and those linked to organisational factors, fostering an environment conducive to KS and organisational growth.

Table 1. Enabling factors for effective LL practices (Source: adapted from [12]).

Ref	Enablers	References
Individual factors		
B1	Sharing culture	[7, 21, 22]
B2	Honouring of commitment	[22–24]
B3	Peer recognition	[22, 24, 25]
B4	Reciprocity and trust	[7, 22, 26]
Organisational factors		
B5	Perceived value	[7, 22, 27]
B6	Financial/ social motivation	[22, 26, 27]
B7	Workplace culture	[7, 27, 28]

Sharing culture is a fundamental enabler of LL practices. When individuals engage with one another and share their tacit knowledge, it creates a learning environment where knowledge is transformed into explicit insights that benefit the organisation. KS not only encourages collaboration within teams but also extends to competitors, a concept known as "coopetition", which allows for the exchange of valuable information, ideas, and technology that can drive innovation and development [7, 21]. A culture that promotes sharing helps individuals improve and boosts overall organisational productivity [22].

Honouring commitment is another crucial enabler. In construction projects, professionals from various departments must work together, and individuals are motivated to stay committed to shared knowledge and solutions. When people honour their commitments to solving issues, it builds trust and fosters collaboration within teams [22, 24]. Leaders who inspire commitment and lead by example help ensure that team members remain engaged and productive, contributing to the project's success [23].

Peer recognition plays a significant role in motivating individuals to contribute to LL practices. Recognition, whether from peers or seniors, encourages individuals to share knowledge and fosters a positive workplace culture [25]. The sense of appreciation for one's contributions boosts confidence and encourages ongoing knowledge sharing. Peer recognition is often more impactful than financial incentives, enhancing the overall collaborative spirit within the organisation [22, 24].

Reciprocity and trust further enhance LL practices. A reciprocal environment, where individuals are willing to share knowledge with those who have supported them, fosters trust and strengthens team relationships. Trust is essential for knowledge exchange; when people trust each other, they are more willing to share valuable insights, reducing conflict and improving collaboration within the organisation [7, 22, 26].

Perceived value also influences KS. Employees are more likely to share knowledge if they perceive it as unique or valuable [27]. The uniqueness of an organisation's KM system can make sharing more attractive, as employees recognise the competitive advantage it offers. A knowledge system that is distinct and difficult to replicate motivates individuals to contribute, as it enhances their personal value and organisational standing [7, 22].

Financial or social motivation serves as another driver. Incentives, whether monetary or social, encourage active participation in LL practices. Financial rewards, such as bonuses or points that can be redeemed for benefits, motivate individuals to contribute to the KM system. This not only improves individual performance but also enhances overall organisational productivity [22, 26, 27].

Lastly, workplace culture is an overarching enabler that shapes the effectiveness of LL practices. A positive workplace culture, where there is shared vision, mission, and commitment to teamwork, encourages individuals to contribute actively. Organisational culture influences behaviour, which in turn affects performance. A culture that values innovation, creativity, and collaboration leads to better outcomes in KS and project completion [7, 27, 28].

Overall, these enablers collectively create an environment that facilitates the effective capture, sharing, and application of LL. By fostering enhanced collaboration, knowledge exchange, and improved performance, they ultimately contribute to the success of construction projects.

2.2 Barriers to Implementing Lessons Learned Practices in the Construction Industry

KM is a widely recognised practice in the construction industry, but not all organisations have fully adopted LL practices. Despite their potential to improve project outcomes, several challenges can hinder the successful integration of LL practices. This section explores the key barriers that impede the effective implementation of LL within the construction sector. Table 2 provides a detailed overview of these barriers. Similar to the enablers, the identified barriers are grouped into two primary categories: individual factors and organisational factors. Understanding these barriers is crucial for addressing obstacles and creating an environment conducive to KS and continuous improvement in construction projects.

Hierarchy within construction organisations helps structure management levels, such as top, middle, and lower levels, each with distinct roles and authority. However, it can hinder KS. Employees may hesitate to share their knowledge due to fears of losing their unique status or job security, especially at lower levels. Hierarchical structures can also lead to inefficiencies, as the transmission of information between levels may be prone to errors, ultimately affecting decision-making and slowing down the knowledge-sharing process [22, 29, 30].

Interpersonal skills, particularly communication abilities, are essential for effective KS in construction projects. A lack of interpersonal skills can hinder the transfer of knowledge within teams. Effective KS relies on the ability to communicate clearly and collaborate with others. Additionally, communication styles can differ across hierarchical levels, which may further limit the exchange of knowledge, affecting project outcomes [22, 29, 31].

Differences in gender and age can act as inhibitors to LL practices in the construction industry. Men and women often approach problem-solving and decision-making

Table 2. Barriers to implementing effective LL practices.

Ref	Barriers	References
Individual factors		
C1	Use of hierarchy	[22, 29, 30]
C2	Interpersonal skill	[22, 29, 31]
C3	Gender and age	[30, 32]
C4	Education and experience level	[30, 31, 33]
Organisational factors		
C5	Resources	[26, 34, 35]
C6	High turnover	[26, 36, 37]
C7	Male sector	[38–40]
C8	Culture	[29, 35, 41]

differently, with women tending to seek more collaboration, while men may prefer solving problems independently. Age differences can also create barriers, as younger employees may struggle to communicate with older colleagues, and older employees may resist adopting new innovations. These generational and gender dynamics can hinder the sharing of valuable LL [30, 32].

Differences in education and experience levels among team members can impact KS. Employees with higher levels of education or more experience may struggle to relate to those with less knowledge or expertise, resulting in difficulties in sharing LL. Overconfidence among experienced workers can also create a barrier, as they may dismiss the input of less experienced colleagues. This gap in perception and understanding can slow down the process of implementing LL practices [30, 31, 33].

Limited resources, such as time, human capital, and financial investment, can be a significant inhibitor to LL practices in construction projects. Many organisations view KS as an inefficient use of resources, especially in a time-sensitive environment. The lack of allocated time for KS or LL processes can prevent effective implementation, as construction projects often operate under tight schedules and resource constraints [26, 34, 35].

High employee turnover in construction organisations can disrupt the continuity of LL practices. When skilled employees leave, they take with them valuable tacit knowledge, which diminishes the organisation's ability to retain and apply LS. This high turnover often leads to increased training costs and can result in lower morale and productivity, further hindering KS within the company [26, 36, 37].

The construction industry is predominantly male, which can present challenges in fostering an inclusive KS environment. Although women may bring valuable perspectives and higher-quality personnel exchanges, their underrepresentation in the sector limits the diversity of thought and collaboration. The male-dominated nature of the industry can therefore act as an inhibitor to effective KM and the successful implementation of LL [38–40].

Organisational culture plays a crucial role in the success or failure of LL practices. A culture characterised by vertical silos and poor communication across departments can prevent knowledge from being shared effectively. Furthermore, if an organisation's culture does not support innovation or knowledge exchange, it can become a significant barrier to implementing LL practices. Organisations must foster a culture of innovation and openness to make KM successful [29, 35, 41].

The range of barriers present significant challenges to the effective implementation of LL practices in the construction industry. Addressing these barriers is essential to creating a more collaborative and efficient KS environment. By overcoming these obstacles, construction organisations can better utilise insights gained from past projects, fostering continuous improvement and enhancing overall project performance and organisational success.

3 Research Methodology

This study adopted a positivist paradigm, employing a deductive approach to objectively examine the practice of capturing LL within the construction industry. A quantitative research design was utilised, with a cross-sectional field survey chosen as a cost-effective and efficient means of gathering data from a wide sample of construction professionals actively working in the industry. This methodology facilitated robust statistical analysis, allowing for the extraction of meaningful insights. The research framework is outlined in Fig. 1.

The data collected were analysed using the Statistical Package for the Social Sciences (SPSS), version 23. Descriptive statistical techniques, including mean scores and standard deviations, were used to prioritise the values of LL and their associated enablers and barriers. These methods are widely utilised in construction management research to rank variables, providing valuable insights into their relative significance and enabling informed decision-making within the industry [20, 42, 43].

3.1 Questionnaire Design

The questionnaire was developed based on insights from the literature review and consultations with industry subject matter experts. Questions were carefully crafted to be clear and concise, ensuring they were easy to understand, while limiting the survey completion time to 15 min in order to avoid respondent fatigue. The questionnaire was divided into four sections. Part I gathered demographic information from respondents, including their educational background, years of industry experience, and the types of projects they have worked on. Part II asked respondents to assess their agreement with the value of LL in construction projects, using a five-point Likert scale ranging from 1 (strongly disagree) to 5 (strongly agree). Part III presented a list of enablers, identified through the literature review (see Table 1), and asked respondents to indicate their level of agreement using the same Likert scale. Part IV focused on the barriers (as outlined in Table 2), with respondents again asked to rate their agreement on the same scale used in Parts II and III.

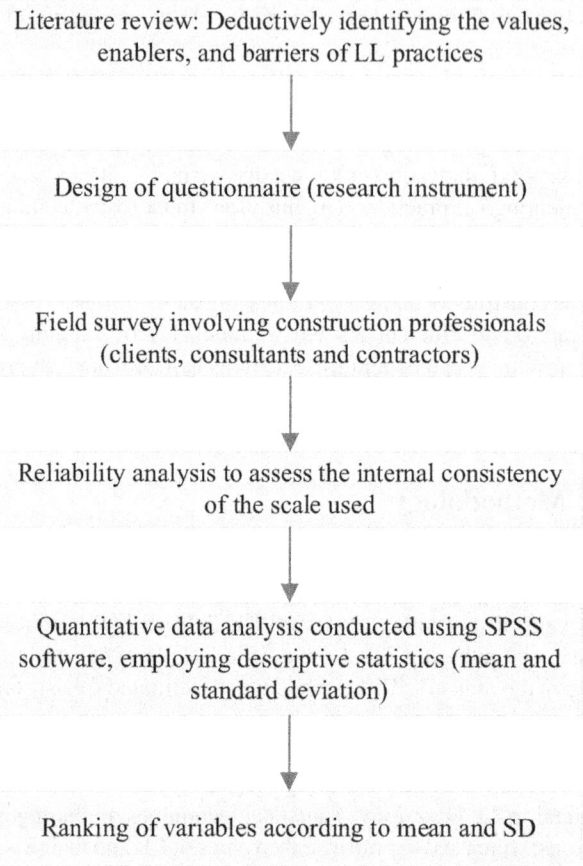

Fig. 1. Research methodological flowchart (Source: adapted from Yap [12]).

3.2 Survey Respondents and Demographics

The sampling frame comprised professionals from the three key parties in construction: clients, consultants, and contractors in Malaysia. Non-probability sampling techniques, including purposive, convenience, and snowball sampling, were employed to select respondents, ensuring a reasonable spread of responses. In this study, the unit of analysis was construction professionals, as they are directly involved in project delivery. Engaging a variety of professionals (i.e., clients, consultants, and contractors) ensured that diverse perspectives on LL practices in construction were captured.

A pilot test of the questionnaire was conducted with 30 targeted construction professionals to ensure clarity and eliminate ambiguity. Following the successful pilot, the questionnaire was unchanged for the main survey, during which 170 questionnaires were distributed electronically. A total of 129 valid responses were collected after follow-up reminders, resulting in a response rate of 64.5%. This sample size (greater than 100) is considered adequate for meaningful statistical analysis [44, 45]. With responses from each group - clients (38), consultants (48), and contractors (43) - exceeding 30, the data meets the requirements of the central limit theorem.

Table 3 presents the demographic profile of the respondents, consisting of 38 clients, 48 consultants, and 43 contractors. Of the 129 respondents, 90% held at least a bachelor's degree, with nearly 50% having over 10 years of experience in the construction industry. Additionally, 57.4% were involved in building projects. These characteristics highlight the expertise and experience of the respondents, ensuring that the study's findings are based on informed insights from qualified professionals within the construction sector.

Table 3. Demographic profile of respondents (Source: adapted from Yap [12]).

Profile	Category	Respondents				Percentage (%)
		Client (N = 38)	Consultant (N = 48)	Contractor (N = 43)	Total (N = 129)	
Academic qualification	Master's degree	13	9	11	33	25.6
	Bachelor's degree	17	21	19	57	44.2
	Diploma	7	17	13	37	28.7
	Certificate	1	1	0	2	1.6
Working experience	0 to 5 years	14	15	12	41	31.8
	6 to 10 years	8	7	11	26	20.2
	11 to 15 years	7	8	8	23	17.8
	16 years and above	9	18	12	39	30.2
Type of project	Building	23	31	20	74	57.4
	Infrastructure	15	17	23	55	42.6

4 Results and Discussions

4.1 Questionnaire Reliability

The α values for the three categories of variables - values, enablers, and barriers of LL - are 0.867, 0.759, and 0.829, respectively. All of these values exceed the 0.70 threshold necessary to confirm the internal reliability of the scale used [45]. This indicates that the research instrument demonstrates strong overall reliability, ensuring the consistency and dependability of the measures employed in the study.

4.2 Mean Scores and Ranking LL Values

Table 4 presents the mean scores and standard deviations (SDs) of values associated with capturing LL in the construction industry, ranked according to their overall significance, based on insights from 129 industry professionals. A closer analysis of Table 4 reveals that all nine values have mean scores exceeding 4.0, indicating a strong consensus on the high importance of these values, with the majority of respondents either agreeing or strongly agreeing. The five most significant values related to capturing LL in construction projects are as follows:

1. A2: Avoiding the same mistakes from happening in upcoming projects (mean = 4.519, SD = 0.574);
2. A5: Better performance or procedure by adopting LL from other projects (mean = 4.519, SD = 0.574);
3. A9: Promote a collective environment to attain the project team's shared goals through the sharing of personal experiences (mean = 4.519, SD = 0.651);
4. A1: Ensuring good practices in previous projects that are successful are being re-used in upcoming projects (mean = 4512, SD = 0.626); and
5. A3: Developing new ideas or methods through LL (mean = 4.496, SD = 0.697).

The data consistently highlights the importance of integrating LL from past projects across various dimensions, with closely aligned mean scores indicating a high level of agreement among respondents [12]. The most highly valued aspect of capturing LL is the prevention of recurring mistakes in future projects. As highlighted by participants in Yap & Skitmore's [14] study, "past experiences will tell you what you can do and enrich one's expert judgment" and "individual needs to learn from his/her mistakes and not repeat the same mistake twice". Given that project mistakes are major contributors to rework and time-cost overruns, capturing and disseminating critical LL can significantly help construction professionals avoid these issues in future projects, improving efficiency and reducing unnecessary repetition of errors.

Another key value highlighted is the role of LL in enhancing productivity and efficiency, driving smarter working practices. By leveraging lessons learned, organisations can build their absorptive capacity, thus fostering continuous performance improvement within the construction industry [46]. This aligns with the broader trend towards increasing operational efficiency by learning from past experiences and applying this knowledge to future work.

Third, LL practices foster collaboration by encouraging project team members to share their personal experiences, which collectively contribute to achieving shared project goals. Knowledge sharing among team members is essential for fostering organisational learning and developing collective competence [47]. This process not only enhances project performance but also builds a culture of collaboration that is critical in complex construction projects. As noted by Teerajetgul & Charoenngam [48], trust and collaboration are fundamental factors for knowledge management in construction projects, enabling teams to work together effectively and optimise project outcomes.

The fourth value pertains to the reuse of successful practices from past projects. LL are valuable sources of project knowledge that can be reused and integrated into future projects, increasing the likelihood of success by reinforcing best practices. The systematic capture and application of these lessons have been shown to improve project delivery outcomes by promoting consistency and reducing the potential for mistakes [7].

Lastly, LL serves as a foundation for innovation, enabling the development of new ideas, methods, and solutions derived from both successes and failures in previous projects. According to Kolb & Kolb [49], individuals learn most effectively through experiential processes such as brainstorming sessions that encourage idea generation. Recent advancements in information and communication technology (ICT) tools have significantly enhanced the way knowledge and ideas are shared, fostering an environment conducive to innovation [3, 50]. These technologies facilitate the easy dissemination of LL, promoting continuous improvement and innovation across the industry.

The findings above indicate that LL are not only crucial for avoiding past mistakes but also for enhancing performance, fostering collaboration, reusing best practices, and driving innovation. The consistent emphasis on these values demonstrates a shared understanding within the construction industry of the strategic importance of capturing and applying lessons learned to achieve long-term success and continual improvement [12].

Table 4. Values of Capturing LL in the Construction Industry (Source: adapted from (Source: adapted from Yap [12]).

Rank	Value Description	Mean	SD
1	Avoiding the same mistakes from happening in upcoming projects	4.519	0.574
1	Better performance or procedure by adopting LL from other projects	4.519	0.574
3	Promoting a collective environment to attain the project team's shared goals through sharing personal experiences	4.519	0.651
4	Ensuring good practices from previous successful projects are reused in upcoming projects	4.512	0.626
5	Developing new ideas or methods through LL	4.496	0.697
6	Transforming individual knowledge to organisational knowledge by sharing LL	4.481	0.663
7	Facilitating project planning (forecasting ability) using LL from previous projects	4.450	0.637
8	Improvising project monitoring and control processes using LL from previous projects	4.326	0.709
9	The quality and quantity of LL in the construction industry are influenced by the size and difficulty of the project	4.326	0.752

4.3 Mean Scores and Ranking LL Enablers

Table 5 presents the enablers of LL in the construction industry, ranked according to their significance. All the enablers have a mean value exceeding 4.00, indicating they are regarded as highly relevant and significant. The top five enablers are as follows:

1. B3: Peer recognition (mean = 4.450, SD = 0.661);
2. B1: Sharing culture (mean = 4.434, SD = 0.705);
3. B2: Honouring of commitment (mean = 4.411, SD = 0.645);
4. B4: Reciprocity and trust (mean = 4.403, SD = 0.724); and
5. B7: Workplace culture (mean = 4.364, SD = 0.706).

Notably, four of these top five enablers are related to individual factors.

Table 5. Ranking of enablers (Source: adapted from Yap [12]).

Enablers	Overall (N = 129)		
	Mean	SD	Rank
B3	4.450	0.661	1
B1	4.434	0.705	2
B2	4.411	0.645	3
B4	4.403	0.724	4
B7	4.364	0.706	5
B6	4.333	0.654	6
B5	4.248	0.729	7

Peer Recognition (Individual). A construction project team is composed of professionals with diverse skills, knowledge, experience, and backgrounds. Despite the hierarchical structure, team members collaborate towards a shared goal. Recognition for contributing knowledge, particularly from senior members, is an important motivational factor [22]. In some cases, a simple "thank you" can affirm a person's contribution, which positively influences the overall workplace culture [22].

Peer recognition from colleagues and superiors enhances self-confidence and motivates further knowledge sharing [51]. This recognition not only supports personal development but also fosters innovation, as individuals feel valued as experts [35]. Research has shown that peer recognition can be more effective than financial incentives, which often have limited scope for sustained recognition [35]. Furthermore, Tan et al. [52], highlighted that peer recognition plays a significant role in problem-solving, boosting individuals' confidence in offering solutions to others.

Sharing Culture (Individual). The interactions among individuals within a team create a learning environment and promote a culture of sharing within the organisation, which brings significant benefits [21]. By sharing tacit knowledge and personal experiences, individuals contribute to transforming this knowledge into explicit forms that benefit the team [31]. However, converting tacit knowledge into explicit knowledge and sharing it effectively can be challenging. Communication plays a crucial role in facilitating knowledge sharing, and informal settings, such as breakfast or lunch gatherings, can serve as valuable platforms for exchanging experiences [53].

Moreover, individuals who can gather, recreate, utilise, and share knowledge provide substantial advantages to the organisation [54]. The concept of "coopetition" - sharing knowledge with competitors - also generates mutual benefits, allowing individuals and organisations to expand their skills, ideas, and technology [55]. When people witness their colleague's sharing knowledge, they are more likely to do the same, thereby fostering a culture of collaboration that enhances productivity and strengthens competitive advantage [56].

Honouring of Commitment (Individual). Construction projects involve a wide range of professionals, including architects, engineers, cost consultants, and project managers. Throughout the course of the project, team members aim to align with the project's objectives and ensure they follow through on their commitment to share knowledge [57]. Once team members engage in addressing issues, they are motivated to continue providing advice, knowledge, or solutions until the matter is resolved [22]. This behaviour often stems from a desire to demonstrate self-worth and earn respect from peers. Furthermore, individuals strive to maintain consistency between their intentions and actions, especially when they have committed to sharing knowledge.

Leaders play a vital role in inspiring team members to uphold their commitments and contribute to the project's success [58]. Effective leadership involves setting clear expectations and actively participating, ensuring that team members remain engaged and committed to the knowledge-sharing process. When leaders honour their commitments, they encourage others to do the same, fostering a culture of accountability [54].

Reciprocity and Trust (Individual). The success or failure of a construction project is heavily influenced by the relationships and environment within the project team. Reciprocity is a key enabler of KS [26]. People are more inclined to share knowledge with those who have previously helped or supported them, creating a reciprocal relationship that fosters mutual benefits and promotes a continuous cycle of knowledge exchange [22]. As the saying goes, "people treat you the way you treat them".

Reciprocity strengthens trust within the team. When individuals trust one another, they are more likely to share valuable knowledge, and knowledge exchange becomes smoother and faster [31]. Trust serves as a catalyst for KS, reducing conflicts and enhancing collaboration [59]. As trust deepens, employees are more willing to share their knowledge and learn from others, resulting in a more effective KM system.

Workplace Culture (Organisational). Organisational culture is one of the most influential factors in the success of a KM system. The adage "working as a team is better than working alone" emphasises the importance of teamwork, which facilitates collaboration, brainstorming, and improved productivity [56]. When all team members align with the organisation's goals, they are more likely to contribute to the project's success [58].

Workplace culture strongly influences individuals' behaviours and attitudes, which in turn affects organisational performance [31]. A positive workplace culture encourages employees to actively engage in activities and share knowledge, whereas a negative environment can discourage such contributions [52]. Just as a student in a positive classroom environment is likely to perform better, employees in a positive workplace culture are more motivated to share knowledge and contribute to the organisation's objectives. A culture that encourages KS and innovation enhances the organisation's ability to remain competitive within the industry [60].

4.4 Mean Scores and Ranking LL Barriers

Table 6 presents the barriers of LL in the construction industry, ranked according to their significance. All the barriers have a mean value above 4.00, except for C7 (Male sector), indicating that they are considered highly relevant and significant. The top five inhibitors are as follows:

1. C2: Interpersonal skill (mean = 4.295, SD = 0.678);
2. C5: Resources (mean = 4.256, SD = 0.763);
3. C4: Education and experience level (mean = 4.248, SD = 0.820);
4. C8: Culture (mean = 4.186, SD = 0.778); and
5. C6: High turnover (mean = 4.178, SD = 0.861).

Two of these barriers are related to individual aspects, while the remaining three are related to organisational factors.

Table 6. Ranking of barriers.

Barriers	Overall (N = 129)		
	Mean	SD	Rank
C2	4.295	0.678	1
C5	4.256	0.763	2
C4	4.248	0.820	3
C8	4.186	0.778	4
C6	4.178	0.861	5
C1	4.093	0.767	6
C3	4.062	0.950	7
C7	3.814	0.908	8

Interpersonal Skills (C2). Interpersonal skills are fundamental for effective communication, collaboration, and KS within construction teams [61]. The lack of these skills can create significant barriers to LL practices. In an industry where team members often come from diverse backgrounds, it is essential that they can communicate clearly, engage with one another constructively, and resolve conflicts efficiently. A high mean score of 4.295 indicates that inadequate interpersonal skills are seen as a substantial barrier to LL practices. If team members struggle to build trust or fail to communicate their ideas, it limits the exchange of knowledge and stifles collaboration [62]. This can result in missed opportunities for learning, ultimately hindering project success. The lack of interpersonal communication hampers the documentation and sharing of lessons, restricting the ability of teams to benefit from past experiences and improve future project performance [7].

Resources (C5). The availability of resources, including time, funding, tools, and human capital, is a critical factor in supporting LL practices. However, resource constraints are a common challenge in construction projects, where time pressures and budget limitations often prioritise immediate tasks over KM activities [63]. The mean score of 4.256 highlights that resource shortages are a significant barrier to LL practices. When resources are limited, teams may find it difficult to allocate the necessary time and personnel to document and share lessons learned effectively [34]. Consequently, valuable insights from past projects may go untapped, preventing teams from capitalising on knowledge that could improve future outcomes [11]. To overcome this barrier, organisations need to prioritise the allocation of resources towards KM activities, ensuring that teams have the tools and support they need to capture, store, and share lessons learned.

Education and Experience Level (C4). Education and experience are fundamental to the ability of construction professionals to recognise, understand, and apply LL from past projects [11, 14]. The mean score of 4.248 indicates that gaps in education and experience are a considerable barrier to LL practices. Professionals with limited formal education or insufficient experience may find it challenging to identify and communicate the significance of LL, thereby reducing the effectiveness of KS efforts [11]. Construction projects often involve complex technical tasks and multifaceted challenges that require both specialised knowledge and practical experience [12]. If professionals lack the education or experience necessary to process and apply LL, they may miss opportunities for improvement. Promoting continuous professional development, including training and mentoring, can help address this barrier, enabling construction teams to more effectively apply LS to future projects [3, 20].

Culture (C8). Organisational culture plays a crucial role in determining how knowledge is shared, valued, and utilised within a team or company [12, 23]. A culture that does not actively support LL practices will likely discourage individuals from sharing their knowledge or learning from past experiences. With a mean score of 4.186, culture is identified as a major barrier to LL practices. When organisations do not prioritise KS, or when employees feel that their contributions will not be recognised or rewarded, they are less likely to engage in LL activities [34]. In contrast, a culture that encourages collaboration, transparency, and KS creates an environment where LL can be effectively captured and disseminated [63]. To address this barrier, organisations need to foster a culture that actively supports KM, with leadership demonstrating a commitment to learning and rewarding contributions to LL practices [34].

High Turnover (C6). High turnover rates within construction projects, especially in field-based roles, present a significant challenge to maintaining continuous KS [64]. The mean score of 4.178 indicates that high turnover is a substantial barrier to LL practices, as the frequent departure of experienced personnel disrupts the flow of knowledge within the team. When employees leave, their knowledge and expertise often leave with them, and new team members must be trained and brought up to speed, leading to knowledge gaps. This turnover disrupts the continuity of KS processes and makes it difficult to capture and retain valuable LL from past projects [65]. To mitigate this issue, organisations should implement strategies for knowledge retention, such as establishing comprehensive knowledge repositories, encouraging mentorship programmes, and creating a system for capturing LL that can be easily accessed by new team members [66, 67].

5 Concluding Remarks

This study identified nine values, seven enablers, and eight barriers of LL practices in the construction industry, based on insights from construction professionals in Malaysia, gathered through a cross-sectional self-administered questionnaire survey. The aim of ranking these values, enablers, and barriers was to highlight the importance of LL practices in the complex construction environment, ultimately increasing the likelihood of project success and fostering a culture of continuous learning and improvement. The findings reveal a strong consensus on the significance of integrating LL from past construction projects, with key values such as avoiding the recurrence of mistakes, enhancing performance through lessons from past experiences, and promoting a collaborative environment where team members share knowledge to achieve common goals. By prioritising LL practices, construction organisations can leverage insights from both successes and failures to optimise project outcomes, reduce costly rework and time overruns, and improve their ability to plan, schedule, and estimate future projects more effectively. This approach enables professionals to drive innovation, increase productivity, and contribute to the long-term success of future projects.

The study further underscores the critical enablers, including peer recognition, a culture of sharing, and the honouring of commitments, all of which play a vital role in fostering a KS environment. These enablers enhance communication, collaboration, and the exchange of valuable insights, ultimately driving the success of construction projects. Peer recognition encourages individuals to share their knowledge, while a culture of sharing creates a supportive learning environment. Honouring commitments not only promotes accountability but also helps build trust, facilitating further knowledge exchange. Organisations that prioritise these enablers can establish a sustainable KS framework that empowers professionals to continuously improve, thereby enhancing project performance and securing a competitive advantage in the industry.

However, the study also identifies significant barriers to the effective implementation of LL practices, particularly interpersonal skills, resource allocation, and variations in education and experience levels. These barriers highlight the importance of both individual competencies and organisational structures in supporting the successful application of LL practices. Deficiencies in interpersonal skills can hinder effective communication and knowledge sharing, while a lack of resources complicates the dissemination of LL. Additionally, disparities in education and experience levels among team members can affect their ability to contribute to and benefit from LL practices. Addressing these barriers requires targeted interventions, such as training programmes to enhance interpersonal skills, investment in resources for KM, and continuous professional development to ensure that all team members possess the necessary education and experience. By overcoming these barriers, construction organisations can improve their capacity to capture, share, and apply LL, leading to better project outcomes and a stronger culture of continuous improvement.

5.1 Implications for Theory and Practice

The integrated model for LL practices in construction as depicted in Fig. 2 offers valuable implications for both theory and practice in construction KM. From a theoretical standpoint, this study enriches the existing literature on LL practices by identifying the enablers and barriers that critically affect their effective implementation in construction projects. In particular, it highlights the need to understand the interrelationship between values, enablers, and barriers, and how these components collectively shape the success of LL practices. The study underscores the importance of fostering an organisational culture conducive to learning, enhancing individual competencies, and ensuring sufficient resource availability - factors that are central to achieving desired KM outcomes.

Practically, the findings provide construction organisations with concrete strategies to strengthen their KM systems. To promote LL practices effectively, it is essential for organisations to not only integrate the core values of LL such as learning from past mistakes and promoting collaboration but also to understand and leverage the enablers that support these values. This includes encouraging peer recognition, cultivating a sharing culture, and honouring commitments, while simultaneously addressing the barriers that hinder LL practices, such as skill gaps, resource constraints, and organisational culture issues. By addressing these enablers and barriers, organisations can create a sustainable environment for continuous learning and improvement, leading to more.

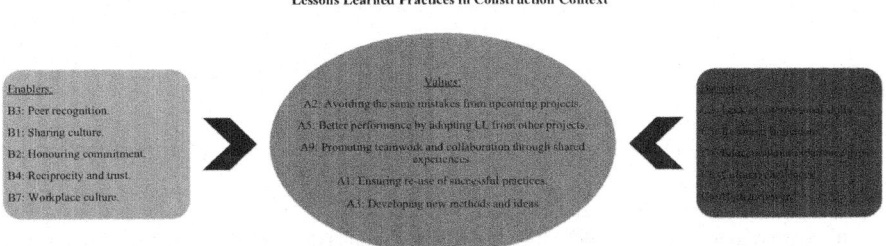

Fig. 2. Integrated model for LL practices in construction.

informed decision-making, reduced project risks, and enhanced project performance. Ultimately, the implementation of these strategies will enable construction organisations to optimise outcomes and secure long-term success in an increasingly competitive and dynamic industry.

5.2 Limitations of the Study

While this study offers valuable insights into LL practices in construction project management, it is limited by its reliance on a single data collection method (i.e. self-administered questionnaires) which may introduce mono-method bias. This limitation has been addressed through the triangulation of findings and cross-referencing with existing literature for theoretical validation. Although self-completion questionnaires are widely used to collect quantitative data from diverse samples, they do not allow for follow-up questions or clarification of responses. Future research could benefit from incorporating more interpretive approaches, such as in-depth interviews or case studies, to capture richer, real-world experiences from construction professionals and further validate the statistical findings.

Additionally, while the use of a five-point Likert scale may lead to subjective differences in how respondents interpret the rating scale, potentially affecting the reliability of the results, it remains one of the most widely used psychometric tools in social science and construction management research. Despite its limitations, the Likert scale provides a simple and effective means of quantifying respondents' attitudes and perceptions. Future studies should explore best practices for capturing LL across various phases of construction project delivery, particularly considering the impact of emerging digital technologies, which can enhance the collection, dissemination, and application of LL. Additionally, future research could investigate how KM and LL practices vary across different cultural and regional contexts, providing valuable insights for multinational construction organisations. These advancements and cross-cultural considerations have the potential to significantly improve the efficiency and effectiveness of KM practices, transforming LL integration in the construction industry.

Acknowledgments. The authors wish to thank the industry professionals who participated in the survey for their valuable insights and contributions.

Disclosure of Interests. No potential conflict of interest was reported by the author.

References

1. CIDB Malaysia, Construction Industry Transformation Programme (2016–2020), Kuala Lumpur, Malaysia (2015)
2. Mischke, J., Stokvis, K., Vermeltfoort, K., Biemans, B.: Delivering on construction productivity is no longer optional. Why the Construction Industry Must Climb out of Its Productivity Rut—and Why It Hasn't yet (2024)
3. Yap, J.B.H., Lim, B.L., Skitmore, M.: Ain Shams Eng. J. **13**, 101790 (2022)
4. Ribeiro, F.L., Ferreira, V.L.T.: Bus. Process. Manag. J. **16**, 361 (2010)
5. Marinho, A.J.C., Couto, J.: Cogent Eng. **9**, 1 (2022)
6. Ribeiro, F.L.: Constr. Innov. **9**, 268 (2009)
7. Yap, J.B.H., Shavarebi, K.: Int. J. Constr. Manag. **22**, 436 (2022)
8. Disterer, G.: J. Knowl. Manag. **6**, 512 (2002)
9. Meredith, J.R., Shafer, S.M., Mantel, S.J.: Project Management: A Managerial Approach, 10th edn. Wiley, Singapore (2017)
10. Bader, M., Jayaraman, R., Antony, J., Goonetilleke, R.S., Linderman, K., Hoerl, R.: Benchmarking (2024)
11. Li, Y., Song, Y., Wang, J., Li, C.: Sustainability **11**, 1 (2019)
12. Yap, J.B.H.: 16th International Joint Conference on Knowledge Discovery, Knowledge Engineering and Knowledge Management (IC3K 2024), pp. 38–47 (2024)

13. Eken, G., Bilgin, G., Dikmen, I., Birgonul, M.T.: Procedia Eng. **123**, 135 (2015)
14. Yap, J.B.H., Skitmore, M.: Int. J. Manag. Proj. Bus. **13**, 767 (2020)
15. Carrillo, P., Ruikar, K., Fuller, P.: Int. J. Proj. Manage. **31**, 567 (2013)
16. Kerzner, H.R.: Project Management: A Systems Approach to Planning, Scheduling, and Controlling, 12th edn. Wiley, Hoboken (2017)
17. Project Management Institute. A Guide to the Project Management Body of Knowledge (PMBOK Guide) and the Standard for Project Management, 7th edn. Project Management Institute, Inc., Newtown Square (2021)
18. Zhang, X., Mao, X., AbouRizk, S.M.: Autom. Constr. **18**, 777 (2009)
19. Abdul-Rahman, H., Yahya, I.A., Berawi, M.A., Low, W.W.: Constr. Manag. Econ. **26**, 15 (2008)
20. Forcada, N., Fuertes, A., Gangolells, M., Casals, M., MacArulla, M.: Autom. Constr. **29**, 83 (2013)
21. Longwe, T., Lord, W., Carrillo, P.: Proceedings of the 31st Annual ARCOM Conference Lincoln, UK, p. 621 (2015)
22. Javernick-Will, A.: J. Manag. Eng. **28**, 93 (2012)
23. Yap, J.B.H., Toh, H.M.: J. Eng. Design Technol. **18**, 55 (2020)
24. Luo, C., Lan, Y., (Robert) Luo, X., Li, H.: Technol. Forecast. Soc. Change **163** (2021)
25. Su, C.: Int. J. Knowl. Manage. Stud. **11**, 41 (2020)
26. Dang, C.N., Le-Hoai, L., Peansupap, V.: Int. J. Constr. Manage. (2019)
27. Wei, Y., Miraglia, S.: Int. J. Proj. Manage. **35**, 571 (2017)
28. Dang, C.N., Le-Hoai, L.: J. Eng. Design Technol. **17**, 515 (2019)
29. Yang, Y., Brosch, G., Yang, B., Cadden, T.: Prod. Plann. Control (2019)
30. Riege, A.: J. Knowl. Manag. **9**, 18 (2005)
31. Rego, A., Pinho, I., Pedrosa, J., Pina M., Cunha, E.: J. Iberoam. Acad. Manage. **7**, 33 (2009)
32. Sanecka, A.: J. Educ. Cult. Soc. **5**, 144 (2020)
33. Virban, P.S.: Procedia Soc. Behav. Sci. **127**, 812 (2014)
34. Shokri-Ghasabeh, M., Chileshe, N.: Constr. Innov. **14**, 108 (2014)
35. Carrillo, P., Robinson, H., Al-Ghassani, A., Anumba, C.: Proj. Manag. J. **35**, 46 (2004)
36. Al-Sadi, B.A.S., Khan, M.F.R.: Humanit. Soc. Sci. Rev. **6**, 52 (2018)
37. Thomas, J.: Int. J. Sci. Res. (IJSR) **4**, 3041 (2015)
38. Amaratunga, D., Haigh, R., Lee, A., Shanmugam, M., Elvitigalage Dona, N.G.: 3rd International SCRI Research Symposium, 3th–4th April (2006)
39. Sewalk, S., Nietfeld, K.: Int. J. Constr. Educ. Res. **9**, 239 (2013)
40. Worrall, L., Harris, K., Stewart, R., Thomas, A., McDermott, P.: Eng. Constr. Archit. Manage. **17**, 268 (2010)
41. Cheng, F., Yin, Y.: Eng. Constr. Archit. Manage. **31**, 957 (2024)
42. Yap, J.B.H., Teh, Y.H., Loo, S.C., Sulaiman, Z.B.: Int. J. Constr. Manage. (2023)
43. Adu, E.T., Opawole, A.: J. Eng. Design Technol. **18**, 230 (2019)
44. Roscoe, J.T.: Fundamental Research Statistics for the Behavioral Sciences, 2nd edn. Holt, Rinehart and Winston, New York (1975)
45. Hair, J.F., Black, W.C., Babin, B.J., Anderson, R.E.: Multivariate Data Analysis, 8th edn. Cengage Learning, Hampshire (2019)
46. Love, P.E.D., Teo, P., Davidson, M., Cumming, S., Morrison, J.: Int. J. Proj. Manage. **34**, 1123 (2016)
47. Yap, J.B.H., Shavarebi, K., Skitmore, M.: Prod. Plann. Control **32**, 875 (2021)
48. Teerajetgul, W., Charoenngam, C.: Eng. Constr. Archit. Manage. **13**, 584 (2006)
49. Kolb, A.Y., Kolb, D.A.: In: Armstrong, S., Fukami, C. (eds.) The Sage Handbook of Management Learning, Education and Development, Thousand Oaks, CA (2009)
50. Carrillo, P.: Engineering. Constr. Archit. Manage. **12**, 236 (2005)

51. Rahman, M.S., Mannan, M., Hossain, A., Zaman, M.H.: Int. J. Educ. Manag. **32**, 761 (2018)
52. Tan, H.C., Carrillo, P.M., Anumba, C.J.: J. Manag. Eng. **28**, 338 (2012)
53. Fong, P.S.: In: Anumba, C.J., Egbu, C., Carrillo, P.M. (eds.) Knowledge Management in Construction, pp. 195–212. Wiley-Blackwell, Chichester (2005)
54. MacNeil, C.M.: Empl. Relat. **25**, 294 (2003)
55. Tsai, W.: Organ. Sci. **13**, 179 (2002)
56. Theriou, N., Maditinos, D., Theriou, G.: Eur. Res. Stud. J. **14**, 97 (2011)
57. Leal, C., Cunha, S., Couto, I.: Procedia Comput. Sci. 998–1005 (2017)
58. Kululanga, G.K., Mccaffer, R.: Eng. Constr. Archit. Manage. **8**, 346 (2001)
59. Levin, D.Z., Cross, R.: Manage. Sci. **50**, 1477 (2002)
60. Duffield, S., Whitty, S.J.: Int. J. Proj. Manage. **33**, 1280 (2016)
61. Loebbecke, C., van Fenema, P.C., Powell, P.: J. Strat. Inf. Syst. **25**, 4 (2016)
62. Razmerita, L., Kirchner, K., Nielsen, P.: J. Knowl. Manag. **20**, 1225 (2016)
63. Othman, A.A.E., ElKady, M.M.: J. Eng. Design Technol. **21**, 23 (2023)
64. Tan, H.C., Carrillo, P.M., Anumba, C.J., (Dino) Bouchlaghem, N., Kamara, J.M., Udeaja, C.E.: J. Manage. Eng. **23**, 18 (2007)
65. Lin, T.C., Chang, C.L., Tsai, W.C.: Manage. Decis. **54**, 1757 (2016)
66. Jamal, A., Khedhaouria, A.: J. Knowl. Manag. **19**, 932 (2015)
67. Ahiaga-dagbui, D.D., Tokede, O., Morrison, J., Chirnside, A.: Eng. Constr. Archit. Manage. **27**, 3341 (2020)

How Does Automation Impact Healthcare Operations? A Model to Describe the Impact of Robotic Process Automation and AI-Enhanced Intelligent Automation in Healthcare

Jani Kaitosalmi[✉] and Milla Ratia

Department of Industrial Engineering and Management, Aalto University, Otakaari 1B, Espoo, Finland
{jani.kaitosalmi,milla.ratia}@aalto.fi

Abstract. Healthcare systems worldwide face increasing challenges due to workforce shortages, rising demands, and administrative burdens. Automation technologies, such as robotic process automation (RPA) and AI-enhanced intelligent automation (IA), offer promising solutions to improve process efficiency and alleviate repetitive manual tasks. However, the impact of automation in healthcare remains underexplored, especially regarding back-office processes that do not directly influence patients. This study investigates the practical utilization and impact of automation through a multi-case study conducted in two large-sized Finnish healthcare organizations. Using the PROVE-IT model, the research identifies key mechanisms by which automation has affected operational efficiency and employee workload. While automation has reduced administrative burdens and improved efficiency, the study underscores the need for systematic monitoring and evaluation of automation benefits. By extending the PROVE-IT model, this research provides a structured approach for healthcare organizations to evaluate the impact of automation. Future research should focus on developing holistic monitoring and evaluation processes for healthcare automation. As part of an ongoing impact assessment process, the PROVE-IT model can aid healthcare organizations in optimizing workflows and proactively addressing possible implementation challenges.

Keywords: Healthcare automation · Impact assessment · Robotic process automation · Intelligent automation · Artificial Intelligence

1 Introduction

European healthcare is in crisis. In 2022–2023, twenty EU countries lacked enough doctors, and fifteen faced nurse shortages [1]. Overall, the deficit of medical staff was about 1.2 million in 2022 [1]. Meanwhile, the aging population is set to nearly double by 2050, driving up healthcare demand [2]. Europe faces a dual challenge: an aging population increasing healthcare demand, and an aging workforce requiring replacements. Even well-funded systems struggle with shortages, as over a third of EU doctors and a quarter of nurses are 55 or older. Meanwhile, interest in nursing careers has declined in over half of EU countries, especially in the Nordics [1].

A key reason for healthcare labor shortages is the field's declining attractiveness, partly due to high burnout rates. In Europe, 22% of physicians expect worsening burnout and staffing issues [3]. Additionally, in nine out of ten developed countries researched, including France, Germany, the Netherlands, Sweden, and the UK, doctors reported dissatisfaction with their work-life balance and excessive administrative tasks [4].

The same trend has been noted in Finland, where social and healthcare personnel availability has declined in recent years, affecting nearly all professional groups [5]. In 2022, nearly all regions reported a "severe shortage" of nurses [6]. By 2040, the share of Finns over 85 will double, driving up demand for elderly care [7]. Additionally, nearly one-third of social and healthcare professionals are set to retire within the next decade, with practical and registered nurses being the largest groups [8]. In response, Finland has launched national programs to improve workforce availability by enhancing well-being, job satisfaction, and retention [9].

Streamlining administrative tasks can reduce physician workload, increasing employee satisfaction and lowering burnout risk [4]. Digitalization offers solutions to manage complex processes, improve clinical productivity, reduce workload, and simplify administrative tasks [10]. In Finland, digitalization has improved staff adequacy in the public healthcare sector by increasing job applicants, enhancing efficiency, and optimizing staff allocation [11]. However, while digitalization can assist healthcare organizations in achieving their aims, it is also known that the results of digital interventions often take time to emerge and may be difficult to quantify [12].

This paper focuses on a specific aspect of healthcare digitalization: the impact of automating digital workflows. Automation solutions are needed in healthcare, where professionals are weighed down by repetitive administrative duties like data entry, documentation, and scheduling, tasks which often distract from patient care. Automation technologies can take over these routine tasks and provide standardized, always-available processes, freeing up clinicians' time for meaningful patient interactions [13–15].

While workflow automation can potentially improve the healthcare sector's effectiveness, it remains unclear how these back-office tools add value [15]. Despite the large-scale adoption, the impact assessment of healthcare automation remains under-researched [13, 16, 17]. The research on automation tends to concentrate on technical aspects, focusing less on exploring their benefits and value-creation mechanisms [15, 18]. While patient-centric assessments have been made [19–22], challenges persist in measuring back-office solutions that indirectly enhance healthcare effectiveness. Moreover, there is a lack research evaluating the effectiveness of conducted implementations.

In Finland's public sector, there is still a lack of systematic evaluations of digitalization efforts [23]. Evidence about the effects of digitalization on healthcare professionals' work has been contradictory, highlighting also the negative impacts [11]. The employees' perception of digitalization has been mixed, with studies in Finland showing increased digital tasks can increase workload and stress [24–26], resulting in more complex work and skills gaps [27]. While Finnish patients have been generally satisfied with digital services, healthcare professionals have been concerned about the increased workload [28].

This study investigates the impact of automation solutions in the Finnish healthcare sector. Specifically, the study focuses on the use of two automation methods: robotic process automation (RPA) and intelligent automation (IA). It analyzes their use in two public healthcare organizations: *the Wellbeing Services County of Pirkanmaa* (PIRHA) and *the Helsinki and Uusimaa Hospital District* (HUS). Although both organizations had implemented several automation solutions, their overall impact has not been fully evaluated.

This paper is an extended version of our initial report [29] presented at the *16th International Conference on Knowledge Management and Information Systems*. In the previous work, we focused on giving an overview of the benefits and risks of utilizing automation solutions in healthcare from the employee perspective. In addition, the research answered broadly, what should be considered when evaluating automation in healthcare. This extended version complements the earlier findings by investigating the mechanisms of how automation creates impact.

The study utilizes the mechanisms presented in the PROVE-IT (Prove Outcomes, Value, and Effectiveness of IT in Healthcare) model by Lillrank et al. [20], which is a relatively new conceptual framework for describing the effects of digital healthcare innovations in Finland. While the model was created in collaboration with Finnish healthcare organizations, it has yet to be tested with automation solutions like the ones analyzed in this study. As such, the model's capabilities of describing back-office automation solutions are tested during the research process. The study concludes by proposing an extension to the PROVE-IT model, making it more suitable for back-office implementations.

Thus, the objective of this research is two-fold. Firstly, to understand how automation impacts healthcare operational processes, and especially, what are the mechanism that creates such impact. Secondly, to test how the impact of automation in healthcare could be described with the PROVE-IT model. The research questions are the following:

RQ1. *How does automation impact healthcare operational processes?*
RQ2. *How the impact of automation in healthcare could be described?*

The paper is structured as follows: Sect. 2 defines the automation solutions, while Sect. 3 describes impact assessment in healthcare and introduces the PROVE-IT model. Section 4 outlines the multi-case study approach and methodology. Section 5 analyzes automation's impact using elements from the PROVE-IT model. Section 6 discusses the evaluation of digital healthcare interventions and considers other impact assessment frameworks. Section 7 concludes with limitations and future research directions.

2 From Paper-Based Processes to Workflow Automation and AI Enhanced Healthcare Operations

2.1 The Role of Workflow Automation in Healthcare

Zayas-Caban, Okubo, and Posnack [30] argue that digital healthcare processes remain partially inefficient because they often replicate outdated paper-based processes instead of rethinking workflows. In fact, some electronic health records (EHRs) have been designed to mirror traditional paper-based methods, creating inefficiencies that contribute to burnout [31, 32].

Thus, simply digitalizing processes differs from automating workflows. In essence, automation reflects the replacement of humans by machines [33]. More precisely, automation describes "the execution by a machine agent (usually a computer) of a function that was previously carried out by a human" [34]. Over the past decade, organizations have increasingly automated software-based business processes [15, 35, 36]. *Workflow automation,* which means streamlining sequences of tasks with technology [37], presents healthcare organizations with opportunities to improve efficiency and enhance staff experiences [30, 38].

Business processes are traditionally optimized by focusing resources strategically on high-value processes [39] using enterprise software or more flexible business process management systems. These solutions often require application programming interfaces (APIs) to integrate with legacy systems [40]. However, many healthcare providers struggle to update outdated IT systems due to closed architectures and weak API support [41]. When traditional methods are too complex, RPA and IA offer a lightweight alternative for rapid automation [42].

2.2 RPA and IA to Improve Healthcare Operational Processes

RPA is a relatively novel software technology that automates simple manual tasks in digital processes, replacing actions humans would otherwise perform [35, 43, 44]. The term 'robotic' refers not to a physical robot but a computer-based process replicating human cognitive work [45]. Thus, RPA bots function as a "virtual human workforce" [46], mimicking human actions at the system interface level [40].

Suitable tasks for RPA automation are repetitive, rule-based, and high-volume [47]. Moreover, the processes should be stable, well-defined, have low exceptions and require only limited or no changes to the existing system [38]. Furthermore, RPA should be implemented in processes with structured digital data and deterministic outcomes [48, 49]. Lastly, the tasks should have low cognitive requirements error [50]. The process characteristics for RPA are summarized in Table 1 below.

RPA robots effectively automate healthcare's routine administrative processes, such as physician credentialing, patient scheduling, billing, and sending patient reminders [46]. During the COVID-19 pandemic, RPA was used to collaborate and communicate critical clinical data, monitor health conditions, handle medical supply orders, and accelerate administrative tasks related to employee onboarding patient registration [51]. In Finland, RPA was employed to handle up to 2,000 COVID-19 vaccinations each day – formerly a task for 10–15 employees [52]. Similarly, HUS reported that RPA saved more than 13,000 workdays in 2021, equaling the workload of 65 full-time employees [53].

Although RPA is a non-invasive and lightweight solution, it is mostly applicable to rule-based structured and standardized tasks [49]. Davenport and Kirby [54] noted that 21st-century automation differs from earlier forms by integrating 'intelligent' computer technologies capable of replacing some human knowledge and service tasks. IA enhances bots with artificial intelligence (AI) elements, such as machine learning and natural language processing, enabling them to replicate cognitive tasks [55]. IA differs from previous forms of automation in that it goes beyond rule-based processes. More precisely, by employing probabilistic algorithms, the AI enhanced IA bots can learn, adapt, and improve their process flow [33, 55, 56].

The possible applications of IA in healthcare are extensive; it can assist in complex scheduling, capacity management, and optimize patient movement between diagnostics and wards [57]. For example, a Nordic university hospital was the first to automate breast cancer follow-ups with IA. Previously a multi-year, labor-intensive, and error-prone task, the new IA solution significantly enhances efficiency, ensures personalized care paths, and improves patient safety [58]. Moreover, HUS has used IA to streamline specialized healthcare referrals, automating 75% of cases, with 50% of RPA-processed referrals verified by IA [59].

Table 1. Summary of RPA process characteristics [38, 47–50].

Process criterias	Description
Rule-based	Processes with well-defined and documented rules
Repetitive and high-volume	Routine tasks that have the potential to introduce time savings.
Stable	Mature processes that stay relatively unchanged
Limited variation	Tasks with low exceptions
Structured digital data	The data should preferably be structured and have readable electronic inputs. For example, Excel sheets are a good fit for RPA robots compared to images.
Low cognitive requirements	The tasks should not require subjective evaluation or creativity

3 Impact in the Healthcare Context

3.1 What is Impact?

Oxford English Dictionary defines impact as "the effect or influence" of an action "of one thing or person upon another" [60]. This means impact can be positive or negative, direct or indirect, and either intended or unintended [61]. In healthcare, the primary metric for impact is *effectiveness*, defined as a meaningful change in health in a population under ordinary (vs. controlled as in laboratory) conditions [62–64].

At the macro level, effectiveness is the result of a healthcare process where resources and costs are used to produce outcomes like services, methods, and deliverables. The quantity, quality, and use of inputs determine the type of output that can be achieved

[65]. Outputs can be measured through various metrics, including process quality, service volume, clinical procedures, patient satisfaction, safety, and accessibility.

Pitkänen et al. [66] argue that impact evaluation in Finland focuses more on measuring outputs than actual outcomes. Similarly, Porter [67] emphasizes that healthcare value should be assessed by patient outcomes rather than the volume of services provided. Thus, Porter and Lee [68] define healthcare value as "maximizing value for patients," meaning the best outcomes at the lowest cost. Simply put, *healthcare value = patient outcomes/total costs* [68]. Although process measurement and improvements are useful strategies, they cannot substitute the necessity of evaluating care outcomes. Given this, what impact do back-office automation solutions have if they do not directly affect patient outcomes?

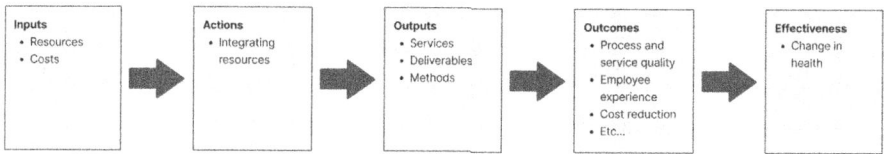

Fig. 1. The value chain of a health system adapted from Sintonen & Pekurinen [64] and Sintonen et al. [65]. Modified by adding outcomes between outputs and effectiveness.

3.2 From Outputs to Automation Benefits

As described above, effectiveness is the primary metric used to evaluate healthcare outcomes. Several other critical metrics can be derived from effectiveness, notably cost-effectiveness and productivity. *Cost-effectiveness* is defined as the ratio of effectiveness relative to costs, while *productivity* refers to the ratio of outputs (results achieved) to inputs (resources or costs used) [65]. Productivity can be enhanced by reducing costs without diminishing outputs or increasing outputs without raising costs. Consequently, improving productivity directly contributes to the enhanced cost-effectiveness of healthcare processes [65].

Automation increases cost-effectiveness by improving productivity. Automation can deliver both tangible and intangible benefits. Tangible automation benefits are measurable by numbers, such as number of transactions, improved process accuracy or execution time [16]. Intangible benefits are harder to measure in monetary terms but can be perceived, such as increased patient satisfaction, employee motivation, or creativity [69]. Because data of intangible benefits is more difficult to collect, automation benefits have had the tendency to be assessed using quantitative rather than qualitative metrics [16]. However, focusing solely on efficiency and cost metrics can fail due to neglecting important perspectives, such as usability or company's readiness for automation [69].

It is clear that any type of automation, with or without AI, can provide a broad range of benefits to the overall system, such as increasing efficiency, reducing costs, and improving employee and patient experience [16, 17]. While the automation benefits are recognized, their systematic impact assessment is however still mostly lacking [16, 23]. Kääriäinen et al. [23] note that organizations often evaluate automation using a limited set of criteria, primarily emphasizing internal cost savings. Many existing assessment frameworks focus on factors such as requirements, feasibility, and a company's readiness for new technology adoption. Examples include the 5D digital technology assessment [69], RPA selection indicators by Kim [45], and the process selection method for RPA proposed by Wanner et al. [70]. However, these frameworks often overlook the importance of continuous and systematic monitoring as well as post-implementation impact evaluation. Additionally, they provide limited insights into how automation solutions affect the specific organizational context beyond the initial readiness to implement the solutions. In other words, time horizon evaluation is typically lacking.

Meironke and Kuehnel [16] identified 62 unique metrics used to assess automation benefits, with most focusing on monetary aspects, e.g. efficiency and cost savings, such as volumes, work hours saved, and process time. Accuracy and error rates are also common for evaluating quality and compliance. However, metrics related to more intangible benefits, such as employee and customer satisfaction or availability of services are less frequently considered. The authors conclude that automation assessments tend to prioritize quantifiable economic factors over qualitative and non-economic benefits [16].

Automation can provide clear benefits and positively influence the health system's outcomes. However, showcasing the measurable impact of automation solutions is hard as these back-office solutions often do not directly impact patients. Thus, they contribute only indirectly to healthcare effectiveness. So, how to measure and evaluate such indirect impact?

3.3 How is the Impact Created?

Inputs are converted into outputs through specific actions, as illustrated in Fig. 1. However, this simplified model does not explain how these actions produce outputs, a limitation that Astbury and Leeuw [70] call the "black box problem." According to Astbury and Leeuw [71], this issue emerges when evaluations focus primarily on program outcomes without considering the underlying processes that generate them. Similarly, in systems theory, organizations are often described as black boxes transforming inputs into outputs [20]. To fully understand how impact occurs, it's necessary to open the black box and examine the mechanisms connecting causes to effects [71].

In healthcare, each level of the system – from individual patient interactions to units, organizations, and national policies – acts as a black box within a larger hierarchy [20]. Digital healthcare interventions penetrate these black boxes and impact various contexts. These interventions can have direct, indirect, and cumulative effects depending on how their impact spreads through different contexts. Ideally, by measuring outcomes within these black boxes, we can model the entire system and better understand its overall impact [20].

Realistic evaluation, introduced by Pawson and Tilley [72], is a theory-driven approach aiming to describe what occurs inside "black boxes." It investigates not only whether an intervention is effective but also how it works, who benefits, under what circumstances, and why. Central to this approach is the Context-Mechanism-Outcome (CMO) framework, expressed by the basic formula: *Outcome = Mechanism + Context*. According to Pawson and Tilley [72], outcomes result from interactions between underlying mechanisms and their contexts. Mechanisms are fundamental processes or structures that, when triggered in a particular setting, lead to specific outcomes.

The original CMO framework has evolved over time. Denyer, Tranfield, and Aken [73] expanded it by introducing the concept of Intervention (I), creating the CIMO framework. The framework bases the expansion on Bunge's [74] technological rule: "If you want to achieve outcome O in context C, then apply intervention type I." [73] Later, Mukumbang et al. [75] and Marchal et al. [76] refined the framework further by adding Actors (A), emphasizing that individuals actively participate in interventions. The resulting ICAMO framework highlights that interventions only become effective when relevant actors engage meaningfully with them or their components [75] (Fig. 2).

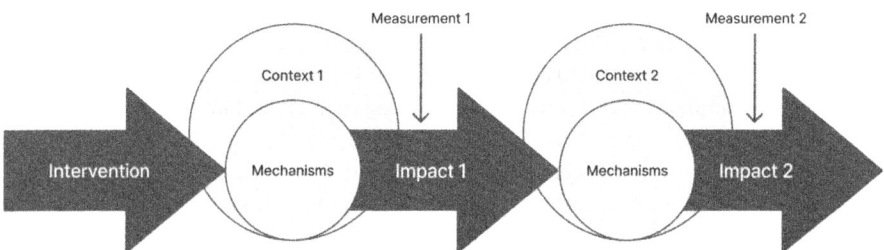

Fig. 2. The impact of a single intervention can accumulate as it extends across different contexts. Adapted from Lillrank et al. [20].

3.4 Utilizing the PROVE-IT Model to Describe the Impact of Digital Healthcare Interventions

CIMO logic has been applied in Finnish healthcare research, particularly through the PROVE-IT model developed by Lillrank et al. [20]. This model offers healthcare professionals a structured method to assess intervention effectiveness by analyzing the contexts, mechanisms, and outcomes involved. By addressing a series of key questions, healthcare managers can better understand how the impact is generated and determine what should be measured.

According to Lillrank et al. [20], a meaningful change occurs only when an actor takes action. For an actor to act, three conditions must be met: the actor must have the necessary resources and capabilities, understand what needs to be done, and possess sufficient motivation to act:

1. *Can do:* Now, something new can be done.
2. *Know what to do:* Now, someone knows better what needs to be done.
3. *Want to do:* Now, someone has the motivation to act.

All three conditions must be met to enable goal-oriented action and activate mechanisms. For example, if an automated referral sorter saves a secretary's time, the secretary must clearly understand how to effectively use this extra time and remain motivated to do so. Lastly, Lillrank et al. [20] identifies key mechanisms that drive successful outcomes, including performing tasks at the appropriate time and organizational level, optimizing resource integration, improving task coordination, strengthening the use of clinical evidence, managing demand more efficiently, and increasing patient involvement through active co-creation of health.

When the impact has been described, the outcomes of interventions should be measured. However, evaluating the effectiveness of a single intervention within a complex healthcare system can be challenging. Therefore, Lillrank et al. [20] recommends focusing on the immediate level of impact, as any observable effects typically first emerge there. If no impact is observed at the first stage, it is unlikely to appear at broader levels. In the context of this research, the immediate level of impact refers specifically to the process step where the automation solution is implemented (Fig. 3).

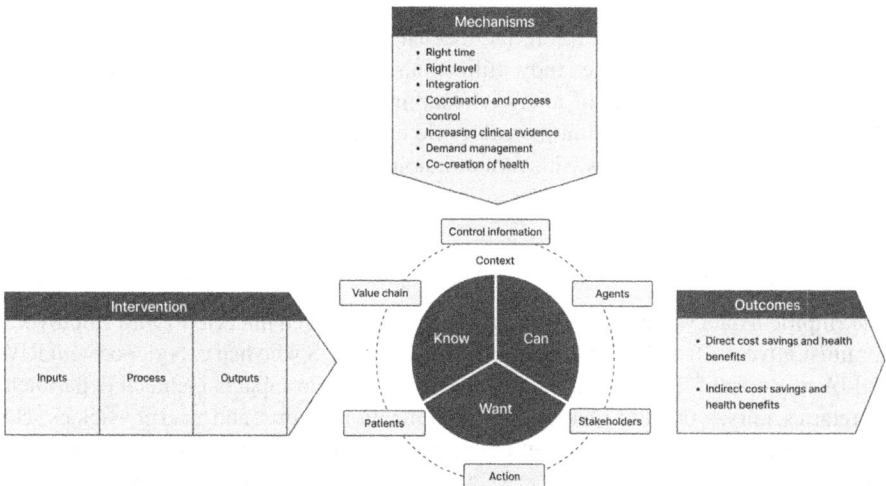

Fig. 3. The PROVE-IT model adopted from Lillrank et al. [20].

4 Methodology

This study explores the impact of automation on healthcare processes by examining its practical utilization in two Finnish public healthcare organizations. Specifically, the study aims to describe the effects of automation and identify the mechanisms through which automation influences healthcare operations.

This research is an extension of our previous report [29], which outlines the key benefits, risks, and evaluation challenges associated with the investigated automation solutions. While building upon those earlier findings, this paper specifically focuses on describing the impact of automation using the PROVE-IT model developed by Lillrank et al. [20]. PROVE-IT is a patient-centric framework created for evaluating digitalization efforts within the Finnish healthcare sector. Although developed collaboratively with Finnish healthcare organizations, the model has not yet been tested with automation solutions such as those examined here. Therefore, our study also assesses the framework's capability to describe the impact of back-office automation solutions that may not directly affect patients.

The empirical part was conducted as a multi-case qualitative study in two Finnish wellbeing services counties: PIRHA and HUS. The two case organizations were ideal for the study due to their large size, needs, and previous experience with automation projects. Both organizations had implemented several automation solutions across different units, aiming to enhance the efficiency of manual processes and improve job satisfaction. However, neither had fully assessed the impact of these solutions. Furthermore, the organizations rank among the largest public healthcare providers in Finland. The two cases allowed for insightful comparisons: PIRHA had primarily implemented RPA, while HUS had experience with both RPA and IA.

A qualitative approach was chosen as it is well-suited for exploring relatively new topics and gaining an in-depth understanding of complex phenomena in real-world settings [77, 78]. Given the limited previous research on automation's effects in healthcare, the approach enabled us to explore the mechanisms behind the automation outcomes more in-depth. Moreover, the study utilized an embedded multi-case study design; it included multiple sub-units of analysis, enabling a rich understanding of the current phenomenon (the 'case') within its real-world context [79]. In plain terms, we investigated employees' experiences with various automation implementations across multiple units.

4.1 Data Collection

The empirical data was collected through 32 semi-structured interviews with employees, administrative staff, and stakeholders in PIRHA and HUS who had experience with RPA and IA as a part of their role in the organization. The participants included department secretaries, nurses, doctors, pharmacists, digitalization experts, and head physicians. The interviewees were from 14 different units, seven from each organization. Additionally, representatives from external IT service providers responsible for implementing the automation solutions were interviewed to capture their perspectives. Table 2 lists the number of participants by their roles.

The data collection took place in two phases: interviews were conducted with PIRHA during spring 2023, focusing on RPA solutions, and with HUS during autumn 2023, covering IA processes. Purposive sampling was used, meaning participants were selected based on characteristics relevant to the research objectives [80, 81]. The study aimed to understand how automation affected employees in various roles and to capture their perspectives on outcomes. Therefore, participants were chosen based on their experience with automation, organizational unit, and role. Although the research team defined selection criteria, the final sample was collected by a designated contact person within each organization, making convenience and availability additional influencing factors. Relevant research permits were gained from both organizations, PIRHA and HUS. In addition, participants were given relevant information about the research in advance as well as their personal consents were collected.

All interviews were conducted remotely via Microsoft Teams with a similar structure. Participants were asked about their perception of automation benefits, potential drawbacks, and future expectations from four perspectives: employees, patients, costs, and operational processes. Additionally, they were questioned about the assessment of automation impact, including challenges related to measuring outcomes. All interviews were recorded and transcribed with participant consent. Before analysis, all interview data were pseudonymized to ensure confidentiality.

Participants discussed five automated processes, but the main focus was on two: referral handling and medical dosage building. A referral is a service request about a patient. It is sent from one healthcare provider to another or between units within the same provider. Referrals can be external, transferring patient care to another organization, or internal, directing patients within the same organization without necessarily transferring care responsibility [82].

Table 2. Participants from both case organizations [29].

Region	Role	Number of participants
PIRHA	Department Secretary	5
	Nurse	2
	Chief Physician/Director	2
	Medical Doctor	2
	Digitalization Specialist	2
	Head/Deputy Head Nurse	2
	Product Owner (External)	1
	Midwife	1
	Service Provider (External)	1
HUS	Pharmacist/Senior Pharmacist	5
	Digitalization Specialist	2
	Department Secretary	2
	Nurse	1
	Product Owner	1
	Deputy Chief Physician	1
	Product Owner (External)	1
	Data Scientist (External)	1
Total		32

Both organizations had implemented a *referral sorter* to reduce the manual workload for nurses and secretaries by automating the classification of incoming referrals. *"Before automation or the electronic patient record system's XDS archive, the paper referrals arriving at the unit were placed on the doctor's desk,"* describes one secretary from HUS in an article from Husari magazine [59]. Today in HUS, a referral sorting robot operates in a virtual referral center, continuously processing new doctors' referral texts. It classifies them into the appropriate queues, allowing physicians to easily access and review referrals for further assessment. HUS had implemented both RPA-based referral sorters as well as IA-enhanced, so-called intelligent referral sorters. These intelligent referral sorters utilize machine learning to interpret symptoms and diagnoses from referral texts.

The referral sorters' task is to place the referral in the right physician's queue for review. If the system's sorting is incorrect, the physician redirects it to the correct department or returns it to the referral center. Correcting the robot's errors helps improve the AI model, allowing the intelligent sorter to learn and improve accuracy over time. Misdirected referrals increase the workload for physicians, as they must review irrelevant cases. The frequency of these errors varies between referral centers, affecting the potential time savings from automation.

In PIRHA, the RPA-based referral sorter automates the referral process using predefined logic. All robots verify patient contact details and, if necessary, complete payment commitment information. Additionally, some PIRHA units use automated referral sorting, directing referrals to the appropriate physician for review. If the robot incorrectly assigns a referral, an employee must manually correct it. However, the implementation of automated sorting varies between units. Some facilities use only one referral category, while others classify referrals into several specialized categories. Consequently, not all units have adopted automated sorting; some have opted out due to challenges like overlapping terminology, which makes accurate classification difficult.

HUS has also implemented an IA solution for filling patients' medication dosage information in the EHR named Apotti. This *medical dosage builder*, primarily used by nurses and pharmacists, converts free-text medication entries into a structured format required by Apotti. By offering automated code suggestions, it reduces the need for manual data entry, streamlining the documentation process. The structured medical data follows a standardized format, ensuring uniform dosage instructions for all patients. The standardized medication information is used to reduce manual input in the future and mitigate the risk of input errors.

4.2 Data Analysis

The data analysis followed a qualitative content analysis, performed with the QDA software ATLAS.ti. The study was conducted as a directed content analysis [83], beginning with existing research findings and preliminary theory-based categories related to automation benefits and risks. The empirical data consisted of two datasets, one for each case, with data collection divided among the researchers. Since none of the researchers participated in all interviews, the final dataset was a combination of primary and secondary data for each researcher.

Given the mix of data, the study followed the set of tactics for an abductive content analysis provided by Vila-Henninger et al. [84]. First, a deductive theory-based codebook was created and later expanded with inductive codes to capture emerging themes. For instance, to highlight the differences in perceived automation outcomes, the benefit dimensions provided by Meironke and Kuehnel [16] were utilized to categorize the mentioned benefits. Additionally, the AI coding feature of ATLAS.ti was utilized for exploratory coding. To reduce the amount of data, codes were combined into broader categories. Here, the 'Query Tool' in ATLAS.ti was used to sort codes based on the four investigated perspectives. Finally, a detailed manual qualitative analysis was conducted to identify emerging themes and compare differences between the two cases.

5 Results

Initiating an impact assessment requires clarity on what should be evaluated and why. This chapter focuses on defining *what to prove* when evaluating automation initiatives. The PROVE-IT model [20] provides a framework for analyzing the impact of healthcare digital solutions by examining key characteristics of the intervention, context, mechanisms, and outcomes. It clarifies what these characteristics are (ontology), how they can be understood (epistemology), and how they interact (dynamics) [20]. By addressing the model's questions, we aim to structure future evaluation efforts and describe the impact of automation in healthcare.

This chapter explores the impact of automation in PIRHA and HUS from the employee perspective by following the structure of the PROVE-IT model: 1) we describe the interventions, 2) define the context, 3) analyze the mechanisms, and 4) outline the outcomes.

5.1 Describe the Interventions

Lillrank et al. [20] suggest describing the Intervention (I) by looking at its three parts: collected *data inputs*, *data processing*, and *outputs*. More precisely, the analysis should focus on what data is collected, how it is gathered and processed into information, how and to whom the results are presented, and what kind of knowledge is created.

Inputs. Automation aims to mimic a virtual human workforce by processing inputs like humans. The referral sorter processes doctors' referral texts, while the dosage builder manages medication data. Both inputs fill the requirements for automation presented in Table 1: they are digital, high-volume, can be processed with rule-based logic, and do not require subjective interpretations.

For accurate results, correct data inputs are needed. Interviewees in both organizations highlight an issue with "complex data." For example, the medical dosage builder often fails to recognize variable dosages over time, providing only a single instruction. *"Well, often if there is a variable dosage, like one tablet in the morning and two in the evening… It can't handle such situations properly, so it just makes a guess,"* notes one pharmacist from HUS (Participant 28). Similarly, even when explicitly stated, the intelligent referral sorter has difficulty processing complex cases, such as referrals indicating treatment outside a patient's home municipality. *"From the referral texts coming to the Meilahti pulmonary clinic, it may clearly state at the end that this referral is intended for the Porvoo pulmonary clinic, but the referral sorter still directs it to the Meilahti pulmonary clinic. So, it doesn't understand more complex referral handing,"* describes Participant 27 from HUS.

Data requirements can broadly affect organizational processes and resources. An interviewee explained that adopting Apotti significantly changed pharmacists' roles, increasing their involvement in technical tasks like structuring medication data. The medical dosage builder was designed to simplify converting medication information into Apotti's structured format. Paradoxically, while automation has helped pharmacists with these new tasks, the new EHR has increased the demand for their expertise: *"Pharmacists have been extensively utilized as support personnel for Apotti. We no longer perform our primary duties but rather engage in the technical work of structuring medication information. A considerable amount of new staff needs to be hired to make the EHR function. Due to Apotti, there must be pharmacists in almost every ward. Otherwise, everything gets documented incorrectly."* (Participant 32).

Data Processing. Automation solutions should only be implemented in stable processes with minimal variation [38]. Participants in both RPA and IA cases identified "lacking processes," rather than the automation itself, as a primary challenge. Common issues included data availability or system inefficiencies. For instance, one PIRHA participant emphasized that effective RPA requires a well-functioning information system; poorly designed or unstable systems make automation unreliable. *"The problems are usually unrelated to the robot or humans but rather to the patient information system. If the system isn't working properly, neither can the robots."* (Participant 12).

Outputs. The studied automation solutions produce two types of outputs: transformed data and performance reports. Automation's cost-effectiveness mainly depends on output quantity and quality, though the importance of each varies depending on context. While the referral sorter increases quantity, it does not necessarily improve quality. Participants emphasized that humans still outperform robots in accuracy, highlighting a trade-off between accuracy and efficiency. *"I don't believe it has improved quality. But it has shifted mechanical work away from humans,"* summarizes Participant 24 from HUS. *"The process is less precise; errors occur more frequently than with a human. However, the robot performs faster and around the clock. That's the trade-off,"* mirrors Participant 31.

In contrast, with the dosage builder, accuracy is a priority. As described above, the solution is prone to errors with variable dosages. As Participant 22, one pharmacist, emphasized: *"Medication safety is a major concern due to potential recurring long-term errors."*. Interviewees noted that medication instructions might remain unchanged for years, meaning unnoticed automation errors could impact treatments long-term. Correcting such mistakes is challenging and requires a "deeper understanding of the system."

Evaluation of the outputs has been hard due to a lack of holistic data and baseline documentation. *"We haven't had any active monitoring. It's been more like we've calculated in advance the potential benefit and how quickly the process would pay for itself,"* summarizes Participant 12 from PIRHA. *"We didn't do measurements before the start of this referral processing, such as how much time we spend now and how much we used to spend. Therefore, it's a bit challenging to assess time savings,"* continues Participant 27 from HUS.

Moreover, the assessment has mainly focused on whether the technology works as intended, not on how people interact with it or how it improves outcomes. *We've tried to gather genuine user feedback, but it hasn't been very successful. Mostly, we just document bugs,"* explains Participant 19 from HUS. Evaluating automation's broader impact has been challenging because automation represents "just a small part" of larger processes, making direct outcomes difficult to identify. So far, feedback has mainly consisted of technical error reports that the participants describe as having limited value in communicating business benefits. *"The reporting is very technical, doesn't resonate with business or operational staff, and may not even reach them,"* Participant 5 from PIRHA summarizes (Table 3).

Table 3. The investigated solutions described according to the PROVE-IT model

Automation solution	Inputs	Data processing	Output: Transformed data	Output: Report
Referral sorter	Doctor's referral texts	In PIRHA, based on predefined business logic and rules. In HUS, the solution also utilizes artificial intelligence to interpret free text	A referral moved to the right doctor *Challenge* Trade-off between quantity and quality. The robot is always available and works 24/7, but makes more errors than humans	A "cold performance report" that doesn't "resonate with the business or operational people" *Challenges* Poor baseline measurements have made evaluation difficult Lack of an evaluation process Difficulties in gathering user feedback
Medical dosage builder	Patient's medication list	Converts free-text medication entries into the required structured format	A transformed medication list for the pharmacist to check *Challenge* Inaccurate medication entries can appear especially with variable dosages. Medication safety risks if the employee is overly confident in the output	

5.2 Define the Context

Context refers to the circumstances in which an intervention operates. For example, the referral sorter is used when transferring patient care between or within healthcare organizations, while the medical dosage builder helps pharmacists structure patients' medication lists correctly. However, the context extends beyond the specific step of the patient journey where the intervention occurs. Lillrank et al. [20] suggests analyzing context through multiple dimensions—patient, agent, stakeholder, action, control information, and value chain—to fully understand the overall situation.

Patient. Participants emphasize that the solutions are not directly visible to the patient. *"It probably doesn't become visible to patients at any point. What the robot outputs, it goes through the doctor, and then the doctor takes it for further processing. Thus, the robot's work results don't really reach the patient, "* Participant 2 summarizes. These backend solutions influence patient experience indirectly, such as increased service quality or more time for patients. Although faster medication processing may offer some benefits to patients, the primary advantage is for employees managing the data input. Furthermore, the medical referral sorter has enhanced service quality by ensuring consistent instructions across the organization. Additionally, the referral sorter operates 24/7 without being affected by "external influences," such as "a bad mood or a rough morning," as one interviewee noted.

Agents. They are individuals or groups directly affected by an intervention who are required to make changes to their activities [20]. In this study, agents are the primary beneficiaries of automation. They are secretaries, nurses, and doctors using the referral sorter and pharmacists and nurses using the dosage builder.

Stakeholders. The term refers to all other relevant actors in the context. The stakeholder perspective carries political weight, as different groups define success differently [20]. We observed a possible mismatch in evaluation expectations between employees using the solutions and other stakeholders. Since no evaluation is visible at the unit level, employees assumed it likely takes place at the "*organizational level*": *"Not in any way, at least in our unit. But I believe, it's measured at the organizational level. I can't answer how,"* describes Participant 15, one secretary from PIRHA. *"At least not at our unit. I don't know if there's any monitoring at the organizational level, but at the unit level, there isn't,"* continues Participant 10.

In contrast, at the higher organizational level, automation is viewed as a minor factor and not actively measured: *"We don't measure automation; we measure the delivery of services. We need to move towards greater impact assessment so that we provide the most impactful services possible, target them correctly, stay within the budget, and deliver health benefits to the customer. Those are our metrics,"* Participant 14 concludes.

Actions. Only actions that directly alter the patient's state or their related information are considered actions [20]. The referral sorter and dosage builder do not directly impact the patient's condition but instead influence the information related to their care.

Control Information. The primary role of both the referral sorter and dosage builder is to organize existing control information rather than to generate new data. The referral sorter categorizes text-based referrals into predefined groups. Similarly, the dosage builder converts free-text medication lists into a structured format needed by the EHR, replacing manual input.

Value Chain. The final step in describing the context is identifying which part of the patient care value chain the intervention targets. The value chain consists of interconnected stages, each representing a specific part of the patient journey. Each stage has a core action that creates value by changing the patient's condition or information. However, performing this action requires preparation, setup, tools, environment, and skilled personnel – all necessary, but none directly create value. For example, surgery creates value, but anesthesia and pre-operative preparations do not; if surgery is canceled, these preparations are wasted [20].

Standardizing setups reduces costs by enabling reuse across cases. Without standardization, setups remain exploratory and, thus, riskier and harder to manage. Automation promotes efficiency and consistency by standardizing processes. Employees from both organizations noted that the referral sorter improved equal access to treatment by applying consistent rules to every referral. Similarly, the dosage builder has helped to standardize medication lists, ensuring consistent medical information across units. Participant 30 highlighted: *"The fact that information is the same for all users. Perhaps that's the best benefit here. It also guides us in standardizing practices across different areas of healthcare."* Participant 21 continues by emphasizing broader benefits: *"It's helpful because it forces a review of service processes and workflows, uncovering issues beyond our initial focus... With automation, we can standardize practices for referrals, especially in units using the intelligent referral sorter."*

5.3 Analyze the Mechanisms

For meaningful action to occur, three logics have to be enabled: 1) an individual must have the necessary resources and skills, 2) know what to do now and next, and 3) be willing to act. If any of these are missing, goal-oriented action is impossible, and impact mechanisms cannot be activated [20].

Can do. The primary goal of automation is to save time, enabling employees to focus on more meaningful tasks. In both organizations, automation has generally been viewed positively. *"Certainly, all secretaries feel that the robot speeds up the process and at least reduces some steps that a secretary is supposed to do, thus leaving time for other tasks,"* describes Participant 2, one secretary from PIRHA. *"We have more time for other work that cannot be handled by automation. Especially, for phone-related tasks,"* adds Participant 26 from HUS.

However, employees struggle to specify exactly how the extra time is used. Nurses and pharmacists report a slight increase in patient care time, improving the overall patient experience. Nonetheless, these time savings per patient are small and difficult to measure. At HUS, doctors have noted a slight increase in workload due to incorrectly handled referrals. The benefits for secretaries are the most tangible; automation has helped them focus on more complex administrative tasks like scheduling and managing calls.

The can do logic cannot be unlocked if the solutions do not work as intended. More specifically, there is a risk that what we call a 'cannot do' counter logic will be unlocked, resulting in additional work. The risk of extra work is notably higher during the early phases of implementation, or what the interviewees describe "infancy stage". PIRHA faced significantly more challenges with its initial RPA solutions than HUS, which had more experience and more advanced automation in place.

The impact of extra workload depends on who bears the burden and to what extent. In PIRHA, most of the extra workload fell on secretaries and nurses, some feeling it "consumed work hours and taken away time from patient care." Participants in PIRHA noted that for the RPA robot to be beneficial, it should handle at least 50% of referrals.

However, one participant reported a success rate of just 27% during a two-week test. Many secretaries and nurses shared similar frustrations, calling automation an "additional burden." *"There is still a substantial amount of manual checking required. In the last report, more than 3/4 of cases had errors,"* Participant 6 explained.

The intelligent referral sorter at HUS appears to be more effective but has still created some extra work for doctors. However, at the organizational level, the overall impact is seen as positive: *"The doctors don't see the advantage yet in the referral handling work. However when I try to consider it from the perspective of the clinic's operation, I see that it creates a positive impact,"* noted Participant 24.

Know What to do. Process management depends on clearly knowing what to do, and automation enhances this through efficiency, availability, and standardization. For instance, in urgent care, faster referral handling can speed up treatment, while the dosage builder has reduced variations in medication data, increasing patient safety.

Faster processing does not necessarily lead to faster treatment. At HUS, an external expert notes that referral processing time has dropped significantly, from 32–35 h to 3–4 h. While this speeds up information delivery to patients, it hasn't necessarily accelerated access to treatment. Participants explained that quicker processing has simply shifted the bottleneck to the next step of patient care, leaving overall treatment time unchanged. However, faster referral handling benefits especially urgent cases, where automation can significantly improve access to care: *"For urgent referrals that take 1–7 days, it makes a significant difference if they can be processed in 2–4 h instead of five working days."* (Participant 1).

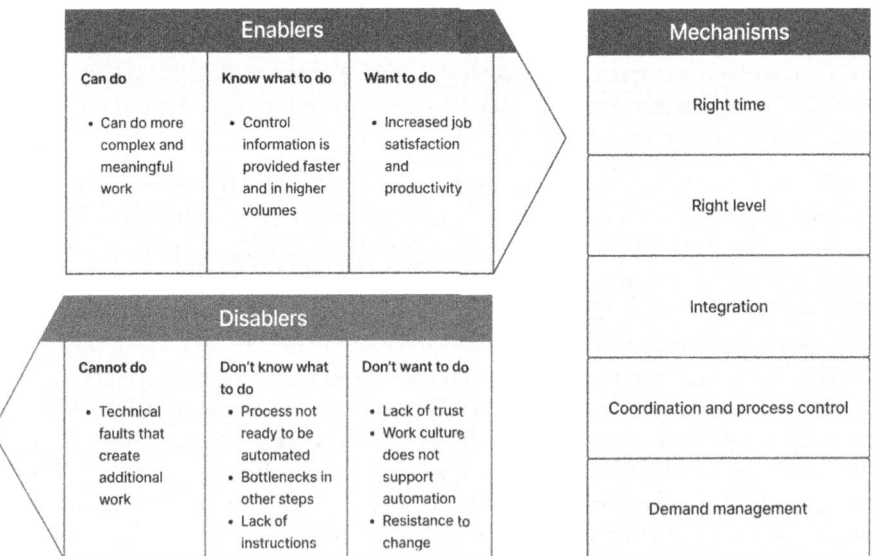

Fig. 4. Can, know, and want to do logics and their counterparts activated in the case studies.

Not all processes benefit from automation. If a process is not well-suited or deviates from the "ideal" workflow, automation may fail to achieve its goals [37]. For example, PIRHA tested automation in a pulmonary clinic, where a robot checked for missing patient lab tests and notified staff to reschedule appointments if necessary. If tests were missing, the system would notify a professional to reschedule the appointment. However, after implementation, it became clear that these notifications disrupted the workflow and created additional work rather than optimized the process. As a result, the automation was discontinued. Although the automation solution functioned technically, it was discontinued until the clinic's workflow could be refined.

Want to do. Considering healthcare professionals' motivation, attitudes toward new technology, and individual support needs are essential for maintaining engagement and job satisfaction [85]. Zhu and Kanjanamekanant [86] highlight that managers should watch for employee burnout in automation projects, especially those targeting high levels of automation. Achieving greater automation often demands increased effort and integration, potentially causing "work intensification" [86]. To prevent this, providing extra support and autonomy is crucial. Secretaries and nurses especially noted a learning curve in utilizing automation solutions. At PIRHA, some secretaries and nurses requested clearer guidance, describing current instructions as "vague" and their understanding of how to work with the robots as "somewhat lacking".

Motivation seems to vary depending on the solution's reliability and the organizational context. Interviewees stress that automation must deliver consistent results to gain trust. For example, some employees expressed hesitation to use the dosage builder because it struggles to accurately manage varying dosages. Participants even shared cases where employees avoided using automation after losing trust in it. *"It would be nice to know the extent to which one can trust it and how much one can actually utilize it,"* for example, Participant 25 summarized.

The work culture in some of the investigated units appears to influence how openly automation benefits are acknowledged. As one participant put it: *"If you have a difficult work atmosphere, you don't go tell your boss you have more bandwidth. You enjoy the fact that you have more space to do things. You don't report that you saved another 5 h of work time this week."* However, systematically collecting impact data could help in motivating the employees to use the solutions: *"It would likely turn even skeptical individuals towards a more positive outlook."* (Participant 31).

Mechanisms. The impact mechanisms of the investigated automation solutions are summarized in Table 4. Digital interventions are most effective when three key logics align, enabling impact through several mechanisms [20]. Each mechanism directly affects costs. Lillrank et al. [20] argues that to control rising healthcare costs without compromising quality and accessibility, one or more of the mechanisms they've listed must be addressed. The studied automation solutions unlock several mechanisms, but not all of them.

Table 4. Activated mechanisms by the two investigated automation solutions.

Mechanisms	Description (Lillrank et al. [20])	Impact of the mechanism: referral sorter	Impact of the mechanism: dosage builder
Right time	Actions are initiated and carried out at the optimal moment – neither too early nor too late.	+ Faster referral processing reduces backlog and allows quicker next steps + Urgent cases are handled quicker + Shifts the bottleneck to the next stage. The impact is dependent on managerial action	No effect
Right level	The least specialized yet sufficient resource is used to optimize costs and expertise. The more specialized the resource, the higher the cost.	+ Reduced the workload for secretaries and nurses – Extra work for doctors	No effect
Integration	Integrating fragmented data provides a full patient view for better decisions and treatment.	+ A standardized referral handling process	+ Standardized medication lists + Standardization reduces the need for subjective interpretations
Coordination and process control	Accurate, real-time data optimizes resource use and scheduling, minimizing waste. Poor coordination causes inefficiency.	+ Improved resource allocation + Time savings + 24/7 process availability – Decrease in output quality	+ Time savings per patient encounter
Demand management	Guiding patients to the right channels reduces unnecessary demand and ensures proper care.	+ Helps to direct patients to the right services	No effect
Increasing clinical evidence	Improving the availability and accessibility of clinical evidence.	No effect	No effect

(continued)

Table 4. (*continued*)

Mechanisms	Description (Lillrank et al. [20])	Impact of the mechanism: referral sorter	Impact of the mechanism: dosage builder
Co-creation of health	Utilizing the patient's resources through active self-care, and personal responsibility.	No effect	No effect

5.4 Outline the Outcomes

The perceived benefits and risks are described in detail in our previous report [29] and summarized in Table 5. In brief, automation at HUS and PIRHA has generally been well-received, with participants highlighting increased efficiency, improved resource use, and better service availability as key benefits. At HUS, referral processing times have notably decreased, particularly benefiting urgent cases, although automation hasn't necessarily shortened overall treatment times. Secretaries experienced the most significant direct time savings, whereas nurses and pharmacists saw only modest improvements in patient care time. Automation has standardized medication documentation, enhancing consistency across specialties and eliminating biases in information handling, promoting equal treatment access. However, cost savings perceptions vary; while digitalization experts highlight scalability, nurses and secretaries note that some of the saved time is spent monitoring and correcting errors.

The main risks participants highlighted involve additional workload from errors and potential declines in process quality, especially in the early implementation stages. PIRHA experienced more issues than HUS, where automation was more advanced. Nearly all nurses and secretaries in PIRHA reported frustration with the rate of referral sorting errors, increasing their workload. In HUS, while doctors faced some extra work due to incorrectly sorted referrals, automation improved the overall efficiency of the units. Participants in both organizations noted a trade-off between speed and accuracy, as robots work faster but with more errors than humans. Automation also struggles with more complex data in both organizations. To ensure patient safety, employees must continue to carefully verify automation outputs considering critical patient information.

6 Discussion on How to Prove It

The following Fig. 5 depicts a modified PROVE-IT model adapted to the context of the two investigated cases. The framework provides a structured approach to answer the question of "what to prove". Due to the notable automation challenges highlighted by participants, we also decided to highlight the risks and key considerations in the framework. Thus, we have expanded the PROVE-IT model with two add-ons; we included the risks as a separate section under outcomes and expanded the framework to include what we call the *disablers* of impact mechanisms: *cannot do, don't know what to do*, and *don't want to do* logics. These enablers and disablers of automation impact mechanisms are illustrated in Fig. 4.

The PROVE-IT model aligns with efforts to assess the impact of digitalization in the public sector. Its strength lies in describing impact from multiple perspectives rather than attempting to evaluate it, making it useful for answering the question: what to prove? Consequently, without concrete metrics, it lacks depth in providing more details on how to prove it.

Various attempts have been made to evaluate the impact of digitalization in the public sector. For instance, WHO [19] has provided step-by-step guidance on monitoring and evaluation efforts of digital health interventions. The COBRA model assesses e-government services from a user perspective, balancing benefits and opportunities against costs and risks [87]. Another possible approach is to focus on public value, evaluating impact based on service delivery, outcomes, trust, and organizational effectiveness [22]. More recently, Heikka et al. [88] introduced the Digitalization Impact Evaluation Model (DIEM), which was tested on a large Finnish healthcare ICT service provider. Though tested in a single case study, it offers valuable new insights for evaluating digitalization in healthcare.

Table 5. The perceived main benefits and risks in HUS and PIRHA [29].

Direct benefits	Description
Process efficiency	Increase in volumes and decrease in throughput times and delays
24/7 availability	The robots are always available
Increased resource utilization	Time savings enable employees to complete more complex tasks
Standardization	Uniting processes and outputs across units
Faster access to treatment (urgent cases)	Automation processes urgent cases faster
Compliance	Helps to meet reporting requirements
Interoperability	Easier data and system linkage
Scalability	Benefits are fast to scale across units
Equal access to treatment	Automation handles information without biases
Indirect benefits	
Increased employee experience	Increased job satisfaction and meaningfulness of work
Increased patient experience	For example, provides the information faster to the patient (referral sorter) and speeds up the treatment visit (dosage builder)
Cost effectiveness	Increase in the value of time gains (difference in cost of process by humans vs automation)

(*continued*)

Table 5. (*continued*)

Direct benefits	Description
Potential risks	
Additional work	The risk of additional work is higher during the "infancy stage" (PIRHA). In HUS, the intelligent referral sorter has been more effective than in PIRHA, but it has also moved extra work to doctors
Decrease in quality	Humans perform tasks more accurately than robots
Risks in patient safety	Outputs considering critical patient information still need to be reviewed by a professional

Our findings highlight the urgent need for a structured impact assessment model for healthcare automation, as no standardized "template or tool" currently exists. While some metrics are in use, employees find the value of implemented solutions unclear: *"The robot works well, but very few feel it's needed in their process."* This lack of perceived benefit has sometimes led to resistance, with employees viewing automation as an added burden: *"Some employees feel that they don't want to adopt automation because they perceive it as an additional burden"*.

Interviews from both PIRHA and HUS suggest that evaluation has been insufficient, primarily because no clear process and metrics have been established for it. Effective assessment should answer two key questions: *Is the project doing things right?* and *Is the project doing the right things?* [89]. In other words, a proper impact assessment consists of two phases: monitoring implementation activities and evaluating the outcomes. *Monitoring* involves regular data collection, review, and analysis—often the most time-intensive part of the process [19]. *Evaluation* systematically assesses whether the implemented solutions have met their objectives and delivered the intended impact [19]. In essence, evaluation assesses whether changes in key metrics result directly from the digital intervention.

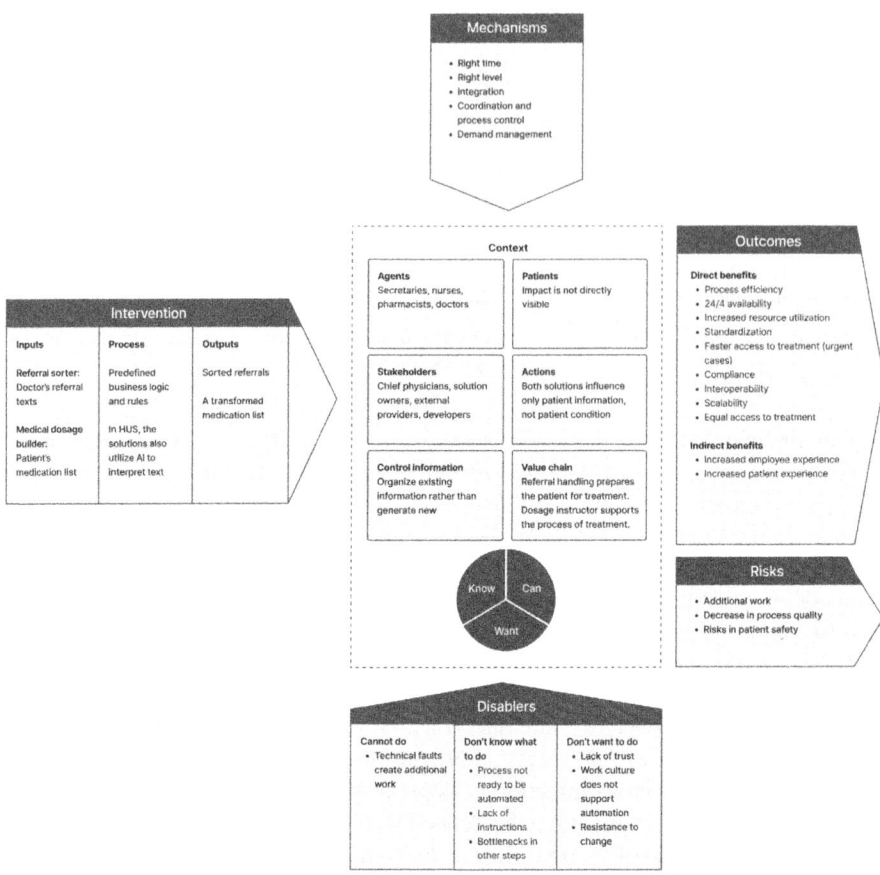

Fig. 5. The modified PROVE-IT model describing the impact of the investigated solutions.

Future research is required to design an appropriate process for evaluating the impact of digital solutions that do not necessarily have a direct impact on patients, such as back office automation in healthcare. Our previous report [29] discusses some of the critical perspectives that should be taken into account in designing an impact assessment framework. Especially in our investigated case organizations, the lack of baseline measurements, inconsistent monitoring, and a narrow focus on technical metrics were perceived as key challenges for future evaluation. Based on the conducted research, clearly there is a need for Finnish healthcare organizations to align on a monitoring process and determine suitable metrics for evaluating automation in the future.

7 Conclusions

This study investigated the impact of automation solutions, specifically RPA and AI enhanced IA, in two major Finnish healthcare districts. The research expanded on the insights of automation benefits, risks, and evaluation challenges presented in our previous report [29]. Especially, the focus of this study was to explore the impact mechanisms of automation. Utilizing the PROVE-IT model by Lillrank et al. [20], this research demonstrated how the impact of back-end solutions can be described and visualized. Thus, the model is valuable in future efforts when healthcare organizations are trying to understand the overall picture of how automation impacts healthcare processes, employees, and patients.

However, the study has its limitations. Firstly, it focused on only two regions with differing levels of automation maturity, which may limit the applicability of the findings. Secondly, the research relied primarily on qualitative data, making it subject to interpretation. While employees provided perspectives on automation's impact, patient feedback was not directly collected, posing a gap in understanding how automation influences patient experiences and outcomes. Method triangulation and quantitative approaches could strengthen the evidence, making findings more reliable and generalizable. Given the scope of the research, quantitative methods such as surveys were not incorporated, though they could help to validate key findings in future studies. Lastly, the use of purposive sampling without randomization may have led to sampling bias, limiting the representativeness of the sample and potentially impacting the study's external validity.

Comparative studies could help validate the use of the PROVE-IT model in describing the impact of automation on other implementations and healthcare contexts. While this research provides valuable insights to answer the question of "what to prove", it does not take a deep dive into how to prove it. Thus, further research is needed on the impact assessment of healthcare automation. Developing a standardized framework for evaluating automation's effectiveness could aid healthcare organizations in optimizing workflows and addressing challenges proactively.

To conclude, this research shows, how evaluation should focus on both the outcomes, and how they are created. Merely focusing on whether technology works is not sufficient. Both cases underline a heavy focus on technical factors and a lack of more holistic data. Thus, we must start to evaluate the impact of our automation efforts more broadly. In the end, the success of the technology depends not only on correct outputs but on meaningful outcomes that motivate to act.

Disclosure of Interests. The first author received a research grant from Digital Workforce, which was used to collect the empirical data. Digital Workforce neither established the research problem nor influenced the direction of the study The donation was received through the Foundation for Aalto University Science and Technology.

References

1. OECD. European Commission: Health at a Glance: Europe 2024: State of Health in the EU Cycle. OECD (2024). https://doi.org/10.1787/b3704e14-en
2. World Health Organization: Ageing and health. https://www.who.int/news-room/fact-sheets/detail/ageing-and-health. Accessed 14 Mar 2025
3. Deloitte: 2024 Global Health Care Sector Outlook (2023)
4. Gumas, E.D., Gunja, M.Z., Shah, A., Williams, R.D., II.: Overworked and Undervalued: Unmasking Primary Care Physicians' Dissatisfaction in 10 High-Income Countries — Findings from the 2022 International Health Policy Survey. (2023). https://doi.org/10.26099/T0Y2-6K44

5. Kirkonpelto, T.-M., Mäntyranta, T., Työryhmä, S.: Terveysalan henkilöstön riittävyyden ja saatavuuden: Tiekartta 2022–2027 : Sosiaali- ja terveysalan henkilöstön riittävyyden ja saatavuuden turvaaminen. https://julkaisut.valtioneuvosto.fi/handle/10024/164634. Accessed 14 Mar 2025
6. Aalto, M.: Terveydenhuolto on akuutissa kriisissä: Nämä lukemat näyttävät, kuinka tiukka umpisolmu on (2022)
7. Croell, K., et al.: Sosiaali- ja terveydenhuollon järjestäminen Suomessa: Valtakunnallinen asiantuntija-arvio, syksy 2024. https://www.julkari.fi/handle/10024/149932. Accessed 14 Mar 2025
8. Keva: Keva. Eläköitymisennuste 2024–2043. 4a. Hyvinvointialueiden eläköitymisennuste ammateittain (2024). https://www.keva.fi/uutishuone/tutkimukset-tilastot-ja-ennusteet/. https://www.keva.fi/uutishuone/tutkimukset-tilastot-ja-ennusteet/
9. Kirkonpelto, T.-M., Mäntyranta, T., Terveysministeriö, S.: Toimeenpanosuunnitelma 2024–2027 : Sosiaali- ja terveysalan sekä pelastusalan henkilöstön riittävyyden ja saatavuuden turvaaminen. https://julkaisut.valtioneuvosto.fi/handle/10024/165315. Accessed 14 Mar 2025
10. Sony, M., Antony, J., Tortorella, G.L.: Critical success factors for successful implementation of healthcare 4.0: a literature review and future research agenda. Int. J. Environ. Res. Public. Health. **20**, 4669 (2023). https://doi.org/10.3390/ijerph20054669
11. Kärkkäinen, E., et al.: Sosiaali- ja terveydenhuollon henkilöstön riittävyyden parantaminen hyvinvointialueiden henkilöstö- ja rekrytointipalvelujen näkökulmasta. https://www.julkari.fi/handle/10024/150034. Accessed 14 Mar 2025
12. Cresswell, K., Anderson, S., Montgomery, C., Weir, C.J., Atter, M., Williams, R.: Evaluation of digitalisation in healthcare and the quantification of the "unmeasurable." J. Gen. Intern. Med. **38**, 3610–3615 (2023). https://doi.org/10.1007/s11606-023-08405-y
13. Patrício, L., Varela, L., Silveira, Z.: Literature review and proposal framework for assessing robotic process automation and artificial intelligence projects in healthcare services. J. Artif. Intell. Auton. Intell. **01**, 155–171 (2024). https://doi.org/10.54364/JAIAI.2024.1111
14. Kedziora, D., Smolander, K.: Responding to healthcare emergency outbreak of COVID-19 pandemic with robotic process automation (RPA). In: Hawaii International Conference on System Science 2022 HICSS-55 (2022)
15. Ratia, M., Myllärniemi, J., Helander, N.: Intellectual capital and robotic process automation (RPA) - a capability perspective. In: Proceedings of the 16th International Forum on Knowledge Asset Dynamics (IFKAD 2021): Managing Knowledge in Uncertain Times, pp. 1810–1824. Institute of Knowledge Asset Management (IKAM) (2021)
16. Meironke, A., Kuehnel, S.: How to measure RPA's benefits? A review on metrics, indicators, and evaluation methods of RPA benefit assessment. In: Wirtsch. 2022 Proceedings (2022)
17. Denagama Vitharanage, I.M., Bandara, W., Syed, R., Toman, D.: An empirically supported conceptualisation of robotic process automation (RPA) benefits. In: Proceedings of the 28th European Conference on Information Systems (ECIS2020). Association for Information Systems, United States of America (2020)
18. Güner, E., Han, S., Juell-Skielse, G.: Robotic process automation as a routine capability: a literature review. ECIS 2020 Research Paper (2020)
19. World Health Organization: Monitoring and evaluating digital health interventions: a practical guide to conducting research and assessment. World Health Organization, Geneva (2016)
20. Lillrank, P., et al.: Terveydenhuollon digitaalisten ratkaisujen vaikuttavuuden osoittaminen (2019). https://research.aalto.fi/en/publications/terveydenhuollon-digitaalisten-ratkaisujen-vaikuttavuuden-osoitt
21. Parviainen, P., Kääriäinen, J., Honkatukia, J., Federley, M.: Julkishallinnon digitalisaatio – tuottavuus ja hyötyjen mittaaminen. https://julkaisut.valtioneuvosto.fi/handle/10024/80883. Accessed 14 Mar 2025

22. Karunasena, K., Deng, H.: Critical factors for evaluating the public value of e-government in Sri Lanka. Gov. Inf. Q. **29**, 76–84 (2012). https://doi.org/10.1016/j.giq.2011.04.005
23. Kääriäinen, J., et al.: Ohjelmistorobotiikka ja tekoäly – soveltamisen askelmerkkejä, https://julkaisut.valtioneuvosto.fi/handle/10024/161123. Accessed 14 Mar 2025
24. Heponiemi, T., et al.: Usability factors associated with physicians' distress and information system-related stress: cross-sectional survey. JMIR Med. Inform. **7**, e13466 (2019). https://doi.org/10.2196/13466
25. Heponiemi, T., et al.: Electronic health record implementations and insufficient training endanger nurses' well-being: cross-sectional survey study. J. Med. Internet Res. **23**, e27096 (2021). https://doi.org/10.2196/27096
26. Kaihlanen, A.-M., et al.: The associations of electronic health record usability and user age with stress and cognitive failures among Finnish registered nurses: cross-sectional study. JMIR Med. Inform. **8**, e23623 (2020). https://doi.org/10.2196/23623
27. Lottonen, T., Kaihlanen, A.-M., Nadav, J., Hilama, P., Heponiemi, T.: Nurses' and physicians' perceptions of the impact of eHealth and information systems on the roles of health care professionals: a qualitative descriptive study. Health Inform. J. **30**, 14604582241234260 (2024). https://doi.org/10.1177/14604582241234261
28. Pennanen, P., et al.: Digitaalisten palvelujen vaikutukset sosiaali- ja terveydenhuollossa. https://julkaisut.valtioneuvosto.fi/handle/10024/165147. Accessed 17 Mar 2025
29. Kaitosalmi, J., Ratia, M.: Evaluating healthcare automation: a multi-case study on the utilization of automation initiatives in healthcare operations. In: Proceedings of the 16th International Joint Conference on Knowledge Discovery, Knowledge Engineering and Knowledge Management, pp. 246–255. SCITEPRESS - Science and Technology Publications, Porto, Portugal (2024). https://doi.org/10.5220/0012947100003838
30. Zayas-Cabán, T., Okubo, T.H., Posnack, S.: Priorities to accelerate workflow automation in health care. J. Am. Med. Inform. Assoc. **30**, 195–201 (2022). https://doi.org/10.1093/jamia/ocac197
31. Fred, H.L., Scheid, M.S.: Physician burnout: causes, consequences, and (?) cures. tex. Heart Inst. J. **45**, 198–202 (2018). https://doi.org/10.14503/THIJ-18-6842
32. Harris, D.A., Haskell, J., Cooper, E., Crouse, N., Gardner, R.: Estimating the association between burnout and electronic health record-related stress among advanced practice registered nurses. Appl. Nurs. Res. **43**, 36–41 (2018). https://doi.org/10.1016/j.apnr.2018.06.014
33. Coombs, C., Hislop, D., Taneva, S.K., Barnard, S.: The strategic impacts of Intelligent Automation for knowledge and service work: an interdisciplinary review. J. Strateg. Inf. Syst. **29**, 101600 (2020). https://doi.org/10.1016/j.jsis.2020.101600
34. Parasuraman, R., Riley, V.: Humans and automation: use, misuse, disuse, abuse. Hum. Factors J. Hum. Factors Ergon. Soc. **39**, 230–253 (1997). https://doi.org/10.1518/001872097778543886
35. Ratia, M., Myllärniemi, J., Helander, N.: Robotic process automation - creating value by digitalizing work in the private healthcare? In: Proceedings of the 22nd International Academic Mindtrek Conference, pp. 222–227. Association for Computing Machinery, New York (2018). https://doi.org/10.1145/3275116.3275129
36. Davenport, T.H., Kirby, J.: Just how smart are smart machines? MIT Sloan Manag. Rev. **57**, 21–25 (2016)
37. Zayas-Cabán, T., Haque, S.N., Kemper, N.: Identifying opportunities for workflow automation in health care: lessons learned from other industries. Appl. Clin. Inform. **12**, 686–697 (2021). https://doi.org/10.1055/s-0041-1731744
38. Ferris, T., Ackers, J., Borhani, M.: RPA in the NHS: guidance for designing, delivering and sustaining RPA within the NHS. National Health Service (NHS) (2022)

39. Dumas, M., La Rosa, M., Mendling, J., Reijers, H.A.: Fundamentals of Business Process Management. Springer, Heidelberg (2013). https://doi.org/10.1007/978-3-642-33143-5
40. Herm, L.-V., Janiesch, C., Helm, A., Imgrund, F., Hofmann, A., Winkelmann, A.: A framework for implementing robotic process automation projects. Inf. Syst. E-Bus. Manag. **21**, 1–35 (2023). https://doi.org/10.1007/s10257-022-00553-8
41. Syed, R., et al.: Robotic process automation: contemporary themes and challenges. Comput. Ind. **115**, 103162 (2020). https://doi.org/10.1016/j.compind.2019.103162
42. Santos, F., Pereira, R., Vasconcelos, J.B.: Toward robotic process automation implementation: an end-to-end perspective. Bus. Process. Manag. J. **26**, 405–420 (2019). https://doi.org/10.1108/BPMJ-12-2018-0380
43. Willcocks, L.P., Lacity, M., Craig, A.: The IT function and robotic process automation. http://www.lse.ac.uk/management/research/outsourcingunit/. Accessed 14 Mar 2025
44. Ivančić, L., Suša Vugec, D., Bosilj Vukšić, V.: Robotic process automation: systematic literature review. In: Di Ciccio, C., et al. (eds.) Business Process Management: Blockchain and Central and Eastern Europe Forum, pp. 280–295. Springer, Cham (2019). https://doi.org/10.1007/978-3-030-30429-4_19
45. Kim, S.-H.: Development of evaluation criteria for robotic process automation (RPA) solution selection. Electronics **12**, 986 (2023). https://doi.org/10.3390/electronics12040986
46. Bhatnagar, R., Jain, R.: Robotic process automation in healthcare-a review. Int. Robot. Autom. J. **5**, 12–14 (2019). https://doi.org/10.15406/iratj.2019.05.00164
47. Doğuç, Ö.: Robotic process automation (RPA) applications in COVID-19. In: Dincer, H., Yüksel, S. (eds.) Management Strategies to Survive in a Competitive Environment, pp. 233–247. Springer, Cham (2021). https://doi.org/10.1007/978-3-030-72288-3_16
48. Aguirre, S., Rodriguez, A.: Automation of a business process using robotic process automation (RPA): a case study. In: Figueroa-García, J.C., López-Santana, E.R., Villa-Ramírez, J.L., Ferro-Escobar, R. (eds.) Applied Computer Sciences in Engineering, pp. 65–71. Springer, Cham (2017). https://doi.org/10.1007/978-3-319-66963-2_7
49. Ng, K.K.H., Chen, C.-H., Lee, C.K.M., Jiao, J., Yang, Z.-X.: A systematic literature review on intelligent automation: aligning concepts from theory, practice, and future perspectives. Adv. Eng. Inform. **47**, 101246 (2021). https://doi.org/10.1016/j.aei.2021.101246
50. Fung, H.P.: Criteria, Use Cases and Effects of Information Technology Process Automation (ITPA) (2014). https://papers.ssrn.com/abstract=2588999
51. Sarker, S., Jamal, L., Ahmed, S.F., Irtisam, N.: Robotics and artificial intelligence in healthcare during COVID-19 pandemic: a systematic review. Robot. Auton. Syst. **146**, 103902 (2021). https://doi.org/10.1016/j.robot.2021.103902
52. Adolfsson, F.: Västerbotten sparar 100 000 timmar med RPA (2021)
53. HUS: HUS. Tarkastuslautakunnan arviointikertomus 2021 Helsingin ja Uudenmaan sairaanhoitopiirin valtuustolle. April. HUS. HUS, Helsinki (2021)
54. Davenport, T.H., Kirby, J.: Beyond automation. Harv. Bus. Rev. (2015)
55. Kedziora, D., Hyrynsalmi, S.: Turning robotic process automation onto intelligent automation with machine learning. In: Proceedings of the 11th International Conference on Communities and Technologies, pp. 1–5. Association for Computing Machinery, New York (2023). https://doi.org/10.1145/3593743.3593746
56. Berruti, F., Nixon, G., Taglioni, G., Whiteman, R.: Intelligent process automation: the engine at the core of the next-generation operating model. McKinsey Digit. (2017)
57. García, J.F., Spatharou, A., Hieronimus, S., Beck, J.-P., Jenkins, J.: Transforming healthcare with AI: the impact on the workforce and organisations. EIT Health & McKinsey Digital (2020)
58. STT: Cancer Care Follow-up automation developed by a Finnish company improves patient safety and aims to save hundreds of millions of euros | Digital Workforce Services Oyj.

https://www.sttinfo.fi/tiedote/70238844/cancer-care-follow-up-automation-developed-by-a-finnish-company-improves-patient-safety-and-aims-to-save-hundreds-of-millions-of-euros?publisherId=69819009&lang=en. Accessed 14 Mar 2025
59. Ahlskog, B.: Ohjelmistorobotit ja tekoäly lähetekäsittelyn apuna I HUS. https://www.hus.fi/ajankohtaista/ohjelmistorobotit-ja-tekoaly-lahetekasittelyn-apuna. Accessed 14 Mar 2025
60. Impact, n. meanings, etymology and more I Oxford English Dictionary. https://www.oed.com/dictionary/impact_n. Accessed 16 Mar 2025
61. Clarke, G.M., Conti, S., Wolters, A.T., Steventon, A.: Evaluating the impact of healthcare interventions using routine data. BMJ l2239 (2019). https://doi.org/10.1136/bmj.l2239
62. Burches, E., Burches, M.: Efficacy, effectiveness and efficiency in the health care: the need for an agreement to clarify its meaning. Int. Arch. Public Health Community Med. **4** (2020). https://doi.org/10.23937/2643-4512/1710035
63. Ikonen, T.: Asiakasryhmäkohtainen tieto laadusta ja vaikuttavuudesta sosiaali- ja terveydenhuollon tiedolla johtamisessa ja ohjauksessa : Laaturekisterien asema palvelujärjestelmässä. https://julkaisut.valtioneuvosto.fi/handle/10024/161976. Accessed 14 Mar 2025
64. Sintonen, H., Pekurinen, M.: Terveystaloustiede. WSOY, Porvoo (2006)
65. Sintonen, H., Blom, M., Roine, R.P., Räsänen, P., Ryynänen, O.-P.: Terveystaloustiede on tärkeää lääkärille. Suom. Lääkärilehti. **76**, 2166–2168 (2021)
66. Pitkänen, L., Haavisto, I., Vähäviita, P., Torkki, P., Leskelä, L., Komssi, V.: Vaikut tavuus SOTE:ssa. Suoritteista tuloksiin. Nordic Healthcare Group NHG, Helsinki (2018)
67. Porter, M.E.: What is value in health care? N. Engl. J. Med. **363**, 2477–2481 (2010). https://doi.org/10.1056/NEJMp1011024
68. Porter, M.E., Lee, T.H.: Harv. Bus. Rev. 50–70 (2013). https://hbr.org/2013/10/the-strategy-that-will-fix-health-care
69. Axmann, B., Harmoko, H.: The five dimensions of digital technology assessment with the focus on robotic process automation (RPA). Teh. Glas. **15**, 267–274 (2021). https://doi.org/10.31803/tg-20210429105337
70. Wanner, J., Hofmann, A., Fischer, M., Imgrund, F., Janiesch, C., Geyer-Klingeberg, J.: Process Selection in RPA Projects – Towards a Quantifiable Method of Decision Making (2019)
71. Astbury, B., Leeuw, F.L.: Unpacking black boxes: mechanisms and theory building in evaluation. Am. J. Eval. **31**, 363–381 (2010). https://doi.org/10.1177/1098214010371972
72. Pawson, R., Tilley, N.: Realistic Evaluation, pp. 1–256 (1997)
73. Denyer, D., Tranfield, D., van Aken, J.E.: Developing design propositions through research synthesis. Organ. Stud. **29**, 393–413 (2008). https://doi.org/10.1177/0170840607088020
74. Bunge, M.: Scientific Research II: The Search for Truth. Springer, Cham (1967)
75. Mukumbang, F.C., Marchal, B., Van Belle, S., Van Wyk, B.: Using the realist interview approach to maintain theoretical awareness in realist studies. Qual. Res. **20**, 485–515 (2020). https://doi.org/10.1177/1468794119881985
76. Marchal, B., van Belle, S., van Olmen, J., Hoerée, T., Kegels, G.: Is realist evaluation keeping its promise? A review of published empirical studies in the field of health systems research. Evaluation **18**, 192–212 (2012). https://doi.org/10.1177/1356389012442444
77. Saunders, M.N.K., Lewis, P., Thornhill, A.: Research Methods for Business Students. Pearson, New York (2019)
78. Antwi, S.K., Hamza, K.: Qualitative and quantitative research paradigms in business research: a philosophical reflection. Eur. J. Bus. Manag. **7**, 217–225 (2015)
79. Yin, R.K.: Case Study Research and Applications: Design and Methods. SAGE, Los Angeles (2018)
80. Andrade, C.: The inconvenient truth about convenience and purposive samples. Indian J. Psychol. Med. **43**, 86–88 (2021). https://doi.org/10.1177/0253717620977000

81. Etikan, I., Musa, S.A., Alkassim, R.S.: Comparison of convenience sampling and purposive sampling. Am. J. Theor. Appl. Stat. **5**, 1–4 (2015). https://doi.org/10.11648/j.ajtas.20160501.11
82. Terveyden ja hyvinvoinnin laitos: Sote-sanastot - Sanasto - Terveydenhuollon tiedonhallinnan sanasto. https://sotesanastot.thl.fi/termed-publish-server/vocabulary/3e597f88-02a0-478d-b65b-35f0fd7eae71/concept/d0ee1239-7440-4653-8e9f-869176587a44. Accessed 14 Mar 2025
83. Hsieh, H.-F., Shannon, S.E.: Three approaches to qualitative content analysis. Qual. Health Res. **15**, 1277–1288 (2005). https://doi.org/10.1177/1049732305276687
84. Vila-Henninger, L., et al.: Abductive coding: theory building and qualitative (re)analysis. Sociol. Methods Res. **53**, 968–1001 (2024). https://doi.org/10.1177/00491241211067508
85. Jedwab, R.M., Manias, E., Redley, B., Dobroff, N., Hutchinson, A.M.: Impacts of technology implementation on nurses' work motivation, engagement, satisfaction and well-being: a realist review. J. Clin. Nurs. **32**, 6037–6060 (2023). https://doi.org/10.1111/jocn.16730
86. Zhu, Y.-Q., Kanjanamekanant, K.: Human–bot co-working: job outcomes and employee responses. Ind. Manag. Data Syst. **123**, 515–533 (2023). https://doi.org/10.1108/IMDS-02-2022-0114
87. Osman, I.H., et al.: COBRA framework to evaluate e-government services: a citizen-centric perspective. Gov. Inf. Q. **31**, 243–256 (2014). https://doi.org/10.1016/j.giq.2013.10.009
88. Heikka, J., Heikkinen, S., Iivari, M., Koivumäki, T.: Digitalization impact evaluation model: a case study. In: Bertolino, A., Pascoal Faria, J., Lago, P., and Semini, L. (eds.) Quality of Information and Communications Technology, pp. 279–294. Springer, Cham (2024). https://doi.org/10.1007/978-3-031-70245-7_20
89. Pritchett, L., Samji, S., Hammer, J.S.: It's All About MeE: Using Structured Experiential Learning ('e') to Crawl the Design Space (2013). https://papers.ssrn.com/abstract=2248785. https://doi.org/10.2139/ssrn.2248785

Uncertainty Analysis in Socio-economic Dynamic Microsimulation Models: A Literature Review

Miia Rissanen[1(✉)] and Jyrki Savolainen[1,2]

[1] Lappeenranta-Lahti University of Technology, Yliopistonkatu 34, Lappeenranta, Finland
Miia.rissanen@keva.fi, jyrki.savolainen@lut.fi
[2] CSC – IT Center for Science, Tehdaskatu 15, Kajaani, Finland

Abstract. This paper investigates the use of dynamic microsimulation (DM) models and the application of Monte Carlo (MC) simulation as an uncertainty analysis (UA) technique in socio-economic policy analysis. Based on a structured review of 44 studies, the analysis identifies key shortcomings in how uncertainty is addressed in existing modeling practices and related reporting of probabilistic outcomes. Key findings reveal also a lack of standardized guidelines for validating simulation results, as well as a use of updated data and finer temporal resolution in models. The paper advocates for a methodological shift toward more agile, transparent, and frequently updated models that can better support timely, evidence-based policymaking. Establishing common standards for UA and related reporting would enhance both the interpretability and policy relevance of DM-based research.

Keywords: Dynamic microsimulation · Socio-economic models · Demographic models · Uncertainty analysis · Monte Carlo simulation · Forecasting

1 Introduction

Dynamic microsimulation (DM) models are analytical tools to simulate the behavior of individual units over time and predict recurring events based on historical data. These models integrate data analysis, computational methods, and computer experiments to support ex-ante policy analysis, government planning and decision making [17, 37, 76, 79, 93, 99]. Throughout the simulation, each micro-unit, representing diverse population characteristics (e.g., age, employment, health status), evolves independently through stochastic processes, with their states updated over time according to current conditions and attributes—a phenomenon referred to as "dynamic aging" [22, 29].

Simulation models can enhance population forecasting by capturing uncertainty thus providing probability-based projections for better decision-making. Probabilistic models aim to answer key questions about the future while quantifying uncertainty through probability distributions [13, 57]. Stochastic methods are a special case of probabilistic methods, focusing on modeling of random processes over time. Over the past decades,

© The Author(s), under exclusive license to Springer Nature Switzerland AG 2026
J. Bernardino et al. (Eds.): IC3K 2024, CCIS 2703, pp. 279–300, 2026.
https://doi.org/10.1007/978-3-032-06878-1_13

so-called "statistical demography" has advanced rapidly, particularly in stochastic population forecasting at the national level (see e.g., [13, 37, 82]). Harding [37] summarizes that many popular, national level dynamic microsimulation applications (see also, O'Donoghue's review study [75]), were initially developed to address concerns about population aging and to assess the affordability of the future social protection system (see also Astolfi et al. [5]). Over the last decade, their applications in health and labour market studies have been growing [77]. Unlike population-aggregating macroscopic approaches, DMs consider individuals separately, which is crucial for understanding the complex interconnections between factors such as demographics, education, employment, and health that influence future economic and health outcomes. In this paper, we do not distinguish between socio-economic and demographic models, but rather use the term socio-economic models, which broadly covers any demographic forecasting models that may be included in the review.

Times of uncertainty, such as the Ukraine war, COVID-19 and past financial crises, have created new demands for real-time simulation and "nowcasting" [79, 101] (see also [30, 74]) to facilitate timely decision-making in rapidly evolving economic landscape. Digital trace data from web browsing and mobile applications provide new type of regional and temporal data granularity, enabling close-to-real time modeling of social phenomena and economic activity, such as predicting disease spread or labor market activity [5, 10, 22, 46, 63, 77, 85]. Nowcasting techniques are commonly applied relying on high-frequency indicators like employment, financial markets, and production to estimate near-term GDP growth [85, 101] (see also [43, 54]). A recent review of Stundziene et al. [101] concludes, however, that the field of nowcasting is still relatively new and evolving.

With more real-time data, decision-support tools such as simulation models could better capture short-term fluctuations instead of producing predictions on an annual level, thus hiding seasonal variations and timely insights, e.g., related to healthcare demands or labour force participation. However, it seems common that administrative data used in many popular DMs targeted to public policy analysis typically has a time lag [79], even if such data is generated constantly as by-products of administrative transactions (see discussion [37, 101]).

The proper accounting of modeling uncertainty remains challenging [82] even though so called "data revolution" has enhanced simulation capabilities [28, 68, 79]. To address the inherent stochasticity when simulating individual behaviour, demographic and economic changes is complex, particularly given (too) high expectations for perfect modeling accuracy [20, 36, 76, 77, 82, 94, 95]. In modeling studies, this often shifts the focus from probabilistic thinking back to traditional, deterministic analysis with single-point estimates (see discussion, [56]), although it is well-known (see e.g., [20, 95, 108]) that for DMs to be useful, they must thoroughly analyze potential impacts on populations under various scenarios (and their associated probabilities). Bijak et al. [13] summarize that in the context of probabilistic methods, probability distributions should be formulated in a way that aids decision-making, as the preference for deterministic methods stems from the easiness of understanding (see also, [82]). That is why probabilistic population forecasting are rarely integrated into official statistics. The authors discussing uncertainty and stochasticity in socio-economic modeling include also Alho and Lassila [1], Raftery [82], Xue et al. [111], Sabelhaus and Topoleski [91], and Lee and Tuljapurkar [62].

Previous literature reviews and surveys on DMs [64, 75, 77] provide a comprehensive overview of DMs developed over decades (see also [5, 98, 112]). In past reviews, the lack of standardization in reporting practices and incomplete validation of models stay as an ongoing topic (see also [20, 61]). O'Donoghue [75], for instance, highlights the need for a better understanding of simulation properties, particularly the role of random numbers. O'Donoghue [76] critically observes for publications on microsimulation studies to primarily report simple point estimates generated by the models despite their incorporation of uncertainty (see also [58, 108]).

Past reviews on simulation studies especially in socio-economic context have not dug deeper into the use of probabilistic methods, specifically Monte Carlo simulation approach and related reporting, although best practices of uncertainty analysis have been proposed by e.g., Burgard and Schmaus [20], Lee et al. [61] and Caro [25]. Another gap pertains to the scarcity of literature examining whether enhanced data accessibility in terms of granularity and timeliness have spurred advancements in models capable of delivering more accurate and timely forecasts, compared to "traditional" DMs those run simulations in yearly intervals and are initialized using historical data with a time lag of several years [79].

The rest of the paper is structured as follows: the next section covers theoretical background by deepening the understanding of the methods of dynamic microsimulations and uncertainty analysis. It also provides a brief theoretical overview of the Monte Carlo technique as an approach, followed by a description of the literature review method. In the Results section, the findings of the review are presented and further discussed in the Results analysis section. The paper concludes with suggestions for future research.

2 Theoretical Background

2.1 Dynamic Microsimulations

Microsimulation models are categorized as dynamic or static, and they involve either deterministic or stochastic approaches to produce predictions [17, 34, 76]. Static models analyze immediate ("morning after") distributional impacts of policy changes, assuming unit characteristics remain constant over time. Dynamic microsimulation usually forecasts long-term impacts, like fiscal and healthcare demands [17], and thus, recognized as a relevant tool for decision-makers who require long-term perspectives [38]. Models are also categorized based on their forecasting nature whether they employ continuous-time or discrete event simulations. Shortly, in continuous-time models the changes of simulated individuals can occur at any point, while for discrete-time the simulation horizon consists of a set of fixed periods [20]. Static model is often deterministic producing the same results given the same inputs, because it doesn't involve randomness or probabilistic transitions. As such, deterministic population forecasts use different scenarios to indicate uncertainty, although these models usually handle all outcomes as equally likely. A criticism of static models is that they assume perfect correlations between demographic components and cannot capture real-world complexity in a realistic manner [21, 42].

In microsimulations, the initial population consists of individuals (micro-units) that represent the population's characteristics across various dimensions. During a dynamic microsimulation, each micro-unit evolves independently according to stochastic processes. Their states are continuously updated based on their current conditions and attributes—a process known as dynamic aging. A model based on static aging simulates the passage of time indirectly through updating and reweighting, without simulating individual life events like dynamic models do. See more discussion and methodological aspects e.g., Dekkers [29] and Burgard et al. [21, 22].

Agent-based models (ABM) extend traditional dynamic microsimulation approaches by incorporating smaller transition matrices and diverse rule sets to simulate agent properties, being however, from a mathematical and computational perspective identical to microsimulations [7, 86]. Agents can represent individuals or groups, making microsimulation highly detailed and specialized [7, 19]. Summarized by Li et al. [63], the agent approach allows simulation first from a microscopic view, after which the macroscopic changes under different scenarios can be quantified in a bottom–up way (see also [75]). With the increasing accessibility for large-scale, individual-based panel data, ABM has become popular for simulating heterogeneity [63, 72, 75]. This method has been used for decades to analyze socio-economic phenomena, such as the effects of social networks on demographic processes [45, 68], and for example, in modeling epidemic spread (see e.g., [63, 100]). However, ABM still remain outside the mainstream in micro-level simulations of social systems although their potential to apply detailed population data [45].

A common criticism of complex dynamic microsimulation models is that they require significant resources to develop and maintain, which is why they are predominantly crafted within policy institutions [33, 37, 77, 87]. While generic software packages like JAS-mine, LIAM2, and SIDD are available, researchers often develop their own models. However, this practice can limit the external validation of simulation results [19, 77, 86, 104]. Common constraints of modeling tasks involve also data availability and computing time issues, although according to O'Donoghue and Dekkers [77], these areas have gone through significant improvements in past decade. Authors [77] also call for the importance of personal skills alongside technical expertise when building simulation models, such as sectoral/policy knowledge and analytical skills. There is also a continued need for methodological approaches to clearly explain simulation results to counter the longstanding "black box" criticism. These debate prompts a recommendation to develop specialized, simpler dynamic models that can be integrated into more complex microsimulation frameworks for detailed interactions (see discussion [37, 112]). The pros and cons of model complexity is also discussed in the survey of microsimulations by Spielauer [98].

2.2 Uncertainty Modeling

Although methods exist for analyzing and communicating uncertainty, it remains one of the most challenging aspects of simulating complex demographic processes which, still, every modeler has to consider [20, 40, 62, 91, 95]. This is especially true in the case of fiscal decision-making in policy evaluation [1, 59]. Sharif et al. [95] assert that the purpose of uncertainty analysis (UA) is to provide uncertainty/confidence intervals around the mean estimate of one or more outcomes. Confidence intervals (CI) of simulation results help to communicate uncertainty in the findings, when a set of simulations are run to capture a spectrum of outcomes. A more comprehensive discussion of UA is given by e.g. Sharif et al. [95] and Briggs [16]. The different forms of uncertainty analysis with the detailed process are described by, for example, Kozlova et al. [56].

The types of uncertainties can be categorized in several ways. Aleatory uncertainty refers to the inherent randomness in the real world [66, 94]. As it arises from natural variability, it cannot be reduced by gaining more knowledge, but it is typically addressed through probabilistic modeling techniques, such as Monte Carlo simulations. Epistemic uncertainty, on the other hand, stems from a lack of knowledge, incomplete information with limited historical data, or model limitations. It is reducible and can be addressed by improving data, models, and the overall understanding [66, 94, 95]. The modeler aims to enhance data collection to better represent the population, as larger samples assist in distinguishing between "real variation" stemming from inherent randomness and random variation caused by sampling error.

Monte Carlo (MC) simulation is a numerical method that involves random sampling from distributions and repeated simulations using the sampled values. It is one of the key methods for handling uncertainty in DMs as it offers a simple, yet robust, approach to systematically explore how variations in inputs affect model outputs, especially when analytical approaches are impractical [95]. As such, the MC simulation mitigates misinterpretations from single simulations by examining a broad spectrum of possible outcomes, thereby capturing the inherent variability in simulated population dynamics [20, 69, 90].

The Markov Chain Monte Carlo (MCMC) method draws mutually dependent samples to generate random sequences of state transitions based on probabilistic rules (for details, see e.g., [57]). The state transitions should follow as closely as possible real-world settings. For example, in demographic simulations, logit models can estimate probabilities of transitions like employment or health status changes. This process is repeated hundreds or thousands of times to simulate the expected behavior of the object of interest over time, with calibration performed at each step using newly generated parameters. As such, the MC simulation mitigates misinterpretations from single simulations by examining a broad spectrum of possible outcomes, thereby capturing the inherent variability in simulated population dynamics [20, 69, 90].

3 Data and Methodology

This paper addresses a research gap specifically related to the use of probabilistic methods, mainly Monte Carlo simulation, in literature reviews on dynamic microsimulation for modeling demographic and social systems. The literature review query was structured as follows: publications from 2000 onwards were searched in the Scopus Database using the terms 'Dynamic Microsimulation' and 'Population' or 'Demography' in the title, abstract, or keywords. This search yielded 158 results, with the majority of studies falling within Social Sciences (27%), Medicine (23%), and Mathematics (10%). There has been a notable increase in the number of publications in recent years, with a peak in 2022, as illustrated in Fig. 1.

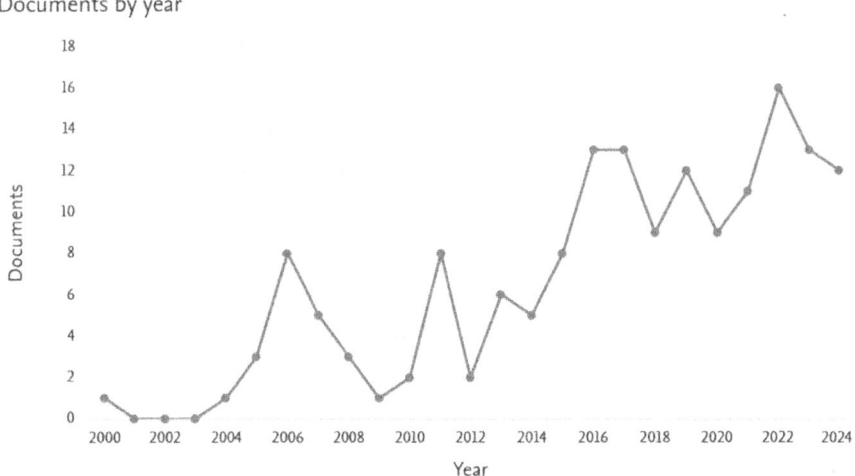

Fig. 1. Results of the literature survey by years (2000–2024) on Scopus search.

A content analysis of the titles and abstracts was conducted, resulting in 44 relevant documents focused on dynamic microsimulation modeling, primarily aimed at modeling demographic dynamics, such as forecasting trends in population growth, aging, and social structures and related economic consequences. We intentionally did not limit the findings to social sciences in order to compare potential differences in publications from different fields (e.g., social sciences, economics and medicine).

In this review, the focus is not on the technical details of the models. Therefore, technical or model introduction reports outlining mainly model construction were excluded, as they do not primarily focus on conducting simulations but rather introduce aspects such as modules and software requirements. Additionally, since the primary interest is on dynamic microsimulations (DMs), publications that utilize combined micro-macro simulations were also excluded. However, the review includes studies in which the models may be partially static and dynamic, typically in modular national models.

The review attempts to aggregate knowledge on the conventions of uncertainty analysis such as number of simulations run and the use of CIs. Additionally, other possible discussion of uncertainty aspects together with its possible mitigation methods are emphasized in the analysis. Secondly, the review inspects the time span of the forecasts (e.g., annual) and the possible specification of being spatial or agent-based model (ABM). These reflect (from one perspective) to the data aspects in terms of timeliness and granularity. The paper aims to identify those studies that aim to utilize near real-time information or continuously updating models (i.e. "nowcasting").

4 Results and Discussion

Table 1 presents basic information of the modeling works (author, year), the brief summary of main modeling purpose and the findings related to the MC simulation and data aspects, as detailed in the previous section. We do not specify whether the MC is used only in some model parts. Also, if the use of MC is not reported, but repeated simulations are applied, it is categorized under the MC. If other related methods are clearly reported, such as bootstrapping, they are marked. The information in Table 1 is based solely on the content of the reviewed articles. Some studies may omit details on modeling methodology but may reference other sources for aspects like model validation or MC related information. However, this review does not examine these additional sources, focusing only on the primary articles identified.

Table 1. Reviewed studies of DMs in alphabetical order. Legend: [*MC*] = Monte Carlo method used (*Yes/No* or "-" if unclear and additional *NR* = not reported, if repeated simulation applied without reporting the method or "*B*" if bootstrapping is applied instead of MC), [*Simrun*] = number of simulations run (*NR* = not reported and "-" if MC not applied), [*CI*] = confidence intervals used (if MC used, otherwise "-") [*Simstep*] = Forecast period (*A* = annual, *M* = monthly, *D* = daily) + Detail (spatial (*S*)/ agent-based (*AB*). *In progress = not yet available since study ongoing but reported to be applied. Adopted from Rissanen & Savolainen [88].

Auth. & Year	Study purpose	MC/Simrun/CI/Simstep + Detail
Aransiola et al. 2024	To assess if expanding Social Assistance could reduce infant and child mortality in Brazil.	Yes/10000/ Yes/A
Archer et al. 2021	To project the prevalence of chronic diseases and their economic impacts using the Future Elderly Model (FEM) in the UK.	Yes/100/Yes/A
Atella et al. 2021	To project future individual health status across OECD countries by applying several FEM models.	Yes/NR/Yes/A
Baldini et al. 2008	To assess the characteristics of the long-term disabled in Italy and the evolution of public expenditure for long-term care.	Yes/NR/No/A
Ballas et al. 2005	To simulate the basic components of population change in Ireland using spatial SMILE model.	Yes/NR/No/A + S
Ballas et al. 2005	To simulate urban and regional populations in UK.	No/-/-/A + S
Becker et al. 2024	To assess the efficiency of COVID-19 mitigation strategies with the CEACOV model in U.S.	-/-/-/D

(*continued*)

Table 1. (*continued*)

Auth. & Year	Study purpose	MC/Simrun/CI/Simstep + Detail
Ben Jelloul et al. 2023	To forecast morbidity of population aged + 60 and identify causing factors in France.	No/-/-/A
Bonin et al. 2015	To model monetary value of family policy measures with ZEW model in Germany.	No/-/-/A
Brouwers et al. 2016	To study the effects of an ageing population on inpatient and elderly care with SESIM-LEV model in Sweden.	No/-/-/A
Böheim et al. 2023	To model the impact of health and education on labor force participation in US and Germany.	Yes/12/No/A
Chen et al. 2019	To model fiscal sustainability of healthcare by projecting the health of future elders using FEM model for Singapore.	No/-/-/A
Craig et al. 2022	To simulate the long-term health impacts in UK.	Yes/10000/Yes, In progress*/A
Ernst et al. 2023	To analyse migration impacts on demographics in Germany.	Yes/NR/No/A + S
Flannery & O' Donoghue 2011	To study the fiscal and redistributive impacts of different higher education finance structures using the LIAM model in Ireland.	No/-/-/A
Fukawa 2011	To project health/long-term care expenditures with the INAHSIM-II model in Japan.	Yes/NR/No/A
Head et al. 2024	To model time individuals spent in different health states in UK.	Yes/100/Yes/A
Horvath et al. 2023	To project healthcare costs over the lifecycle using microWELT model in Austria.	No/-/-/A

(*continued*)

Table 1. (*continued*)

Auth. & Year	Study purpose	MC/Simrun/CI/Simstep + Detail
Jiang & Li 2024	To project the population size and share of late middle-aged/older people with difficulties/dependence on activities of daily living (DL) and instrumental activities of DL with the CHARISMA model in China.	Yes, NR/ 1000/No/A
Keegan 2011	To simulate the distributional impact of pension policy scenarios on superannuation savings using the APPSIM model in Australia.	No/-/-/A
Khalil et al. 2024	To predict demographic dynamics in Canada with STELARS model.	No/-/-/A + AB
Kingston et al. 2018	To predict the survival and (risk/disease) characteristics and related health expectancies in UK using PACSim model.	Yes, NR/10/-/A
Kirn &Dekkers 2023	To simulate with MIDAS_CH model the distribution of pension income and its underlying processes in Switzerland.	No/-/-/A
Knoef et al. 2013	To analyse the income distribution of the Dutch elderly.	Yes/NR/No/A
Kopasker et al. 2024	To project changes in psychological distress given predicted economic outcomes. From a tax-benefit UKMOD model with SimPaths model in UK.	Yes, NR/ 1000/Yes/A
Lawson 2016	To model how demographic change is likely to affect household spending patterns in the UK.	Yes/5/Yes/A

(*continued*)

Table 1. (*continued*)

Auth. & Year	Study purpose	MC/Simrun/CI/Simstep + Detail
Li et al. 2024	To model the spread of COVID-1 in China.	Yes, NR/10/ Yes/D + S, AB
Maitino et al. 2022	To study the future socio-demographic structure and the effects of social security programmes in Italy.	Yes/NR/No/A + S
Marois & Aktas 2021	To project the health of cohorts for selected EU countries to study the effects of risk factors and education on future health trajectories using ATHLOS-Mic model.	Yes/NR/No/A
May et al. 2022	To project the health and service use among elderly in Ireland using TILDA model.	Yes/25/No/A
Milne et al. 2015	To model child development from birth to age 13 with MELC model and studying e.g., changes in family circumstances and early education in New Zealand.	Yes, NR/10/Yes/A
Nadeau et al. 2013	To model physical activity to inform population health policies using POHEM-PA model in Canada.	Yes, B/40/ Yes/Annual
Patxot et al. 2018	To model the impact of retirement decision and demographics on pension sustainability in Spain.	-/-/-/A
Rasella et al. 2021	To analyse the prospective effects of fiscal policies on childhood health in the EU countries and in Italy.	Yes/1000/Yes/A
Rephann & Holm 2004	To model economic-demographic effects of immigration in Sweden using the SVERIGE model.	Yes/NR/No/A + S

(*continued*)

Table 1. (*continued*)

Auth. & Year	Study purpose	MC/Simrun/CI/Simstep + Detail
Spielauer & Dupriez 2019	To apply DYNAMIS-POP model to study and project child vaccination in Nepal.	Yes/NR/No/A
Spooner et al. 2021	To model epidemics with spatial SPENSER model in UK.	Yes,NR/1000 /Yes/D + S
Tamborini et al. 2022	To analyze socioeconomic gaps in retirement benefits using the MINT model in U.S.	No/-/-/M, A
Tikanmäki et al. 2015	To analyse impacts of the pension reform on working lives using ELSI model in Finland.	Yes/NR/No/A
van Sonsbeek & Gradus 2006	To simulate the budgetary impact of the 2006 regime change in the Dutch disability scheme.	Yes/NR/No/A
Walker 2004	To model the likelihood that more Australians aged 65–70 will work + 15 h per week in a changing employment environment.	Yes/NR/No/A
Wu et al. 2011	To model several demographic processes under various scenarios with a Moses in UK.	Yes/NR/No/A + S, AB
Zhang & Miller 2024	To predict the location of new housing supply in U.S.	No/-/-/- + S, AB
Zhang et al. 2023	To model the processes of developing depression and care-seeking behaviors among U.S children and adolescents.	Yes, NR/20/ Yes/M

4.1 Results

In most of the reviewed studies (30 out of 44) MC/repeated simulations were applied (see, Table 1), and in rest of the studies (see, e.g., [15, 18, 41, 47, 51]) the model was run following with "traditional", what-if-type of, scenario analysis methods and different future scenarios were commonly tested through "optimistic/pessimistic" settings, modeling commonly 3–5 alternatives. In the set of these 30 studies applying MC reporting practices varied: seven works did not directly report on using the MC method, but it was shown that the simulation had been run repeatedly. In 13 entries the number of simulations run was not reported and notably, 16 studies (out of 30) did not report CIs. Yet only two studies [3, 27] reported using 10 000 and four studies [44, 55, 83, 100] 1000 simulation runs. In the remainder, the number of simulations vary mainly from five to forty.

Additionally, there is a notable variability in depth across publications about the discussion of the sources and mitigation of uncertainty. Many studies indirectly or directly, yet briefly, address uncertainty when discussing issues like data availability and sample size [11, 51, 84] or mention it broadly as parameter/statistical/MC uncertainty. These issues are by their nature related to epistemic uncertainty (although no such "uncertainty terminology" were observed in the studies). In some works, aleatoric uncertainty is also addressed indirectly, for example, when authors discuss the inherent complexity of the topic under investigation (see, e.g., [2, 24, 63]). As a notable exception to the others, Archer et al. [4] provides a thorough discussion on uncertainty issues, classifying their sources and outlining mitigation methods. Authors commonly discuss of "model error" or "model-based bias", which intersects with the uncertainty concept [6, 44, 53, 55, 60, 69, 99].

Another goal of this work was to explore how advancements in data availability, in terms of granularity and timeliness are reflected in dynamic microsimulation models conducted in demography studies. The time span of the simulation results produced by the reviewed studies was analyzed to see if the applied models offered shorter than annual results being able to reveal short-term cyclical changes of discovered phenomena, such as health or employment dynamics.

Only epidemiological models [11, 63, 100] seem to offer sub-annual observation periods, reaching daily level accuracy in simulation results. Exception in addition to these studies are Zhang et al. [114] and Tamborini et al. [102] whose models provide monthly-level results: the authors of [114] introduced a model to analyze the depression and care-seeking behaviors among children and adolescents, whereas the authors of [102] developed cohort-specific projections that predict in addition to lifetime measures, monthly social security retirement benefits in U.S. settings. Notably, in their multi-morbidity modeling study, although simulation results are presented at yearly intervals, Kingston et al. [50] updated individuals' characteristics monthly over the simulation period "to achieve a more realistic evolution for characteristics which jointly influence each other." A similar approach was used by Böheim et al. [24] for modelling labour force status.

Based on the review only epidemiology models by Becker et al. [11] and Spooner et al. [100] seem to target to produce forecasts using near-real-time data with updates. In rest of the models covered, it appears to be common to use administrative statistics with a time lag of at least 2–3 years in model initialization.

Regarding the level of detail in models, seven studies are by their nature spatial [9, 31, 67, 84, 110], including two already pointed out epidemiological studies [63, 100]. Three studies [49, 63, 110] combined the ABM method with dynamic models out of which all of them are also spatial. Publications on projecting population change at the sub-county level consider also employment and migration questions, for example [9, 10, 84, 100].

4.2 Results Analysis

Uncertainty Analysis. Monte Carlo simulation is a commonly used uncertainty analysis technique, however, there is a lack of common format of reporting the methodological aspects of probabilistic simulations, and its results. In our opinion, this calls for mutually agreed standards and/or strategies to improve the transparency and comparability of demographic models in this given research field, which would not only improve the accuracy of individual studies but also would facilitate more robust analyses and comparisons across different research efforts in demographic modeling. This claim can be motivated by the often inadequate depth of the discussion (and missing information) of modeling related details, such as the number of simulation rounds (along with the rationale behind this choice) and lack of CIs. This aligns also with Smithson [97], who noticed that different disciplines vary considerably how frequently they report CIs in published research (see also [58, 76, 77]). Kingston et al. [50] observed that the lack of CIs as one of their study limitations, although they also highlighted that, in their study, running the simulation iteratively revealed a small range of prevalence for multimorbidity (less than 1 %) - even when the error in transition rates was disregarded. Knoef et al. [53] reported not using CIs due the "computational reasons". Lappo [58], however, states that the omission of reporting confidence intervals (CIs) may be due to the fact that many microsimulation users are not statisticians. Perhaps the same applies in the case of social sciences, from which most of the studies originate. These findings indicate a general lack of established practices in employing methods to convey information on result variability across research disciplines [64].

We also come back to the discussion of how the results, especially based on the probability distributions, should be displayed in order to facilitate decision making (see [13, 56]). Weinstein et al. [108] present the best practices for decision analytic modeling emphasizing that model outputs should never solely rely on point estimates. Instead, a proper sensitivity analysis should be conducted to examine the effects of alternative data and assumptions on the results. Further discussion and findings on the topic are also addressed by Astolfi et al. [5].

To further explore practices related to the MC method, some authors provide information related to model validation, such as the basis (or tests made) for selecting the number of simulations. In their study on the prospective effects of fiscal policies on childhood health in the EU countries, Rasella et al. [83] states that a thousand simulation iterations was chosen after ensuring that the estimates were stable and additional runs did not alter the point estimates (see also [105]). Spielauer and Dupriez [99] claimed that 24 iterations make MC variation neglectable when applying dynamic microsimulation to study immunization rates in Nepal, whereas Aransiola et al. [3] performed 10k rounds to ensure the variation of the parameter values when studying the effect of social pensions and cash transfers on child mortality in Brazil.

Overall, the selection of the number of MC simulation runs has received only limited attention even though it is a crucial factor for generating meaningful predictions [23, 48]. In general, the choice of the number of MC simulation runs is, of course, much dependent on the complexity of models. The findings above relate to the varying extent to which model robustness is discussed and how validation is conducted and reported. As an exception, the paper by Aransiola et al. [3] provides comprehensive details on both internal and external validation of the model (see also e.g., [4]), and the modeling procedures followed the international model reporting guidelines (ISPOR-SMSM). On the other hand, some articles (see e.g. [11]) also refer to secondary sources for modeling details, which may provide specific information on the methodology and validation. Overall, we can concur with O'Donoghue and Dekkers [77] who noted that alignment techniques (not a focus of this study) are that common in DMs that most reports do not even mention them, despite their significant impact on simulation results. This oversight is similar to the treatment of the MC method [23, 48, 65].

When analyzing the big picture regarding the use of the MC approach, the studies covered reveal differing perspectives on the objectives of modeling: some prioritize analyzing current systems without accounting for variations or forecasting goals, thus considering repeated simulations unnecessary [12, 32]. In contrast, the majority (30 out of 44) employ the probabilistic method to understand system functionality under uncertainty. Studies focusing on individual behavior and future trends through predefined scenarios and single-point estimates may fail to capture the full spectrum of potential outcomes or convey the inherent uncertainty of modeled phenomena. Such approaches might overlook rare yet impactful events, whereas the MC accounts for these events and their potential consequences [34, 36, 69, 76, 90].

Bijak et al. [13] elaborate the advantages and challenges of using probabilistic methods, particularly regarding attitudes and understanding of the approach. They suggest that to demonstrate the value of uncertainty analysis and overcome institutional inertia, insights from other fields—such as meteorology, aviation, and economic regulation—could be applied. These areas have developed ways of effectively communicate probabilistic forecasting and uncertainty that could also benefit population forecasting. In addition, research papers published in e.g., medicine or mathematics on the best modeling practices could provide useful guidelines for works in the social sciences as well, such as the work of Weinstein et al. [108].

As a last point, one should bear in mind that the variability in the reporting styles together with overlapping issues with validation and data availability issues noted in the literature analysis makes it challenging to uniformly categorize how "comprehensively" the researchers have included uncertainty analysis into their studies. The sources of uncertainties are typically shortly mentioned or found "indirectly mentioned" in well-standardized sections such as used data or the study's limitations.

Data Granularity and Timeliness. Considering data aspects, the shortcomings of the models running yearly intervals have been recognized. Salonen et al. [92] emphasise that modeling transitions in one-year intervals poses challenges in capturing gradual changes, such as increases in pension age or short social security spells (see also discussion: [37, 50, 112]). They [92] continue that, for example, administrative registers show that the average duration of sickness and unemployment spells to be only one week, although these periods often accumulate over an individual's life course (see also [81]). Chen et al. [26] acknowledges the limitation of not modeling shorter disease dynamics similarly than Andreassen et al. [2], who suggest that with improved data access and today's computing power, monthly time units could be preferable in the MOSART model (renowned for evaluating the Norwegian pension system) to avoid aggregating data annually which potentially can lead to overlooking important nuances.

In an ideal world, employing close-to-real time data for model calibration would reduce the risk of obsolete information affecting transition probabilities – an issue that is especially important when addressing rapidly evolving matters, such as changes in labour market status during economic crises (see e.g., [79]). The finding of the absence of close to real time data aligns with O'Donoghue and Loughrey [78] who observed already ten years ago that microsimulation models tend to use historical data (see also, Klevmarken, 2008), limiting researchers' ability to analyze recent changes e.g., in income distribution and policymakers' capacity to monitor recent developments.

Forecasting models must meet the needs of the user group to be useful (see discussion, Bijak et al. [13]). We remind that not all the models require daily/monthly forecast accuracy and frequent updates typical e.g., in pandemic research. The requirement of prediction "time span" is thus both, user and phenomena related. It is necessary to know the basic essence of the modeled system, whether the target to be predicted is typically such that it undergoes rapid changes with a wide range of variation, or whether the development is more stable in nature. In such cases high updating frequency of the model with new data likely does not bring any added value, especially in a strategic level decision making. An analogy can be drawn to the cyclical or defensive behavior of the stock market. On the other hand, when choosing an appropriate modeling interval for a social phenomenon, it may be relevant to assess whether its pattern of development has shifted from the steadier progression observed historically to a more rapid cycle, e.g., in the case of labor force dynamics.

It is also worth considering that the "traditional" social policy models could aim to reduce the delay between data collection and utilization, moving from a lag of several years to using more recent statistics. This shift would better reflect contemporary issues, such as the interconnections between labour force participation and health status [79]. As a recent example related to enhanced data utilization is The Finnish Dataroom –project led by VATT Institute for Economic Research [106]. It aims to produce more accurate and fast-paced analyses of the effects of social and political solutions than before, using up-to-date register data, serving as an inspiring example in the more agile use of public register data.

Admittedly, increased granularity and the use of more timely data to update transition probabilities (together with MC method) add to model complexity with regards to model calibration and computational demands. Nevertheless, many renowned models in this field already require substantial computing power and resources for maintenance due to their high modularity. Today's technological capabilities, such as cloud computing and big data analytics help overcoming this issue [2, 77, 87].

In the near future, it is not surprising that there would be a trend towards simpler models that allow for agile calibration with detailed, current data, albeit sacrificing some modularity [37, 64, 112]. For instance, localized projections (with ABM approach) are vital for addressing regional disparities and tailoring policies to specific areas. They enhance the relevance of simulations and allow for more detailed evaluations of policy impacts [9, 10, 14, 31]. Agile calibrated models providing timely forecasts could potentially be recognized also at the tactical decision-making level.

Other Findings. Many of the studies covered in review highlight the issues of complex settings where causalities between variables are hard to address. As an example,

Kopasker et al. [55] discuss that the effects of economic determinants of mental health manifest over multiple periods and through complex pathways, which makes it difficult to analyse the input – output relationship. It is often unclear whether improvements in population health trends can be most effectively achieved through immediate policy changes or through the use of policies implemented over several years (see also [44]). Kopasker et al. [55] note that the inherent assumption of continuity within trend prediction arises as a study limitation since the present relationship between, in this case, diseases and functioning is assumed to persist unaltered. Weinstein et al. [108] summarizes that a model's value lies not just in its results but in its ability to make the connection between inputs and outputs transparent, reducing its "black box" nature.

Machine learning (ML) techniques, in addition to being utilized in model calibration tasks, can aid in addressing complexity arising from models' non-linearities, a topic of ongoing discussion [44, 51, 52, 55, 109]. The integration of ML could enable the development of more dynamic and predictive models, which could better address complex societal challenges and facilitate faster decision-making. These methods could uncover unobserved, detailed behavioural patterns among individuals thus improving simulation granularity and supporting, e.g., ABM constructions (see discussion of Margetts & Dorobatu [68]). There are only a few demonstrated applications of ML within the reviewed works including Khalil et al. [49] who provide an innovative application of explainable artificial intelligence (xAI) with the aim to interpret ML models. The ML is utilized here to elucidate input-output relationships in complex settings. This study can be regarded as a pioneering effort in integrating ML within DM schemes in this research domain. Other studies like Rodriguez et al. [89] in healthcare (see also Shi et al. [96]) offer also insights into applying advanced methods, potentially inspiring social science research. However, in the age of artificial intelligence, it is important to recall Weinstein et al.'s [108] suggestion that a model should maintain a high level of transparency to ensure that the reasoning behind its results is intuitively comprehensible. The logic of the model must be explainable, even when utilizing more complex computational methods.

5 Conclusions

This article provided a literature review on the use of the probabilistic Monte Carlo (MC) method as an uncertainty analysis (UA) technique in socio-economic decision models (DMs), as well as the related reporting practices of probabilistic outcomes. To the best of our knowledge, this is the first review attempt in this field. The study revealed significant limitations in current modeling practices and a lack of standardized guidelines for implementing MC simulation-based modeling. Furthermore, the literature analysis highlighted inconsistencies in model validation and in the reporting of probabilistic outcomes, particularly regarding the use of confidence intervals. Therefore, the study suggests that common guidelines for probabilistic simulations and standardized reporting practices should be established to enhance the transparency of such analyses.

The main limitation of this study lies in its methodology: although the literature review was structured, it may not have captured all relevant studies. In addition, this review did not treat bootstrapping separately from the MC method and did not explore, for example, alignment techniques or specific statistical practices.

Despite advances in modeling and data analytics, we found no evidence that DMs are currently being developed toward nowcasting with real-time datasets. We observed that the time lag between data generation and its utilization in models typically spans several years. Most simulation efforts remain constrained to annual time steps, even though many socio-demographic phenomena evolve over shorter periods. Addressing the gap in (near) real-time modeling would require a paradigm shift—from large-scale DMs to simpler and more agile models that still preserve the overall dynamics of existing DMs.

Disclosure of Interests. The authors have no competing interests to declare that are relevant to the content of this article.

References

1. Alho, J., Lassila, J.: Assessing components of uncertainty in demographic forecasts with an application to fiscal sustainability. J. Forecast. **42**, 1560–1568 (2023)
2. Andreassen, L., Fredriksen, D., Gjefsen, H.M., Halvorsen, E., Stølen, N.M.: The dynamic cross-sectional microsimulation model MOSART. Int. J. Microsimul. **13**, 92–113 (2020)
3. Aransiola, T.J., et al.: Current and projected mortality and hospitalization rates associated with conditional cash transfer, social pension, and primary health care programs in Brazil, 2000–2030. JAMA Netw. Open **7**, e247519 (2024)
4. Archer, L., Lomax, N., Tysinger, B.: A dynamic microsimulation model for ageing and health in England: the English future elderly model. Int. J. Microsimul. **14**, 2–26 (2021)
5. Astolfi, R., Lorenzoni, L., Oderkirk, J.: Informing policy makers about future health spending: a comparative analysis of forecasting methods in OECD countries. Health Policy **107**, 1–10 (2012)
6. Atella, V., et al.: The future of the elderly population health status: Filling a knowledge gap. Health Econ. **30**, 11–29 (2021)
7. Axtell, R.: Why agents?: on the varied motivations for agent computing in the social sciences. Center Soc. Econ. Dyn. **17** (2000)
8. Baldini, M., Mazzaferro, C., Morciano, M.: Assessing the implications of long-term care policies in Italy: a microsimulation approach. Politica economica **24**(1), 47–72 (2008)
9. Ballas, D., Clarke, G., Dorling, D., Eyre, H., Thomas, B., Rossiter, D.: SimBritain: a spatial microsimulation approach to population dynamics. Popul. Space Place **11**, 13–34 (2005)
10. Ballas, D., Clarke, G.P., Wiemers, E.: Building a dynamic spatial microsimulation model for Ireland. Popul. Space Place **11**, 157–172 (2005)
11. Becker, J.E., et al.: Using simulation modeling to inform intervention and implementation selection in a rapid stakeholder-engaged hybrid effectiveness-implementation randomized trial. Implementation Sci. Commun. **5**, 70 (2024)
12. Ben Jelloul, M., Bozio, A., Perdrix, E., Rain, A., Toulemon, L.: Dynamique du processus de perte d'autonomie dans les populations vieillissantes/Dynamic of the Disablement Process in Ageing Populations. Economie et Statistique **538**, 13–31 (2023)
13. Bijak, J., et al.: Probabilistic population forecasts for informed decision making. J. Official Stat. **31**(4), 537 (2015)
14. Birkin, M., Wu, B., Rees, P.: Moses: dynamic spatial microsimulation with demographic interactions. New Front. Microsimul. Model. 53–77 (2017)
15. Bonin, H., Reuss, K., Stichnoth, H.: Life-cycle incidence of family policy measures in Germany: evidence from a dynamic microsimulation model (2015)
16. Briggs, A.: Economics notes: handling uncertainty in economic evaluation. BMJ (Clin. Res.) (1999)

17. Brown, L., Harding, A.: Social modelling and public policy: application of microsimulation modelling in Australia. J. Artif. Soc. Soc. Simul. **5**(4) (2002)
18. Brouwers, L., Ellegård, L.M., Janlöv, N., Johansson, P., Mossler, K., Ekholm, A.: Simulating the need for health-and elderly care in Sweden–a model description of Sesim-LEV. In: New Pathways in Microsimulation, pp. 41–60. Routledge (2016)
19. Burka, D., Mohácsi, L., Csicsman, J., Soós, B.: Supporting pension pre-calculation with dynamic microsimulation technologies. In: ECMS, pp. 562–568 (2017)
20. Burgard, J.P., Schmaus, S.: Sensitivity analysis for dynamic microsimulation models. Research Papers in Economics, No. 15/19 (2019)
21. Burgard, J.P., Krause, J., Merkle, H., Münnich, R., Schmaus, S.: Conducting a dynamic microsimulation for care research: data generation, transition probabilities and sensitivity analysis. In: Stochastic Models, Statistics and Their Applications: Dresden, Germany, March 2019, vol. 14, pp. 269–290. Springer, Cham (2019)
22. Burgard, J.P., Krause, J., Schmaus, S.: Estimation of regional transition probabilities for spatial dynamic microsimulations from survey data lacking in regional detail. Comput. Stat. Data Anal. **154**, 107048 (2021)
23. Byrne, M.D.: How many times should a stochastic model be run? An approach based on confidence intervals. In: Proceedings of the 12th International Conference on Cognitive Modeling, Ottawa (2013)
24. Böheim, R., Horvath, T., Leoni, T., Spielauer, M.: The impact of health and education on labor force participation in aging societies: Projections for the United States and Germany from dynamic microsimulations. Popul. Res. Policy Rev. **42**(3), 39 (2023)
25. Caro, J.J., Briggs, A.H., Siebert, U., Kuntz, K.M.: Modeling good research practices—overview: a report of the ISPOR-SMDM Modeling Good Research Practices Task Force–1. Med. Decis. Making **32**(5), 667–677 (2012)
26. Chen, C., et al.: The long-term impact of functional disability on hospitalization spending in Singapore. J. Econ. Ageing **14**, 100193 (2019)
27. Craig, P., et al.: Evaluation of the mental health impacts of Universal Credit: protocol for a mixed methods study. BMJ Open **12**(4), e061340 (2022)
28. Crato, N.: From lack of data to data unlocking: computational and statistical issues in an era of unforeseeable big data evolution. In: Handbook of Computational Social Science for Policy, pp. 125–139. Springer, Cham (2023)
29. Dekkers, G.: The simulation properties of microsimulation models with static and dynamic ageing–a brief guide into choosing one type of model over the other. Int. J. Microsimul. **8**(1), 97–109 (2015)
30. di Bella, E., Leporatti, L., Maggino, F.: Big data and social indicators: actual trends and new perspectives. Soc. Indic. Res. **135**, 869–878 (2018)
31. Ernst, J., Dräger, S., Schmaus, S., Weymeirsch, J., Alsaloum, A., Münnich, R.: The influence of migration patterns on regional demographic development in Germany. Soc. Sci. **12**(5), 255 (2023)
32. Flannery, D., O'Donoghue, C.: The life-cycle impact of alternative higher education finance systems in Ireland. Econ. Soc. Rev. **42**(3) (2011)
33. Fredriksen, D., Holmøy, E., Strøm, B., Stølen, N.M.: Fiscal effects of the Norwegian pension reform–a micro–macro assessment. J. Pension Econ. Financ. **18**(1), 88–123 (2019)
34. Fuchs, J., Söhnlein, D., Weber, B., Weber, E.: Stochastic forecasting of labor supply and population: an integrated model. Popul. Res. Policy Rev. **37**(1), 33–58 (2018)
35. Fukawa, T.: Household projection and its application to health/long-term care expenditures in Japan using INAHSIM-II. Soc. Sci. Comput. Rev. **29**(1), 52–66 (2011)
36. Gilbert, N., Ahrweiler, P., Barbrook-Johnson, P., Narasimhan, K.P., Wilkinson, H.: Computational modelling of public policy: reflections on practice. J. Artif. Soc. Soc. Simul. (2018)

37. Harding, A.: Challenges and opportunities of dynamic microsimulation modelling. In: Plenary Paper Presented to the 1st General Conference of the International Microsimulation Association (2007)
38. Harding, A., Keegan, M., Kelly, S.: Validating a dynamic population microsimulation model: Recent experience in Australia. Int. J. Microsimul. **3**(2), 46–64 (2010)
39. Head, A., Birkett, M., Fleming, K., Kypridemos, C., O'Flaherty, M.: Socioeconomic inequalities in accumulation of multimorbidity in England from 2019 to 2049: a microsimulation projection study. Lancet Public Health **9**(4), e231–e239 (2024)
40. Hilton, J., Bijak, J.: Design and analysis of demographic simulations. In: Agent-Based Modelling in Population Studies: Concepts, Methods, and Applications, pp. 211–235. Springer, Cham (2016)
41. Horvath, T., Leoni, T., Reschenhofer, P., Spielauer, M.: Socio-economic inequality and healthcare costs over the life course–a dynamic microsimulation approach. Public Health **219**, 124–130 (2023)
42. Härdle, W.K., Mysickova, A.: Stochastic population forecast for Germany and its consequence for the German pension system (2009)
43. Itkonen, J., Juvonen, P.: Nowcasting the Finnish economy with a large Bayesian vector autoregressive model (2017)
44. Jiang, Y., Li, L.: Projections of functional dependence among the late middle-aged and older population from 2018–2048 in China: A dynamic microsimulation. Glob. Health Res. Policy **9**(1), 15 (2024)
45. Kashyap, R.: Has demography witnessed a data revolution? Promises and pitfalls of a changing data ecosystem. Popul. Stud. **75**(sup1), 47–75 (2021)
46. Kashyap, R., Zagheni, E.: Leveraging digital and computational demography for policy insights. In: Handbook of Computational Social Science for Policy, pp. 327–344. Springer, Cham (2023)
47. Keegan, M.: Mandatory superannuation and self-sufficiency in retirement: an application of the APPSIM dynamic microsimulation model. Soc. Sci. Comput. Rev. **29**(1), 67–84 (2011)
48. Kennedy, M.C.: Experimental design principles to choose the number of Monte Carlo replicates for stochastic ecological models. Ecol. Model. **394**, 11–17 (2019)
49. Khalil, M.A., Fatmi, M.R., Orvin, M.: Developing and microsimulating demographic dynamics for an integrated urban model: a comparison between logistic regression and machine learning techniques. Transportation 1–35 (2024)
50. Kingston, A., Robinson, L., Booth, H., Knapp, M., Jagger, C.: Modem project: projections of multi-morbidity in the older population in England to 2035: estimates from the population ageing and care simulation (PACSim) model. Age Ageing **47**(3), 374–380 (2018)
51. Kirn, T., Dekkers, G.: The projected development of the gender pension gap in Switzerland: introducing MIDAS_CH. Int. J. Microsimul. **16**(3), 100–129 (2023)
52. Klevmarken, A.: Dynamic microsimulation for policy analysis: problems and solutions. In: Simulating an Ageing Population: A Microsimulation Approach Applied to Sweden, 31–53. Emerald Group Publishing Limited (2008)
53. Knoef, M., Alessie, R., Kalwij, A.: Changes in the income distribution of the Dutch elderly between 1989 and 2020: a dynamic microsimulation. Rev. Income Wealth **59**(3), 460–485 (2013)
54. Kohns, D., Bhattacharjee, A.: Nowcasting growth using Google Trends data: a Bayesian structural time series model. Int. J. Forecast. **39**(3), 1384–1412 (2023)
55. Kopasker, D., et al.: Evaluating the influence of taxation and social security policies on psychological distress: a microsimulation study of the UK during the COVID-19 economic crisis. Soc Sci Med **351**, 116953 (2024)

56. Kozlova, M., Piano, S.L., Yeomans, J.S.: Methodological landscape of sensitivity analysis and the place of SimDec. In: Sensitivity Analysis for Business, Technology, and Policymaking, pp. 3–26. Routledge (2024)
57. Krüger, F., Lerch, S., Thorarinsdottir, T., Gneiting, T.: Predictive inference based on Markov chain Monte Carlo output. Int. Stat. Rev. **89**(2), 274–301 (2021)
58. Lappo, S.: Uncertainty in microsimulation. Master's thesis, University of Helsinki (2015)
59. Lassila, J., Valkonen, T., Alho, J.M.: Demographic forecasts and fiscal policy rules. Int. J. Forecast. **30**(4), 1098–1109 (2014)
60. Lawson, T.: How the ageing population contributes to UK economic activity: a microsimulation analysis. Scottish J. Polit. Econ. **63**(5), 497–518 (2016)
61. Lee, J.T., et al.: Methods for health workforce projection model: Systematic review and recommended good practice reporting guideline. Hum. Resour. Health **22**(1), 25 (2024)
62. Lee, R., Tuljapurkar, S.: Stochastic population forecasts for the United States: beyond high, medium, and low. J. Am. Stat. Assoc. **89**(428), 1175–1189 (1994)
63. Li, Z., et al.: An urban trajectory data-driven approach for COVID-19 simulation. IEEE (2024)
64. Li, J., O'Donoghue, C.: A survey of dynamic microsimulation models: uses, model structure and methodology. Int. J. Microsimul. **6**(2), 3–55 (2013)
65. Lorscheid, I., Heine, B.O., Meyer, M.: Opening the 'black box' of simulations: increased transparency and effective communication through the systematic design of experiments. Comput. Math. Organ. Theory **18**, 22–62 (2012)
66. Mahadevan, S., Sarkar, S.: Uncertainty analysis methods. US Department of Energy, Washington, DC, USA (2009)
67. Maitino, M.L., Mariani, M., Patacchini, V., Ravagli, L., Sciclone, N.: Employment effects of Reddito di cittadinanza, before and during the Covid-19 pandemic. IRPET Working Papers 06/2022, Florence: IRPET (2022)
68. Margetts, H., Dorobantu, C.: Computational social science for public policy. In: Handbook of Computational Social Science for Policy, pp. 3–18. Springer, Cham (2023)
69. Marois, G., Aktas, A.: Projecting health-ageing trajectories in Europe using a dynamic microsimulation model. Sci. Rep. **11**(1), 1785 (2021)
70. May, P., Normand, C., Matthews, S., Kenny, R.A., Romero-Ortuno, R., Tysinger, B.: Projecting future health and service use among older people in Ireland: an overview of a dynamic microsimulation model in The Irish Longitudinal Study on Ageing (TILDA). HRB Open Res. **5** (2022)
71. Milne, B., Lay Yee, R., McLay, J.M., Pearson, J., Von Randow, M., Davis, P.: Modelling the Early life-course (MELC): a microsimulation model of child development in New Zealand (2015)
72. Mitton, L., Sutherland, H., Weeks, M.: Microsimulation Modelling for Policy Analysis: Challenges and Innovations. Cambridge University Press, Cambridge (2000)
73. Nadeau, C., et al.: Development of a population-based microsimulation model of physical activity in Canada. Health Rep. **24**(10), 11–19 (2013)
74. Navicke, J., Rastrigina, O., Sutherland, H.: Nowcasting indicators of poverty risk in the European Union: a microsimulation approach. Soc. Indic. Res. **119**, 101–119 (2014)
75. O'Donoghue, C.: Dynamic microsimulation: a methodological survey. Braz. Electron. J. Econ. **4**(2), 77 (2001)
76. O'Donoghue, C. (ed.): Handbook of Microsimulation Modelling. Emerald Group Publishing (2014)
77. O'Donoghue, C., Dekkers, G.: Increasing the impact of dynamic microsimulation modelling. Int. J. Microsimul. **11**(1), 61–96 (2018)
78. O'Donoghue, C., Loughrey, J.: Nowcasting in microsimulation models: a methodological survey. J. Artif. Soc. Soc. Simul. **17**(4), 12 (2014)

79. O'Donoghue, C., Sologon, D. M.: The transformation of public policy analysis in times of crisis-a microsimulation-nowcasting method using big data. (2023)
80. Patxot, C., Solé Juvés, M., Souto Nieves, G., Spielauer, M.: The impact of the retirement decision and demographics on pension sustainability: a dynamic microsimulation analysis. Int. J. Microsimul. **11**(2), 84–108 (2018)
81. Perhoniemi, R., Blomgren, J., Laaksonen, M.: Identifying labour market pathways after a 30-day-long sickness absence: a three-year sequence analysis study in Finland. BMC Public Health **23**(1), 1102 (2023)
82. Raftery, A.E.: Use and communication of probabilistic forecasts. Stat. Anal. Data Min.: ASA Data Sci. J. **9**(6), 397–410 (2016)
83. Rasella, D., et al.: Developing an integrated microsimulation model for the impact of fiscal policies on child health in Europe: the example of childhood obesity in Italy. BMC Med. **19**, 1–12 (2021)
84. Rephann, T.J., Holm, E.: Economic-demographic effects of immigration: results from a dynamic spatial microsimulation model. Int. Reg. Sci. Rev. **27**(4), 379–410 (2004)
85. Richardson, P.: Nowcasting and the use of big data in short-term macroeconomic forecasting: a critical review. Economie et Statistique **505**(1), 65–87 (2016)
86. Richiardi, M., Richardson, R.E.: Agent-based computational demography and microsimulation using JAS-mine. In: Agent-Based Modelling in Population Studies: Concepts, Methods, and Applications, pp. 75–112 (2017)
87. Richiardi, M., Bronka, P., van de Ven, J., Kopasker, D., Katikireddi, S. V.: SimPaths: an open-source microsimulation model for life course analysis. Available at SSRN 4808042 (2023)
88. Rissanen, M., Savolainen, J.: Uncertainty analysis in population-based dynamic microsimulation models: a review of literature. In: Proceedings of the 16th International Joint Conference on Knowledge Discovery, Knowledge Engineering and Knowledge Management - Volume 3: KMIS, pp. 74–84. SciTePress (2024). ISBN 978-989-758-716-0
89. Rodriguez, P.J., Veenstra, D.L., Heagerty, P.J., Goss, C.H., Ramos, K.J., Bansal, A.: A framework for using real-world data and health outcomes modeling to evaluate machine learning–based risk prediction models. Value Health **25**(3), 350–358 (2022)
90. Rutter, C.M., Zaslavsky, A.M., Feuer, E.J.: Dynamic microsimulation models for health outcomes: a review. Med. Decis. Making **31**(1), 10–18 (2011)
91. Sabelhaus, J., Topoleski, J.: Uncertain policy for an uncertain world: the case of social security. J. Policy Anal. Manage. **26**(3), 507–525 (2007)
92. Salonen, J., Tikanmäki, H., Lappo, S.: Partition of the life course: an extended dynamic microsimulation analysis (2021)
93. Sauerbier, T.: UMDBS-a new tool for dynamic microsimulation. J. Artif. Soc. Soc. Simul. **5**(2) (2002)
94. Sharif, B., Wong, H., Anis, A.H., Kopec, J.A.: A practical ANOVA approach for uncertainty analysis in population-based disease microsimulation models. Value Health **20**(4), 710–717 (2017)
95. Sharif, B., et al.: Uncertainty analysis in population-based disease microsimulation models. Epidemiol. Res. Int. **2012**(1), 610405 (2012)
96. Shi, Y., Zeng, W., Wang, N., Wang, S., Huang, Z.: Early warning for human mental sub-health based on fMRI data analysis: an example from a seafarers' resting-data study. Front. Psychol. **6**, 1030 (2015)
97. Smithson, M.: Confidence Intervals, no. 140. Sage (2003)
98. Spielauer, M.: Dynamic microsimulation of health care demand, health care finance and the economic impact of health behaviours: Survey and review. Int. J. Microsimul. **1**(1), 35–53 (2007)

99. Spielauer, M., Dupriez, O.: A portable dynamic microsimulation model for population, education and health applications in developing countries. Int. J. Microsimul. **12**(3), 6–27 (2019)
100. Spooner, F., et al.: A dynamic microsimulation model for epidemics. Soc Sci Med **291**, 114461 (2021)
101. Stundziene, A., Pilinkiene, V., Bruneckiene, J., Grybauskas, A., Lukauskas, M., Pekarskiene, I.: Future directions in nowcasting economic activity: a systematic literature review. J. Econ. Surv. **38**(4), 1199–1233 (2024)
102. Tamborini, C.R., Reznik, G.L., Iams, H.M., Couch, K.A.: The growing socioeconomic gap in lifetime Social Security retirement benefits: current and future retirees. J. Gerontol. Ser. B **77**(4), 803–814 (2022)
103. Tikanmäki, H., Sihvonen, H., Salonen, J.: Distributional effects of the forthcoming Finnish pension reform: a dynamic microsimulation approach (2015)
104. Van de Ven, J.: Exploring the importance of incentive responses for policy projections. Int. J. Microsimul. **10**, 134–164 (2017)
105. Van Sonsbeek, J.M., Gradus, R.H.: A microsimulation analysis of the 2006 regime change in the Dutch disability scheme. Econ. Model. **23**(3), 427–456 (2006)
106. VATT Institute for Economic Research. https://vatt.fi/en/data-room. Accessed 15 Jan 2025
107. Walker, A.: Impact of health on the ability of older Australians to stay in the workforce-with possible contributions to economic sustainability (2004)
108. Weinstein, M.C., et al.: Principles of good practice for decision analytic modeling in healthcare evaluation: report of the ISPOR task force on good research practices—modeling studies. Value Health **6**(1), 9–17 (2003)
109. Wolfson, M., Rowe, G.: HealthPaths: using functional health trajectories to quantify the relative importance of selected health determinants. Demogr. Res. **31**, 941–974 (2014)
110. Wu, B.M., Birkin, M.H., Rees, P.H.: A dynamic MSM with agent elements for spatial demographic forecasting. Soc. Sci. Comput. Rev. **29**(1), 145–160 (2011)
111. Xue, X., Chen, F., Zhou, D., Wang, X., Lu, M., Wang, F.Y.: Computational experiments for complex social systems—Part I: The customization of computational model. IEEE Trans. Comput. Soc. Syst. **9**(5), 1330–1344 (2021)
112. Zaidi, A., Rake, K.: Dynamic microsimulation models: a review and some lessons for SAGE. Simulating Social Policy in an Ageing Society (SAGE) Discussion Paper, vol. 2 (2001)
113. Zhang, Y., Miller, E.J.: Analyzing housing supply location choice: a comparative study of the modelling frameworks. Sci. Rep. **14**(1), 1435 (2024)
114. Zhang, C., Zafari, Z., Slejko, J.F., Camelo Castillo, W., Reeves, G.M., Dosreis, S.: Impact of different interventions on preventing suicide and suicide attempt among children and adolescents in the United States: a microsimulation model study. Front. Psych. **14**, 1127852 (2023)

Utilizing ER Model Extraction for an Industry Data Validation Use Case

Philipp Schmurr[1](✉)[iD], Andreas Schmidt[1][iD], Maiko Friedrich[2],
Karl-Uwe Stucky[1][iD], Wolfgang Suess[1][iD], and Veit Hagenmeyer[1][iD]

[1] Institute for Automation and Applied Informatics, Karlsruhe Institute of Technology,
Kaiserstr. 12, Karlsruhe, Germany
`philipp.schmurr@kit.edu`
[2] Siemens AG, Werner-von-Siemens-Straße 1, Munich, Germany
`https://www.iai.kit.edu/english/index.php`

Abstract. In order to enable domain experts to perform data integration independently, we present a method which involves data integration based on Entity-Relationship (ER) models that are semi-automatically extracted from various data sources. We propose strategies to extract ER models from standard data sources such as relational databases, XML files, and OWL data, with a concept to extend this extraction to other data sources. In case the automatic extraction yields insufficient results, we present an enhancement approach that allows the user to manually adjust the generated ER model. The extracted models support data integration into an ontology-based model, contributing to harmonized knowledge management in heterogeneous data environments. A graphical visualization of the ER models is introduced that allows to review and enhance the extracted models. Moreover, we present exemplarily an industry use case of an extracted model that serves as a foundation for data validation of power grid models. An ER model-based data integration paves the way for FAIR energy data.

Keywords: Entity relationship model · Model extraction · Data integration · Structural metadata · FAIR principles

1 Introduction

New projects often require the gathering and integration of data from various sources, which can be internal or external, and stored in different systems, formats, and locations. Manual data integration is common, especially with limited budgets and staff, because it allows to get started without doing research for a suitable tool or process first. Advanced projects may use assisted or automated data integration solutions, but these often require the involvement of internal experts or external contractors.

The energy transition demands data-driven solutions, but smaller power companies often lack the necessary data experts. Within the energy domain, software is frequently delivered as turnkey solutions with proprietary models and interfaces, leading to vendor lock-in due to the complex or not openly accessible interfaces. Further challenges in the energy domain include that cloud solutions are often not feasible for critical infrastructure, and many software systems have legacy issues and custom data sources. These statements are based on the authors' working experience in the energy domain.

FAIRlead [24] is a data integration and management system tailored for the energy domain, designed to be open source and suitable for smaller budgets. It features a graphical user interface based on entity-relationship (ER) models [4], providing an easy-to-understand interface for all data sources. The system supports semi-automatic extraction of ER models with the ability to include user enhancements. It further integrates data sources into target models that are based on ontologies, and allows data access through a virtual knowledge graph. Additionally, code generation methods are employed to simplify data access.

The present paper demonstrates a strategy to extract ER models from data using structural metadata when available, and presents a user interface that enables the user to introduce enhancements to the model. The paper shows the extraction process for the Mondial database [17], the Siemens PSS®E RAW file format and the PSS®SINCAL database. For the first two this extraction was previously presented in a conference publication [25]. The paper is now further extended with example data from PSS®SINCAL and additionally presents the strategy for integrating user enhancements to the extracted ER model. The integration of user enhancements is implemented using a model merging algorithm that will be explained later on. Moreover, the user interface to edit the generated ER model is demonstrated for the PSS®SINCAL model, as this step helps the domain experts from Siemens to visualize relations of the model and therefore provides a means to find new validation rules. In the future, the data integration capabilities of FAIRlead shall be utilized to extend the existing validation application to other data sources beyond PSS®SINCAL.

This paper is organized as follows: The paper begins by discussing related work on model extraction in Sect. 2, therefore providing a foundation for understanding the current state of the field. This section also introduces existing concepts for model merging. In Sect. 3 it delves into the data sources used for the experiments, highlighting the variety and relevance of the data involved. Following this, the concepts of ER model extraction are introduced in Sect. 4, explaining the theoretical basics and practical applications within FAIRlead. Initial results from the model extraction are presented in Sect. 5, showcasing the effectiveness and potential of the proposed methods. The paper also explores the mechanism for user model enhancements in Sect. 6, emphasizing the importance of user involvement in refining the models. A real-life use case for power grid model validation is described in Sect. 7, along with the implementation of the current user interface, demonstrating the practical application of FAIRlead in an industry context. Finally, in Sect. 8 the paper concludes with a summary of the findings and an outlook on future research directions, suggesting areas for further exploration and development.

2 Related Work

Extraction or reverse engineering of ER models or conceptual models in general, has been performed for several data formats, but to the authors best knowledge not generically across many different types of data formats.

Previous work includes the extraction of ClassSheet models from spreadsheets [8]. Integrating them directly into spreadsheet files is possible, which provides accessible structural metadata [9], and creates a baseline for comparing them with relational schemas [7]. Key benefits include the detection of table headers and relations between tables. However, challenges exist with the legacy code base and a focus on only Open Office spreadsheets.

Research by Chiang et al. [6] and Alalfi et al. [1] has focused on the extraction of extended entity relationship (EER) models from relational databases. The first, did further evaluate the performance of the presented approach [5], while the latter presented an export to UML diagrams. Their logic is partially reused in FAIRlead, but with a stronger focus on a lightweight semantic representation of ER models.

Various approaches have been proposed for extracting models from XML files and their schema representations like Document Type Definitions (DTD). Shiu and Fong have presented an approach to extract DTDs from XML data [26], further introducing a new graph format called *Extended DTD Graph* which allows finding references based on the XML document structure as well as potential *ID/IDREF* pairs. Next to DTD there exist many other schema specifications for XML data like XML Schema (XSD), RelaxNG and schematron. A survey of available schema extraction methods was collected by Klímek et al. [16]. An existing approach for ER model extraction from DTDs is presented by Yang et al. [27]. Their focus is on making DTDs more understandable, which is following the same idea as FAIRlead: to use ER models as a simple abstraction. Mello et al. also present a conceptual model extraction strategy for DTDs, but with the focus on semantic data integration for XML data [19]. This strategy is closely related to FAIRlead, however, they employ a rule-based approach to achieve this instead of a hard coded algorithm. Della Penna et al. have presented the extraction of ER models from an XSD schema [10]. Existing software for DTD or XSD extraction can be utilized as a pre-processing step for the ER model extraction solution presented in this paper.

ER models can also be extracted from Resource Description Framework (RDF) data, which usually has an ontology (for example in OWL format) as a model. Conceptual modeling (e.g. with ER models) is often used as a strategy to understand a certain domain when creating new ontologies [13]. Ontologies can also be used to describe conceptual models directly and is then called *ontology-based conceptual modeling*. An example of this is the Unified Foundational Ontology (UFO) [14]. A rule-based approach for extracting conceptual models from ontologies has been proposed by El-Ghalayini et al. [11]. The goal of this approach is to facilitate the merging of multiple ontologies into an overarching domain ontology. Another approach to directly extract ER models is presented by Han et al. [15]. The Conceptual Model Ontology (CMO) [18] is used to annotate ontologies with conceptual model concepts, aiming to integrate different data sources using common natural language terminology. In contrast to FAIRlead, this requires manual annotation of the data sources that shall be integrated.

A further topic that is touched by this paper is the enhancement of a generated ER model with additional information. To achieve this, a model merging approach has been implemented. Model merging has been widely discussed for relational databases where it is also often called schema merging. For example, Buneman et al. [3] describe the useful properties commutativity and associativity of schema merging algorithms. Those properties allow finding exactly one correct schema regardless of the order of the given input schemas. For example, the following constraint for merging the schemas A and B

$$A \text{ merge } B = B \text{ merge } A$$

is only true if the *merge* algorithm provides commutativity. Moreover, using three schemas A, B and C with the constraint

$$(A \text{ merge } B) \text{ merge } C = A \text{ merge}(B \text{ merge } C)$$

is only valid if the algorithm is associative. Later on, Brunet et al. extended these properties of models with idempotency, monotonicity and totality as well as a means to define inverse operations [2]. Furthermore, their publication defined all the relevant operations that are needed for model merging.

Example implementations of various model merging algorithms have been published. For example, Quix et al. present their generic model merging algorithm [22], that uses a detailed role-based metamodel (GeRoMe) which abstracts away the properties of different pyhsical schema types (e.g. relational, XML schema, etc.) while still being detailed enough to capture all relevant properties. This effectively means that the algorithm can be used for almost any existing schema type, as long as the conversion to GeRoMe is implemented. After the merge, the schema metamodel needs to be converted back to a physical form, to be used in an application. Some of the merging issues are therefore deferred to this conversion step, e.g. what happens if the physical target model does not allow multiple labels for an entity. Sabetzadeh et al. have presented an application (TReMer) with a user interface to visually define models and perform merging using different algorithms from a library [23]. This implementation does focus specifically on the relations between the models and the fact that depending on the development stage, a different algorithm may yield better results. The authors have applied this tool to the example of state machines.

When schemas are merged to create an overarching schema it can also be called mediated schema. This especially applies when almost unrelated schemas are merged for data integration purposes. Algorithms how to create such a mediated schema are presented in A. Pottinger's dissertation [21]. This publication also describes algorithms, that are used for query processing against such a mediated schema to convert them to queries against the individual data sources, which will be interesting for future work to allow data integration with FAIRlead.

3 Demonstration Data Sets

The Mondial database [17] is a collection of data about countries, cities, geographic features, and demographic features. Its availability in several data formats is an advantage for demonstrating an ER model extraction approach. It contains more than 15 entities and over 20 individual relations, including concepts relevant for ER models such as weak and strong entities, key attributes, and various relation cardinalities. Additionally, a reference ER model exists for comparison.

The SAVNW Example Power Grid Model from the Siemens PSS®E power system simulator represents the topology and component attributes of an electrical power grid, serialized as a text file (RAW format) with tables for each power grid element type. It may contain comments for column labels, but these are not mandatory. Additional user inputs are required for ER model extraction due to the lack of structural metadata in the file format.

As a second energy domain example, a demo model of the Siemens PSS®SINCAL power system planning and analysis software is used, which is mostly stored in an SQLite database file. The general extraction of the ER model is therefore similar to the Mondial database in SQL form. The model is a lot larger than the previous two as it contains 264 entities roughly covering the same content as PSS®E does, but it provides more content with regard to types of analysis and modeling details. Notable is the lack of foreign key definitions which technically results in a list of completely unrelated entities by default. So, again, this serves as a good example to integrate user enhancements and also to showcase a strategy to infer relations from a model that does not specify them directly.

4 ER Model Extraction

This section provides an overview of ER model components and their extraction from data sets and optional schema information. A more detailed explanation can be found in the original conference paper [25]. ER models are abstract representations of important concepts and relationships often used for database modeling. They consist of entity types, relation types, cardinalities, and attribute types. In this paper, they are visualized using the Chen notation [4]. However, the newest diagrams started to adopt a newer syntax for cardinalities from UML, because it is more expressive, and it is possible to distinguish between *exactlyOne* and *noneOrOne*, as well as *any* and *atLeastOne*. If this newer syntax is used, it is explicitly stated in the figure description. Figure 1 shows example diagrams on the right-hand side, containing rectangles as representation of entity types and diamond shapes for the representation of relation types. Cardinalities of a relationship are given as edge labels and attribute types (not depicted in the figure) are visualized using oval shapes. The diagrams of Fig. 1 will be explained in more detail in Sect. 5.

The Chen notation contains some more detailed visualizations like double borders for entity types and relation types depicting the so-called *weak entities* and *identifying relations* respectively. A *weak entity* can not exist on its own and is dependent on another entity that it is related to through an *identifying relation*.

The term entity is often used ambiguously in natural language. Generally, an entity is the instance of an entity type and all the instances together form an entity set. Within an ER diagram only the entity types are depicted. However, in natural language the words *type* and *set* are often omitted, causing the term *entity* to be used synonymously for all of them.

In tabular data (e.g. CSV or relational databases), entity types are represented by tables. Additional logic is necessary to filter out potential $n : m$ relations that are also often modeled as tables in tabular data. Relational databases provide schema information that can help to make this decision while CSV does not. For OWL data, entity types are represented by nodes that have the *rdf:type owl:Class*. Ontologies do not require the designer to specify every aspect of the model, which makes it harder to extract an ER model from it. In these cases, a reasoner is important to fill in the missing class definitions to generate a complete ER model. Reasoners do infer additional triples based on a rule catalog, for example if A *rdfs:subClassOf* B then both A and B must be of *rdf:type owl:Class*. These additional triples are added by the reasoner if they have not been specified explicitly in the ontology. In XML, entities are represented by elements with attributes or child elements (*complexType* in XSD). In JSON, all objects are considered entities, but it can be hard to detect what objects do have the same entity type as many object properties can be optional. Available schema information makes assigning objects to entity types more precise.

Relations indicate that one entity references at least one other entity. For object notations (like JSON), a property that has another object as its value or stores an ID as value is the expression of a relation. In OWL, the *owl:ObjectProperty* class specifies relations, it allows tracking of domains (subject), ranges (object), and cardinality constraints (*owl:Restriction*). Tabular data does not provide a direct way of detecting relations, and it usually requires additional logic to do so. In CSV, common naming patterns (e.g., ID columns) can help to identify relations. With relational databases, foreign key constraints represent relations. Additionally, it is possible to evaluate the value sets of primary key columns. If another column's values are a partial set of any of the primary key column value sets, it could indicate a relation. If the information about primary keys is available for CSV data, then the same logic can apply there.

Cardinalities represent quantity constraints between connected entities. In plain table data, it is difficult to infer cardinalities without additional schema information. For relational databases, cardinalities are inferred through modeling patterns and constraints. In OWL, the *owl:Restriction* concept with cardinality predicates for exact or minimum/maximum conformity is used. For the extraction of cardinalities from hierarchical object notations, an external schema that specifies quantity constraints is necessary. This includes the *minOccurs* and *maxOccurs* attributes in XSD, and for JSON schema arrays can have minimum or maximum counts and all properties in general can be required or not.

In relational databases and other tabular data, attributes are represented by columns. However, the columns used to represent relations are no longer considered attributes in ER models. For OWL, the *owl:DatatypeProperty* concept is used for encoding attributes. Object notations consider an attribute to be a primitive property that does not represent another entity's ID. In XML, elements without attributes and primitive content, as well as explicit XML attributes, are considered ER model attributes.

Due to the varying level of available structural metadata among the different described data sources, the quality of extracted ER models can be quite different. And even for the highest quality models, user enhancements are often needed to achieve accurate ER models.

5   Examples from the FAIRlead ER Model Extraction

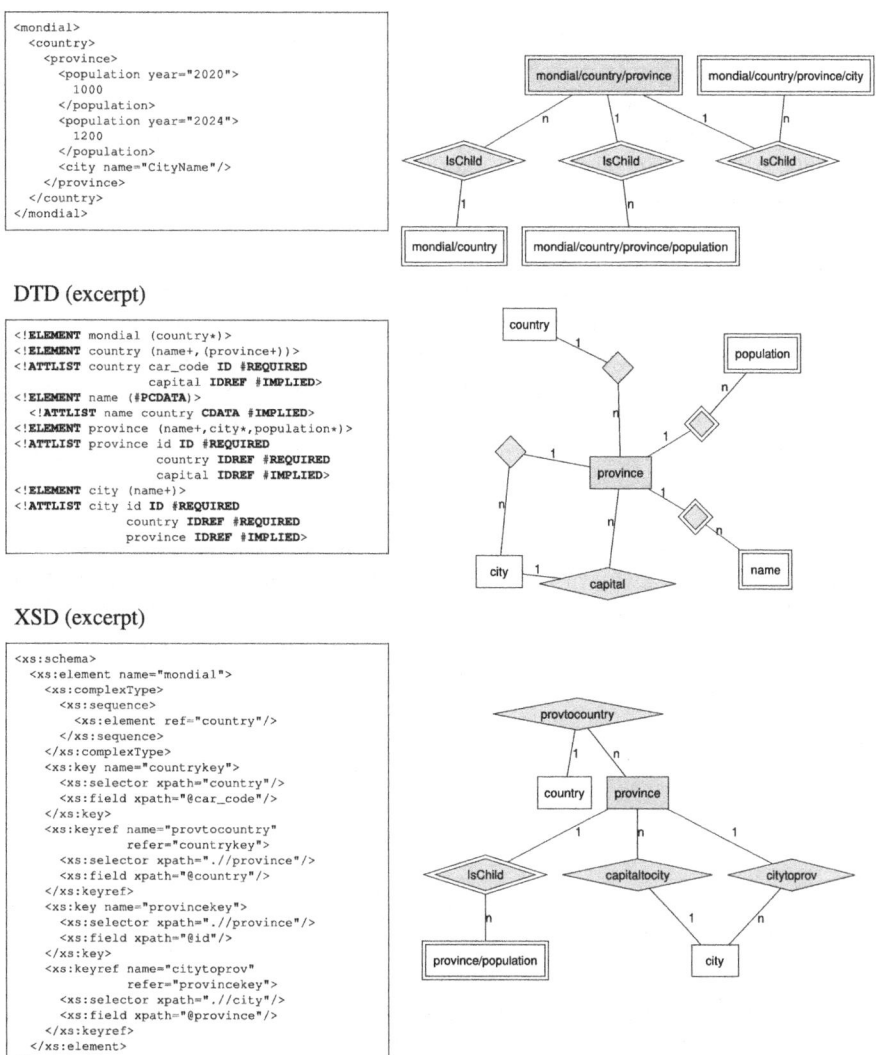

Fig. 1. ER extraction of the province entity from Mondial XML data in three processing types (diagrams from [25]).

5.1 Mondial

Figure 1 illustrates the relevant XML and schema sections as well as the respective ER diagram of the province entity in three versions: only the XML file without schema, with DTD and with XSD.

The schemaless version uses compound naming, which is used to indicate the hierarchical position of entities within the XML file, such as *mondial/country/province/city* and *mondial/country/city* (not visible in the diagram) which both represent a city entity that is found at different locations within the structure (within a country or a province). Furthermore, the hierarchical structure is represented through the *IsChild* relation.

For the next two diagrams, schema information in form of DTD and XSD was available, which allowed the extraction process to become more accurate. For instance, the province entity is treated as a unique entity, which has been inferred by the *xsd:key* or *ID* type in the respective schema. So, the entity no longer uses compound naming, and all occurrences at different locations inside the XML file are considered to be of the same entity type. The relations extracted with schema information differ from those without it, providing a more accurate representation e.g. by using descriptive names. However, even with the most detailed schema (XSD), some entities may still lack quality due to the limitations of the schema specification, when comparing it to the relational or OWL based models of Mondial. For example, the *provtocountry* relation is, in fact, an identifying relation, making province a weak entity, which is not visible in the extracted model.

Figure 2 shows a pattern in XSD-extracted models where entities could be relations, highlighting the complexity of accurately extracting ER models from schema-based data. More precisely, the *river/located* entity can be expressed as an *n to n* relation. This case could be implemented with an automated schema enhancement that is applied to all schemas regardless of the data source as a post-processing step (see Sect. 6.2).

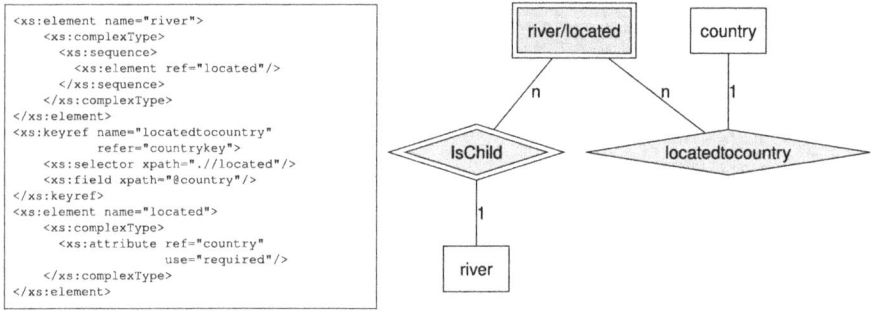

Fig. 2. Extracted ER model from the XSD schema that could be contracted with a post-processing step (diagram from [25]).

Figure 3 demonstrates cardinality extraction from OWL data, with the *isBorderOf* relation as a *2-to-n* and the *locatedIn* relation as *n-to-n*, showcasing the ability to capture complex relationships and cardinalities.

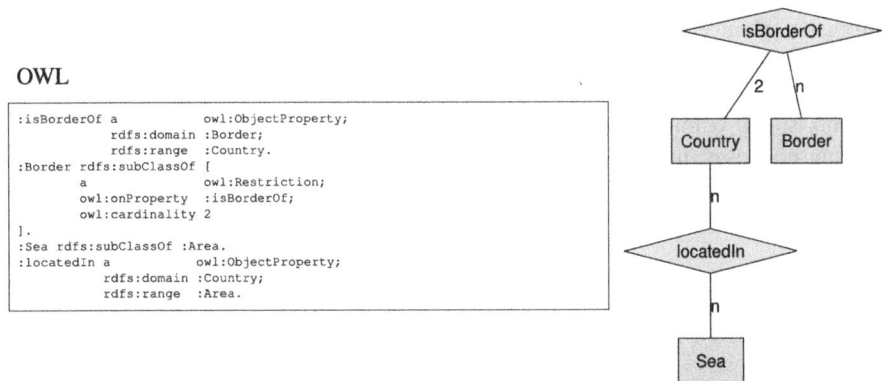

Fig. 3. Extracted ER model of the OWL data set that showcases the cardinality possibilities in an ontology (diagram from [25]).

5.2 PSS®E

The Siemens PSS®E data presents unique challenges for ER model extraction due to its format and optionality of structural metadata. The RAW file format used by PSS®E contains tables for each power grid element type, such as busbars, transformers, and generators. It is necessary to perform a preprocessing step, that helps in organizing the data into a more manageable format.

In this case, the input file was split into several CSV files. In the worst-case scenario, the extracted ER model contains only generic entity and attribute names like *Table 1* to *TableN* and *Column1* to *ColumnN*, making it difficult to interpret. As a result, user enhancements are essential for refining the ER model. For example, the users can provide meaningful names for entities and attributes, ensuring the extracted model accurately represents the underlying data. One benefit of the creation of enhancements is that it is not mandatory to modify everything at once, but do so incrementally every time new data needs to be processed for a use case. Figure 4 provides an example of such a user-enhanced ER model.

First, it shows the extracted ER model as described above in the top left. The entity names could be used from the CSV file names, but for the columns no information was available, so they are just enumerated. Next to that diagram on the right, is the specification of the user enhancements in the format used internally in FAIRlead. It includes the renaming of all the columns as well as the introduction of two relations *BusInArea* and *LoadLocatedAt* which can be seen in the final diagram on the bottom of the figure.

5.3 PSS®SINCAL

The PSS®SINCAL data set does not provide foreign key relations in its SQLite database, so the extraction process by default delivers a list of unrelated entities. However, the database schema uses a predictable pattern if one column refers to another entity, for example a column name *Element_ID* will reference the respective column in the *Element* table. To create a more meaningful ER model for the users, a semi-automatic enhancement strategy was created that is described in detail in Sect. 6. The output ER model of this strategy can be seen for the *Infeeder* entity in Fig. 5.

The strategy does not have the information needed to create a good name for the relation, so the column name is used instead. In contrast to the previous figures, the diagram now uses the UML syntax for the cardinalities. This allows to show whether

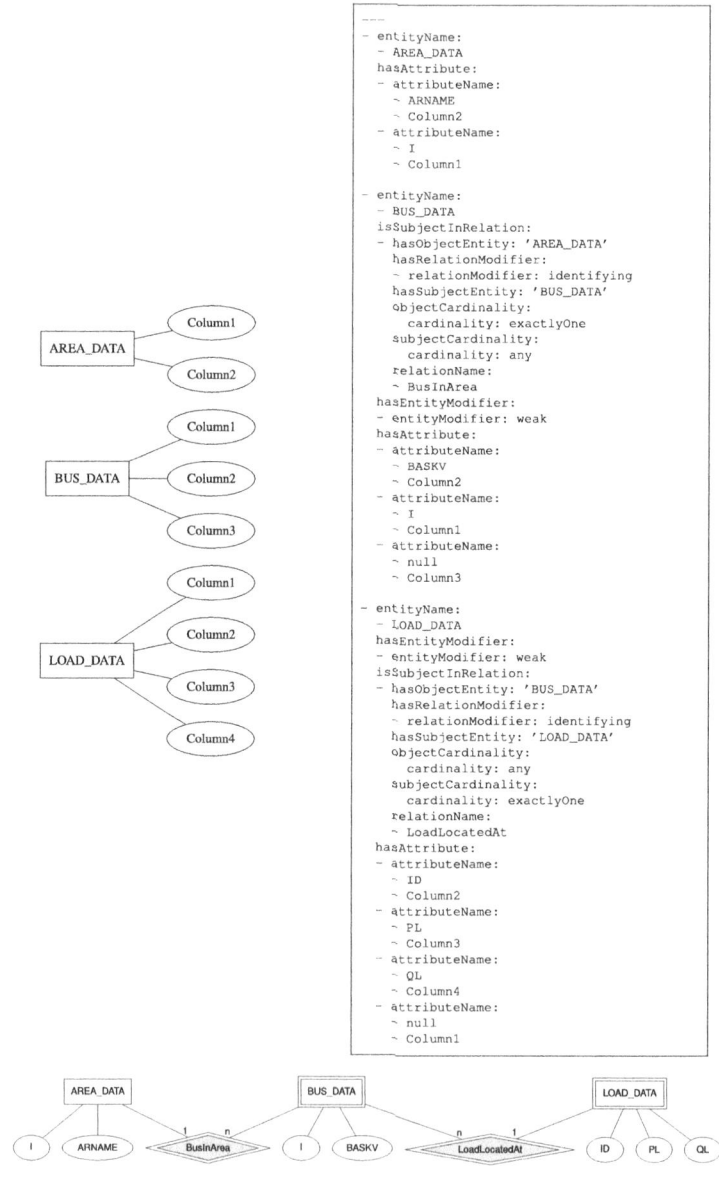

Fig. 4. User corrected ER model of the PSS®E data set (bottom diagram from [25]).

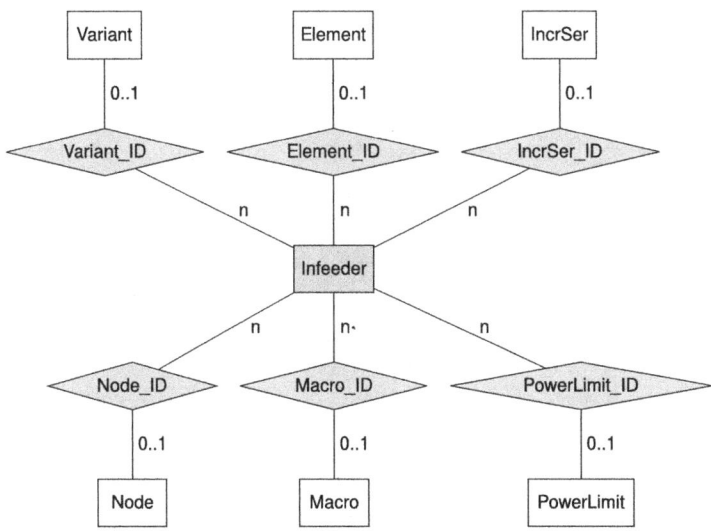

Fig. 5. Automatically optimized ER model of the PSS®SINCAL data set (Using improved cardinality syntax from UML).

a cardinality must be *exactly-one* or it can be *none-or-one*. In addition, some of the attributes that also have the *ID* suffix have not received the respective relation automatically. This is due to small name differences between the column and table names that have been introduced by the database designers, which can not be handled deterministically by the semi-automatic strategy. This can be improved if the user does add renaming operations to the entity type before the logic tries to find matches. Technically, it would also be possible to rename the attribute instead. However, in this case, the user has to rename all occurrences of that name to produce a consistent result. Applying user enhancements is also helpful after the automatic process was conducted, to rename the relation names to a more meaningful text. Figure 6 shows an enhanced version of the previous diagram, where the user supplied names for the relationship types are visualized. This updated figure also shows the changes in cardinality for the *belongsToVariant* and *specializationOf* relations, such that an *Infeeder* must have exactly one referenced *Variant* and exactly one referenced *Element*.

5.4 Summary

The extracted models from both the Mondial database and Siemens energy domain examples demonstrate the variability in accuracy depending on the availability of schema information and the need for user enhancements. While the extracted models may not match the ER diagrams that have originally been used to create the data sets to 100% due to specific modeling decisions of the respective physical models, this lack of exactness is not problematic. The domain experts will perform visual data integration on the extracted models, and possess the necessary knowledge to make appropriate changes or work with the model as is. The semi-automatic approach requires

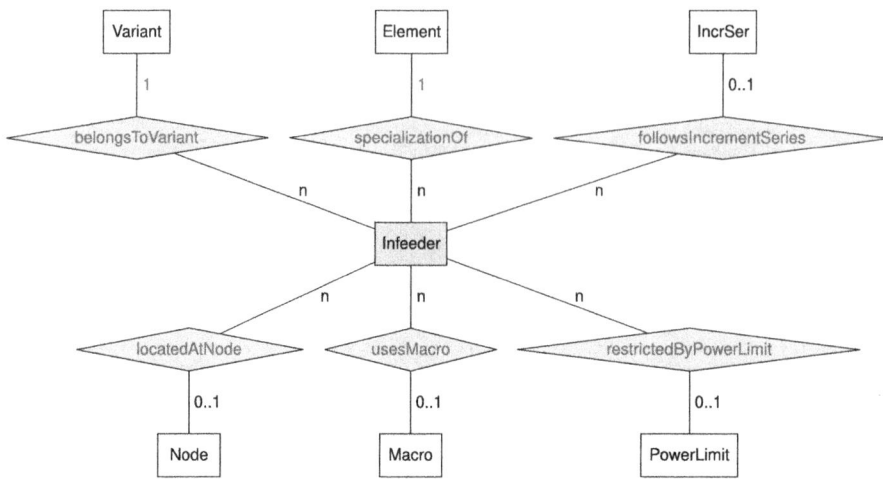

Fig. 6. Optimized ER model of the PSS®SINCAL data set using both user and automatic optimization - changes highlighted in red (Using improved cardinality syntax from UML).

user enhancements for extreme cases, such as XML without schema and schema-less PSS®E data, ensuring the final ER models are both accurate and useful for data integration purposes. This has been shown as an example with the PSS®E data set and the ER model in Fig. 4. Moreover, it has also been shown that running additional logic to automatically improve the generated model is possible. This has been showcased with the PSS®SINCAL dataset which employed both the automatic and user-based ER model enhancements. The ER diagrams shown in this section can directly be created with the REST API and Command Line Interface (CLI) of FAIRlead. It uses the Graphviz [12] visualization tool for this purpose. The following section will discuss the mechanism used for improving the model with user input and automatically executed logic.

6 Model Enhancement

The development of FAIRlead has introduced new approaches in the following order: At first, the previously presented ER model extraction has been implemented. Then, a model merging approach was added, that allows to integrate user enhancements to the previously extracted model. At last, an additional automated process has been introduced to further enhance the extracted ER model. The execution of these steps follows the workflow depicted in Fig. 7. The three steps are visualized using a light gray color and also show the numbers from one to three. The figure uses full-stroke arrows to indicate the flow of actions (rounded boxes), while the dashed arrows indicate the flow of data assets (rectangles).

The content of the original conference paper [25] only included the first workflow action and produced the *ExtractedModel*, while all further steps and models are new content of this paper. The workflow indicates that enhancements in general, as well as the user and automatic enhancements can be enabled or disabled individually. This is expressed with the hexagon shapes that represent conditionals. This allows to easily access the model in all the forms given in the diagram, namely *ExtractedModel*, *UserEnhancedModel* and *EnhancedModel*. Depending on the settings, the *EnhancedModel* can be built upon either of the previous two models. When generating the ER models via the API, the settings to control the enhancement process are passed using query parameters.

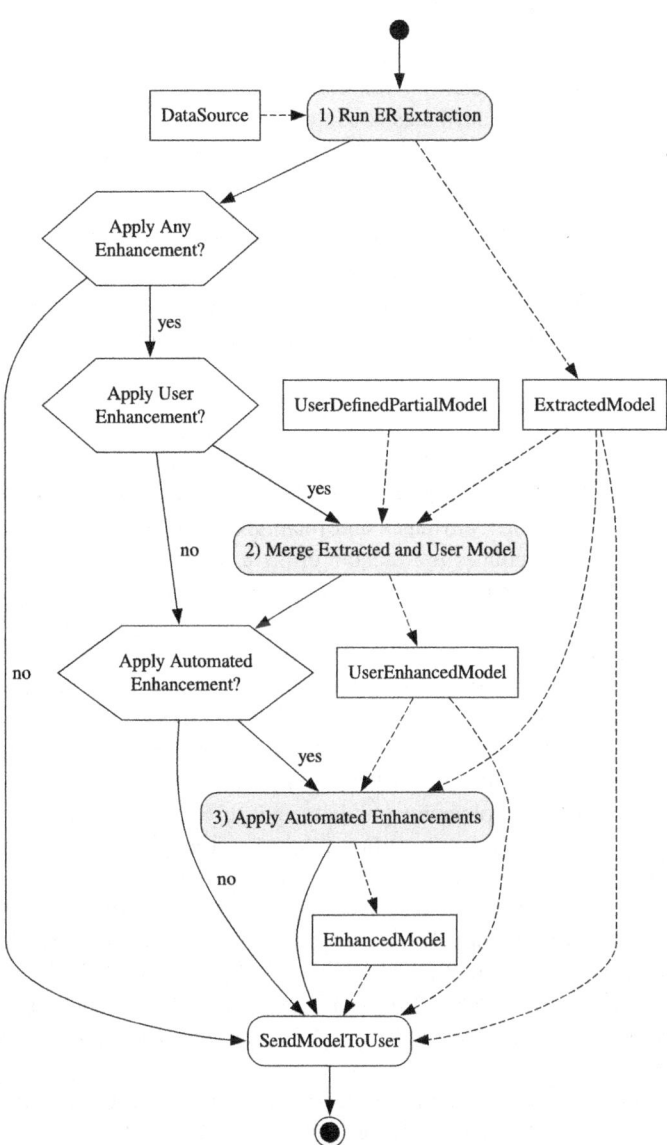

Fig. 7. Workflow of applying ER model enhancements from manual user input and an automatic process.

The process of model merging for the user enhancements is described in the following subsection and the automated enhancement follows afterward.

6.1 User Input Based Model Enhancements

A user should be enabled to perform any necessary step to enhance a generated model. Therefore, the following set of operations was implemented to fully modify the model:

- Renaming of entities, attributes and relations
- Deletion of entities, attributes and relations
- Creation of new entities, attributes and relations
- Changes of entity, attribute and relation modifiers (e.g. entity weakness)
- Changes of relation cardinalities

The approach to introduce the user enhancements was implemented using a model merging strategy. This means, the user defines a secondary model that is then merged with the originally extracted model to produce the final result. As the metamodel for the ER models is quite verbose in respect to the individual enhancements a user might want to make, it was decided to use so-called *Partial Models* to store the secondary user defined model. This further allows maintaining user changes while the main extraction logic can still be updated. If the user would instead create a full model or even edit a copy of the extraction, it would quickly diverge from any improved models generated by the extraction logic. A partial model is characterized by the fact, that almost all properties of the entities, attributes and relations can be left blank (except for the name properties). This reduces the manual effort to create these user defined partial models. The merge algorithm will only consider the properties of the partial user model that have been explicitly defined. This allows, for example, to rename an entity by just giving a new name to the entity without the need to duplicate all other properties of an entity like attributes and relations. An example of a full model and the respective partial user model can be seen in Fig. 8. It shows two fully specified entities *Transformer* and *Generator* from the extraction process on the left and the partial model that shall rename the *Transformer* entity to *TwoWindingTransformer* on the right.

Names are currently implemented as lists and only the first element in the list is used as the actual display name of entities, relations, or attributes. This allows to track name changes through the creation of a history of consecutive changes to the name. It also allows the deletion of an object by setting its name to *null*. All of the enhancements can be applied directly via the REST API, that is used to extract the ER models. The specification of the API can be found on GitHub[1]. The API is used within a web user interface (which will be introduced in Sect. 7.2) to provide the capabilities to rename entities directly in a rendered view of the ER diagram instead of manipulating files or calling the API manually.

For the merging process the term *object* will be used as the base class of entity, relation, and attribute. The merge of the generated ER model with the user defined partial model uses a custom merging algorithm, that uses the name list of the respective

---

[1] https://cpprentice.github.io/FAIRlead-user-interface/api-documentation/.

Extracted Model

```
- entityName:
    - Transformer
  hasAttributes:
    - attributeName: Attribute1
      hasAttributeModifier: []
    - attributeName: AttributeId
      hasAttributeModifier:
        attributeModifier: key
  entityModifier: []
  isSubjectInRelation: []
  isObjectInRelation: []
- entityName:
    - Generator
  hasAttributes:
    - attributeName: Attribute20
      hasAttributeModifier: []
  entityModifier: []
  isSubjectInRelation: []
  isObjectInRelation: []
```

Partial User Model

```
- entityName:
    - TwoWindingTransformer
    - Transformer
```

Fig. 8. Extracted model on the left with a partial user model for a renaming operation on the right (both in the FAIRlead internal YAML syntax).

objects to detect which objects need to be merged. This is done by checking if one list of names is a super set of the other. For example, the name list *(ProperName, ShortName)* is considered a super set of *(ShortName)*. The actual object merge favors the value of the user enhancement object, unless it is undefined. This effectively only overwrites the fields of the original object, that are specified in the partial user object, keeping all other field values intact. Considering the example from Fig. 8, only the first entity on the left is selected for merging with the partial user model on the right, because the *entityName* of the partial user model *(TwoWindingTransformer, Transformer)* is a super set of that entity's name list. As all other properties of the partial entity except for the name are undefined, the resulting entity will have all the values from the first entity on the left, but with the *entityName* value from the right side. Moreover, the second entity on the left is not touched at all, so it will be included as-is in the output model.

6.2 Automatic Model Enhancements

While theoretically, many automatic enhancements are possible to improve the generated ER model, only one is currently implemented. This automated enhancement was introduced due to the missing relations (foreign keys) of the PSS®SINCAL database. While the database does not directly model the foreign key constraints, it still uses a pattern that can be used to generate relations automatically. This pattern is as follows: When the database schema expresses a reference from a column to another table, it uses the referenced table name and appends the suffix *_ID* as the column name. Moreover, a primary key column also follows the pattern *<Tablename>_ID*. This means, it is possible to link all occurrences of the column *Element_ID* to the *Element_ID* column of the *Element* table. This pattern can also be applied directly to the extracted ER model, because each column is represented by an attribute. Therefore, the automatic enhancement logic will detect all these cases and replace the respective ID attribute with a relation. The outcome of this process has previously been shown in Fig. 5.

6.3 Issues with the Current Enhancement Approach

While each of the presented ways of adding enhancements to the ER model works great on its own, the combined use produces issues that shall be discussed in this section. Consider the following example: The automated logic to create relations from attributes relies on matching attribute names - so if a user change is applied beforehand, the algorithm might not detect this case anymore. A more advanced example can be seen in Fig. 9.

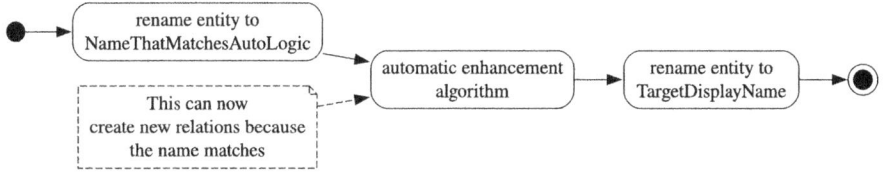

Fig. 9. Scenario of renaming an entity twice.

The entity is renamed twice, first to a matching name to make the automated process find an additional relation, and second to give it a more representative name in the output ER model. In the example of the figure, the entity is renamed to *NameThatMatchesAutoLogic* such that the algorithm will add the respective relations towards that entity, and then it is renamed to a more suitable display name *TargetDisplayName* that is used for visualizing the ER model, while the created relations stay intact. However, that implies that either it must be specified when to apply a change or there needs to be another solution that can perform all the operations in the optimal order.

For the first approach, an easy solution would be to maintain two separate sets of user enhancements, one to be applied before and one after the automatic processing. However, the user should not be required to have this level of understanding about the inner workings of the ER model creation. Therefore, the code would need to determine the correct execution order automatically. Which directly leads to the second solution again, as the correct order needs to be determined automatically.

This second solution is harder to implement but does grant the benefit, that it is possible to even apply user enhancements in between multiple automatic enhancement steps. To achieve an ordering of all individual enhancements, the algorithm needs to be able to infer an order from the given input data. In general, if an ordering of all enhancements can be created deterministically, it would allow for associativity and commutativity of the entire process, which would be a major improvement over the current implementation as the current one cannot guarantee that at the moment. This does in fact cause issues right now, as some of the requested operations can not be applied in the correct order using the current algorithm.

In the following, some solution ideas are discussed, but it is not fully evaluated which of them will be implemented in the end. The first idea for that could be to not perform schema merging in the first place, but rather store a set of operations that work like the atomic CPU operation *compare and swap (CAS)*. A *CAS* is defining the condition that is expected, and is only executed if that condition evaluates to true. If the condition does not match, the operation is tried again at a later time. This is for example used to implement locks in parallel computing, where the lock operation would be a CAS that expects the locked state to be zero and only if that is the case the operation would replace the zero with a one atomically. The application code must therefore retry the operation if the lock state is not zero when the operation is attempted. To transfer this idea to the correct enhancement of a model, it would mean that each change operation can check if the object to be modified already is in the state that is expected by the change operation, and if not it will be attempted after other changes have been applied.

A similar but slightly different idea is to use the fact that most metaclasses do have a name property that is implemented as a list to support renaming. This name list can be used to ensure the proper order of merge operations. However, this seems to have the limitation that a change to the attribute modifiers would not be handled correctly. This would currently only work if a modifier change is executed together with a renaming operation, which allows to precisely define the execution order. Obviously, that is not a feasible solution.

Another idea, which is heavily different from the current implementation, could be to implement the schema optimization with SHACL shapes and respective inference rules to be executed on match. This could work the same way for both manual user enhancements and the automated process. This synergy could be beneficial to streamline the application of all rules with the same algorithm / reasoner. An example of how this could be done is given by Pareti et al. [20].

7 Utilizing an Extracted ER Model to Improve Power Grid Validation

7.1 Motivation

More than ever, electric grid planners are reliant on the data that power systems generate, as an input for designing solutions for the future. But these solutions are only as good as the underlying data and models. A reliable evaluation, whether the data being processed are consistent and valid - in other words, whether there are conflicts with physical, technological, or standards-related limits, is necessary. To identify and solve data quality issues, Siemens Power Technologies International (PTI) is using a semantic data validation engine, which is based on a predefined, but individually adjustable, validation rule set, which covers standards, physical limits, and experienced-based ranges.

This application converts selected entities from the PSS®SINCAL SQLite database to an RDF model based on their ontology. This RDF model is used to apply a set of predefined validation rules generically. It generates a list of constraint violations as an output that can be exported in JSON or CSV format. Each violation references its respective entity and affected property. However, no data changes are performed by the data validation engine. Hence, the user can decide whether power grid specific deviations from the rule set are acceptable. For false-positives the validation rules can be adjusted or moved to a user specific whitelist, whereas verified issues can be corrected in the respective input grid model by the network planer. In contrast to any manual data validation process, the application of the data validation engine saves time and costs, brings reliable transparency on level of data quality, and improves data quality.

Currently, the power grid model used for the validation is only available as an RDF file and a documentation that lists entities and data attributes. A non-standardized mapping between the PSS®SINCAL and the RDF model does exist, but it is hard to understand. As a result, it is hard to get an overview of the available entities and their respective attributes from the data source. The visualization of FAIRlead and the planned data integration solution can help to improve the accessibility of the source data model for the engineers and, in a future release, enable the visual mapping between the two models. For example, to easily see what information is available in PSS®SINCAL and which parts of it are already used for the definition of validation rules. Moreover, FAIRlead can be used in the future to simplify the process of adding new supported data formats as inputs for the validation engine.

7.2 FAIRlead User Interface

FAIRlead does provide a web based user interface, that currently has the capability to both visualize ER models and allow the user to introduce the enhancements without manually editing files or making API calls manually. The visualization uses a framework[2] for flow-based programming. Although it seems counterintuitive to use such a framework for the visualization of ER diagrams, this choice was made deliberately to provide an easy way to show data previews while creating a data mapping for integration and to perform consistency checks when creating new mappings. However, this has not yet been implemented and will follow in a later release.

An example entity visualization in this web user interface can be seen on the left side of Fig. 10 which shows an entity with a list of attributes. A further example can be seen in Fig. 11 which does not show the attributes but does display the relations between entities with the blue lines. Both figures will be explained in more detail in the next subsection.

Within the framework, the main UI elements are called nodes, which represent entities in FAIRlead. In addition, it uses different types of sockets to represent inputs (on the left side) and outputs (on the right side) of a node, which can be connected with an edge between input and output sockets of the same type. In this context, each entity does only have exactly one input, which is used to connect a relation that has this entity as its target. However, the number of outputs is dynamic and depends on the number of attributes (orange sockets) and outgoing relations (green sockets) the entity has.

While this visualization is not an ER model in respect to the traditional notations (like the Chen notation), it still carries the meaning. And it is ready to enable the data previews and validations mentioned above, to make any kind of interaction with the models and a future data integration more approachable. Moreover, the information

---

[2] https://retejs.org/.

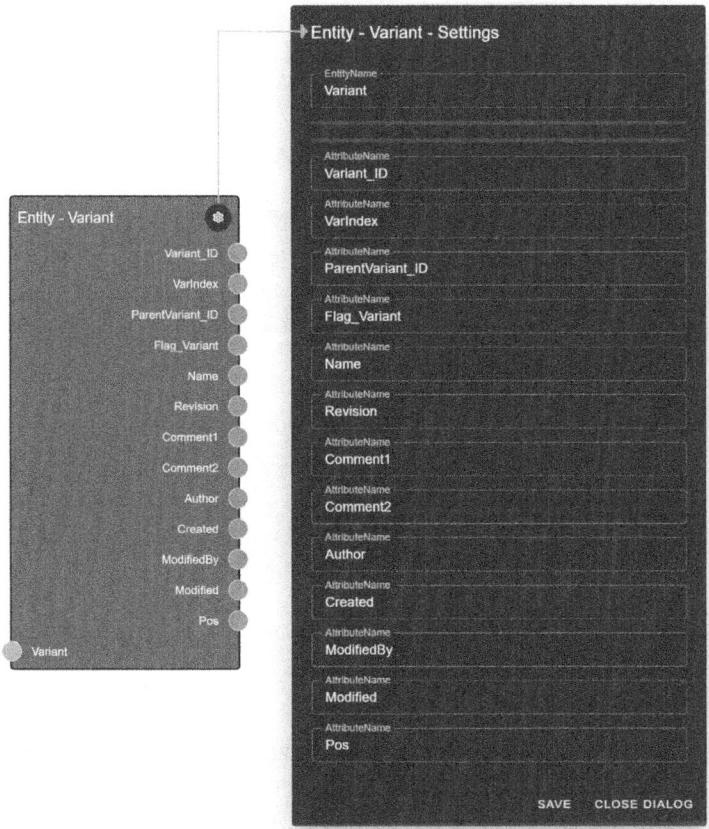

Fig. 10. User Interface for viewing and modifying the ER model - the latter is a popup that is triggered by the small black settings button on the left.

that is not visualized, such as cardinalities and modifiers (e.g. entity weakness), does not play an important role for the data integration workflow intended for the future of FAIRlead. The visualization is already helpful to the Siemens engineers in its current form. For the sake of completeness, those missing features might be implemented in a future version of the FAIRlead user interface, but they are not in the authors' current focus. The next subsection will describe how this FAIRlead user interface was used to view and enhance the ER model of the PSS®SINCAL database that is used for this data validation use case.

7.3 PSS®SINCAL ER Model Enhancements

As mentioned before, without automatic and user enhancements to the ER model, the result for PSS®SINCAL is just a plain list of unrelated entities. Figure 10 shows the *Variant* entity in the model view on the left and the user interface for changing the identifiers of the entity and the attributes on the right. The black dialog for the renaming

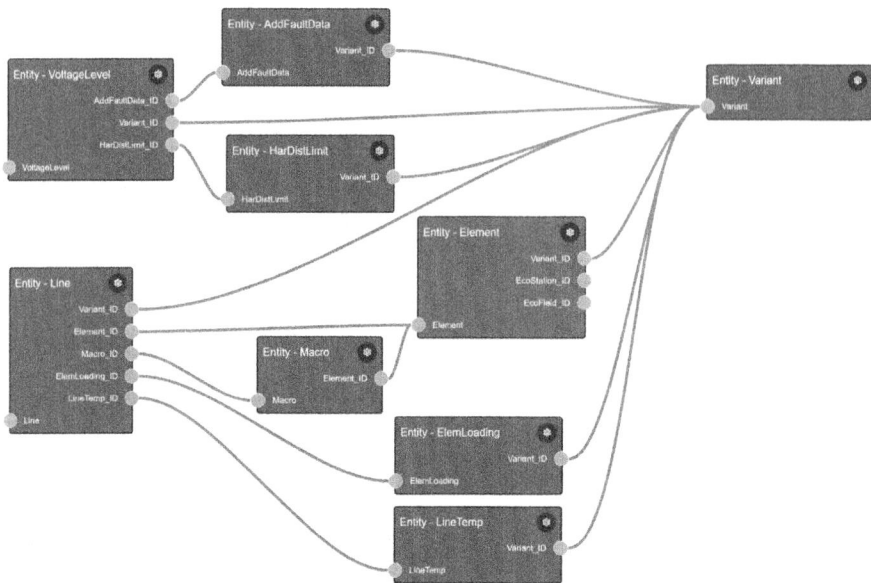

Fig. 11. User Interface displaying the *Line* and *VoltageLevel* focus entities (not rendering attributes).

operations does allow the user to change the names of the entity itself and all of its attributes and relations (In this example no relation does exist, so no green sockets are displayed on the right side). The *Variant* entity is the most referenced entity in the database as it reflects the possibility to store multiple variants of almost any grid model component and functionality, and even if the network doesn't consist of any variants each model component and functionality is per default referred to the base variant with ID 1. This allows quick changes between slightly different scenarios to perform high quality analysis.

For the implementation of this demonstration use case, a new difficulty was encountered: Rendering an ER model with more than 260 entities, some of which have around 100 attributes, is quite a challenge. This is not just the case for the FAIRlead visualization but for any graph visualization of that size. As a solution, two approaches have been implemented.

The first uses a partitioning strategy that forms partitions of a predefined maximum number of entities. The strategy analyzes the ER model in the form of a graph where an entity is a node and a relation is an edge. It does split the graph in a list of unconnected sub graphs. Small sub graphs are combined until the maximum allowed entity count is reached. For sub graphs that are larger than the allowed size, the algorithm does remove the entity/node with the highest node degree from the sub graph, and repeats the procedure with the size limit reduced by one. In the end, the partitions are built up by adding the previously removed entity to all the sub graphs that its removal has produced. This approach has shown two flaws: First, the number of entities is a bad metric for the partition size as a large number of attributes still produces a large diagram. The second flaw is that it is extremely hard to find a certain entity in all the partitions, as there is no indicator in which partition to look. And some entities like the above-mentioned *Variant* are part of almost all partitions.

The second strategy attempts to improve on these flaws. It expects the user to select the entity that shall be rendered (called focus entity), and will only render its direct neighbors. The fact that multiple focus nodes can be selected simultaneously makes it easy to traverse the graph from one entity to another.

A rendered view of entities from the PSS®SINCAL dataset that uses the focus entity strategy can be seen in Fig. 11. It shows the *Line* and *VoltageLevel* focus entities with their relations that have been generated by the automatic model enhancement logic that was introduced in Sect. 6.2. This example has disabled the rendering of attributes to reduce complexity. It only shows the relations (visualized through the green sockets and the blue connections).

The automatic relation detection does not work if the names are different between the primary key column and table name, according to the pattern discussed in Sect. 6.2. So, it seems in Fig. 11 that the *VoltageLevel* entity does not have incoming relations. Figure 12 does show the same focus entities, but additionally the user enhancements are also included. Comparing the two diagrams, it can be seen that the *VoltageLevel* entity does in fact have incoming relations, they have just not been automatically detected without the additional user enhancements. To achieve this, the entity needed to be renamed from *VoltageLevel* to *VoltLevel* as the column name used is *VoltLevel_ID*. Additionally, the relation between the *Line* and *CoupData* entities is new, following the same logic as above. Aside from the new visible relations, the diagram also shows modified relation names. This allows to remove the stub names from the automatic enhancement strategy, with more meaningful relation names like *belongsToVariant* or *hasVoltageLevel*.

Reviewing the ER model with the domain expert yielded three other notable cases, that are, however, not visualized here. The first two follow a similar pattern as above where the name of the primary key does not match the given pattern. This applies to *GraphicAreaTile* with the *GraphicArea_ID* primary key column and the *NetworkGroup* entity that just uses the *Group_ID* primary key column. The first describes a list of graphics that are displayed within the user interface of PSS®SINCAL and the latter specifies the different groups of electric components that shall be grouped for performing power grid analysis. At last, the column *MasterElm_ID* which can be found in several entities, references the *Element* table to represent that the control systems of the current entity follow the lead of another grid element referenced by this column. In this case, the entire relation needs to be added by the user manually, as this is not covered by the automatic process.

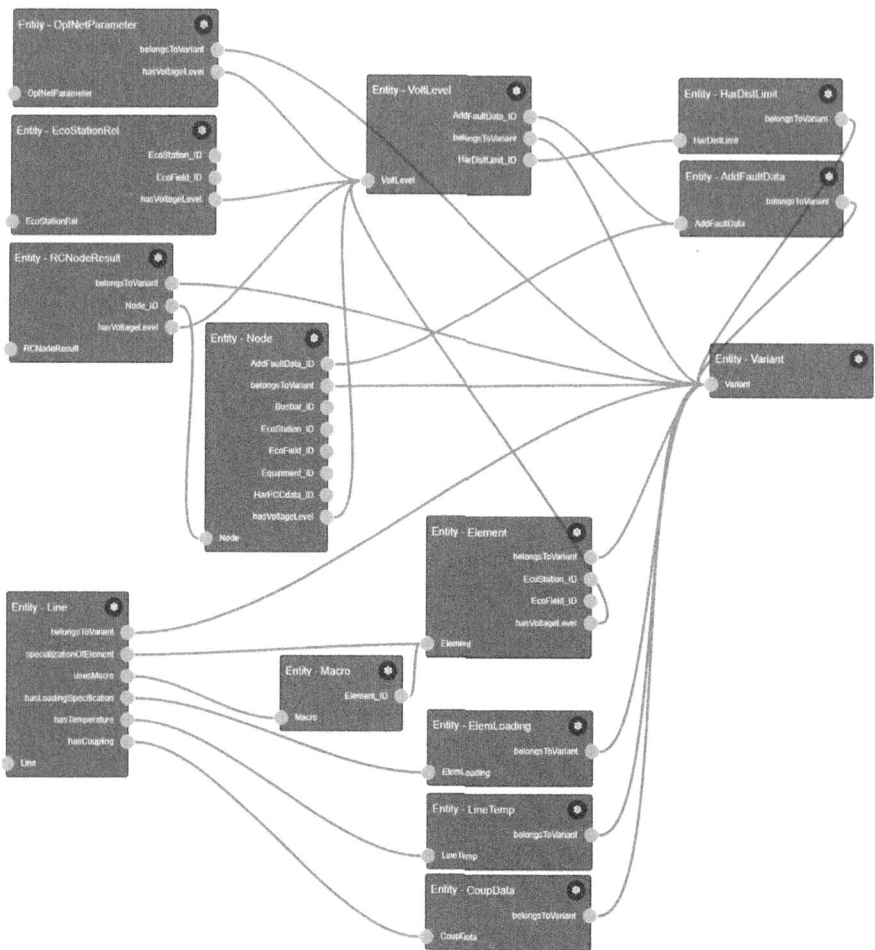

Fig. 12. User Interface displaying the *Line* and *VoltLevel* focus entities including user enhancements (not rendering attributes).

8 Conclusion and Future Work

The present paper has presented strategies to extract ER models from various data sources and demonstrated this with several example data sets. It further introduced a solution to integrate user and automatic enhancements to the extracted ER model, to provide a high quality model for future data integration efforts. Moreover, an industry use-case was presented that makes use of extracted ER models to improve a power grid validation solution. All presented features are part of the open-source solution FAIRlead, which enables domain experts to improve the FAIRness of their data through self-performed data integration. To extend the support for further data sources, either new converters can be implemented using a plugin system for FAIRlead, or a small preprocessing step can be used to convert the data to an already supported format. Examples such as the PSS®E RAW file and the PSS®SINCAL database show the need for user model enhancements due to incomplete structural metadata. A user interface has been demonstrated for rendering simplified ER models and allowing user enhancements.

Future work will address shortcomings in the current model enhancement solution, continuously improve the implementation for accurate ER models, and integrate existing schema generation tools. Next to the current diagram export format (Graphviz), it is planned to create direct export capabilities for other modeling languages like UML. The further development of FAIRlead to facilitate data integration from multiple heterogeneous data sources using the RDF Mapping Language (RML)[3] is ongoing. The authors intend to automatically generate RML mappings alongside the ER models, to directly generate a virtual knowledge graph as an access layer for the underlying data sources. The user interface will be extended to actively use flow-based programming to visually link original data source entities to ontological concepts of a target model.

Acknowledgments. The authors would like to thank the German Federal Government, the German State Governments, and the Joint Science Conference (GWK) for their funding and support as part of the NFDI4Energy consortium. Funded by the Deutsche Forschungsgemeinschaft (DFG, German Research Foundation) – 501865131 within the German National Research Data Infrastructure (NFDI, https://www.nfdi.de/).

This publication was also supported by the Helmholtz Metadata Collaboration (HMC, https://www.helmholtz-metadata.de/), an incubator-platform of the Helmholtz Association within the framework of the Information and Data Science strategic initiative.

Disclosure of Interests. The authors have no competing interests to declare that are relevant to the content of this article. However, the first author is a former employee of Siemens AG, which initiated the collaboration for this publication, in which the Siemens AG employee and co-author Maiko Friedrich is also involved.

A Appendix

Appendix

The FAIRlead code for both the ER model extraction and the visualization and enhancement user interface can be found on GitHub:
https://github.com/Cpprentice/FAIRlead-model-extraction
https://github.com/Cpprentice/FAIRlead-user-interface

Furthermore, the API specification for the ER model extraction API is available as an OpenAPI specification online:
https://CPPrentice.github.io/FAIRlead-user-interface/api-documentation

---

[3] https://rml.io.

References

1. Alalfi, M.H., Cordy, J.R., Dean, T.R.: SQL2XMI: reverse engineering of UML-ER diagrams from relational database schemas. In: 2008 15th Working Conference on Reverse Engineering, pp. 187–191 (2008). https://doi.org/10.1109/WCRE.2008.30
2. Brunet, G., Chechik, M., Easterbrook, S., Nejati, S., Niu, N., Sabetzadeh, M.: A manifesto for model merging. In: Proceedings of the 2006 International Workshop on Global Integrated Model Management, GaMMa '06, pp. 5–12. Association for Computing Machinery, New York (2006). https://doi.org/10.1145/1138304.1138307
3. Buneman, P., Davidson, S., Kosky, A.: Theoretical aspects of schema merging. In: Pirotte, A., Delobel, C., Gottlob, G. (eds.) Advances in Database Technology — EDBT '92, pp. 152–167. Springer, Berlin, Heidelberg (1992). https://doi.org/10.1007/BFb0032429
4. Chen, P.P.S.: The entity-relationship model–toward a unified view of data. ACM Trans. Database Syst. **1**(1), 9–36 (1976). https://doi.org/10.1145/320434.320440
5. Chiang, R.H.L., Barron, T.M., Storey, V.C.: Performance evaluation of reverse engineering relational databases into extended Entity-Relationship models. In: Elmasri, R.A., Kouramajian, V., Thalheim, B. (eds.) Entity-Relationship Approach — ER '93, pp. 352–363. Springer, Heidelberg (1994). https://doi.org/10.1007/BFb0024379
6. Chiang, R.H.L., Barron, T.M., Storey, V.C.: Reverse engineering of relational databases: extraction of an EER model from a relational database. Data Knowl. Eng. **12**(2), 107–142 (1994). https://doi.org/10.1016/0169-023X(94)90011-6
7. Cunha, J., Erwig, M., Mendes, J., Saraiva, J.: Model inference for spreadsheets. Autom. Softw. Eng. **23**(3), 361–392 (2016). https://doi.org/10.1007/s10515-014-0167-x
8. Cunha, J., Erwig, M., Saraiva, J.: Automatically inferring classsheet models from spreadsheets. In: 2010 IEEE Symposium on Visual Languages and Human-Centric Computing, pp. 93–100 (2010). https://doi.org/10.1109/VLHCC.2010.22
9. Cunha, J., Fernandes, J.P., Mendes, J., Saraiva, J.: Extension and implementation of ClassSheet models. In: 2012 IEEE Symposium on Visual Languages and Human-Centric Computing (VL/HCC), pp. 19–22 (2012). https://doi.org/10.1109/VLHCC.2012.6344473
10. Della Penna, G., Marco, A.D., Intrigila, B., Melatti, I., Pierantonio, A.: Interoperability mapping from XML schemas to ER diagrams. Data Knowl. Eng. **59**(1), 166–188 (2006). https://doi.org/10.1016/j.datak.2005.08.002
11. El-Ghalayini, H., Odeh, M., McClatchey, R., Solomonides, T.: Reverse Engineering Ontology to Conceptual Data Models (2004). https://doi.org/10.48550/ARXIV.CS/0412036
12. Gansner, E.R., North, S.C.: An open graph visualization system and its applications to software engineering. Softw. Pract. Exper. **30**(11), 1203–1233 (2000)
13. Gómez-Pérez, A., Fernández, M., de Vicente, A.: Towards a method to conceptualize domain ontologies. In: Proceedings Workshop: Ontological Engineering | 12th European Conference on Artificial Intelligence (ECAI'96) | 13Ago 1996 | Budapest, Hungría. Facultad de Informática (UPM), Budapest (1996)
14. Guizzardi, G.: Ontological Foundations for Structural Conceptual Models. Ph.D. thesis, University of Twente (2005)
15. Han, L., Xu, J., Yao, Q.: Entity-Relationship semantic meta-model based on ontology. In: 2010 International Conference on Computer Application and System Modeling (ICCASM 2010), vol. 11, pp. V11–219–V11–222 (2010). https://doi.org/10.1109/ICCASM.2010.5623220
16. Klímek, J., Nečaský, M.: Reverse-engineering of XML Schemas a survey. In: CEUR Workshop Proceedings, vol. 567, pp. 96–107 (2010)
17. May, W.: Information Extraction and Integration with Florid: The Mondial Case Study. Technical Report 131, Universität Freiburg, Institut für Informatik (1999)

18. McCusker, J., Luciano, J., Mcguinness, D.: Towards an ontology for conceptual modeling. In: CEUR Workshop Proceedings, vol. 833 (2011)
19. Mello, R.d.S., Heuser, C.A.: A rule-based conversion of a DTD to a conceptual schema. In: S.Kunii, H., Jajodia, S., Sølvberg, A. (eds.) Conceptual Modeling — ER 2001, pp. 133–148. Springer, Heidelberg (2001). https://doi.org/10.1007/3-540-45581-7_12
20. Pareti, P., Konstantinidis, G., Norman, T.J., Şensoy, M.: SHACL constraints with inference rules. In: Ghidini, C., Hartig, O., Maleshkova, M., Svátek, V., Cruz, I., Hogan, A., Song, J., Lefrançois, M., Gandon, F. (eds.) The Semantic Web – ISWC 2019, pp. 539–557. Springer International Publishing, Cham (2019). https://doi.org/10.1007/978-3-030-30793-6_31
21. Pottinger, R.A., Bernstein, P.A., Halevy, A.Y.: Processing Queries and Merging Schemas in Support of Data Integration. Ph.D. thesis, University of Washington, USA (2004)
22. Quix, C., Kensche, D., Li, X.: Generic schema merging. In: Krogstie, J., Opdahl, A., Sindre, G. (eds.) Advanced Information Systems Engineering, pp. 127–141. Springer, Heidelberg (2007). https://doi.org/10.1007/978-3-540-72988-4_10
23. Sabetzadeh, M., Nejati, S., Easterbrook, S., Chechik, M.: A relationship-driven framework for model merging. In: International Workshop on Modeling in Software Engineering (MISE'07: ICSE Workshop 2007), p. 2 (2007). https://doi.org/10.1109/MISE.2007.4
24. Schmidt, A., Koubaa, M., Liu, N., Schmurr, P., Stucky, K.U., Süß, W.: FAIRlead: a conceptual framework for a model driven software development approach in the field of FAIR data management. In: Proceedings of the 16th International Joint Conference on Knowledge Discovery, Knowledge Engineering and Knowledge Management, pp. 323–330. SCITEPRESS - Science and Technology Publications, Porto (2024). https://doi.org/10.5220/0013013700003838
25. Schmurr, P., Schmidt, A., Stucky, K.U., Suess, W., Hagenmeyer, V.: Performing entity relationship model extraction from data and schema information as a basis for data integration. In: Proceedings of the 16th International Joint Conference on Knowledge Discovery, Knowledge Engineering and Knowledge Management, pp. 316–322. SCITEPRESS - Science and Technology Publications, Porto (2024). https://doi.org/10.5220/0013012600003838
26. Shiu, H., Fong, J.: Reverse engineering from an XML document into an extended DTD graph. In: Siau, K. (ed.) Theoretical and Practical Advances in Information Systems Development: Emerging Trends and Approaches, pp. 101–119. IGI Global (2011). https://doi.org/10.4018/978-1-60960-521-6.ch006
27. Yang, W., Zhan, M., Wang, Q., Shi, B.: A conversion of a DTD to conceptual model by using UML. In: The Fourth International Conference on Computer and Information Technology, 2004. CIT '04, pp. 303–308 (2004). https://doi.org/10.1109/CIT.2004.1357212

Design and Validation of a Digital Mindset Model: A Combination of Organizational Culture Theory and Design Science

Seyma Kocak[1,2](✉) and Jan Pawlowski[2]

[1] Faculty of Information Technology, University of Jyväskylä, Jyväskylä, Finland
seyma.kocak@hs-ruhrwest.de
[2] University of Applied Sciences Ruhr West Institute of Computer Science, Bottrop, Germany
jan.pawlowski@hs-ruhrwest.de

Abstract. Digital transformation (DT) is a crucial challenge for modern organizations that requires cultural and structural adjustments. A digital mindset, which includes digital competencies, personal characteristics, entrepreneurial orientation, personality traits, and motivation, is a key factor for a successful transformation. This study develops and evaluates a comprehensive digital mindset model, filling research gaps that often focus on individual characteristics. Using the design science research approach and a mixed-methods design, Schein's organizational culture theory is integrated to examine how artifacts, values, and assumptions influence digital readiness. The model includes six dimensions: Digital mindset, digital competencies, personal competencies, personality traits, motivation, and entrepreneurial orientation. A five-level maturity framework, from "Digital Outsider" to "Digital Master," enables companies to assess their digital readiness. The results highlight agility, communication, and technological competencies, while negative interactions, such as conflicts between results orientation and error acceptance, are addressed. Expert reviews confirmed the completeness and practicality of the model and suggested refinements for traits such as 'extraversion' and 'generosity'. Recommendations include industry-specific applications, particularly in traditional sectors, and the need for broader samples to improve generalizability. By operationalizing the digital mindset with measurable dimensions and maturity levels, this research provides a robust framework to support sustainable Digital transformation.

Keywords: Digital Mindset Organizational Culture Theory · Digital transformation · Design science · Organization

1 Introduction

Digital transformation is one of the key challenges facing modern companies and significantly impacts their competitiveness. Companies are increasingly benefiting from the opportunities offered by digitalization and implementing them to survive in a constantly changing, agile environment [76]. However, they must make far-reaching organizational changes to meet the new requirements. Corporate culture, which shapes a company's values, norms, and ways of thinking, plays a crucial role [6]. At the same time, corporate culture is influenced by Digital transformation, resulting in a reciprocal relationship between the two [82].

Despite the increasing importance of digitalization, many companies lack the necessary digital competencies, organizational competencies, and a suitable mindset to drive Digital transformation successfully [58]. Digital competencies are essential for using new technologies, working in networks, and effectively transferring knowledge [3]. However, these competencies alone are not enough to accelerate complex change. Instead, a suitable digital mindset is required that promotes the willingness to adapt and change [30].

Mindset plays a decisive role in the Digital transformation process, as it influences the attitudes and mindsets of individuals and organizations [32]. The mindset's flexibility and change orientation is critical to successfully shaping transformations [31]. Studies show that companies with a positive digital mindset are better able to drive change actively [68]. At the same time, the mindset is closely linked to the digital competencies of employees and managers, which also form an essential basis for the digital performance of organizations [7].

Although the literature emphasizes the importance of a digital mindset for Digital transformation, there is a research gap: Many existing models either focus on the individual level [14, 35, 42, 68]. A comprehensive view at the organizational level that integrates all relevant dimensions is still lacking. These limitations make it difficult for companies to develop a complete understanding of the digital mindset and embed it strategically in their transformation processes. To close this gap, a comprehensive model is required that integrates the dimensions of the digital mindset and considers companies' specific requirements and challenges. The lack of such a model significantly hinders Digital Transformation [67]. Digital change can only be driven forward slowly or inefficiently without a suitable digital mindset. Organizational culture plays a key role in fostering a digital mindset, as cultural barriers within organizations [20] often must be overcome to implement Digital Transformations [43] successfully. Norms and values significantly impact the development of a digital mindset [43], making integrating cultural factors into a comprehensive model essential [83]. While the model primarily focuses on organizations, it is complemented by the cultural dimensions of the Organizational Culture Theory to strengthen the connection to the individual level and its influence on the organization [1].

This study aims to develop and evaluate a digital mindset model for companies. The design science method [33, 56] creates a practicable and scientifically sound model. In addition, a mixed-methods approach is used [19, 75] to integrate qualitative and quantitative perspectives. This study is an extended version of [41]. It builds on their conceptual foundations, deepens central aspects, and expands the scope of application both theoretically and empirically.

The work is structured as follows: First, the concept of digital mindset and the research gaps are presented. The methodological approach follows, including the sample and the study process. The model developed is then introduced, and the evaluation results are presented. The paper concludes with a discussion in which the results are critically reflected upon and perspectives for future research are outlined.

2 Organizational Culture Theory as a Conceptual Foundation for the Development of the Digital Mindset Model

Since digital technologies determine Digital Transformation and people are at the center of numerous changes and innovations, a digital mindset is necessary [35]. The term "Digital Mindset" has been used in different ways and perspectives in the Information Systems (IS) literature, or seen as part of digital competencies [35, 37]. In addition, various definitions of the Digital Mindset describe the application and use of digital technologies, which are vaguely defined [5, 34, 44, 55]. After intensive research, [34] define a Digital Mindset as follows: "A Digital Mindset describes thinking patterns, epitomized through cognitive processes, filters, and core convictions of humans constituted of cognitive mechanisms and knowledge structures that affect and foster the use and applications of digital technologies and cope with their consequences in the context of individuals, organizations, or society." From this, it is deduced that, in addition to attitudes, competencies also play an essential role in realizing Digital Mindset. This paper uses the definition of [34].

Companies' Digital Transformation still has a long way to go because sometimes they are trapped in a cultural heritage that has worked for a long time. In this context, organizations play an essential role in the digital age and require a robust Digital Mindset [25]. In this regard, a Digital Mindset is a factor of exponential development that makes companies successful in the long run. It is essential to communicate the importance of Digital Transformation and Mindset to companies [40]. The first step is to assess the organization's mindset, enabling tailored measures or learning paths [40]. Accordingly, the success of Digital Transformation measures depends on the targeted involvement of employees in the change process [68], whereby employees with a pronounced Digital Mindset see themselves as self-reliant, independent, and willing to learn [61].

Understanding the organization's Digital Mindset is crucial, as its role in Digital Transformation requires further research and skilled leadership [76]. Evidence shows that a Digital Mindset is a critical success factor in Digital Transformation [40, 44]. However, different concepts, models, or measurement tools are needed to investigate the extent to which a Digital Mindset determines the success of people and companies [35].

Digital mindset concepts and models define essential competencies and attributes such as collaboration, critical thinking, creativity, openness, and responsibility, but often lack precise dimensions or specific organizational contexts [5, 16, 80]. Some approaches, such as those of Kocak and Pawlowski [42], focus on digital competencies and attitudes that are crucial for Digital Transformation in organizations. In contrast, others, such as Lessiak [46] and Hildebrandt & Beimborn [35], emphasize dimensions such as personal innovativeness and collaborative thinking. Models such as that of Bredendiek and Knorr [15] combine digital competencies and attitudes with characteristics such as agility and proactivity, but do not sufficiently address all dimensions. Studies by Dombrowski and Bogs [22] add relevant leadership characteristics such as networking and trust, which underline the importance of leadership for Digital Transformation. To develop a comprehensive digital mindset model for organizations, approaches were selected that integrate central dimensions, competencies, attitudes, and personality traits to cover holistic requirements [15, 35, 42].

There is a large body of research on the impact of a Digital Mindset [80]. The Digital Mindset affects companies by increasing value creation or competitiveness [40, 44]. Openness, agility, proactivity, criticality, customer centricity, and entrepreneurial action orientation effectively increase value creation through digitalization [40]. A Digital Mindset also influences a digital leader's communication and people management [22]. Attitudes and digital competencies also significantly affect self-efficacy [59]. In the DCI (Digital Competence Indicator) validation study, proactivity and customer centricity were identified as two critical influencers of employee job satisfaction [15]. Openness and the ability to deal with uncertainty bring new concepts and novel solutions to a company. Heilmann and Zimmerhofer [32] found that using the survey method in HR, team orientation, and entrepreneurial action orientation leads to quick problem identification and, thus, problem-solving. In addition, a digital mindset is helpful in today's work environment in understanding and recognizing digital contexts [82]. As the digital mindset matures, people become more confident in learning and trying new things [80].

The conceptual framework for the Digital Mindset Model is based on Schein's Organizational Culture Theory [64], which encompasses three levels: artifacts, values, and basic underlying assumptions [65]. Artifacts deal with the visible elements of culture, which can be considered digital competencies, such as training programs or digital tools that foster development. Values relate to motivation and personal competencies, as organizational values, such as recognizing innovation and a feedback culture [12], can enhance individual motivation for a digital mindset within the organization [43]. Personal competencies can also influence the organizational level, as values like openness, teamwork, or flexibility are crucial [54]. The Digital Mindset Model can thus be expanded by identifying specific values. The underlying assumptions of OCT represent the most profound level and consist of unconscious beliefs, perceptions, and feelings that guide organizations [65]. These assumptions may relate to digital thinking, uncovering ingrained beliefs about technology, innovation, or risk [36]. Another assumption could involve entrepreneurial orientation, as organizational cultural values regarding risk-taking, autonomy, and agility are directly linked to entrepreneurial behavior [41]. Similarly, personality traits, which primarily exist at the individual level, are significant at the organizational level since organizational assumptions influence the traits deemed ideal, such as openness to change or creativity [2]. The Organizational Culture Theory serves as a framework to make the Digital Mindset Model applicable at the individual level, as in previous models, and at the organizational level. A digital mindset is critical for an organization's successful Digital Transformation. While existing approaches have identified critical dimensions, there remains a need to translate these to the organizational level and integrate them into a comprehensive model. This study aims to fill this gap by developing a practical and scientifically grounded model to support organizations in their transformation process.

3 Digital Mindset Model

The development of the model began with creating a concept matrix [79] to analyze existing models and evaluate their applicability to organizations. The analysis of various approaches to the digital mindset reveals a wide diversity of dimensions and factors. However, several weaknesses also emerge, complicating holistic application. Ala-Mutka [3] focuses on technical competencies and critical thinking but neglects cultural and contextual factors crucial for practical implementation. [80] and [53] emphasize individual adaptability and willingness to learn, but remain theoretical, offering few actionable recommendations for organizations. Similarly, [68] focuses on individual beliefs while ignoring organizational transformation processes (Table 1).

Table 1. Literature Review of Existing Models.

Sources	Factors of the Dimensions	Area	Lack/Weakness
[3]	Information management, critical thinking, problem-solving, collaboration, and technical skills	Both	Overemphasis on technical skills, lack of cultural and contextual integration, and limited focus on practical application.
[80]	Adaptability, openness to learning, and digital collaboration	Both	The theoretical approach lacks empirical validation and actionable insights for workplace integration.
[53]	Digital fluency, adaptability, problem-solving, and collaboration	Individuals	Focus on educational preparation; lacks organizational context and long-term impact analysis.
[68]	Perception of technology, openness to change, innovation, and resistance to change	Individuals	Limited focus on organizational-level transformation; lacks practical implementation strategies
[46]	Curiosity, risk-taking, openness to change, and digital literacy	Individuals	Conceptual focus; lacks actionable strategies for organizational application
[44]	Vision, adaptability, Digital Transformation, team management	Organization	Leadership-centric; neglects broader workforce and cultural dimensions
[40]	Agility, entrepreneurial orientation, critical thinking, and innovation	Organization	Focus on competitiveness; limited applicability to individual-level mindset development.

(*continued*)

Table 1. (*continued*)

Sources	Factors of the Dimensions	Area	Lack/Weakness
[22]	Communication, adaptability, team management, and strategic thinking	Organization	Leadership-specific lacks broader workforce application and insufficient focus on individual mindset aspects.
[16]	Onboarding strategies, employee engagement, and cultural alignment	Organization	Limited empirical evidence, primarily a theoretical focus, and a lack of cross-industry applicability
[15]	Proactivity, customer centricity, digital collaboration, and problem-solving	Organization	Focus on quantifiable metrics, lack qualitative insights, and limited focus on cultural and individual-level factors.
[5]	Technology adoption, critical thinking, leadership skills, and problem-solving	Organization	Focused on the education sector, limited transferability to other industries, and insufficient attention to cultural differences
[4]	Proactivity, opportunity recognition, adaptability, risk-taking	Individuals	Limited focus on organizational application, lack of empirical validation, and overemphasis on individual traits.
[42]	Leadership, collaboration, adaptability, and problem-solving	Both	Limited scalability across industries; focus on specific managerial contexts
[35]	Cognitive flexibility, openness to innovation, and digital awareness	Individuals	The conceptual framework lacks empirical validation and limited organizational integration.
[26]	Cultural awareness, adaptability, leadership, and digital tools integration	Organization	Focus on cultural transformation; lacks detailed operationalization for individual-level application.
[34]	Cognitive tools, opportunity recognition, and innovation fostering	Individuals	Focus on cognitive aspects lacks practical application for teams or organizations.
[43]	Technical competencies, adaptability, leadership, teamwork, problem-solving	Both	Sector-specific focus, limited generalizability to other industries, and a lack of cultural integration.
[49]	Leadership skills, innovation, agility, decision-making, and cultural intelligence	Both	Emphasis on European context; limited scalability outside leadership-focused scenarios

(*continued*)

Table 1. (*continued*)

Sources	Factors of the Dimensions	Area	Lack/Weakness
[41]	Innovative thinking, customer focus, agility, problem-solving, and digital literacy	Organization	Focus on the industrial craft sector; limited empirical validation; lacks scalability across diverse organizational contexts.

Models such as those by Forsythe and Rafoth [26] highlight cultural aspects but do not offer detailed operationalization for individual applications. Hildebrandt and Beimborn [34, 35] provide a conceptual understanding of the digital mindset but lack empirical validation and stronger integration of organizational perspectives. Kollmann [44] and Dombrowski and Bogs [22] focus on leadership competencies while neglecting the inclusion of the broader workforce. Some sector-specific models, such as those by Kocak and Pawlowski [43] and Knorr [40], are practice-oriented and consider individual and organizational dimensions. However, their application is often limited by industry-specific focus. Notably, [41] provides a solid foundation by integrating competencies, attitudes, and agility, while [40] emphasizes the value of a digital mindset for competitiveness.

In summary, most models cover only partial aspects of a digital mindset, focusing on technological, individual, or organizational dimensions. [40] and [41] approaches were selected to develop a comprehensive model. These focus on the organizational level and encompass various digital mindset dimensions. They provide a robust foundation for effectively supporting organizations in their Digital Transformation. Thus, the dimensions of digital thinking, digital competencies, personal competencies, and personality traits from [41, 75] were selected as they address the organizational level and include a variety of sub-factors. Additionally, the dimensions of motivation and entrepreneurial orientation from [40] are crucial and cover organizational levels (Fig. 1).

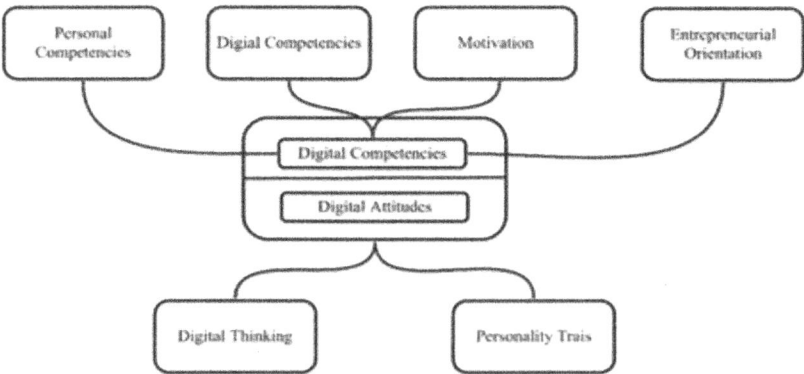

Fig. 1. The Digital Mindset Model.

Finally, these two approaches integrate Schein's [64] Organizational Culture Theory (OCT), which includes the following (Table 2):

Table 2. Description of the Dimensions and Meaning of OCT.

Dimension	Description	Meaning for OCT
Digital thinking	Describes the ability to strategically and innovatively use digital technologies to enhance problem-solving and decision-making processes.	The Organizational Culture Theory emphasizes how deeply rooted assumptions and values influence strategic and innovative thinking in digital contexts.
Personality traits	Describes openness, adaptability, and resilience, influencing how individuals respond to Digital Transformation	Cultural norms and values shape which personality traits (e.g., openness or resilience) are fostered or preferred within an organization.
Motivation	Describes the internal willingness and commitment to embrace digital changes and actively contribute to Digital Transformation	Organizational values and recognition systems influence motivation to accept and drive Digital Transformations.
Entrepreneurial orientation	Describes an entrepreneurial mindset characterized by innovation, risk-taking, and initiative.	Organizational culture can promote or hinder risk-taking, innovative thinking, and entrepreneurial action.
Digital competencies	Describes competencies in using digital tools and technologies to work productively, securely, and efficiently in digital environments.	Artifacts such as digital tools and training programs within the organization reflect and foster the development of digital competencies.
Personal competencies	Describes interpersonal and organizational competencies such as teamwork, communication, and self-management, which are essential in digital contexts.	Values and norms within the organization determine how much competencies such as teamwork, communication, and self-management are valued and developed in digital contexts.

The digital mindset is assessed at the organizational level by collecting data via a standardized questionnaire, calculating and visualizing results using software aligned with the 5-level model, and classifying results. Level 1 reflects a lack of digital competencies, while Level 5 represents the full integration of a digital mindset. The model helps organizations evaluate digital maturity, align personality traits, competencies, and attitudes, and develop a future-oriented digital strategy.

3.1 5-Stage Model

In addition to the Digital Mindset model, a 5-step model developed to determine companies' current state helps assess maturity. The stage model contains five stages: the digital outsider, digital beginner, digital intermediate, digital advanced, and digital master. The description of the level model is shown in the figure (Table 3):

Table 3. The Stage Model.

Stages	Description
Stage 1 Digital Outsider	The digital outsider describes an organization or team that lacks the characteristics outlined in the Digital Mindset model. Such an organization has not yet integrated the foundational principles of Digital Transformation into its operations, culture, or strategy. It requires a fundamental understanding of what Digital Transformation entails and how it can impact organizational success.
Stage 2 Digital Beginners	A digital beginner describes an organization in the early stages of Digital Transformation. It has adopted some essential characteristics and principles of a digital mindset, but still lacks many key features. The organization is starting to learn digital processes and strategies, but still requires targeted measures to enhance its digital maturity.
Stage 3 Digital Intermediary	A digital intermediary describes an organization that already clearly understands Digital Transformation and possesses the essential characteristics of a comprehensive digital mindset. This organization has integrated relevant digital competencies and attitudes in many areas. However, further development is still needed to implement and fully optimize all necessary attributes.
Stage 4 Digital Advanced	A digitally advanced organization has understood and implemented all relevant characteristics of a digital mindset. It integrates digital principles into its strategies, processes, and culture, leveraging them effectively to gain competitive advantages. However, there may still be potential to strengthen specific areas further.
Stage 5 Digital Master	A digital master describes an organization that has fully integrated and confidently mastered all qualities of the digital mindset model. This organization is entirely digitally transformed and applies digital strategies at the highest level. It is a leader in the digital economy, capable of responding flexibly to new technological developments while actively driving innovation.

3.2 Description of the Factors

The Digital Mindset model has several sub-factors and six main dimensions. The table inserts and describes these sub-factors, which help one understand the meaning behind the technical terms (Table 4).

Table 4. Description of the Factors.

Personality traits (PT)	
Extraversion	Trait of being dominant, talkative, determined, adventurous, and energetic [21]
Openness	Trait of being willing to take on new challenges, try out different activities, and be intellectual [21]
Conscientiousness	Traits of showing high willpower are organized, planful, careful, effective, and responsible [21]
Curiosity	Trait of interest in understanding and discovering the unknown that is not part of the experience [46]
Compatibility	The trait of being helpful, behaving cooperatively, and having a positive attitude towards others. [48]
Flexibility	Property to adapt to change and, above all, the anticipation of future innovation [68, 78]
Enthusiastic	Trait of possessing passionate zeal, a heightened interest in a specific topic or task [77]
Resistance	Trait of dealing with stressful situations, and getting back on one's feet quickly after crises, thus being less at risk of burnout [67]
Communicative	Quality to communicate requirements for new ideas for digitalization [67]
Digital competencies (DC)	
Communication competency	Ability to communicate constructively, effectively, and consciously [63]
Development competence	Ability to master procedures and techniques used in computer science and information systems management [70]
Technological competency	Ability to assess the consequences of technological developments - both positive and negative - learn and understand concepts of digital technology [46]
Information processing competence	Ability to collect, process, and apply information is considered a common element of information-processing competencies [69]

(*continued*)

Table 4. (*continued*)

Personality traits (PT)	
Professional competence	Ability to organize own work, team-oriented work, communicative, social, and problem-solving competencies [70]
Digital Thinking (DT)	
Being comfortable with curiosity	Attitude to being able to act permanently in curiosity mode [16]
Embracing diversity	Attitude of knowing, sharing, and valuing people from different sectors, actors, organizations, cultures, or age groups [46]
Agility	Attitude to react creatively and opportunity-oriented to market changes and to bring them about innovatively and proactively [70]
Being more open to failure	Attitude of seeing failures and defeats as further development and acting on them [43]
Intercultural attitude	Attitude to empathize with other cultures that have different patterns to find and adopt a comprehensible interaction [3]
Being up-to-date	Attitude to collect information about new digital technologies and innovations [24]
Self-control	Attitude of behaving consistently and self-controlled maintains or brings about a state by trying to counteract distractions from a goal [8]
Self-confidence	Attitude to recognize and evaluate the strengths and weaknesses of the individual and the group [8]
Competitive and innovative mindset	Attitude to recognize opportunities to improve performance by changing methods, processes, products, and services [57]
Broad mindset	Attitude of embracing the unknown, looking at things from multiple perspectives, and focusing on positive aspects [57]
Openness to learning	Attitude to continuously develop knowledge, competencies, and abilities through tasks and experiences in dealing with others [57]
Visioning	Attitude to imagine the future, plan, develop a vision, turn ideas into reality, and create future scenarios to guide efforts and actions [51]

(*continued*)

Table 4. (*continued*)

Personality traits (PT)	
Result-oriented mindset	Attitude of focusing on the result, thinking about areas, trying timesaving strategies, and prioritizing tasks [57]
Motivation (M)	
Creativity	Ability to develop different ideas and opportunities to create value, combine knowledge and resources to achieve valuable effects, and research and experiment with innovative approaches [8]
Design Motivation	Ability to change work processes, eliminate deficiencies, implement own ideas, and show a solid willingness to exert influence in one's environment [40]
Mastering digital technology challenges	Ability to take on the challenges of digital technologies, learn to work with new digital technologies, integrate, and introduce them into traditional implementation [32]
Motivation to shift	Ability to change conventional processes and bring in new ideas [55]
Entrepreneurial orientation (EO)	
Proactivity	Ability to take responsibility, act on own initiative, and be goal and future-oriented [70]
Customer centricity	Ability to develop in a user-centric way, provide customer insights, and inform and support customers through the use of digital tools [82]
Critical thinking	Ability to accept, question, and improve criticism [3]
Taking responsibility	Ability to make decisions whose outcome is unpredictable to reduce the risk of failure and to manage fast-moving situations in a timely and flexible manner [8]
Action-orientation	Ability to show willingness and commitment to providing active and comprehensive benefits to the organization [43]
Acting on your initiative	Ability to make independent decisions within a limited framework, as well as to create active information [82]
Personal competencies (PC)	
Emotional intelligence	Ability to recognize and control one's feelings and understand the feelings of others [27]

(*continued*)

Table 4. (*continued*)

Personality traits (PT)	
Risk-taking	Ability to deal with ambiguity and make calculated decisions in the face of uncertainty [57]
Trusting instinct	Ability to build a relationship of trust between staff and stakeholders [42]
Autonomous	Ability to be independent, not needing to show consideration for others, and free from control to make their own decisions [42]
Inspirational competencies	Ability to attract others through words, actions, and beliefs [39]

4 Method

This study's methodology is based on the **Design Science Research (DSR)** method as described by [56], with extensions through a mixed methods approach [75]. The aim is to develop a digital mindset model that is both theoretically sound and practically applicable. The methodology was inspired by the approach of [52], who identified seven dimensions and corresponding characteristics to describe design principles.

The study aims to develop and validate a digital mindset model at the organizational level with three components: a framework integrating key dimensions like digital thinking and competencies, a survey tool for measuring and identifying strengths and weaknesses, and a maturity model for assessing development levels and planning transformation. This provides a practical, scientifically grounded basis for advancing the digital mindset (Table 5).

Table 5. Meta Requirements.

Dimensions	Characteristics				
Perspective	Supportive		Reflective		
Research Design	DSR	ADR	Qualitative	Quantitative	Mixed
MR Source	Derived		Extracted		Responsive
DP Design	Literature	Theory	Interviews	Workshops/ Focus Group	Non
Iterations	Single			Multiple	
Evaluation	Expert		Field Testing		Argumentation
Formulation	Free			Based on Template	

The meta-requirements for the artifact were derived based on a comprehensive literature review and key theories [28]. Existing concepts on digital competencies, attitudes, and organizational factors were considered [35], while the phased approach of [56] structured the research process. The process involves six steps, from analyzing barriers and defining goals to developing, testing, and communicating a digital mindset model, survey tool, and maturity framework for practical validation and future research. A mixed-methods approach [75] was chosen to comprehensively analyze and evaluate the digital mindset model by combining qualitative expert interviews and quantitative online surveys. The qualitative phase provides detailed insights and enables the identification of weaknesses and potential for improvement. At the same time, the quantitative validation statistically checks the results and increases the model's generalizability. This iterative process ensures that the model meets scientific standards and is practically applicable.

The digital mindset model was evaluated in three rounds: experts reviewed its completeness, prioritized dimensions using feedback tools, and assessed its organizational impact to enhance practical relevance. This iterative process ensured the model's theoretical soundness and practical applicability. Three central artifacts were developed as part of the study, forming a comprehensive basis for analyzing and promoting the digital mindset in organizations. The first artifact is the digital mindset model, which integrates key dimensions such as digital thinking, entrepreneurial orientation, and competencies and provides a theoretical basis. The second artifact is a survey instrument that makes the various dimensions of the digital mindset measurable and allows targeted measures to be derived. The third artifact is a maturity model that helps organizations assess their digital mindset's development status and plan strategic steps for further development.

Problem Identification

The central issue addressed by this study is the lack of integration of a digital mindset at the organizational level, which is essential for a successful Digital Transformation. While many companies adopt modern technologies and aim for Digital Transformation, they often lack a comprehensive organizational digital mindset that forms the foundation for sustainable change [35]. This deficiency manifests in a slow adaptation to new technologies and work practices and insufficient flexibility in responding to changing market conditions [62]. Existing models and concepts of the digital mindset predominantly focus on individual perspectives and do not sufficiently address the organizational level [15, 42]. There is a lack of specific dimensions and a systematic approach to measuring the extent of a digital mindset at the organizational level, as well as targeted methods to foster this mindset [46, 53]. This gap makes it difficult for companies to evaluate their organization's digital competencies, attitudes, and perspectives and derive targeted actions to promote the digital mindset. Furthermore, **Organizational Culture Theory** emphasizes how deeply embedded assumptions and values within an organization influence strategic and digital thinking in digital contexts (see Chapter: Organizational Culture Theory as Conceptual Foundations). This study addresses this problem by developing a comprehensive model that defines the key dimensions of the digital mindset at the organizational level and establishes a transparent process for measuring and fostering this mindset. The goal is to provide a practical and scientifically grounded tool that helps companies address the challenges of Digital Transformation and remain competitive in the long term.

Defining Objectives of a Solution, Design Development, and Demonstration

In the context of design science methodology (DSM), goal definition, design development, and demonstration are critical phases in the solution development process. The goal is to provide a structured approach to developing a model that captures the dimensions of the Digital Mindset, considering digital competencies and personality traits. The model incorporates mindset-related elements that reflect the organization's approach to digitalization. Digital competencies are also identified and included, and employees within the organization should possess them to foster a digital mindset. Personality traits that influence the adoption and sustainability of a Digital Mindset are also included. The model uses a stage-based measurement approach to assess the organization's digital mindset level. The development of the design involves the creation and refinement of the Digital Mindset Model. This phase includes several key steps. First, essential digital attitudes and competencies are identified. This step builds on the work of [42], who categorized these elements into dimensions. To support the design, existing models of the digital mindset, such as those by [41] and [35], were analyzed. These models provide valuable insights and characteristics that can be integrated into the new model. The model's dimensions were also defined and adapted using **Organizational Culture Theory** (see Chapter: Digital Mindset Model). After identifying the relevant dimensions and aspects, they were described in detail to ensure clarity and understanding for subsequent phases. A five-level model was developed to measure an organization's maturity or acceptance of a digital mindset. Each level represents a specific stage of maturity or implementation of the digital mindset.

The demonstration stage involves presenting the Digital Mindset model and collecting feedback for evaluation. In this particular case, the following steps were taken. The demonstration was conducted via a virtual Miro board that provided a common platform for participants. Participants were invited to evaluate the developed model using open-ended questions. Their insights and feedback are critical to the further development of the model. A survey was conducted to gather information on the descriptions and potential interactions of the factors in the model.

Evaluation and Communication

We chose the **exploratory mixed methods approach** to evaluate the model, which involves a sequential temporal progression of qualitative and quantitative methods [19, 75]. A mixed-methods approach allows for the investigation of a research question from multiple perspectives [17, 72]. This study uses a mixed-methods design to evaluate the Digital Mindset model for business [17]. It is an extended mixed-methods design in which the researcher simultaneously collects and examines quantitative and qualitative data as part of a traditional quantitative or qualitative design [18]. The research strategy chosen for the design is exploratory and confirmatory, meaning that a theory is developed and tested in the same study [84]. The priority of the methodological approach is the dominant design, which means that the qualitative component has a much higher priority than the quantitative phase [60, 73]. A qualitative research methodology [60] is used to answer the open-ended questions based on expert interviews to generate specific operational knowledge and determine the factors' completeness, understandability, and impact. External validity refers to the quality of the results obtained from the literature

[60]. Quantitative research is used to evaluate factor descriptions and examine the comprehensibility of the factors and priority. Quantitative data is collected and statistically analyzed [23]. For this purpose, a Likert scale [47] is used, and the interviews take place on a virtual Miro board. The open question and answer session is recorded and transcribed using an audio device. As a necessary condition for the analysis, we rely on the statements of [38, 45, 81]. They state that the central limit theorem is valid if the samples are large enough, usually defined as n > 30. Sample sizes of less than 30 are generally considered too small for representativeness [9].

4.1 Sample

Sample I

A **basic sampling** procedure is chosen to identify and compare the characteristics of the groups. The same participants took part in the qualitative and quantitative phases of the study, using an identical sample [17, 72]. To achieve the objectives associated with the research question, the experts were selected to be particularly informative in answering the research question. They were chosen from different sectors and the university environment to obtain different perspectives. Experts have technical, process-related, and explanatory knowledge about their areas of specialization. They possess systematically structured expertise and an in-depth understanding of specific experiences derived from their activities, responsibilities, and tasks within their specific professional status within an organization [13]. The focus is on narrative data, although numerical data was also generated [74]. The scope of respondents in this research follows the study by [19]. With a uniform population [29], a sample size of 12 qualitative interviews is recommended, while phenomenology studies usually involve 3–10 interviews. The sample was N = 10, as experts were selected based on their experience and expertise in digitization. The study was conducted in 2022 between January and May. The ages of the experts ranged from 23–33 years, and the individual interviews lasted approximately one hour. Experts E1 and E2 come from the IT sector; four experts are from the public sector, i.e., from a university specializing in Digital Transformation. One expert came from the consulting and development sector (E3), one from the telecommunications sector (E7), one from the production sector (E10), and one from the craft sector (E9) (Table 6).

Sample II

In the **quantitative survey**, there were 50 participants, of which 46 were valid cases. After identifying the valid values, N = 33 records were used for analysis. The participants were from the IT sector (39.4%), public sector (27.3%), construction sector (6.1%), industry (3.0%), production industry (6.1%), and others (18.2%), and had experience in the field of digitalization. The age of the participants ranged from 23–59 years ($M = 31$) (Fig. 2).

4.2 Process of the Study

The study follows a multi-stage process that combines qualitative and quantitative methods. The aim is to develop and evaluate a comprehensive understanding of the dimensions and characteristics of a digital mindset at the organizational level.

Table 6. Sample I of the Experts (E).

E	Gender	Age	Experience	Position	Number of employees
E1	M	30	4 years	IT-Project manager	3000
E2	M	33	8 years	IT-In-house Consulting	2000
E3	M	29	6 years	IT-Consultant	1500
E4	F	23	2 years	Research Assistant (Digital Transformation)	400
E5	M	30	5 years	Research Assistant (Digital Transformation)	400
E6	M	27	6 years	Research Assistant (Digital Transformation)	400
E7	F	29	5 years	User Experience Researcher	16.000
E8	M	27	4 years	IT-Software-Manger	E8
E9	F	30	4 years	Project Manager	400
E10	M	27	3 years	ERP-Consultant	E10

Fig. 2. Sample II.

In the **first round (sample I),** questions about the comprehensibility and completeness of the digital mindset model and the 5-step model were asked through expert interviews (N = 10). The interviews took place online and were presented using an online Miro Board, lasting around 40 min. The questions on comprehensibility and completeness are as follows: (Table 7).

In the **second round (sample I),** expert interviews (N = 10) were conducted to assess the transparency and clarity of the factor descriptions for each dimension in the Digital Mindset Model and the priority of the factors. The aim was to eliminate irrelevant factors from the model. The questions for this phase are as follows (Table 8):

In round 3 (sample I), the experts (N = 10) were asked about the possible positive and negative effects of the respective factors in the digital mindset model to gather new insights for future research.

In round 4 (sample II), an online survey was conducted to determine the prioritization of the factors and the comprehensibility of the factor description. This was done with N = 33 participants to wrap up the qualitative part of the study. A Likert scale of 1 = not

Table 7. Guiding Questions I.

Categories	Guiding question
Understandability	Is the model with the six dimensions understandable?
Completeness	Are there any dimensions that should be added to the model? Are the sub-factors sufficient, or are aspects still missing that should be integrated?
Suggestion for improvement	Do you have any other comments on the Digital Mindset model?

Table 8. Guiding Questions II.

Categories	Guiding question
Clarity	In your opinion, are the descriptions of the factors clear? How could the descriptions be improved or expanded?
Priority	Which factors have a high priority and a low priority? Why are the factors with high priority of great importance and those with a low focus of less significance for the model?
Notes	Do you have any further comments or suggestions for improvement?

understandable and 5 = entirely understandable was selected for this purpose. In order to prioritize the factors, respondents were asked whether they had a positive or negative impact. There were 25 questions, and respondents were asked about various topics, including demographic data, descriptions of the digital mindset factors, and prioritization of these factors. The survey aimed to compare the quantitative data with the qualitative results and to validate the robustness of the dimensions and characteristics of the digital mindset.

4.3 Data Analysis

The study's data analysis is based on a sequential qualitative and quantitative approach, complemented by a quantitative analysis (sample I) [73, 75]. The qualitative analysis follows Mayring's [50] approach, a structured qualitative method for analyzing text-based data. A coding procedure assigns the data materials to categories and breaks the research question into individual aspects. This approach combines a deductive procedure, in which a theoretically based category system is used, with an inductive procedure, in which categories are developed directly from the data material.

Various measures ensured the validity and reliability of the qualitative analysis. Construct validity was checked based on expert interpretations to ensure the results were consistent with the theoretical principles. Semantic validity was tested through expert judgment by checking whether text passages with similar meanings were assigned to the same categories [11, 66]. To ensure inferential validity, the strategy of [73] was used, which relies on participant feedback and confirmability audits.

The interviews' results were presented using the approaches of [10, 71]. Tambling and Lee [71] recommend continuous text to explain differences in the experts' expectations, while [10] proposes a text matrix to present the most important statements. This combination of methods enabled a clear and differentiated presentation of the qualitative results.

The quantitative analysis (sample II) was based on the survey results, which validated the qualitative findings and supplemented them with measurable data. A frequency analysis was conducted to determine the distribution and priorities of the sub-factors covered in the survey. The frequencies with which specific sub-factors appeared in the responses were calculated and presented in a percentage distribution [11]. The aim was to investigate the comprehensibility and relevance of the sub-factors and their prioritization by the participants.

By combining the qualitative and quantitative analyses, this study offers a comprehensive and well-founded investigation that integrates in-depth insights from the interviews and statistically validated results from the survey. This enables a detailed answer to the research question and developing a solid insight model based on text-based and numerical data.

5 Results

5.1 Understandability and Completeness of the Digital Mindset Model (Sample I)

The results show that the model is generally comprehensible, as experts E1, E2, E7, E9, and E10 confirmed. Experts praised the subdivision into Digital Competencies, Digital Attitude, and Entrepreneurial Action Orientation (E4), though E5 criticized the lack of clarity in the "digital thinking" dimension. While most experts agreed that the model captures essential characteristics, they noted the need to add legislative factors (E2) and analytical competencies (E10). E9 further suggested refining "New Thinking" and "Innovative" factors to align entrepreneurial action orientation with entrepreneurship better (Table 9).

After discussing the low-priority factors, the experts provided recommendations and insights for improvements to evaluating the Digital Mindset. Most experts agree that certain factors, such as development competencies, are not essential for a digital master. One expert pointed out, "What is meant by that is, yes, development area, more development" (E1). Another expert noted, "I am not sure if all those who call themselves digital masters necessarily have to have development competencies" (E6). This highlights that while valuable in specific contexts, development competencies are not a core requirement for fostering a Digital Mindset. Generosity was another factor rated as less relevant by the experts, as it does not align well with the practical demands of a digital environment. One expert illustrated this with an example: "We have situations in the company where, if the customer has made a request and then realized afterward that they want something different, it happens that, out of generosity, someone says, 'Come on, we will change it again,' but it involves an effort" (E3). This underscores that excessive generosity may hinder efficiency rather than contribute to a productive digital culture. Compatibility and extraversion, often considered important personality traits, were less critical for a

Table 9. Table of the Important Statements.

E	Understandability	Completeness
E1	"The model and the terminology are understandable and presented understandably."	"The most important competencies were mentioned, and in the lower part, I think that would be enough. Otherwise, it becomes too much. The key points have been described".
E2	"The model is understandable."	"Integrate legislative factors into technological competence."
E3	„Often you could take one thing for other groups as well." often you could take one thing for other groups as well." often you could take one thing for other groups as well."	"This is already very extensive. I would not have thought of some aspects at all."
E4	"I would divide the model into three areas: Digital Competencies, Digital Attitudes, and Entrepreneurial Orientation."	"I think the factors are already very comprehensive. Spontaneously, when I look over, I cannot think of any dimension that is still missing".
E5	"Digital Thinking is meant in a digital context. The individual points in these dimensions are not digital".	"Spontaneously, actually, no other factors or dimensions."
E7	"I like the model. I cannot think of anything where I would say I do not understand it or I cannot think of it that way".	"What does not fit at all does not exist."
E9	"It is understandable to point to the division between competencies and attitudes."	"What strikes me is the entrepreneurial orientation. I also associate that with entrepreneurship, new thinking, and being innovative. That should still be included here in the dimension."
E10	"A great many points were covered."	"Analytical mindset is missing. I would add this to the Digital Mindset".

Digital Mindset. Experts emphasized that an introverted individual can possess strong digital attitudes and excel in digital environments. For example, one expert stated, "In my opinion, someone can have a good Digital Mindset even if they are introverted" (E4). Another expert added, "You do not necessarily have to be extroverted to have a Digital Mindset" (E10). Self-confidence, similarly, was viewed as having limited relevance to a Digital Mindset. According to one expert, "For me, it is very personality-dependent, and everyone is different. Maybe the not-so-self-confident can develop perfect designs or concepts" (E7). This reflects a broader understanding that digital capabilities are not tied to specific personality traits but to competencies, adaptability, and mindset.

5.2 Transparency and Clarity: The Assessment of Factor Descriptions in the Digital Mindset Model (Sample I)

When evaluating the factor descriptions, most experts said that the description for "taking responsibility" needs to be shortened because it is very long (E1, E4, E5, E6, E7, E10). The description "extraversion" also does not fit the factor and should be adjusted (E4, E5, E7).

Experts suggested clarifying "development competencies" as software development or work-specific practices (E4, E5) and recommended rewriting factors like "embracing diversity" and "design motivation" (E4, E6). Additionally, they advised separating "self-control" and "self-confidence" (E6) and improving descriptions of "customer centricity" and "intercultural attitude (Table 10)."

Table 10. Results of the Transparency and Clarity.

Factor	Clarity
Taking-responsibility	"The point "taking responsibility," I would make the description a bit shorter" (E1).
Motivation to shift	"Motivation to shift and the description "ability to change" are two different things for me" (E3)
Extraversion	"For me, the description does not fit extraversion; possibly choose a different generic term" (E4).
Development Competencies	"It is about software development or concepts and practices that should be applied in the IT field" (E4).
Embracing Diversity	"Upper category does not quite fit the description" (E4)
Self-Control and Self-Confidence	"Both are separate points. After that, you have three different descriptions. I would shorten them" (E6).
Design-Motivation	"The description only refers to the change of processes. I would not have assigned that to "design motivation" (E6).
Customer-centricity	"Rewrite as user-oriented development with interactive testing and customer insights" (E7)
Intercultural attitude	"I would rather use this to mean that I can put cultures into perspective, to understand the different patterns that find interaction, to adapt accordingly" (E6).

5.3 Impact of the Factors (Sample I)

Experts identified agility, communication competencies, and technological competencies as positively impacting other factors. Agility influences flexibility, development competencies, proactivity, emotional intelligence, and communicative traits, while communication competencies enhance intercultural competence, customer centricity, and openness. However, some factors, like risk-taking and visioning, were noted to have potentially harmful effects, such as reducing openness to learning or critical thinking (Fig. 3).

Fig. 3. Impact of the Factors.

5.4 Prioritization of the Key Factors of the Digital Mindset Model (Sample I)

The low prioritization of certain factors reflects a consistent perspective across multiple experts. Most experts deem development competencies relatively unimportant, given that only a subset of professionals engage in development or concept creation. For example, one expert noted, "what is meant by that is, yes, development area, more development" (E1). Another expert emphasized, "I am not sure if all those who call themselves digital masters necessarily have to have development competencies" (E6). This highlights that developing competencies is not a prerequisite for being considered a "digital master." Similarly, the factor of "generosity" is rated as low priority, as it does not align closely with the characteristics of a Digital Mindset. While generosity occasionally plays a role in customer interactions, it often entails additional effort without significant benefits. An expert illustrated this by stating, "We have situations in the company where, if the customer has made a request and then realized afterward that they want something different, it happens that, out of generosity, someone says, 'Come on, we will change it again,' but it involves an effort" (E3). Furthermore, traits such as compatibility and extraversion, which are often considered essential personality factors, are viewed by most experts as less critical for a Digital Mindset. They emphasize that an introverted individual can still possess strong digital attitudes and that compatibility is not mandatory. For instance, an expert explained, "In my opinion, someone can have a good Digital Mindset even if they are introverted" (E4). At the same time, another added, "You do not necessarily have to be extroverted to have a Digital Mindset" (E10). Self-confidence is also seen as having little relevance to a Digital Mindset. According to one expert, "For me, it is very personality-dependent, and everyone is different. Maybe the not-so-self-confident can develop perfect designs or concepts" (E7). This underscores that personal characteristics, such as introversion or lower self-confidence, do not preclude individuals from excelling in digital environments or contributing meaningfully to digital innovation (Table 11).

Table 11. The low Priority of the Factors.

Factors	Low priory of factors
Being comfortable with curiosity	"Curiosity must already be there at the beginning. For this reason, I have rated it low" (E1)
Taking-responsibility	"Is it now related to the management level or the whole company or for one area?" (E1)
Visioning	"Because for me, it depends on the role you are in. I think it is essential for managers from a certain level in the company. I think you would have to adapt this to roles. For classic workers, I do not think visioning is so important" (E4).
Factors	Low priory of factors

5.5 Evaluation of the Priority (Sample II)

The frequency distribution shows that many factors are prioritized as high. The factors of the dimension personality traits such as openness (M = 4.58, SD = .708), flexibility (M = 4.70, SD = .529), and communication (M = 4.70, SD = .637) were prioritized as very high. The factor generosity is relatively low (M = 2.73, SD = 1.281). In the dimension of digital competencies, the factor development competence is rated as medium priority (M = 3.73, SD = 1.442), and the factor technical competencies as high priority (M = 4.70, SD = .637). The dimension of personal competencies shows a high priority among the factors in the evaluation. In particular, the factors "emotional intelligence" (M = 3.64, SD = 1.410) and "autonomous" (M = 3.73, SD = 1.306) are rated as a high priority. The factors of the entrepreneurial orientation dimensions generally have a high priority. The factor "critical thinking" (M = 4.36, SD = 1.055) is prioritized most. When ranking the priority, the factors "design motivation" (M = 3.97, SD = 1.104) and "motivation to shift" (M = 3.85, SD = 1.372) of the dimension motivation are rated as rather average. Finally, the digital thinking dimension results show that most factors are highly prioritized. Above all, "agility" (M = 4.55, SD = .938) is the highest priority. The factors "being comfortable curiosity" (M = 3.55, SD = 1.371), "embracing diversity" (M = 3.97, SD = 1.104), and "intercultural attitude" (M = 3.82, SD = 1.261) are prioritized as average.

5.6 Evaluation Survey. Description of the Factors (Sample II)

The survey evaluation shows that the descriptions of the factors are generally understandable and should only be changed in some places. The figure shows the frequency distribution of the factor descriptions. Many descriptions are understandable. Since the study is a mixed method and the experts come from the field of digitalization, different results will be given, and other samples will not be taken. The descriptive evaluation showed that most of the descriptions of the factors are understandable. The description of the factors "openness" ($M = 4.55$, $SD = .938$) and "communicative" ($M = 4.67$, $SD = .595$) is seen as very understandable by the participants. On the other hand, the factor "generosity" is seen as moderately understandable ($M = 3.97$, $SD = 1.159$). The factors "proactivity" ($M = 4.58$, $SD = .708$) and "acting on your initiative" ($M = 4.55$, $SD = .794$) of the dimensions of entrepreneurial orientation and personal competencies are rated as very understandable, and "taking responsibility" ($M = 3.97$, $SD = 1.104$) is only rated as understandable. The description of the factors "creativity" ($M = 4.55$, $SD = .754$) and "motivation to shift" ($M = 4.58$, $SD = .708$) are very understandable for the participants and should not be changed. All factors of the dimension of digital competencies are seen as understandable. The "technological competency" factor is rated as particularly understandable ($M = 4.58$, $SD = .708$). The characteristics of the dimension of personal competency are also seen as understandable. The factor "trusting instinct," in particular, is rated as very understandable ($M = 4.55$, $SD = .754$). Finally, the results of the characteristics of the dimension of digital thinking show that they are predominantly understandable. Especially the factors "openness to learning" ($M = 4.58$, $SD = .751$), "visioning" ($M = 4.55$, $SD = .711$), and "result-oriented mindset" ($M = 4.64$, $SD = .699$) are very understandable and do not need any improvement (Table 12).

6 Discussion

The study aimed to develop and evaluate a digital mindset model for organizations to measure their digital maturity and advance and foster Digital Transformation. The objective was to create a model that integrates digital competencies, attitudes, and personal and organizational aspects. The study addresses research gaps by combining an organization-specific perspective with dimensions such as digital thinking, personality traits, digital competencies, motivation, and entrepreneurial orientation.

For the model's development, the Design Science Research (DSR) approach was chosen, with Schein's Organizational Culture Theory [65] providing support in defining and adapting the dimensions of the digital mindset model. A mixed-method approach was selected for the evaluation, with expert interviews ($N = 10$) conducted during the qualitative phase to assess the model's comprehensibility, completeness, and prioritization of dimensions. During the quantitative phase, online surveys ($N = 33$) were carried out to validate the descriptions of the factors and their prioritization. The developed model with six dimensions was rated as comprehensible and complete. It highlights key factors like agility, openness, communication, and technological competencies while addressing positive and negative impacts. Integrating Organizational Culture Theory provides a systematic foundation to assess the digital mindset and strategically manage Digital Transformation.

Table 12. Mean Value of the Descriptions.

Factors	Mean value	Std. - Devitation
Extraversion	4,09	1,071
Conscientiousness	4,30	,810
Curiosity	4,18	,983
Compatibility	4,36	,962
Flexibility	4,39	,933
Enthusiastic	4,03	1,045
Resistance	4,30	,984
Communication competency	4,42	1,032
Development competency	4,52	,795
Information processing competence	4,33	,854
Professional competence	4,64	,742
Being comfortable curiosity	4,09	1,071
Embracing diversity	4,24	,867
Agility	4,52	,712
Being more open to failure	4,52	,667
Intercultural attitude	4,21	,992
Being up-to-date	4,52	,795
Self-control and self-confidence	4,15	1,004
Competitive and innovative mindset	4,45	,666
Broad mindset	4,48	,834
Customer centricity	4,48	,939
Critical thinking	4,18	2,518
Action-orientation	4,52	,795
Creativity	4,55	,754
Design Motivation	4,18	,917
Mastering digital technology challenges	4,33	,957
Motivation to shift	4,58	,708
Emotional intelligence	4,45	,971
Risk-taking	4,36	,859
Autonomous	4,39	1,029
Inspirational competencies	4,45	,971

The findings of this study on developing a digital mindset model largely align with existing theoretical concepts while offering new perspectives and extensions. It reaffirms that a digital mindset is critical for successful Digital Transformation [31, 32]. The highly prioritized factors, such as agility, openness, and critical thinking, reflect the core characteristics of a digital mindset, which are described in the literature as conducive to change processes [68]. Contrary to existing theories, the study emphasizes the importance of personality traits (e.g., resilience and communication competencies) and their integration into organizational culture. This aspect has been less considered in prior research [35].

The study extends Schein's Organizational Culture Theory [64, 65] by demonstrating how artifacts (e.g., digital tools), values (e.g., promotion of innovation), and underlying assumptions (e.g., openness to change) influence the development of a digital mindset at the organizational level. This aligns with the theory's assertion that deeply rooted cultural assumptions shape an organization's strategic direction and mindset [65]. The study operationalizes OCT for Digital Transformation processes by embedding specific dimensions and factors, such as digital and personal competencies, into the cultural context. This provides a detailed methodology for how organizations can overcome cultural barriers [20, 43].

The results highlight the role of individual personality traits such as flexibility, openness, and resilience. According to the study, these factors are significant individually and influenced by organizational values and norms. This aligns with approaches emphasizing the connection between individual and organizational levels [2, 36]. While theory often focuses on the personal level [35], the study demonstrates that these traits can be fostered through targeted cultural initiatives at the organizational level. Linking personality traits with organizational values represents a significant theoretical advancement.

The study's analysis reveals both positive and negative interactions between factors. For instance, risk-taking behavior can hinder openness to learning, while agility promotes flexibility and emotional intelligence. These findings expand the theoretical understanding, which has predominantly explored the positive influences of mindset factors on Digital Transformation [22, 40]. Identifying adverse effects, such as conflicts between outcome orientation and acceptance of failure, provides new insights and complements existing literature, which has scarcely addressed such interactions.

The development of a five-stage model for assessing digital maturity (from "Digital Outsider" to "Digital Master") addresses a frequently criticized issue in theory: the lack of operationalization for concepts like digital mindset [35, 42]. The study offers a practical methodology by integrating clearly defined dimensions and measurable criteria. Using a Likert scale and detailed factor descriptions enables more precise measurement of digital maturity, refining theoretical approaches such as the Digital Competence Indicator [15].

6.1 Theoretical Contributions

This study contributes to the literature by introducing a multidimensional model for analyzing the digital mindset. It offers a comprehensive perspective that addresses research gaps and advances theories on Digital Transformation.

Another significant theoretical contribution lies in including entrepreneurial orientation and personality traits alongside digital competencies and attitudes. This holistic perspective provides a nuanced basis for identifying the critical elements for successful Digital Transformation. Moreover, the study offers precise descriptions and operational definitions of the relevant factors within each dimension, establishing a robust foundation for future research on developing and assessing the digital mindset.

The research also emphasizes the interactions between the model's dimensions. For example, the positive influence of agility, communication, and technological competencies on other dimensions is examined in detail. At the same time, the study considers potential adverse impacts, an aspect primarily overlooked in the literature, which opens up new avenues for research.

Another theoretical advancement arises from applying and further developing the Organizational Culture Theory (OCT) (Schein [64, 65]. The study integrates this theory into the context of the digital mindset, demonstrating how cultural values, norms, and deeply rooted assumptions influence the development and implementation of a digital mindset. Particular emphasis is placed on the role of artifacts (e.g., digital tools and training), values (e.g., promotion of innovation), and underlying assumptions (e.g., openness to technology) in either supporting or hindering Digital Transformation.

Moreover, the research highlights how cultural barriers within organizations can impede the development of a digital mindset. Simultaneously, it underscores that cultural factor such as flexibility, openness, and teamwork are key enablers. These insights provide organizations with new approaches to address cultural changes and proactively support Digital Transformation.

The study shows how individual traits like openness and adaptability impact organizations when aligned with their norms and values. It provides a theoretical basis for understanding how cultural assumptions influence dimensions like "Digital Thinking" and "Entrepreneurial Orientation," shaped by risk-taking, autonomy, and innovation.

A final contribution lies in the detailed operationalization of cultural dimensions using OCT as a framework. The study concretely demonstrates how artifacts (e.g., digital training), values (e.g., a feedback culture), and underlying assumptions (e.g., openness to technology) operate at different levels and sustainably influence organizational transformation. This linkage between cultural elements and Digital Transformation represents an extension of OCT and opens up new perspectives for its application.

Finally, the study contributes to the advancement of OCT by extending its application to Digital Transformation processes. The proposed digital mindset approach provides theoretical foundations and practical tools to help organizations measure and manage cultural changes. This strengthens the promotion of digital competencies and mindsets, creating an important bridge between theory and practice.

6.2 Practical Contributions

This study makes a significant practical contribution by providing organizations with a hands-on tool for assessing the maturity of their digital mindset using a five-stage model ranging from "Digital Outsider" to "Digital Master." This model not only helps companies measure their current level of development but also identifies priority areas for further improvement.

Another practical benefit lies in the development of a detailed survey tool. This instrument allows organizations to analyze the digital mindset across various dimensions systematically. The insights gained provide a solid foundation for designing training programs, developing HR strategies, and implementing strategic initiatives.

Furthermore, the five-stage maturity model offers a structured approach to evaluating an organization's Digital Transformation readiness. It also serves as a guide for crafting targeted strategies to enhance digital competencies. The ability to identify key factors such as agility, communication competencies, and technological competencies is particularly noteworthy. This prioritization enables organizations to focus their resources on the areas with the most significant impact on their Digital Transformation.

Another contribution of the study is the integration of entrepreneurial orientation and personal competencies into the model. This provides valuable guidance for leadership development and cultural change, which are critical to the success of Digital Transformation. At the same time, the model's flexibility allows for industry-specific adaptations, making it applicable even in traditional or less digitized sectors.

Finally, the rigorous evaluation process ensures the model's practical relevance and scientific validity. This combination enhances organizations' confidence in its applicability and supports them in making strategic decisions and developing effective measures for Digital Transformation.

6.3 Limitation

The study was limited by a small sample size, particularly in the quantitative phase, which restricts the generalizability of the findings across different industries. Including experts from various sectors may have diluted sector-specific insights, highlighting the need for further research with a clear industry focus. Additionally, the comprehensive scope of the research model posed challenges for participants, suggesting that future studies should adopt a more streamlined approach. Finally, cultural and organizational differences between regions were not examined in depth, limiting the model's applicability to specific cultural contexts.

7 Conclusion and Future Work

This study deals with developing and evaluating a Digital Mindset model to determine how comprehensible and complete the model is. For this purpose, the priority and effects of the factors on each other were examined. The study follows the design science approach, complemented by the mixed method. The results show that the model is generally understandable and complete. Many factors are highly relevant, and there can be many positive effects among the factors. The results clearly show that the descriptions of the factors need to be improved and expanded.

Furthermore, the presentation and development of a Digital Mindset model for a specific industry, such as craft enterprises, is essential. They are still very traditionally positioned and have a great need for a gap in digital transformation. Also, developing measures for the 5-step model is necessary to drive companies forward in Digital Transformation, primarily focusing on people. A quantitative study with a specific sector can investigate the expression of a Digital Mindset. Finally, the relationships between the dimensions should be conducted through a quantitative research methodology with a more appropriate sample.

Declaration of Interest. We have no conflicts of interest to disclose, and all authors declare no conflicts of interest.

References

1. Abawa, A., Obse, H.: Organizational culture and organizational performance: does job satisfaction mediate the relationship? Cogent Bus. Manage. **11**(1), 2324127 (2024)
2. Abdul-Halim, H., Ahmad, N.H., Geare, A., Thurasamy, R.: Innovation culture in SMEs: The importance of organizational culture, organizational learning and market orientation. Entrepreneurship Res. J. **9**(3) (2019)
3. Ala-Mutka, K.: Mapping digital competence: towards a conceptual understanding. Sevilla: Inst. Prospective Technol. Stud. (2011)
4. Aliabina, E.: The concept of digital mindset in the context of entrepreneurship. Sci. Eur. **61**(2), 15–19 (2020)
5. Allen, S.J.: On the cutting edge or the chopping block? fostering a digital mindset and tech literacy in business management education. J. Manag. Educ. **44**(3), 362–393 (2020)
6. Alvesson, M., Sveningsson, S.: Changing Organizational Culture: Cultural Change Work in Progress. Routledge (2015)
7. Aral, S., Weill, P.: IT assets, organizational capabilities, and firm performance: how resource allocations and organizational differences explain performance variation. Organ. Sci. **18**, 763–780 (2007)

8. Bacigalupo, M., Kampylis, P., Punie, P., Van den Brande, G.: EntreComp: the entrepreneurship competence framework. Luxembourg: Publication Office of the European Union, 10, 593884 (2016)
9. Bahrenberg, G., Giese, E., Nipper, J.: Univariate und bivariate Statistik. (1985)
10. Birklbauer, V.: Frauen und Bier trinken. Auf der Suche nach Motiven und Gewohnheiten [Women and beer drinking. In search of motives and habits]. In R. Buber, & H. Holzmüller, Qualitative Marktforschung, pp. 805–822. Wiesbaden: Gabler (2009)
11. Blaikie, N.: Analyzing Quantitative Data: From Description to Explanation. Sage (2003)
12. Blanka, C., Krumay, B., Rueckel, D.: The interplay of digital transformation and employee competency: a design science approach. Technol. Forecast. Soc. Chang. **178**, 121575 (2022)
13. Bogner, A., Littig, B., Menz, W.: Introduction: expert interviews—an introduction to a new methodological debate. Interviewing Experts, 1–13 (2009)
14. Bredendiek, M., Knorr, J.: Digital Competence Indicator (2020). https://www.dci.digital
15. Bredendiek, M., Knorr, J.: Digitales Mindset–Wertschöpfungstreiber für die Zukunft. Ökonomische und unternehmerische Potentiale (2020)
16. Chattopadhyay, S.: A new way of thinking to onboard digital culture in your company (2020). https://blog.signaturit.com/en/a-new-way-of-thinking-to-onboard-digital-culture-in-your-company
17. Creswell, J.W., Creswell, J.D.: Research Design. SAGE Publications, Inc, California (1994)
18. Creswell, J.W., Klassen, A.C., Plano Clark, V.L., Smith, K.C.: Best practices for mixed methods research in the health sciences. Bethesda: National Institutes of Health, pp. 541–545 (2013)
19. Creswell, J.W.: Research Design: Qualitative, Quantitative, and Mixed Methods Approaches, 4th edn. Sage Publications, Los Angeles (2013)
20. Deep, G.: Digital transformation's impact on organizational culture. Int. J. Sci. Res. Arch. **10**(2), 396–401 (2023)
21. Dehne, M., Schupp, J.: Persönlichkeitsmerkmale im Sozio-oekonomischen Panel (SOEP) Konzept, Umsetzung und empirische Eigenschaften [Personality Traits in the Socio-Economic Panel (SOEP) Concept, Implementation, and Empirical Properties.]. Res. Notes, **26**(1), 1–70 (2007)
22. Dombrowski, H., Bogs, N.: Digital- Leadership- Index- Führung im digitalen Umfeld anschaulich und messbar machen [Digital Leadership Index - making leadership in the digital environment clear and measurable.]. In M. h. Dahm, & S. Thode, Digitale Transformation in der Unternehmenspraxis (pp. 103–122). Wiesbaden: Springer Gabler (2020)
23. Döring, N., Bortz, J.: Forschungsmethoden und evaluation [Research methods and evaluation]. Springer Verlag, Wiesbaden (2016)
24. Dweck, C.S.: Mindset: The New Psychology of Success. Ballantine Books, New York (2008)
25. Eggers, B., Hollmann, S.: Digital Leadership–Anforderungen, Aufgaben und Skills von Führungskräften in der „Arbeitswelt 4.0 "[Digital Leadership - Requirements, Tasks and Skills of Managers in the "Working World 4.0]. Wiesbaden: Springer Gabler (2018)

26. Forsythe, J., Rafoth, J.: Being digital: why addressing culture and creating a digital mindset are critical to successful transformation. Insight **25**(1), 25–28 (2022)
27. George, J.M.: Emotions and leadership: the role of emotional intelligence. Hum. Relat. **53**(8), 1027–1055 (2000)
28. Gregor, S., Hevner, A.R.: Positioning and presenting design science research for maximum impact. MIS Quarterly, 337–355 (2013)
29. Guest, G., Bunce, A., Johnson, L.: How many interviews are enough? An experiment with data saturation and variability. Field Methods **18**(1), 59–82 (2006)
30. Gupta, A.K., Govindarajan, V.: Cultivating a global mindset. AMP, **16**, 116–126 (2002)
31. Hartl, E., Hess, T.: The role of cultural values for digital transformation: insights from a delphi study. In: Twenty-third Americas Conference on Information Systems, AMCIS 2017, pp. 1–10 (2017)
32. Heilmann, K., Zimmerhofer, A.: Agilität und Diagnostik: Personalauswahl für agile Organisation [Agility and Diagnostics: Personnel Selection for Agile Organization]. In A. Ternes, & C. D. Wilke, Agenda HR- Digitalisierung, Arbeit 4.0, New Leadership, pp. 211–223. Wiesbaden: Springer Gabler (2018)
33. Hevner, A., Chatterjee, S.: Design research in information systems. Des. Res. Inf. Syst. 9–22 (2010)
34. Hildebrandt, Y., Beimborn, D.: A cognitive conveyor for digital innovation-definition and conceptualization of the digital mindset. In: Wirtschaftsinformatik 2002 Proceedings 12 (2022)
35. Hildebrandt, Y., Beimborn, D.: The intangible key for digitalization: conceptualizing and measuring the" digital mindset. In: Proceedings of the 2021 on Computers and People Research Conference, pp. 89–91 (2021)
36. Hoffman, E.P., Sergio, R.P., Chabani, Z.: Understanding organizational culture in the context of digital transformation to pursue sustainable growth. In: Bilgin, M.H., Danis, H., Demir, E., Vale, S. (eds.) Eurasian Business and Economics Perspectives. EBES 2023. Eurasian Studies in Business and Economics, vol. 29. Springer, Cham (2024)
37. Kane, G.C., Palmer, D., Nguyen-Phillips, A., Kiron, D., Buckley, N.: Achieving digital maturity. MIT Sloan Manage. Rev. **59**(1) (2017)
38. Kendall, M.G.: The Advanced Theory of Statistics: Inference and Relationship. Vol. 2 (Vol. 2). C. Griffin (1961)
39. Kessel, L., Graf-Vlachy, L.: Chief digital officers: the state of the art and the road ahead. Manage. Rev. Q. 1–38 (2021)
40. Knorr, J.: Digital Mindset zur Steigerung der Wettbewerbsfähigkeit [Digital Mindset to increase competitiveness]. In: Dahm, M.H., Thode, S., (eds.) Digitale Transformation in der Unternehmenspraxis, pp. 45–59. Wiesbaden: Springer Fachmedien (2020)
41. Kocak S., Pawlowski J.: Crafting the future: developing and evaluating a digital mindset competence model for the industrial craft sector. In Proceedings of the 16th International Joint Conf. on Knowledge Discovery, Knowledge Engineering and Knowledge Management - Volume 3: KMIS, pp. 108–119. SciTePress (2024). ISBN 978-989-758-716-0
42. Kocak, S., Pawlowski, J.M.: A Qualitative Study on the Categorisation and Prioritisation of Digital Competencies and Attitudes for Managers and Employees. International joint conference on knowledge discovery, knowledge engineering, and knowledge management. SCITEPRESS-Science and Technology Publications, pp. 52–63 (2021)

43. Kocak, S., Pawlowski, J.: Characteristics in digital organizational culture: a literature review. J. Knowl. Manage. Pract. **23**(2) (2023)
44. Kollmann, T.: Digital Leadership. Springer Fachmedien Wiesbaden GmbH, Wiesbaden (2020)
45. Kwak, S.K., Kim, J.H.: Statistical data preparation: management of missing values and outliers. Korean J. Anesthesiol. **70**(4), 407 (2017)
46. Lessiak, C.: The digital mindset as a prerequisite for successful digital transformation: definition, attributes, and approach for measurement. In: Workshop specifického výzkumu 2020, pp. 120–127 (2020)
47. Likert, R.: A technique for the measurement of attitudes. Archives of psychology (1932)
48. Ling, Y., López-Fernández, M.C., Serrano-Bedia, A.M., et al.: Organizational culture and entrepreneurial orientation: examination through a new conceptualization lens. Int. Entrep. Manag. J. **16**, 709–737 (2020)
49. Manolova, M., Wang, R.: Future Skillsets als kritischer Erfolgsfaktor: Ein neues Framework mit einem innovativen Quantifizierungsmodell des Digital Mindsets in KMU. In Kompetenzen für die Arbeitswelten der Zukunft: Impulse des European Year of Skills für Wirtschaft, Bildung und Personalwesen [Future skillsets as a critical success factor: A new framework with an innovative quantification model of the digital mindset in SMEs. In Skills for the Working Worlds of the Future: Impulses of the European Year of Skills for Business, Education and Human Resources], pp. 161–184. Wiesbaden: Springer Fachmedien Wiesbaden (2024)
50. Mayring, P.: Qualitative content analysis. A companion to qualitative research, vol. 1, no. 2, pp. 159–176 (2004)
51. Mihardjo, L.W., Sasmoko, S.: Digital Transformation: Digital Leadership Role in Developing Business Model Innovation Mediated by Co-Creation Strategy for Telecommunication Incumbent Firms. Strategy and Behaviors in the Digital Economy (2019)
52. Möller, F., Guggenberger, T.M., Otto, B.: Design principles for route optimization business models: a grounded theory study of user feedback. In Wirtschaftsinformatik, pp. 1084–1099 (2020)
53. Morman, L.M.: How do we prepare the next generation for a career in our digital era? Computer **52**(5), 72–74 (2019)
54. Nuraeni, N., Nuruly, S., Harun, S.H., Susanto, P.C.: Organization development projection: analysis of leadership style, teamwork, competence employee and recruitment process. J. Econ. Manage. Entrepreneurship, Bus. (JEMEB), **2**(2), 139–145 (2022)
55. Oswald, G., Kleinemeier, M.: Shaping the Digital Enterprise. Springer, Switzerland (2017)
56. Peffer, K., Tuunanen, T., Rothenberger, M.A., Chatterjec, S.: A design science research methodology for information systems research. J. Manag. Inf. Syst. **24**(3), 45–77 (2007)
57. Petter, S., Barber, C.S., Barber, D., & Berkley, R.A.: Using online gaming experience to expand the digital workforce talent pool. MIS Q. Executive, 315–332 (2018)
58. Plattfaut, R., Borghoff, V.: Developing digitalization mindset and capabilities: preliminary results of an action research study. International Conference on Wirtschaftsinformatik, pp. 155–161 (2021)
59. Prior, D.D., Mazanov, J., Meacheam, D., Heaslip, G., Hanson, J.: Attitude, digital literacy, and self-efficacy: flow-on effects for online learning behavior. Internet High. Educ. **29**, 91–97 (2016)
60. Qu, S.Q., Dumay, J.: The qualitative research interviews. Qual. Res. Account. Manag. **8**(3), 238–264 (2011)
61. Rauch, R.: Digital Mindsets: Wie die Digitalisierung Beschäftigte bewegt [Digital Mindsets: How digitalization moves employees]. In S. Kaiser, A. Kozica, F. Böhringer, & J. Wissinger, Digitale Arbeitswelt, pp. 93–117. Wiesbaden: Springer Gabler (2021)

62. Rusly, F.H., Taliba, Y.Y.A., Abd Mutaliba, H., Hussina, M.R.A.: Developing a digital adaptation model for Malaysian manufacturing SMEs. In: Proceedings of the 4th UUM International Qualitative Research Conference (QRC 2020), vol. 1, no. 3, pp. 225–229 (2020)
63. Salleh, L.M.: Communication competence: a Malaysian perspective. Pac. Asian Commun. Assoc. **11**(3), 303–312 (2008)
64. Schein, E. H.: Organizational Culture and Leadership 4 ed. (2010)
65. Schein, E.H.: Organizational Culture and Leadership, 2nd edn. Jossey-Bass, San Francisco (1992)
66. Schmal, S.: Analyse der Berichterstattung über die Einführung des EU-Energielabels für Fernsehgeräte [Analysis of the coverage of the introduction of the EU energy label for televisions.]. In S. Schmal, Involvement mit Produkteigenschaften, pp. 45–78. Wiesbaden: Springer-Gabler (2016)
67. Singh, A., Hess, T.: How chief digital officers promote the digital transformation of their companies. MIS Q. Exec. **16**(1), 1–17 (2017)
68. Solberg, E., Traavik, L.E., Wong, S.I.: Digital mindsets: recognizing and leveraging individual beliefs for digital transformation. Calif. Manage. Rev. **62**, 105–124 (2020)
69. Son, M., Jeong, D., Son, J.: Analysis of middle school students' difficulties in science inquiry activity in view of knowledge and information processing competence. J. Korean Assoc. Sci. Educ. **38**(3), 441–449 (2018)
70. Tahvanainen, S., Luoma, E.: Examining the competencies for the chief digital officer. In: Twenty-fourth Americas Conference on Information Systems, pp. 1–10 (2018)
71. Tambling, R., Lee, J.N.: Client expectations about couple therapy. Am. J. Fam. Ther. **38**, 322–333 (2010)
72. Tashakkori, A., Creswell, J.W.: The new era of mixed methods. J. Mixed Methods Res. **1**(1), 3–7 (2007)
73. Tashakkori, A., Teddlie, C.: Mixed Methodology: Combining Qualitative and Quantitative Approaches. Sage Publications, Thousand Oaks (1998)
74. Teddlie, C., Tashakkori, A.: The Foundations of Mixed Methods Research: Integrating Quantitative and Qualitative Techniques in the Social and Behavioral Sciences. Sage Publications, Thousand Oaks (2009)
75. Venkatesh, V., Brown, S.A., Sullivan, Y.: Guidelines for conducting mixed-methods research: an extension and illustration. J. AIS **17**(7), 435–495 (2016)
76. Vial, G.: Understanding digital transformation: a review and a research agenda. J. Strat. Inf. Syst. **28**(2), 118–144 (2019)
77. Von Ohain, B.P. Leader attributes for successful digital transformation. In: Fortieth International Conference on Information Systems, pp. 1–17 (2019)
78. Wagner, M., Heil, F., Hellweg, L., Schmedt, D.: Working in the digital age: Not an easy but a thrilling one for organizations, leaders and employees. In P. Krüssel, Future Telco. Management for Professionals, pp. 395–410. Springer, Cham (2019)
79. Webster, J., Watson, R.T.: Analyzing the past to prepare for the future: Writing a literature review. MIS Q. xiii–xxiii (2002)
80. White, C.: We may have digital literacy and skills sets but do we have the digital mindset to succeed in a digital workplace? In: Proceedings of the 24th Asia-Pacific Decision Science Institute International Conference (APDSI), pp. 126–133 (2019)
81. Wilcox, R. R.: Statistics for the Social Sciences. Academic Press (1996)

82. Wörwag, S., Cloots, A.: Human Digital Work- Eine Utopie. Springer, Wiesbaden (2020)
83. Xiao, J.: The digitalization dialectic: a critical analysis of technology's role in cultural formation and social change. Adv. Soc. Behav. Res. **6**, 38–42 (2024)
84. Zhang, X., Venkatesh, V.: A nomological network of knowledge management system use Antecedents and consequences. MIS Q. **41**(4), 1275–1306 (2017)

Artificial Intelligence for Improving Drivers' Emotional Intelligence: An Innovative Approach for Safer Roads

Ana Todorova(✉), Irina Kostadinova, and Svetlana Stefanova

University of Ruse "Angel Kanchev", Ruse, Bulgaria
{attodorova,ikostadinova,sstefanova}@uni-ruse.bg

Abstract. Road fatalities caused by road accidents and risky driving are a worrying global problem. The World Health Organization reports over 1 million deaths per year, with these accidents being the leading cause of death among children and young people aged 5 to 29. Many studies argue that drivers' emotional intelligence can prevent risky driving. The current study proposes an AI-based model that, through continuous assessment and training, aims to improve drivers' emotional intelligence. The model uses virtual reality to simulate situations that help drivers recognize and manage their emotions and respond appropriately on the road. It is expected that this will reduce aggression and intolerance on the road and make roads safer.

Keywords: Artificial intelligence · Emotional intelligence · Safer driving · Virtual reality

1 Introduction

Road traffic accidents have emerged as a significant and somewhat insurmountable global health crisis. They are currently the eighth leading cause of death worldwide. The Global Road Safety Report 2023 shows that the annual number of road traffic deaths has fallen slightly. Efforts to improve road safety are having an impact, and some reductions in road traffic deaths have occurred [1]. Still, more proactive and innovative strategies are needed to effectively address this global crisis that affects every citizen of the world. No one is safe.

Just under 1.2 million people die on the roads each year. Most of the deaths occur in developing countries. Children, older people and people with low incomes are particularly vulnerable [2]. The number of road accidents is so alarming that it is imperative to study the behavior of drivers. A key factor influencing their behavior is emotional intelligence (EI) [3]. The latter encompasses various factors that support an individual's ability to understand, manage and respond to different emotions, including as an active participant in the traffic situation [4].

A number of studies have shown that different emotional states of drivers have different effects on their behavior and are directly related to risky driving [3]. Scientists warn that drivers' emotions can have a powerful influence on their destructive driving behavior. The link between different emotions (e.g. anger, intolerance and sadness) and risky driving is highlighted [5].

In overcoming this crisis, the application of advanced information and communication technologies (ICT) is becoming imperative. Artificial intelligence (AI), for example, has relatively quickly declared its potential to affect various areas of social life and economic activities, finding applications in autonomous vehicles, finance, smart cities, and healthcare [6]. Its interaction with other technologies, such as virtual reality, augmented reality, and blockchain, has not yet been fully explored. However, the effect of such synergy will be significantly greater than their distinct capabilities.

This article is based on and represents a substantial extension of a conference paper entitled "Developing an Artificial Intelligence Model to Enhance the Emotional Intelligence of Motor Vehicle Drivers for Safer Roads" [5], which was presented in November 2024 at the 16th International Conference on Knowledge Management and Information Systems (KMIS). Based on existing scientific knowledge in the field of EI and AI, the authors propose a prototype of a model that uses simulated scenarios in a virtual environment to assess and train drivers. Building on the findings presented in the report, this present study focuses more deeply on the presented innovative AI-based model that aims to improve the EI of drivers and reduce risky behavior on the road.

The main goal of the model is to improve the ability of drivers to recognize and manage their own and others' emotions, as well as to respond adequately to different situations on the road. Through ongoing assessment and subsequent training, the model seeks to reduce risky driving, aggression and intolerance on the road, thereby contributing to safer roads.

The article is structured as follows. A theoretical overview of the factors leading to road accidents is presented: EI and its relationship to road safety, the development of information and communication technologies in the recognition of human emotions, and a brief overview of the capabilities of automated emotion recognition systems. Then, the research methodology and the prototype of the AI-based model are described. The discussion section analyzes the feasibility and effectiveness of the model. Finally, the limitations of the study and the model are discussed, and directions for future research in this area are proposed.

2 Theoretical Background

In September 2020, the UN General Assembly adopted a resolution entitled "Improving Global Road Safety". It essentially proclaimed the Decade of Action for Road Safety 2021–2030 and set an ambitious goal of preventing at least 50% of road deaths and injuries by 2030. The Global Plan is consistent with the Stockholm Declaration, emphasizing the importance of a holistic approach to road safety and calling for continuous improvements in road and vehicle design, improving laws and enforcement, and providing timely life-saving emergency care to victims [7].

The Global Plan also reflects the Stockholm Declaration's encouragement of policies to promote walking, cycling and the use of public transport as inherently healthy and environmentally friendly modes of transport. The lack of progress made during the previous Decade of Action for Road Safety 2011–2020 set the stage for accelerated action in the years ahead. Achievements include mainstreaming road safety into the global health and development agenda, disseminating scientific evidence on what works, strengthening partnerships and networks, and mobilizing resources. This new Decade of Action provides an opportunity to build on the successes and lessons of previous years and to save more lives [8].

Large-scale studies show that, to date [7]:

- The number of road traffic deaths globally has decreased by 5% since 2010;
- The global share of deaths has decreased by 1% among users of four-wheeled vehicles and 2% among users of two and three-wheeled vehicles since 2010, but has increased from 5% to 6% among cyclists;
- 108 countries have seen a decrease in the number of deaths between 2010 and 2021, including for the first time in low-income countries.

However, the price paid for mobility remains too high. Motor vehicle crashes and suicide are two of the leading preventable causes of death among 13–19-year-olds [9]. At the same time, road traffic accidents remain the leading killer of children and young people aged 5–29. More than half of these deaths occur among pedestrians, cyclists and motorcyclists, especially those living in low- and middle-income countries [7, 10]. Worryingly, if current trends continue, road deaths are expected to become the fifth leading cause of death by the end of 2030 [1]. Therefore, in order to have an organized society, special attention must be paid to vulnerable road users such as pedestrians and cyclists at the planning stage itself in order to reduce road accidents [11].

A study suggests that the most effective way to prevent road deaths is a systems approach that shifts responsibility from drivers and pedestrians using the roads to city planners and the officials who design them [2]. But how sustainable is this shift in responsibility? And how fair is it to absolve the primary road users – motor vehicle drivers – of responsibility?

A survey of 400 commercial vehicle drivers published in 2025 revealed worrying trends. In the past five years, 34% of respondents had been involved in a crash, while in the past decade, this figure had risen to just over 43%. These data suggest that a significant portion of the workforce may be prone to risky behavior or lack adequate training in defensive driving techniques. Furthermore, over 42% of drivers reported engaging in driving violations each month, further highlighting the need for better compliance with traffic laws and regulations [1].

Therefore, the concept of roads without fatalities and serious injuries is a vision that must be achieved through a holistic approach [1]. It is not enough for one party to take responsibility alone. Every individual must strive for road safety, and this maxim must guide their behavior. The convenience of mobility should not be paid for with human lives. Achieving this requires innovative strategies capable of causing a profound change not only in the culture of traffic safety but also in the personal responsibility of all stakeholders. And as such, every citizen of the world is.

Factors Determining Road Accidents.

Road safety research focuses on understanding the factors that underlie risky driving behavior. It has also been identified as a significant factor in road traffic injuries. In this sense, a number of authors have emphasized the importance of considering multiple contributing factors to a crash. This approach recognizes that crashes are the result of failures at different levels of the system rather than a single factor. It acknowledges human error and the inevitability of human error in the context of road transport, emphasizing the need for a holistic view of road safety [12]. Therefore, the presence of quality infrastructure does not guarantee a world without road accidents. Nor does it guarantee fewer road deaths.

The holistic approach recognizes that multiple factors are associated with road crashes, including vehicle defects, the environment (i.e. road and weather conditions), and dangerous driving behavior. Despite this recognition, a study of the causes of motor vehicle crashes from 2005 to 2007 found out that 94% of crashes were caused by risky driving behavior. Other factors contributed only marginally [4].

McCarty and Kim also found that human behavior is the dominant factor in road accidents, contributing to more than 70% of these incidents. Striking in their study was the insight that 77% of crashes occurred within 15 miles (24 km) of home and 33% occurred within 1 mile (1.6 km) of home, further demonstrating that roads within 7 miles (11 km) of home accounted for half of all trips and 62% of all crashes [13]. This is likely due to routine, which dulls attention and makes drivers confident but inattentive to the route they are taking.

In a study in Toronto, a statistical analysis of accidents showed that the following factors were responsible for fatal accidents: reckless driving, lack of concentration while driving, and speeding. It was found that reckless driving, speeding, and red light running accidents and their respective fatal accident rates were over 62%, 21%, and 10%, respectively [11].

Shamoa-Nir argues that road rage is a social phenomenon that involves risks for drivers and also affects road safety. Aggressive driving is one of the leading causes of road accidents, so it is essential to study the factors that may encourage both identifying and avoiding aggressive driving and road behavior. Furthermore, the researcher argues that anger in drivers can lead to the expression of overt hostility. The standard explanation for driver aggression is based on the frustration-aggression model, in which, for example, a driver who has been blocked from reaching his destination expresses feelings of frustration and anger. That can lead to aggressive behavior, such as injuring another driver [14].

Another significant factor is the aging of the population. This is a global phenomenon, with the elderly demographic growing faster than any other age group. At the same time, driving is crucial for the mobility and quality of life of older people. As the population ages, so too has the number of older drivers. This demographic shift has raised public concerns about the safety of older drivers. The latter experience a higher rate of crashes per distance traveled and are disproportionately involved in intersection crashes. According to data from the National Police Agency of Japan, for example, while the annual number of traffic fatalities among drivers aged 65 or older decreased between 2012 and 2019, the proportion of traffic fatalities in this age group remained above 50%. It showed a slight increase over the period. Older drivers often exhibit physical weakness and reduced tolerance to injury, making them more susceptible to severe injury or death in the event of a crash [15].

In a comprehensive literature review, McCarty and Kim [13] identified the following leading factors that influence the risk of causing a traffic accident. These are human behavior, vehicle speed, alcohol consumption, driver fatigue, distracted driving, reckless driving, personality traits, age, and gender. The authors refer to a report that emphasizes the prevalence of behavioral causes, including unreasonable actions, driver errors, reactions, distraction, inexperience, and emotions such as aggression, nervousness, uncertainty, and panic. Distracted driving, although accounting for less than 6%, is not negligible. It includes the use of a mobile phone, as well as various internal and external distractions. Inexperience and reckless driving, on the other hand, play a more significant role, contributing to 28% of accidents. This includes 5% from inexperience, 1% from slow driving and a substantial 22% from various subcategories such as following too closely and stopping suddenly. Emotional factors such as aggressive driving and feeling nervous add another 7%, making them a significant aspect to consider. Together, these categories provide a comprehensive picture of up to 83% of recorded road accidents.

Risk Propensity and Risky Behavior.

Risky driving behavior is defined as any inappropriate driver activity that increases road hazards and the likelihood of a vehicle crash. Previous studies have classified risky driving, aggressive driving, driving with dangerous errors, and driving under the influence of negative emotions as risky behavior [4].

Risk perception refers to an individual's subjective assessment of the likelihood and severity of potential negative consequences associated with a particular behavior or situation. It can be measured using self-report scales that assess an individual's subjective assessments of the likelihood and severity of potential negative consequences associated with risky driving behavior. These scales typically include items that assess the perceived likelihood of adverse outcomes (e.g., crashes, fines, injuries) and the perceived severity of these outcomes. Risk perception can be influenced by a variety of factors, such as personal experience, social norms, and individual differences in risk-taking and risk-taking attitudes [1].

Another reason for engaging in risky behavior is peer pressure. It refers to individuals who are motivated to act and think in specific ways because they have been prompted, encouraged, or pressured by peers to do so. The bulk of the literature shows that peer pressure is associated with substance use, sexual activity, and bullying, as well as increased levels of risky driving among young drivers [16]. Similarly, a study in Cambodia found that beliefs about peer driving behavior accounted for over a third of the variance in risky driving among teenage motorcyclists [1].

Cultural factors also play a role in the relationship between social norms and risky driving. A comparative analysis of 32 countries found that gender differences in risky driving behavior and attitudes vary according to cultural context, possibly due to different social expectations related to gender roles [1]. Last but not least, specific behaviors may differ to some extent in other parts of the world due to local factors, such as the prevalence of alcohol or drug use and whether and how these behaviors can be controlled [12].

In addition, there is a strong relationship between whether people consider risky driving acceptable and whether they engage in it. When people see that their family and friends are doing it and approving it, they are more likely to do it. This creates a sense of social norm that puts pressure on the individual. If risky driving is widespread in society, the individual may feel compelled to engage in it. Conversely, if society does not approve of dangerous driving, people are more likely to drive safely. Therefore, it is essential to change public opinion to reduce risky behavior on the road [1].

These results highlight the importance of working to change public attitudes and perceptions to reduce risky driving. Measures that challenge the idea that dangerous driving is acceptable and promote positive social norms may be more effective in changing driver behavior [1]. However, to achieve changes in social norms and society as a whole, it is necessary to target changes into the individual or significant groups in society, such as drivers.

Emotions, Emotional Intelligence and Risky Driving.

The earliest definition of "emotion" states that emotions are sensations of physical change and that physiological changes, such as facial expressions, muscle tension, and visceral activity, inevitably accompany any emotion. This means that emotional expression plays a crucial role in human life and work [17]. The basic theory of emotions postulates that emotions are distinct and brief states that include physiological, subjective, and expressive components that allow people to respond in ways that are usually adaptive to evolutionarily relevant problems [18].

Emotions, along with a number of other physiological and psychological variables such as gender, experience, and age, inevitably influence driver behavior. At the same time, driving can be defined as a psychomotor skill, as it involves body movement and a cognitive task. This skill can take many forms, but the technique that the driver uses depends on his personality and behavioral profile [5].

The conventional classification of emotions as positive and negative is also essential. Positive emotions are acceptable and lead to a positive outcome. On the other hand, negative emotions are unfavorable and include stress, guilt, sadness, aggression, and fear [3]. Emotions can undoubtedly arise at any particular moment during driving and have an unpredictable emotional impact on the driver's behavior. Since people differ in the way they react to situations, various emotional states can affect driving differently [5].

Negative emotional states such as stress, depression, anger, fatigue, and confusion impair an individual's ability to perceive risks on the road accurately. This finding is consistent with previous research showing that emotional disturbances can lead to cognitive biases and impairments in decision-making processes, which ultimately affect risk perception. Drivers who experience high levels of negative mood are more likely to underestimate the severity of potential risks or misjudge the risks associated with specific driving behaviors. This intense emotional state can interfere with their ability to effectively process and interpret risk-related information, leading to poor risk assessment and potentially increasing the likelihood of risky driving. Negative mood can stem from a variety of sources, including work-related stress, personal problems, fatigue, or external factors such as road conditions or bad weather. These emotional challenges can impair cognitive functions that are critical for safe driving, including attention, decision-making, and risk perception [1]. This makes emotional self-regulation (an active element of EI) imperative in driving situations.

The concept of EI is associated with both emotions and intelligence. Emotions are organized responses that cross the boundaries of multiple psychological subsystems, including cognitive, physiological, experiential, and motivational systems. Controlling emotions for positive benefits involves being intelligent, which is a measure of the ability to observe and control one's mental processes in a way that shows a positive response to any circumstances. Intelligence is the ability to receive and process vital data from various sources in addition to deriving meaningful results. Emotions are a great source of data and thus influence people's decision-making and actions, thinking, behavior, or communication, so the ability to control one's own emotions and those of others has a significant impact on one's life [3].

In this sense, EI is defined as a person's ability to recognize, identify, use, express, and regulate one's own and others' emotions [5]. There are two broader ideas about EI, known as the ability and trait models. Bar-On also proposes a mixed model that includes non-cognitive abilities (e.g., adaptability, optimism) that also influence a person's emotional ability to succeed by coping with the environment and stressors [4].

In the context of risky and aggressive driving behavior, especially in the context of young drivers, the relationship between emotions, EI, and driving behavior is a subject of growing interest. It has been found that drivers' emotions are among the main factors contributing to dangerous driving behavior. Accordingly, emotions can be measured, understood, and regulated most effectively through the EI concept [5].

Large-scale studies confirm the relationship between EI and dangerous driving behavior to varying degrees. Emotion affects drivers due to its influence on the degree of self-regulation, thus influencing the way they drive. A 2019 study found that people who drive every day have a low EI coefficient, which hinders safe driving. This gives reason to argue that training drivers in emotional regulation can contribute to safer roads [5].

It is known that driving is influenced by the environment (e.g. weather, traffic) and the activities of other road users, which affect the emotional states of drivers, as well as social (e.g. cooperation with different drivers) and personality (e.g. impulsivity) components. Therefore, considering EI as a trait is more appropriate in the context of driving. EI combines key factors that influence behavior. These include *self-regulation* (e.g. impulse control or emotional regulation), emotionality (e.g. emotional awareness, emotional expression) and sociability (e.g. social awareness, managing emotions in a group). Although Arnau-Sabates *et al.* (2012) found that some components of EI – emotional regulation, empathy and impulse control – are negatively associated with risky driving behavior [19], numerous other studies have demonstrated their positive correlation with risky driving behavior [11, 20, 21].

Smorti *et al.* found that EI was associated with risky and aggressive driving but did not explain which individual subscales were associated with driving behavior [20]. Similarly, Hayley *et al.* found that lower scores on emotional recognition and expression led to aggressive driving (e.g., speeding, weaving in and out of traffic) and driving with negative emotions. Research has also shown that lower emotional regulation ability significantly predicts aggressive driving [21]. In comparison, drivers with higher emotional regulation abilities demonstrated more adaptive and safe driving behavior. At the same time, drivers with higher scores on social awareness and relationship management had significantly fewer driving violations and errors [4]. Social awareness and relationship management essentially require the presence of developed empathy.

In addition to self-regulation, *empathy* has also been established as an essential element of various EI constructs [5]. It involves the ability to understand another person's internal affective state and to respond appropriately. It is often defined as emotional communication between people that allows individuals to interact effectively in different social contexts [22, 23]. It is important to note that lower levels of emotional awareness (or alexithymia) and the associated reduced empathy are central concepts in the understanding and study of human behavior, including criminal behavior [22]. In this sense, empathy is also an essential element in the analysis of risky driving, although not all risky driving can be classified as criminal behavior.

Empathy is usually divided into emotional empathy and cognitive empathy. Emotional empathy means that a person is emotionally moved by a given situation. Cognitive empathy involves understanding the thoughts and emotions of others, and this is considered perspective-taking [23]. In the context of nervous, aggressive, and intolerant driving, adequately taking the perspective of others (i.e. other road users) is of vital importance. Driving behavior is generally considered to be a pattern chosen by the driver himself. Therefore, the specific style and skills that a motor vehicle driver applies at a given place and time are strongly influenced by his emotions and the relationship between stimulus and response. The relationship between *stimulus-response*, or rather the bridge between them, represents the individual's EI [5].

The primary motivation to look for a relationship between EI and driving is that it is the driving style of many drivers that is responsible for a significant number of accidents that occur. Higher EI, especially the ability to regulate emotions, is associated with a lower tendency to risky driving. The regulation, understanding, and evaluation of one's own and others' feelings are EI abilities, which are in-depth studies that can predict the number of potential road accidents. It has been empirically proven that EI influences driving behavior [11, 20, 21].

Such a conclusion is hardly surprising, given that, as indicated, emotions are a fundamental part of human behavior. They guide attention, memory, motivation, and even the decision-making process of an individual. However, in risky contexts, emotions are of vital importance, given the time (momentary) pressure and significant emotional consequences that these situations often involve.

The integration of emotional factors in the processing of risky behavior has also been demonstrated at the neural level, including in the context of driving. As noted, driving is an activity in which emotions often arise – traffic jams, accidents, risky road users, etc. All of these situations can provoke fear, as well as retaliatory aggression, intolerance, and dangerous behavior. In many cases, these emotions are the basis of human behavior, but their consequences in risky driving are particularly significant and often deadly [5].

The synthesis of information on EI and driving behavior allows us to understand the effect of EI on driver behavior. It provides grounds to generalize that drivers with higher reported EI scores engage in less dangerous driving, which is reflected in fewer crashes and fatalities [3]. Therefore, promoting and improving EI may be helpful in preventing risky driving, aggressive behavior on the road, and intolerance among stakeholders.

Artificial Intelligence and Emotional Intelligence.

Incorporating EI into driver education, on-the-job training, and licensing procedures can help develop safer drivers. However, traditional methods of assessing EI are vulnerable to subjectivity. The problem lies in the human factor, i.e. the self-interest or subjective opinion of the trainer. The latter can be a prerequisite for intentional or unintentional errors and corrupt practices in such a crucial area as road safety. With the help of large language models and the inclusion of AI during the training phase of young drivers, it can be beneficial to assess and train them based on their EI. Their behavior can be, if not more objectively, then more impartially evaluated by an AI agent and then compared with the *ideal* behavior. This will allow the elimination of negative traits in human behavior that are already in the initial stages before they pass their driving test and become experienced drivers. Such negative behavior is challenging, if not impossible, to change after years and years of driving experience, so it should start as early as in training courses [5].

Advances in ICT, and more specifically in the field of AI, have created numerous opportunities in all areas of human society [25]. AI has enjoyed exponential interest due to its ability to improve productivity, automate processes and stimulate innovation. In general, AI is perceived as a tool for making decisions based on logic and data, handling structured tasks faster and more accurately than humans. Its influence has gradually grown in areas that are believed to require uniquely human traits – such as creativity, empathy and EI [24].

At the heart of the debate about AI and its relationship to emotions is once again the idea of EI. However, given that emotions are sensations of physical change [17], can we argue that AI can understand and objectively interpret these sensations?

Overall, there is academic dissonance about how emotions are expressed or interpreted. A large-scale 2019 study aimed to determine whether emotions can be read from facial movements alone. The authors summarized the content of more than 1,000 articles, concluding that it is not possible [26]. In this case, is it possible for AI to be helpful and practical not only in reading emotions but also in cultivating EI?

A potential answer lies in the increasing investment in and adoption of these transformative technologies. The global market for AI related to human emotions is projected to grow from US$2.74 billion in 2024 to US$9.01 billion by 2030. It is significant how quickly AI is evolving to recognize and respond to human emotions with increased efficiency – a field known as affective computing [24]. The quest to bridge the gap between human emotions and machine intelligence has naturally led to the creation of Emotional AI. The technology aims to understand, interpret, and even reproduce human emotions, enabling more empathetic and effective *human-machine* interactions. In its broadest sense, it is advanced technology designed to recognize, analyze, and respond to human emotions. This field combines elements of psychology, cognitive science, and computer science to create systems that can understand and simulate human emotional responses [27].

This ability is crucial in various fields, especially in improving human-computer interactions, delivering personalized experiences and improving customer service outcomes. By using machine learning, AI can [24]:

- *analyze* facial expressions to detect emotions such as happiness, disappointment, and surprise;

- *track* pupil dilation to detect arousal or emotional intensity;
- *interpret* voice tone, pitch, and speech patterns to gauge emotional states;
- *uses* sentiment analysis to assess emotional intent in written text, such as reviews or social media comments;
- *examine* physiological signals, such as heart rate variability, to detect stress or anxiety.

AI-driven simulations and role-playing exercises train people in empathy, negotiation, and conflict resolution. By reflecting emotional data to individuals, AI has the potential to bridge emotional gaps, making EI a more tangible and teachable skill in an increasingly digital world. Human emotions are certainly fluid, contradictory, and subject to personal and cultural interpretation. Variables like sarcasm, cultural norms, past experiences, and unconscious biases are complex to encode in data-driven models. This leads a team of researchers to conclude that this makes AI less reliable in contexts that require deep empathy or moral understanding [24]. But less reliable does not mean useless.

AI relies on vast datasets of labeled emotional expressions and pattern-identifying neural networks to recognize emotional cues, predict responses, and simulate human interactions. Beyond consumer and workplace applications, AI is even helping people improve their own EI. Mood-tracking apps provide users with insight into their emotional patterns [24]. Through AI systems, input and output data (such as test questions and their corresponding answers) will be more integrated and flexible, which will not only reflect in an improved educational experience but will also increase the accessibility of resources [28]. Therefore, objective and timely analysis of driver-generated test data will make the materials developed to improve driver EI more tailored and effective.

Automated Emotion Recognition Systems.

As it has become clear, emotion is a dynamic cognitive and physiological state that develops in response to input, such as experiences, thoughts, or interactions with people. It includes subjective experience, mental processes, behavioral influences, physiological reactions, and communication. Therefore, emotion recognition is of crucial importance in application areas such as marketing, human-robot interaction, healthcare, mental health monitoring, and security [29], including road safety.

Emotions are not only physiological states that integrate sensations, thoughts, and behaviors but also psychological reactions generated by various external stimuli. As a result, researchers in many fields have recognized the importance of accurately identifying emotions [17]. Therefore, the development and implementation of automated emotion recognition has found applications in many fields, such as healthcare, e-learning, and surveillance [30]. In recent years, research on emotion recognition has been mainly applied in fields such as psychology, affective computing, and clinical therapy [17]. The development of computer-aided diagnostic tools is also at the heart of the automated recognition of human emotions [30].

Automated emotion recognition systems involve several steps to predict accurate emotional states [29]:

- *Source*: This first step refers to the part of the body used to measure responses to various inputs. Such sources can be eyes, speech, brain, heart, skin;
- *Stimuli*: Stimuli are any elements, events, or conditions that cause an individual to respond. Stimuli are commonly used in psychology and research to elicit reactions

or behaviors to study and understand various psychological processes. Stimuli can include situations, scenarios, or social interactions that elicit emotional, cognitive, or behavioral responses. Well-known stimuli for eliciting the target emotions are virtual reality (VR), images, video games, music, audio/video clips, audio, and/or video;

- *Input signals*: Input signals are preprocessed for practical analysis. Preprocessing refers to the steps or procedures performed on raw data before analysis or further processing. Preprocessing is critical in data analysis as it improves data quality, reduces noise or extraneous information, and prepares the data for practical analysis and modeling. The specific steps of preprocessing are determined by the nature of the data and the objectives of the study. Typically, the steps involved in preprocessing are cleaning, integration, transformation, sampling, and scaling of the data;
- *Feature Extraction*: In data analytics and ML, feature extraction refers to the transformation of raw data into a set of relevant and representative features that can be used for further modeling. It seeks to extract meaningful information or patterns from the data that encapsulate key features or properties of the underlying phenomenon. The goal of feature extraction is to find and select a subset of attributes that best capture the fine details in the data while discarding redundant or unnecessary data. This procedure reduces the dimensionality of the data, making it more understandable and suitable for analysis or modeling activities.
- *Feature Selection*: The process of selecting a subset of relevant features from a set of features that are present in a dataset is known as feature selection. It attempts to choose the most discriminative and informative features that contribute the most to the analysis or prediction while avoiding duplicate or unnecessary features. Feature selection is crucial as it can speed up computations, reduce re-fitting, improve interpretability, and improve model performance;
- *Classification*: This is a crucial step in an automated discovery system that is used to categorize variable values into subsequent classes. This involves decision-making using machine learning (ML) or deep learning (DL) techniques;
- *Model evaluation*: Performance measures assess the quality and efficiency of an ML or classification model. These metrics provide numerical estimates of the model's performance in terms of predictions and generalizability to new data. The specific challenge, type of data, and required evaluation standards influence the selection of performance metrics.

There is no doubt that emotion recognition technologies provide a number of advantages. They allow for quick and convenient emotional testing via smart devices, replacing paper questionnaires and increasing user engagement. They also enable the continuous monitoring of emotional states, which helps to understand the factors that influence them. The participants can provide immediate feedback. Automation of data storage and processing facilitates access and analysis of emotion information, which allows for better personalization of recommendations for developing EI. The use of multimedia elements in emotional tests would increase user interest and participation.

3 Methodology

Based on the theoretical analysis, the developed model for improving the EI of motor vehicle drivers introduces three *basic variables*. With the help of ICT and human control, the following dimensions will be prioritized for research, analysis and improvement:

- *self-regulation (x)* or control of emotions,
- *empathy (y)* or recognition of emotions (in others and oneself), and assessment of
- *emotional intelligence (z)* as a construct.

The measurement and assessment of *variable z* follow one of the three schools of EI: cognitive abilities, personality traits, or a mixed model. The choice is still being refined and validated. Based on the chosen general construct, *additional variables*, such as self-knowledge or social skills (elements of the mixed model of EI), can be introduced.

Existing research on the relationship between the specified basic variables and the driving model applied by the individual justifies the need to introduce baseline variables.

It is essential to explain why the *basic* variables, such as *empathy* and *self-regulation*, are specified explicitly in the algorithm instead of examining only the EI construct as a whole. Or why the general EI construct is specified at all, and not only the relationships between empathy and self-regulation of drivers and their aggressive and angry behavior, which puts them in risky situations, are studied. As mentioned earlier, self-regulation and empathy are part of the general EI construct. Although in the pilot AI model presented, as well as in many other studies, they are studied as independent competencies, in reality, it is not possible to fully develop these two abilities without the other EI competencies, regardless of which of the three EI models will be followed. For example, the mixed model includes self-regulation and empathy, as well as self-knowledge, motivation and social relationships. Goleman himself, one of the creators of the model, points out that it is not possible to achieve *self-regulation* without self-awareness since each of the sub-competencies of self-management relies on self-awareness [5]. This necessitates the study, assessment, and improvement of the overall EI construct by examining the constituent components of the construct separately, i.e., it is crucial to approach the problem deductively.

In the future, the application of additional variables will search for underestimated or previously neglected correlations between EI components and driving behavior. At this stage, these variables are not built into the model and its algorithm and are not subject to analysis.

The developed AI model is related to *aggression* and *risky driving*. Therefore, the algorithm will search for correlations between the basic and potential additional variables introduced so far and the characteristics of the motor vehicle driver identified in the literature that influence the genetic driving style. These characteristics are introduced as key variables: *aggression (a), intolerance (b)* and *risk-taking (c)*. Figure 1 presents the conceptual model of the study.

To develop the methodology and model of AI, a team of Bulgarian university scientists with expertise in various fields, including management, entrepreneurship, social sciences, and information and communication technologies, was formed. The team's goal is to detail the main elements, the algorithm, and the overall process from development to implementation and validation of the AI model.

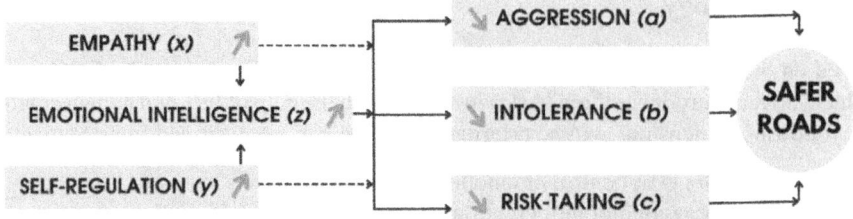

Fig. 1. Conceptual model of the study. Source: Own development.

4 Model Technology and Algorithm

From an ICT perspective, the model adheres to a toolkit of three technologies: *artificial intelligence, virtual reality* and *blockchain technology*. Table 1 describes the need for their applicability. Specifically, the application of AI technology in the proposed emotion regulation model (Fig. 2) includes:

1. *Machine Learning* (Classification, Regression, Clustering):

By applying classification methods, the participants' responses will be categorized into different personality types or traits, such as extroversion or introversion. Regression analysis will be used to predict the values of variables related to the learner's personality, which include basic, additional, and key factors. Cluster analysis will be applied to group participants with similar personality profiles.

2. *Deep learning* (neural networks, recurrent neural networks):

Neural networks, which mimic the functioning of the human brain, are effective at recognizing complex patterns in data. They are used for natural language analysis, image recognition, and processing large amounts of unstructured information. Recurrent neural networks are beneficial for analyzing sequential data, such as text responses in personality tests, because they can capture contextual information and extract deeper meanings.

3. *Natural Language Analysis* (sentiment analysis, keyword extraction, semantic content analysis, personalized recommendations, computer vision, physiological signal processing):

AI models will be used to interpret large volumes of text responses from personality tests to identify keywords, phrases, and emotional reactions characteristic of certain personality traits. In some cases, AI will also be used to analyze non-verbal signals, such as facial expressions and gestures, to obtain additional information about the individual's personality.

Facial recognition and emotion detection software are key components of emotional AI. Sensors measure physiological signals such as heart rate, skin conductance, and brain activity to determine emotional states. This data adds context that improves the AI's accuracy in assessing emotions. As a result, based on the test results, the AI will

Table 1. Type and applicability of implemented ICT. Source: [5].

ICT Type	Application
Artificial Intelligence (AI)	AI focuses on creating systems that can perceive, analyze, and respond to their environment to achieve specific goals. AI models aim to replicate and even surpass human cognitive abilities, such as learning, problem-solving, pattern recognition, and natural language understanding. They can process large volumes of data faster and more accurately than humans, detecting complex patterns that are difficult or impossible for human perception. In addition, although their accuracy is still debated, AI models offer greater objectivity as they are less susceptible to subjective bias. These advantages, along with process automation and resource savings, make AI models an effective alternative to human resources.
Virtual Reality (VR)	Virtual reality is a technology that creates immersive and interactive environments that mimic real or fictional situations. Users use VR headsets that display three-dimensional images and sounds, and sometimes controllers or gloves, to interact with the virtual world. VR allows for the creation of realistic and engaging experiences that can trigger different emotions, thoughts, and actions. The development of EI is believed to be closely linked to personal experience, which is why a connection is often made between EI and wisdom. Through VR technology, participants will be placed in simulated real-life situations that have been proven effective in developing EI competencies.
Blockchain Technology (BT)	Blockchain technology is a distributed database that records transactions in a secure, transparent, and immutable manner. Information is stored in blocks that are linked by cryptographic hashes. Once data is added to the blockchain, it is virtually impossible to change it, ensuring its reliability. This technology is decentralized, meaning that there is no single central authority controlling the network. Instead, the network is managed by multiple computers, making it resistant to censorship and manipulation. The inclusion of blockchain in the AI model is essential for protecting the personal data of training participants. Although personality test results are not medical information, they contain personal and sensitive data that require a high level of protection.

generate personalized recommendations for developing the individual's EI and offer virtual experiences that are most suitable for the learning goals.

The study of driver participation and engagement will be conducted using a combination of automated, semi-automated and manual methods. Automated systems will analyze images, body sensor data, and log files. Semi-automated systems will monitor

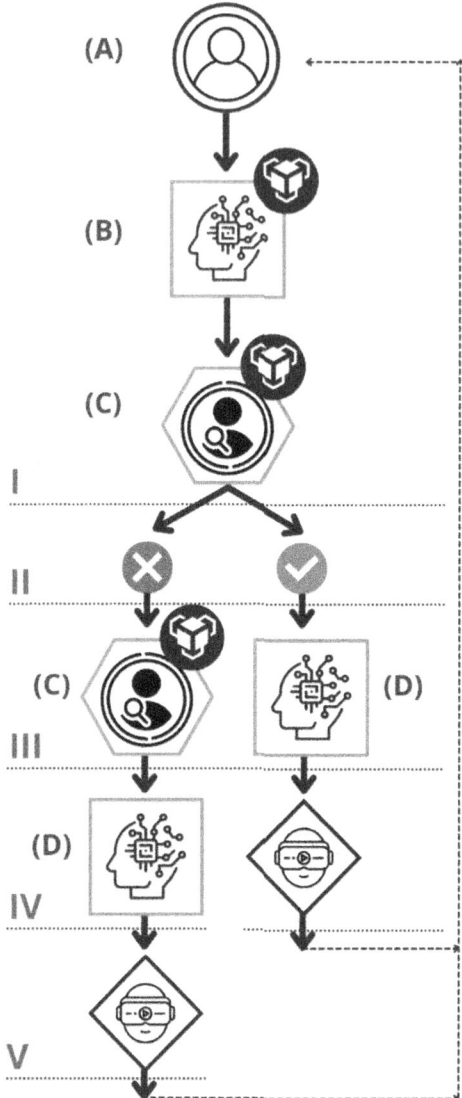

Fig. 2. Working algorithm of the developed AI model for evaluating and improving the EI of motor vehicle drivers for safer roads. Source: [5].

drivers' reactions and performance during tests. Manual methods will include checklists and self-assessment forms.

Figure 2 presents the algorithm of the developed AI model. The whole process is divided into four main stages:

Stage I) Measurement and evaluation of the introduced *basic (x, y, z)*, *key (a, b, c)* and *additional variables*;

Combining AI with the ability to recognize emotions aims to improve the ability of machines to understand and respond to human feelings. This will lead to a deeper understanding and a better user experience. This will be achieved through the following:

1. *Data acquisition.* Data collection and extraction are done from a variety of sources, including text, voice, visual, and physiological. This is key to training AI to recognize and interpret emotions. This data allows for an objective and accurate assessment of the variables at stake. Emotion recognition is defined as the ability to make correct inferences about human emotions by analyzing a variety of sources and modalities, including questionnaires and physical and physiological signals [29]. These signals will be collected from both the driver trainee and their instructor. The behavior of the instructor, who is also a passenger in the vehicle, will be taken into account when assessing the driver's behavior.
2. *Detecting and interpreting emotions. Generating a response.* Machine learning enables emotion detection by identifying patterns that correspond to feelings such as happiness, sadness, anger, or surprise. Once emotions are detected, they are interpreted in the context of a specific interaction, allowing the AI to understand the driver's emotional state and possible causes for it. Based on this interpretation, the AI model generates an EI score for the driver.

Stage II) Verification of the results obtained by a person – it is envisaged that this person will be with expertise in EI assessment and/or psychoanalysis. It is essential that the initial test data be interpreted with caution and that the evaluation is not one-sided – the work of an artificial or natural agent (defined below);

Stages III) and IV) Depending on the results of *Stage II* – respectively unsatisfactory or satisfactory from the point of view of human assessment, in the next stage either a human specialist makes a new measurement and assessment of the variables, or the AI determines the virtual experience that the subject will be subjected to.

The model also introduces four work agents: *(A) – learner, (B) – AI trainer/assessor, (C) – trainers/assessors/supervisors* and *(D) – AI-defined virtual experience.*

In Stages I and III, the blockchain encryption of the data generated by the tests measuring the sought variables is introduced. This, as stated earlier, is imperative from the perspective of the confidentiality of the subject and the protection of their data. The results of such tests, if publicly available, may have an adverse impact on the individual's personal and professional development in the future. Also, blockchain technology will neutralize the possibility of the records of the results being tampered with and manipulated.

The role of virtual reality is to act as an imaginary learning environment where learning does not mean learning phrases or behavioral responses. The goal is to gain life experience quickly. Still, in a protected (virtual) environment, this experience is directly related to the development of key variables – self-regulation and empathy – and the reduction of key variables – aggression, intolerance, and risk-taking. Recent studies have shown that virtual reality (VR) and augmented reality (AR) are immersive technologies that are effective in developing empathy. The main reason behind this assumption is that immersive technologies allow people to experience perspective-taking [23]. In virtual reality, the individual will be trained to respond most effectively to the stimulus-response interdependence. This effective response is achieved thanks to the developed EI ability.

On the other hand, virtual reality is implemented not only as a training environment but should also be perceived as an option for the individual to be placed in the shoes of the other – the person to whom he would cause harm in the caused traffic accident. In other words, to feel the pain, to feel the grief that he caused with his reckless behavior on the road. This is like a movie script in which the driver of a vehicle not only participates as an active participant but also indirectly develops the script himself. That is, the goal is to achieve awareness on the part of the driver that the decisions he makes at the moment affect not only his own life but also the lives of all other road users.

The use of VR requires careful planning and design, as well as the use of appropriate techniques. Table 2 presents some of the design features of the AI model. The main goal is to provide people with the opportunity to experience their mistakes in advance in a protected virtual reality, which would potentially allow them to see the gaps in their behavior and avoid them in real life. In most cases, emotional reactions are not only predictable but also adjustable as long as the individual is aware of what to expect from himself and other road users. This is precisely the role of virtual reality. Achieving the déjà vu effect – from a virtual to a real environment – will help drivers learn to respond adequately to as many situations as possible that they encounter as drivers of vehicles. Therefore, by increasing their EI, drivers will also improve the quality of their driving skills. The overall quality of driving for other drivers on the road around them will also improve.

The role of the expert psychologist in the developed AI model is key, precisely from the point of view of the experience in the virtual environment. It must be individually created not only according to the EI of the specific driver but also according to his temperament. The goal is not to deny drivers from driving in general but to remind them in an acceptable way that they are not alone on the road. Also, they are not insured against mistakes, emotional instability, intolerance, aggression – be it their own or others'. As can be seen from the explanation of the algorithm and the application of VR technology, the goal of the model is to work on the correction of the two basic variables – empathy and self-regulation. Changing their coefficients down or up on predefined assessment scales will also have an impact on the coefficient of the entire EI construct. This will reflect in a better response from the driver when a stimulus-response situation occurs in life. It will make him more adaptive and less reactive. In the future, as mentioned, additional variables, similar to the other EI competencies, will be introduced: self-awareness, optimism, and social relationships.

The AI model does not aim to directly influence the variables of aggression and risk-taking behavior of drivers, as it is assumed that they are too complex behavioral traits that hide different reasons in themselves. Like aggression and risk-taking, intolerance is also a complex concept. The lack of empathy, i.e. the lack of acceptance of another person's point of view and the fact that the other party also has the right to express an opinion, is the cause of a number of negative manifestations on the road. Intolerance can manifest itself in different forms and distinguish people by gender, age, ethnicity, and social affiliation.

Shamoa-Nir [14] explains driver aggression with the *frustration-aggression* model, which essentially represents a negative expression of the *stimulus-response* relationship.

Table 2. Scenario for the virtual application in the development of the AI model. Source: own development.

Scenario	Purpose / Application
Empowerment	VR will allow users to put themselves in situations that are outside their usual experience. For example, a person can experience what it is like to be homeless, live with a disability, or be a victim of discrimination. By experiencing these situations firsthand, users can develop a deeper understanding and empathy for others. By experiencing different emotional states firsthand, a person can learn to recognize and understand their feelings. At the same time, VR can simulate situations that trigger strong emotions, such as fear, anger, or anxiety. By repeatedly experiencing these situations in a controlled environment, a person can learn to manage their emotional reactions.
Storytelling	VR can be used to tell stories that evoke an emotional response. By immersing users in other people's stories, they can connect with their emotions and develop empathy. In addition, they can learn to cope with different emotional situations.
Interactive Scenarios	VR can be used to create interactive scenarios in which users have to make decisions that affect other people. By experiencing the consequences of their actions, users can develop greater responsibility and empathy. They will also be trained in emotional reactions to the different scenarios/situations they are involved in.
Using Emotional Feedback	VR can be used to provide emotional feedback to drivers. For example, if an individual shows a lack of empathy in a given situation, VR can show them how the other person is feeling. This will improve their tolerance for other road users. VR can provide feedback on the effectiveness of emotional regulation strategies. This can help the person learn to use more effective techniques to manage their emotions.
Social VR	Social VR allows people to interact with each other in a virtual environment. It can be used to create opportunities for intercultural dialogue and understanding, to practice social skills, and to develop EI.

As indicated in the theoretical background, the correct response to everyday stimulus-response situations lies in a well-developed EI.

Butrus and Witenberg empirically prove that the most critical predictor of tolerance in the dimensions of speech and action is precisely *empathic concern* [31] or *empathy*. Again, the goal of the AI model for regulating drivers' emotions is to show the person behind the wheel not only that he is not the only participant in the movement but that everyone else has the same right to be a participant in this process. Like aggression, the roots of intolerance can be diverse and challenging to identify. Therefore, the authors of the AI model direct their efforts not to the causes of its existence but to the skill that is capable of making people more tolerant – empathy and empathic concern.

On the other hand, there are real situations in which negative emotions such as aggression and intolerance cannot be blunted without eradicating their causes. But more important remains the reaction—the individual's learned reaction to negative feelings. In this sense, the AI model also emphasizes the development of the second key variable – *self-regulation* and how the individual reacts to their negative emotions. That is, it aims for an adequate response to the stimulus-response model in the context of road traffic.

As the graph in Fig. 2 shows, the process does not stop after the learner's experience in virtual reality. New measurements and evaluation of the main variables are required, as well as the additional and key variables adopted in the Methodology. Therefore, the algorithm starts again from Stage I. The following steps, i.e. whether to stop or continue the training, depend on the evaluation of agents B and C and the decision of agent B. Realistically, the process of increasing EI may never stop. It may even be applied to refresher driving courses (similar to periodic psychological tests) for experienced drivers.

Although not yet proven conclusively, some EI researchers believe that this ability and its inherent competencies have the potential to develop positively over time, one reason being precisely the accumulated life experience. The model of EI developed and presented in this study is based precisely on the claim that EI can be developed and that it undergoes evolution with age [32].

5 Discussion

Analyzing the algorithm, a natural question arises: What is the reason for human monitoring and control over the evaluation of the AI model? Conversely, if human capabilities are sufficient, why introduce AI?

The paradigm today is not one of man versus machine. People should start to think of AI as a complementary technology to human competencies. Machines are very good at analyzing large amounts of data; they can listen to voice inflections and begin to recognize when those intensities correlate with stress or anger. Machines can analyze images and pick up subtleties in the micro expressions of people's faces that may occur even too quickly for humans to recognize [33]. In other words, the potential of AI lies primarily in its ability to process vast amounts of data at speeds beyond the reach of a human. This ability is tested and proven daily by millions of users who use generative AI. However, it is not only the speed that matters but also the accuracy of the results. Subjectivity and unintentional errors in data analysis are inherent in humans. But the same goes for the imperfect (yet) AI, which, like its creator, is also not immune to biases and errors in its algorithm. In fact, the AI model being developed to increase the EI of drivers shows precisely how natural and AI should cooperate – in balanced synergy, but also with good-natured distrust of the abilities of one or the other. It should also not be forgotten that the objectivity of AI lies in the objectivity of the data it is fed from. In this sense, the quality of data is also a key element of the AI model being developed.

On the other hand, it is essential to note that AI models cannot and are not expected to replace human assessors. In the overall model, the human factor is equal to the participation of AI. This further justifies the intervention of blockchain technology in the algorithm. Encryption of data from the tests and training will ensure the confidentiality and objectivity of the process. Therefore, AI models should be used as an additional tool to justify and support final decision-making. In order to ensure the validity and reliability of the results of tests based on AI, careful validation studies should be conducted.

The issue of applying VR technology in such a profound way that it literally changes the human psyche is also delicate. In addition, the effectiveness of VR for developing empathy may vary depending on individual differences. Some people may be more inclined to immerse themselves in virtual reality and develop empathy and self-regulation, while others may be more skeptical, and this may hinder interaction.

Society tends to perceive empathy as something that you either have or don't. However, many studies show that empathy is not just a trait. It is something that can be purposefully worked on and increased or decreased according to the situation. The specific thing about the AI model being developed is the precision of the boundary at which a person can be placed in the shoes of another. When the goal is to feel someone else's pain and suffering, care must be taken that this virtual experience does not cause real disturbances in a person's mental state. In other words, each virtual scenario must be set according to the driver's individual indicators.

Similarly, a virtual reality experience developed at Stanford called "*Becoming Homeless*" is helping to expand research on how this new immersive technology affects people's levels of empathy. According to the study, people who saw in virtual reality what it would be like to lose their jobs and homes developed longer-lasting compassion for people experiencing homelessness compared to those who studied other media versions of the VR scenario, such as text [34]. Taking the perspective of others in a VR environment produced more empathy and prosocial behavior in people immediately after going through the experience and over time compared to simply imagining what it would be like to be in someone else's shoes [34–36].

In their study, Susindar *et al.* demonstrated that using VR can be an effective method for eliciting emotions when studying emotionally influenced decision-making. As stated in the theoretical framework, this is highly inherent in drivers of motor vehicles, who are exposed to emotionally arousing situations on a daily basis and have to make immediate decisions and respond to the stimulus-response relationship according to their current mood [35].

The study by Susindar and his co-authors focused on the extraction and generation of situations that evoke fear and anger – emotions that drivers also encounter on the road. At the same time, the authors of the cited study add that it is not entirely clear how the virtual environment affects performance (or learning) and the degree to which emotions are evoked. This means, on the one hand, that it is not categorically clear whether an individual would react in the same way in a real and virtual environment, and on the other hand, that more in-depth research is needed in this direction [35]. However, the latter in no way belittles the possibilities of VR technology, as can be seen from similar studies on the topic [37, 38].

Attention to detail throughout the process is essential, as irreparable damage can be done to the learner's psyche, which is not the goal of the AI model. It is extremely important to create and implement "training" in virtual reality according to the results of the test of the introduced variables. A hypersensitive person would perceive such experiences in one way, while an individual who is more selective in his feelings would have a radically different perception of what is happening. Therefore, any virtual environment for training in EI proposed by AI and approved by a person must be perfect and maximally adapted to the personal qualities of the respective learner. In this sense, it is essential to be careful not only with the implementation of AI but also with VR technology for developing empathy and self-regulation. Improper use can lead to emotional trauma or unintentionally turn into manipulation. It is necessary to ensure that VR experiences and AI applications are ethical and responsible and that the overall procedure is transparent but without compromising the confidentiality of the person's data.

From this, it can be concluded that the application of technology for emotion recognition, behavior assessment and generation of appropriate virtual learning environments involves a number of challenges. First of all, access to data emerges as a critical issue, as the early stages of technology development require a significant amount of data for training models for prediction and decision-making. Although public databases are widely used by researchers, common problems with research datasets, such as data imbalance and limited data set size, can lead to inconsistencies between the data used for training and experimentation.

No less important is the assessment of costs and who would be saddled with this burden: driving school owners, scientific organizations, drivers, and government institutions. Data extraction, storage, and analysis, along with the use of human resources and hardware, can be financially burdensome and require significant investment. They also require collaboration between as many stakeholders as possible.

Differences in education levels are also likely to affect the quality of the data generated and require validation efforts. Last but not least, there is a notable lack of consensus on security, ethics, and privacy issues in this context, further complicating the implementation of emotion recognition and behavioral assessment technology in driving lessons. Addressing these challenges is essential to harness the full potential of this technology while ensuring the confidentiality of participant-generated results, the quality of input-output data, and cost-effectiveness.

Study limitations

A significant drawback of the present study and the developed model is the lack of clear evidence for the effectiveness of some of the ICTs used. Existing analyses and studies are insufficient and often yield contradictory results. Therefore, the application of the described technologies cannot guarantee the desired effect.

Another limitation of the study is the lack of practical data from the actual application of the developed model. The presented model is purely theoretical and has not been tested in actual conditions, which limits the possibility of assessing its reliability and predictive validity. To overcome this drawback, an empirical study with a large and diverse group of participants is necessary. Our interdisciplinary team plans to conduct extensive research and tests in this direction, and the purpose of this model is to lay the foundation.

Last but not least, the implementation of such an AI algorithm in an environment ostensibly controlled by the state but dominated by private interests, such as driving schools in Bulgaria, requires significant will and consent from multiple (non)stakeholders. In this sense, just creating the AI model is not enough. Therefore, the future efforts of the author team will be directed towards the experimental implementation of the model and seeking validation of the algorithm and the expected results.

Applicability

Since drivers' emotional states influence their behavior, transportation companies must track drivers' emotional states at the time they are scheduled to drive. In addition, all transportation company management and organizational policies should consider EI important, as EI training programs can improve EI.

The research team's goal is for the algorithm to be implemented as a priority in driving skills courses. This is an environment in which an individual most actively reveals himself – as more aggressive, more intolerant, more selfish, or vice versa. Bulgaria ranks first in the EU in road deaths in 2023. The European Commission published preliminary data for last year – the EU average is 46 deaths per one million inhabitants. In Bulgaria, the ratio is 82 victims per million inhabitants [5]. In this sense, the developed AI model is expected to lead to significantly greater self-awareness and self-regulation of one's own emotions in both inexperienced and experienced drivers on the roads.

At the same time, the developed AI model can be used in a number of other areas where poor emotion self-regulation leads to conflict situations or where it is necessary to reduce aggression levels. The implementation results will validate the results and allow the model to be incorporated into educational programs and applied in the fight against hate speech, intolerance of differences, selfishness, cruelty towards the weaker, etc. The authors will conduct future research on this subject.

The developed model and its active application will improve efforts to achieve SDG3 – *Good Health and Wellbeing – ensuring healthy lives and promoting wellbeing for all at all ages* from the UN Global Goals for Sustainability and Development. Specifically, SDG3.6 is supported, which aims to halve the number of global deaths and injuries from road traffic accidents, and its leading indicator is "Road traffic fatalities". SDG 3 aims to prevent unnecessary suffering from preventable diseases and premature death by focusing on key targets that improve the health of all populations. Regions with the highest burden of disease and neglected population groups and regions are priority areas. Goal 3 also calls for more significant investment in research and development, health financing, and health risk reduction and management [38].

6 Conclusion

Road safety is a global issue that affects millions of people every year. Risky driver behavior, often influenced by emotional factors such as aggression and intolerance, is among the leading causes of road accidents. In the modern world, where technology plays an increasingly important role in our lives, the use of AI to improve road safety represents a promising opportunity.

Death on the roads as a result of serious road accidents is one of the saddest facts of our time, which we must either accept or overcome. Over 1 million people die on the road, a significant number of them being children and young people. The purpose of the developed AI model to increase driver EI is precisely this – fighting statistics and risky driving, but above all, saving lives before they are even in danger.

The proposed model should be considered as an integral part of the holistic approach to road safety proposed by the UN and the Stockholm Declaration. This approach involves continuous improvements in road and vehicle design, improved laws and enforcement, and timely life-saving emergency care for victims. It is essential to clarify that in this "battle", neither EI nor AI is a panacea. The human factor remains a significant unknown, along with the cultural and social characteristics of one or another country. However, let us assume that it is almost impossible to change cultural and social conditions. In this case, only the way in which the individual reacts to the stimulus-response relationship is within his capabilities.

The authors of this study recommend that the presented AI model be included as a significant social innovation aimed at improving the individual driver without neglecting all other factors affecting road performance. However, while the quality of infrastructure and adequate legislation and health care are the responsibility of public authorities, road behavior is a personal responsibility and, as such, should be encouraged in a tone of empathy, tolerance and avoidance of unnecessary risk.

In conclusion, the developed AI model is a small step towards achieving high EI of motor vehicle drivers and reducing risky behavior on the road. Although additional research and efforts are needed to implement this technology, it is essential to find a way to save human lives and reduce the socio-economic costs directly related to road accidents.

Acknowledgments. This study is financed by the European Union-NextGenerationEU through the National Recovery and Resilience Plan of the Republic of Bulgaria, project №BG-RRP-2.013-0001.

Disclosure of Interests. The authors have no competing interests to declare that are relevant to the content of this article.

References

1. Damadi, M., Haghighi, F.: Multidimensional influences on risky driving and crash risk among commercial drivers in developing countries: Structural equation model approaches. Transp. Res. F: Traffic Psychol. Behav. **109**, 809–839 (2025). https://doi.org/10.1016/j.trf.2025.01.007
2. Welle, B., et al.: Sustainable and Safe: A Vision and Guidance for Zero Road Deaths. World Resources Institute (2026). https://www.wri.org/research/sustainable-and-safe-vision-and-guidance-zero-road-deaths. Accessed 15 Mar 2025
3. Aniah, E.: The influence of emotional intelligence on driving behavior in the transportation sector: a literature review. J. Contemp. Issues Bus. Gov. **27**(6), 1524–1537 (2021). https://cibgp.com/au/index.php/1323-6903/article/view/2255. Accessed 15 Mar 2025
4. Ahmed, J., Ward, N., Otto, J., McMahill, A.: How does emotional intelligence predict driving behaviors among non-commercial drivers? Transp. Res. F: Traffic Psychol. Behav. **85**, 38–46 (2022). https://doi.org/10.1016/j.trf.2021.12.013

5. Todorova, A., Kostadinova, I., Stefanova, S.: Developing an artificial intelligence model to enhance the emotional intelligence of motor vehicle drivers for safer roads. In: Proceedings of the 16th International Joint Conference on Knowledge Discovery, Knowledge Engineering and Knowledge Management – KMIS 2024, pp. 339–346. SciTePress (2024). https://doi.org/10.5220/0013051400003838
6. Kirova, M., Boneva, M.: Artificial intelligence: challenges and benefits for business. In: New Trends in Contemporary Economics, Business and Management. Selected Proceedings of the 14th International Scientific Conference "Business and Management 2024", pp. 253–260. https://doi.org/10.3846/bm.2024.1277
7. World Health Organization: Global status report on road safety 2023. https://iris.who.int/bitstream/handle/10665/375016/9789240086517-eng.pdf?sequence=1. Accessed 15 Mar 2025
8. World Health Organization: Decade of Action for Road Safety 2021–2030. https://www.who.int/teams/social-determinants-of-health/safety-and-mobility/decade-of-action-for-road-safety-2021-2030. Accessed 15 Mar 2025
9. Ehsani, J. P., Duren, M., Grant, B., Wilcox, H.: Suicidal thoughts, risky driving, and crashes among U.S. Adolescents. J. Saf. Res. 93, 12–14 (2025). https://doi.org/10.1016/j.jsr.2025.01.001
10. International Transport Forum, Road Safety Annual Report 2023, OECD Publishing, Paris (2023). https://www.who.int/publications/i/item/9789240086517. Accessed 15 Mar 2025
11. Athiappan, K., et al.: Identifying influencing factors of road accidents in emerging road accident blackspots. Adv. Civ. Eng. **2022**(1), 9474323 (2022). https://doi.org/10.1155/2022/9474323
12. Somoray, K., White, K.M., Watson, B., Lewis, I.: Predicting risky driving behaviours using the theory of planned behaviour: a meta-analysis. Accid. Anal. Prev. **208**, 107797 (2024). https://doi.org/10.1016/j.aap.2024.107797
13. McCarty, D., Kim, H.W.: Risky behaviors and road safety: an exploration of age and gender influences on road accident rates. PLoS ONE **19**(1), e0296663 (2024). https://doi.org/10.1371/journal.pone.0296663
14. Shamoa-Nir, L.: Road rage and aggressive driving behaviors: the role of state-trait anxiety and coping strategies. Transp. Res. Interdiscip. Perspect. **18**, 100780 (2023). https://doi.org/10.1016/j.trip.2023.100780
15. Zhu, Y., Jiang, M., Yamamoto, T.: Personality, functional performance, and travel patterns related to older drivers' risky driving behavior: a naturalistic driving study. Accid. Anal. Prev. **209**, 107833 (2024). https://doi.org/10.1016/j.aap.2024.107833
16. Li, Y., Sun, L., Guo, J.: Psychometric properties of the peer pressure on risky driving scale in young Chinese drivers and its associations with risky driving behaviours and safe driving climate among friends. Transp. Res. F: Traffic Psychol. Behav. **110**, 118–127 (2025). https://doi.org/10.1016/j.trf.2025.02.011
17. Guo, R., Guo, H., Wang, L., Chen, M., Yang, D., Li, B.: Development and application of emotion recognition technology – a systematic literature review. BMC Psychol **12**, 95 (2024). https://doi.org/10.1186/s40359-024-01581-4
18. Herrero, J., Donoso, F., Vila, R.: The first steps for adapting an artificial intelligence emotion expression recognition software for emotional management in the educational context. Br. J. Edu. Technol. **54**, 1939–1963 (2023). https://doi.org/10.1111/bjet.13326
19. Arnau-Sabatés, L., Sala-Roca, J., Jariot-Garcia, M.: Emotional abilities as predictors of risky driving behavior among a cohort of middle aged drivers. Accid. Anal. Prev. **45**, 818–825 (2012). https://doi.org/10.1016/j.aap.2011.07.021
20. Smorti, M., Andrei, F., Trombini, E.: Trait emotional intelligence, personality traits and social desirability in dangerous driving. Transport. Res. F: Traffic Psychol. Behav. **58**, 115–122 (2018). https://doi.org/10.1016/j.trf.2018.06.012

21. Hayley, A.C., Ridder, B.D., Stough, C., Ford, T.C., Downey, L.A.: Emotional intelligence and risky driving behaviour in adults. Transp. Res. F: Traffic Psychol. Behav. **49**, 124–131 (2017). https://doi.org/10.1016/j.trf.2017.06.009
22. Koufouli, A., Tollenaar, M.S.: Empathy and emotional awareness: an interdisciplinary perspective. In: Gavrielides, T. (ed.), Offenders No More: An Interdisciplinary Restorative Justice Dialogue, pp. 101–122 (2016). Nova Science Publishers
23. Lacle-Melendez, J., Silva-Medina, S. Bacca-Acosta, J.: Virtual and augmented reality to develop empathy: a systematic literature review. Multimed. Tools Appl (2024). https://doi.org/10.1007/s11042-024-19191-y
24. ESCP Business School: Artificial Intelligence and Emotional Intelligence: The New Frontier of Human-AI Synergy (2025). https://escp.eu/news/artificial-intelligence-and-emotional-intelligence. Accessed 15 Mar 2025
25. Kalmukov, Y. Evstatiev, B., Kadirova, S.: Individual cow identification using non-fixed point-of-view images and deep learning. Int. J. Adv. Comput. Sci. Appl. (ijacsa) **15**(10), 2024. https://doi.org/10.14569/IJACSA.2024.0151066
26. Veljkovic, J.: Emotional AI: Can technology grasp emotions? How AI is changing the way we work. Rydoo (2023). https://www.rydoo.com/cfo-corner/emotional-ai/. Accessed 15 Mar 2025
27. Shrivastav, R.: The Mechanics and Impact of Emotional AI in Modern Technology. Convin (2024). https://convin.ai/blog/emotion-ai-in-modern-technology. Accessed 15 Mar 2025
28. Stefanova, P., Ibryamova, E., Smrikarov, A., Ivanova, G.: Development and integration of audio and visual micro-resources in the learning process through the use of artificial intelligence systems. Strateg. Policy Sci. Educ. **32**(5s), 233–243 (2024). https://doi.org/10.53656/str2024-5s-23-dev
29. Khare, S.K., Blanes-Vidal, V., Nadimi, E.S., Acharya, U.R.: Emotion recognition and artificial intelligence: a systematic review (2014–2023) and research recommendations. Information Fusion **102**, 102019 (2022). https://doi.org/10.1016/j.inffus.2023.102019
30. Maithri, M., et al.: Automated emotion recognition: current trends and future perspectives. Comput. Methods Programs Biomed. **215**, 106646 (2022). https://doi.org/10.1016/j.cmpb.2022.106646
31. Butrus, N., Witenberg, R.T.: Some personality predictors of tolerance to human diversity: the roles of openness, agreeableness, and empathy. Aust. Psychol. **48**(4), 290–298 (2013). https://doi.org/10.1111/j.1742-9544.2012.00081.x
32. Todorova, A.: Examining emotional intelligence evolution with age: insights from Bulgarian digital entrepreneurs of different generations. IIMT J. Manag. **1**(1), 5–23 (2024). https://doi.org/10.1108/IIMTJM-12-2023-0075
33. Somers, M.: Emotion AI, explained. MIT Sloan School of Management (2019). https://mitsloan.mit.edu/ideas-made-to-matter/emotion-ai-explained. Accessed 15 Mar 2025
34. Stanford University: Virtual reality can help make people more compassionate com-pared to other media, new Stanford study finds (2018). https://data.unicef.org/sdgs/goal-3-good-health-wellbeing/. Accessed 15 Mar 2025
35. Susindar, S., Sadeghi, M., Huntington, L., Singer, A., Ferris, T.K.: The feeling is real: emotion elicitation in virtual reality. Proc. Hum. Factors Ergon. Soc. Annu. Meet. (2019). https://doi.org/10.1177/1071181319631509
36. Huang, X., Macgilchrist, F.: From physical feelings to empathy: an immersive virtual reality approach to facilitate physical empathy. Comput. Educ. Open **7**, 100215 (2024). https://doi.org/10.1016/j.caeo.2024.100215

37. Mancuso, V., Bruni, F., Stramba-Badiale, C., Riva, G., Cipresso, P., Pedroli, E.: How do emotions elicited in virtual reality affect our memory? A systematic review. Comput. Hum. Behav. **146**, 107812 (2023). https://doi.org/10.1016/j.chb.2023.107812
38. UNICEF: Goal 3: Good health and well-being. https://data.unicef.org/sdgs/goal-3-good-health-wellbeing/. Accessed 15 Mar 2025

Systemic View on Creating Knowledge Maps: Putting the Pieces Together

Tatiana Gavrilova[1], Anna Kuznetsova[2](✉), and Irina Leshcheva[1]

[1] Graduate School of Management, St. Petersburg State University, St. Petersburg, Russian Federation
{gavrilova,leshcheva}@gsom.spbu.ru
[2] Lyceum No. 408, St. Petersburg, Russian Federation
anna.romantseva@gmail.com

Abstract. The paper discusses the possibilities, techniques and prospects for creating a visual guide of diagrams describing the intellectual assets of the organization (university, enterprise or company). Such a systematic repository is called a corporate atlas of knowledge maps. It may be used as a classifier. These maps present expertise, knowledge and technologies and visualization, provide information transparency of communications in universities making any collaboration smart and effective. Knowledge and data visualization solve the problem of eliminating barriers between information flows of university departments, as well as between the university and the external environment. The research described in this paper was a part of METACARTA project – "MEthodology and Technology for developing digital knowledge mAps for eduCAtion and Research TeAms". It is based on mapping the university business school knowledge and competences. The research framework was based on the ontology engineering, where ontologies as conceptual skeleton build the base of faculty knowledge maps. The novel FOCUS-KM ontology (Framework for Organizing Comprehensive Understanding and Structure of Knowledge Maps) was developed. It generalizes a set of knowledge maps attributes and properties. This ontology reflects and unveils the structure of the knowledge landscape and the most essential features of knowledge maps. The most popular ones are suggested to be included into the knowledge atlas from which the decision makers can select relevant maps for their work. This text is an extended, enriched and revised version of the article presented in the proceedings of "The 16th International Conference on Knowledge Management and Information Systems". In general, the approach can be adapted to business companies and government organizations if they are interested in disclosing their intellectual capital.

Keyword: Ontology · Knowledge Maps · Visualization System · Knowledge Transfer

1 Introduction

Business and academic work require cooperation. Learning includes access to influencers and experts. It can be difficult to find colleagues and potential partners in an over loaded world of redundant and contradictory information. Even within a department, the activities of a particular teacher may be unknown. The same problem arises at the scale of institutes and universities.

But companies and universities are in no hurry to share their intellectual assets, and often companies themselves do not know about their "treasures". Acquisition and systematization of such information resources are useful primarily for the companies themselves, in addition, they are invaluable in the market. Internal portals of universities are often built on formal artifacts of teaching and research activities of employees, which does not allow conclusions to be drawn about the expertise of specific teachers and their readiness to implement consulting projects. The established formal approach to the presentation of university expertise does not allow it to be demonstrated in a language understandable to the external audience and complicates the interaction of universities with potential external counterparties. The paper discusses the possibilities and prospects for creating the atlas of corporate knowledge maps – visual guide to the intellectual assets of the enterprise based on the case of a university business school.

Visual knowledge maps are a powerful tool for enhancing understanding and fostering collaboration in a company setting. These maps can be used to visually represent information, ideas, and relationships in a clear and concise manner, making it easier for faculty and students to grasp complex concepts and share knowledge with their colleagues.

Visualization allows to present complex data and identify patterns, trends, and structures, which facilitates deeper exploration of the data. Diagrams allow all the employees and newcomers to expand less cognitive energy deciphering the meaning of the text they are reading, which means they will have more cognitive energy available for the critically important tasks of understanding, assessment and reflection [1, 2]. The main benefits of knowledge visualization are related to: stakeholder engagement, flexibility, knowledge transfer, signaling role, agility and interactivity [3]. Using knowledge representation and mapping help to organize the smarter collaboration. The term was coined by H. Gardner [4] when she described the need for highly-specialized experts to come together in order to tackle more complicated issues than any of them could do on their own.

The paper discusses some results obtained as part of the METACARTA project (MEthodology and Technology for developing digital knowledge mAps for eduCation and Research TeAms) where the methodology visualizing teaching and research activity of the faculty members was developed.

The paper structure is as follows: the current Sect. 1 provides the motivation for creating a new approach, Sect. 2 presents a brief literature review and highlights the existing research gap, the attributive ontology design is described in Sect. 3, while Sects. 4 and 5 provide a demonstration of this approach in a decision-making process.

2 A Brief of Knowledge Mapping

To solve the problem of eliminating barriers between information flows of university departments, as well as between the university and the external environment, data and knowledge visualization can be used [5]. Knowledge maps are powerful information visualization techniques that allow storing, describing knowledge assets, connecting experts, accessing and disseminating knowledge over time, existing knowledge resources and knowledge gaps [6–8]. The main tools that are widely used in knowledge mapping, require the participation of both experts and analysts who develop visual diagrams reflecting.

- Sources of knowledge;
- Location of knowledge elements;
- Owners of knowledge elements;
- Links and relations between them, etc.

Knowledge maps are closely related to competency maps and employee competency management, which are denoted as skills and competencies in corporate decisions [9]. Such maps turn enterprise data into valuable and insightful information. Knowledge maps are one of the tools used in knowledge engineering for organizing and presenting knowledge, forming a graphical framework and landscape in visualizing complex concepts, decision support, knowledge sharing, etc. [10, 11].

However little attention is paid to the development of a well-structured set of visual representations of key concepts, relationships, knowledge owners of a knowledge domain of the organization encouraging the employees to see the big picture, promote collaboration, and improve organization and focus.

The development of knowledge maps starts with the definition of goals and stakeholders. For each level, a basic atlas (visual set) of types of knowledge maps was created.

2.1 Why Mapping?

In the field of management, the following goals may be solved using the developed knowledge maps:

- optimization and activation of resources, including the formation of project teams or working groups taking into account the principle of complementarity, ensuring the transfer of knowledge from experts to employees who have gaps [12] (in this case, an employee development plan is formed based on such tools as coaching and mentoring) and strategic planning for the development of assets [13] (based on the analysis of the map for various areas of knowledge, a decision is made to close gaps or change the focus of activity);
- identification of the hidden potential of employees. The principle of completeness, implemented in the construction of ontologies of subject areas, provides a comprehensive analysis and allows for the formalization of those areas of knowledge that were previously not in the field of view when assessing employees. By discovering previously unknown competencies and publications of subordinates, a manager can make a more informed (and therefore less risky) decision about developing new areas of activity [14].

2.2 Who are Using K-Maps?

The creation of any visual model makes sense only in the context of a certain management goal, when the organization's management has formulated a request for solving specific problems. In this case, the visual model is designed to present the information necessary for this in a form and shape that facilitates quick, informed decision-making. Another important component is the definition of key users of visualization – when establishing several groups with different needs this can lead to the emergence of different approaches to visualizing the same data.

Before the knowledge mapping study, a stakeholder analysis was conducted. Stakeholders who influence academic and research teams and benefit in one way or another from access to the knowledge map data may include both external and internal users and can be divided into three categories:

- managers (administrators),
- experts, and
- ordinary employees, including newcomers [11].

Experts, using knowledge maps, can increase their innovative activity by forming initiative groups, for example, for research and development by uniting people with complementary skills and knowledge. Transferring and receiving knowledge also creates additional opportunities for self-development of experts. Ordinary employees, including newcomers, are interested in using knowledge maps in order to obtain knowledge from experts to develop competencies in specific areas and quickly find the necessary information, increasing the efficiency of work processes by reducing deadlines and improving performance.

Thus, for each of the stakeholders, a separate set of visual representations of the knowledge map may be formed, meeting the above stated tasks. According to this division, the subject of mapping also changes: the company's management needs a high-level overview of assets, mapping the entire organization to identify common features and growth areas. An expert needs to focus on his/her subject/professional area and current trends within it; an ordinary (and especially new) employee needs a detailed description of the individual knowledge of colleagues.

2.3 Levels and Steps in Knowledge Mapping

In modern universities, the roles described above are represented by internal stakeholders: administration (managers), research and teaching staff, including young scientists and postgraduates (experts and ordinary employees). Based on the fundamental differences between these three groups of knowledge map recipients, a classification was proposed at three levels: general, focused, and detailed, as described in previous publications [15]. These three levels in the described case correspond to

- institution level,
- department level,
- individual level.

Within the project several pilot maps were developed [16]. They mostly illustrate the teaching activity and expertise of the faculty.

In this paper the emphasis is put on the research activity and analysis of secondary data. The next two figures illustrate school and department levels for shaping the research activity by mapping the bibliometric data extracted from Google Scholar.

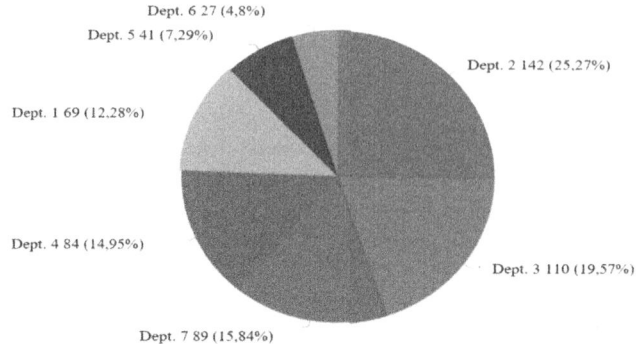

Fig. 1. Distribution of all the publications among the school departments.

Figure 1 shows the general level distribution of all the publications listed in the database among the university school departments. Here the information on the percentage of the total amount of publications of the university school departments is stated. That helps to evaluate the more and less active departments in terms of publications.

Figure 2 shows focused and detailed levels of generalization describing a portrait of the faculty from department X and gives the information on the number of publications for each of the faculty members, their H-index, the number of citations of each of the teacher.

Mapping is not an operation but a process and this process includes 5 phases at least.

- Choosing a focus, level and a target for developing maps;
- Development of ontologies, that describe the milestone concepts;
- Formation of a knowledge maps atlas;
- Data and knowledge collection;
- Their Visualization via Maps;
- Analysis of the results.

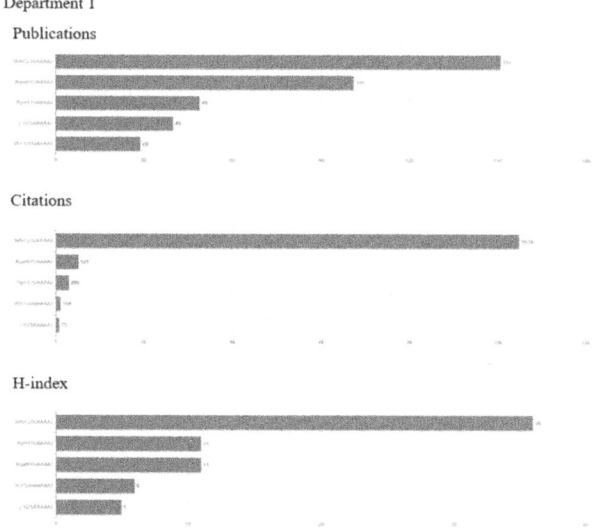

Fig. 2. Scientometric profile of department X.

3 Attributive Ontology Design for Systemic View

3.1 Why Ontologies?

Digital technologies provide the opportunity to better understand the internal processes in organizations and the needs of stakeholders and, based on this, to formulate effective strategic initiatives [17]. But digital approach is only an effective tool.

In order to describe the intellectual information landscape of an organization we need the solid methodological framework. Such framework will help to compress and to generalize corporate administrative and scientific knowledge in organizations.

Ontologies or conceptual models can create the potential for significantly improving the quality of information support and management efficiency [18–20]. Such conceptual models are one of the most promising approaches to the development of knowledge bases and knowledge graphs that allow to describe knowledge structurally, systematically and visually.

However, at the moment, the relationship between the needs of organizations and new technologies in the field of knowledge engineering and visual ontological engineering is rather weak [21].

Although the theoretical basis for ontology-based knowledge mapping (OBKM) was laid more than a decade ago, it was the digitalization boom that attracted the attention of practitioners. Currently, an increase in the number of articles is observed in which the process of constructing a knowledge map is described as a process that should include knowledge engineering approaches [22]. The second driver of OBKM migration to the applied area is the development of such tools [23] as OLAP tools; automated metadata; automated annotation and intelligent agents.

Ontologies in the described project serve as a system-forming theoretical and methodological framework for knowledge maps.

3.2 Describing Knowledge Maps

To orchestrate a set of diagrams (or atlas elements) the novel FOCUS-KM ontology (Framework for Organizing Comprehensive Understanding and Structure of Knowledge Maps) was developed.

Using ontologies as a basis for knowledge mapping allows researchers to trace the holistic and systemic skeleton of knowledge integration [24].

This ontology presents a systematic description of various characteristics (attributes) of knowledge maps – basic tools for managing the intellectual potential of a company. Through this set of attributes, one can describe any of the almost hundred visual diagrams included in the atlas.

FOCUS-KM ontology is (see Fig. 3) summarizing the numerous characteristics of knowledge maps into three categories:

a. Content of the map;
b. Form or map's shape and
c. Purpose of the map.

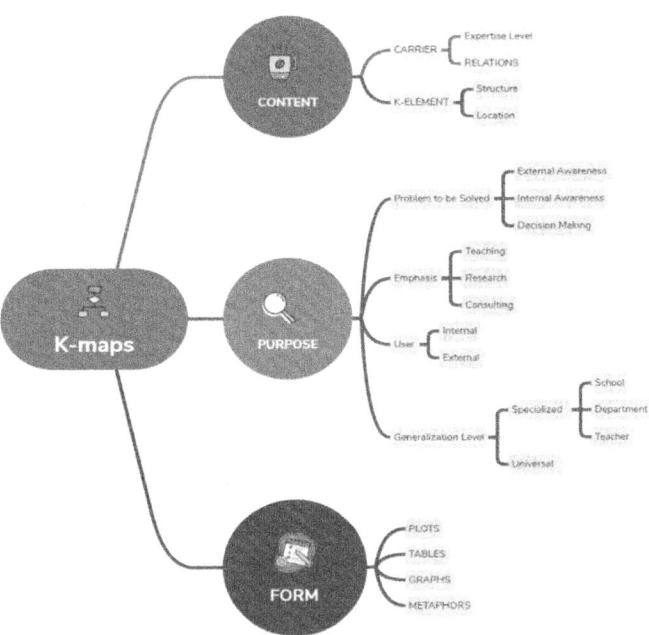

Fig. 3. Structure of FOCUS-KM ontology: upper level.

These three categories will be described below.

This upper level of ontology gives the general and understandable view on the domain of knowledge mapping for experts and other stakeholders. Simpler models such as mind maps and concept maps can be used as a visualization tool for ontologies.

The ultimate Focus-KM ontology view can be seen at Fig. 4. Next, its three upper level components will be considered in more detail below.

a) Content of Knowledge Maps

The content of knowledge maps plays a key role in determining effectiveness in different contexts. It includes two main aspects: the producer and the elements of knowledge.

In the context of an educational institution, a *knowledge producer or carrier* (teacher) is an entity responsible for the accumulation and transfer of knowledge. The main feature of the attribute "producer" is its "potential".

The *potential* of a knowledge producer reflects his or her combined level of expertise, knowledge, skills and experience in certain areas.

The *dynamics* of the carrier reflects the changes in his potential over time: the teacher's self-improvement, as well as the continuous updating of knowledge. Relationships between carriers are a network of interactions for the exchange of knowledge and experience, including various forms of cooperation, such as the exchange of educational materials, research projects, etc. These relationships play an important role in shaping the educational environment and improving the professionalism of teachers.

Knowledge elements include specific learning materials and pieces of information belonging to the producers. Elements can be organized into different structures, also they have priorities, locations and formats.

Structure of knowledge elements describe the ways of classifying, organizing and linking individual elements of knowledge to ensure their accessibility and understanding interconnections for navigation.

The location of knowledge elements includes the geographical location of the teacher (for example, in a branch of a university), an academic unit (department, faculty) and the program (bachelor or masters).

b) Knowledge Map Shape (Form or Representation)

The shape of knowledge map is an important aspect of its visual representation, which determines the way information is displayed. The Fig. 4 illustrates the main groups of patterns like graphs, tables, charts, as well as metaphoric drawings (like sunburst diagrams, fishbone, rock hill).

Tables are familiar and widely used. They structure and present data that can be single-level or multi-level, depending on the number of hierarchy levels. Tables can be represented in different dimensions, from two-dimensional to multi-dimensional, allowing to work with different types of data.

Graphs are one of the most basic ways to visualize data and can be one-dimensional, two-dimensional, or three-dimensional, depending on the number of dimensions they represent. One-dimensional graphs present information in one dimension and can include line graphs, which show relationships between variables, and dot plots, which use points on a coordinate plane to represent data. Two-dimensional graphs present information in two dimensions and can include plots and bubbles. Three-dimensional graphs present information in three dimensions, which provides a more complete visual representation of the data. They can be dimensional or color-based, depending on how the third dimension is used.

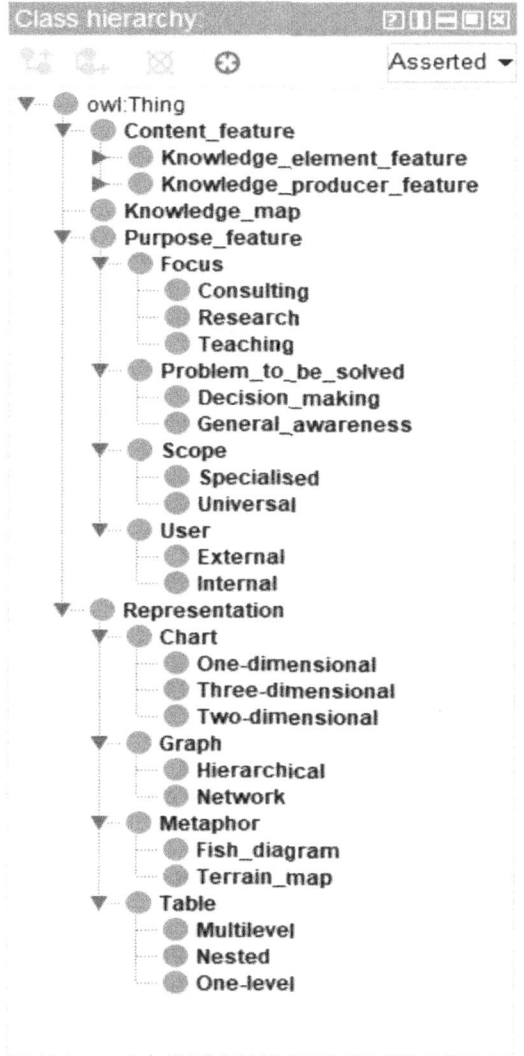

Fig.4. FOCUS-KM ontology.

Graphs represent structured networks of relationships between knowledge elements and can be hierarchical or network. Hierarchical graphs show structured relationships between knowledge elements in the form of a tree structure.

Chart (plot) or function graph is a visual representation of a function on a plane that helps a person to understand the various properties of a function.

Metaphor drawings such as terrain maps, pyramids and fish diagrams are used to illustrate key concepts and relationships between knowledge elements.

To sum up, the form of knowledge maps represents a variety of information visualization techniques that play a key role in structuring and understanding knowledge in various fields. From one-dimensional and two-dimensional plots to tables and graphs, each of these types of data representation has its own unique characteristics and applications.

For example, 3D graphs allow for deeper exploration of data by presenting information in three dimensions, while tables provide a structured and systematic presentation of data for easy comparison and analysis. Graphs, in turn, help visualize the relationships between different knowledge elements, making them a useful tool for analyzing complex data networks. Finally, drawings and metaphors, such as a terrain map or a fish diagram, help illustrate key concepts and relationships between knowledge elements, making them more accessible and understandable to users.

c) **Purpose of Knowledge Maps**

The purpose of knowledge maps plays an important role in determining the goals and specifics of their use in various contexts, especially in educational institutions. The characteristics of the purpose include: problem to be solved/emphasis/users/level of generalization.

"Focus" refers to the main focus of the use of the knowledge map. Within the framework of the study of the experience of teachers in three areas, the following types of focus can be distinguished: teaching/research/consulting. While teaching faculty focused on developing and teaching courses, on preparing course materials, teaching classes, and assessing students. Faculty actively engaged in research track to publish research articles, participate in conferences, and receive grants. Faculty focused on solving practical business cases and engaged in consulting use their knowledge and experience to help solve specific problems for clients or partners.

The problem to be solved by knowledge mapping plays a key role and can be considered in different contexts, e.g. – decision-making/raising general awareness within the company.

Users consist of *external* and *internal* ones expressing interests and expectations that are important to consider in order to develop an effective knowledge map. In an educational context, such maps can be used for decision making, determining the educational institution's positioning in the market, and raising awareness within the organization. External users include applicants, business partners and customers who can use knowledge maps to obtain information about the educational institution, projects and employees and students. Internal users incorporate administration, colleagues and students.

In general, all users of the knowledge map expect that it provides convenient and transparent access to information about the knowledge and expertise of teachers, facilitates collaboration, exchange of knowledge and experience, and enriches their professional development and expands opportunities for research activities. Professional knowledge maps help not only to assess intellectual capital, but also to see gaps and anticipate potential threats.

The *level of generalization* of knowledge maps is also vital, which is determined by the purpose and task of mapping. It can be either universal or specialized. Universal knowledge maps are applicable in various fields of knowledge and disciplines, showing the general picture of what is happening (for example, a faculty scientific citation map).

Specialized knowledge maps can be focused on specific areas or levels, such as faculty, graduate school, department, or individual faculty.

4 The Knowledge Mapping Atlas

One of the ultimate results of METACARTA project was the atlas systematizing the variety of knowledge maps templates and identifying their significant features (or properties). The term "atlas" was borrowed from classical definition: "Atlas is a bound collection of maps often including illustrations, informative tables, or textual matter" [25].

When creating an atlas of knowledge maps that describes modern diagram templates and recommendations for their use, a huge amount of work was carried out to generalize and structurally describe the existing diagrams.

Information design in knowledge maps aims to avoid confusion by presenting data in a way that's easy to understand. Based on the study of researchers Lengler and Eppler who compiled a table similar to the periodic table, consisting of more than 100 different visualization techniques, divided by type of use [26] more than 20 visual diagrams are included into the atlas.

Also atlas systematizes the recommendations for their use, it describes modern diagram templates and structurally summarize describe the existing diagrams in a form of a table. The use of the developed atlas creates an additional advantage for all its users and the project stakeholders.

The KM atlas itself includes representations of various knowledge maps and helps the choice depending on:

- the interested party;
- the task at hand;
- the chosen level of generalization for mapping (institute/department/individual) or
- some other factors.

Table 1. Fragment of the KM-Atlas.

Graphs	Hierarchical	Hierarchical tree		Graphical representation of hierarchically organized data in the form of a tree.	
	Net-work non-directed	Radar		A graphical representation of data in the form of lobes, usually used to compare different categories or aspects.	
		Radar with markers		A petal diagram that displays markers for specifying values in addition to petals.	
		Filled radar		A petal diagram in which the areas between the petals are filled with color for better visualization.	

Part of the atlas involves interactive maps, the content and form of which will change automatically, allowing administration, students and teachers to view knowledge maps, search on various topics and get information about the links between different fields of knowledge. The atlas is designed in the form of the table (performed by Ms. Elvira Grinberg) with a description of the difficulty level of the diagram, the preview of the pictogram, its design and the main characteristics and purpose (see Table 1).

The atlas of the knowledge maps presents systemic vision of possible diagrams that scaffolds the understanding of university intellectual assets from a range of perspectives. The paper tries to provide comprehensive insight into the ways in which university and faculty members visualize their bibliometric and teaching intellectual assets.

5 Knowledge and Data Capture Remarks

The described approach was totally based on the collected data and knowledge. Management research in general relies heavily on both primary and secondary data to understand complex organizational phenomena, inform decision-making, and contribute to the existing body of knowledge. However, analysis of each type of data and knowledge requires distinct approaches, techniques from data and knowledge science.

The primary data collection (executed by Dr. Alkanova) on teaching was shortly described in [27]. The data was acquired from the current full-time faculty who teach at least 1 course per year via online questionnaire.

That self-assessment questionnaire was developed as part of larger project for internal self-assessment of the targeted school full-time faculty. A well-known traditional scheme was used for the development of the questionnaire (goal – questions and their order – simplification of questions and their minimization – answer format – testing – re-design [28, 29]. The respondents answered a series of binary questions whether they consider themselves as an expert in a particular area of knowledge from the predefined set of ontologies.

In case of a positive answer for a particular area a set of questions regarding teaching, research and applied consulting experience followed. Consequently, the dataset was organized in a "matrix" logic – the assessment of experience in each type of activity was carried out for each area of knowledge noted by the employee [30]. The average number of knowledge areas reported by employees as areas of expertise was about 3–5.

Secondary (bibliometric) data about research was acquired from Google Scholar data base (performed by M. Kubelskiy and V. Shvankin) and was discussed in [16]. To collect bibliometric data, it was necessary to create access to the register of collaborating authors in connection with the departments for which information would be collected and searched.

The provided register contained links to employee profiles on the main open scientific bibliometric resources. This fact made it possible to significantly reduce the labor intensity while implementing this part of the project, because there was no need to manually search for the links to employee profiles. The register includes reference information about employees and contains a set of fields, for example.

> Name, family name / Department /Position /
> Degree Elibrary_SPIN / Scopus_AuthorID /
> WoS_ResearcherID/ WoS_link/ Orcid /
> Google Scholar /Pure_link.

Thus, Google Scholar was chosen as the main source of data on the scientific activities of teachers, which meets all the formulated criteria:

- It is possible to automatically upload both via the API and using freely distributed libraries;
- The access is free and available from Russia, the faculty' papers are still continued to be indexed;
- Most faculty have profiles in this system, links to which are presented in the register.

For future studies the choice between primary and secondary data, or a combination of both, depends on the research question, available resources, and desired level of control over the data. By carefully considering the specific analysis techniques and relevant considerations for each type of data, management researchers can generate valuable insights and contribute meaningfully to the field.

It's vital to choose the most appropriate method based on the research question, understand its strengths and limitations, and apply rigorous analysis techniques to ensure the validity and reliability of the findings. Finally, ethical considerations must always be at the forefront of the research process, regardless of the data source or analytical approach.

6 Conclusion

Organizations today are drowning in information. The sheer volume makes finding, organizing, and understanding crucial data a significant challenge, consuming vast amounts of time and resources. A visual approach, leveraging knowledge maps and atlases, offers a powerful solution to this information overload. This approach allows for the compression and contextualization of complex information, presenting a systemic overview instead of a fragmented view.

This paper details the development of a prototype knowledge map atlas specifically designed for a university business school. This atlas provides invariant representations of knowledge maps, dynamically adapting to different stakeholders (students, faculty, administration), tasks, and levels of detail (institute, department, individual). Crucially, the maps are not static; they are designed to evolve and reflect the ever-changing landscape of the institution's intellectual assets – encompassing educational programs, research projects, and consulting engagements.

The atlas functions as a sophisticated, interactive directory, revealing the intricate connections between various aspects of academic life. For example, a student could utilize the atlas to quickly identify relevant courses, faculty experts, and ongoing research projects related to their chosen field of study. Faculty members can leverage it to understand collaborations, identify potential research partners, and visualize the contribution of their work to the larger departmental and institutional goals. Administrators can use the atlas to report on the business school, assess resource allocation, and identify areas for improvement or further investment. The granular level of detail allows for a comprehensive overview of the business school's intellectual capital while simultaneously providing context-specific details as needed.

The development of this atlas was part of the METACARTA project (Methodology and Technology for developing digital knowledge mAps for eduCAtion and Research TeAms), which focused on creating a robust methodology for building and managing these dynamic visual representations. The project relied heavily on ontology engineering, employing ontologies – formal representations of knowledge – as the conceptual backbone for structuring the knowledge maps. Specifically, a novel ontology called FOCUS-KM (Framework for Organizing Comprehensive Understanding and Structure of Knowledge Maps) was developed. This ontology provides a generalized framework, capturing a wide range of attributes and properties relevant to knowledge maps, ensuring consistency and facilitating interoperability across different types of maps and data sources. The FOCUS-KM ontology is designed to be extensible and adaptable to future changes and additions to the university's intellectual landscape. Further research is needed to evaluate the long-term impact and effectiveness of this atlas, potentially incorporating user feedback to further refine its functionality and usability. Future work could also explore the integration of other data sources, such as performance metrics and student feedback, to provide a more holistic and comprehensive view of the business school's activities. The ultimate aim is to create a dynamic, self-updating system that provides real-time insights into the evolving landscape of the university's intellectual assets, fostering smarter collaboration, improved decision-making, and ultimately, enhanced educational and research outcomes [31].

Acknowledgments. Authors thank Dr. Dmitry Kudryavtsev, who was the initiator of the project and proposed the research design, Dr. Olga Alkanova for organizing the survey of faculty teachers, Miroslav Kubelsky for the digital support of bibliometric maps, and Ms. Elvira Grinberg for the visual analysis.

Disclosure of Interests. The authors have no competing interests to declare that are relevant to the content of this article.

References

1. Miller, F.: The power of Diagrams. https://www.francismiller.com/articles/
2. Moody, D.: What makes a good diagram? Improving the cognitive effectiveness of diagrams in IS development. In: Wojtkowski, W., Wojtkowski, W.G., Zupancic, J., Magyar, G., Knapp, G. (eds.) Advances in Information Systems Development, LNCS, pp. 481–492. Springer, Boston, MA (2007). https://doi.org/10.1007/978-0-387-70802-7_40
3. Troise, C.: Exploring knowledge visualization in the digital age: an analysis of benefits and risks. Manag. Decis. **60**(4), 1116–1131 (2022). https://doi.org/10.1108/MD-01-2021-0086
4. Gardner, H.: Smart Collaboration: How Professionals and Their Firms Succeed by Breaking Down Silos. Harvard Business Review Press, Sholamadevi (2017)
5. Liang, X., Luo, L., Hu, S., Li, Y.: Mapping the knowledge frontiers and evolution of decision making based on agent-based modeling. Knowl.-Based Syst. **250**(C), 108982 (2022)
6. Faisal, H., Rahman, A., Zaman, G.: Knowledge mapping for research papers. Int. J. Comput. Sci. Netw. Secur. **19**(10), 158–164 (2019)
7. Ding, X., Yang, Z.: Knowledge mapping of platform research: a visual analysis using VOSviewer and CiteSpace. Electron. Commer. Res. **23**(3), 787–809 (2020)
8. Cordeiro, M., Puig, F., Ruiz-Fernández, L.: Realizing dynamic capabilities and organizational knowledge in effective innovations: the capabilities typological map. J. Knowl. Manag. **27**(1) (2022)
9. Anthony, Jr, B.: Information flow analysis of a knowledge mapping-based system for university alumni collaboration: a practical approach. J. Knowl. Econ. **12**(2), 756–787 (2021)
10. Balaid, A., Abd Rozan, M.Z., Hikmi, S.N., Memon, J.: Knowledge maps: a systematic literature review and directions for future research. Int. J. Inf. Manag **36**(3), 451–475 (2016)
11. Pereira, V., Bamel, U., Temouri, Y., Budhwar, P., Del Giudice, M.: Mapping the evolution, current state of affairs and future research direction of managing cross-border knowledge for innovation. Int. Bus. Rev. **32**(2), 101834 (2023)
12. Liebowitz, J.: Linking social network analysis with the analytic hierarchy process for knowledge mapping in organizations. J. Knowl. Manag. **9**, 76–86 (2005)
13. Zack, M., McKeen, J., Singh, S.: Knowledge management and organizational performance: an exploratory analysis. J. Knowl. Manag. **13**(6), 392–409 (2009). https://doi.org/10.1108/13673270910997088
14. Butt, S.A., et al.: A knowledge map for ICT integration in the silver economy. Procedia Comput. Sci. (181), 93–701 (2021)
15. Kuznetsova, A., Gavrilova, T., Alkanova, O.: Building atlas of knowledge maps: towards smarter collaboration. In: Proceedings of the 16th International Joint Conference on Knowledge Discovery, Knowledge Engineering and Knowledge Management - Volume 3: KMIS, pp. 130–136 (2024). ISBN 978-989-758-716-0, ISSN 2184-3228
16. Kubelskiy, M., Kuznetsova, A., Leshcheva, I., Gavrilova, T., Shvankin, V.: Ontology-based approach for research activity mapping. In: International Symposium on Knowledge-Ontology-Theory KNOTH2024 as Part of IEEE International Multi-Conference on Engineering, Computer and Information Sciences (SIBIRCON), pp. 334–339 (2024). https://ieeexplore.ieee.org/document/10758489
17. Tsenzharik, M.K., Krylova, Y.V., Steshenko, V.I.: Digital transformation of companies: strategic analysis, influencing factors and models. Bull. St. Petersburg Univ. Econ. **36**(3), 390–420 (2020)
18. Choi, N., Song, I.Y., Han, H.: A survey on ontology mapping. ACM Sigmod Record **35**(3), 34–41 (2006)
19. Sure, Y., Staab, S., Studer, R.: Ontology engineering methodology. In: Staab, S., Studer, R. (eds.) Handbook on Ontologies. International Handbooks on Information Systems, pp. 135–152. Springer, Berlin, Heidelberg (2009). https://doi.org/10.1007/978-3-540-92673-3_6

20. Romanenko, E., Calvanese, D., Guizzardi, G.: Abstracting ontology-driven conceptual models: objects, aspects, events, and their parts. In: Guizzardi, R.S.S., Ralyté, J., Franch, X. (eds.), Research Challenges in Information Science: 16th International Conference, RCIS 2022, Barcelona, Spain, 17–20 May 2022, Proceedings. LNBIP, vol. 446, pp. 372–388. Springer, Cham (2022). https://doi.org/10.1007/978-3-031-05760-1_22
21. Osman, M.A., Noah, S.A.M., Saad, S. Ontology-based knowledge management tools for knowledge sharing in organization—a review. IEEE Access **10**, 43267–43283 (2022)
22. Qin, Q., Zhang, S.: Visualizing the knowledge mapping of artificial intelligence in education: a systematic review. Educ. Inf. Technol. **30**(1), 449–483 (2025)
23. Duan, Y., Liu, Y.: Ontology-based knowledge graph construction and application for large workpiece forging. In: 2022 IEEE 8th International Conference on Computer and Communications (ICCC), Chengdu, China, pp. 2033–2037 (2022). https://doi.org/10.1109/ICCC56324.2022.10065699
24. Zheng, Y., Törmä, S., Seppänen, O.: A shared ontology suite for digital construction workflow. Autom. Constr. **132**, 103930 (2021). ISSN 0926-5805. https://doi.org/10.1016/j.autcon.2021.103930
25. Merriam Webster dictionary https://www.merriam-webster.com/dictionary/atlas
26. Lengler, R., Eppler, M.J.: A Periodic Table of Visualization Methods (2007). https://www.visual-literacy.org/periodic_table/periodic_table.html
27. Gavrilova, T., Kudryavtsev, D., Alkanova, O.: Using knowledge maps to create a business school faculty portrait. In: Proceedings of 15-th International Conference on Knowledge Management and Information Systems (KMIS), within the 15-th International Joint Conference on Knowledge Discovery, Knowledge Engineering and Knowledge Management (IC3K), Rome, 13–15 November 2023, vol. 3, pp. 185–193 (2023). https://doi.org/10.5220/0012181000003598
28. Mooi, E., Sarstedt, M., Mooi-Reci, I.: Market Research: The Process, Data, and Methods Using Stata. Springer, Cham (2018). https://doi.org/10.1007/978-981-10-5218-7
29. Aithal, A., Aithal, P.: Development and validation of survey questionnaire & experimental data—a systematical review-based statistical approach. Int. J. Manag. Technol. Soc. Sci. (IJMTS) **5**, 233–251 (2020)
30. Gavrilova, T.A., Kuznetsova, A.V., Alkanova, O.N., Grinberg, E.Y.: Visualization of employees' competencies using knowledge maps. Russ. Manag. J. **22**(1), 86–112 (2024). https://doi.org/10.21638/spbu18.2024.104
31. Bell, E., Warren, S., and Schroeder, J.: Introduction: the visual organization. In: The Routledge Companion to Visual Organization, pp. 1–16. Routledge (2014)

Author Index

A
Aka Uymaz, Hande 37
Al-Dausari, Nada 93
Antakli, André 199

B
Belo, Orlando 3
Benfenati, Domenico 106
Bermeitinger, Bernhard 22
Blöthner, Simon 177
Brito e Abreu, Fernando 121

C
Cavalcante, Claudio 150
Coenen, Frans 93
Cosme, Diogo 121

D
Duarte, Ana 3

F
Friedrich, Maiko 301

G
Galvão, António 121
Gavrilova, Tatiana 386

H
Hagenmeyer, Veit 301
Handschuh, Siegfried 22
Hrycej, Tomas 22

K
Kaitosalmi, Jani 249
Kocak, Seyma 326
Kostadinova, Irina 360
Kumova Metin, Senem 37
Kuznetsova, Anna 386

L
Larch, Mario 177
Leshcheva, Irina 386
Lifschitz, Sergio 150

N
Nandini, Durgesh 177
Nepomuceno, Joao 150
Nguyen, Anh 93
Nguyen, Duong 57
Nguyen, Thu 57

P
Pawlowski, Jan 326

R
Ratia, Milla 249
Rinaldi, Antonio Maria 106
Rissanen, Miia 279
Ruberg, Nicolaas 150
Russo, Cristiano 106

S
Sahota, Harkiran 199
Savolainen, Jyrki 279

Schmidt, Andreas   301
Schmurr, Philipp   301
Schönfeld, Mirco   177
Seabra, Antony   150
Shantsila, Eduard   93
Spieldenner, Daniel   199
Spieldenner, Torsten   199
Spörer, Jan   22
Stefanova, Svetlana   360

Stucky, Karl-Uwe   301
Suess, Wolfgang   301

T
Todorova, Ana   360
Tommasino, Cristian   106

Y
Yap, Jeffrey Boon Hui   229

Made in the USA
Monee, IL
03 May 2026

49438651R00234